UNIVERSITY OF NORTH CAROLINA STUDIES IN COMPARATIVE LITERATURE

Founded by Werner P. Friederich

William J. DeSua, *Editor*

Robert S. Mayo, *Assistant Editor*

Editorial Committee:

Edwin L. Brown	Eugene H. Falk	Aldo D. Scaglione
Alfred G. Engstrom	Dan W. Patterson	Siegfried Wenzel

THE CLASSICAL THEORY OF COMPOSITION

Number 53

Foreign Sales (outside U. S. A. and Canada):
FEFFER AND SIMONS, INC.
81 Union Square
New York, N. Y. 10003

THE CLASSICAL THEORY
OF COMPOSITION
FROM ITS ORIGINS TO THE PRESENT

A HISTORICAL SURVEY

by

ALDO SCAGLIONE

CHAPEL HILL
THE UNIVERSITY OF NORTH CAROLINA PRESS
1972

PRINTED IN THE U. S. A. BY J. H. FURST COMPANY,
BALTIMORE, MARYLAND

Tantum series iuncturaque pollet

Such is the importance of word arrangement!

HORACE, *Ars poetica* 282

D'un mot mis en sa place enseigna le pouvoir

(Malherbe) taught us the great power of a word well placed

BOILEAU, *Art poétique* I, 133

TABLE OF CONTENTS

ABBREVIATIONS

IPo	Initial or Front-Position
EPo	End-Position
MPo	Mid-Position
VMPo	Mid-Position of the Verb (i. e. between the Subject and the Complements)
S	Subject
P	Predicate
V	Verb fV finite Verb
C	Complement CC Complements iC indirect C
O	Order dO Direct Order
WO	Word Order
Ob	Object dOb, iOb direct, indirect Ob
Cl	Clause Cls Clauses mCl main Clause
	sCl secondary or subordinate Clause
ex.:	$(S+)V+CC-O =$ a (word) order characterized by the sequence of Subject (if expressed), Verb, Complements; the parenthesis indicates that when, as often in Latin, the subject is understood, the clause is still regarded as falling into this type.

INTRODUCTION

We all remember the scene in Molière's *Bourgeois gentilhomme* [Act II, Sc. 4], where the eager pupil is attempting a more effective phrasing ('more gallant and gently turned') for the thought: "Belle Marquise, vos beaux yeux me font mourir d'amour." After having tried all sorts of rearrangement of word order, and eventually the most drastic of them all: "Me font vos yeux beaux mourir, belle Marquise, d'amour"—desperately seeking poetry through inversion—, he hears from his philosophy teacher that the spontaneous version was best. More recently, the weekly *Time* delightedly reminded its readers of a long list of colorful stylistic criticisms it had been enduring over the years. "A favorite butt of early *Time* baiters was [its] distinctive and mannered style. . . . In a famous 1936 *New Yorker* parody, the late Wolcott Gibbs captured that style in the classic line: 'Backward ran sentences until reeled the mind.'" [1]

Concern with sentence composition and, as part of it, word order has affected, in one way or another, every generation in many a language. It is, of course, much older than Molière. Like so many basic notions of ours, it is no wonder that it should go back—for the West at least—to the ancient Greeks. Within some geographical and bibliographical limitations, the present study intends to be the story of this concern.

Today the more sophisticated sense of 'composition' involves the principles of internal cogency, the inner logic underlying the unitary development of plot through all its particular incidents in any given literary work (especially if not an oration). But the term in question was used by the ancients in a rather microscopic sense. For 'poetic' or 'structural' composition, the organic, total envisioning of the work as a unit, they had no word. Indeed they seldom expressed such a sense theoretically. This may be one reason for the limited impact of Aristotle's *Poetics* in antiquity, for in that work something resembling our requirements for overall struc-

---

[1] *Time* magazine, August 5, 1966. Incidentally, fresh and spontaneous as they may appear to us, the grammatical lessons to the "Bourgeois" singularly testify to the subtle impact of the technical production with which we are about to concern ourselves. In Act II, Sc. 6 Molière was echoing word by word the phonetic descriptions he found in Cordemoy's *Traité physique de la parole* (about which more later). Cf. M. Grammont, *Traité de phonétique* (Paris, 1933, 1950⁴), p. 13 fn.

ture was present through the notion of " plot," with its demand for a close relationship between the parts and the whole (ἐν καὶ ὅλον). The term οἰκονομία did come fairly close to the notion of overall management (at least the way Dionysius of Halicarnassus used it); yet it was conceived more 'physically' than we might wish it, and, at any rate, it received only limited attention.

This lack of plan may seem paradoxical in the works of writers as artistic as the Greek men of letters. So, indeed, it is; but it is explained by the quite different conception that the Greeks—at least those of the decadence— have of the beauty of a discourse. For them the whole value is in the detail. The perfecting of the whole is secondary; they have no taste for it. [I should find it safer to state that their expressed theoretical consciousness of it was rather limited.] By a sort of deliberate intellectual myopia they restrict their field of vision to the analysis of a paragraph, a period, a phrase, even a word. Their esthetic sense, so to speak, is fragmentary.[2] [And fragmentary, one might add, the aesthetic sense remained in the West until the ripening of Romantic ' organicism.']

More recently, E. R. Curtius substantially confirmed such a judgment, with some added qualifications:

What we mean today by ' composition' has no equivalent in antique and medieval literary theory. Antiquity knew the concept of composition in its strict sense only in epic and tragedy, for which Aristotle prescribed a limited action. . . . As a result, modern critics have frequently deplored the lack of composition in antique literature. But what we perceive as elements of composition in late antique and medieval literature are for the most part taken from the traditional succession of the five sections of an oration.[3]

Indeed, the organization of the whole literary artifact was seldom conceived in other terms than those derived from the traditional sequence of the five parts of an oration (introduction, narration, proof, refutation, peroration).[4]

True enough, it is only fair to qualify this generalization further by

---

[2] This direct, if perhaps too peremptory judgment is found in Marcel Guignet, *St. Grégoire de Nazianze, Orateur et épistolier* (Paris, 1911), p. 214, cited and translated by Ch. Baldwin, *M. R. and P.*, p. 21.

[3] Curtius, *European Literature . . .* , p. 71.

[4] What Curtius was not taking into consideration is the exact equivalent of part of our notion of composition, namely its linguistic and stylistic dimensions. For this there was, indeed, a well-articulated speculative tradition, which alone concerns us here, together with its continuous impact on Western ideas concerning literary and acceptable writing form.

mentioning the celebrated passage where Plato spoke of every well-composed *logos* or discourse as a living organism, ζῷον (*Phaedrus*, 264C; also *Rep.* IV, 420C-D, as applied to statuary). Likewise, we all remember Horace's insistence, ostensibly from the vantage point of 'appropriateness' of the parts to the overall purpose, on the need to fit every incident into a logical and natural unity (beginning of *Ars poetica*, with the conclusive dictum: *Denique sit quod vis, simplex dumtaxat et unum*, l. 23; again, later on: *primo ne medium, medio ne discrepet imum*, l. 153, reminiscent of Aristotle's ἓν καὶ ὅλον). And there is, too, the singular position of the Epicurean philosopher Philodemus, Cicero's Greek contemporary. Isolated, generally unheeded, and perhaps even unique though he may have been, his thought remains nevertheless an impressive critique of the views on art prevalent in all antiquity. He condemned the traditional fragmentation of works of poetry and literature perpetrated by the critics in the exercise of analytical methods, and vigorously asserted the unity of the poem, which must be judged as a whole, taking account of all its aspects at once. But more on him later.

On the other hand, the ancients had an elaborate heading on 'composition' within rhetorical theory, and this is the subject of the present study, namely the stylistic criteria of sentence structure as first theorized in antiquity under that term and, as such, regularly transmitted through the centuries down to our own day.

Linguistic or grammatical speculation had begun under the aegis of logic with Plato and Aristotle, after the very first attempts at morphological analysis by the Sophists. But that initial hegemony of logic did not last very long. Still running strong within the Stoico-Pergamene schools, the logical approach was opposed by the influential Alexandrian schools. And toward the end of the Empire, grammar found itself in a highly autonomous position. By then, logic had generally decayed from the prominent position it had once held in Greek education. In particular, syntax, the area of linguistic study most susceptible to yield to logical orientations, had found little development in all of antiquity, and only two major texts survive to witness even its limited vitality, Apollonius Dyscolus' four syntactic books, for Greek, and the two last books of Priscian's *Institutions*, for Latin. These only two full-fledged treatments of syntax bequeathed by antiquity are not unrelated to each other: Priscian (teaching in Constantinople, early sixth century A. D.) was, in this domain, a late disciple of Apollonius (fl. ca. A. D. 150).

The intensive development of the syntactical approach and of syntax itself as a part of grammar starts with full rights only in the Middle Ages (beginning at the end of the twelfth century). But syntax was limited to *analyse logique*: the function of the parts of speech and the flectional system (cases, words, verbal aspects etc.). It never, or almost never reached the *syntaxe de la période* (sentence beyond the clause), and had only little to say on word order.

Such twentieth-century scholars as the American E. K. Rand and the German E. R. Curtius have earnestly endeavored to prove and illustrate the continuity of the classical tradition down to 1800 in general terms or, more specifically, in such domains as the rhetorical. It is, however, less known that the grammatical tradition was even more continuous and durable, in its narrower compass. Let me cite a few rather trivial examples. We are so thoroughly accustomed to the word 'etymology' in the acceptation of study of word roots and derivations (preferably from ancient languages), that we are surprised to find that 'etymology' was used consistently from late antiquity to at least the 1890 ed. of Kennedy's manual to indicate what we now call, with no less Greek a term, 'morphology.' Indeed Kennedy still gave as grammar's "two chief divisions" etymology and syntax (respectively, "true word formation"—in a rather forced interpretation of ἔτυμον, which meant simply "the true meaning"—and "construction," Priscian's *constructio*). To these he finally added prosody (Quantity, Rhythm, and Meter) as one "which is not a necessary part of Grammar, but is usually appended to it" (p. 5). So it had been, indeed, from late antiquity, as all other major divisions and subdivisions. Similarly, but in a notably conservative vein, substantives, adjectives, and pronouns were still treated by Kennedy as three kinds of nouns (*The Public School Latin Grammar*, 7th ed., 1890, pp. 70-71), plus the numerals. And number, gender, person, and case of nouns, as well as voice, mood, tense, number, and person of verbs, were still called, with persistent Aristotelianism, "accidents" of nouns and verbs (p. 72)—and they still are, occasionally, to this date, at least in English.

But a matter of greater interest to the modern student is that the major portions of both *syntaxe de la période* and word order (this latter now definitely part of grammar, precisely within syntax) developed through the centuries clearly within the domain of rhetorical theory, and from that rather exalted position these subjects occasionally branched out into grammar proper at the same time that they drew inspiration from logic.

All this we shall see as our story unfolds. In the meantime, since we are dealing with the organization of sentences and parts thereof, some genetic data may be in order. Although, as we have already noted, the sentence as an organized whole was studied *de facto* only within rhetoric, it was the grammarians who defined its nature and linguistic functions.[5] Dionysius Thrax neatly termed it as "a whole made of words and expressing a complete thought," [λόγος ἐστὶ ...] λέξεως σύνθεσις διάνοιαν αὐτοτελῆ δηλοῦσα. He placed its treatment (not actually given in his manual) as logically posterior to that of words as parts of speech, i. e. the basic categories of the elements of the clause. The first extensive treatment of the sentence from a linguistic point of view has been preserved for us in the *Syntax* of Apollonius Dyscolus. Modern students of language have emphasized the notion that the sentence or syntactic construction has a natural priority over its elements and parts, since "isolated words are in fact only linguistic figments,"[6] but it appears that only some ancient Indian linguists, out of the whole recorded history of linguistics, placed the sentence first in their analysis of language.[7]

The opening statement in Aristotle's *Rhetoric* declares that rhetoric is a "counterpart" (ἀντίστροφος) of dialectic. Poetry, in turn (or, rather, poetics), could be said to be, in a sense, a counterpart of rhetoric. Both oratory and poetry depend on grammar, while lyric poetry, in particular, is associated with music. When, several centuries later, the system of the arts became crystallized within the framework of the seven liberal arts, we find four of those companions neatly arranged in a harmonious progression: from grammar to rhetoric to dialectic (= trivium), with music in the next group (= quadrivium); if poetry was not assigned an individually autonomous place in the system, it was because one saw it as a byproduct of the first two arts—although in the practice of the curriculum its study was frequently viewed as an appendage of grammar.

I have already stated that we are now about to witness a rare, exemplary case of symbiosis between the three arts of the Trivium. Music will also come in for its share, although we will not give it all its due for reasons of economy which will become evident. If poetry will not intervene in its own right, it will constantly be in the background inasmuch as all-pervasive stylistic considerations will extend the notion of style beyond

---

[5] C. C. Fries, *The Structure of English* (New York, 1952), pp. 9-16.
[6] B. Malinowski, *Coral Gardens and Their Magic* (London, 1935), II, 11.
[7] Cf. R. H. Robins, "Dionysius Thrax and the Western Grammatical Tradition," *Transactions of the Philological Society, 1957* (Oxford, 1958), 67-106; see p. 91.

oratory through the whole domain of literature, including poetry itself.

A few more preliminary steps are now needed to bring us closer to the issues involved in our inquiry. As early as 1852 Ernst Curtius and L. Lange affirmed that subordination arises from coordination, and all clauses were originally main clauses. In line with this principle, and in the light of the psychological resolution of many a thorny question traditionally afflicting the philosophy of language (a solution inaugurated by H. Steinthal, "Grammatik, Logik, Psychologie," 1855), we could tentatively adopt the view that periodic style is essentially a literary, intellectual artifact superimposed on the popular syntax, which is naturally unperiodic, *grosso modo* '*style coupé.*' Periodic, however, does not mean logical, but neither does *coupé* mean logical, the basic difference between them being that in the latter the logical relationships are perceived psychologically, intuitively, whereas in the former they are pictured formally, crystallized in linguistic morphemes.

Should we find this initial approach acceptable, we would already have posited a number of the key concepts around which the following story will revolve. Yet, if only to exorcise it, it will not be inopportune to evoke one of the persistent ghosts of the now vanishing traditional education; the prejudice, that is, that the Latin language, for one, distinctively shines for the logical character of its periods. There is, of course, some precious glimmer of truth in that belief, but whatever logic we will find in the Latin sentence will be a very special kind of formalized, internal logic. In particular, we shall do well to remember that in the special realm of word order Latin is, relatively to such modern languages as French and English, not logical but impressionistic (in a sense that will soon become clear).

We are entitled to retain the expressions 'natural' and 'logical' if only we keep in mind that what we actually mean is not that it is 'natural' or 'logical' for words to be arranged in a given way (in the clause or in the sentence), but that the reason and function of that arrangement may be found in the (logical) sequence of thought according to the thinking habits of speakers of the language in question. The distinction may seem oversubtle and abstract; it must nevertheless remain basic, for it will avoid confusion of language with logic while acknowledging logic's due in the language process as at least one of its constitutive factors.

Public school students of Latin first started to have the modern view on these matters neatly placed before them in Kennedy's grammar:

"Logic and grammar are akin to one another; but their spheres are different. Logic is the Grammar of reasoning: it develops 'the laws of thought.' Grammar is the logic of language: it displays the rules and idioms of discourse. The correlation and the terms of Subject-Predicate are necessary to both sciences. But the scope of these terms is not the same in both " (7th ed., 1890, p. xii).

I cite this once famous manual because it is exemplary in other respects also. But for this we shall have to take one step back. Sentence structure and word order, which now appear to us as a set of problems belonging to linguistics and eventually bordering on stylistics, have really evolved at the borderline between several disciplines or, shall we say, at the crossroads where the three liberal arts of the Trivium converged. This province of syntax concerning both language and the intensive use of language that we call style, has, through the centuries, shown itself to partake of grammar, logic, and rhetoric as well.

CHAPTER ONE: ANTIQUITY

A. GENERAL

As general background to our story, we must take into account some related historical factors, beginning with the grammatical issues which arose out of speculation on the nature of language. Owing to our imperfect records of ancient positions on such complex matters, the following reconstruction must be regarded as partly conjectural.

Starting from the early controversy on *physis* vs. *nomos*, the Sophists divided themselves on the question whether human expression and communication, i. e. language, was as it was 'by nature,' communication being possible thanks to an objective relationship between words and things, our language and the outside world (*nomina sunt consequentia rerum*, to use Dante's stringent formula), or whether language was simply a result of arbitrary convention sanctioned by usage and popular agreement. Aristotle espoused the latter view, as Plato before him seemed to imply he also did, and the Alexandrian philologists followed Aristotle on this point. When the new and more sophisticated controversy of analogy versus anomaly erupted, the Alexandrian grammarians conceived their art as a search for the regularities (analogies) which underlie the basic structure of language in a way that resembles the laws of human intellection and of the very world of nature. But they did so without implying that such regularities were based on a primitive correspondence going back to the origin of language—since they remained true to their conventionalist or 'nominalist' position. The Stoics, on the other hand, and the Pergamene philologists influenced by them, adopted an empirical attitude toward the realities of language, recognizing in it no visible trace of a necessary relation between the sounds and their meanings—the things for which the sounds stand—, and, furthermore, denying that the current linguistic forms, with their pervasive exceptions and multiplicity of patterns, justified a basic claim of canonic regularity. They were, therefore, anomalists. Yet they satisfied their need for rationality by assuming that the relationship to nature lay somewhere else in the language, to wit in its past, at a stage now hidden by forms which, through the corruption

8

COMPOSITION   9

introduced by human arbitrariness and choice, had decayed and departed
from their original state. This latter could be rediscovered through the
study of word-roots, the *etyma*, and precisely through etymology one
could attain to a state of the language that was 'natural' and characterized
by 'regularity.'[1]

If we now turn our attention to the first recorded positions on matters
of literary style which were consciously taken in Roman circles, we shall
notice that the first Roman 'Atticists,' the circle around Scipio and Laelius,
were known to be strongly influenced by Stoicism, and the later Atticists,
without necessarily being professed Stoics, continued to be influenced by
the ideas of the Stoic orators, now generally described as follows: "The
virtues of the Stoic style were correctness of language, clearness, conciseness, aptness, ornament that rose above the level of vulgar speech. The
Stoic tendency was toward unimpassioned oratory, marked especially by
the quality of conciseness."[2]

We owe to Morris W. Croll a rather influential interpretation of the
impact of ancient rhetoric on modern stylistic theories and practices. Since
I shall have to refer to this hypothesis repeatedly, the reader will allow
me a few anticipatory notes on the matter. The following points are part
of Croll's conclusions: The baroque 'Atticists' of the seventeenth century
harked back, as their authorities and inspiration, to the Roman 'Atticists'

---

[1] Cf. Francis P. Dinneen, S. J., *An Introduction to General Linguistics* (New York
. . . London, 1967), pp. 70-97.

[2] Cf. J. F. D'Alton, pp. 36, 216-217.
In referring to the Scipionic circle I have placed 'Atticist' within quotation
marks because the term is acceptable in that context only with qualifications. Although Cicero alludes to them once or twice in a way that suggests the use of
the term, the writers of that circle did not think of themselves as Atticists or as
imitating Attic models specifically. But they were interested in purity (or *Latinitas*)
and clarity of style and influenced by Stoic grammatical studies. The soberer use of
the term Attic among modern historians tends to restrict it to Calvus and his
friends in the period from 55-45 B. C. as well as their later Latin imitators, and to
the Greek movement in Rome of which Dionysius of Halicarnassus and Caecilius
of Calacte were the leading members, and which led to the kind of Atticism seen,
e. g., in Aristeides and Lucian in the second century. Asianism, on the other hand,
remains a more general and vague concept. I am thankful to Professor George A.
Kennedy for these points. I must add, however, that the special sense of 'Atticism'
as applied to Seneca's group in the critical tradition established by M. W. Croll
(see below), although generally unfamiliar to classical scholars, is of proven value
in the light of that group's impact on Renaissance and baroque prose.
Cf. G. C. Fiske, "The Plain Style in the Scipionic Circle," in *Classical Studies
in honor of Ch. Forster Smith* (Madison, 1919), pp. 62-105, esp. 62-76.

of the first century A. D. These latter were intimately linked to Stoic thought (Seneca) and to the stylistic theories of the plain style in the curt, occasionally obscure form of Tacitus as well as in Seneca's 'loose' but lucid modes. They opposed themselves to the 'Asianism' of Cicero's grand style. Stimulating as it may appear by virtue of its impressive internal cogency, Croll's picture of complex historico-theoretical relationships presents an initial difficulty, in that it does not take into account the grammatical side of the ancient theories on style, and more specifically, the full-fledged *querelle* of analogists and anomalists.

The Alexandrians, who were at the origin of the analogical approach, had adopted a rather dogmatic stand based on their rationalistic method of analysis. The Stoics, on the other hand, standing at the origin of anomalism, were, may I repeat, empiricists in the area of language and appreciated experience, observation, and the particular facts of actual usage. Herein lay the opposition between Crates' and Aristarchus' schools.[3] Now, in apparent contradiction to Croll's identification of Stoicism (therefore, implicitly, anomalism) with Atticism, a strong inclination among modern philologists remains, ever since Norden's early attempt, to establish a direct rapport between analogists and Atticists, on the one hand, and anomalists and Asianists, on the other. One could graphically represent the problem with the following diagram:

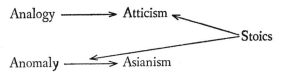

In other words, we may wonder, in what way or sense could the Stoics be at the same time anomalists and Atticists if anomalism normally led toward Asianism, whereas it was analogism which normally led to Atticism?[4] A. Dihle has found, however, that the equation of analogy and

    [3] See H. J. Mette's studies: *De Cratete Mallota seu Pergameno*, diss. (Berlin, 1931); *Sphairopoïïa, Untersuchungen zur Kosmologie des Krates von Pergamon* (Munich, 1936); and, especially, *Parateresis, Untersuchungen zur Sprachtheorie des Krates von Pergamon* (Halle a. S., 1952).
    [4] See E. Norden, *Kunstprosa*[3], I, 184. F. della Corte, *La Filologia latina dalle origini a Varrone* (Torino, 1937), 61-99. E. Castorina, *L'Atticismo nell'evoluzione del pensiero di Cicerone* (Catania, 1952). S. F. Bonner, "Roman Oratory" (1954). P. Giuffrida, in *Maia*, VII (1955). José Guillén, in *Arbor*, XXXI (1955). A. D. Leeman, in *REL* (1955). Albrecht Dihle, "Analogie und Attizismus," *Hermes*,

Atticism is not valid regardless of specific circumstances of time and place, but that it acquires a special meaning in Rome starting in the first century B. C.[5]

By the end of the century the partisans of Asianism had lost much ground. Yet we must take cognizance of the presence in Rome and Greece, at the time of Augustus, of Theodorus of Gadara and his followers, allegedly a brilliant school of Stoically-inclined rhetoricians and literary critics apparently not immune to some sympathies toward Asianism. We shall have to turn our attention to them later on, since the golden booklet *On the Sublime* has been interpreted as possibly an offshoot of that school.

By and large, in the first century of our era the Atticist orientation had become so general that Quintilian could refer to Asianism as a thing of the past and to the Atticists as " by far the best school by universal consent" (XII, x, 16-39, esp. 16-26). And this prevailing taste undoubtedly bore the mark of Stoic notions of style. Yet Quintilian's 'Atticism' was very different from Seneca's, whose style he utterly disliked for its 'baroque' qualities. The real problem here is perhaps that Croll's presentation somewhat transfers back to the first century A. D. a sense of 'Atticism' which was the result of a peculiar reconstruction by seventeenth-century critics. He might have avoided this false impression concerning Seneca's 'Atticism' by stressing the different value of the term in the two widely removed periods, and by pointing out that both Seneca and the Stoics generally were not 'Atticists' at all in more than one respect.

Having merely skimmed over all these delicate questions, one cannot leave unmentioned an aspect of the opposition between rhetorical and

---

LXXXV (1957), 170-205, esp. 202-203. J. Collart, "Analogie et anomalie," in "Varron, Six exposés et discussions par C. O. Brink . . . A. Michel," *Entretiens sur l'antiquité classique IX,* Fondation Hardt, Vandœuvres-Genève, 1962 (Geneva, [1963]), pp. 119-132, followed by discussion, pp. 133-140. G. Calboli, *Studi grammaticali* (Bologna, 1962), esp. p. 227.

[5] Desmouliez has taken a stand on the question of cause and effect between the terms of the equation: "Atticistes parce qu'ils étaient des analogistes? Disons plutôt: analogistes parce qu'ils étaient atticistes." Cf. A. Desmouliez, "Sur la polémique de Cicéron et des atticistes," *Revue des Études Latines,* XXX (1952), 168-185, esp. 172. Cf. G. Calboli, op. cit., p. 226. For some of these and a few other references, see the *bibliographie raisonnée* by J. Collart, "Varron grammairien et l'enseignement grammatical dans l'antiquité romaine: 1934-1963," *Lustrum,* IX (1964, but 1965), 213-241.

philosophical orientation—a battle whose arguments changed remarkably little from the time Socrates opened it till at least the end of the fifteenth century and which bears directly on the notion of the nature of language and the definition of the different modes of speech, or literary styles. The Sophists had offered a unitary view of rhetoric as a science that supposedly developed both the thinking faculty and the expressive faculty together: Gorgias' principle that rhetoric λέγειν ποιεῖ δυνατούς . . . καὶ φρονεῖν (it makes one capable to speak as well as to understand what is being said: Plato, *Gorg.*, 449E) was developed by Isocrates (*Antidosis*, § 277) and eventually assimilated, in its essence, by Cicero, who pointed out in *De oratore* that to deny this principle is tantamount to introducing a *discidium quasi linguae atque cordis*, a sort of dichotomy between our speech and our mind (*De or.* III, xvi, 61). In other words, logic and language could appear to be essentially one and the same, so that the art of reasoning and the art of speech (meaning all linguistic expression) would practically coincide. For Cicero (or rather Crassus, his interlocutor in the dialogue), it was Socrates who laid the foundation for that *discidium* by separating *sapientia* from *eloquentia* and defining philosophy and rhetoric as distinct, mutually exclusive methods. True enough, such a distinction reflected a real state of affairs at his time, in that teachers of eloquence had become abstractly technical and devoid of true virtue and knowledge.

It is not necessary in this context to recall in any detail these controversial issues in the history of rhetoric. They have to do with the delicate interpretation of the true relationship between the third book of the Aristotelian *Rhetoric* and the earlier parts [6] and, consequently, with the distinction between the two contrasting currents, the Sophistic and the genuinely Peripatetic. We shall only briefly concern ourselves with this latter, broader question, since it bears directly on the true place of elocution and *ornatus*, of which our subject is a relevant part.

Rhetoric was born as a *Janus bifrons*, 'two-faced Janus,' since it had a 'logical' side, pertaining to the τέχνη of persuasion, and an aesthetic, 'artistic' side, grounded in the doctrine of *ornatus* as the basic aspect of style and, for the artistically pleasing presentation of the content, in a

---

[6] Cf. Hendrickson, "Origin and Meaning of the Characters of Style," *Am. Journ. of Philol.*, XXVI (1905), 249-290, esp. 254-255. Norden, *Ant. Kunstprosa*, I, 125-126, found the same inconsistency between the *Rhetoric* and other works of Aristotle.

cogent arrangement (*distributio* of the parts of the judiciary oration first proposed, perhaps, by Corax of Syracuse as proem, arguments or ἀγῶνες, and peroration).

But the *ornatus* has been frequently misunderstood, since the best tradition viewed the logical and the aesthetic aspects of rhetoric as inseparable. For the effective style consists of *ornatus* not in the sense of a more or less gratuitous, artificial, and conventional adjunct to the plain, direct, 'natural' expression, but in the sense of any expressive form that the effective use of language will necessarily assume. The insertion of some figures of speech into the grammar course was indicative of the fact that language and style, *langue* and *parole* if we may borrow a modern distinction, were, though rather vaguely, sensed as ultimately inseparable.

In catering to a society plagued by litigation after the establishment of democracy in Syracuse (466 B. C.), Corax started from the point of view of the practicing lawyer. The topic of general probability (εἰκός) which he illustrated, next to the divisions of the speech, served his purpose directly and eminently well. Plato's *Phaedrus* shows the further development of this successful weapon at the hands of Corax's disciple Tisias. The Sophists, however, engrossed as they soon became in success for its own sake, lost track of any essential commitment to intellectual and moral honesty. Formal brilliance and ephemeral effect were given priority above the true and the good. Aristotle took it upon himself to postulate the true and the good as the end of the art of speaking, and accused rhetors of having theretofore concerned themselves mainly with the arousing of emotions. The true aim should be, instead, to prove, or at least seem to prove, your point. Thus rhetoric as the art of persuasion became, for him, the 'popular' branch of logic or, rather, dialectic. Only the master of logic will be truly qualified as master of rhetoric—which assumes that logic be understood broadly, including and even stressing the *topica*. Indeed, the full extent of the realm of rhetoric cannot be properly grasped in its historical tradition without including within it, beyond Aristotle's treatise on Rhetoric, Aristotle's own *Topics* also, since the theory of probable reasoning lies between dialectic and rhetoric or, rather, in both, for different functions. From the vantage point of his ethically-inspired approach, Aristotle, rather than neglecting the psychological or, specifically, emotional element in persuasion, did true justice to it, since the rhetorical side of dialectic does take explicit account of the emotional potentiality of arguments and topics, enthymemes and *exempla*.

Despite the limited direct impact of the Aristotelian treatise on the rhetorical tradition through the centuries, its vigorous reassessment of the art was far more than a noble philosopher's dream. It remained the determined orientation of the most responsible proponents of the art as a solid foundation of paideia, as was the case with Cicero and Quintilian. The popular conception of rhetorical training as concerned only, or chiefly, with brilliance of exposition, empty formalism, and unconcern for the intrinsic validity of the issues at hand, derives from the most common actual practice as exemplified by the Second Sophistic and in times when the literary application was the only task extant, while public oratory was obliterated by changed socio-political conditions. This development does injustice to the authentic part of the tradition.[7]

The most constant features in the systematic treatment of the art of rhetoric, starting with the earliest and most illustrious of the extant treatises, that of Aristotle, down to Martianus Capella (early 5th c. A. D.), consisted of the three kinds or *genera orationis*, the five functions of the orator (*officia oratoris*), and the parts of a speech, *partes orationis*. The kinds or types, which concerned the subject matter or *materia artis*, were: judicial or forensic oratory (*genus iudiciale*, γένος δικανικόν), deliberative (*g. deliberativum*, γένος συμβουλευτικόν or πολιτικόν), panegyrical or epideictic (*g. demonstrativum*, γένος ἐπιδεικτικόν or πανηγυρικόν). The functions were: discovery or invention (*inventio*, εὕρεσις), disposition (*dispositio*, τάξις), elocution or diction (*elocutio*, λέξις), memory (*memoria*, μνήμη), and delivery (*actio*, ὑπόκρισις). The parts, usually six or, in Quintilian, five (*exordium, narratio, probatio, confutatio, conclusio*), do not concern us here. The functions were also called parts (of the art).

With the extinction of freedom in Greece and, later, in Rome, changes occurred on the score of parts as well as kinds, the result being a gradual concentration of emphasis on elocution and the triumph of panegyric— even though the rules of judicial oratory continued to dominate the theory, especially through the five parts of the judicial speech. Both the judicial and deliberative or political kind continued to thrive, but chiefly

[7] The unfortunate neglect of this most vital and relevant aspect of the tradition has prompted a contemporary philosopher to propose a modern theory of argument (a "New Rhetoric") based on what he regards as the true spirit of the rhetorical tradition itself. See Chaim Perelman and L. Olbrechts-Tyteca, *La Nouvelle Rhétorique: Traité de l'argumentation* (2 vols., Paris, 1958). On the extensive discussions occasioned by this work and for modern views on rhetoric see, now, the special issue "Le Istituzioni e la retorica" of *Il Verri*, 35-38 (1970).

in the downgraded form of literary displays and school exercises, usually called (as in the Elder Seneca) *controversiae* and *suasoriae*, respectively (and collectively, *declamationes*).

The restriction of ancient *inventio* was especially impoverishing, and through the Middle Ages it ended in total neglect of that branch and others, with the resulting reduction of rhetoric to the treatment of elocution. The art of speech thus became a sort of stylistics. Not a minor aspect of the humanists' reaction against medieval education and science in the field of rhetoric lay in their reviving the lost or neglected *partes* of the art, first and foremost 'invention,' even though this latter eventually ended up as the topical part of another art, i. e. dialectic.

Elocution is, nevertheless, the part which concerns us, and, specifically, the section thereof that was often labeled: *Elocutionis virtutes et vitia,* which later on became expanded even to cover the basic divisions of elocution as a whole. The identification of specific virtues of style goes back to Aristotle, in whose *Rhetoric* one found, in a rather germinal, non-schematic manner, the notions of correctness (τὸ ἑλληνίζειν, III, v, 1407A), clarity, and appropriateness (σαφήνεια, πρέπον, III, ii, vii, xii; also *Poetics,* xxii, 1458A-B).[8] We must add that clarity was for him the main requisite, the only one truly deserving the name of 'virtue.' When technical treatment had finally become crystallized, possibly under the impulse of Theophrastus, the divisions of elocution were often presented under successive headings best exemplified by Diogenes Laertius' Stoic classification (probably early 3ᵈ c. A. D.). I shall give it with Cicero's corresponding terminology (*De oratore*):[9]

---

[8] See, e. g., the formula λέξεως ἀρετὴ σαφῆ εἶναι, Rhet., III, ii, 1404B. In the passages indicated Aristotle also mentions other qualities of style, and especially what one could render as 'distinction' (variedly called σεμνόν, ξενικόν, or with the negatives τὸ μὴ ἰδιωτικόν, τὸ μὴ ταπεινόν). Generally speaking, clarity is produced by ordinary words, distinction by unusual words: good style is a judicious mixture of both. See Poetics xxii.

[9] For a variant plan, see Clark, *Rhet. in G.-R. Ed.,* 83-84 (83-107 on *elocutio*). Theophrastus' lost work *On Style* seems to lie at the source of this systematic classification, at least in the fourfold division echoed by Cicero, who quoted and used Theophrastus (*Orator* 79). Cf. the fragments published by August Mayer, *Theophrasti περὶ λέξεως libri fragmenta* (Leipzig, 1910), and the reconstruction by Johannes Stroux, *De Theophrasti virtutibus dicendi* (Leipzig, 1912), summarily accepted by Clarke, *Rhetoric at Rome,* p. 6, but challenged by G. M. A. Grube, "Theophrastus as a Literary Critic," *Transactions and Proceedings of the Am. Philol. Ass.,* LXXXIII (1952), 180 ff. See, now, A. Michel, *Rhétorique et philosophie*

Diog. Laert. VII, 59 (Life of Zeno)		De oratore
1) ἑλληνισμός	purity of language, correctness	latine dicere §§25-47
2) σαφήνεια	clarity	plane dicere 48-51
3) συντομία	brevity	
4) πρέπον	appropriateness	apte congruenterque dicere 210-212
5) κατασκευή	distinction through embellishment	ornatus 52-209

Purity or correctness was sometimes called *puritas*, more commonly *Latinitas*, in correspondence to 'hellenismós' (*Graecitas*). The vices corresponding to it were *barbarismus* and *soloecismus*, usually treated, however, within the grammar course. This closeness to the grammatical training (which included the linguistic, exegetic, and critical reading of the good authors) is shared by both the first and the second virtues on our list, so that both the *Rhetorica ad Herennium* and Cicero's *De oratore*, for example, barely touch upon these subjects.[10] We shall see

chez Cicéron (1960), pp. 327 ff. For Quintilian's classification, see *Inst. Or.*, I, v, 1; VIII, Prooemium 31; i, 1-2; ii, 22-24.

[10] In Cicero's *Brutus*, Atticus speaks of Caesar's eloquence as if his style, based on the preoccupation with purity or correctness (one sort of Atticism), did not really concern rhetoric but more properly grammar. His *De analogia* is quoted as *De ratione latine loquendi*, 'on the principles of correct Latinity'; he is said to be the purest user of the Latin tongue, "omnium fere oratorum Latine loqui elegantissime," and to have held that choice of vocabulary is the foundation of eloquence, "verborum dilectum originem esse eloquentiae" (252-253). Purity thus becomes the foundation of oratory, and Caesar strove to restore this now lost purity with the help of an explicit, formal theory: "Solum et quasi fundamentum oratoris vides, locutionem emendatam et Latinam, cuius penes quos laus adhuc fuit, non fuit rationis aut scientiae, sed quasi bonae consuetudinis" (258); . . . "Caesar autem rationem adhibens consuetudinem vitiosam et corruptam pura et incorrupta consuetudine emendat" (261). In other words, in older generations it was inherited, but now it must be learned through grammar (= *litterarum scientia*; see *litteras nesciebat* 259, applied to Titus Flamininus). Caesar is thus praised for *brevitas* and simplicity, "omni ornatu orationis tamquam veste detracta" (262). The text makes it sound as though Caesar himself had separated correctness and eloquence when he praised Cicero in an introductory remark to his own *De analogia*: "Ac si, ut cogitata praeclare eloqui possent, non nulli studio et usu elaboraverunt, cuius te paene principem copiae atque inventorem bene de nomine ac dignitate populi Romani meritum esse existimare debemus, hunc facilem et cotidianum novisse sermonem

how they will be fully absorbed back into the general practice of stylistic analysis in due course of time—but this will not take place before the eighteenth century. Though separated from the others by curricular and disciplinary division of the *artes*, these 'virtues' did not ccasc to bc considered of paramount importance. Quintilian, for one, echoed Aristotle in rating clarity (referred to by him with the more common label of *perspicuitas*) as "the first virtue of style"; he associated it with both *apta conlocatio* and *rectus ordo*, which refer to sentence structure and word order (*Inst.* VIII, Prooemium 31; i, 1-2; ii, 22-24).[11] Quintilian's basic criterion for correctness was usage (that of the cultivated, not that of the majority). He saw this foundation strengthened by the rational confirmation of analogy and etymology, by antiquity, and by the example of good authors, or, to put it in our own terms, by the scientific method, the historical or linguistic approach, and the argument from authority (*Inst.* I, vi).

Aside from their specific nationalistic orientation, 'hellenismos' and *Latinitas* generically meant 'correctness,' and in this non-nationalistic, non-puristic acceptation they were developed by the Stoics as part of their far-reaching grammatico-rhetorical approach to the main question of analogy-anomaly in language.[12]

num pro relicto est habendum?" (253); "And if, to the task of giving brilliant and oratorical expression to their thought, some have devoted unremitting study . . .—wherein we must recognize that you, as almost the pioneer and inventor of eloquence, have deserved well of the name and prestige of Rome—yet are we therefore to look upon a mastery of the easy and familiar speech of daily life as a thing that now may be neglected?" (Hendrickson trans.) Similarly, Quintilian placed the treatment of purity in his Book One, that is within the grammatical part of his *Institutio oratoria,* as he repeats in VIII, i, 2.

[11] Cf. Robins, p. 44 fn.: "Since the time of Aristotle there had developed the conception of the 'correct Greek' ('Ελληνισμός), as against debasements (βαρβαρισμός, σολοικισμός), the care of the Greek language belonging especially to the grammarians and rhetoricians (Lersch, I, 48-50, Steinthal, 365-74). For similar views among the Romans cf. Seneca, *Epist.* III, 95, 65: 'grammatici, custodes latini sermonis.' Some remarks on this point in the general history of language study will be found in Bloomfield, *Language,* Ch. 1."

[12] Morris W. Croll, "'Attic Prose' . . .," p. 85, reduces the Stoic 'virtues' and their Aristotelian ancestry to clearness, brevity, appropriateness. He must admit, with Diogenes Laertius VII, 59, that these were preceded by purity of language, but he merely relegates this detail to a footnote. For he seems to identify Aristotle's purity with ἐλληνισμός and, once it reached Rome, *Latinitas*: hence he claims that it was practically dropped by the 'Attics' of the first century A.D. because it was alien to their Stoic mentality. I believe he is neglecting the more basic sense in order to reduce the term to its nationalistic-puristic application.

'Brevity' was not regularly subsumed under the general group of the virtues, but the Atticist Stoics became so fond of it in the defense of their favorite style, that they first placed the topic of brevity under the heading of the three *genera elocutionis* or *genera dicendi* (types of style or, as the Greeks rather put it, 'characters' of style, χαρακτῆρες τῆς λέξεως) and finally made of it a fifth virtue of style. *Ornatus* and *aptum* were the most treated categories among the virtues.

To the Stoics, as we have seen, language was usage, ξυνθήκη (convention), a νόμος, law, not φύσει, by nature, but by man's arbitrary and unstable decision and collective, implicit agreement. The job of the grammarian-critic in the exercise of his *téchne* was, therefore, not to classify and codify the laws (the favorite task of the Alexandrian analogists, who had no room for *vitia et virtutes*), but to stress the collective character of usage by warning against individual idiosyncrasies in the form of κακίαι τοῦ λόγου: hence the Stoics' favorite relying on the doctrine of κακίαι καὶ ἀρεταὶ τοῦ λόγου, *vitia et virtutes orationis*. Indeed, Crates of Mallos, the Stoic, had prepared the ground for this development through his treatise Περὶ ἀττικῆς διαλέκτου, wherein he is believed to have treated precisely of ἑλληνισμός. Yet, the same individual idiosyncrasies which were unacceptable from the linguistic point of view, could be part of the literary tradition when used functionally, i. e. for an acceptable specific reason, by recognized poets. This gave rise, in the grammatical treatises, to the counterparts of barbarisms and solecisms, namely metaplasms and schemata.

The emphasis on logic as the main exercise of the grammarian-critic and on stylistics within the linguistic concern is the trademark of the Stoic; this is the direction he favors rather than the development of morphology as such.[13] Similarly, in the realm of rhetoric, the strongly moralistic motivation of the Stoic moved him toward evaluation, and nothing in the *téchne* perhaps lent itself so well to the exercise of his value judgments as the theory of stylistic virtues and vices.[14]

We are also concerned here with the much-debated question of the *genera elocutionis*, which could be referred to both the category of *aptum* and that of *ornatus*. Plato's and Aristotle's response to the Sophistic

---

[13] See A. Pagliaro, *Sommario di linguistica arioeuropea*, esp. the acute summary on p. 15 (on the *Cratylus*) and p. 24.

[14] On the contrast between the linguistic and the stylistic orientations of the two schools of Alexandria and Pergamon (Stoic), and their repercussions down to the fifteenth century, see A. Scaglione, "The Humanist as Scholar and Politian's Conception of the *Grammaticus*," *Studies in the Renaissance*, VIII (1961), 49-70.

paideia had sharply opposed the search for truth (which underlies the method and style of science or philosophy) to the preoccupation with effect (typical of the political or judicial orator facing audiences). Based as it was, especially, on that response, the technical distinction of kinds of style, *genera elocutionis*, appears to have originated with Theophrastus, who specifically distinguished the straightforward or 'plain' language of argumentation and factual exposition from an elaborate, 'ornate' style more suitable to the expression and production of emotion.[15] The diverging modes of 'dialectic' and 'rhetoric' were thus potentially categorized. The partisans of the former mode, however, soon started to insist on the principle that the plain style could, in its own way, be just as 'effective' as the grand style, though it operated by reasoning and persuasion rather than by arousing the emotions. And it was far from 'simple,' since it possessed its own array of figures and devices appealing to the rhetorically-minded analyst of fine speech. The doctrine of style genera is related to that of composition since the taste for particular types of sentence movement is directly affected by the variety of 'grand' or 'plain' style the author desires, and the question of word order is, even down to the modern age, constantly under the influence of the clash between the dialectical and the rhetorical formation, the appeal to reason and the appeal to emotion.[16]

Allowing for each author's peculiar variations, in the traditional schema

---

[15] On the doctrine of the *genera dicendi* and its derivation from Theophrastus see the discussion in George A. Kennedy, "Theophrastus and Stylistic Distinctions," *Harvard Studies in Classical Philology*, LXII (1957), 93 ff. and, again, Kennedy's discussion and rich bibliography in his *The Art of Persuasion*, pp. 278-282 and fn. 25, pp. 278-279. Kennedy challenges the once authoritative study by Hendrickson, "Origin and Meaning . . ." (1905), who denied that Theophrastus had originated the style genera. See, also, G. M. A. Grube, "Thrasymachus, Theophrastus, and Dionysius of Halicarnassus," *Am. Journal of Philol.*, LXXIII (1952), 251-267, and Grube, *Greek . . . Critics*, pp. 107-109. Grube assigns to Theophrastus no more than the notion of a threefold distinction in levels of diction: the poetic language of Gorgias (grand), the simple or plain of Lysias, and the middle one which he attributed to Thrasymachus. Also, briefly on the negative, Clarke, *Rhetoric at Rome*, p. 6.

[16] The first two books of Aristotle's *Rhetoric*, systematizing the ideas of Socrates and Plato, were the starting point of subsequent 'modern' theories of style in that they worked out for the first time a theory of rhetoric as prose composition "not on the basis of the susceptibilities of audiences, and the aural effect of language, but . . . (of) the processes of reasoning and in strict relation with the science of logic." "Speaking roughly, we may say that the *Rhetoric* treats for the first time the art of writing, as opposed to the art of speaking." Croll, "'Attic Prose,'" p. 86.

ornatus, the third among the four basic virtues, is subdivided into figures of speech and composition or general arrangement of words.[17] Figures are usually classified as figures of thought (*figurae sententiarum* or *schemata dianoias*) and figures of word, sound, or elocution (*figurae elocutionis vel verborum* or *schemata lexeos*, sometimes *schemata lógou*). Sometimes, however, these latter include the arrangements of words, so that *compositio* is not formally set aside as a major subdivision of *ornatus*.[18] A more elaborate mode of classification [19] separates choice of single words from choice of groups, the former being split into choice of vocabulary (*electio*) and attribution of special meanings to words (*tropi*), the latter being split into figures and composition, according to the following overall paradigm:

ELOCUTIONIS VIRTUTES ET VITIA:

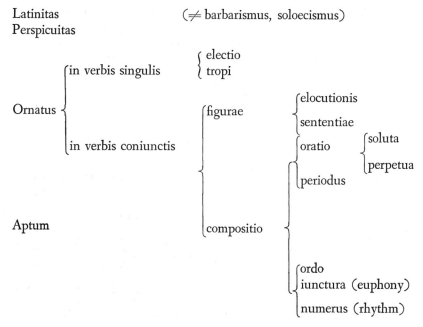

Latinitas   (≠ barbarismus, soloecismus)
Perspicuitas

in verbis singulis — electio / tropi

Ornatus —
     in verbis coniunctis

figurae —
     elocutionis
     sententiae
     oratio / soluta, perpetua
     periodus

Aptum

compositio —
     ordo
     iunctura (euphony)
     numerus (rhythm)

---

[17] Cf., for instance, Quint. VIII, iii, 59: "Sunt inornata et haec, quod male dispositum est, quod male figuratum, quod male collocatum. . . ."

[18] Word arrangement is thus classified as part of *figurae verborum* in the first ed. of Lausberg's *Elemente*, but in the second ed., as well as in Lausberg's own *Handbuch*, it is placed under a separate heading parallel to that of *figurae*.

[19] This further mode, but without the *tropi*, is represented in the second ed. of Lausberg's *Elemente*.

The basic outline of our study will be more easily followed by keeping in mind the subdivisions of *compositio* in this paradigm.

When matters pertaining to *compositio* were simply treated among the figures (as, for instance, in Martianus Capella's *Rhetoric*, to cite a late and, for the later tradition, somewhat conclusive authority), the simplest manner of organization was the following: On the assumption that the figures of words can be distinguished from those of thought in that a change in word order necessarily alters or destroys the former but not the latter (Quintilian's test: *Inst.* IX, i, 17), all questions of composition would be included in the figures of word; sentence structure would then be defined by distinguishing between periodic and non-periodic sequences; finally the characteristic reciprocal relationships between parts of the sentence (mostly of the periodic variety) would be indicated. This corresponded chiefly to the famous Gorgianic figures, the earliest and most characteristic artifices in word arrangement and composition, aiming at psychological effect through melodic, acoustic devices. These figures were four: ἰσόκωλον, equality of members, when the clause-like units within the sentence are equal in length (e. g., classem speciosissimam et robustissimam instruxit, / exercitum pulcherrimum et fortissimum legit, / sociorum maximam et fidelissimam manum comparavit); πάρισον, equality of sound, when the lengths are only relatively equivalent, but words in corresponding positions in different members correspond to one another in morphology or in sound (Cicero: causa quae sit, videtis: nunc quid agendum sit, considerate); ὁμοιόπτωτον, when the case-endings (πτῶσις = case) of words closing the cola or clause-like units are identical or quasi-identical (huic socios vestros criminanti et ad bellum vos cohortanti et omnibus modis ut in tumultu essetis molienti); ὁμοιοτέλευτον, when the endings in such words are identical or at least similar in sound, though not in morphological value.[20] To these and other figures were usually added the most elaborate artifice of all, the παρόμοιον,[21] parallelism in sound, i. e. assonance at beginning or

[20] Cf. Capella in Halm, xxxix-xli, pp. 479-483. Diodorus Siculus (XII, 53, 4) attributed antithesis, too, to Gorgias: "He was the first who made use of schemata which were far-fetched and characterized by artificiality: antithesis, isocolon, parison, homoeoteleuton and others of that sort. . . ." Engelbert Drerup, "Die Anfänge der rhetorischen Kunstprosa," *Jahrbücher für Klassische Philologie*, Supplementband XXVII, 2 (1902), 219-351, interpreted the taste for antithesis as the fountainhead for all the figures used by Gorgias: see pp. 258-259, and 260 ff. specifically on sýnthesis onomáton.

[21] The current Latin equivalent was *paromoeon* (which includes what we are

end of cola, or even throughout them (alliteration); the πολύπτωτον, repetition of stems with different suffixes (particularly popular in the Middle Ages as *figura etymologica*); and, last but not least, the ἀντίθετον (in pace ad vexandos cives acerrimus, in bello ad expugnandos hostes inertissimus), considered here for its value in contributing a dramatic type of symmetry.

Somewhat more methodically, and with the exception of hyperbaton which he placed among the *tropi*, Quintilian divided the *figurae verborum* into: (1) variations of syntax (*Inst.* IX, iii, 3-27); (2) modes of iteration (28-65); (3) word-play (66-73); (4) balance (*paria, similia*), and antithesis (74-86). The last group, the one especially cultivated by the Sophists, included the Γοργίεια σχήματα, which Quintilian introduced as follows: "Magnae veteribus curae fuit gratiam dicendi paribus et contrariis acquirere. Gorgias in hoc immodicus: copiosus, aetate utique prima, Isocrates fuit. Delectatus est his etiam M. Tullius" (74). He traditionally proceeded to divide balance into πάρισον, ὁμοιοτέλευτον, ὁμοιόπτωτον, ἰσόκωλον, then went on to treat ἀντίθετον. All of these figures, with or without 'antithesis,' have usually been subsumed under the heading of 'balance,' as by Quintilian.

All syntactic aspects of sentence movement were often treated under the heading of *concinnitas* ('being well-ordered, elegant'), basically the category implying structural symmetry. In its most specific sense, *parallelismus* (παραλληλισμός) could refer to the perfect symmetry of the isocolon.

If Gorgias was the first to theorize and exemplify the virtues of methodic composition,[22] Isocrates was praised as the first great practical master of it, whose lasting influence (not to mention the 'Attic' Demosthenes) was felt even on his later critics, such as Dionysius of Halicarnassus, or on Latin orators, including Cicero himself.[23] Isocrates was the

---

wont to call alliteration). Capella uses the term *homoeoprophoron* (ch. xxxiii, § 514: Halm, pp. 474-475—Halm's *homoeprophoron* is a misprint).

[22] Of course, such far-reaching practices cannot be the invention of any single writer or theorist: Norden, *Kunstprosa* I, 25-29, pointed out that Gorgianic figures were in use in both verse and prose before Gorgias, and rhythmical prose before Thrasymachus.

[23] "Balanced clauses, antitheses, similar endings, though he [Isocrates] was not their discoverer but only the skilful user of what had already been discovered, he put his mind to, and also to copiousness, rhythm, sentence-movement, sonorousness. These things prepared the way to the elocution of Demosthenes, who was, to be sure, a pupil of Isaeus, but a disciple of Isocrates. . . ." Philostratus I, xvii, 503-504 in W. C. Wright, ed., Philostratus and Eunapius, *The Lives of the Sophists*, with an Eng. trans. (London, Engl., and Cambridge, Mass., Loeb Lib., 1952²), p. 50. The trans. is mine. See, also, Baldwin, *Medieval R. and P.*, p. 6.

original master of the smooth or florid style (γλαφυρὰ, ἀνθηρὰ ἁρμονία), characterized by the 'hedonistic' application of the rhythmic and acoustic resources of composition according to the verbal figures, Gorgianic and others. His sentences were fastidiously balanced and methodically periodic. It was the kind of oratory *in sole et pulvere*, to say it with Cicero, which could ideally cater to popular, mass audiences. It was, indeed, a 'popular' art. This audio-oral approach ran directly counter to the taste for the visual and intellectual approach which became embodied in the 'Attic' current and which, starting once again in the seventeenth century, remained essentially prevalent through modern times.

Both First and Second Sophistic tended to stress composition above all else; paradoxically, this very emphasis could cause some confusion in the use of the traditional terminology. Τάξις, which originally meant *dispositio*, the second major division of rhetoric presiding over the arrangement of the elements 'discovered' in the process of *inventio*, is a term used by Philostratus for nothing more than *compositio*, σύνθεσις, since this is all he specifically treated. His term ξυνθήκη [24] also does not extend beyond the sentence, as a perfect equivalent of σύνθεσις, just as νόημα means *sententia*, here understood as the material content of the periodic sentence. In praising Isocrates for his "brilliant composition," ἡ ξυνθήκη λαμπρά, he specifically refers to his handling of rhythm, "for thought after thought (νόημα) concludes upon a balanced period." [25] The fact is thus confirmed that the Sophists had little explicit consciousness of overall composition in the sense of organic structure or plot.

The actual distribution of subject matter by the individual *technigraphi* was subject to greater fluctuations than in other technical disciplines. Consequently any organization of the field into something approaching a coherent, general and detailed system, necessary and expedient though it may be for our own orientation in such a scattered and prolific discipline, is bound to be arbitrary. This is also true in our case. In stressing the distinction between figures of sound and figures of thought (or wit), modern students have often regarded emphasis on the former as characteristic of the Sophistic tradition, emphasis on the latter, of Atticism and Stoicism. This neat division is useful and illuminating. Yet we must

[24] This term is reported by Lausberg in his index, and in the more common form συνθήκη, but without further elaboration.
[25] Philostratus, *The Lives of the Sophists*, I, xvii, 505 (p. 54 in Wright's ed.). Cf. Baldwin, *M. R. and P.*, pp. 20-21.

not overlook the wide variations and the general lack of comprehensive definitions among the actual treatises extant. The *Rhetorica ad Herennium,* for one, placed the *sententia* (conceived as apophthegm, pithy or witty saying, the chief figure of thought in Croll's plan) among the figures of word (IV, xvii). On a more general level, whatever referred to sentence rhythm could be treated either within the figures or, more systematically, as part of composition. However this may be, whether or not figures and composition were kept distinct and separate, as the two parts of *ornatus* pertaining to groups of words they were ideally interrelated. We will have to keep this fact in mind, and from time to time refer to the theories of figures according to the *genera elocutionis* in order to see in a better perspective what goes on in the following section. Our proper study here is, then, the theory of composition which, let us note, has never received until rather recent times the degree of attention that was commensurate with its obvious importance within the system of rhetoric. One part of it, however, namely the doctrine of harmony and especially rhythm, has been studied extensively and rather satisfactorily. This part I shall, therefore, not treat directly, while I shall concentrate on the remainder, which happens to cover the genuinely syntactical aspect of style.

But before we proceed with our investigation, I should point out that in their way of applying the technical categories the literary critics often used a method of analysis in which composition played a significant role. One of their typical formulas consisted of proceeding through the four stages of *inventio, dispositio, dictio, compositio.* The first two stages were supposed to cover content (πραγματικὸς τόπος), the other two, form or style (λεκτικὸς τόπος), each group being analogously organized by tackling single items first (*inventio* = single topics, *dictio* = single words), their combinations next.

B. SENTENCE STRUCTURE

I. A Systematic Presentation

Compositio,[1] also called *structura,* is the Greeks' σύνθεσις, which studies the relationship or, rather, the structural order of the parts of the sentences,

[1] The following is partly based on Lausberg's masterful manuals: see *Elemente*

hence primarily an aspect of syntax (an aspect, as we have seen, never treated by grammarians), but seen from the rhetorician's particular vantage

(1949), §§ 48-66; *Elemente* (1963), 448-463; *Handbuch*, I, §§ 911-1054, but esp. 911-953, pp. 455-471.

Since these three texts do not correspond to one another in treatment, I have chosen and merged from all three the material that appears to be representative of the prevailing ancient views, with some additions and modifications from other standard surveys of the field as mentioned (Baldwin, Curtius, Croll, Clark, etc.). I have omitted all that is not directly relevant to the problems of the present study, and added source material that appeared useful and appropriate.

Generally speaking, the disposition of subject matter in Lausberg's *Handbuch* fairly corresponds to the second ed. of his *Elemente*, not to the first. In this second ed. the discussion of types of sentence structures is close to the *Handbuch*, but in abridged form, although it contains rich examples from French and English in addition to the classical ones of the *Handbuch*. The first ed. developed the syntactic structures to greater length (§§ 48-50, 1st ed., are rejected to the end of the 2nd, in small print, §§ 450; 452; 455, IIA—pp. 147, 148, 150). The second part of composition beginning with *ordo* is succinctly treated in the *Handbuch*, but has no real equivalent in the *Elemente*, where there is, in its stead, a brief "phonetic" section, mainly on *clausulae* (see 1949 ed., §§ 50-51; 1963 ed., §§ 457-463). I must add that the whole arrangement of *figurae* in *Elemente*, 1949, seems rather arbitrary. The most serious gap in Lausberg's sources—an odd one at that—is the absence of Dionysius of Halicarnassus under the headings we are considering.

The chief sources for the ancient treatment of *compositio* are the following (most of them also used by Lausberg).

1. Alexander, *Perì schemáton* (Spengel, *Rhetores Graeci* III, 1856, pp. 7 ff.), esp. pp. 27-28.

2. Anonymous, *Perì schemáton* (first in the series of three treatises with that heading successively edited in Spengel, III, pp. 110 . . . , 171 . . . , 174 . . .), esp. pp. 113, 157.

3. Anonymous, *Téchne rhetoriké* (Spengel I, 1894, 352 ff.), p. 395.

4. Anonymous, *Perì hýpsous* (see Loeb ed. in 11. below and other eds. passim).

5. Aquila Romanus, *De figuris sententiarum et elocutionis* (Halm, *Rhetores Latini Minores*, pp. 22-37), §§ 18-19, pp. 27-28 (also §§ 20-48 on *figurae elocutionis*).

6. Aristeides, *Perì politikoû kaì apheloûs lógou* (Spengel II, 1854, 457 ff.), esp. p. 507. Also available as Aelius Aristides' *Téchne rhetoriké* in *Aristidis . . . libri rhetorici II*, ed. W. Schmid (Leipzig, 1926): see pp. 63-65, §§ 167-173.

7. Aristotle, *Rhetoric* III, ix, 1-3 and 5-9.

8. Auctor ad Herennium (ed. H. Caplan, 1954), esp. IV, xix.

9. *Carmen de figuris vel schematibus* (Halm, pp. 63-70), vv. 4-12.

10. Cicero, *Brutus* viii, esp. § 34.
    De oratore III, xlviii, 171-198, esp. 186.
    Orator lxi, §204—lxvii, 226.

11. Demetrius, *Perì hermeneías* (Spengel III, 257 ff., and the Loeb Class. Libr. vol. Aristotle *The Poetics*, 'Longinus' *On the Sublime* . . . H. Fyfe, Demetrius *On Style* . . . W. Rhys Roberts: London, Eng.—Cambridge, Mass., 1953, 294 ff.), I, 1-29; 34-35.

point, namely one which transcends the grammatical criteria of *recte dicere* to rise to the level of *bene dicere*.[2] The major authority on this subject, Dionysius of Halicarnassus (taught at Rome in the late first century B. C.), posited ἐκλογή (*electio*, choice of vocabulary) and σύνθεσις as the two parts of style, and considered the latter *more* important than the former.[3]

Composition was treated from the two viewpoints of sentence structure and word order. The theory of the sentence took into consideration, last, the periodic style, first, the non-periodic style, which often could be further distinguished into *oratio soluta* and *oratio perpetua*. The former of these, διαλελυμένη λέξις, defined sentences made of casual series of phrases and clauses, usually artless and arbitrarily juxtaposed, as characteristic of spoken language and of its imitation in informal epistolary style.[4] It could be used artistically in the plain style when *brevitas* and life-like effects were wanted. One of the traditional precepts to achieve

12. Dionysius of Halicarnassus, *Perì synthéseos* (ed. W. Rhys Roberts).

13. C. Chirius Fortunatianus, *Artis rhetoricae l. III* (Halm, pp. 79-134), III, §§10-12, pp. 126-128.

14. Hermogenes (*Opera*, ed. H. Rabe, Leipzig, 1913), *Perì ideón lógou*, pp. 213-413, passim; also *Perì methódou deinótetos*, pp. 429-431 "on hyperbaton."

15. Isidorus Hispalensis (Lindsay), ii, 18.

16. Longinus, *Téchne rhetoriké* (Spengel I, 179 ff.), p. 193.

17. Martianus Capella, *Liber de arte rhetorica* (Halm, pp. 449-492), ch. xxxix, §§526-530 (also ch. xl on the main *figurae elocutionis*).

18. Quintilian, II, xx, 7; VIII, ii, 22; vi, 62-67; IX, iv, 19-32 and 58-60 and 116 and 122-130; X, i, 79 (but all of IX, iv, 1-147 is concerned with *compositio*).

19. *Rhetorica ad Alexandrum*, ed. H. Rackham (London, Eng.–Cambridge, Mass., 1937), ch. xxiv.

20. Rufinus, *Versus . . . de compositione et de metris oratorum* (Halm, pp. 575-584).

21. Sacerdos Grammaticus (Keil VI, pp. 427-495), 459.

22. St. Augustine, *De Doctrina Christiana*, Book IV, esp. chs. vii, xvii-xxviii.

23. C. Iulius Victor, *Ars rhetorica* (Halm, pp. 371-448), ch. xxii, p. 439, ll. 20-31.

[2] Lack of composition was designated as κακοσύνθετον. Cf. Quint., VIII, iii, 59: "Sunt inornata et haec: quod male dispositum, id ἀνοικονόμητον, quod male figuratum, id ἀσχημάτιστον, quod male conlocatum, id κακοσύνθετον vocant."

[3] This striking judgment was underlined as early as 1844 by H. Weil in his fundamental linguistic study of word order.

[4] Aquila 18, in Halm, *Rhetores Latini Minores*, p. 27: "Oratio . . . soluta, nulla inter se necessitate numerorum neque composita membris quibusdam vel determinata certa circumscriptione verborum; ea plerumque in sermone assiduo et in epistolis utimur. . . . Interponitur autem et iudicialibus orationibus, ubi aliquid simile et proximum sermoni volumus effingere." Also Quint. IX, iv, 19-21.

clearness came from Aristotle (who used it in the context of *hellenismos*: *Rhet.* III, v), and amounted to a caveat against the abuse of *oratio soluta* by the unskilled: Avoid overlong suspensions of thought through abuse of weakly connected or frankly parenthetical insertions.

Oratio perpetua, εἰρομένη λέξις (= ordered by successive, coordinated alignment) or διηρημένη ἑρμηνεία (= fragmented, chopped-up style), consists of consciously coordinated sequences where the natural order of ideas is immediately reflected by the order of the corresponding linguistic elements in semantic and syntactic linearity. Its syntactic trademark is parataxis, with a limited use of hypotaxis in such relatively simple forms as relative clauses. Instead of being organized around a center, with accessory notions radiating out like the branches from a trunk, the intellectual content of the sentence is exposed in straight, successive articulation. There is a chronological beginning but not an ideal end, to be anticipated through a degree of active suspense. It is becoming to the historian and to descriptive prose as well.[5] One is reminded of Aristotle's singling out of Herodotus to exemplify the disorganic character of archaic narrative prose (*Rhet.* III, ix, 2). Likewise the nervous, *coupé* articulations preferred by some adherents of the plain style, especially in the first centuries B. C. and A. D. in Rome, were branded by critics with such derogatory terms as *fracta compositio*, or *disiuncta*.[6]

---

[5] Martianus Capella, *De rhetorica* xxxix, §526 in Halm, p. 479: " (εἰρομένη λέξις) ita conectitur, ut superiorem elocutionem semper proxima consequatur: et historiae convenit et narrationi, et non conversum neque circumscriptum eloquendi genus desiderat, sed fusum atque continuum." See also, for the source, Aquila 18 in Halm, p. 27: "oratio perpetua . . . ita conectitur, ut superiorem elocutionem semper proxima sequatur, atque ita seriem quandam significatus rerum explicet. . . ."

[6] Cf., for *fracta compositio*, the Elder Seneca's *Suasoria* II, 23, with reference to the broken sentences of Arellius Fuscus. Tacitus' *Dialogus de oratoribus*, 18 refers to a now lost correspondence between the chief Atticist Calvus and the pro-Atticist Brutus on the one hand, and Cicero on the other. While Calvus branded Cicero's style as "loose and slack" (*SOLUTUM et enervem*) and Brutus dubbed it worse than "feeble and emasculated" (*FRACTUM atque elumbem*)—in a curious perversion of the terms more technically used against the non-periodic style—, Cicero countered with an equally damaging "tedious and disjointed" (*otiosum atque DISIUNCTUM*) addressed to Brutus (and "bloodless and worn," *exsanguem et attritum*, for Calvus). Cf. G. L. Hendrickson, "Cicero's Correspondence with Brutus and Calvus on Oratorical Style," *Am. Journal of Philol.*, XLVII (1926), 234-258.

Quintilian, VIII, iii, 57, also defined *compositio fracta* as the breaking up of periods into exceedingly small commata, and regarded it as a *vitium* by excess against *ornatus*. Cf. Lausberg, *Handbuch*, §1073.

Quintilian advised the orator to make good use of the *oratio concisa*
(somewhat related to the *soluta*) in the dialogue parts of his speech and in
the *argumentatio*, whereas the *oratio perpetua* was adapted to the mono-
logue and the *narratio*.[7] Indeed, we may wish to hark back to Socrates'
polemic against Gorgias, to his defense of straightforwardness of philosophic ('plain' or 'loose') style to which the *o. soluta* seems well suited
as the style of dialectic interchange, as against the sustained, elaborate,
but unwieldy and ultimately deceptive rhetorical style of continued
oratory. True enough, we do not have exact equivalences here; contextual differences may intervene as we move from the syntactic to the
rhetorical and logical levels. The rhetorical categories are so broad and
abstract that they seldom fit any specific individual style. The style
postulated by philosophers never exactly corresponded to any pattern
accepted and described by the rhetoricians.

Finally, we come to the periodic style. This was the most cherished
flower in the rhetorician's garden, yet we must not infer that it was unconditionally and indiscriminately seen as a summit of the art. The rule of
aptum, καιρός, forbad such a sweeping conclusion: not only is the *periodus*
not suitable for all kinds of writing, but even in the appropriate place it
must never be used exclusively and in a prolonged way. For the acme
of the art lies in the clever mixing of all compositional styles, and satiety
arises inevitably from clinging too long to the same formula.[8] Every
schoolboy was familiar with this outstanding piece of advice—which had a
longer life than ancient rhetoric: many a college composition book for the
English language, among others, still repeats it to this date.

The period is an organic, membrated whole, to wit a semantic and
syntactic sequence in which the constituents are differentiated yet organ-

---

[7] It must be noted, however, that the traditional distinction between *soluta* and
perpetua was often vague and ambiguous. Quintilian, for one, apparently beclouds
the issue by recalling Zeno's famous dictum of the open and closed fist, and hereby
applying the term *oratio perpetua* to the orator's speech ("perpetua, quae rhetorice
dicitur"), *concisa* to the dialectician's (II, xx, 7).

[8] Cf. Cic., *Or.*, lxi-lxii, 207-209: "In history and epideictic oratory, it is desirable
to have everything done in the periodic style of Isocrates and Theopompus, so that
the language runs on as if enclosed in a circle until it comes to an end with each
phrase complete and perfect. . . . But this style of prose is not to be taken over
bodily into forensic speeches, nor is it utterly to be rejected. If you use it constantly . . . it takes the feeling out of the delivery . . . and utterly destroys the
impression of sincerity." Trans. H. M. Hubbell (Cicero, *Brutus, Orator*, Loeb
Cl. Libr.).

ized according to their unified functions toward a common end. This type of sentence is designated in Latin by sundry equivalents of περίοδος (='rounded'): cf. Cic., Or. lxi, 204: "in . . . circuitu illo orationis, quem Graeci περίοδον, nos tum ambitum, tum circuitum, tum comprehensionem aut continuationem aut circumscriptionem dicimus." Quintilian prefers the more direct ambitus or circumductum (IX, iv, 22). It gives rise to a style that is called λέξις or ἑρμηνεία κατεστραμμένη ('compacted': cf. Aristotle, Rhet. 1409A; Demetrius I, 12) and by Quintilian oratio vincta atque contexta and connexa series (here Quintilian recognizes only two types of structure, this and the soluta: IX, iv, 19). The period is characterized by its 'roundness,' since the circle is as symbolic of it as the line was of oratio perpetua. To a basically analytic and cumulative process there succeeds a basically synthetic and climactic one. This is achieved by a sort of suspense whereby everything in it tends toward the end: before the end is reached everything seems to be left hanging (Isid., Et. II, 18, 2: adhuc pendet oratio). In other words, the conclusion of the o. perpetua is regulated by the content, whereas the conclusion of the period is regulated by the form. These facts were already clearly recognized by Aristotle when he remarked that elocution (λέξις) can be either 'loose' and continuous (εἰρομένη) and united by conjunctions (τῷ συνδέσμῳ μία), or 'compact' (κατεστραμμένη), namely unperiodic or periodic.[9]

---

[9] Arist., Rhet., III, ch. ix, 1409 A-B: λέγω δὲ εἰρομένην, ἣ οὐδὲν ἔχει τέλος καθ' αὑτήν, ἂν μὴ τὸ πρᾶγμα λεγόμενον τελειωθῇ; . . . λέγω δὲ περίοδον λέξιν ἔχουσαν ἀρχὴν καὶ τελευτὴν αὐτὴν καθ' αὑτὴν καὶ μέγεθος εὐσύνοπτον . . . etc. See Ch. S. Baldwin, A. R. and P., pp. 27-30. In this context, one must keep in mind the problem of conflict between the treatment of rhetorical matter from a basically traditional viewpoint in Book III and the program stated in Books I-II in polemic against the amoral emotionalism and the empirical technicalities of the sophistic manuals. The difficult solution of this question has been part of a conjectural reconstruction of Aristotle's evolution and of the genesis of his writings. Cf. Werner Jaeger, Aristotle: The Fundamentals of the History of his Development, trans. R. Robinson (Oxford, 1934); Friedrich Solmsen, "Die Entwicklung der aristotelischen Logik und Rhetorik," Neue Philologische Untersuchungen, 4 (Berlin, 1929); Felix Grayeff, "The Problem of the Genesis of Aristotle's Text," Phronesis, I (1956), 105-122.
 The doctrine of the period and its divisions, colon and comma as indicated below, was Peripatetic. For a careful and up-to-date analysis of the whole theory of figures and style in Aristotle's Rhet. III see G. Kennedy, The Art of Persuasion, pp. 103-114. With particular reference to the chapter on periodicity, which Kennedy asserts has been generally misunderstood, see T. B. L. Webster, Art and Literature in Fourth Century Athens (London, 1906), pp. 75 ff.; G. A. Kennedy, "Aristotle on the Period" (1958); and most recently Guido Morpurgo Tagliabue, Linguistica e

The former, which he compared to the dithyrambic preludes, is apt for narrative prose, as in Herodotus: " it has no end in itself and only stops when the sense is complete." Because it is endless, it is unpleasant, " for all wish to have the end in sight." Only the latter (which he compared to the antistrophes of ancient poets) is suitable for oratory because each diction (sentence) thereby acquires " a beginning and an end in itself and a magnitude which can be easily grasped. Such sentence movement is both satisfying to the ear and easily followed by the mind; satisfying as being the opposite of endless and as giving the hearer the sense of always having hold of something . . . ; easily followed . . . because periodic diction has number ($\dot{\rho}\upsilon\theta\mu\acute{o}s$). . . ." He had elsewhere emphasized the rhythmic character of good diction, and now he was ready to enter into technical details: " A period is either in members ($\kappa\hat{\omega}\lambda\alpha$) or simple. Composed in members, it . . . makes a rounded whole and yet it is distinct in its parts." It is simple when made up of one member. Members should be neither too long nor too short.[10]

The basic implicit law of the period is, then, one of progressive or ascending movement. In particular, the procedure often identified by linguists under the name of ' law of the growing sections ' (" Gesetz der wachsenden Glieder ") applies here, to the effect that the longest, at least the weightiest ' colon ' or periodic section comes at the end, and must be such as to complete the sentence semantically and logically by summarizing and integrating, as it were, all the preceding. Demetrius imaginatively transferred the concept to the athlete's arena; he found Aristotle's definition good and fitting " for the very use of the word ' period' implies that there has been a beginning at one point and there will be an ending at another, and that we are hastening toward a definite goal as runners do when they leave the starting place." (*On Style*, I, 11—Roberts trans.)

Formally speaking, the circular unity of the period can be achieved

---

stilistica di Aristotele (Rome, Edizioni dell'Ateneo, 1967), esp. pp. 226-236, with interesting analysis of broad systematic implications.

[10] Arist., *Rhet.*, III, ix, 1409B. Morpurgo Tagliabue, op. cit., p. 227, underlines the passages " easily grasped . . . ," " easily followed . . . ," as implying a process of anticipation as well as memorization. Aristotle exactly says: $\epsilon\dot{\upsilon}\mu\alpha\theta\dot{\eta}s$ $\delta\grave{\epsilon}$ $\ddot{o}\tau\iota$ $\epsilon\dot{\upsilon}\mu\nu\eta\mu\acute{o}\nu\epsilon\upsilon\tau\sigma s$, ' easily learned because easily remembered '—1409B. Later on (pp. 230-231), the same scholar states that the $\epsilon\dot{\iota}\rho\sigma\mu\acute{e}\nu\eta$ $\lambda\acute{e}\xi\iota s$ may be viewed as coinciding with what we call parataxis, while the $\kappa\alpha\tau\epsilon\sigma\tau\rho\alpha\mu\mu\acute{e}\nu\eta$, but less so, may correspond to hypotaxis.

through the employment of such structural devices as the antithesis, which serves this formal purpose excellently because by its nature it distinguishes and opposes only to bind together more effectively and dramatically. (When the French writers of the seventeenth and eighteenth century will have discarded most of the structural features of the period, they will retain the antithesis and exploit it to the fullest for its intuitive unifying value; indeed, the methodical extension of this device will, as it were, compensate for the other 'losses.' A similar evolution is observable in English. Compare the classic example of sentence 'balance" from Pope: "To err is human, to forgive, divine.")

The antithesis as a basic device for structural balance may well have been the earliest invention of rhetorical practice and is probably characteristic of the earliest formal style of Greek art prose, preceding Gorgias' imitation of poetic, verse-like movement and Thrasymachus' adoption of rhythms.[11] When, after those early masters, the full-fledged periodic style came to fruition, we recognize the antithesis (which Quintilian latinized as *contrapositio*) as really a conspicuous case of a basic law underlying the dynamics of the period: the 'cola' or constituent parts of the period are interrelated by an inner tension in which the form can reflect the contrast between the contents, the language can mirror the thought. Aristotle dubbed the sharper variety ἀντικειμένη λέξις (locution by antithesis—cf. Demetrius, I, 22: ἐξ ἀντικειμένων κώλων περίοδοι), as distinct from the milder variety of διῃρημένη λέξις (locution by distinction).[12]

Syntactically speaking, the transformation of an *oratio perpetua* into a *periodus* is essentially a matter of subordinating the logically or factually secondary. The narrative sequence: "homines defoderunt in terram . . . ignemque circumposuerunt, ita interfecerunt" will become a period if

---

[11] Cf. Hollingsworth's and Kenyan's studies of antithesis in the Greek orators and historians. Also, on the mental processes implied in the earliest uses of antithesis, Ben Edwin Perry, "The Early Greek Capacity of Viewing Things Separately," *Transactions and Proceedings of the Am. Philological Assoc.*, LXVIII (1937), 403-427. For early discussions and examples of formal antitheses in Aristotle and *Rh. ad Al.*, see following fn.

[12] Ar., *Rhet.* III, ix, 7-8, 1409B-1410A, with examples, and *Rhetorica ad Alexandrum*, 1435b, 27 ff. Cf. Aquila's example in Halm, p. 30: "In pace ad vexandos cives acerrimus, in bello ad expugnandos hostes inertissimus"; an ex. repeated by M. Capella. From Dionysius of Halicarnassus, *Lysias*, 14, we learn of Theophrastus' threefold definition of antithesis (in his *On Style* now lost): When contraries are predicated of the same thing, or the same thing of contraries, or contraries of contraries (also Ar., ad loc. cit. above).

reset as follows: "homines in terram defossos igni circumposito interfecerunt."[13]

Cicero provides an eloquent example of this kind of garbling exercise
when he corrects a passage from a pleading delivered in 124 B. C. by
Gaius Gracchus so as to "square it" and turn "looseness" into functional
coherence ("*in quadrum* redigere, efficere *aptum* quod fuerat antea dif-
fluens ac *solutum*"). As Gracchus had it: "Abesse non potest quin
eiusdem hominis sit probos improbare qui improbos probet." Cicero's
revision provides a tighter analytical cohesion and, at the same time, a
suspenseful ascendant movement toward the climax of the main statement:
"Abesse non potest quin eiusdem hominis sit, qui improbos probet, probos
improbare."[14] An example of this sort seems to reveal that the ancients
had at least as keen a sense (though not entirely conscious) of genuinely
syntactic and logical criteria ('logical' in the sense of psychologically
cogent according to the order of thought) for the composition of the
sentence as they had for the internal arrangement of the clause—although,
for the latter, they tended to yield to all-pervasive considerations of musicality, as we are about to see.[15]

Equally characteristic is another form of compositional balance, an
aesthetic, architectonic principle which begins with the division of the
matter into a 'protasis' and an 'apodosis' (in this case the period is,
once again, structurally dualistic, the first half being suspended until
integrated by the second). Quintilian, IX, iii, 80 and Aquila, 18 offer an
example from Cic., *Pro Caec.*, I, 1: "Si, quantum in agro locisque desertis
audacia potest, tantum in foro atque iudiciis inpudentia valeret, non
minus nunc in causa cederet Aulus Caecina Sexti Aebuti inpudentiae,
quam tum in vi facienda cessit audaciae."[16] Quintilian went on to
stress the presence here of isocolon, homoioptoton (in both halves), and
(in the second half) homoioteleuton. It was a successful example, to
be repeated as late as in the polemics on style in the seventeenth and
eighteenth centuries. It showed the kind of balance which was most
satisfying to the ancient ear: a 'square' structure, with protasis and
apodosis clearly joined in the middle of the period and equally subdivided

[13] Lausberg, *Elemente*, 1949 ed. §48, 1963 ed. p. 147.
[14] Cicero, *Orator*, lxx, 233.
[15] See below, however, for what Cicero himself had to say about his reasons for
thus correcting Gracchus.
[16] Lausberg, *Handbuch*, p. 459, quotes the example from Aquila in a different
textual form.

into two parallel, correlative clauses. Such clauses fulfill the function of 'cola' ('colon,' κῶλον, Lat. *membrum* [17]), the basic rhetorical unit within the period. The colon, however, does not necessarily coincide with a clause: it may be made of less or even more than one full clause.[18]

The question of periodic structure exemplifies the general phenomenon whereby the basic concepts of linguistic analysis have historically been derived from logic and, even more, rhetoric. The student of late Renaissance and baroque rationalist linguistics is familiar with the far-reaching theory of ellipsis (starting with Sanctius). This theory had its distant origins in the classical rhetorical figures: a period lacking some of its constituent elements was said to form a figure, a permissible *vitium*, specifically the figure of ellipsis, ἐλλειπτικὸν σχῆμα, as when the apodosis is missing (ἀνανταπόδοσις, ἀνανταπόδοτος).[19] If only a syntactic element, a particle, is missing, the term *anacoluthon* would be invoked, with three possibilities: either the particle introducing the apodosis is missing, or the one introducing the protasis, or both.[20]

The period, Aristotle pointed out, can be simple or complex. It is simple when it consists of one colon only—although some critics deny this possibility.[21] Whatever the type, its minimum and maximum lengths are controlled by reasons pertaining to physiology (the speaker's breath), semantic (self-contained intellectual content adapted to the hearer's ability to grasp it), mnemonics (the speaker's ability to memorize it): "Modus eius a Cicerone aut quattuor senariis versibus aut ipsius spiritus modo terminatur. Praestare debet, ut sensum concludat: sit aperta, ut intellegi possit, non immodica, ut memoria contineri." [22]

Its cyclical or circular character will be determined by placing the main

[17] Lat. *membrum* for 'colon' is first found, it appears, in the *Rhet. ad Her.*
[18] The term and concept of colon seems to have originated by analogy with the human body, although it came to rhetoric from the art of music.
[19] Cf. Anon., *Perì schemáton*, Spengel III, p. 157, 10; 17.
[20] Cf. Lausberg, *Handbuch*, p. 459 for references.
[21] The monocolon period is still regarded as an unclear notion by recent philologists. Kennedy, *The Art of Persuasion*, p. 288, e. g., complains that the nature of their "rounding" is not explained. Yet Demetrius, I, 17, makes it clear that the rounding of monocola is chiefly a matter of cadence-like ending (whereas the roundness of a complex period is a more pervasive structural affair).
[22] Quint., *Inst.* IX, iv, 125. Also cf. Cicero, *Orator*, lxvi, 221: "Constat enim ille ambitus et plena comprehensio e quattuor fere partibus, quae membra dicimus, ut et auris impleat et neque brevior sit quam satis sit neque longior . . . ut aut citius insistendum sit aut longius procedendum, ne brevitas defraudasse auris videatur neve longitudo obtudisse"; and Aristotle, *Rhet.*, III, ix, 3-6, 1409B.

statements last and the conditional ones first. This peculiar, suspense-producing arrangement will affect clauses in the complex period, complements and parts of speech in the simple, or monocolon period: in the latter case we may have, therefore, hyperbaton, while such devices as chiasmus, either within the clause or between clauses, may also serve the above purpose. Let us remember, for instance, the typical opening periods: *Arma virumque cano . . . ; Quid faciat laetas segetes . . . , hic canere incipiam* (*Georg.*), and many others.[23] The order is 'indirect,' the sentences start with complements or secondary clauses. And since prose and poetry develop their own corresponding patterns along such lines, metrical enjambments will have a similar periodic value by establishing a circular motion which transcends the metrical boundary. For the verse corresponds to the colon (Cic., *Or.*, lxvi, 223), just as the minimum unit of the period, to wit, the comma (κόμμα), roughly corresponds to the hemistich, while, at the other end of the scale, the period itself corresponds to a strophe or stanzaic sequence.

Cola have a self-sufficiency of their own: as a matter of fact, they can exist outside the period, and as independent coordinated clauses they can form the juxtaposed units of the *oratio perpetua*, in which case one speaks of *membratim dicere*. Cicero gives the following example of *membratim dicta*: "incurristi amens in columnas, in alienos insanus insanisti" (*Or.*, lxvii, 224). The chiasmus would seem to make it a unitary period, yet this is a case of *oratio perpetua* because the key procedural movement of suspense is lacking.

Periods made of more than four cola were usually regarded as potentially excessive, and in need of parenthetic interruptions or comma-like appendages to reduce the tension and thus save the equilibrium of the whole. The golden mean was always recognized to be the four-cola period, τετράκωλος περίοδος, the structural square whereby the noble style reaches the peak of its artistic perfection. It encompasses in its full course the length of four metrical lines, and the 4-line stanza is therefore, in a way, its poetic analogue. This easily reminds us of the most frequent use of the quatrain in many literatures, from Europe to China, as a natural way of expressing thought in an elegant form graced with simple and perfect balance.[24]

[23] Lausberg includes examples from modern literatures, such as *Buona pulcella fut Eulalia; Nel mezzo del cammin di nostra vita . . . ; Per correr migliori acque . . . ; Of man's first disobedience*, etc. (*Handbuch*, p. 469).
[24] Cf. Cic., *Or.* lxv, 221-222: "The full comprehensive period consists of approxi-

The smallest constituent of the period is called 'comma' (κόμμα, 'chip,' comma, caesum, incisum, particula, articulus):[25] it is generally shorter than the colon, less complete or self-sufficient, somewhat close to the linguistic notion of phrase, since it may be with or without finished sense. The borderline between the two becomes vague when we reach particularly full 'commata' or particularly slim 'cola,' so that, theoretically, a period can also be made entirely of commata (or substandard cola). Nevertheless, there is, on principle, a clear distinction between the two, which introduces us to the musical, or 'acoustic,' aspect of composition: the colon characteristically ends according to a recognizable rhythmic pattern, namely with a cadence, clausula, the comma does not. "Membrum . . . est sensus numeris conclusus," "incisum, quantum mea refert opinio, erit sensus non expleto numero conclusus" (Quint., IX, iv, 123 and 122).

Commata are also put to good use in the 'laconic' style, which (like the Spartans' speech) is characterized by brevity and sententious concentration or wit. In this variety of plain style the comma comes in handy as a pithy independent clause. Apophthegms are of this order, and a series of comma-length coordinate clauses produces the variety occasionally referred to as incise dicta (analogous to the membratim dicta seen above): "'Domus tibi deerat? At habebas; pecunia superabat? At egebas.' Haec incise dicta sunt quattuor."[26] More particularly, a series of parallel single-word commata in a clause or sentence determines a caesa oratio, as in "acrimonia, voce, vultu adversarios perterruisti" (Ad Her. IV, xix, 26).[27] Sequences strung together without use of connective particles such as conjunctions (generally σύνδεσμοι) are called asyndeton: "asyndeta and repetition of the same word are rightly disapproved in written speech, but in public debate, even rhetoricians make use of them."[28]

mately four parts which we call membra . . . , each approximately equal to a hexameter verse." They are held together by the nodi continuationis (ibid.), perhaps an unclear allusion to transitional particles and conjunctions also recommended by the Greeks. Although we are inclined to think in terms of distichs for the alexandrine, Lausberg points out sequences of four alexandrines in Corneille and Racine somewhat embodying the heritage of the classical period (Handbuch, p. 464).

[25] Incisum for 'comma' was first proposed as a technical term by Cicero, Or. 211, although he also used rather less formally the other terms.

[26] Cicero, Or. lxvii, 223.

[27] Cf. also Aquila, 18, in Halm p. 28, 5 for more examples and for renewed use of the same term, caesa oratio.

[28] Arist., Rhet. III, xii, 1. One aspect of the definition of the period, namely

*   *   *

Clearly the three types of sentence structure, though related to them, do not coincide with the three kinds of style. The *oratio soluta* is usually regarded as most limited in literary possibilities, and all warnings in favor of variation may imply a balanced mixture of the three styles, but only of the two 'upper' compositional formulae, namely the *perpetua* and the *periodica*: these two are sufficient to produce the perfect mix by balancing the complication of sustained hypotaxis with the relative simplicity of smooth-flowing parataxis. Variation of styles, however, differs on the different literary levels: it might be recommended and even required in oratory, but in the fictional genres it was usually shunned—thanks to a sense of formal unity which is germane to the 'classic' view of rigid genre-divisions. Medieval and Renaissance poetics often quoted Horace's dictum to this effect: *Amphora coepit / Institui currente rota: cur urceus exit?* [29] So did, e. g., Geoffrey of Vinsauf: [30] "Considerandum est ut stylum materiae non variemus, id est ut de grandiloquo stylo non descendamus ad humilem. Quod (Horatius) notat his verbis: *amphora est. . . .* Servemus uniformitatem styli et hic declinemus a vitio styli, quod dicit Horatius hoc versu: *Denique sit quod vis, simplex dumtaxat et unum (A. P., 23)*." Looking at the matter from the narrower point of view of rhythm, Dionysius of Halicarnassus recommended variation: "A style is finest of all when it has the most frequent rests and changes of harmony; when one thing is said within a period, another without it; when one period is formed by the interweaving of a large number of clauses, another by that of a smaller; when among the clauses themselves one is short, another longer, one roughly wrought, another more finished. . . ." [31]

---

the stress on rhythm (Aristotle) or on thought (Demetrius), on which we have not lingered, is bibliographically discussed in the admirable fn. 116 of G. Calboli's ed. of the *Rhetorica ad C. Herennium* (Bologna, 1969), pp. 329-334, with references to, among others, A. Du Mesnil, "Begriff der drei Kunstformen der Rede" (1894), J. Zehetmeier, "Die Periodenlehre des Aristoteles" (1929), L. Voit, DEINOTHΣ (1934), J. Lücke, *Beiträge zur Entwicklung der genera dicendi und genera compositionis* (Diss. Hamburg, 1952), W. Schmid, *Über die klassische Theorie und Praxis des antiken Prosarhythmus* (1959), and esp. D. M. Schenkeveld, *Studies in Demetrius on Style* (1967).

[29] *Ars poetica*, 21.

[30] *Documentum de arte versificandi*, §157 (Faral p. 315).

[31] *De compositione*, xix, pp. 196-197 of Roberts' ed. Trans. by Roberts. The advice to mix the three styles for elegant variation, already present, e. g., in Cicero's

The power inherent in a judicious alternation of copiousness and shock-tactics by varying sentence length is one of Demosthenes' high lessons. A splendid example of this pattern for Greek is the language of the Pseudo-Longinus, which it is particularly appropriate to recall because as a case of expository prose it shows that the lessons of oratory could transcend their own immediate genre.[32] All in all, however, Demosthenes' lesson was better learned by the Roman masters (like Cicero) than by the Greeks.

Besides and beyond the danger of over-stressing the appeal to the popular audience, or, which amounts to the same, the appeal to the audience's emotions through display of the speaker's 'pathos'—a danger vigorously denounced by Aristotle on moral and philosophical grounds—, the fault of the Gorgian-Isocratean tradition and of its intemperate heir, the Asianic school, was to have used certain compositional ingredients of the grand style too persistently, to the point of monotony and satiety. Cicero, for one, attempted in his riper years to mitigate the excesses of the *genus grande* and thus placate the Atticist adherents of the *humile*, according to the teachings of the Rhodian school.

*   *   *

Now that the basic outline of the 'system' lies clearly before us, we must pause for a moment and inquire how and when it started to take shape, and what historical circumstances caused its moving in a direction which remained consistent to the very end. The original motivations are relevant to the proper understanding of the systematic outcome of ancient rhetoric.

The most persuasive approach seems to be afforded to us by considering that rhetoric was nothing more than an implicit application to prose (signally the prose of the public speaker) of what was felt to be the secret power and beauty of poetic discourse. In particular, the rhythmic nature of poetry was something that transcended mere versification, and the ancients felt it as an aspect of the all-pervasive, civilizing power of music. Aristotle had stressed the value of rhythm for art prose on the basis of a rather Pythagorean view of number dominating all things as a supreme principle of order: "All things are limited by number, and the

Orator, became canonical: cf. Quintilian, *Inst.* X, ii, 22; XII, x, 58 ff.; and Pliny, *Epist.* vi, 33; ii, 5; iii, 13.
[32] Cf. H. D. Blume, *Untersuchungen zu Sprache und Stil der Schrift περὶ ὕψους* (Göttingen, 1963).

number pertaining to the form of elocution is rhythm, of which the meters
[= prose feet] are divisions." [33]

Cicero put it thus (*De oratore*, III, xliv, §§ 173-174): "The old Greek
masters [i. e. the Sophists of the 5th c. B. C.] held the view that in our
own prose it is proper for us orators to use something almost amounting
to versification, that is, a rhythmic movement. . . . These two things,
therefore, namely modulation of the voice and the arrangement of words
into periods, they thought proper to transfer from poetry to oratory, so
far as the severe character of the latter could tolerate." More specifically,
Gorgias was thought to have bequeathed to his school the principle of
counting syllables for the sake of parallelism and quantitative balance,
which from the standard practice of Aeolic lyric became the rhetorical
figure of *parisosis*.

Indeed, Cicero himself still clung to the habit of referring indiscriminately to the units of both prose and poetry as "verses" (e. g. *Orator*,
lxvi, 223). And the parallel between hexameters or *senarii* and cola, on
the one hand, hemistichs and commata, on the other, was current in
rhetorical literature (e. g. Demetrius, *On Style* I, 1). Clearly moving on
the theoretical plane, Quintilian peremptorily equated composition itself
with the art of versification as its direct parallel: "Quem in poemate
locum habet versificatio, eum in oratione compositio" (IX, iv, 116). Elementary as this may sound on the surface, its consequences can hardly
be overstated. The result was that elements of rhythm, formal arrangement, and physiological division (on the basis of delivery according to
breathing capacity) remained, to ancient ears, more basic than considerations of logical content and organization. Thus, for instance, both complete periods and parts thereof (mainly cola) are sometimes hard for us
to reconstruct, because they do not necessarily correspond to our sentences
and clauses or even phrases—which are essentially logical and, concurrently, syntactic units. A concrete example is needed here, and we shall
take it from an exordium of a Ciceronian oration—following Quintilian's
hint that "the full periodic style is well adapted to the exordium of
important cases" (IX, iv, 128).

The exordium to the third Catilinarian might be read as if made up

---

[33] Περαίνεται δὲ ἀριθμῷ πάντα· ὁ δὲ τοῦ σχήματος τῆς λέξεως ἀριθμὸς ῥυθμός ἐστιν,
οὗ καὶ τὰ μέτρα τμήματα: *Rhet.*, III, viii, 1408B. This passage is also interesting for
the analogy it shows between Gr. 'rhythm' ῥυθμός and Lat. *numerus* through Gr.
'number' ἀριθμός.

of seven periods, which could be divided into cola and commata as
follows:

(1) Rem publicam, Quirites, vitamque omnium vestrum,
    bona, fortunas, coniuges, liberosque vestros
    atque hoc domicilium clarissimi imperi
    fortunatissimam pulcherrimamque urbem:
(2) hodierno die
    deorum immortalium summo erga vos amore,
    laboribus, consiliis, periculis meis
    e flamma atque ferro ac paene ex faucibus fati ereptam
    et vobis conservatam ac restitutam videtis.
(3) Et si non minus nobis
    iucundi atque illustres sunt
    ei dies quibus conservamur
    quam illi quibus nascimur:
(4) quod salutis certa laetitia est,
    nascendi incerta condicio,
    et quod sine sensu nascimur,
    cum voluptate servamur:
(5) profecto
    quoniam illum qui hanc urbem condidit
    ad deos immortales benevolentia famaque sustulimus,
    esse apud vos posterosque vestros in honore debebit is
    qui eandem hanc urbem conditam amplificatamque servavit.
(6) Nam toti urbi, templis, delubris, tectis ac moenibus
    subiectos prope iam ignes circumdatosque restinximus,
    idemque gladios in rem publicam destrictos rettudimus
    mucronesque eorum a iugulis vestris deiecimus.
(7) Quae, quoniam in senatu
    illustrata, patefacta, comperta sunt per me,
    vobis iam exponam breviter, Quirites,
    ut
    et quanta et quam manifesta
    et qua ratione investigata et comprehensa sint
    vos qui et ignoratis et exspectatis scire possitis.[34]

[34] I have adopted the method of division used for this exemplary passage by

What we must not fail to notice here is, first, that the periods do not necessarily end with a full stop: indeed, they do not even have to contain a complete *logical* statement, since they may be deprived of a subject or predicate or both—as one can best see in number (1). Nor do they have to contain a main clause: (3) and (4) are subordinate clauses, (3) being concessive and (4) parenthetic of a causal nature. Moreover, the example shows how the favorite kind of period was the square one, which, let me repeat, derives from and corresponds in physiological and aesthetic function to the lyrical quatrain, with longer or shorter lines according to the emotional weight of the argument. Simultaneously, the tension of the audience and the delivery effort of the speaker are occasionally relieved by the appropriate dosage of relative

---

Charles J. Robbins, "Rhetoric and Latin Word Order," *Classical Journal*, XLVII (1951), 78-83: see p. 81. Of course the passage might also be read differently, with (1) and (2) together as one period, and likewise for (3), (4), and (5). But the square units, either as autonomous wholes or as parts of larger entities, remain clearly distinguishable in either case. Robbins expounds the principles of parallelism with poetry in an original and stringent manner, but I believe he tends to over-emphasize its implications to the point of obliterating the logical rhythm of prose; more seriously, he sets up the middle section of cola as being their most important part, thus subverting the basic laws of emphasis at beginning and end. His example, a reading of Cicero's *Oratio in Catilinam tertia*, 3, 22, seems to me dangerously misleading and, overall, unacceptable:

> Quo
> etiam maiore sunt *isti* ' *odio* supplicioque digni
> qui non solum *vestris* ' *domiciliis* atque tectis
> sed etiam *deorum* ' *templis* atque delubris
> sunt funestos ac *nefarios* ' *ignes* inferre conati.

He maintains that the words in italics bear the brunt of the period as delivered, even while he divides each colon in the middle with a caesura-like pause as indicated by the apostrophe, like a line of two hemistichs: "We have, then, four cola, each of them about the length of a dactylic hexameter, each with a well defined caesura. We notice, furthermore, that the important and emphatic words are all clustered about the caesura in the middle of each line" (p. 79). The example is well chosen for such a purpose, and may well lend itself to being delivered in the way indicated, but the attempt to offer it as an illustration of a general trend seems far-fetched and not corresponding to actual practice.

Based as it is on the evidence of some ancient Mss. of Virgil, Norden's valuable analysis of ancient punctuation as it bears on periodic articulation appears to confirm my demurrers against Robbins' readings: cf. E. Norden, ed., P. Vergilius Maro, *Aeneis VI* (Leipzig, 1903; repr. Stuttgart, 1965), Appendix II, pp. 369-381 (on periodic structure in poetry). See also Appendices III and IV, on word order and homoioteleuton.

lengths, alternations and variations of form—even though the use of the
period is sustained throughout the exordium. In conclusion, the physiological reasons, that is the speaker's ability to deliver each unit in one
breath at ease, are a paramount consideration. No wonder that Cicero
spoke of constantly exercising his lungs.

Concomitantly with the imitation of poetic forms, it is important to
realize one aspect of the Sophists' impact on the elaboration of rhetorical
schemas. Far from departing from an 'objective' stress on the linguistic
elements of expression toward a merely subjective appreciation of individual stylistic peculiarities, the Sophists were guided, in their search for
the secret of success in the use of speech, by the same positive empiricism
which also prompted them to attempt precise measurements in the fields
of astronomy, geometry, and music. Thus the so-called Gorgianic figures
were thoroughly conditioned by the criterion of symmetry and equivalence: it was felt that there was beauty and persuasive effectiveness in
the use of parallel and equivalent sequences—on a basis of repetition of
parts, especially the last, but also of similar lengths in the successive
clauses, even to the point of carefully counting syllables. The very
roundness of the period, which seems to satisfy in such a deep way the
aesthetic sense of the ancients, responded to precise solicitations deriving
from an empirical identification of beauty with mathematical, measurable
regularity. Such an approach did not entirely convince the humanistically-
inclined critics of the Sophists, like Socrates. This critical reaction is
shrewdly represented in the satire we read in Aristophanes' Frogs: Preparing himself to the contest with Aeschylus as to who deserves the
tragic palm, the Sophists' disciple Euripides asks Pluto's servants to bring
in rules, scales, and circles, so that his competitor's productions can be
evaluated not in an emotional and intuitive manner, but with an exact
method.

One must also keep in mind the gradual evolution of the ancient notion
of period. The most advanced stage in that evolution—the one we ordin-
arily have in mind when we use the term—implies a high degree of
syntactical complexity, hinging on methodical use of subordination (as
in Isocrates). But critics have pointed out that early theorists' examples of
periods (including Aristotle) are seldom of that kind, since they often
consist of two coordinated members, and may be even smaller than a
complete 'sentence.' It is true, on the other hand, that balance and
rhythm, though essential to the period, do not by themselves make one.

Suffice it to recall that Dionysius attributed to Thrasymachus (the inventor of prose rhythm) only compactness, not periodicity.[35]

The material about to be analyzed in greater detail could be integrated with ancient statements within the rhetorical division of 'delivery' (actio, pronuntiatio). Cicero and Quintilian, among others, spent much time to describe the manner of 'suspending' the discourse at each division between phrases, i. e. commata and cola, even beyond the more conspicuous distinctiones equivalent to our punctuation marks. Their analyses amount to precious indications as to the way the ancients felt about the inner organization of their sentences as well as the successive ordering of their parts. But such material would add little of concrete value to our inquiry, and even less to the knowledge to be derived from the remarks normally included in the direct treatment of elocution.[36]

II. A Historical Presentation

We have seen how the question of the manifold uses of compositional structures and of their specific aptness for different levels of speech had already been clearly raised by Aristotle. Its canonical codification was perhaps most authoritatively summarized by Cicero in his Orator. The gap between Aristotle and Cicero is, unfortunately, easy to close, owing to the loss of practically all the rhetorical manuals produced between the two with the sole exceptions of the pseudo-Aristotelian Rhetorica ad Alexandrum and the Rhetorica ad Herennium, the first of which was apparently written shortly after Aristotle's death, the second during Cicero's youth.

This, of course, assumes that the περὶ ἑρμηνείας attributed to Demetrius does not antedate Cicero (of the two main datings proposed, ca. 280-250

---

[35] Cf. G. A. Kennedy, "Aristotle on the Period"; G. M. A. Grube, "Thrasymachus, Theophrastus and Dionysius of Halicarnassus," Am. Journal of Philology, LXXIII (1952), 251-267. I wish to express here my gratitude to Professor Grube of the University of Toronto for his careful and helpful reading of this whole Chapter.

[36] The treatment of distinctiones within the theory of delivery has been carefully analyzed, with numerous and ample quotations of relevant texts, by Maurice P. Cunningham, esp. in his paper on "Some Phonetic Aspects of Latin Word Order," Proc. Amer. Philos. Soc., CI (1957), 481-505, and his previous "Some Principles of Latin Phrasing . . . ," Classical Weekly, XLVII (1953), 17-22, and "Latin Word Order . . . ," Year Book of the Amer. Philos. Soc., 1954 (1955), 360-370.

B. C. and end of first century A. D., the former has been recently defended by Grube but rejected by most specialists).[1]

The *Rhetorica ad Alexandrum*[2] presents little interest for us. Within the rules for clarity it discusses sentence structure and discourages hyperbata (ch. xxv); it then goes on to examine antithesis (xxvi), parisosis (parallelism of structure, xxvii), and paromoeosis (parallelism of sound, xxvii). These are the only considerations on composition—although the explicit heading of *synthesis* appears solely in ch. xxv—, and the figures are included (just about the only ones discussed in the treatise).

The *Rhetorica ad Herennium* (ca. 86-82 B. C.) is a very different matter. This work, which Spengel did not hesitate to praise as "more precious than gold," was a first, brilliant attempt to introduce rhetoric to Rome in a systematic way and with a Latinized nomenclature.[3] The result was, all in all, exquisitely idiosyncratic, and although later Romans felt less and less squeamish about adopting the Greek terms outright, some of the *ad Herennium* terminology remained—thanks in part to the indirect help of Cicero's somewhat snobbish abhorrence from technical jargon. The *Ad Herennium* also interests us particularly on account of the widespread impact it had during the Middle Ages, especially through its fourth book.

It immediately strikes the reader by starting out with *inventio* (two

---

[1] For an acceptance of the early dating, cf. Kennedy, *The Art of Persuasion*, pp. 284-286, resting on Grube, *Demetrius* . . . (1961), pp. 39 ff. Grube has again argued for his dating in "The Date of Demetrius on Style," *Phoenix*, XVIII (1964), 294-302. See, also, my fn. 40 *infra*.

[2] See H. Rackham's ed. in Aristotle, *Problems*, II, ed. and trans. W. S. Hett . . . (Loeb Cl. Libr., 1937). This text is a good example (the only one extant *in toto*) of the fourth-century technical treatises so much despised by Plato and Aristotle. Ever since L. Spengel and P. Wendland it has been ascribed to Anaximenes of Lampsacus. This ascription has recently been challenged by Vinzenz Buchheit, *Untersuchungen zur Theorie des Genos epideiktikon von Gorgias bis Aristoteles* (Munich, 1960), but these objections have been refuted by Manfred Fuhrmann, *Untersuchungen zur Textgeschichte der pseudo-aristotelischen Alexander-Rhetorik* (der τέχνη des Anaximenes von Lampsakos), Abh. d. Akad. d. Wiss. Mainz, Geistes– u. soz.–wiss. Kl., Heft 7, 148 (1964), and, finally, Kark Barwick, "Die 'Rhetorik ad Alexandrum' und Anaximenes, Alkidamas, Isokrates, Aristoteles und die Theodekteia," *Philologus*, CX (1966), 212-245 (to be continued).

[3] I use H. Caplan's ed. Translations are mine, except for some of the technical terms. See the splendid new ed. by G. Calboli (Bologna, 1969).

The whole span of Roman stylistic theory and practice from the *Ad Herennium* to A. Gellius is the subject of Leeman, *Orationis Ratio* (1963). A superbly competent study, this thoroughly historical and largely explanatory exposition will be found of limited use by those who seek a consistently systematic treatment of specific technical categories—which is our main interest here.

full books) instead of with the parts of the oration. It thus reconciles the Aristotelian approach and the manualistic method. Book III encompasses a discussion of Deliberative and Epideictic Causes, Arrangement (*dispositio*), Delivery (*pronuntiatio* for traditional *actio*), Memory (*memoria*).

At the beginning of Book IV the style genera are recognized as three and presented through famous made-up examples, each being matched by another passage exemplifying the opposite vice (the grand style can fall into the swollen, the median into the slack, the plain into the vulgar). All these examples interestingly exhibit uses and abuses of sentence forms. We are then offered a streamlined presentation of the doctrine of 'virtues': *elocutio* is made apt and finished by the following (IV, xii, 17-on):

elegantia = *Latinitas* and clarity together
conpositio = euphony and avoidance of: alliteration or paromoion, repetitions, internal rhymes (homoeoptoton), inelegant transpositions, prolonged sentences which do violence to both the listener's ear and the speaker's breathing: IV, xii, 18—this treatment is clearly more negative than constructive, and is notable by its distrust of Gorgianic schemes as prerequisite for a sound notion of composition
dignitas (= figures).

The meagerness of this treatment is simply due to the fact that our anonymous author scatters the various aspects of composition and word order among the figures. These are divided into 35 figures of words, *exornationes verborum*, 10 tropes (set aside but without a common label, only as a special group of the above), and 19 figures of thought, *exornationes sententiarum*.[4] Among the first group we find, in this order though not in immediate succession:

antithesis, here called *contentio* (IV, 21)

contrarium (25-26), a contrastive presentation or exhibition of opposite alternatives, intended to be built into a period

colon, *membrum* (26), a literal and successful translation which, we shall remember, first appears in this text. It does not express a complete thought except when combined in sequences of two or—which the author finds best of all—three

comma, *articulus* (26), generally a short phrase, but mostly consisting

---

[4] The figures in the *Ad Her.* can be easily located by referring to one of the paradigms prepared by editors (like Caplan in the Loeb. Cl. Libr.) and historians (like Baldwin).

of single words set apart by pauses in chopped-up speech (cum singula verba intervallis distinguuntur caesa oratione, hoc modo: " Acrimonia, voce, vultu adversarios perterruisti ")

period, *continuatio* (27), a closely-knit, uninterrupted structure with complete meaning.

Three basic literary situations are said to require the period: the *sententia* (the elaborate, articulate maxim, as distinct from the 'laconic' apophthegm); the *contrarium* (extended, elaborate antithesis in the form of reasoning by contraries); the conclusion (summing up of an argument). The passage from the golden booklet is worth quoting *in extenso* for the shrewd way in which one example, twice revised, is made to show the three cases:

Continuatio (= the period) est densa et continens frequentatio verborum cum absolutione sententiarum; ea utemur commodissime tripertito . . . : IN SENTENTIA hoc pacto: ' Ei non multum potest obesse fortuna, qui sibi firmius in virtute quam in casu praesidium conlocavit.' IN CONTRARIO hoc modo: ' Nam si qui spei non multum conlocarit in casu, quid est quod ei magnopere casus obesse possit? ' IN CONCLUSIONE hoc pacto: ' Quodsi in eos plurimum fortuna potest qui suas rationes omnes in casum contulerunt, non sunt omnia committenda fortunae, ne magnam nimis in nos habeat dominationem ' (IV, xix, 27).

isocolon, *conpar* (27)

homoeoptoton, *similiter cadens* (28)

homoeoteleuton, *similiter desinens* (28)

climax, *gradatio* (34): climactic building up of movement until tension is relieved by releasing the decisive and weightiest element in the end. This effect is the highest achievement of the period, but note that the terms *climax* and *gradatio* were used, as here, in a technical sense to mean a gradually ascending movement through iteration of some element. E. g., *Africano virtutem industria, virtus gloriam, gloria aemulos conparavit.*

disiunctum and *coniunctio* meaning syntactical separation or combination, respectively

asyndeton, *dissolutum* (41), when conjunctions are suppressed

aposiopesis, *praecisio* (41), incomplete sentence.

Among the tropes we find transposition, *transiectio*, a violation of word order like, also, anastrophe, *perversio*: both together constitute *transgressio* (a term destined to a long success in the Middle Ages as a variant of

hyperbaton): " transgressio [= exception to normal order] est quae verborum perturbat ordinem perversione [= inversion] aut transiectione
[= disjunction] " (IV, xxxii, 44).[5] When not obscure, these devices are
useful to round out the periods and properly seal their rhythm.

As was to be expected, nothing under the heading of figures of thought
concerns composition. One finds here a second treatment of antithesis,
contentio (58), now being viewed as *exornatio sententiae,* and the virtue
of *brevitas* also treated as a figure (68).

Turning now to Cicero, we shall begin with his most definitive text,
the *Orator.*[6] The three styles recognized by Cicero are the *genus tenue,
medium, grande.* They arise from the orator's three tasks: to prove, to
win sympathy, to move: "ita dicet ut probet, ut delectet, ut flectat"
(269).[7] These three tasks, however, specifically define judiciary or forensic and public or deliberative oratory ("in foro causisque civilibus")
as distinct from all of the following kinds of speech: the sophistic (specifically, epideictic oratory), the philosophic, the historical, the poetic. What
these share with the practical orator is only a degree of rhythm in their
use of language, plus a minor degree of elevation in speech (choice of
vocabulary). The real difference lies in the combination of the three tasks
above (61-68).

Observe that this threefold set of tasks revives in a more compact,
aphoristic formula the three manners of proof recognized by Aristotle:
the analytical or logical, based on fact and aiming at truth; the ethical
(persuasion by display of the speaker's good character), the pathetical
(appeal to the emotions). The third was the hardest to justify philo-

---

[5] Transposition, anastrophe, and hyperbaton are also Caplan's renderings; the ones
in brackets are Marouzeau's: cf. Marouzeau, *L'Ordre des mots,* I, p. 1.

[6] Cf. *Orator* v, 20—ix, 32; xi, 37—xiii, 42; xix, 61—xxxi, 112. The last section,
xxxix, 134—lxxi, 238, deals with figures and harmony. See a digest of these
sections on style in Baldwin, *A. R. and P.,* 57-61, with the following discussion.
Also J. E. Sandys, ed., *M. Tulli Ciceronis ad M. Brutum Orator . . .* (Cambridge,
1885), digest on pp. lxxiv-lxxvi. The *Orator* is largely devoted to elocution and
is, therefore, complementary to the *De oratore,* which dwells more amply on
invention. About Cicero's ideas on style, cf. Hendrickson, "Cicero's Correspondence
with Brutus and Calvus on Oratorical Style" (1926); Id., "Cicero de optimo
genere oratorum" (1926). On the broader aspects of Cicero's position on rhetoric,
see A. Michel's work (1960). The *Orator* and *De oratore* are studied in their
relationship to Horace's *Ars poetica* by G. C. Fiske and M. L. Grant. For an
analysis of the section of the *Orator* dealing with *compositio* see, in particular,
Leeman, *Orationis Ratio,* I, pp. 149-155.

[7] This formula corresponds to the terms used elsewhere by Cicero, but the
sequence *probare, conciliare, movere* in *De or.* II, 115 was perhaps more felicitous.

sophically: indeed, Aristotle's treatise had opened with an attack on the traditional manuals for being overly concerned with emotions. Consequently, it had been excluded, together with the second (unworthy of an honest man), by the Stoics, who accepted only the first, the 'didactic.' Quintilian, almost as unsympathetic as Cicero toward their position on the matter, implicitly reminds us of the Stoics' strictures without naming them (V, Prooemium, 1), and clings to Cicero's position (*doceat, moveat, delectet: Inst. or. III, v, 2*). But it may be an echo of the Stoics' impact as well as a sign of his philosophical concern, that Cicero felt impelled to justify the use of pathos by warning the orator that genuine pathos will be produced in the audience only if the speaker is sincere, for he cannot communicate what he does not feel, as is also true of the actors on the stage (*De or.* II, 189-204).[8]

The Sophists introduced the grand style by using a special sort of it in their panegyrics (38-42). Cicero defends Isocrates as the best in this kind, and is content with Socrates' concurring opinion (Plato, *Phaedrus,* 279A), while he criticizes the others of that school, wittily referred to by Socrates as λογοδαίδαλοι, 'cunning artificers of speech' or speech-Daedali (*Phaedrus,* 266E). The periodicity of the early Sophists was still elementary, lacking as it was in circularity. Gorgias of Leontini (the first to have applied art to speech) and Thrasymachus of Calchedon are "concisi minutis numeris," 'cut up into short rhythmical phrases,' while Theodorus of Byzantium was "praefractior nec satis . . . rotundus," 'too rugged and not round enough.' Isocrates, instead, first undertook to "expand his phrases and round out his sentences with softer rhythms."[9] Thus the achievements of this school, with due exception for its greatest exponent, coincide with its limitations, namely the use and abuse of the Gorgianic figures, which Cicero describes as follows: "indulge in a neatness and symmetry of sentences, . . . well defined and rounded periods . . . words correspond to words as if measured off in equal phrases, frequently things inconsistent are placed side by side, and things contrasted are paired [= antithesis]; clauses are made to end in the same way and with similar sounds."[10]

---

[8] Cf. Kennedy, *The Art of Persuasion,* p. 292.
[9] "Primus instituit dilatare verbis et mollioribus numeris explere sententias." *Or.,* § 40. I adopt, for this and the following passage only, Hubbell's trans. (Loeb Cl. Libr.)
[10] "Datur enim venia concinnitati sententiarum et argutiis, certique et circumscripti verborum ambitus conceduntur, . . . ut verba verbis quasi demensa et paria

The *genera dicendi* for oratory proper are defined and described in the
second third of the work (69-on). A style is apt when it is adjusted to
its object as well as to the speaker and hearer: this carries with it a
demand for a particular mixture of the 'three tasks' (*tripertita varietas*).[11]
The low style is particularly fit for proof, the median for winning sympathy, the high for arousing the audience. This last encompasses the
peak of the art.[12]

But even the plain style (that some call the 'Attic'), though more
ordinary, demands attention. It will do well to avoid all the Sophistic
devices described above, while it will be allowed a judicious use of all
other figures, provided the speaker is particularly parsimonious in his
periods, which must not be overlong and too elaborate ("continuationem
verborum modo relaxet et dividat," 85). Otherwise, it is untrammeled by
preoccupation with euphony, rhythm, and cadences (77), it is free without rambling. It admits a careful use of wit through a wise dosage of
sententiousness (87-90). The median style is for pleasing, *conciliare*, the
psychological key to winning sympathy, and for acting on the audience's
ἦθος, or mood, by means of its *suavitas*. The high style, finally (97), aims
specifically at πάθος (moving by emotional appeal); it must not, however,
be used exclusively—just as the periodic style must not consist entirely of
periodic sentences—, for the perfect orator is master of all three (100).
The three styles may be modified (103) and combined for variety's sake,
and variety is always necessary (109).

This general statement is, however, somewhat qualified later on, where
Cicero reiterates his assigning of the continuous use of periodic style to
historiography and epideictic oratory, after the examples of Isocrates and
Theopompus (207), while he repeats the advice to mix the forms in
forensic use. The reasons he gives are curiously pertinent: An unbroken
ministering to the pleasure of the listener's ear is bound, in the long run,
to arouse his suspicion that he is about to be deceived by the tricks of art

---

respondeant, ut crebro conferantur pugnantia comparenturque contraria et ut pariter
extrema terminentur eundemque referant in cadendo sonum." *Or.*, § 28.

[11] For the following, see Baldwin, *A. R. and P.*, p. 69. On the judicious mixing
of the three levels of style, see also Cicero at the beginning of *De optimo genere
oratorum*.

[12] " Sed quot officia oratoris tot sunt genera dicendi; subtile in probando, modicum
in delectando, vehemens in flectendo; in quo uno vis omnis oratoris est. Magni
igitur iudici, summae etiam facultatis esse debebit moderator ille et quasi temperator
huius tripertitae varietatis." *Or.*, §§ 69-70.

away from a stern adherence to truth of fact. The impression of sincerity and the holding of sympathy are thus endangered—a serious predicament in a court of law. The danger does not hold for an audience attending a formal public ceremony, as in epideictic oratory (208-209).

The last third or so of the *Orator* specifically deals with composition, which Cicero, with his peculiar disdain for technical terms and fondness for Latinizations (often such as to steer him toward elegant but not exceedingly clear periphrases), prefers to call *collocatio* (147-238). His approach allows genuinely syntactical considerations to play a very limited role in this area, which is thoroughly slanted in the direction of harmony. This means, incidentally, that Cicero treats all the traditional issues of *compositio* together as matters of word arrangement, although he leaves out altogether one of the major questions, that of word order proper. More importantly, Cicero's method is typical of a general trend he so brilliantly sums up, that is one of including periodicity and stylistic syntax among the treatment of style genera (the uses of compositional patterns), the virtues of style, and the figures of speech rather than within a specific treatment of composition itself, where they more properly belong. This should justify our own excursuses into those distinct but related provinces of the art.

Collocatio is defined and divided (149) into: 1) euphony—"quasi structura quaedam," avoidance of hiatus, sudden stops, awkward junctures (147-203); 2) formation of periodic structure through balance and symmetry—"ut forma ipsa concinnitasque verborum conficiat orbem suum" (204-end); 3) rhythm—that is, *numerus*, mostly cadences or *clausulae* (treated together with 2). Cicero does not distinguish between *oratio soluta* and *oratio perpetua*; he identifies only two broad possibilities: the loose sentence (*soluta*) and the periodic (either continued or, more wisely, balanced off by intermingling periods with *incise* and *membratim dicta*—211). In a most significant passage the great Roman orator reveals how thoroughly aesthetic his orientation was on matters of style—one must add that this elegance and brilliance of artistic form was most valuable to Cicero for its practical impact on the audience—:

Hence these procedures—call them composition or finish or rhythm as you may please—must be used if you want to speak elegantly. The reason is not only that the sentence must not drift along like an endless stream, as Aristotle and Theophrastus put it: the sentence must come to an end not just so that the speaker may breathe, or because the copyist has placed a punctuation mark, but because the cadence brings it necessarily to a close.

More importantly still, periodic sentences are far more effective than the loose.[13]

As one can easily see, there is no appeal to reasons of logic or anything having to do with cogent, orderly, or methodical representation of the train of thought, although we had heard earlier (168) that the crowds respond promptly to well-cadenced periods because "the ear expects the words and the sense to march together." The effectiveness or forcefulness (*vis*) invoked here has to do, chiefly, with the impact on the audience. In concluding his study of *collocatio* Cicero alludes to the ordering of words and the use of *traiectio* (inversion) as if the main goal of all these operations were nothing more than the achievement of rhythm (esp. 227-230). In point of fact, he submits three examples from his own orations to stress the point that the slightest change in word arrangement would destroy their whole compositional value as a well-knit period, but the garbling he practices in order to show this principle concerns only the final *clausulae*. He also gives a fourth example, that of Gracchus we have seen above (p. 32). It had then seemed to us, I trust, that Cicero's correction was so brilliantly convincing because it produced a more cogent overall structure. And so it did. Yet, his stated reason for making those changes is, quite simply, that in his revised version the period *falls* better! Having been able to hammer out a more satisfying cadence, he feels no need to explore the matter any further.

More generally, Cicero adds that there is a distinct rhythm for prose which can be explained, even though it appeals to sense rather than to reason, and is less basic than in verse. It was lacking in early writers, for instance in Herodotus (186). This, Sandys maintained in glossing the text, was due to the fact that their style was unperiodic, and there can hardly be rhythm without periodicity. The frequent association of historians with oratory reminds us that narrative rhythms of prose fiction were not much discussed separately at a time when imaginative prose was undeveloped. Those who affect to despise rhythm, Cicero continues, call themselves Attic (234), but they ineptly ignore the rhythm of Demosthenes. If they prefer a loose style, let them follow it if they can show even in their parts the beauty that is lacking in the whole (235).

---

[13] "Hanc igitur, sive compositionem sive perfectionem sive numerum vocari placet, [et] adhibere necesse est, si ornate velis dicere, non solum, quod ait Aristoteles et Theophrastus, ne infinite feratur ut flumen oratio, quae non aut spiritu pronunti-

This whole discussion, the modern reader might well conclude, confirms that, when all had been said and done, RHYTHM rather than LOGIC remained the most basic characteristic of the period.

Though less extensively, Cicero had already dealt with our subject in his previous works *De oratore* and *Brutus*. Like the *Orator*, only with greater succinctness, the *De oratore* treated composition mostly from the vantage point of euphony (words must be woven together like the tesserae in a fine mosaic, avoiding clashing encounters of vowels or consonants between end-syllables and front-syllables of successive words) and rhythm (overall and in cadences).[14] The *Brutus* carried on Cicero's polemic against the self-styled Roman Atticists of his time, confirming the judgment that the plain style of Stoic oratory lacked in popular appeal, for it was "too closely knit and too compact for a popular audience."[15] But the polemic between the two opposed points of view became somewhat exasperated in the *Orator* (23-32), where Cicero went to the defence of his own style by disclaiming any guilt by association with the *genus asiaticum*. In the *Brutus*, however, he could still offer an objective, rather dispassionate analysis of Asianism, which he divided into two kinds: one given to balanced but curt, pointed, epigrammatic cola (*sententiae*), the other, to emotional, copious, flowery ornamentation (325 ff.). This distinction is extremely significant: in the following century much of Stoic Atticism will be hard to tell from the curt variety of Asianism.

We have already seen (p. 3) how Cicero's contemporary, the Greek Epicurean philosopher Philodemus, detached himself from the most established currents of literary scholarship by insisting that the work of art can only be understood and appreciated when seen in the totality of its aspects. This is as close as ancient theory ever came to an 'organic' view of art, aside from Plato's famous passage on a good discourse being like a living organism.

Rostagni has given an interpretation of Philodemus' thought that is centered on his alleged view of art as imaginative intuition.[16] This has been challenged as going beyond the evidence, especially because he referred to the modern notion of intuition within the Crocean context.

antis aut interductu librari sed numero coacta debet insistere, verum etiam quod multo maiorem habent apta vim quam soluta." *Or.*, § 228.

[14] *De oratore*, III, §§ 171-198.

[15] "Stoicorum astrictior est oratio aliquantoque contractior quam aures populi requirunt." *Brutus* xxxi, 120; Hendrickson's trans.

[16] A. Rostagni, "Filodemo contro l'Estetica classica" in *Scritti Minori*, I, esp. 356-371.

In fact Philodemus seemed to stress the intellectual side of poetic activity, at least in polemic against those (the κριτικοί) who *de facto* appeared to reduce the appreciation of the artifact to a play of feeling and sensory perception.[17] This fascinating element in Philodemus' thought throws some light on the originality of his method even in dealing with a more specific matter of direct concern to us. In discussing style (*plásma*), Philodemus describes four kinds (the first such description in antiquity, strongly reminiscent of the later one by Demetrius): the copious or forceful, ἀδρογραφία; the plain, ἰσχνότης; the grand, μέγεθος; the elegant or smooth, γλαφυρότης.[18] *Plásma* is the last of the three subdivisions of ornamentation, the others being tropes and *schema*. *Schema* refers to sentence structure: periods, cola, and commata. Our author's sympathy clearly goes to the plain style, the simple, direct, beautifully unadorned manner of expression that is typical of philosophical discourse. It is also the "natural" way, although artistic, φύσει καλὸς λόγος, as opposed to the artificial way of the rhetors.[19]

Ornamentation appears, traditionally, as the last of the four virtues, thus following upon correctness, clarity (discussed through criticism of its opposite, ἀσάφεια 'obscurity'), and appropriateness. As anyone can see, the traditional patterns of the art are there, but while Philodemus moves within their technical framework, he has emptied them of all serious significance. They are nothing more than expository rubrics; the spirit of the exposition, the inner drift of speculation is elsewhere. Indeed Philodemus despises the rhetors and their predecessors the Sophists: to their art he denies the scientific rank of *téchne*.

[17] See Grube, *Greek . . . Critics*, pp. 192-206, esp.. 197. Grube recalls Philodemus' *Poetics*, XX, 21-26 and XXIII, 30-35 (Jensen ed., pp. 47 and 53), for Philodemus' "clearly stated" view that criticism is a function of reason as intellect, λόγῳ. Yet this would not by itself demolish Rostagni's contention, since from a Crocean point of view criticism is clearly an intellectual and rational exercise, even though art is 'intuition.' In fact, 'intuition' itself is intellectual insofar as it is an act of cognition, although it radically differs from the 'logical' activity.

For another sober philological analysis of Philodemus, cf. C. O. Brink, *Horace on Poetry* (1963), pp. 43-76. And see the most recent studies by Marcello Gigante, *Ricerche filodemee* (Naples, Macchiaroli, 1969).

[18] The largely restored texts of Philodemus' extant writings are available in Sudhaus' ed. for the *Rhetoric*, Jensen's ed. for the *Poetics*. There is a translation of the former, by H. M. Hubbell. These texts are notoriously uncertain at many points: for one thing, it is not to be excluded that only three styles be implied here. See Sudhaus, vol. I, p. 165, col. IV, ll. 2-5.

[19] Sudhaus I, 149 (IV); 151-153 (VII-X); and, on *schema*, 164-165 (III, 18-25).

Given these premises, the position of the Epicurean philosopher toward rhetorical questions acquires broader meaning when set against the background of his *Poetics*, where indeed we find the most pertinent material for our purpose. This is especially the case with his polemic stance vis-à-vis the rather mysterious school of the κριτικοί, who seem to have conceived of literary criticism as centered on composition. Against this sort of 'stylistic critics' *avant-la-lettre* Philodemus retorts, first, that composition cannot be separated from the other aspects of the work without damaging the organic unity of the work. This is the main point of his aesthetics. Moreover, he maintains that stressing composition as it was then conceived (that is, as mostly euphony) amounts to reducing the work of art to an exercise by and for the senses and the emotions, so that such 'euphonists' end up by delivering literature to the sole judgment of the ear, thus removing it from the realm of the intellect.[20]

While stressing the intellectual value of poetry (and of criticism as well, which proceeds by reason, λόγῳ), Philodemus was in no danger of confusing it with philosophy: they are two essentially different activities, even though the best style for poetry, indeed for all literature is simple, direct, and adherent to the thought, like the language of philosophy. He insists on the importance of technique: a form cannot be good without good composition (σύνθεσις τῆς λέξεως: Jensen, 43, XVIII, 1-17). Yet it needs more than that to be good: it needs fusion of thought, diction, and composition. Their deep unity is so basic that the garbling method as advised by the grammarians to show that a change in word order destroys the art (*metathesis*, soon destined to be eminently practiced by Dionysius), is inconclusive: it is only another instance of the fragmentary approach of criticism, whereby one forgets that by changing its arrangement one transforms the total poem, even its thought.[21] Thus, form and content, style and thought cannot be separated, since a change in one means a change in the other.[22] Consequently, again, all rules (θέματα) are inadequate and misleading, because they abstract from the actual, unique relationships between the parts of the particular poem at hand.

Dionysius of Halicarnassus, the eminent literary critic and historian, settled in Rome in 30 B.C. and taught there. In his critical approach to the work of art he came perhaps as close as anyone in antiquity to our

---

[20] See Jensen, 47-49 (XX, 22–XXI, 22).
[21] Cf. N. A. Greenberg, "Metathesis as an Instrument in the Criticism of Poetry," *Transactions and Proc. of the Amer. Philol. Ass.*, LXXXIX (1958), 262-270.
[22] Jensen, 27-29 (X, 33–XI, 4).

demands for global composition (taking this term in the modern sense of basic structure) by insisting that *dispositio* (οἰκονομία, = more traditionally, τάξις) ought to rank above *inventio* (εὕρεσις).[23] This unusual preference (disposition received only limited attention in ancient treatises, practically swallowed up as it was by the extensive treatment of invention) was paralleled by his rating of *compositio*, σύνθεσις, above *electio*, ἐκλογή. With the former of these two main divisions of elocution or style is entirely concerned Dionysius' epochmaking Περὶ συνθέσεως ὀνομάτων, *De compositione verborum*, for which we will also have much use when we deal with word order in our next section. For the moment we are only interested in this work for its ideas on sentence structure.[24]

Considering the importance of the work and its uniqueness for a complete treatment of *compositio* (within the limitations to be indicated below), a sketchy outline may be in order. I shall concentrate on definitions and omit questions of word order, to be dealt with later.

---

[23] Cf. Baldwin, *A. R. and P.*, p. 107 and fn., with reference to Dionysius' essay *De Demosthene*.

J. W. H. Atkins, *Literary Criticism in Antiquity* (2 vols., Cambridge, Engl., 1934), I, ch. vi, esp. pp. 170-177, outlines a spectrum of critical opinion in the third century B. C. (after the death of Theophrastus) going from the contentualists to the formalists, Heracleodorus being a representative of the latter in that he showed the way to Dionysius of Halicarnassus by attaching a fresh importance to composition. Neoptolemus of Parium, Horace's model for his *Ars poetica*, allegedly established a sort of compromise between the two schools.

[24] The basic ed. is D. of H., *On Literary Composition*, ed. W. Rhys Roberts (1910), with excellent trans., introduction, apparatus, and notes. See, also, D. of H., *The Three Literary Letters*, ed. W. Rhys Roberts (1901). Dionysius' rhetorical system was conjecturally reconstructed and tabulated by G. Ammon, *De Dionysii Halicarnassensis librorum rhetoricorum fontibus* (Munich, 1889), pp. 4-76. Also cf. Baldwin, *A. R. and P.*, 104 ff. for some of the following data. The most recent and competent analysis of *De compositione* is found in W. B. Stanford, *The Sound of Greek* (1967), esp. pp. 15-17 and 51-73. Prof. Stanford, however, is satisfied with extracting from our author all the documentation on theory and practice of Greek linguistic euphony, and therefore stops at consideration of only one of the aspects which concern us here. See, also, Bonner's work on Dionysius' literary ideas and Grube, *Greek . . . Critics*, pp. 207-230, especially for the relationships with other works on literary criticism by Dionysius. Of course we all remember Pope's slightly extravagant praise: " See Dionysius Homer's thoughts refine, / And call new beauties forth from every line." *An Essay on Criticism*, III, 106 f.

Also cf. the bibliographic note in Roberts' Introd. to his ed. of the *De compositione*, pp. 32-33, where he briefly characterizes the contributions of H. Weil, T. O. Goodell, Charles Short, H. L. Ebeling, Th. Harmsen, Ph. Both, J. J. Braun, F. Darpe, Hilberg, V. Clavel, J. W. H. Walden, A. Bergaigne, besides the studies of word order in Thucydides by Spratt and in Plato by Riddell.

Ekloghé and *synthesis* exhaust the treatment of expression as distinct from treatment of subject matter or " thought " (ch. i, ll. 12-13, p. 68). Ekloghé, diction or choice of words, is the less important of the two (ii, p. 72). The value of composition will be illustrated by passages from the *Odyssey* and Herodotus owing their beauty to *synthesis* rather than diction (iii). More examples follow, with garbling being exercized on them in order to show by its disastrous effects the truth of the above statement. The *Iliad* is chosen for poetry, and the opening of Herodotus' *History* for prose, this latter being then rewritten in two different manners (iv). The author engages in a sweeping indictment of all Greek writers of roughly the last three centuries B. C., for they utterly neglected that art of composition which had been the pride and glory of the old authors. Among the " unreadable " moderns he singles out such men as the historian Polybius and the philosopher Chrysippus the Stoic. This, incidentally, is an example of Dionysius' broad literary range, since he does not limit his stylistic analysis to oratory but extends it to all provinces of literary and even non-literary writing (iv, pp. 92-98). We go on to examine the grammatical theories of word order (v) and the three functions of *synthesis* (vi), then the ways of arranging cola into periods (vii) and of shaping them by revision (viii). Expansion and abridgment of cola and periods for the sake of rhythm comes next (ix), and finally, the question of the two aims of *synthesis*, namely charm and beauty, ἡδονή and τὸ καλόν: only Herodotus has both, Thucydides has mostly beauty, Xenophon mostly charm (x). The main sources of these two basic qualities are four: μέλος melody, ῥυθμός rhythm, μεταβολή variety, and πρέπον appropriateness. The remaining sources are, of charm: freshness, grace, euphony, sweetness, persuasiveness; of beauty: grandeur, impressiveness, solemnity, dignity, mellowness (xi). Here we encounter the conclusive assertion that " the science of public oratory is, after all, a sort of musical science, differing from vocal and instrumental music in degree, not in kind " (p. 125). The secret of sustained harmony lies in variation (melodic as well as rhythmic and lexical, etc.). The judge of this difficult art is good taste (Roberts thus translates καιρός), or sense of opportunity (xii). The same elements produce both charm and beauty, depending on how they are used (xiii). Then begins the phonetic treatment of the basic elements of melody, namely sounds, divided into letters (xiv) and syllables (xv). Words chosen by great writers are expressive, and this can be due to their imitative (onomatopoeic) sound (xvi). Rhythm and meter are studied next (xvii), and their effects (xviii). Since variety is a supreme prerequisite for excellence, the Isocratic authors deserve criticism for their lack of a sufficient degree of variety (xix). Appropriateness is analyzed mostly on the basis of sound—meaning correspondences, with a view to the particular action being imitated (xx). Composition has three modes (xxi): The author begins with the judicious demurrer that styles cannot be reduced into classes because they are as personal as our physiognomies. Yet we can, somewhat metaphorically, use three generic characterizations: αὐστηρά [διαφορά or ἁρμονία] rough or austere composition, γλαφυρά (or ἀνθηρά) smooth (or florid), εὔκρατος harmoniously blended (xxi). The first is plain but noble and forceful, uses few connectives and conjunctions, leans chiefly on cola rather than periods, these latter coming about, if at all, in an unstudied, natural manner and almost by accident. Pindar, Thucydides, Aeschylus, the orator Antiphon are some examples of the austere mode for different genres (xxii). We note that the detailed analyses of examples are heavily weighted on the side of 'phonetics': euphony is the chief preoccupation, or rather the lack of it, which seems to be the case with this mode. Even the choice of models clearly shows that this mode is not looked upon with disfavor. Dionysius claims it is characterized by a constant stress on each element of discourse, each word of the sentence. On the other hand the smooth mode (xxiii) "does not intend that each word should be seen on every side": its parts move freely, "sweeping along one on top of another," always "combined and interwoven," "like the onflow of a never resting stream"; indeed, the general effect is "one of continuous utterance." The junctures admit "of no appreciable time interval between the words," like pictures in which the lights melt insensibly into the shadows," "soft as a maiden's cheek." Through the full glow of its rich, felicitous imagery, this famous passage vibrates with the critic's enthusiasm toward the better achievements of this mode. It is marked by balanced, many-colon periods. But the method of binding periods together is opposite to that of binding words inside the periods, which has just been described. Just as the latter flow evenly and continuously, without ever standing apart, the periods, on the contrary, do acquire full individuality, "wishing that they may be seen, as it were, from every side" (p. 237). Among the models we find here Hesiod, Sappho, Euripides, Isocrates, and no historian. The blended mode (xxiv) deserves the first prize because it is a sort of mean, which the Peripatetics equate with perfection. Homer, Sophocles, Herodotus, Demosthenes, Plato, and Aristotle are in this group.[25] Returning to meter and rhythm, it is now time to watch how artistic prose resembles poetry (xxv) and, similarly, how good poetry resembles artistic prose, chiefly when meter determines the general movement but verses do not correspond to clauses (or cola), so that through enjambment poetry also enjoys a freedom of movement comparable to that of beautiful prose, though more rigorously controlled. Likewise, clauses and periods should vary in length and form, even in poetry (xxvi).

From the point of view of the writer's praxis in moving through drafts and revision, Dionysius' composition operates in three ways—or, to put it differently, has three 'functions'—: [26]

---

[25] In his famous commentary on the De comp., Batteux placed in this class Fénelon, Racine . . . and, surprisingly, La Fontaine and even Voltaire. For a compact discussion of the problem posed by Dionysius' application of this distinction to Demosthenes in his separate and contemporaneous essay on the great orator, see Grube, Greek . . . Critics, pp. 222-225.

[26] Baldwin, A. R. and P., pp. 111 and 113-122; Grube, Greek . . . Critics, pp. 217-222.

(1) discernment of what elements go naturally with what in order to make a satisfying combination; (2) knowledge of how to fit the parts together in order to obtain a harmonious whole; (3) revision in view of introducing the final modifications required: " abridging, expanding, altering in order to adapt."

De comp., vi, p. 104

The first operation is based on a criterion of 'natural' arrangement (chiefly logical) but ends up by aiming at the sensuous and hedonistic satisfaction of the aesthetic sense. The second is decidedly musical. The third roughly corresponds to the classical notion of *concinnitas*, elegance, to be achieved through revision by abridgment (*brevitas*), amplification (*amplificatio*), etc. This third point is important with regard to 'applied' rhetorical training, that is, the practical exercise of achieving satisfactory sentence emphasis by adapting the style and transposing terms, phrases, or clauses (vii).

One may feel tempted to indulge in a brief digression with regard to modern development of the practice under discussion here. The righting of sentences by transposition has been widely practiced in the past, but perhaps never so successfully as in the eighteenth century in France, as we shall see, and not only as a school exercise, but as a sophisticated form of stylistic criticism. Baldwin noted (p. 114) that a defect of modern text-books was to set forth this important process as if it were purely logical (and the heritage of Cartesian linguistics undoubtedly bore a heavy responsibility for this), and offered Dionysius' approach as a valid corrective. One could hardly disagree, provided one does not lose sight of the danger inherent in the Greek master's equal, though opposite, one-sidedness.

Dionysius' method is also notable for the linking of his subject matter with the grammatical inquiry on the one hand and the dialectical approach on the other. His use of the term colon, for example, is so close to the grammatico-logical notion of clause and proposition that Roberts invariably translates it as "clause." More importantly, his definition of composition—which neatly covers both structure and order—envisages a progression of subject matter which is clearly set in grammatical (and logical) terms: from words to clauses ("cola") to sentences ("periods"), this last stage of arranging cola into periods, a part of syntax, being called harmony. The text is worth quoting. After a survey of the progress of grammatical identification of parts of speech (from Theodectes and Aristotle to the Stoic school—beginning of ch. ii), we read: "The function of composition is to put words together in an appropriate order, to assign a suitable connexion to clauses, and to distribute the whole discourse properly into periods." [27]

The use Dionysius makes of the dialectical approach is, however, entirely negative. We shall realize the detailed implications of this when we deal with word order in the following section. On a more general level, we must register here a severe stricture as to the weakness of De compositione with respect to an explicit appreciation of anything transcending 'harmony.'

This is not to say that Dionysius was unaware of the existence of another governing principle of composition. When we turn, e. g., to his essay on Isocrates (ch. 2), we find there a tellingly conclusive judgment: Isocrates, we read, by paying excessive heed to formal balance and rhythm, composed so that "the thought is often the slave of rhythmical expression, and truth is sacrificed to elegance. . . . But the natural course is for the expression to follow the ideas, not the ideas the expression." [28] In other words, he is said to have sacrificed logical connection for the sake of harmony and formal structure. Once we have recognized Dionysius' open-mindedness on principle, we must take notice of the actual narrowness of his approach as it is worked out. At the bottom of his attitude there probably lies the very notion of composition as it was often understood. Dionysius' real subject is the formal relationship between words in their structural arrangement, NOT the relation of words to the ideas they express. Hence the author is not interested in words as symbols but only as sounds, not in logic and semantics but only in phonetics broadly understood. Thus he might have claimed that all matters we find so essential in a well-rounded discussion of composition such as clarity, emphasis, economy, expressiveness, and so on, were not part of his subject but either of the doctrine of ornatus or of that of subject matter, the πραγματικὸς τόπος he expressly excluded, limiting himself to part of the λεκτικὸς τόπος (ch. i, p. 66).

[27] ii, Roberts, pp. 72-73: ἔστι δὴ τῆς συνθέσεως ἔργα τά τε ὀνόματα οἰκείως θεῖναι παρ' ἄλληλα καὶ τοῖς κώλοις ἀποδοῦναι τὴν προσήκουσαν ἁρμονίαν καὶ ταῖς περιόδοις διαλαβεῖν εὖ τὸν λόγον.
[28] Roberts' trans. in De comp., p. 11. This judgment appears particularly significant in the light of Dionysius' complex position vis-à-vis Isocrates. His enthusiastic admiration for this orator goes to the philosophical and moral foundations of his work, but as an Atticist he cannot approve of his style: no direct praise of his famous balanced periodic composition is to be found in Dionysius' essay on Isocrates. Cf. Grube, Greek . . . Critics, p. 215.

Dionysius then divided the study of *compositio* into consideration of its nature, force, processes (respectively in commata, cola, periods), charm (ἡδονή, the pleasure-giving, sympathy-winning factor of oratorical practice) and beauty (τὸ καλόν), kinds, finally verse- and prose-form. In particular, while distinguishing charm from beauty (the subjective from the objective element, so to put it), he found that they arose from four factors: melody, rhythm, variety, aptness.[29] The last-but-one category above ("kind") refers to the three typical modes of sentence movement: the rough or austere, the smooth or florid, and finally the harmoniously blended. The first mode seeks rather the force of each part than the harmony of the whole, it aims at emotion, πάθος, and can be exemplified by Pindar and Thucydides. The words stand out separately, without fear of hiatus or other clashing of sounds, and without care for periods.[30] It is clear that the analogy between compositional forms and style genera could go so far as to blur the distinction, as is definitely the case here. Indeed, Dionysius' threefold division has something in common with some modern interpretations of the profound meaning of the three ancient styles (and, particularly, with that of the baroque theorists of the 'point'): the modern view of 'Attic' and 'humble' style as sententious, pointed, sharp, and eventually not alien to meaningful obscurity reminds us, in a sense, more of Dionysius' "rough" sentence than of the literal ancient definitions of genera, within which Attic and 'humble' meant essentially simple and clear.[31] The smooth mode (xxiii) is periodic in its sentences and nicely articulated in its clauses and phrases. "It tries to combine and interweave its component parts, and thus give, as far as possible, the effect of one continuous utterance. This result is produced by so nicely adjusting the junctures that they admit no appreciable time-interval between the words."[32] Aiming at the easiest transitions within the period,

---

[29] Chs. x—beginning of xi. See, also, Dionysius' letter on Demosthenes (Roberts' ed.), xlvii.

[30] *De compositione* xxi, pp. 208-210. The following chs. discuss the three modes in great detail. See Baldwin, p. 119.

[31] See, in fact, Baldwin, p. 120. When actually referring to the plain style, as he does in his essay on *Lysias*, ch. viii, Dionysius specifically points out that Lysias composed un-periodically for the rendering of character (ἠθοποιία), an accomplishment in which that orator excelled over all others and for which the period is not suitable: καὶ συντίθησί γε αὐτὴν [λέξιν] ἀφελῶς πάνυ καὶ ἁπλῶς ὁρῶν ὅτι οὐκ ἐν τῇ περιόδῳ καὶ τοῖς ῥυθμοῖς ἀλλ' ἐν τῇ διαλελυμένῃ λέξει γίγνεται τὸ ἦθος: Usener and Radermacher, eds., *Dionysii Halicarnassei Opuscula* (Leipzig, Teubner, 1899-1904, 1909, 2 vols.), I, 15, 21-22.

[32] xxiii, p. 234. As usual, I give Roberts' trans.

it is careful to distinguish between periods. The parts coalesce; the units stand out.[33] All this is in line with Aristotle (*Rhet.* III, ix, 1409A) and with Cicero's own practice. The third mode was only vaguely distinguished.

One can conclude that this system, just like that of the style genera, was more basically twofold than threefold. Moreover, even the two major classes, ingenious as their definitions were, necessarily entailed a certain degree of abstraction. The system, based as it was on facts of style, did not go much beyond Aristotle's rather casual distinction between the unperiodic style and the periodic (*Rhet.* III, viii, 1408B), of which it was little more than an elaborate extension—but with the important difference that 'unperiodic' has dropped its rather negative value as referring to a primitive, elementary, pre-periodic mode of writing. Furthermore, Dionysius went far beyond the great Stagirite in questions of sound and rhythm.

It is clear that Dionysius moves outside the narrow sphere of the *technigraphi*, since in all of his literary works he occupied himself with practical criticism and literary theory rather than rhetorical theory. He is of course closely indebted to the latter, as most ancients were, and most of the time keeps close to its patterns. But he often becomes uneasy with the abstractness of these patterns, and strives to brush them aside, as when he organizes his essays on the orators and historians around the doctrine of stylistic virtues and genera only to step beyond them as soon as they threaten to outgrow their usefulness and become mere straitjackets for the concrete critical judgment. He is, in sum, a good example of the limitations of such doctrines when they became conceived as rigid, a priori systems merely reflecting the technicians' addiction to formulaic simplifications—what Grube has wittily spurned as "formulaitis."

Dionysius was not alone in this. After all, most of the shrewdest critics of antiquity avoided overstating the reality of the genera—an error into which the classicists of the late Middle Ages and of the late Renaissance often fell, as they also did with the similarly dangerous hypostatization of the literary genres.

The weaknesses and limitations of the system were most genially exposed in the treatise on Sublimity (Περὶ ὕψους) of the Pseudo-Longinus.[34]

---

[33] xxiii, p. 236. See Baldwin, p. 120.
[34] See the masterful Introduction in A. Rostagni's ed. for the theoretical background of this book. Also cf. Baldwin, pp. 124-129.

The anonymous author exerted his unparalleled critical gifts to show that oratorical amplification (αὔξησις, a characteristic feature of the *genus grande*), which is complementary to compression, of itself never rises to the heights of expression. "Therein lies the difference, that sublimity depends on elevation, while amplification is also a matter of copiousness: whereas the former is mostly found in a single thought, the latter is inseparable from a certain quantity and abundance."[35] This clearly implies that heightening of style (δίαρμα, the foundation of ὕψος, the 'sublime') lies on the other side of both the main conventional style genera. Generally speaking, it is single and intensive, as in poetry or in the orations of Demosthenes, while amplification is iterative and extensive, as in Plato or Cicero.

It is interesting to note that medieval theory, in its characteristic tendency to confuse the principles of rhetorical prose and those of poetic discourse, applied the techniques of amplification to poetry more unscrupously than had ever been done in antiquity; with total disregard for the point of view which the Pseudo-Longinus so eminently represents, amplification became in the Middle Ages one of the chief ingredients of 'elevation,' both in theory and in practice.

Sentence movement (σύνθεσις) is then said by the Pseudo-Longinus to subsume handling of figures and noble diction, though formally distinct. Together, these three factors (figures, noble diction, and synthesis) are the *acquired* sources of height in style, whereas intellectual power of conception and force of emotion ('pathos,' not specifically treated by the author) are the *native* sources (viii, 1). In oratory the purpose of imagery is typically intellectual, in poetry, emotional; although oratory too may use it for emotional effect.

The author serves notice that having already in another treatise in two books (now lost) gone exhaustively into the theory of *synthesis*, he will treat it here only insofar as it is relevant to the subject at hand (xxxix, 1). The pervasive emotional effect of harmony needs to be stated, but no more than that; it is too evident to require proof. Conversely, a wrong rhythm may drag down or distract (xli-xlii). The whole section occupied by these four chapters is characterized by a 'harmonic' sentence structure (or composition in the narrower sense) which will be more properly under-

---

[35] . . . κεῖται τὸ μὲν ὕψος ἐν διάρματι, ἡ δ' αὔξησις καὶ ἐν πλήθει . . . (xii, 1). See Roberts' trans., literally different from mine, in *On the Sublime*, ed. W. R. Roberts (Cambridge, 1899), p. 77.

stood after we have dealt with the question of word order, since in the
general scheme I follow in this exposition, harmony and rhythm are more
directly associated with word order than with sentence structure. Indeed,
the anonymous author boldly defines composition itself as a sort of harmony or music applied to language (. . . τὴν σύνθεσιν, ἁρμονίαν τινὰ οὖσαν
λόγων . . . , xxxix, 3), and in quasi-mystical tones reminiscent of the best
of Plato he asserts its subtle but irresistible powers over our minds and
souls. He unhesitatingly relates this compositional harmony to sublimity
itself (καὶ εἴσῃ, πόσον ἡ ἁρμονία τῷ ὕψει συνηχεῖ.— xxxix, 4). This is easily
shown by the loss of all truly persuasive power in any passage where the
slightest garbling has destroyed even a single prosodic measure. Still
more important is what he calls the connecting of the parts (ἐπισύνθεσις,
xl, 1). Consequently, the whole in an artistic speech unit is more than
the sum of its parts, and sublimity or excellence is the result of a conspiring of organically tied elements: "It is my view that greatness in the
periods lies in the collective contribution of a multiplicity of elements"
(σχεδὸν ἐν ταῖς περίοδοις ἔρανός ἐστι πλήθους τὰ μεγέθη, ibid.). The overwhelming import of this harmonic factor in the arrangement of the parts
of speech as a separately distinguishable cause of heightening can be seen
in many an author, most strikingly in Euripides, who is a poet rather
by his *compositio* than by his thought (xl, 3).[86]

The independence of our author from the more literal precepts of the
schools is seen in the succeeding warning against relying too much, as
it were, on physical measurements of the sentence. Value is in the spirit
of the thing and its inner justification: for the moment he will only stress
that meagerness of expression is as impotent as conciseness is good, and
the same is true of their opposites, since the sublime can be rich but
never indulges in prolixity (xlii). In a related context we had already

---

[86] I render thus a difficult passage that is usually translated as "Euripides is a
poet of arrangement rather than of ideas." Russell, in the latest ed. of the *Sublime*
(1964), p. 177, objects to this interpretation and proposes: "It is the arrangement
rather than the sense of which Euripides is the poet," and adds: "i. e., it is the
σύνθεσις which shows the great poet."

Allen Tate, *The Forlorn Demon* (Chicago, 1953), "Longinus and the 'New
Criticism,'" 131-151, esp. 147-149, holds that of all the five sources of Longinus'
sublime the fifth, namely "'composition and distribution of words and phrases
into a dignified and exalted unit' heads up the entire argument. 'It is a unity
of composition,' he says, 'attained through language.'" And it is equivalent to
"harmony" (p. 145): at least, it includes rhythm (148-149). Cf. William K.
Wimsatt, Jr. and Cleanth Brooks, *Literary Criticism: A Short History* (New York,
1966²), 108-109.

witnessed the independence I am alluding to, when, earlier in the treatise
(xx-xxi), even while he defended the use of pathos (of which the Asians
were generally more fond than their counterparts), he criticized the
followers of Isocrates. There, also, an isolated remark on the syntactic
use of conjunctions to transpose the unperiodic or 'plain' into the
periodic or 'florid' acquires all its flavor when placed in the context of
composition theory: "You can thus see that what is hurried and rough-
ened by emotion, if you smooth it out to a level by conjunctions, loses
its sting and fire" (xxi, 1). The example used is a passage from Demosthenes which is characterized by powerful asyndeta strengthened by ana-
phoras. If you follow the example of the Isocrateans, the author warns
his pupil (also that of the Ciceronians, we might add), and add conjunctions with all possible connectives to round out the period, you will take
away that supreme freedom that passion needs to express itself, as if you
were tying a runner's limbs just as he makes ready to thrust himself
forward.[37]

[37] Much ingenuity has gone into the effort of giving the author of the *Sublime*
a local habitation and a name. He remains anonymous, and nearly as elusive as
his own subject, for after all, to say it with Pope, he "is himself the great sublime
he draws." Yet, we might feel entitled to accept a suggestion, tentative and conjectural though it might be, if a convincing one were offered us. A very attractive
suggestion was once formulated by the eminent classicist Augusto Rostagni, and I
should like to summarize it even though it is now rather discredited as unsupported
by the available evidence. Rostagni's reconstruction of the historical milieu and
scholastic affiliations of the treatise was based, in turn, on the hypotheses of M.
Schanz (1890) and H. Mutschmann (1913). See Rostagni's edition: Anonimo,
Del Sublime (Anonymi De Sublimitate), esp. pp. xiii-xxv.
   According to this interpretation, the position of the Pseudo-Longinus on the
matters seen above can be best understood in the historical setting and cultural
background which conditioned his unusual work. For its meaning clearly transcends
that of a treatise on rhetoric to encompass poetics (as the theory of how poetry must
be both made and judged) and aesthetics (as the principles of artistic values). The
views of our author (who probably lived between the age of Augustus and that
of Claudius) stem from the polemics that raged at the time in Greece and Rome
between the followers of Apollodorus of Pergamum, a teacher of public speaking
to Augustus (second half of 1st c. B.C.) and Theodorus of Gadara (a teacher
at Rhodes around the turn of our era, and teacher of Tiberius). The *Apollodorei*
derived from the Peripatetic school, but had emptied the Aristotelian position on
rhetoric of its philosophical implications by fixing its principles into dry and rigid
rules. In point of fact, Apollodorus conceived of his discipline as a science, ἐπιστήμη:
the aims of persuasion were to be attained by rational means, hence by proof, argument, and facts (πίστεις, πράγματα) rather than psychological suggestion (ψυχα-
γωγία) and 'illusion.' The type of problems he raised determines the framework
of those polemics and the personal solutions offered by the Pseudo-Longinus: the

Although he did not contribute a technical treatment or even extensive discussions of our matters, Seneca cannot be left unmentioned because of his deep and wide impact on later theorists. He immediately strikes the observer with an approach that is strongly reminiscent of both Philodemus and the Pseudo-Longinus, in that he despises the established scholasticism of the rhetors even while he counters their blind faith in abstract rules by insisting that style is individual, indeed it is a mirror of the writer's moral personality. Doubtless he would have agreed with Buffon's dictum: *le style, c'est l'homme même.* The supreme Stoic precept

negative part of the doctrine combated the very ideals his later opponents would stand up for, principally the expression and arousing of passion, enthusiasm, and ecstasy (πάσχειν, ἐνθουσιᾶν, ἐξιστάναι). In direct reaction, the *Theodorei* (whom M. Schanz dubbed "the anomalists of rhetoric") stressed the conception of rhetoric as art, τέχνη, not science: its supreme criterion is that of καιρός, the convenience of a particular form to its unique circumstances, since all principles involved are relative and flexible, and no absolute rules, no natural laws can be thought to hold fast. Pathos is the key to persuasive discourse in every aspect and part (Apollodorus had relegated it to the 'external' parts in every genre, the proem and the epilogue). Πάθος is the irrational, emotional faculty, it is feeling that overrides all bounds and norms; working through imagination (φαντασία) it attains to the full evidence of actual life-like-ness (ἐνάργεια) by means of imagery (σχήματα), physical forms endowed with spiritual dynamism. If Apollodorus was affiliated with the philology of the Alexandrians, Theodorus was in line with the Platonic background of the Stoically-dominated Pergamene philologists. The Apollodoreans were Atticists on style, analogists and purists on language; the Theodoreans looked with more favor on Asianism, were basically anomalists, and fought against purism. The outstanding personalities who come under the influence of the opposite schools do not, however, espouse a neat party-line. While, for instance, the Atticist leader Caecilius of Calacte is at the antipodes of the exquisitely Theodorean treatise *on the Sublime,* the latter occasionally treats the Isocrateans with disdain, just as Dionysius of Halicarnassus, another leading Atticist, was a fervent admirer of *both* Isocrates and Lysias. Rostagni's arguments are now re-examined in a sympathetic light by Giuseppe Martano in his new ed.: Pseudo-Longino, *Del Sublime* (Bari, 1965).

In a recent study of the question, Grube has challenged the more systematic implications of such approaches as Rostagni's: cf. G. M. A. Grube, "Theodorus of Gadara," *Am. Journal of Philol.,* LXXX (1959), 337-365; Id., *The Greek and Roman Critics* (Toronto, 1965), pp. 272-274 and 340-341, where the question is curtly disposed of. The Introduction to the new textual ed. by D. A. Russell, '*Longinus*' *On the Sublime* (Oxford, 1964), declines to tackle the question. See, also, Grube, "Notes on the περὶ ὕψους," *AJP,* LXXVIII (1957), 335-374. Even if it should ultimately be regarded as an unwarranted deduction from the too limited evidence at hand, it has seemed worthwhile to me to present once again this suggestive theory, both because it has received too little attention outside Germany and Italy, and because Grube's presentation of it is polemically tinged. In addition to the preceding see, now, Winfried Bühler, *Beiträge zur Erklärung der Schrift vom Erhabenen* (Göttingen, 1964). On the influence of the treatise on modern criticism, see the studies by S. H. Monk, A. Scaglione, J. Brody.

of living according to nature, κατὰ φύσιν, holds good for style, meaning
that we must avoid the 'unnatural' extremes of both Asianism and narrow
Atticism, excessive attention to formal devices and neglect of them to
the point of dryness (*ieiuna et arida*), a composition made effeminate
through artificial musical modulations as well as one made jerky through
chopped-up, minutely minced sentences. But Seneca was especially dis-
dainful of balance and symmetries, which he regarded as an unmanly
sort of ornamentation: *non ornamentum virile concinnitas*—a phrase often
cited in the seventeenth century. His taste favored a type of segmented
style suitable to the rendering of the dynamic flow of spontaneous and
ever-changing feeling through a continuous movement of speech—unlike
the Ciceronian scanning of broad formal and artificial units by way of
conspicuous *clausulae*. In his most articulate analysis of stylistic "sins"
as attributable to specific, historically identifiable styles (*Epist.* 114, 15-
16), besides the above strictures against Cicero he also warned against
the excessive sensuality of the Asianists, who could be said to "set their
words to music rather than composing them" (*non est compositio, modu-
latio est: adeo blanditur et molliter labitur*). Likewise he censured the
excessive suspension through transposition and separation of grammatically
bound terms, which are held up to the very end (*verba differuntur et diu
expectata vix ad clausulas redeunt*), but also the excesses of those who
"are all for abruptness and unevenness of style purposely disarranging
anything which seems to have a smooth flow of language. They would
have jolts in all their transitions; they regard as strong and manly whatever makes an uneven impression on the ear."[38] (See *Epist.* 100, 6-7,

---

[38] Trans. by Leeman, *Orationis Ratio*, II, p. 476 fn. 99. See *Ep.* 114, 15:
"Quidam praefractam et asperam probant; disturbant de industria, si quid placidius
effluxit; nolunt sine salebra esse iuncturam: virilem putant et fortem, quae aurem
inaequalitate percutiat." The principal document is Seneca's *Letter to Lucilius*
114, 1-22. See also his *Letters* 40, 75, 100, 115. Cf. C. N. Smiley, "Seneca and
the Stoic Theory of Literary Style," *Classical Studies in honor of Ch. Forster Smith*
(Madison, 1919), 50-61. A. Guillemin, "Sénèque directeur d'âmes: Les théories
littéraires," *Revue des Études Latines*, XXXII (1954), 250-274, shows the profound
impact of the *Sublime* on Seneca. Also Grube, *Greek . . . Critics*, pp. 268-272. It
is interesting that to Quintilian's sensitive ear Seneca's sentences sounded as un-
bearably fractured as those he himself criticized in his warnings against extremes:
"Si rerum pondera minutissimis sententiis non fregisset . . . comprobaretur"—*Inst.*
X, i, 130.
Leeman, *Orationis Ratio*, I, pp. 274-276 compares *Ep.* 100, 6-7 with *Ep.* 114,
15-16, and points out, in particular, how the former shows appreciation of Cicero's
smooth flow by contrast to Asinius Pollio's abrupt divisions between sentences, where-

with reference to Asinius Pollio, to whom Leeman adds Cestius Pius and Domitius Afer.) Order can also be unnatural if immoderately inverted. For these reasons, and especially for the sake of being true to oneself, imitation must be discouraged, even if the models could be happily chosen.

Smiley has conclusively shown how Seneca conformed in his own writings to the Stoic ideals on style: he was 'pure,' 'clear,' 'brief,' and 'ornate' in thought-figures exclusively, although these 'virtues' were conspicuous above all in his diction and composition without necessarily extending to his handling of subject matter, which, with regard to 'brevity,' could be far from concise. In particular, he delighted in the 'baroque' effects produced by pointed *sententiae*, antitheses (with their special, 'concentrated' variety known as oxymora), and paradoxes of various kinds: something, we may recall, in the order of one of the two kinds of *genus Asiaticum* condemned by Cicero in his *Brutus*. This was part of the taste of his age and an aspect of Silver Latinity. If, from a certain point of view, these developments were just as 'unnatural' as those he criticised, they did not thereby cease to be one of the main secrets of his prodigious success in the seventeenth century, when such devices were also admired by those who preached a 'natural,' 'plain,' and 'Attic' style. True enough, the unprepared contemporary reader was likely to be shocked by some aspects of Seneca's style. It is reported that Caligula found it to be like *arena sine calce,* sand without lime, meaning that the parts of the loose sentences were felt as lacking cohesion.

Quintilian's views on sentence structure have been tapped point by point in the systematic presentation above, and his more detailed section on word order will be extensively put to use in the following sub-chapter. Most of this material appears in a lengthy chapter of his *Institutio* devoted to *compositio* (IX, iv, 1-147); every point is presented in a precise manner that remained in certain respects definitive, as far as it went. The chapter opens with an interesting preamble: some have raised the objection that the art of composition is to be discarded for the sake of speaking in a "manly and natural way." The answer is that this way of being "natural" would entail discarding not only this part of art, but all art, nay civilization itself, and returning to live in woods and caves (iv, 6). This argument is taken up again at the end of the work (XII, x, 40-44). Quintilian also discusses the Attic and Asianic movements and the chief styles (two, three, or four as they might be), but at the very end of the

as the latter sees Cicero's style under a different angle and censures it for its Asianic rotundity.

work (XII, x, 10-80), almost as an afterthought, and rather succinctly. The tone lacks strong conviction, and the drift of reasoning seems to be that such categories are more abstract than not, and not applicable with precision. His basic, empirical good sense tells him that the concreteness of true style is a personal matter: If you look closely enough, you will find that talents are individual, and that there are as many spiritual physiognomies in literature as there are physical bodies: " totidem paene reperias ingeniorum quod corporum formas" (XII, x, 10). Besides, and this concerns us more, he does not characterize styles by compositional patterns.

Quintilian was equally wary of the chaos in the denominations of tropi (cf. IX, iii, 1-99). Indeed his attitude toward the figures in general is one of moderate scepticism, reflecting his adherence to the philosophical school of thought which stressed dialectical and moral purpose as against the sophistical concentration on elocution or form. In this, however, he missed the close connection between form and content when the inner nature of dialectical or persuasive discourse is viewed from a higher vantage point. For him figures are important but the validity of proof does not rest on the type of figures chosen for the formal presentation. In this sense he remained within the confines of the prevailing opinion, consisting of a view of figures as mere ornaments artificially added and to be moved around at will. When an orator like Latro professed the un-orthodox view that figures had not been " invented " as ornaments, his opinion was regarded as remarkably idiosyncratic.[39]

Of especial interest to us is Quintilian's justification of the fondness of the eminent Roman orators for the grand style on the ground of its being more congenial to their language than it was for the Greeks (cf. esp. XII, x, 63). This is related to the fact that the apt use of Latin

---

[39] Cf. Seneca the Rhetor, *Controversiae et Suasoriae*, ed. Henri Bornecque (Paris, 1932, 2 vols.), I, Book I, Preface, § 24. And see Perelman, *Traité de l'Argumentation* (1958), vol. I, pp. 226-227, with reference to Jean Paulhan, " Les figures ou la rhétorique décryptée," *Cahiers du Sud*, XXXVI, 295 (1949), 361-395, esp. 387. For a correct perspective on the importance of our subject to Quintilian it must be remembered that he explained how his limited treatment of composition was due to his agreement with most of Cicero's handling of it, which he did not deem necessary to duplicate (*Inst. Or.*, IX, iv, 2). But he did disagree with him on some details, e. g. on Cicero's wrongly stating that such old Greek authors as Lysias, Herodotus, and Thucydides had little regard for rhythm (IX, iv, 16-18). And he had different views on some points of prose metrics, which he treated more extensively and elaborately than Cicero in the *Orator* (*Inst. Or.* IX, iv, 45-147). Cf. Leeman, *Orationis Ratio*, I, pp. 307-310.

requires greater care than that of Greek, which is somehow better endowed by nature with pleasing sounds (XII, x, 27). Which is tantamount
to saying that the Romans should logically pay greater attention to composition than the Greeks were obliged to do, and this, Quintilian had
pointed out before (IX, iv, 145-146), is precisely what happened. All in
all, however, Quintilian looked upon Asianism as practically dead. This
statement is rather surprising if we only think of the numerous testimonies
of alarm and hostility against the "popularity" of Asian bombast and
declamatory display through the century, including Seneca the Elder's
warnings and Petronius' identification of Asian bad taste with the needs
of the masses (esp. *Satyricon*, iii).

The treatise *on Style* (Περὶ ἑρμηνείας) attributed to Demetrius (probably end of first century A. D.) is far from a complete manual of the art,
since it is rather a treatise of literary criticism and stylistic theory on the
basis of the style genera. But this very nature of the work makes it possible for the doctrine of composition to loom large through its five books.[40]
The author did not sin by excessive orderliness or critical depth, yet the
plan of the work appears, somewhat deceptively, to be careful and
methodical.

The first book tackles the question of periodicity, apparently taking
clues from Aristotle. Expression or style (ἑρμηνεία) is simply divided, from
the viewpoint of structure, into 'compacted' or periodic (κατεστραμμένη)
and 'disjointed' or 'loose' (διῃρημένη, also διαλελυμένη) (I, 12). For
Demetrius' taste, the optimum upper limit of the period is the tetracolon—
the ideal 'square' that marks the last stage in the progression from
Aristotle's rather elementary insistence on the two parts of his basically
antithetic period. The periodic style can be classified, according to its
uses, into dialogical, narrative or historical, and oratorical, in this ascending order, the first being quite close to the loose sentence (I, 19-21). The
remainder of the work takes on the questions concerning the four style
genera, each one of these being treated in a separate book. Every time the
author includes a specific treatment of the type of composition appropriate to each style. One must note that composition here also includes,

---

[40] Cf. Aristotle . . . , Longinus . . . , Demetrius *On Style*, ed. and trans. W.
Rhys Roberts (1953). This ed. was preceded by the one prepared by the same
editor: Demetrius *On Style* . . . (Cambridge, 1902), with a fuller apparatus. On
the dating of the work, basically in agreement with Roberts and against Grube's
thesis, see, now, D. M. Schenkeveld, *Studies in Demetrius 'On Style,'* Diss.
(Amsterdam, 1964); J. M. Rist, "Demetrius the Stylist and Artemon the Compiler," *Phoenix*, XVIII (1964), 2-8.

as it happened in several other texts, all questions of figures of speech and virtues of style; all the questions, that is, which we have decided to separate from the narrower sense of our term, although we are compelled by the texts and the tradition to take into account the close interrelatedness of all these matters. Demetrius rather methodically treats each style under the three headings of its specific sources, namely composition (σύνθεσις), subject matter (πράγματα or διάνοια), and diction (λέξις, meaning choice of words, vocabulary) (II, 38).[41] The "characters of style" are, then, four: plain, grand, elegant, forceful (ἰσχνός, μεγαλοπρεπής, γλαφυρός, δεινός). Demetrius judiciously adds: They all mix together freely, except the plain and the grand, which are irreducible extremes. Interestingly enough, though somewhat mysteriously, he informs us that this sequence was interpreted in a particular way by some critics, who tended to reduce all styles to two basic ones, plain and grand (II, 36). These writers insisted on associating the elegant with the plain and the forceful with the grand. Could we then not take the liberty of going one step further, establishing a methodic ascending sequence, thus: Plain–Elegant–Forceful–Grand, or, more significantly, P→E–F→G. Whether this inference corresponds or not to the intentions of "those critics," Demetrius rejects their views as absurd; but I believe they make more sense out of his terminology than he was able to draw from it.

At any rate, the actual order of treatment in the text is still another, that is to say Grand (typically characterized by the use of a harmonious period), Elegant (typically, loose sentence), Plain (mostly cola), Forceful (using comma rather than colon as its basic unit). The last is the most interesting from the point of view of composition. If periods must be used in it, then let them be two-colon periods, the pithiest and most forcible variety. This style puts the virtue of Laconic brevity to good use. This is why it prefers phrases to full-fledged, articulated clauses, for "length paralyzes intensity, while much meaning conveyed in a brief form is the more forceful" (V, 241). It "must avoid antitheses and exact symmetry (paromoion) in the periods, since instead of force they produce a labored frigidity" (V, 247). On the other hand, it can use inversions to great advantage: Demetrius does not use the term, but refers to the principle that end-position carries a special weight, so that "to place the most striking element at the end produces a forceful expres-

[41] See Roberts' synopsis, pp. 290-293, where these distinctions are placed in evidence.

sion," and quotes an eloquent example ending with a startling participle
(V, 249). We will then not shy away from an appropriate abruptness,
which can be the felicitous effect of dropping the transitional conjunctions
(μέν . . . δέ and similar) (V, 269) or even of bluntly ending the sentence
with the conjunctions δέ or τέ—something sternly disapproved of in the
manuals teaching normal correctness and fluency (V, 257).

In discussing the doctrine of style genera after Theophrastus, G. Kennedy [42] has attempted to define the relationship between this doctrine and
the ancient views on composition as part of his identification of the various
ingredients of the concept of style. He points out that " though the author
of the *Ad Herennium* speaks of composition, he seems to regard the
diction [choice of words, vocabulary], or the diction and the figures (iv,
16), as the basic difference." Cicero's account in the *Orator* differentiates
the styles on the basis of diction, composition, and subject (20 f.).
Dionysius' threefold distinction (xxi) would be based on composition
in the *De compositione,* and on diction in his essay on Demosthenes,
with Isocrates as an example of the smooth style in composition, but
of the middle style in diction. Quintilian (XII, x, 58) would have
" conflated these two schemes into the plain (ἰσχνός), the grand and
forcible (ἁδρός), and a third which some call middle, others florid
(ἀνθηρός). He does not find any set of three categories satisfactory
(XI, x, 66)." Demetrius' four styles were " all based on diction and subject, which is roughly similar to [literary] genre, but also each has a
characteristic composition." Finally, " a set of types found in some late
rhetoricians is austere (Thucydides, Antiphon), middle (Demosthenes,
Hyperides), plain (Lysias, Isocrates)."

This concise summary indicates the absence of standardization in
such a sensitive area of ancient critical canons and formulaic principles.
Kennedy attributes this flexibility to the critics' shifting points of view
" depending on whether they wanted to stress diction, composition, or
thought." Convincing as this analysis appears to me, I find Kennedy's
isolation of the various 'ingredients' a bit vague and unclear. This is
not entirely his fault: his terminology significantly depends, I believe, on
that of Demetrius, which we have found somewhat misleading, since his
' composition' includes figures and virtues. Ancient conceptions of styles
were always a shifting mixture of several elements, but in conclusion I
feel these latter can be more precisely and meaningfully analyzed as

[42] G. Kennedy, *The Art of Persuasion,* pp. 278-282, esp. 281-282.

diction, figures, virtues of elocution, and composition. Subject matter or thought entered the picture only, though importantly, under the perspective of the uses of genera.[43]

In the literature of the early Christian Fathers we might reasonably expect a lack of appreciation for the declamatory rhetoric and heavy emphasis on form brought about by the Second Sophistic.[44] We would be right in our expectation, albeit those among the Fathers who enjoyed the privileges of an advanced formal education were as much the products of Sophistic education as anybody else at their time. They could not escape it, since it was almost the only lore of available training in the public use of speech—an activity of paramount importance to them as preachers of the new Gospel.

Augustine, for one, had not only learned it; he had taught it.[45] But if we turn to his *De Doctrina Christiana*, a true foundation of Christian preaching and one of the most influential treatises on rhetoric for the Middle Ages, we will find out how the great Bishop of Hippo could apply the most effectively devastating tactic toward the rejection of Sophistic. Instead of attacking it, he ignored it. This does not mean that he rejected classic rhetoric. To the contrary, he brought it back to its purest original sources, in the spirit of the best tradition as Aristotle, Cicero, and Quintilian had truly envisaged it, namely, as the formative training of the speaker who masters the art not for the sake of amoral personal triumph but for that of communicating moral and scientific truth in such a manner as to move the audience beyond conviction to persuasion, from approval to action.

Yet, what interests us more particularly in this treatise is the almost total concentration on the compositional aspects of rhetorical doctrines,

[43] For general studies on the doctrine of styles, see Augustyniak (1957) and Quadlbauer (1958).

[44] On aspects of the Second Sophistic in the Greek and Roman worlds, see the works of A. Boulanger (1923) and R. Marache (1952). Also Barwick, *Probleme* and *Martial*.

[45] On the uses of popular Latin and the language of the Scriptures as sources for Augustine's own style in addition to the norms of contemporary rhetoric, see Christine Mohrmann, *Études sur le latin des Chrétiens* (Rome, 1958-61), I (1958), "Saint Augustine and the 'Eloquentia,'" 351-370, and the earlier Edith Schuchter, "Zum Predigtstil des hl. Augustinus," *Wiener Studien*, LII (1934), 115-138. Augustine's preaching style was adduced by Auerbach, *Literary Language and its Public* (1965), pp. 27-66 as the point of departure for his masterful analysis of the early medieval *sermo humilis*, the original Christian formula which combined features of the plain style with verbal and phonetic patterns to achieve sublimity in simplicity.

whenever it turns to discussion of style and critical analysis. More specifically still, we hear about sentence movement almost exclusively, aside from a few remarks on figures or tropes. Then, Augustine goes on to relate all his observations to the traditional theory of style genera, which he borrows directly from Cicero's *De oratore* and *Orator*, disregarding all other precedents as marginal and otiose.

The relevant passages occur in chs. vii and xvii-xxviii of Book IV. In IV, vii three examples are offered to show how Christian eloquence is to be analyzed.

(1) Romans V, 3-5: " [Non solum autem, sed et] gloriamur in tribulationi bus, scientes quia [Vulgate and Versio antiqua = quod] tribulatio patientiam operatur, patientia autem probationem, probatio autem [as in V. a.; Vulg. = vero] spem. Spes autem non confundit: quia charitas Dei diffusa est in cordibus nostris per Spiritum sanctum, qui datus est nobis."
(2) 2ᵈ Corinthians xi, 16-30.
(3) Amos vi, 1-6.[46]

In the first passage, Augustine recognizes a case of *gradatio* or *klimax* (to which terms he adds a Latin equivalent, *scala* 'ladder'), in that words or meanings are connected by proceeding from one another through repetition (and this process of linking iteration, incidentally, was a favorite of Sophistic method). But all three passages he closely analyzes on the basis of breaking them up into the traditional components designated as *caesa, membra, ambitus* or *circuitus,* of which he also gives the Greek equivalents of *kómmata, kóla, períodos.* Baldwin (*M. R. P.,* 61) holds that in Augustine's use *caesa* denoted phrases and subordinate clauses, *membra* coordinate clauses, which would place him in a rather idiosyncratic po- sition vis-à-vis the established tradition. I believe it is more correct to say that Augustine uses *membra* as divisions of periods, whereas he tends to refer to phrases and clauses used in isolation or in non-periodic sequences as *caesa*—which is personal enough but more in keeping with the tradi- tion. He points out the value of *caesa* for the sake of variety and of breaking the monotony of periodic successions. Yet he is not entirely

⁴⁶ Baldwin, *M. R. P.,* 55-73. Augustine follows the " Versio antiqua " of Paul's text. I place in brackets the variants according to the Vulgate. The punctuation varies markedly in the different versions. See Augustine's text (with slightly different punctuation) in Sister Thérèse Sullivan, S. *Aureli Augustini De Doctrina Christiana Liber Quartus,* Catholic Univ. of Amer. Patristic Studies, XXIII (Washington, D. C., 1930), p. 66, with fns., and the textual comparisons on p. 19. The ex- tensive commentary in this edition is the best guide for rhetorically-minded users of this text.

consistent in this, for he also refers to *membra* outside the period. In such cases *membra* become hard to distinguish from *caesa,* as he uses the terms, but then the difference between *membra* inside and *membra* outside the period lies entirely in the method of delivery. This is significant, in that the emphasis on delivery was indicative of the oratorical orientation of this ancient body of stylistic analysis, since the objective value of the text as written down and physically punctuated was only a secondary matter for purposes of identification of its periodic units and other subdivisions.[47] Thus, in the Pauline passage quoted above *in extenso,* Augustine regards only the last part as a period (starting with *Spes autem*): all the preceding is a succession of *caesa* and, above all, *membra.* The difference between a non-periodic sequence and a periodic one is that, in the former, all units are "pronounced with the same expression," while in the latter "the *membra* are held suspended by the speaker's voice until the last one is completed" (hence it "cannot have fewer than two clauses"). In other words, the difference is one of musical movement or rhythm, and the manner of definition throws the emphasis on delivery.

In one way Augustine's terminology does depart from classical habit: although he speaks of periods, his examples are all from texts which the more rigorous rhetorical schooling would have classified within the 'plain style' (even if, by 'Longinian' standards, they could be cases of 'sublimity'), and of a kind to which nothing could be thought to be more alien than the oratorical period. This surprising approach is due to the very nature of his undertaking, since he is showing the Christian preacher how to use and interpret Biblical texts—which were laid down in verselike units excluding the longer, more complex, and more sustained rhythmical reaches of true periodicity. One can see, for instance, that the movement of the Pauline sentence under discussion is not the ascending and circular one of the classical period. It sounds more like Gracchus' passage *before* Cicero's revision. Augustine thus foreshadows a time when the feeling for the classical periodicity had disappeared—a time that practically covers all of the Middle Ages. He has a thesis to prove: the cultured and poetic value of the religious texts, inferior to none of the secular ones even by literary standards. He succeeds brilliantly, but at the same time he reveals more than he perhaps intended.[48]

[47] See the Third Catilinarian analyzed above.
[48] On the use of rhetorical theory in the *De Doctrina Christiana* see Auerbach, op. cit., esp. 33-39.

C. WORD ORDER

The other aspect of the theory of word arrangement or, more broadly, 'literary composition' (as W. R. Roberts called it with reference to Dionysius of Halicarnassus' treatise), concerns word order, to which we shall now turn.

It is pertinent for us to assert once again that the two questions of sentence structure and word order are collateral and contiguous, not only in the sense that these major aspects of sentence building were usually treated as the two main subdivisions of *compositio,* but also in that they presented several common problems of method and treatment—not the last of these being the appeal to considerations of musical harmony as we are about to see.

Word order could be envisaged from three basic points of view, namely: 1) what the ancients designated as *ordo* proper; 2) the art of joining the sounds and sound-groups harmoniously (*iunctura,* euphony); 3) the rhythmical arrangement of word sequences and the scanning and marking of functional pauses by the use of cadences (*numerus,* rhythm). A perfectly ordered composition meets all three requirements equally, but this happy degree of perfection is most difficult.[1] Although we conceive of word order in a narrower sense, which corresponds basically to part only of the first of these three concepts, the ancient theorists usually encompassed all three of them in their treatment of the subject.

We have seen how Dionysius rated composition above diction. He proved the validity of this preference by analyzing a long passage from *Odyssey* XVI, 1-16 (*De compositione* iii, Roberts ed. pp. 76-78) and another from Herodotus I, 8-10 (*De comp.* iii, pp. 80-82), concluding in the end: "The fascination of his style does not . . . lie in the beauty of the words but in their combination" (p. 85). He ingeniously confirmed this by his peculiarly effective method of garbling, purporting to show how one could more drastically destroy the aesthetic quality of the text by shifting its words around than by changing the words themselves.

---

[1] Quint., *Inst. or.,* IX, iv, 22 and 27: "In omni porro compositione tria sunt genera necessaria: ordo, iunctura, numerus." "Felicissimus . . . sermo est, cui et rectus ordo et apta iunctura et cum his numerus opportune cadens contigit." On word order see Lausberg, *Handbuch,* esp. pp. 469-471. As already indicated, Dionysius of Halicarnassus is curiously missing among Lausberg's sources under the headings we are considering.

More specifically, what he thus strove to reveal is that sound rather than thought was often, to the ancient reader-hearer, the major ingredient of the beautiful style.[2]

One of Dionysius' examples may yield interesting observations (in line with the Latin example we have seen above) on the way a non-periodic sentence could be syntactically reworked into a period simply through a reordering of its words. It will also show that the Greek language was less tolerant of inversions than Latin. The first of the following sentences is the opening of Herodotus' *History* (with slight dialectal changes). Dionysius then recasts it into a less "natural," less "linear" but "rounder" manner, in imitation of Thucydides' style. The third rendering of the same narrative passage, however, in the "affected, degenerate, emasculate" manner of Hegesias, is objectionable to Dionysius as unrhythmic and unnecessarily inverted to the point of obscurity and disorderliness—a case of bad Asianism.

Κροῖσος ἦν Λυδὸς μὲν γένος, παῖς δ' Ἀλυάττου, τύραννος δ' ἐθνῶν τῶν ἐντὸς Ἅλυος ποταμοῦ· ὃς ῥέων ἀπὸ μεσημβρίας μεταξὺ Σύρων τε καὶ Παφλαγόνων ἐξίησι πρὸς βορέαν ἄνεμον εἰς τὸν Εὔξεινον καλούμενον πόντον.

Κροῖσος ἦν υἱὸς μὲν Ἀλυάττου, γένος δὲ Λυδός, τύραννος δὲ τῶν ἐντὸς Ἅλυος ποταμοῦ ἐθνῶν· ὃς ἀπὸ μεσημβρίας ῥέων μεταξὺ Σύρων καὶ Παφλαγόνων εἰς τὸν Εὔξεινον καλούμενον πόντον ἐκδίδωσι πρὸς βορέαν ἄνεμον.

Ἀλυάττου μὲν υἱὸς ἦν Κροῖσος, γένος δὲ Λυδός, τῶν δ' ἐντὸς Ἅλυος ποταμοῦ τύραννος ἐθνῶν· ὃς ἀπὸ μεσημβρίας ῥέων Σύρων τε καὶ Παφλαγόνων μεταξὺ πρὸς βορέαν ἐξίησιν ἄνεμον ἐς τὸν καλούμενον πόντον Εὔξεινον. (cf. iv, Roberts p. 90)

The term *ordo* was used generically by the Romans with regard to the disposition of words, and it could specifically apply to series of single coordinate words or to organized groups.[3] In the former case, it could imply that the series must follow the rule of planned progression ("Gesetz der wachsenden Glieder") and avoid any sort of anticlimax. Most eloquent is Quintilian's way of phrasing and exemplifying the rule: "Cavendum, ne decrescat oratio, et fortiori subiungatur aliquid infirmius, ut sacrilego fur, aut latroni petulans; augeri enim debent sententiae et insurgere, ut optime Cicero: 'tu' inquit 'istis faucibus, istis lateribus, ista gladiatoria totius corporis firmitate': aliud enim maius alii supervenit."[4]

---

[2] See also his *De Demosthene*, ch. li. Cf. D. L. Clark, *Rh. in G.-R. Ed.*, p. 94, and Baldwin, *A. R. and P.*, p. 107 and fn.

[3] Cf. Quint., *Inst. or.* IX, iv, 23: "(de ordine) . . . eius observatio in verbis est singulis et contextis."

[4] The quote is from Cic., *in M. Antonium Philippica* II, 25, 63. Lausberg,

This law applied, then, to coordinated word sequences, typically including *asyndeta*, just as it also applied to the periodic circuit of the sentence, as we have noticed above.[5] Again, this fundamental rule extends, most interestingly, to the phonetics of the phrase and sentence: thus it will not do to end a sentence with an unintegrated monosyllable instead of with a weightier unit, such as a colon or at least a comma. (Cf. Martianus Capella, 35, 520.) Indeed, a final monosyllable has a comic effect (Horace, *Ars poetica*, 139), unless it is consciously used to express suddenness (*Aen.* I, 105: *insequitur cumulo praeruptus aquae mons*). At only apparent variance with this is the rule that the more general must precede the more specific: " Qui est compositionis ordo? Ut ante ponamus genera quam species, communia quam propria, remota quam proxima; leviora verba ut non nimis longe differamus . . ." (Fortunatianus, III, ii, p. 127 ll. 25-27). More specifically, the term *naturalis ordo*, which was destined to arouse such wide and deep controversies, rather modestly referred to the respect of 'natural,' customary, and mainly 'chronological' order in enumeration and enumerative nexus, as in *viri ac feminae, dies ac nox, ortus et occasus.*[6] This principle could be stretched by some to the extent of desiring every event to be assigned, in the exposition and specifically in the sentence, to its place according to chronological order. It was going pretty far, indeed too far, even to the point of a ' superstition' in Quintilian's opinion, because, as he suggested, certain events which occurred earlier must be mentioned first not really for that reason, but because they happen to be more important: " Nec non et illud nimiae superstitionis, uti quaeque sint tempore, ea facere etiam ordine priora; non quin frequenter sit hoc melius, sed quia interim plus valent ante gesta, ideoque levioribus superponenda sunt " (IX, iv, 25).

Coming to the more momentous question of the place of each grammatical part in the clause, we find here that the key term was *rectus ordo*, whose meaning was manifold, its first acceptation being very close to one of 'natural' order. To begin with, one finds, rather interestingly, that

---

Handbuch, 470 fn., aptly notes that what is implied here is that in an enumeration the collective, if any, must close the series.

[5] See Weil, p. 7, on *versus rhopalici* and earlier, on " Beauzée's law."

[6] " Est et alius naturalis ordo, ut *viros ac feminas, diem ac noctem*, . . . dicas potius quamquam et retrorsum. Quaedam ordine permutato fiunt supervacua, ut *fratres gemini*; nam si *gemini* praecesserint, *fratres* addere non est necesse." Quint. IX, iv, 23-24. This passage and what follows (23-27) clearly echoes Dionysius, *De comp.*, v.

the ancients (especially the Romans) were aware of the possibility that one could view their way of ordering parts of speech as being, in some way, artificial and unnatural. Let us hear Quintilian (IX, iv, 3): "I am well aware that there are certain writers who would absolutely bar all study of composition and contend that language as it chances to present itself in the rough is more natural and even more manly." In its context, this also appears to reflect on word order in the clause and, indirectly though significantly, to point up the relative closeness of *spoken* Latin to the analytic order of, say, modern languages.

The ancients had produced a number of inquiries into our subject which are now lost. Dionysius refers, in his *De compositione*, to Stoic treatises of a dialectical orientation, and especially to Chrysippus' two works "on the grouping of the parts of speech" (Περὶ τῆς συντάξεως τῶν τοῦ λόγου μερῶν), cautioning his reader that they contain "not a rhetorical but a dialectical investigation, dealing with the grouping of propositions, true and false, possible and impossible, admissible and variable, ambiguous, and so forth" (iv, Roberts, pp. 96-97).

Now in ch. v he squarely faces, perhaps for the first time, a number of hypotheses with which he claims to have taken his first steps in investigating the laws of word order. He ended up, so he tells us, by discarding them all as contrary to experience. "I used to think that we ought to follow nature as far as possible in adjusting the parts of a discourse, . . . for instance, to put nouns before the verbs. . . . This idea is plausible; but I came to think it was not true."[7] What no one seems to have underlined or even noticed is that Dionysius attributes all such prejudiced approaches to the very kind of "manuals on dialectic" exemplified above by the reference to Chrysippus: Such manuals, he concludes, "are not relevant to the present inquiry, therefore they are not worth studying" (v, p. 104). To them he opposes the rhetorical point of view, which aims at beauty and effectiveness. We shall see presently what these hypotheses were, but let us note in passing that they will all become part of the rhetorical tradition starting with Quintilian (who summarized them in *Inst*. IX, iv) but, again, without any expressed reference to their non-rhetorical, dialectical, logical, or grammatical origin and nature. Indeed, some of them will be fully reconsidered and become central to investigation of word order in more modern times, precisely when stylistic

---

[7] *De comp.*, v, p. 98. On this and the following see Baldwin, A. R. *and* P., 109-114: the trans. above is Baldwin's (p. 109).

analysis will start to transcend the area of rhetoric and come directly under the influence of logic.

Dionysius, then, tells us that he had first thought the following principles of word order were to be observed because they were taught to us by nature itself (τῇ φύσει: v, p. 98): Duly place nouns before verbs (p. 98); verbs in front of adverbs (100); respect the chronological sequence of events (100); again place substantives before their appositions or adjectives, as well as pronouns referring to them, appellatives before substantives, pronouns before appellatives, primary verbal forms and moods before secondary forms and moods (102). The reason for the first stated rules is that in the nature of things nouns indicate substance, verbs accidents, adverbs circumstances, and just as substance takes precedence over its accidents, so does action over its modalities and circumstances.[8] This terminology from Aristotelian logic recurs from Dionysius to Apollonius in terms that seem to indicate a common source, and it was later echoed, through Priscian, by many medieval glossators.[9]

Indeed it would appear that Dionysius, just like all other rhetorically-oriented critics (we are about to witness a similar ambiguity in Cicero's *Partitiones*), was unable even to understand the full implications of the grammatico-logical viewpoint, since "noun before verb" clearly did not mean, for him, subject before predicate; his examples clearly show this, since they give *any kind* of noun, mostly in oblique cases, therefore not in subject position. The first two examples are, in point of fact, the first words from *Iliad* and *Odyssey*: ἄνδρα μοι ἔννεπε, Μοῦσα and μῆνιν ἄειδε, θεά (The hero to me sing, o Muse; The wrath sing, o goddess): neither has anything to do with SIPo. The examples he gives of "exceptions" are equally irrelevant from the logical viewpoint, since they are imperative constructions with the perfectly 'normal' VIPo. This context seems to disprove the once current translation of Dionysius' τὰ ὀνόματα πρῶτα . . . τάττειν τῶν ῥημάτων (ibid.) as "placing the subject before the verb," even though Aristotle did use ὄνομα to mean subject.[10]

---

[8] "Since the noun indicates substance, the verb accident, it is according to nature that substance should come before accident": τὰ μὲν γὰρ (ὀνόματα) τὴν οὐσίαν δηλοῦν, τὰ δὲ (ῥήματα) τὸ συμβεβηκός· πρότερον δ' εἶναι τῇ φύσει τὴν οὐσίαν τῶν συμβεβηκότων—De comp., v, p. 98.

[9] See Weil, p. 9 fn.

[10] Interpreters have tended to overlook this distinction and have identified the grammatical and the logical categories in the ancient parlance. Cf. Baldwin, *A. R. and P.*, p. 110, who explains Dionysius' meaning thus: "The order in a given

The lack of recognition of a 'normal' order carries with it the absence of any reference to the phenomena of transposition and inversion—a surprising omission if we only think of the frequent mention of hyperbaton in ancient theory. Yet Dionysius rather cursorily points out, a propos of 'appropriateness,' that our emotions (anger, joy, sorrow, fear, etc.) make us use different patterns of word order from those issuing from a calm state (ch. xx). He gives no name to such changes in order, but the failure to dwell on these important matters must perhaps be blamed on the intentional rejection of the semantico-logical areas from the narrow definition of composition which characterizes Dionysius' treatise, as we have seen in the preceding section.[11]

What is missed in Dionysius will be found very explicitly stated in the *Sublime,* as part of a typical equation of pathos with naturalness and depth of expression. In dealing with the figures, the Pseudo-Longinus underlined the effect of naturalness produced by infractions of the normal order in the process of expressing emotion, most typically through hyperbata, because strong passions make us deviate from an orderly behavior. Hence "the best authors imitate the working of nature by way of hyperbata. For it is then that art is in its perfection, when it seems to be nature itself, and nature, in turn, is happiest when it contains art hidden in it." (*Sublime,* ch. xxii.) Demosthenes was a great master at creating this kind of suspense through inversion: "The idea from which he started is often kept in suspense, and meanwhile he piles up extraneous matter in the middle of his sentence in an ostensibly strange and improbable order; he throws his hearers into a panic lest his whole argument collapse as his realistic vehemence compels them to run that risk with him; then, unexpectedly and after a long interval he comes to the long-awaited conclusion at the end, just at the right moment."[12] Indeed

sentence is not determined abstractly by the logical idea of putting the subject before the predicate, or the substance before the accident."

[11] Ὑπερβατός, adj., is first applied to transposition by Plato, *Protag.* 343E. The *technigraphi* treat hyperbaton sometimes as a figure, sometimes, as Quintilian does (VIII, vi, 62; IX, i, 3), as a trope. See modern discussions in Volkmann, *Rhetorik,* 436; J. P. Postgate, "Some Flaws in Classical Research," *Proc. of the Brit. Acad.* (London, 1907-1908), 161-211; R. J. Getty, Introd. to his ed. of Lucan; J. D. Denniston, *Greek Prose Style,* 47 ff. On the rhetors, see T. Schwab, "Alexander Numeniu, περὶ σχημάτων . . . ," *Rhetorische Studien* 5 (Paderborn, 1916), esp. 87-97.

[12] *Sublime,* xxii, 4. For this last passage I adopt Grube's effective trans.: *Greek . . . Critics,* p. 349.

Demosthenes uses such devices so masterfully that he "seems to be improvising," but Herodotus and Thucydides are just as adept at this sort of vehemence.

Starting with the problem of word arrangement, the ancients somewhat obscurely realized the existence of three factors in composition, both within the proposition and within the whole sentence: intellective motivation (the rendering of the rational, analytical part of the thinking process), psychological stress (the extra-logical emergence of the impact of thought on the mind through feeling and imagination), and the sensuous appeal (the hedonistic, aesthetically approved element). True enough, they were unable to define these different aspects sharply and to place them in their proper relationship to one another; above all, they tended to let their rhetorical orientation take the upper hand by overstressing the third aspect and understressing the second.

As we have seen, Dionysius' answer to the main question on word order was that sound rather than thought is the chief determinant in this sphere, since order is widely variable and, most typically, is partly controlled by rhythm. In conclusion, order has little to do with logical classification, or any thought-directed orientation. His sources went back as far as Aristotle himself, *De interpretatione*, ch. 2 (where ὄνομα appeared to mean nominative noun, subject).[18] Quintilian will repeat this demurrer against the grammatico-logical position: "Illa nimia quorundam fuit observatio, ut vocabula verbis, verba rursus adverbiis, nomina appositis et pronominibus essent priora; nam fit contra quoque frequenter non indecore" (IX, 4, 24). Of course Greek and Latin presented completely independent problems with respect to basic order and especially the position of the verb, yet we can place the theorists of the two languages side by side: not only do they succeed one another in a continuous tradition, but they use strikingly similar terminology in their historical succession.

At the end of the first century, we find explicit references to the logical approach in Demetrius. He recommends what he calls "the natural order," ἡ φυσικὴ τάξις, in narrative passages using the plain (ἰσχνός) style. Such

---

[18] See H. Weil, p. 9 fn. (p. 18 fn. in Super's trans.), with a hint at Dionysius' "misunderstanding" of Aristotle. Cf., in *De interpretatione*, ch. 2, esp. p. 16B. Interpreting Dionysius as referring to the thesis that nouns however inflected ought to precede verbs as substance precedes accident, Jellinek, *Geschichte der neuhochdeutschen Grammatik* (1914), I, p. 431 fn. defends Dionysius from Weil's charge of having misunderstood his sources.

sentences should begin with the "subject" or "nominative case" (τὸ
περὶ οὗ, . . . ἀπὸ τῆς ὀρθῆς; the accusative in objective infinitive clauses),
then proceed with the other words in due succession. This method, to
him, is the secret of clarity, a necessary virtue in the plain style. He
continues: "Of course the order might be reversed. . . . We do not unconditionally approve the former order nor condemn the latter; we are
merely setting forth the natural method of arrangement, τὸ φυσικὸν εἶδος
τῆς τάξεως." [14]

Apollonius Dyscolus (fl. ca. A. D. 150) occupies in this area a peculiar
and rather unique position: while he presents the grammatical point of
view on the matter, he is also the first and in a way the only Greek
grammarian to produce a complete syntactical treatise extant for us.
Furthermore, his concern with syntax was related to his extensive involvement in the logical approach to language.[15]

Apollonius distributes his syntactical material according to the order of
the parts of speech, and starts out his analysis with an intriguing explanation of that order. He first defines syntax as the whole of the principles
underlying the structural qualities of the sentence, or, in his words, as
the properties of the sentence inasmuch as it can be a coherent and
complete whole ("constructio . . . unde nascitur congruens absolutumque
enuntiatum," ὁ αὐτοτελὴς λόγος).[16] He then declares the parts of speech
to be ordered on a rational basis: in the "ordo partium orationis" (cf.
I, § 13, pp. 15-16), he feels "nomen et verbum ceteris orationis partibus
antecedere debere" (cf. I, §§ 14-15, pp. 16-18), because they are the
necessary parts of the clause. Since, as is well known, Priscian relied
heavily on Apollonius in his own syntactical books (Institutiones Grammaticae XVII and XVIII, "De constructione"), it will be in order to
compare here the corresponding passages showing Priscian's derivations
and interpretations of his source. At this point Priscian echoes the latter

[14] Demetrius, On Style, IV, 198-201. Moreover, he charges lack of clarity when
the sentence does not begin with the subject; the hearer as well as the speaker
are then put to the rack, βάσανον παρέχει. See the whole section 190-206 on use
of clear constructions in plain style.
[15] Much of his work is unfortunately lost, but we know that, taken as a whole,
it constituted the most comprehensive treatment of Greek grammar for the ancients
(the grammar of Dionysius Thrax, for instance, had no section on syntax).
[16] Apollonius, De constructione Libri IV (Περὶ συντάξεως), Book I, 1, p. 1 of
Uhlig's ed. Apollonius' text being notoriously difficult and involved, I shall support
my interpretation with the aid of Uhlig's translations and interpretations, here
represented by my Latin quotations.

closely (XVII, §§ 12-13, p. 116 Keil): "Sicut igitur apta ordinatione perfecta redditur oratio, sic ordinatione apta traditae sunt a doctissimis artium scriptoribus partes orationis, cum primo loco nomen, secundo verbum posuerunt, quippe cum nulla oratio sine iis completur, quod licet ostendere a constructione, quae continet paene omnes partes orationis. A qua si tollas nomen aut verbum, imperfecta fit oratio; sin autem cetera subtrahas omnia, non necesse est orationem deficere. . . ." More specifically, then, the noun, Apollonius tells us, comes before the verb because "corpora nominibus notata id agunt aut patiuntur, quod verbis significatur. . . . Neque fieri affectio posset, nisi corpus esset" (I, §§ 16-17, pp. 18-19). And Priscian (XVII, § 14, p. 116 Keil): "Ante verbum quoque necessario ponitur nomen, quia agere et pati substantiae est proprium, in qua est positio nominum, ex quibus proprietas verbi, id est actio et passio, nascitur." The following paragraphs in Apollonius carry on the analysis of the other parts of discourse.

Yet, when we take a more careful look at the text, we wonder what is really meant by this rational order. For it is far from crystal clear whether Apollonius is really referring to sentence or clause construction at all. Is he not speaking merely of the "grammatical" order, the special sequence in which the *artigraphi* must methodically take up the parts of speech one after the other in their chosen technical method? And yet the implied possibility was there of inferring from that sequence a schema of priorities and relative values pertaining to the nature of speech.

At any rate, a lot of water went under the bridge between Apollonius and Priscian. With the latter one has the first clear impression that notions concerning word order and composition, once exclusive property of the rhetorician, have definitely entered the realm of grammatical treatment under the heading of syntax, at least in germinal form. Indeed he starts out (Book XVII: see Keil, III, pp. 106 ff.) with considerations on word sequence and sentence structure by analogy with letter and syllable, and, interestingly enough, briefly dwells on the 'pre-syntactical' phase, that of apparently incomplete sentences where ellipsis or conciseness (*defectio orationum*) seems to present closed word-sequences of an 'unordered' and 'uncomposed' type, as it were, as in the eloquent example from Terence, *Eunuchus* I, 1, 20: "Egone illam, quae illum, quae me quae non?" In the course of Priscian's exposition, the fusion of Aristotelian logic and syntax has become clear: "RECTA ORDINATIO exigit, ut pronomen vel nomen praeponatur verbo . . . quippe cum substantia et persona ipsius agentis vel patientis, quae per pronomen vel

nomen significatur, prior esse debet NATURALITER quam ipse actus,
qui accidens est substantiae" (XVII, § 105, p. 164 Keil). The 'right'
(*rectus*) order, therefore, is the 'natural' (*naturalis*): it is that because
of this, right because natural, and it is natural because it is LOGICAL.
A simple enough statement, to be sure, apparently self-evident, but
fraught with far-reaching, controversial consequences.

To begin with, as soon as he cast his eyes on a written page, the
Latin linguist, more than the Greek, could not but recognize the
formidable obstacles confronting him. For the Latin sentence shows
little regard for the principle just stated. So that Priscian must hasten
to add: "Licet tamen et praepostere ea proferre auctorum usurpatione
fretum" (XVII, § 105, p. 164 Keil). Indeed, "the authors' usage" imposes an acceptable (though embarrassingly frequent) licence, involving
inversions that are a rather drastic subversion of that order. The difficulty derives in part from the limited development of a terminology
that would have clearly and consistently distinguished the morphological
from the syntactical context, noun from subject. This fundamental distinction was a belated invention of the medieval *modistae*. But we
shall not have to dwell on such particulars, for the time being, committed as we are to pursue the main points of our authors' speculations.

The Latins were obviously aware that in point of fact the irresistible
trend of their language (especially in its literary uses) was to put the
verb quite far from any place near the beginning, indeed, most often
at the very end of the clause. This was so much so that the fact had
to be recognized as *the* basic rule of Latin construction, and they found
its explanation not in the area of phonetics or harmony, obviously of no
relevance here, but in the principle of semantic fulfillment. To say it
with Quintilian, pithily definitive as usual: "Verbo sensum claudere
multo, si compositio patiatur, optimum est; in verbis enim sermonis vis
est." [17]

So this seems to be the final rule, at this point, on the factual basis
of the spirit of the language, regardless of rational or logical order: at
the beginning the noun-subject, at the end the verb-predicate, all
complementary parts in between. Once stated in this way, the rule has
clearly shifted from the level of logic to a very different one, essentially

---

[17] Quint. IX, iv, 26. Fortunatianus will echo him, less effectively: "verbis plerumque in conclusione quam nominibus utamur, . . . nisi . . . maiorem vim habeant
novissime conlocata." (Fort. III, 11, p. 127, l. 27.)

a psychological one. Dimly aware of this difference, the ancients attempted to define it, and could find no better principle than that of "importance": From the point of view of the recipient of speech, the most important places in the clause are the first and the last, because they function as the opening and the conclusion, the two conspiring ends of a closed system. Hence S and P, being the two most "important" elements, must come first and last (in that order because of, this time at least, logical reasons, the same ones already observed in the definitions of the *rectus ordo*). *Vis*, force, meant precisely the psychological impact on the audience.

From this follows, however, that IPo and EPo invest the parts placed there with that special *vis*, making them important by the very nature of the position per se. If, therefore, the hearer should find something other than subject and verb in those respective places, he will automatically recognize the somewhat unexpected parts as having acquired a special importance, an emphasis deserved by their role in that particular sentence. They have acquired that, as it were, unusual place because in the speaker's mind they had a special force. The rhetoricians agreed on this stylistic principle: Quintilian had pointed out the value of *postridie* in Cicero's *Phil*. II, 25, 63: "ut tibi necesse esset in conspectu populi Romani vomere ⟨postridie⟩," as an example of the norm: "Saepe tamen est vehemens aliquis sensus in verbo, quod si in media parte sententiae latet, transire intentionem et obscurari circumiacentibus solet, in clausula positum adsignatur auditori et infigitur" (IX, iv, 29). On the general principle involved here Quintilian himself speaks very explicitly: "Nam ut initia clausulaeque plurimum momenti habent, quotiens incipit sensus aut desinit, sic in mediis quoque sunt quidam conatus iique leviter insistunt. Currentium pes, etiam si non moratur, tamen vestigium facit" (IX, iv, 67). Demetrius was no less explicit: "We all especially remember the things that come first and last; we are moved by these, and to a lesser extent by those that come in between, almost obscured or hidden" (*De eloc*. II, 39). While we take note of Quintilian's lingering on the recognition that MPo may not go entirely without emphasis, we must also add that Latin and Greek diverged somewhat on the pattern of main emphases, since EPo was generally less strong for Greek than for Latin, while IPo tended to be stronger. Likewise, in Fortunatianus' words (III, 11, p. 127, 27) the rule whereby EPo belongs to the verb will suffer a necessary exception whenever a different part of the clause is so important that it must usurp that place ("nisi

. . . maiorem vim habeant novissime conlocata "). This realization of
semantic emphasis was natural in observers who, like the rhetoricians,
were committed to analyze speech on a basis of audience-directed function. From an objective viewpoint, it enabled them to distinguish implicitly between basic linguistic habits and expressive variations, between
grammar and rhetoric, i. e. linguistics and stylistics.

Still at the borderline between language and style there came the
observation that the *rectus ordo* could also be subverted for reasons of
clarity, that is, to avoid ambiguity (ἀμφιβολία): "amphiboliam quoque
fieri vitiosa locatione verborum, nemo est qui nesciat" (Quint. IX, iv,
32); "caveamus, ne ordo faciat ambiguitatem" (Fortunatianus III, 11,
p. 127, 29). On the other hand, we are decidedly in the realm of style
when we come to the manifold exceptions to *rectus ordo* due to the
musical aspect of speech. When a *clausula* is needed, and the verb does
not lend itself, it will graciously yield its place to anything suitable for
the purpose: "Si id asperum erit, cedet haec ratio (i. e. the norm of
rectus ordo) numeris, ut fit apud summos Graecos Latinosque oratores
frequentissime" (Quint. IX, iv, 26); "verbis plerumque in conclusione
. . . utamur, nisi et melius cadant nomina" (Fortun., III, 11, p. 127,
27-29). The verb will likewise change place when required by reasons
of euphony (εὐφωνία)—the art of avoiding clashing contiguous sounds
and of producing melodic word couplings, as its Latin name *iunctura*
implied.

Emphasis, then, as well as rhythm and euphony bring about those
inversions, *hyperbata*, on which rhetoricians and rhetorically-oriented
analysts of speech and style lavished such fond care from early antiquity
to modern times. The ancients' ear was incomparably sensitive to the
musical qualities of speech, and most rhetoricians, including the leading
authorities from Cicero and Dionysius to Quintilian, were agreed that
iunctura and *numerus*, euphony and rhythm, took precedence over logical
order. As Quintilian put it: ". . . Sine dubio erit omne, quod non cludet,
hyperbaton, set ipsum hoc inter tropos vel figuras, quae sunt virtutes,
receptum est. Non enim ad pedes verba dimensa sunt, ideoque ex loco
transferuntur in locum, ut iungantur, quo congruunt maxime . . ." (IX,
iv, 26-27).[18] And Dionysius: "The science of public oratory is, after

---

[18] And see the general trend in Cicero's *Orator*, 61-236 on style, esp. 168-236 on
rhythm. Cf. D. L. Clark, *Rh. in G.-R. Ed.*, p. 94: "Speakers and theorists . . .
were dealing with the spoken word or the written word addressed to the mind's ear."

all, a sort of musical science, differing from vocal and instrumental music in degree, not in kind." [19] Again, Quintilian conceived of literary composition as an effect of art imposed on nature—a technical approach somewhat at variance with the philosophical notion of art as imitation of the ways of nature. The contrast that may result is due to our musical needs: words do come to our mind in a certain order, the other of things, so to say, but this primitive order must be changed according to the satisfaction of our aesthetic sense, *ratio compositionis et decor* (VIII, vi, 62). If we always followed a spontaneous order, "si ad necessitatem ordinis sui verba redigantur, et, ut quodque oritur, ita proximis, etiam si vinciri non potest, alligetur" (ibid.), disharmony might ensue: "fit . . . frequentissime aspera et dura et dissoluta et hians oratio." (Beauzée, *Grammaire générale* quoted below, 1819 ed., p. 708 translated these eloquent terms as "malsonnante et dure, sans harmonie et sans suite.")

This is the justification for the famous device of *transgressio*, hyperbaton, which of course, besides its due place within the treatment of *compositio*, was also treated formally and separately among the figures or, as in Quintilian VIII, vi, 62-67, among the *tropi* as distinct from figures. Nothing contributes to rhythm as much as such transpositions: "nec aliud potest sermonem facere numerosum, quam opportuna ordinis permutatio" (VIII, vi, 64). True enough, Quintilian repeated here his distinctive plea for moderation and cautioned that composition may sin by falling into obscurity through prolonged complication by inversion— the vice recognized as *synchysis* but destined to remarkable popularity in later times: "Quaedam vero transgressiones et longae sunt nimis, . . . et interim etiam compositione vitiosae . . . quales illae . . . 'inter ⟨se⟩ sacra movit aqua fraxinos'" (IX, iv, 28).

Thus, *rhythmus* in particular can interfere with the arrangement of words within the clause. Its principle is, of course, broader than the application to VEPo might make it appear. One could say that, if seen strictly from the angle of distribution of intensity, rhythmic movement works its way backward, *starting* from the final cadence of the period or the clause and gradually investing the whole sentence. The theorists may appear so vague in defining rhythm for any other parts than the very last, that most students have restricted it to cadences, while refusing to recognize the presence of regular rhythmic patterns in any other position than at the end of a colon or even of the whole period. Such

[19] *De comp.*, xi, p. 124. Trans. Roberts.

difficulties notwithstanding, one can also hear sensible opinions to the contrary, like those advanced, for example, by H. D. Broadhead and F. Novotný half a century ago. The latter reasserted the interrelatedness of periodic structure and prosodic rhythm in a way that transcends the cadences, so that the whole unfolding of discourse is conditioned by a pervasive rhythm which can be described, but only in an abstract, non-literal fashion, by using metrical, foot-like units.[20]

At any rate, the beginning and especially the middle of both clause and sentence were often said to be relatively free, in that the rhythm there could be felt by a trained ear but not defined according to fixed patterns; whereas the end part of clauses and especially of the whole period was expected to scan in precise manners. As Cicero put it in his *De oratore* (III, 50, 192): "Nam versus aeque prima et media et extrema pars attenditur, qui debilitatur, in quacumque est parte titubatum; in oratione autem pauci prima cernunt, postrema plerique, quae quoniam apparent et intelleguntur, varianda sunt, ne aut animorum iudiciis repudientur aut aurium satietate." It is well known that the practice of cadences was not restricted to classical times. Although the metrical *clausula* of antiquity gave way in the Middle Ages to accentual *cursus*, this latter proved to be one of the most creative aspects of prose style in its time, until well into the fifteenth century, when classical rhythms started to be restored, consciously or more or less intuitively through sheer imitation.

The remarks just recalled, as exemplified by Cicero, confirmed from their special perspective the general importance, for the ancient speaker and hearer, of the conclusive part of the statement—a phenomenon which can be more fully appreciated when contrasted with the modern

---

[20] In a review of Broadhead's *Latin Prose Rhythm* (Cambridge, 1922), Novotny stated that he found himself in agreement with the author's method (though not with his way of applying it) and described it as based "on two principles. One regards a dismemberment of speech into periods, 'cola,' and smaller members, the second postulates that accent alongside with quantity is the basic element in Latin prose rhythm" (p. 115). This qualification of rhythm by quantity as well as natural phonic stress is important, and means that the rhythm in the whole sentence is based on words being pronounced as in ordinary speech. Cf. *Philologica: Journal of Comparative Philology*, II (1923-24), 115-119. Also quoted by A. W. de Groot, *La Prose métrique*, p. 14. Broadhead gave the following example of prolonged rhythm: tū tămēn | sālvōs | ēssĕ vŏlŭ | īstĭ = cretic + spondee + resolved cretic + dissyllabic end (= csc²2), while Novotny scanned Cic., *Planc.* 13 thus: "quám petitiónem cúm reliquísset, si hóc indicásti, tánta in tempestáte té gubernáre non pósse, || de virtute túa dubitávi, si nólle, de voluntáte."

sense of stress often bearing on the middle portion, logically as well as melodically.

We have seen how the ancients had the notion of a normal order in word arrangement—even though they defined it neither too categorically nor quite clearly—and of a less normal, or 'inverted' order which could be brought about by a number of legitimate reasons. In view of the later developments of this important notion it is interesting to note that, despite their also using the technical term *naturalis ordo* in a different sense—and one rather irrelevant for our study—, they did associate the normal order with the way dictated by nature. We are about to witness this once again in a Ciceronian passage worthy of our attention also because it contains a synonym of *rectus ordo* (*directe*) which was destined to a remarkable success in later times. Furthermore, in this passage from the *Partitiones oratoriae*, vii, 24,[21] we find a methodical description of the ways in which the order could be 'transformed':

" In coniunctis autem verbis [= in word arrangement] duplex [22] adhiberi potest commutatio, non verborum, sed ordinis tantummodo [concerning order alone, not the terms]; ut, cum semel dictum sit, DIRECTE, sicut NATURA ipsa tulerit, invertatur ordo et idem quasi SURSUM VERSUS RETROQUE dicatur, deinde idem INTERCISE atque PERMIXTE.[23] Eloquendi autem exercitatio maxime in hoc toto convertendi genere versatur."

To begin by anticipating an episode of the complex controversy which grew out of these ancient texts in modern times, one can identify here three methods, as Beauzée was to do in his *Grammaire générale* of 1767:[24] the direct or natural; the drastic, complete inversion which turns the former, so to speak, upside down and backwards; or the partial inversion by use of parenthetic or incidental insertion—one may assume that Cicero had especially in mind the separation of the modifier from the

---

[21] See Bornecque's ed.: Cicéron, *Divisions de l'art oratoire . . .* , pp. 11-12. I have changed the punctuation slightly. This manual in dialogue form ostensibly written by Cicero for the instruction of his own son, contains little of interest for us aside from this illuminating passage. Within the section on *elocutio*, composition occupies §§ 18-24 (pp. 9-11 of Bornecque ed.). The material is divided and explained in an elementary and untypical manner.

[22] Bornecque reads *duplex*, but all codices except the two Paris ones have *triplex*, which was Beauzée's reading discussed below.

[23] Another reading, *perincise*, not recorded by Bornecque, is found in quotations of this passage in lieu of *permixte*.

[24] I use the original ed., Paris, J. Barbou, 1767, 2 tomes: see II, pp. 548-549. Pp. 710-711 of Paris, 1819 ed.

modified.[25] Beauzée took this unusually explicit text as a witness to his
contention that the ancients did recognize the 'direct' order as the
'natural' one.

However Charles Batteux, Beauzée's adversary, promptly retorted that
what Cicero meant by *directe* could not be the same as the 'grammatical' or direct order of French, since Cicero's language was absolutely
unfamiliar with anything of the sort. By 'direct' he simply meant, as
he textually put it, 'natural'—natural, of course, to Latin, including
the placing of the verb at the end, which by French standards would
be an 'inversion.' This must also have meant that whatever came naturally by following the basic law of word order in all languages, that is
the *ordre d'intérêt,* could be inverted slightly or extensively for special
reasons, such as the search for rhythm or euphony or an artificial
elegance of some kind.[26] In a way, these objections would appear to be
borne out by Dionysius' referring to the doctrine which claimed first
place for nouns without thereby implying the equivalence noun =
subject, as we have adduced above.

The technical terms seen so far were the basic ones. The range of
the terminology, however, was richer. In Priscian, for one, *ordinatio
partium orationis* was synonymous with *constructio,* meaning syntax, as
the title and subtitle of his Books XVII and XVIII indicate. And syntax
meant the relationship and linking of parts, mainly words rather than
clauses. But *ordinatio sequentium,* just like *ordo, structura, coniunctio
sequentium* did mean word arrangement: see his *Partitiones versuum
duodecim Aeneidos principalium,* where possibly ambiguous cases (e. g.:
is *arma* in *arma virumque cano* nom. or acc.?) were eventually solved
by analytically construing the lines: "hoc certum est a structura, id est,
ordinatione et coniunctione sequentium." This method of scholastic
explication was likewise exemplified in Servius' commentary on the
Aeneid and Donatus' on Terence.

We have seen, in our initial diagram, that the most methodical schema

---

[25] In quoting this text in his ed. of Rivarol's *Discours,* appendix XV, Suran
translated, not too technically nor clearly, this last possibility as "*fragmentaire* et
haché." We will see that these modern terms have traditionally acquired a rather
different meaning from that which Cicero must have intended. Bornecque
translates: "séparer des mots qui se construisent ensemble et même faire permuter
des mots entre eux."

[26] Batteux, *Nouvel Éclaircissement sur l'Inversion pour servir de réponse aux
objections de M. Beauzée,* ed. 1774 pp. 379-380.

would have comprised as part of the second major division of *compo-sitio*, and alongside *ordo*, also *iunctura* and *numerus*. A study of *iunctura* and *numerus* in antiquity is really necessary to support our contention that, in theory as well as practice, harmonic and hedonistic considerations were of paramount importance in determining the pre-vailing taste for compositional forms. Yet, important as they are, we have decided not to cover these last two subjects, assuming that these aspects of the question can be taken for granted as having already been demonstrated by students of such matters. We must also remind our-selves that, as usual, the divisions were not always systematic nor, even when so intended, carefully observed. We have noted, for example, that Cicero did not recognize word order as such, and treated harmony within sentence structure, the only aspect of composition he actually developed. Furthermore, the avoidance of cacophonous encounters of vowels and consonants, obviously an aspect of *iunctura*, was at times treated under *structura*, at others under *ordo* itself.[27] Such considerations often brought along the treatment of prosodic sequences to be avoided, as in Martianus Capella. In brief, we shall remain content with what we agree to consider a workable definition of *ordo*, and proceed on that basis.[28] I shall, nevertheless, refer to this aspect of compositional theory occasionally, when it becomes relevant to the understanding of principles directly related to the uses of syntactic structures—which will remain the subject of the present study.

If we now turn to an evaluation of all the material just surveyed, we must begin with two broad, and somewhat contrasting, observations. In the first place, it is evident that the ancients were able to define and analyze difficult linguistic and stylistic questions in such clear and com-prehensive terms that they remained basic until very recent times. At the same moment, they were partly mistaken and, as it were, confused in their understanding of the nature of their own language. For one thing, one fails to perceive the precise connection between their rational notion of a spontaneous, instinctive order (in which words would appear to the

---

[27] See, e. g., C. Julius Victor, ch. xx, Halm pp. 432, l. 32-433, l. 29 (*structura hiulca*); Mart. Capella, chs. 33-34, Halm pp. 474-476 (particularly on *iotacismus, mytacismus, labdacismus, et similia*).

[28] The literature on the 'acoustical' part of rhetoric, and especially cadences, is large and detailed with respect to both ancient and modern languages; among the best studies I wish to recall M. W. Croll's (see the last section of his *Style, Rhetoric, and Rhythm*, eds. Patrick and Evans, with particular reference to the relationship between Latin and English).

mind according to the rational hierarchy in which logic would arrange
the things they symbolize) and, on the other hand, their (especially
the Romans') realization that the verb or predicate did not normally come
second, as it should according to that reasoning; it came last, and did so
because of the strategic value of EPo. In other words, the order of importance in their language(s) was not one of linearly 'descending' arrangement starting with the most important. Their views on *rectus ordo*
could apply more satisfactorily to many modern languages than to the
classical languages, characterized as these were by sentences 'hollow'
in the middle. Deeply rooted in the ancient mind was the intuitive notion
that the important elements of the phrase have their place at the beginning and end, and that it was only 'natural' that it be so. We find
perhaps a confirmation of this by analogy in the rhetorical and dialectical
notion that the strongest arguments in the demonstration of a case must
be placed first and last (Cicero, *De oratore*, II, lxxvii). This, to them,
appeared as 'natural' as the traditional order of *exordium, narratio, con-
firmatio*, etc.

Secondly, and most importantly, their extraordinary sensitivity to the
musical qualities of speech caused them to leave on the margin other
factors whose role in determining 'artificial' patterns in word arrangement
was more decisive than euphony, harmony, and rhythm—namely, the
expressive needs of emphasis and impressionism. The consequence of this
relative blindness was that what they saw as the 'natural,' instinctive
phase of expression ('direct' order), was a notion introduced ex post
facto by analysis and abstractly superimposed on the actual forms of expression. In point of fact, the 'inverted' patterns so common in classical
literary use served purposes of impressionistic relief the audience-directed
speaker needed for a more persuasive, therefore emotional, impact—a pre-
logical, pre-rational process even if it was so very often exploited by
conscious artificers. Paradoxical as it may sound, in exaggerating the
importance of music the ancient theorists underrated what their rhetorical
training ought to have made so easy for them to discover, that is to say,
the semantic value of so many special patterns. For example, such insertions of a governing word between a noun and its modifier had the function of stressing the modifier by temporarily isolating it as in EODEM
usi consilio (*De bello gallico*, I, 5, 4), *propterea quod aliud iter haberent*
NULLUM (ibid., I, 7, 3).[29] Besides the emphatic value of EPo, the effect

[29] Cf. W. G. Hale and C. D. Buck, *A Latin Grammar*, § 627, p. 338.

of *nullum* is enhanced by its being held in suspense. The ancient rhetorician would have acknowledged the value of the EPo in this case, but perhaps not that of separation from nexus—a very common occurrence in written Latin. Such 'suspenseful' separations were analyzed, when really extreme and compounded, as synchysis, but their value was seen as mainly decorative, as if to distinguish the literary style from common speech by the sheer weight of the difficulty it presented to the hearer. When successful, the true value of the device was, instead, expressive, quite independently from considerations of musicality, which might play no role whatever.

Modern grammarians have recognized in the Latin sentence a 'normal' pattern which adds something to ancient speculation, and which, with its more advanced and refined articulateness, will be of some use for later stages in our story. The main principle of order is one of general grammar, and can be considered valid beyond its application to a specific language. It lies, rather than in any conceivable logic, in a psychological fact: "Emphasis may be obtained either by putting an important thing before the hearer immediately, or by holding it back for a time, to stimulate his curiosity." [30] This rule applies to Latin in a specific way as follows. First, "the most emphatic places in a sentence, clause, or group, are the first and last." Furthermore, and consequently, "the places next to these are relatively next in emphasis, and so on." "If no *special* emphasis is to be given to any part, the subject and the act are the most important things. Hence they stand first and last respectively. Their modifiers naturally stand near them."

Accordingly, the normal order of the clause is:

Subject, modifiers of the subject, modifiers of the verb, verb.

The third group can be broken down as follows: Remoter modifiers (time, place, manner, etc.), indirect object, direct object, adverbs.

As distinct from the NORMAL order (meaning: statistically more frequent), 'rhetorical' order comes from the frequent need to place some special emphasis upon some part of the sentence. Any part of the clause, may I add, will increase its *vis* by being placed differently than in the 'normal' schema, either by virtue of the relative shock deriving from its

---

[30] Hale and Buck, p. 334. I cite this excellent manual, now again available (1966), because it contains one of the earliest (1903) 'popular' presentations of the modern view on word order expounded in solid, detailed paragraphs (pp. 334-340).

unexpected position, or by its moving closer to the more strategic positions. This broadly applies as well to the ordering of clauses within the sentence, considering that the basic sentence movement, at least in the periodic manner, is progressive, that is, one of increasing emphasis.

To determine the precise value of an unusual position may, however, be a rather delicate decision, since the requirements of *numerus*, for one thing, may directly compete with reasons of emphasis. Given, for instance, the following Ciceronian terminal portions we may decide that they are determined by emphasis: . . . *tu illum amas mortuum?* (*Ph.* II, 110, l. 4, Clark-Peterson ed., Oxford Classics): . . . *tota denique rea citaretur Etruria* (*Mil.* 50. 13, same ed.); . . . *officiosam amicitiam nomine inquinas criminoso* (*Pl.* 46. 2, same ed.), instead of the 'normal' *mortuum amas, Etruria citaretur,* etc. But it will only be the establishment of *numerus* in the cadence that conditions the departure from the norm in this other case: *quae nunc paucis [verbis] percurrit oratio mea* (*Cl.* 166. 24, same ed.).[31]

Similarly, the following *clausulae* from Book V, Ch. 1 of Lactantius' *Divinae Institutiones* contain transpositions visibly due to rhythm:

> sententiam differat in extremum.
> sciunt se facile superari.
> irretire possunt suavitate sermonis.
> ad populum sunt locuti.
> ponderat sed ornatu.[32]

---

[31] Cf. Willy Rönsch, *Cur et quomodo librarii verborum collocationem in Ciceronis orationibus commutaverint* (Weidae Thuringorum, 1914). This interesting Dissertation studied the tendency of medieval scribes to transpose the order of words in Cicero's orations when it departed from the expected norm. Rönsch found (p. 70) that this inclination to reconstruct by falsely restoring a simpler word order determined almost all cases of discrepancy among codices even in a text which offers few discrepancies in the tradition, such as Pliny's letters (where he counted about 80 cases). I find particularly interesting those cases where modifier and modified were rejoined, against a common rhetorical tendency of the authors, classical as well as medieval; thus *his ex causis* could be copied as *ex his causis, auctoritati debeam tuae* as *auctoritati tuae debeam.*

[32] These examples were chosen by F. Di Capua, *Il "Cursus" e le clausule nei prosatori latini e in Lattanzio* (Bari, Adriatica, 1948-49 academic course), p. 43. Di Capua also mentions the following passages as the clearest and most important statements by grammarians concerning the interference of rhythm on word order: *Ad Her.* IV, xxxiv, 44; Cic., *Or.* xlix, 168; Quint., *Inst.* V, vi, 62-65; IX, iv, 20-30; 68; 109-110; St. Aug., *De Doctr. Chr.* IV, xx, 40; Pompeius, *Commentum artis Donati:* Keil V, 295.

One of the most striking cases of systematic transpositive patterns is that of the celebrated historian and orator Asinius Pollio (fl. after 35 B. C.). Although his work is now completely lost except for the famous 'necrology' of Cicero preserved by Seneca the Elder, modern critics tend to agree that even this short passage suffices to document both the characteristic just mentioned (and perhaps derived from the example of Thucydides) and Seneca the Younger's judgment of his *compositio* as eminently 'jolty' (*salebrosa*). This is particularly interesting in the light of Pollio's being an extreme case of Atticism, which would show the possibility of a high degree of artificiality in word order even while the same writer laid stress on naturalness, simplicity, and directness in sentence structure (the early Atticist ideal of *sanitas* made up of *puritas, perspicuitas,* and *proprietas*).[33]

Whether the word order of primitive popular Latin, and possibly Greek, was somewhat akin to the 'direct order' of modern Western languages, remains largely a matter of educated conjecture. At any rate, in classical times it was 'natural' for the spoken language to arrange itself in this more 'direct' manner and thus not to conform to the highly artificial, even if widely practiced, arrangement of rhetoric and literature. One kind of proof lies in such well-known texts as the 'triumphal' rhythms of Caesar's soldiers (*Ecce Caesar nunc triumphat, qui subegit Gallias; Nicomedes non triumphat, qui subegit Caesarem*), and another in the early examples of popular Christian hymns. St. Ambrose († 397), for instance, could use the rhetorical style with the greatest ease, yet a prayer written in the following manner has also been attributed to him:

Rex virginum et amator castitatis et integritatis,
caelesti rore benedictioni tuae
extingue in corpore meo fomitem ardentis libidinis
ut maneat in me tenor castitatis corporis et animae.[34]

Even St. Augustine could offer movements such as the following, which are found in a sermon delivered before a council of bishops in Carthage, on May 5, 418:

Quoniam placuit Domino Deo nostro, ut hic constituti praesentia corporali etiam cum vestra Charitate illi cantaremus Alleluia, . . . laudemus

---

[33] Cf. Leeman, *Orationis Ratio*, I, esp. pp. 187-190 and 275. Leeman fully reports the passage preserved from Pollio.
[34] This passage is cited by Charles J. Robbins, *Cl. J.*, XLVII, p. 82. I reproduce it divided into cola according to Robbins.

Dominum, fratres, vita et lingua, corde et ore, vocibus et moribus. . . . Hic
ergo cantemus Alleluia adhuc solliciti, ut illic possimus aliquando cantare
securi. . . . "Condelector enim, inquit, legi Dei secundum interiorem
hominem, video autem aliam legem in membris meis repugnantem legi
mentis meae et captivantem me in lege peccati quae est . . . in membris
meis." [35]

The cogency of the preceding argument also tends to invalidate a frequently heard theory, according to which the acquisition of the direct
order in the vernacular languages was the consequence of the loss of
inflectional endings. This phenomenon certainly played an important
role, but was neither the sole determinant nor, perhaps, even the principal one.

Rules of order for classical Greek are much harder to come by, and less
relevant to the historical development of Western languages. For these
reasons I have so far refrained from lingering on this question. I shall
only refer to the most recent investigation by K. J. Dover and summarize
his results.[36] Having centered his attention on the early centuries, in order
to catch the language in its most 'natural' stages before the onset of
Kunstprosa, Dover concludes that "in Greek prose of the fifth and fourth
centuries B. C. the S tends to precede its V. . . . The ratio OV:VO shows
greater fluctuation . . . ." (p. 25). Admittedly, all his statistics "are very
far indeed from establishing for 'Classical Greek' *simpliciter* anything
worth calling a syntactical rule of word order." If extended further, the
inquiry would likely display "the vagaries of individual preference—and
thereby suggest with increasing force that all patterns of order which
are describable in syntactical terms are secondary phenomena" (31).
Dover points out the decisive role of 'emotive,' 'emphatic' determinants,
and especially what he chooses to call 'logical' determinants as distinct
from structural forms (syntactic). We shall see in the theoretical part
at the end of this study how such distinctions are to be understood. For
the moment it seems expedient to quote Dover's conclusion *in extenso*:

It appears from the history of other Indo-European languages that syntactical principles of order have a greater endurance than logical principles,
and I have suggested that in Greek itself the primary logical principles
weighted the scales in favor of an increasing dominance by syntactical
patterns of order. If the Greeks had not possessed so intense a degree of

---

[35] This sermon is numbered 256 in the Maurist edition. See the first two pages
reprinted in Auerbach, *Literary Language and its Public* (1965 ed.), pp. 27-28.
[36] Dover, *Greek Word Order* (1960).

artistic self-consciousness, it may be thought likely that syntactical patterns would have established themselves much earlier and much more firmly. (P. Barth, in *Philosophische Studien*, XXIX, p. 26, seems to imply—rightly, I think—that it was conscious art which maintained the elasticity of Greek word order for so long.) We find, in fact, that in the language of the New Testament rules of order are much more easily defined in syntactical terms than they are in Classical Greek. (Cf. Barth, p. 48; W. Wundt, *Völkerpsychologie* I, p. 369, on the part played by colloquial language in enforcing formal analogy.) It appears that Greek literature, by attaching value to variety of form, maintained a resistance to that drift towards syntactical uniformity which has been the fate of other languages, and that pagan post-Classical literature diverged increasingly from the colloquial language of its own day by reasserting the primacy of logical rules of order.

CHAPTER TWO: THE MIDDLE AGES

A. SENTENCE MOVEMENT

Once again, in the medieval period we naturally look for material relevant to our purpose in the grammatical and the rhetorical writers. Medieval rhetoric, to take the last first, is divided, in practice, into the two major categories of arts of poetics (chiefly rhetoric applied to verse) and *artes dictaminis*. Each of the three resulting areas is exemplified in the critical collections of Ch. Thurot, E. Faral, and L. Rockinger, respectively. We can easily and quickly dispose of the second, for, aside from some occasional elements I shall pick up presently, the medieval treatises on poetics contain next to nothing that bears on composition, this being, at least in theory, almost exclusively restricted to prose. It is imperative to note that on the didactic plane the medieval arts of poetry could belong either in the grammatical curriculum within the system of the Trivium, as seems to have been the case with the poetics of Matthew of Vendôme and Eberhard the German, or in the rhetorical part of the curriculum, as with those of Geoffrey of Vinsauf and John of Garlandia. This distinction affects the respective treatments of composition. Thus the discussion of " natural and artificial order " which is found in Geoffrey and John is replaced by the treatment of zeugma and hypozeuxis in Matthew and Eberhard. The terms " natural and artificial order " could refer to word order, as we shall see; but the authors of poetics normally applied them to *dispositio*, the arrangement of plot and argument either in chronological and logical sequence or by plunging *in medias res*. *Compositio*, then, just like in antiquity, was not conceived in the more general sense of unity of plot, but as a criterion of sequence and material arrangement. The still narrower sense of choice and arrangement of words can be expected to find its place in the grammatically-oriented treatises of poetics, as specifically in Matthew—a step in the process whereby these matters were adopted by linguists away from rhetoricians.[1]

---

[1] Cf. Douglas Kelly, " The Scope of the Treatment of Composition in the Twelfth- and Thirteenth-Century Arts of Poetry," *Speculum*, XLI, 2 (1966), 261-278, esp. 261 and 264. See, also, Giovanni Mari, ed., *Poetria magistri Johannis anglici* [de Garlandia] *de arte prosayca metrica et rithmica*, in *Romanische Forsch-*

Likewise, though for different reasons, the field of *dictamen* might on first analysis appear generally barren for us; this on account of the technical preoccupation with the setting up of bureaucratic schemas and formularies into which the masters of this art soon channeled all their material. Yet it is precisely this that, together with the grammatical literature, will turn out to be rich in revelations, some more surprising than others, even if all of them seem to throw only scarce beams of light on areas we would wish to see more fully lit.

The extraordinary importance acquired by the *cursus* in both medieval practice and theory indicates a subtle but far-reaching transformation in sensitivity to sentence forms. We have witnessed how the divisions of the ancient period were chiefly based on delivery, with its acoustical and physiological demands. Even the method of scanning biblical verse-like units could contribute to, and be a reflection of, this way of sensing the oratorical caesurae, as vouchsafed by St. Augustine's detailed analyses. But the first major discovery which occurs to the observer is that the divisions of the medieval sentence (perhaps beginning around 1100) are strictly syntactic; the cadences practiced according to the *cursus* fall at the end of clauses and sentences, so as to scan the periodic whole logically and reconcile, in an enviable harmony, the hedonistic need for rhythm with the developing scholastic taste for logical divisions and subdivisions. In other words, the medieval *cursus* marks the progress of the logical patterns in composition. The medieval writer and reader are more aware than ever before of the *clauses* as basic units of discourse, even while the way of linking them together has become noticeably more haphazard. In fact, in what must be recorded as a major shift away from ancient taste, the authors of the *artes dictaminis* suggest that the function of rhymes and *clausulae* might be that of rhythmic DIVISIONS of discourse; this matches their expressed inclination to discourage periodicity in favor of brevity and pithiness. What had been used, rather sparingly, to underline the symmetric balance within the period, now becomes a device to break up overlong sentences.[2]

---

ungen, XIII (1902), 883-965, besides the texts in Faral. It must be noted, however, that, whatever the use of the *Poetria nova,* Vinsauf was rather a grammarian than a rhetorician.

  [2] Cf., e. g., Lisio, *L'Arte del periodo* . . . , "Teorie rettoriche e grammaticali," pp. 69-77, esp. 77. On the broader implications of *cursus,* with particular reference to Boncompagno da Signa (taught at Bologna, ca. 1200-1220), cf. Pio Rajna, "Per il *cursus* medievale e per Dante," *Studi di Filologia Italiana,* III (1932), 7-86;

The increasing attention being paid to punctuation in the course of the Middle Ages serves a similar purpose. One of the divisions of *ars grammatica* was *prosodia*, prosody, which treated not quantity but accent (*accentus*) and pauses (*pausationes*). These latter, graphically expressed by punctuation (*positurae* or *distinctiones*), referred to sentence scansion and derived their basic terminology (*comma, colon, periodos*, still literally preserved in such languages as English) from the rhetorical divisions of the periodic parts which, precisely, they serve to scan by marking their ends. So one of the lasting authorities, Isidore of Seville, had it (*Et.* I, 19), and such influential authors as Hugh of St. Victor in France and Thomas of Capua in Italy, confirmed him.[3] The fact that the signs used vary from time to time, as they also vary both from ancient and from modern usage, need not concern us here. Nor are we concerned with terminological variations temporarily introduced by such authors as Peter Helias, Alexander of Villedieu, and other lesser ones. The relevance of medieval innovation in dividing the sentence, as witnessed through the use of punctuation, could hardly be overstated. As Father Ong has remarked, not until Isidore of Seville in the seventh century was it suggested that punctuation marks off the sense as well as the rhythm.[4] Indeed, the ancients did not really need punctuation because their cadences scanned the sentence's inner and outer divisions clearly enough for their well attuned ears. It was only toward the end of the Empire that punctuation, once a *confirmation* of rhythmical elements, became a *substitute* for them, since the ability to sense cadences became dulled by the increasing loss of metrical and prosodic sensitivity. This explains both the shift of pauses from rhythmical moments to semantical divisions and the replacing of metrical *clausulae* with accentual *cursus*.

The criteria of punctuation are also covered by several masters of *dictamen* such as, for instance, the anonymous Northern Italian writer of the after-1140 *Rationes dictandi* once attributed to Alberic of Montecassino (fl. 1057-1088), and Konrad von Mure (1210-1281), who appeared

---

F. Di Capua, *Il Ritmo prosaico nelle lettere dei Papi* . . . (Rome, 1937-1946, 3 vols.); Id., "Per la storia del latino letterario medievale e del *cursus*," *Giornale Italiano di Filologia*, IV (1951), 97-113 (sub-ch.: "Una lezione di Boncompagno sull'artistica disposizione delle parole," 100-108) and VI (1953), 19-34; and, on *cursus* specifically in Italy, G. Lindholm, *Studien zum mittellateinischen Prosarhythmus* (Stockholm, 1963).

[3] Cf. Thurot, pp. 407-417. For Hugh, see his *De grammatica*, ed. R. Baron (1966), pp. 123-125.

[4] Ong, *PMLA* (1944). See p. 353.

to follow the *Rationes* in this matter.[5] Konrad underlined the correspondence between signs, pauses, and basic periodic divisions according to the
traditional terminology, Greek and Latin. His terms, as close as any to
the more current practice, are *distinctio* [*seu pausa*] *suspensiva seu media*
(= *metrum, colon, membrum*); *constans seu subdistinctio* (= *punctus,
coma, incisio*); *finitiva seu plena* (= *versus, periodus*). The first is written
;, the second ., the third ;.[6]

The preoccupation with form in much of medieval writing produced
many a text which could be traced back to the Sophistic tradition of
'Gorgian' imprint. Let us look at a characteristic tenth-century cere-
monious letter: " Summae sanctitatis, scientiae, pietatis et ordinis culmine
sublimato domino. . . . Nunc ergo puerum istum, viscera mea, filium
consobrinae meae, solam et maximam curam meam, commendo [. . . vobis]
ut vestram vitam et vos 'primis miretur ab annis,' mansuetudinem vigore
decoratam, doctrinam operibus commendatam, austeritatem dulcedine tem-
peratam, taciturnitatem modestam, locutionem utilem vel necessariam, vic-
tus et somni parcitatem, mediocritatem vestibus . . . ." An eloquent sample,
indeed, of the highly structured 'grand style,' it carries on with similar
juxtaposed isocola using homoioteleuton, homeoptoton, parison—all the
equipment of the Gorgian arsenal. But note how the procedure may strike
the hearer or reader as somewhat mechanical, since the 'fragmented'
movement has displaced the authentic periodicity of older days.[7]

A special problem is posed by the versified and rhymed prose transmitted

---

[5] Conradus de Mure, canonicus thuricensis, *Summa de arte prosandi*. See text
in Rockinger, pp. 403-482; pp. 443-445 on punctuation. Incidentally, Konrad cites
both *Doctrinale* and *Graecismus*. See Rockinger, pp. 25-26 for the text of the
Rationes dictandi. For a better reference, see the recent ed. of Konrad's *Summa*
by W. Kronbichler (1968), pp. 107-109. Together with the post-dating of the
Rationes dictandi, which Rockinger and many after him still attributed to Alberic,
recent scholarship has exploded the traditional myth of Alberic as the 'founder'
of the *ars dictandi*, that should more properly be traced to Adalbertus Samaritanus of
Bologna (fl. ca. 1110-1120). See bibliography in my *Ars grammatica*, p. 139 fn.

[6] About the second, Konrad simply says it is marked *cum puncto plano*. This
dot was often written on top of the line, or even in the middle. Ludolf von Hildesheim in his *Summa dictaminum* gives a very similar picture of the matter, but for
the *constans* he prescribes two successive dots on top of the line: · ·. See text in
Rockinger, p. 369. I give these examples of the practices of *dictatores* because
they are at variance with those of the *grammatici* expounded by Thurot. See, also,
for the same terminology, Gervais von Melkley, *Ars poetica*, ed. Hans-Jürgen
Gräbener (Münster, 1965, litho.), pp. 217-218. Gervasius' *Ars* was composed in
1208-1216.

[7] Text from *MGH*, Legum sectio V, formulae, 409 (Collectio Sangallensis Salo-
monis III tempore), cited in Baldwin, *M. R. P.*, p. 144 fn.

through the Isidorian and Hilarian canons. This style is placed at the summit of art prose by John of Garlandia: " Iste stilus valde motivus est ad pietatem et ad letitiam et ad intelligentiam."[8] He defined it thus: "In stilo ysidoriano, quo utitur Ysidorus in libro *Soliloquiorum*, distinguuntur clausule similem habentes finem secundum leonitatem et [vel] consonantiam: et videntur esse clausule pares in syllabis, quamvis non sint." Note that clausula here means colon or clause, *leonitas* rhyme ("rectas consonantias in fine dictionum que dicuntur leonitates a Leone inventore "),[9] and that isocolon is also mentioned. John's example is clear: "Pre timore genus humanum obstupeat, de communi dampno quilibet abhorreat; admirentur servi, stupescant liberi; dum vocantur ad cathedram elingues pueri, conformantur magistris leves discipuli."[10] The practice of this highly artificial style, which achieved its balanced effects chiefly through parallelisms, spread after the year 1000 and reached its peak around 1200.[11]

Because of its relevance in the light of future developments, I should like to call attention to a seemingly marginal remark in Matthew of Vendôme's *Ars versificaria*.[12] We find documented here the incipient realization that conjunctions (some of them at least) are words of a special kind in that they fulfill a 'secondary' (in the *modista* terminology, a co-signifying) function—of a merely logical nature, Matthew could have added. For this reason there is very little room for them in the lyrical language of poetry. Later stylists will see to it that their role is also restricted in prose, since their excessive popularity had been due to abuse of periodicity, whereas the swiftness of plain style relies more on the intuitive association suggested by simple word sequence and sentence structure. As Matthew rather picturesquely put it:

[8] *Poetria magistri Johannis anglici de arte prosayca metrica et rithmica,* ed. G. Mari in *Romanische Forschungen,* XIII (1902), p. 929, for this and the following quote. See, also, Rockinger, I, 502; Faral, pp. 40 ff. and 378 ff. Cf. F. Di Capua, *Scritti minori,* II, 230-231 on Isidore's *Soliloquia* as model of *stilus ysidorianus.* I correct Mari's "Augustinus" to Rockinger's "Ysidorus," which is the reading of Munich Ms. 6911.

[9] Giovanni Mari, "I trattati medievali di ritmica latina," *Memorie del R. Istituto Lombardo di Scienze e Lettere: Classe di Lettere,* XX, fasc. 8 (1899), 373-496. Quote on p. 419. Also published as sep. monograph (Milan, 1899, 124 pp.).

[10] *Poetria magistri . . . ,* p. 929.

[11] On the Latin styles in the Middle Ages see the detailed sections in Norden, *Antike Kunstprosa,* and, particularly for the Roman style, the ample and learned study by F. Di Capua, *Il ritmo prosaico nelle lettere dei Papi* etc.

[12] Matthieu de Vendôme, *Ars versificaria,* Book II, Ch. 46: Faral, p. 167.

Sunt quaedam dictiones panniculosae quae quasi anathemizatae et indignae ceterarum consortio a metrica modulatione debent penitus absentari: ut istae: *porro, autem, quoque,* et hujusmodi sincategoreumata, id est consignificantia, quae, quia totius metri derogant venustati, a metro penitus debent eliminari. Paucae etenim sunt conjunctiones et adverbia quae in metro debent collocari, nisi necessitatis incubuerit articulus.

Much of the detailed material contained in medieval rhetoric can be clarified by the simple reminder that one of the most pervasive influences during all these centuries was exerted by the *Rhetorica ad Herennium.* But it must be added that the boldly Latinized terminology used there— rather idiosyncratic from the viewpoint of the prevailing tradition—was replaced with the more durable Greek equivalents starting with the *Doctrinale* and the *Graecismus* at the beginning of the thirteenth century— such works reflecting in this manner the new preoccupation of the age.[13] All in all, aside from matters of nomenclature, the organization of the material did not change drastically from the earliest medieval codifications. Isidore's example was paradigmatic: He analyzed *elocutio* under the headings of the three styles, then the subdivisions of colon, comma, and period, some typical " vices," and finally the figures (*Et.* II, xvi-xxi).

As to the ripest production of the High Middle Ages, we may content ourselves with a closer analysis of the *Candelabrum,* a text attributed to Bene of Florence and one of the most exemplary texts of *dictamen* both for its detailed and systematic character and for its affiliation with the school of Bologna.[14]

Books III and IV deal with the traditional parts of the oration or, rather, letter, Book V contains a summary of all the preceding, while Books VI-VIII present the material again as seen from the point of view

---

[13] See the valuable tables in Faral, pp. 52-54.

[14] The *Candelabrum* was dated after 1208-1213 by Baldwin, *M. R. P.,* p. 217 fn., on account of the quote it contains from Geoffrey of Vinsauf's *Poetria nova,* ll. 1051-1060. It was cited by Thurot (esp. p. 415), who used Ms. B. N. Paris, Lat. 15082; mentioned by Gaudenzi, Manacorda, Clark, and finally Baldwin esp. pp. 213 and 216-223, with a detailed digest based on a Plimpton Ms. The relationship of this text with other French and Italian manuals bespeaks its central position in the culture of its century. On Bene and the School of Bologna, with particular reference to the sententious style, see now G. Vecchi, " Il ' Proverbio ' nella pratica letteraria dei dettatori della Scuola di Bologna," *Studi Mediolatini e Volgari,* II (1954), 283-302. See, also, Giuseppe Vecchi's brief study *Il Magistero delle ' artes ' latine a Bologna nel medioevo* (Bologna, 1958) and his ed. of Bono da Lucca's *Cedrus Libani* (Modena, 1963). A critical ed. of the *Candelabrum* by a young scholar, Giancarlo Alessio, is announced as forthcoming, with " Prolegomena " to it scheduled to appear in *Italia Medioevale e Umanistica.*

of the French schools. The first two books are devoted to the basic principles of style, commencing with the theory of the three styles, then dividing elocution into diction (elegant vocabulary), *compositio*, and *ornatus*. This last, the theory of figures, occupies Book II. We are concerned with the larger portion of Book I dealing with composition. This is defined as *ordinatio verborum equabiliter perpolita*, 'word-ordering smoothly polished,' a formula which reminds us immediately of the *aequaliter perpolita* in the *Rhetorica ad Herennium*, while, in turn, both the thirteenth-century Cremonese grammar edited by Fierville and Faba's *Ars dictaminis* (see below) echo Bene's text closely with their own *aequabiliter perpolita* (Fierville p. 116). The kind of even polish in question will be achieved by such changes in word order as to give our speech an appealing and not vulgar *cursus*—a general acceptation of this term which seems again reflected in the Cremonese grammar. We shall turn to this section when dealing with word order.

A little further on there follows one of the clearest medieval statements of that preoccupation with DIVISIONS that we have witnessed in the treatment of punctuation. In fact we find here the terms for punctuation transferred bodily to the realm of composition without any need for intermediaries: just as *cursus* is enlarged from the specific formulas for sentence or clause endings to encompass the whole flow of discourse as punctuated by cursus-type cadences, so is the term *distinctiones* bent to mean the clauses themselves, while *clausula* refers to the whole sentence. "Clausula igitur est plurium distinctionum continuatio ambitum perfectum sentente comprehendens." [15]

The central passage on periodic 'divisions' bears quoting *in extenso*:

We have spoken often of *distinctiones* since no discourse can please that is indistinct. . . . A *distinctio*, then, is an integral member of one sentence, weaving its words in apt order and releasing its thoughts from any tangle of doubt. . . . There are three kinds: . . . (1) *dependens* [later styled by its ancient name *comma*, or *caesum*], (2) *constans* [a statement complete in itself, but carrying on—*colum, membrum*, also called *distinctio media*], (3) *finitiva*, that *distinctio* in which the whole sentence is finished, *totalis clausula terminatur*, called by the Greeks *periodus*, i. e., *circuitus*, or *finalis*.[16]

---

[15] Plimpton Ms., f. 6. See Baldwin, p. 218, fn.: "The author adds that [the term *clausula*] is otherwise used *abusive*. His definition agrees with Fierville, 119."
[16] Trans. Baldwin, pp. 218-219.

The author takes cognizance of the more prevalent system of punctuation (*modus punctandi*), whereby a *coma* must end in actual utterance with a raising of the voice tone (*per arsin, id est elevationem vocis*), and this is marked with the sign ⁙. *Cola*, on the other hand, end in a lowered pitch (*accentu gravi*), marked with a simple dot. The sign ; , finally, marks the end of the sentence, to be pronounced with an even lower tone: "periodum censetur graviori accentu pronunciari debere." The author, however, holds with the use of the Curia, which he prefers as simpler: All periodic divisions will end with arsis, the sentence itself, and it alone, ending with a thesis (except when reading aloud in the church), and all punctuation marks are reduced to the plain dot, the modern semicolon being reserved for the end of the whole speech.[17]

Toward the end of this Book I Bene considers the length of sentences and recommends against prolixity, while stressing again his concern with clarity, judicious brevity, and aptness of *ornatus*.

At this point we cannot afford to forego at least a quick glance at Dante's treatise on language and style, a theoretical aspect of the most momentous development in the evolution of the medieval stylistic experience. The varied medieval attempts to revive the sublime style of antiquity had usually been foredoomed to failure. Such a style contrasted with, and was generally replaced by, the unique blend of purposeful sublimity and popular, everyday simplicity embodied in the *sermo humilis* which had been originally proposed by St. Augustine to the Christian preacher. Those attempts were finally resumed and brought to fruition in a newly creative way by Dante—though not in Latin, but in the vernacular.[18] Now it is pertinent to note that Dante assigned to the "noble" style, that of the poet of ideal love, virtue, and salvation, precisely four ingredients, one of them being a sweeping sentence structure:

Stilo equidem tragico tunc uti videmur, quando cum gravitate sententiae tam superbia carminum, quam constructionis elatio et excellentia vocabulorum concordat.[19]

And Auerbach sagaciously noted that "This smacks of pedantry, but it covers the ground completely." [20]

---

[17] Text in Thurot, p. 415.

[18] For the preceding remarks on the relationship between ancient grand style and the Christian *sermo humilis*, see Auerbach, *Literary Language and Its Public,* esp. the Ch. "Camilla, or, The Rebirth of the Sublime."

[19] Dante, *De vulgari eloquentia,* II, 4. 7.

[20] *Literary Language and Its Public,* p. 220. Auerbach went on to elaborate on

The example Dante offered of a "tragic" sentence structure strikes us for its antithetic isocolon:

Eiecta maxima parte florum de sino tuo, Florentia, nequicquam Trinacriam Totila secundus adivit.[21]

(Charles of Valois, the second Totila, succeeded in casting out of thy bosom the greatest part of thy flowers, O Florence, but then he failed in his assault on Sicily.)

B. WORD ORDER

Remigio Sabbadini was perhaps the first to call attention to a text falsely attributed to Terentius Scaurus, as containing the first clear traces of a medieval view of *constructio*. This text, which is found in a Ms. of the ninth or tenth century, proposes a definitely idiosyncratic ordering of narrative speech as follows: Indicative Verb, Adverb, Infinitive, Nominative, Pronoun, Participle, and Oblique Cases.[1] Sabbadini was quick to notice how the only instructive element in this scheme is the drastic anteposition of the verb. Otherwise, its only application is to the following type of phrase, clearly unrelated to precepts destined to prevail later: "Cupiebat strenue pugnare dux ille, defensurus libertatem patriae." [2] The eminent classicist found the new order better represented in the tenth-century codex Ashburn. 4 (Paoli 3) of the *Aeneid*, where the passage from II, 347-353 is thus glossed—the letters of the alphabet indicating the order of construction—: "O iuvenes (a) fortissima (b) pectora (c) videtis (d) quae sit (e) fortuna (f) rebus (g) excessere (h) omnes (i) dii (k) relictis (l) adytis (m) aurisque (n) quibus (o) steterat (p) imperium hoc (z) frustra (q) succurritis (r) incensae (s) urbi (t) si vobis (u)

the four ingredients: "The lofty subject; a meter that has nothing trivial, hurried, or playful about it . . . ; further, a sentence structure that is neither primitive and paratactic nor, like nearly all the Latin rhetoric of his time (*ars dictaminis, stilus altus*), purely pedantic and epideictic, but richly diversified, grand, and passionate; and, finally, a noble, strong, high-sounding vocabulary, neither crude, nor childish, nor too glib." (Ibid.)

[21] Ibid., pp. 220-221. Cf. *De vulg. el.*, II, 6. 5.

[1] Keil VII, 33: "In contextu historiae vel latinitatis primum verbum indicativi modi, deinde dicimus adverbium, postea infinitivum, deinde rectum casum idest nominativum, deinde pronomen, postea participium et postea obliquos casus. Siquis recte historiam legat, secundum hunc ordinem omnes partes orationis examinabit."

[2] Sabbadini, "Sulla *constructio*," *Rivista di Filologia e d'Istruzione Classica*, XXV (1897), 100-103; see p. 100.

cupido (x) audiendi (y) extrema (z)." Leaving aside the mistaken
position of *frustra* and the obscure collocation of *imperium hoc* on account
of the repeated (z), we find again here the Pseudo-Scaurus' anteposition
of the verb.

For most of our documentation on word order we must turn to the
artes grammaticae. This was another decisive step forward, in that the
theory of syntax was gradually coming into its own by incorporating
matter that was naturally due to it even if the ancients had hardly allowed
it to transcend the narrow confines of rhetoric. We have noticed how
constructio, the Latin equivalent of Greek 'syntax,' had signified little
more than the theory of links between (single) words, only rarely rising
to comprehend some scattered relationships between phrases and clauses.
Peter Helias and Hugh of St. Victor took over the definition "constructio
est congrua dictionum ordinatio" from Priscian II, 15 (who in his turn
was following Apollonius): "Oratio est ordinatio dictionum congrua,
sententiam perfectam demonstrans." [3] In the later language of the *modistae*
this sounded thus: "Est constructio congrua constructibilium unio ex
modo significandi causata" (*Glosa Admirantes*).[4] In Priscian the term
had also assumed the practical meaning of "construing" as a school
exercise designed to explicate difficult constructions by placing words in
a 'normal,' analytical order.[5] These two meanings remain current in
medieval terminology together with a new one which makes its appearance possibly around the year 1000: the term *constructio* becomes then
transferred from the abstract operation to its concrete outcome, thus
becoming equivalent to our 'clause.' [6]

The most interesting documents of such developments are perhaps to
be found in a few anonymous manuscripts collected by Thurot, and
dated between the eleventh and the fifteenth century.[7] Let us look

---

[3] Keil II, 53, 28.

[4] C. Thurot, pp. 83, 218-219.

[5] The current Latin term for this rearrangement for the purpose of parsing was
ordo est (used, e. g., by Diomedes). The Greek equivalent among scholiasts and
glossators was τὸ ἑξῆς οὕτω. It must be noted that the scholiasts' parsing would
seldom do more than bring together the elements of the same grammatical group.
In such cases is showed an analytical trend only in a microscopic way.

[6] See also, e. g., Golling in Landgraf, art. cit., p. 33 on meaning of *constructio*
in medieval syntax.

[7] Ms. Bibl. Nat. Paris, Lat. 7505, 11th c.: f. 3ᵛ contains precepts on word order
inscribed at the head of a Ms. of Priscian: Omnis constructio ex substantia et
actu fit—inter quas et aliae possunt intromitti constructiones, ut supra diximus.

closely at the earliest of these.[8] It is a good example of the way the theory of the two basic types of *ordo, naturalis* and *artificialis,* became part of syntax (then called *diasynthastica* or *diasyntactica,* a medieval deformation of *de syntactica*), together with the theory of cases or government (*regimen*) and that of concord (*congruitas, concordantia*): it was usually placed between these two as the second of three subdivisions. This was also to become Alexander de Villedieu's plan.[9] When treated thus, *ordo* was part of *constructio* narrowly conceived, namely as linkage of terms in a given order.

Our text begins by distinguishing in the transitive construction the agent, the act, the patient (*agens, illius actus, in quo fit paciens*), often accompanied by 'adjective' elements of qualities and quantities referred to both the substance and the act (*et qualitates et quantitates substancie vel actui adiecte positae*), plus several possible complements (*et ubi et quando et quare*). The logical terminology used in these definitions is indicative of the speculative trend which was to blossom between 1250 and 1350 in the major works of the *modistae.* Our Ms. can then be considered, according to the dating we adopt, one of the earliest examples of 'philosophical' grammar, this being not the least of its singular merits. The anonymous author goes on to assign places to each part: first the subject, then the predicate, finally the object, while the 'adjectives' mostly tend to precede their parts: " In omni . . . constructione anteponitur agens, qui nominativo vel vocativo profertur, dehinc vero illius actus, postea

---

Ms. B. N. Paris, Lat. 7553, 15th c., containing Joh. Tortellius Aretinus, *Diphthongorum tractatus;* Apuleii *Diphthongi;* Guarinus Veronensis; Gasparinus Pergamensis, *Diphthongi* and *De modo punctandi;* finally, an anonymous treatise on the method of construing and on punctuation: f. 123 Rem parvam adortus sum, sed non inutilem de lectionis explanandae ordine—129ᵛ quae, si diligentes esse voluerimus, ab eruditissimo quoque usurpata inveniemus. Τέλος. (The approach is logical, in line with the *modistae.*) Ms. B. N. Paris, Lat. 10922, 15th c.: f. 58ᵛ on punctuation, followed by precepts on word arrangement, f. 59: Nota quod volentibus discere compositionis vel cursuum documenta—63ᵛ ut aio te Romanos vincere posse. Et hec sufficiant. The three Mss. were used by Thurot (descriptions on pp. 16, 57), who refers to them in the course of his analyses as K*n*, OO, PP, respectively.

[8] See complete text in Thurot, pp. 87-89. Thurot dates the Ms. 11th c., but it seems to me a copy from an earlier text on account of several ungrammatical accidents of the kind imputable to slips by a negligent scribe. For a brilliant discussion of the increasing reciprocal interference between grammar and dialectic from the late tenth century onwards see L. M. de Rijk, *Logica Modernorum,* vol. II, part 1 (Assen, 1967), pp. 95-125.

[9] Cf. Thurot, pp. 237-239.

autem in quo fit paciens; . . . adiectiva plerumque anteponuntur cui adiciuntur." And the example is: FORTIS JOHANNES MULTUM PERCUSSIT DEBILEM PETRUM. The 'adjectives,' however, will follow their term in some cases, especially when they are made of adjectival complements in oblique cases or they govern an oblique case of their own, as in: JOHANNES FORTIS BRACHIUM vel DIGNUS LAUDE PERCUSSIT PETRUM MULTAE AUDACITATIS (CUM) VIRGA. Then comes the question of how to arrange internally a sequence of several complements. Since most ablatives unaccompanied by prepositions (our author calls them 'loose,' *ablativi absoluti*) have the force of adverbs (*vim adverbiorum habent*), they can either precede or follow the verb. Anteposition will avoid ambiguity or awkward encounters if another is naturally postponed, as in JOHANNES MANIBUS APPREHENDIT PETRUM FUGIENTEM PEDIBUS. "Quare vero et ubi et quando, si adsunt frequentius, . . . postponuntur," to wit: the complements of cause, place, and time are postponed when there are several of them; but their reciprocal arrangement is free (*inter se autem quovis ordine poni possunt*), like: JOHANNES MAGNAE VIRTUTIS MULTUM PERCUSSIT PETRUM HODIE IN ECCLESIA OB FURTUM, or, at will, . . . OB FURTUM HODIE IN ECCLESIA. *Unde*, however, that is, the complement of movement from place, often follows, as in JOHANNES HODIE VENIT DE CIVITATE.

This is a precious text insofar as discussion of multi-complement sequential arrangement is relatively rare before the early eighteenth century. Yet nothing in our text resembles the important orientation which will become known as Beauzée's law, if I may anticipate a fruitful development of a later time.

Then in a passage which shines as an anticipation of the one decisive step still needed for syntax to become master of the complete range of problems that are its due, the author goes on to announce the study of the relationship between clauses in a complex sentence. Just as single words, he says, are aptly ordered into clauses, so clauses are tied together by way of hypotaxis or subordination, to which he will now turn: "Quemadmodum apte sunt dictiones in constructione ordinande, ita et constructiones sunt in oratione ponende quae ex multis perficitur constructionibus." Incidentally, this and what follows is a lucid sample of the use of *constructio* in the new acceptation of 'proposition' or 'clause.'

Now subordination can be introduced by means of participles, relatives, and conjunctions. In particular, a simplified (rather *over*simplified) system is shrewdly attempted concerning location of subordinates with conjunctions (*coniunctiones*—they are later called *adverbia*): whereas participial and relative clauses can be set in the middle of the ruling clause, clauses with conjunctions precede or follow their regimen, with the possibility of being separated from it by other participial or relative clauses. Take the following example, which will show both the middle- and the ante- or post-position: JOHANNES IDEO SCRIPSIT LIBRUM, QUEM [inset between main and secondary] PRISCIANUS, VOLENS [participle, interposed inside a (secondary) clause] RELINQUERE EXEMPLUM ALIIS, COMPOSUIT . . . , QUONIAM EXINDE ACCEPIT PRECIUM. Specifically, clauses with *quoniam* and *quia* follow their regimen, those with *cum* precede or follow, those with *si* (*causalis vel racionalis*) always precede.

The scholastic reasons given for the principle whereby noun and pronoun should precede the verb are in keeping with Aristotelian metaphysics, that is: because the substance is naturally prior to the act. This terminology was already to be found in Priscian, even in a passage (XVII, 105) which did not derive from Apollonius. Peter Helias did not discuss this passage, and Robert Kilwardby just paraphrased it without further ado. Unlike these influential interpreters of Priscian, our fragmentary and anonymous author distinguishes himself even in this so clear anticipation of a favorite topos of scholastic linguistics.

This module of rationalization was reflected once again in the 'Treatise of St. Gall,' which also applied it one step further, specifically to the reciprocal arrangement of predicate and complements: " Prius semper actio et deinde passio: in verbo enim actio est, in obliquo casu fit passio; et ideo medium locum tenet verbum inter nominativum et obliquum quia nominativus dirigit verbum." Hence the verb precedes its complement.[10]

It is worth noting that the well-organized examples offered by our text are all methodically made up. This contrasts with the habit pre-

---

[10] The Treatise of St. Gall is cited by Jellinek, *Gesch. der neuhochdeutschen Gr.*, Bd. II, p. 431, with part of the passage I have reported. The text of this interesting grammatical treatise, with Incipit " Quomodo VII circumstantiae rerum in legendo ordinandae sint," and dealing with several aspects of word order and sentence composition, is part of a composite Brussels codex. It is transcribed in Paul Piper, *Die Schriften Notkers und seiner Schule*, I (Freiburg i. B. and Leipzig, 1895), pp. XIII, 7–XLIX, 2, from which I quote.

vailing in earlier times, of quoting literary *auctores,* ancient or even
medieval, and foreruns the method of scholastic speculation on language.
(In a similar manner, seventeenth-century French grammarians will
make up their examples on the basis of 'logic' and of selected contemporary usage, thus departing from the inveterate habit of the Italian
Accademia della Crusca, which always quoted older authors.) [11]   The
exquisitely medieval flavor of these examples invariably reminds us of the
syntactic style characteristic of the newly formed Romance languages:
S (+ adjectival C) + V + dC + iCC, in the principal as well as in all
dependent clauses. We may add, as an afterthought, that the usual
order: P→iC in dative case→dC in accusative case, can be viewed as
corresponding to the Romance tendency to place the indirect object
before the direct one (indeed, even before the verb) when the indirect
object is an enclitic (atonous) pronoun. At any rate, one senses a 'logical'
approach in the background reasoning but a 'natural' effect in the
phrasing of the examples—this, of course, in the light of the characteristic
vernacular-like movement of medieval Latin, especially in the form soon
to be adopted by scholastic philosophers. Furthermore, there is here no
consideration of expressive extra-logical factors such as (rhetorical) devices
underlining emphasis for affective reasons, or even logical reasons of an
exceptional order.

   Of course one must bear in mind that we are here confronted with
an extension of the didactic method of parsing or 'construing,' which
originally did not mean that the writer or speaker should follow such
criteria of ordering, but that the student would find them useful in order
to clarify for himself the system of relationships implicit in the actual
sentence. Nonetheless in such a text as the one at hand one has reached
the borderline at which explicative construing *has* become a scientific and
practical norm for current expression and even for good style. The hidden
reasoning seems to be: If a sentence could be expediently explicated and
clarified by construing, why not construct it in a self-explanatory and
CLEAR way in the first place? Indeed the step was already taken, implicitly and inadvertently; the bridge was *de facto* closed. Yet, regardless
of the actual habits acquired or to be acquired by users of expository
prose, the fact remained that a lot of ancient prose and of contemporary
imaginative prose was still such as to need construing in the classroom.

---

[11] Cf. B. Migliorini, *Che cos'è un vocabolario?* (Florence, 1951², 1961³), pp. 53-57.

It was the turn of the rhetoricians and of more advanced grammarians to account for precisely those extralogical and affective reasons responsible for such complications. This is what took place in the following period, roughy between 1100 and 1400, while linguistic speculation was, on the one hand, elaborating most of the points raised by the exemplary manuscript we have just scanned. At any rate, the doctrine of 'construing' may well have been, at least in part, fostered by the didactic need to compare vernacular word order with Latin. Classroom practices thus brought linguistic study back from scientific speculation into the domain of 'empirical' observation. As Sabbadini shrewdly observed, the vernacular was becoming, through the back door, the true master, and Latin the servant.[12]

The 'new order' is pointed out by Sabbadini in what he regarded as a 'firm and most precious document,' the twelfth-century Sallust of Ashburn. 3 (Paoli 2).[13] See, for an example, Sall., Iug., 102, 5: "Rex Bocche, magna laetitia nobis est, cum te talem virum di monuere, uti aliquando pacem quam bellum malles." Ms. Ashburn. 3, f. 54ᵛ: "Rex Bocche, magna laetitia est nobis, cum dii monuere te talem virum uti aliquando malles pacem quam bellum."

With his customary gift of concise statement, Alexander de Villedieu gave a first complete formulation of the theory of 'construction' by prescribing that first should come the nominative (preceded, if the case be, by the vocative), then the personal verb (to wit, in finite mood, which will be first if the aforementioned is lacking, just as the impersonal verb comes first). Afterwards the adverbs, if any, otherwise the dative (iOb) and the accusative (dOb), in this order. The genitive follows immediately its regimen (i. e., the modifier follows the modified). Prepositions accompany, apparently in the final places, either an accusative or an ablative.[14] Thurot suggested that such instructions were meant to be taken,

---

[12] On grammatical coverage of word order between 1100 and 1400 cf. Thurot, pp. 341-350, on which is based the following analysis.

[13] Sabbadini, " Sulla Constructio," p. 101.

[14]   Construe sic: casum, si sit, praepone vocantem;
         Mox rectum pones; Hinc personale locabis
         Verbum, quod primo statues, si cetera desint.
         Tertius hinc casus et quartus saepe sequuntur,
         Aut verbo subdes adverbia. Subde secundum
         Casum rectori. Debet vox praepositiva
         Praeiungi quarto vel sexto, quem regit illa.

Doctrinale, ch. ix, ll. 1390-1396.

once again, as an explanatory method, not as rules for the writer and speaker; he inferred this from relevant passages as to the use of the term *construere* in the thirteenth-century *Glosa Admirantes,* one of the most authoritative and popular commentaries on the *Doctrinale.*[15] This was most likely their " literal import." But the same *Glosa* refers (f. 106) to that passage in Alexander as " debita et communis forma constructionis, . . . communis modus in contextu partium orationis," a rather ambiguous annotation. As *communis modus* refers to regular order, so *contextus partium* stands here for ' construction,' not just ' construing,' since the author goes on to treat of exceptions to the basic order as " impedimenta quae contingunt aliquando contra istum contextum " (ibid.). The implication clearly shifts to the actual compositive level in a fifteenth-century *Glossa,*[16] where the Aristotelian logical terms of substance and action are brought back to justify the " order," the possibility of a verb opening a sentence is explained on the ground that the verb may implicitly contain its subject (" quia verbum habet suppositum expressum vel intellectum "), and heavy stress is placed on the principle that the determinant follows the determined (" illud quod determinat dependentiam alicuius, sequitur illud . . . ; determinatio sequitur suum determinabile, et quia adverbium est determinatio verbi et verbum est determinabile, ideo . . ."). A note of interest to the linguist here is the censuring of Alexander for repeatedly holding that the preposition RULES its noun, whereas, according to the anonymous glossator, it only determines the case.[17] But most significant to us in this manuscript is the reference to the possibility of an inverted order, for which the commentator chooses the example of a qualifier *preceding* its term, *ab solis ortu.* He motivates it on the ground of stylistic embellishment: " dico quod ibi ponitur causa ornatus," hence it can be dismissed as irrelevant to the basic rule.

To the texts adduced by Thurot I should add, for its explicitness, the Treatise of St. Gall cited above, where the methodic use of the ' natural '

---

[15] *Glosa Admirantes,* cited by Thurot as R, Ms. 252 of the Orléans City Library, cf. ff. 76, 77, 106, 111, 113: Thurot, p. 342 and fn. 5.

[16] Ms. B. N. Paris, Lat. 14747, referred to by Thurot as Ms. St.-Victor 867 (II), f. 152ᵛ.

[17] " Dicit actor [viz. auctor] quod prepositio ante accusativum et ablativum situatur, quos ipsa debet gubernare. . . . Nota primo quod prepositio non regit nec gubernat, sed disponit casuale. Quod est contra actorem, qui tenet hoc in pluribus locis." This prejudice of Alexander's continued to enjoy favor among the humanists down to the Latinists of the nineteenth century. R. Sabbadini combated it at the turn of the century (see, e. g., his *Metodo degli umanisti,* pp. 10-11).

order is reserved to didactic exposition, while writers and speakers are considered free to choose the type of order they prefer: "ordinem autem naturalem . . . in eruditione tantum scholastica tenemus. . . . Scribentibus autem et loquentibus ex arbitrio suo licet quamlibet earum [scil. 'orders'] alteri preponere" (xvi-xvii).[18]

Departures from the normal order may or may not involve a choice, that is to say, may be linguistic or stylistic. Free and, therefore, individually expressive, the latter possibility was of direct concern to the rhetorician, while the former was within the grammarian's domain. Indeed the masters of grammar, in the wake of the *Doctrinale*, dutifully defined the various cases of this sort, which they termed *impedimenta*. A few commentaries on the *Doctrinale*, and especially the *Glosa Admirantes,* are of paradigmatic significance in this respect. The result of this careful effort was an elaborate and, one must add, largely irrelevant theory which need not detain us, whereby were considered as 'obstacles,' in order: infinitives, participles, absolute ablatives, double-nominative verbs, interrogative and relative clauses, verbal ellipses, conjunctions, etc. As examples of these "grammatical inversions," *homo habilis currere placet mihi* and *nititur currere* were regarded as *impedimenta* because in the first case the infinitive *currere* instead of a 'personal' (finite) verb follows immediately the subject, and in the second an infinitive instead of a dative or accusative follows the verb. The approach is, of course, naïve, and is a consequence of the well known fact that late-ancient and medieval linguistics had betrayed the true intent of the early Greek linguists by tending to identify noun, nominative case, and subject, on the one hand, and finite verb and predicate on the other. That is to say, one came to identify some separable aspects of morphology, syntax, and logic and to categorize the parts of speech into semantico-logical functions (the *modistae* marking the culmination of this trend), whereas the ancient (Aristotelian) distinction of ὄνομα and ῥῆμα was not exactly equivalent to our 'noun' and 'verb,' but vaguely referred to any parts of speech which, in a given sentence, function as subject and predicate, respectively. Thus a verbal form (as an infinitive, a gerundive, or a participle) used nominally (especially as 'nominative' or 'accusative') came to be mistakenly viewed as an 'exception,' since it 'displaced a noun.'

Similarly, an absolute ablative, a participial construction, and any sub-

---

[18] Cf. Jellinek, op. cit., II, 427.

ordinate clause could be regarded as infringing on the normal order if
they were not appended at the end of the main clause as regular complements. Less gratuitous, but no more sensible, was the observation that a
conjunction could mark a break in the rule which wanted the noun
(subject) in first place. More sensible was, however, the realization that
relative pronouns could constitute *impedimenta* in that they normally
start out the clause even in oblique cases.

The *artes dictandi* also occasionally referred to questions of order, although it is still difficult to judge the extent of the rhetoricians' involvement in such matters on account of the incomplete form in which the
texts (and only some of them) have so far been published. Just like all
other rhetoricians, so the *dictatores* used the term *ordo* with reference to
both arrangement of subject-matter (in which case the technique of starting *in medias res* was traditionally offered as example of *ordo artificialis*)
and word arrangement. In the latter case, they usually called the ' direct
order' *ordo naturalis*. From the beginning of the thirteenth century it fell
to the authors of *artes dictandi* to contemplate the differences between
the two basic orders.[19] But the notions became familiar much earlier
than a regular terminology could be introduced.

One of the earliest, yet most original and detailed presentations of
norms on word order appears in the *Rationes dictandi* once attributed
to the first great master of *dictamen*, Alberic of Montecassino (fl. 1057-
1088), but now generally regarded as a Northern Italian anonymous
treatise from after 1140.[20] The author begins by designating what will
be later called *ordo naturalis* and *ordo artificialis* as *recta et simplex constructio* and *appositio*, respectively. He quickly disposes of the former
(the 'analytical' order) as appropriate to an audience with minimal
literacy: "cum minus peritis sive ydiotis sermo dictantis porrigitur." The
latter is directed to the more advanced (*perfectioribus*), and is defined as

---

[19] Konrad von Mure gives a neat definition, and an exemplary one for the analogy
between word order and topical disposition: "NATURALIS hic est ORDO,
quando nominativus precedit et verbum cum suis determinationibus et attinentibus
subsequitur. Et iste ordo rem, prout gesta est, ORDINE RECTO, PLANO MODO
declarat et exponit. ARTIFICIALIS ORDO est, partibus materie artificialiter trans-
positis, rei geste aut ut geste narratio per verba polita decenter et ornata. Quasi
diceretur: Artificialis ordo est, qui rem gestam vel ut gestam a medio incipit narrare,
et postea res narratas de principio ducit ad finem. Et hoc ordine Virgilius utitur in
Eneide." Text in Rockinger, p. 441, and Kronbichler, p. 67.
[20] Text in Rockinger, vol. I, pp. 10 and 26-28. On Alberic's role vis-à-vis the
ars dictandi, and on the authorship of the *Rationes*, see fn. 5 above, Ch. II, A.

a suitable word arrangement which is removed from the sequence we
follow when we simply 'construe': "est appositio apposita dictionum
ordinatio a constructionis serie remota." [21] It must be characterized by
care for sound effect and a 'flowing' arrangement of distinct units:
"sonoram et distinctam id est quasi currentem fieri oportet." Although this
approach clearly echoes the ancient notion of *ornatus*, one immediately
senses a new stress on art as artifice, which removes its product from the
popular, 'vulgar' spontaneity and directness of actual speech.

Both orders are learned and judged more by cultivated ear and experience in good writing than by any rigid doctrine. But with this
qualifying premise, one can proceed to fix some basic norms as follows.
Vocatives shall be placed either at the end of their clauses or toward the
middle. Nominatives must follow the oblique complements directly tied
to them, just as they precede these in 'construing' (*iudiciorum causa,
iudicantis discretio*)—although the rule is not to be rigorously respected.
When we have a combination of different oblique cases, they will be
placed in the paradigmatic sequence of declension: "ita eos ordinamus quo
videlicet ordine in declinationis serie conponuntur," as in this example:
*Narrationis ordini necessarias solummodo causas subtili discretione adhi-
bemus* (gen.–dat.–acc.–abl.). If a nominative is also present, it shall
precede all other cases. (Note how this neat, though very curious mechanical rule, partly contradicts the one that wanted the nominative after
its complement or modifier.)

Once again, all these norms are flexible. In particular, it is elegant to
separate a noun from its adjective by interposing a different case or
an adverb (as in *vestre prudentiam probitatis*). Impersonal verbs have a
free position, but personal verbs appropriately come at the end of their
clause (*distinctio*), unless the cursus demands otherwise. As is well known,
the *cursus* (in its canonical Roman expression) was firmly established by
Alberic's disciple, John of Gaeta. Without using the term, the author of
the *Rationes dictandi* indicates here the tension that may arise between

---

[21] This terminology became canonical among many authors. Cf., e. g., Gervais
de Melkley, *Ars poetica*, ed. H.-J. Gräbener (1965), p. 217: Prose is of two
kinds, one "per simplicem constructionem fit" (i. e. "cum scribimus ydiotis et
minus peritis"), the other "fit per appositionem." "Appositio est dictionum ordinatio a constructionis serie remota." Likewise Boncompagno da Signa (ca. 1180-ca.
1249), *Palma*, p. 106 of C. Sutter, *Aus Leben . . . Boncompagno*: "Appositio est
congrua et artificiosa dictionum structura que varium set non penitus diversum
retinet modum cum constructione."

general ordering principles and the need for a pleasing cadence as part
of the "sonority" he considers essential to eloquent prose. To this effect
he specifies what amounts to a theory of *cursus in nuce*: trisyllables (or
longer words) are preferred for end-positions. This stage of transition to
full-fledged cadence may be an extension of the ancient abhorrence from
ending sentences with syntactically self-sufficient monosyllables. Adverbs
appropriately cling to their verbs, conjunctions fall into three groups: those
which open the clause, those which must be postponed to some initial
words (*ergo, igitur, quidem, equidem, quippe, tamen, quoque, autem,
enim, vero*), and those that can be placed freely.[22] Finally, one must note
that some adverbs and conjunctions are mere filling (*conpletive*), to be
used for sound reasons and especially between noun and adjective (e. g.
vestram utique probitatem).

The *Candelabrum* we have already glanced at introduces us to the
more mature phase in rhetorical speculation. In analyzing the different
methods to achieve the polished smoothness of which art consists, the
author distinguished three sorts of *compositio*: the *naturalis*, the *fortuita*
(casual), and the *artificialis* (Book I). The first simply follows the natural
order and is proper to expository prose, while the second applies some
criteria of arrangement, but simple ones, as manuals usually do and the
Scriptures (followed in this by the style of sacred writing). But it is in
the third that we find true method of arrangement, although there are
several schools of writing which differ among themselves in this respect,
such as the one of Orléans (which relies on regular successions of units
made of one proparoxytonous and one paroxytonous word—a dactyl plus
a spondee); the 'Tullian' or Ciceronian one, still respectful of the ancient
laws of metrical feet; and, last but most authoritative and simplest to
follow, the Ecclesiastical style of the Roman Curia.

The author then comes to the question of the proper order for the
parts of speech in the clause as well as types of phrases and clauses in the
sentence (nominative and complements, relative clauses, infinitives, etc.),
and concludes with a pertinent quote from the *Poetria nova*: "Surgit
item quaedam gravitas quando / Quae sociat constructio, separat ordo." [23]

---

[22] Rockinger, I, p. 28.

[23] Vv. 1051-1060. See the discussion below in this chapter, pp. 118-122. This
quote may well have served to bring that important principle to the attention of
such Italian vernacular poets as Panuccio del Bagno, who made an exceedingly
heavy use of all manners of disjunctions and hyperbata. See M. Musa, ed., *The*

In an anonymous *Summa dictaminis* of the early thirteenth century [24] one similarly witnesses the shift to the rhetorical viewpoint. The *artificialis ordo vel dispositio* becomes more desirable: "quando partes proprie TRANSPONUNTUR et PULCRIUS ordinantur, ut *Petrum sincera dilectione prosequor et amplector.*" Thus the modifiers can precede, as in *de Petri bonitate confido,* and with disjunction *de vestra confido non modicum bonitate.* True enough, such possibilities are subject to limitations: excessive separations and awkward transpositions are blamable, "non tamen bene dicetur *bonitate loquor de Bernardi.*" Again, "verborum etiam transpositio turpis et incongrua fugiatur . . . quia non est pretextu alicuius ornatus deformis transpositio facienda." Yet the search for *venustas* will justify many a transposition, including verb first and noun last, or a relative clause being placed before the correlative main clause: "Ad venustatem pertinet ut nominativum et obliquum sequantur et verba nunc primum nunc medium nunc ultimum locum debeant possidere. . . . Item ad pulcritudinem et ornatum pertinet ut relativum coniunctione non egens suum preveniat antecedens; exemplum: *Qui penitentiam non egerit in presenti peccatorum venia negabitur in futuro* . . . (sic!)" etc., with a paragraph on excesses (*vitia*) following.

Likewise the *Summa dictaminis* by Guido Faba or Fava of Bologna (ca. 1200–ca. 1250–the *Summa* was probably composed in the third decade of the century) explicitly identifies the indirect order with art, beauty, elegant and expressive oratory, and the official administrative style: "In constructione duplex est ordo, scilicet naturalis et artificialis. Naturalis est ille qui pertinet ad expositionem, quando nominativus cum determinatione sua precedit et verbum sequitur cum sua, ut EGO AMO TE. [Note that the direct object is defined as the verb's determinant.] Artificialis ordo est illa compositio que pertinet ad dictationem, quando partes pulcrius disponuntur, qui sic a Tullio [read: Auctore ad Herennium] diffinitur: 'Compositio artificialis est constructio dictaminis equabiliter perpolita.'" [25]

Poetry of Panuccio del Bagno (Bloomington, Ind., 1965). The ed. does not attempt to trace the origins of Panuccio's devices.

[24] Y2, Ms. Sorbonne 449 in Thurot. It is now Ms. Bibl. Nat. Paris, Lat. 16253: see f. 1ʳ⁻ᵛ. Delisle cat. ("Inventaire des Manuscrits Latins . . . ," *Bibl. de l'École des Chartes,* XXXI, 1870, p. 50): Laurentius Lombardus, *de dictamine* (1-38) . . . 14th c. (but it looks 13th c.), 38ʳ ". . . explicit Tractatus de composicione epistolarum." See Thurot, 343-344.

[25] See Faba's (Fava's) text in A. Gaudenzi's ed., *Il Propugnatore,* n. s., III (1890), p. 338.

A text of the fourteenth century [26] briefly repeats these definitions and adds: " Naturalis [ordo] est ille qui pertinet ad expositionem.... Artificialis ordo vel compositio est illa [27] que pertinet ad dictationem, quando partes pulcrius disponuntur." *Rhetorica ad Herennium* IV, xii, 18 is then cited as " Tullius ": " Compositio artificialis est constructio equaliter polita." [28]

The use of the term *ordo naturalis* might suffice to obviate the doubt that we are confronted with little more than an extension of the scholastic construing. Realization of the inherent ambiguity of this doctrine was not late in coming to the fore. As we have just seen, in noting that *constructio* is twofold Guido Faba perspicaciously admonished that the 'natural' (EGO AMO TE) serves didactic purposes (*ad expositionem*), while the 'artificial' is the one actually used in composition (*compositio ad dictationem*). More explicitly than anyone, Dante, in distinguishing four grades of *constructiones* (*gradus insipidus, sapidus, venustus, excelsus*), assigned the one typical of the paedagogic exercise of construing to the lowest, " gradus . . . insipidus, qui est rudium, ut *Petrus amat multum dominam Bertam* " (*De vulgari eloquentia*, II, 6). [29]

Admittedly the habit of transposing words could give way to excesses, if unchecked by the criterion of good taste and clarity. Especially noticeable in some writers of the decadent Latinity, but also implicitly contained in the Asianists' love of complication, this vice eventually became recognized as " synchysis," an extreme type of hyperbaton. Speaking generally of the virtues of inversion, Quintilian had warned that there is vice in

---

[26] Ms. B. N. Paris, Lat. 11386, f. 30: Delisle (*Bibl. Éc. Ch.*, XXIV, 1863, 232) gives it as Ponce, *Traité sur l'art épistolaire* (ff. 13-60); 15th-c. Ms.

[27] Thus Thurot, p. 344; but I read (middle of f. 30ʳ): " Artificialis est illa verborum [?] compositio est illa que pertinet. . . ."

[28] Thus Thurot; but I read: ". . . est constructio dicionum equaliter. . . ." Very similar reading of the whole passage in Ms. B. N. Paris, Lat. 8652, f. 14ʳ, which is identified as G. Faba's *Summa dictaminis*.

[29] In this same chapter of his *De vulgari eloquentia* (II, 6) Dante indicated " hanc quam supremam vocamus constructionem," that is the one worthy of the national *illustre* or 'tragic' vernacular, through a series of examples drawn from Provençal and Italian poets. He then added: " fortassis utilissimum foret " to study the excellent Latin poets, such as Virgil, the Ovid of the *Metamorphoses*, Statius, and Lucan, as well as the noblest Latin prose (Livy, Pliny, Frontinus, Paul Orosius, " and many others "). Only thus could one achieve that elect construction: for the closest we come to the masters in imitating them, the more apt will our poetic and artistic activity become. As for himself, he concluded in *Inf.* I that Virgil alone had been his sufficient master: " Tu se' solo colui da cui io tolsi/ lo bello stilo che m'ha fatto onore." Cf. Scaglione, " Periodic Syntax," p. 5.

excess both by inordinate length and obscure complication (*Inst.* IX, iv, 28). He had accordingly censured as *peior mixtura verborum* (VIII, ii, 14) the line *saxa vocant Itali mediis quae in fluctibus Aras* (*Aen.* I, 109), an awkward and hardly intelligible one to say the least (construe: *saxa [sunt] in mediis fluctibus quae Itali vocant Aras*). It frequently recurred in the standard grammarians as an example of *synchysis* or 'thoroughly confused hyperbaton' (as in Donatus "maior," Keil IV, 401, 18-19: "Synchysis est hyperbaton ex omni parte confusum").

But the hermetic, cabbalistic, and pseudo-Asianist Virgilius Maro (early 7th c.) was fascinated by such aberrant phenomena, and treated them, idiosyncratically as usual, under the worthy heading of *scinderatio phonorum,* with the rather monstrous example of Cato's *mare oceanum classes quod longae saepe turbatur simul navigant* (= *mare oceanum saepe turbatur, quod classes longae simul navigant*).[30] To *scinderatio* Maro assigned three goals: display of wit, search for oratorical embellishment, and hermeticism (*sagacitatis adprobandae, decus eloquentiae, ne mystica repperiantur*), thus giving away both his inherent Asianism and low-grade hermeticism. It was somewhat similar to the more limited anastrophe, as in *Italiam contra* for *contra Italiam,* and parallel to the practice of "tmesis," since not only words, but syllables and even letters could be separated, as in *Hiero quem genuit Solymis, Davidica proles* (= *Hierosolymis*), an example of what was destined to blossom into a favorite medieval sport.[31] Mai appropriately assimilated these practices to "slang cryptography" (*parlare in gergo ossia furbesco* and *scrivere in cifra*), which may well have been, at least in part, the background of Maro's wittily irresponsible exercises, and which shows long and wide extensions into the later vernacular literatures. At any rate, the last of the three goals assigned by Maro to *scinderatio* was closer to the spirit of later *ornatus difficilis* and Provençal *trobar clus.* The first was an echo of the Asianic cult of wit (a cult destined to reemerge and climb to glorious levels in the seventeenth-century 'metaphysical poetry' and its later heritage). The second was to be more specifically analyzed by Geoffrey of Vinsauf: "Surgit item quaedam gravitas ex ordine solo/ Quando, quae sociat constructio, separat ordo/," 'a noble gravity comes from order itself when what is joined by syntax is separated by word order'—an observa-

---

[30] Cf. text in A. Mai, ed., *Appendix . . .* (1871), 153-154.
[31] See further examples of such practices in E. de Bruyne, *Études d'Esthétique médiévale* (3 vols., Bruges, 1946), I, 122 ff.

tion which was later taken very literally, and perilously so, by many a
rhetorically trained vernacular poet.[32] Indeed, separation of contextual
parts of the sentence to achieve the gravity of the noble style was a widespread practice in medieval literature, both in Latin and in the vernacular
languages. Geoffrey went on with examples:

> Ut sit in hac forma perversio: *Rege sub ipso;*
> *Tempus ad illud; Ea de causa; Rebus in illis;*
> Aut huius generis trajectio: *Dura creavit*
> *Pestiferam fortuna famem; Letalis egenam*
> *Gente fames spoliavit humum.* Sic ordine distant
> Quae constructa tamen prope stant. Structura propinqua
> Declarat levius sensum; sed plus sedet auri
> Plusque saporis habet moderata remotio vocum.[33]

The stress, then, was on moderation and on the need to avoid obscurity,
even within the treatment of *ornatus difficilis* to which this whole passage
belongs: "Sic tamen esto gravis ne res sub nube tegatur." [34]

Beyond Maro's three goals, all more or less limited to an effort toward
formal artistry, one must single out a not infrequent medieval phenomenon
within the conscious use of literary Latin, namely the eminently " expressive" use of hyperbaton. E. R. Curtius,[35] and after his example E.
Auerbach,[36] have underlined the significance of laborious word order
patterns for the emergence, in the tenth century, of what they called
medieval Latin "mannerism." It is particularly noteworthy for us that the
most brilliant master of this style, Rather of Verona (Ratherius, ca. 887-
974), displayed a clear theoretical consciousness of this device as being
central to the worth of his stylistic achievement.

In the introduction to *Phrenesis* Rather offered this precious bit of
stylistic analysis of his own writings: [37]

Generat praeterea hoc et difficultatem intellectus eis, quos fecit, libellis,
quod creberrime posita illic cernitur parenthesis et, ut liquidam faciat orationem, mirabilem dictionum facit saepius ordinationem, difficillimam quae
pariat, optimam licet intelligentibus, constructionis materiem.

---

[32] *Poetria nova,* vv. 1051-1052, in E. Faral, *Les arts poétiques,* p. 229.
[33] *Poetria nova,* vv. 1053-1060 in Faral, pp. 229-230. Note the specific uses of
technical terms: *perversio, trajectio, ordo, constructio, structura, remotio vocum.*
[34] Ibid., v. 1063.
[35] E. R. Curtius, *European Literature,* pp. 273-301 Amer. ed., esp. 274-275.
[36] E. Auerbach, *Literary Language and its Public,* pp. 133-152.
[37] Rather, *Phrenesis,* § 3: P. L., CXXXVI, 369, cited by Auerbach, pp. 143-144.

Which R. Manheim renders as follows:

The difficulty of understanding his [Rather's] writings is further increased by his frequent use of parentheses; furthermore, he employs an astonishing word order, which is exceedingly difficult to construe, but altogether excellent for those who understand it.

This passage is ample illustration of the drastic inversions and disjunctions spoken about. What makes them so effective is that throughout his work they seem to be expressive of the author's moral ordeal and dialectic emotional tension. The reader will undoubtedly savor some further examples from the treatise *Qualitatis coniectura cuiusdam* (ca. A. D. 965):

[Rather has himself described by an adversary as follows:] Epicurus ac veluti alter, summum in voluptate bonum qui censeat esse, si ventri bene est, si latere, si pedibus, si sibi est suisque sufficiens soli, contentus.
. . . scurrilitatem vero vel verba otiosa, risumque moventia, omni proferre, sive sit laetus sive iratus, paratissimus hora.[38]

To be construed more or less as follows:

Ac velut Epicurus alter, qui censeat summum bonum esse in voluptate, contentus si bene est ventri, latere, pedibus, [et] si est sufficiens soli sibi suisque.
. . . omni hora paratissimus proferre scurrilitatem vel verba . . . sive sit laetus. . . .

Auerbach concluded by observing that

Rhetorical artifice plays a dominant part almost throughout, and, as usual with Rather, the finest effects are achieved by the idiosyncratic word order; it seems to me that for all its oddity, it springs directly from his nature. Manneristic fashions are known to have existed also in Irish, Anglo-Saxon, and Carolingian Latin; they were inherited by the Liège school, in which Rather received his training. . . . But whereas in the three centuries preceding Rather these and similar devices may be regarded as sterile, pedantic games, he (as far as I know) was the first to have lent such mannerism the dignity of a style.[39]

On the more moderate and healthy level, these practices were subsumed by the rhetoricians under the headings of *trajectio* (Geoffrey's *perversio*) and *transgressio*, the main figures which aimed at breaking up the customary syntagmatic units, as in the examples *ea de causa* and *negotium exer-*

---

[38] Auerbach, 147-148.
[39] Ibid., 150 and 152. See, also, Benny R. Reece, *Learning in the Tenth Century* (Greenville, S. C., Furman Univ., 1968), esp. pp. 70-80 on Ratherius' style.

citatur humanum, respectively. Romance philologists have traced to these basic phenomena the literary yet frequent vernacular practices of separating participles and infinitives from the governing verbs or auxiliaries, as, most typically, in Dante's *l'ora ne la quale m'era questa visione apparita;* . . . *era la quarta della notte stata;* . . . *ciò che io avea nel mio sonno veduto* (*Vita Nuova* iii, 8-9); *non sofferse lo nome de la mia donna stare* (*VN* vi, 2), where we also perceive the lingering Latin habit of sending the verb to the end. An analogous occurrence was that of separating and end-positioning adjectives with a predicative (or quasi-adverbial) connotation, such as: *e li sospiri m'assalivano grandissimi e angosciosi* (*VN* xxxvii, 3); *andavano, secondo che mi parve, molto angosciosi* (*VN* xl, 2); *povero mi pareva lo servigio e nudo* (*VN* xxxiii, 1), this last being a particularly sophisticated, but far from unusual, case of separation, and all of the preceding being quite typical trademarks of Dante's juvenile prose (of a particularly expressive type, through emphasis).[40]

C. GENERAL OBSERVATIONS

The contributions of medieval culture to the development of our subject are more far-reaching than the preceding analysis may have revealed. They lie, more deeply than in particular technical discoveries, in the new spirit pervading the whole approach to the problems of expression. A decisive step forward was taken by shifting gradually and subtly away from the prevailing hedonistic and sensualistic orientation of ancient thought and sensibility toward a basic intellectualism which, however we might view it from a scientific vantage point, was destined to leave a lasting mark on modern taste.

We must stop for a moment to envisage our material in the light of its more general implications. To begin with, scholastic thinking was inspired by the effort to see the general rather than the particular. Thus the grammatical investigator was interested not so much in the individual forms as, rather, in the grammatical concepts, the 'universals.' The notion prevailed that these latter existed before the individual forms of Latin and the other languages. Hence language was an invention neither of 'the

---

[40] Cf. Benvenuto Terracini, *Pagine e appunti di linguistica storica* (Florence, 1957), "Analisi dello 'stile legato' della *Vita nuova,*" pp. 247-263, esp. 263. See, also, ibid., "Analisi dei toni narrativi nella *Vita nuova* e loro interpretazione," pp. 264-272.

people' nor of the linguists or grammarians, unless one conceives the original grammarian as a *grammairien-philosophe*: "Philosophus grammaticam invenit." However unfounded, and unilateral at best, this assumption helped syntactical theory, which is what concerns us here. Consequently, the grammatical principles were held to be essentially similar in all languages (as the eighteenth-century *grammairiens-philosophes* will, once again, hold). Roger Bacon (1214-1294) was exemplarily specific on the matter: "Grammatica una et eadem est secundum substantiam in omnibus linguis, licet accidentaliter varietur."[1] Individual realizations that there are as many grammars as there are languages, as Peter Helias, for one, maintained, were bound to be submerged in the stronger thrust of generalizing speculation. Indeed, might we not venture to assume that this very attitude preannouncing the *grammaire générale* of later times lay at the basis of Bacon's far-reaching and genial reform of Greek grammar?[2] For it was his knowledge of the Latin paradigmatic system of declensions and conjugations that must have prompted him to provide a division of the Greek categories more simplified and workable than the ancients had even been able to formulate.

Beside this purported universality of linguistic structures, in the Middle Ages one held fast to another basic notion, that of language as a product of art, coming into being through reflection. Let us listen to Peter Helias explaining the origin of genders, and we will have a taste of how this notion operated: "Videntes itaque auctores alterum de his sexibus in quibusdam rerum esse, in quibusdam neutrum, tales invenerunt voces, quibus sic substantias notarent, ut secundario significarent an aliquis sexuum inesset eis, an neuter."[3]

Not in spite of such 'prejudices,' but thanks to them, this was the age which gave us a consistent theory of cases; which first distinguished sharply between nouns and adjectives, and gave us a whole string of important terms, such as the new notion of apposition. Alberic of Montecassino (fl. 1057-1088) and Peter Helias (teaching at Paris in 1142, still living in 1166) made standard the expression *ablativus absolutus*.[4] Abelard

---

[1] Cf. E. Charles, *Roger Bacon, sa vie* . . . (Paris, 1861), p. 263. See the *Summa gramatica* in *Opera hactenus inedita R. Baconis*, ed. Robert Steele (Oxonii, 1940).

[2] Cf. A. Pertusi, "'Ερωτήματα. Per la storia e le fonti delle prime grammatiche greche a stampa," *Italia Medioevale e Umanistica*, V (1962), 321-351; and see now Scaglione, *Ars Grammatica* (The Hague, 1970), pp. 72-75.

[3] Thurot, p. 122.

[4] See my *Ars Grammatica*, pp. 131-139.

introduced the term *copula* in syntactic function with respect to the verb *sum*. One learned to distinguish between concord and regimen. Baudry de Bourgueil, around 1098, gave the first example of a methodic use of *regere, regimen* as a fixed technical term, whereas the ancients had nothing more precise than *coniungi, adiungi, construi, desiderare, exigere, sequi, trahere, servire. Regere,* never seen in Priscian, became frequent with Hugh of St. Victor.[5] Although no one thought that tenses and moods could relate to one another in the sentence, since one treated only the construction of the noun with the verb and no other principle of construction was found but those concerning person and number in the relationship between subject and predicate, the very introduction of Subject and Predicate into grammar was a medieval novelty—one of the by-products the leaning toward dialectic brought along with it, and one on which Peter of Spain († 1277) left the indelible marks of his logical orientation.[6]

On the negative side, however, some serious blame attaches to the medieval grammarians for developments which bear directly on our subject. It is known that the approach to questions of expression and style became increasingly sterile in that long period on account of a conventionalized, formalistic use of rhetorical categories emptied of their vital meaning. In particular, within the realm of *ars grammatica* a basic, though not too explicit distinction had introduced itself in the treatment of "barbarisms": whatever was taught as linguistic "correctness" was subject to exceptions, but these were treated with sharply opposite judgments according to whether the departure from the correct rule was formally justified or not. In practice, the rule was expected to stand fast in prose, whereas poetic language (still a central concern of grammatical instruction) was recognized as open to an unlimited number of 'licences.' This dichotomy—for which, it must be said, the theorists of late antiquity were directly responsible—was unsound and dangerous. The particular argument of "metrical necessity" as justification for deviating from the norm (whereby metaplasms and schemata had been defined and distinguished from barbarism and solecism ever since Donatus) was an abuse

---

[5] Thurot, p. 82.
[6] On some of the preceding material, see Golling in Landgraf's manual, III, esp. pp. 27-49, and Wackernagel, *Vorlesungen*, I, esp. p. 23. On the literature of the Trivium arts down to the end of the twelfth century cf. Max Manitius, *Geschichte der lateinischen Literatur des Mittelalters*, I (Munich, 1911), 119-152 and 452-536; II (ibid., 1923), 638-725; III (1931), 175-220.

which betrayed the progressive loss of touch with the reality of the language in its natural, actual word order, at the same time that synchysis, disjunctions, inversions became pure embellishments without content (as already in Claudian). Cicero, who knew better, had foreseen and tried to forestall such inevitable aberrations: "Nobis . . . in scribendo atque in dicendo necessitatis excusatio non probatur. Nihil enim est necesse." (*Or.* 229.) Indeed, nothing happens "by necessity," either in prose or verse, because the apt user of the language always freely chooses the most appropriate means of expression. Style is always choice.

However that may be, the greatest single merit of the medieval students of language was perhaps their concern with syntax. This also brought about a widening of the terminological horizon, consequently an ambiguous use of the ancient all-inclusive term *constructio*. Ambiguous, first of all, because it was often unclear whether it was to be taken as mere 'construing' or as true composing. More ambiguous still because often the term no longer included all of syntax but only a particular portion of it. I shall give one outstanding example. One of the few complete treatments of syntax among the *modistae* appears in the *Grammatica speculativa* by Thomas of Erfurt, chs. 45-54. It is divided into four parts: *principia construendi; constructio; congruitas; perfectio.*[7]

---

[7] Karl D. Uitti, *Linguistics and Literary Theory* (Englewood Cliffs, N. J., 1969), pp. 28-62, offers an interesting analysis of linguistically relevant thought from Priscian through the medieval period, with emphasis on the essentially 'Platonic,' literary-poetic slant in Dante's ideas on language as contrasted with the essentially 'Aristotelian,' philosophico-logical slant in the speculative grammarians.

CHAPTER THREE: THE RENAISSANCE

A. LATIN PHILOLOGY

Viewed from the technical angle that concerns us, what took place in the Renaissance was not all progress. Humanism itself was not an un-mixed blessing. For one thing, as R. Sabbadini pointed out with his customary acumen, syntax moved from the "formal, scientific, or his-torically-oriented" method it had attained in the Middle Ages back to the "empirical" level. The former method, according to this distinction, starts from the forms to extract from them their functions or meanings. It made its first appearance in the glorious essay of case-syntax in the *Doctrinale* (but with roots in Charisius, Diomedes, and Priscian).[1] The humanists fell back to deriving forms from functions (in a different way than that of the modistae), and one cause for this was the progressive introduction of the vernacular in the schools. The habit of translating from Italian to Latin (an exercise usually introduced with the formula *si datur thema*) made them take their point of departure from "elements related to functions" (the meanings of Italian forms) to move towards the (Latin) forms.[2]

All this was part of the diminished interest in the technical systematic aspect of syntactic theory among the humanists. Nevertheless, in a more particular context the humanists sensed the danger of the medieval notion and practice of '*constructio*' taken as 'construing,' first among them being Gasparino Barzizza (*De compositione*, ca. 1420) and Guarino Veronese (author of a little treatise on *compositio* in memorial verses), who sum-marily banned it.[3] Yet the practice of parsing or construing, which amounts

---

[1] Cf. R. Sabbadini, *Il Metodo degli Umanisti* (Florence, 1920), pp. 10 ff.

[2] See, also, R. Sabbadini's papers on logic in grammar, "Dei metodi nell'insegna-mento della sintassi latina (Considerazioni didattiche e storiche)," *Rivista di Filologia e d'Istruzione Classica*, XXX (1902), 304-314, and, on Charisius, Diomedes, Priscian as sources of the medieval 'scientific' syntactic method, "Elementi nazionali nella teoria grammaticale dei Romani," *Studi Italiani di Filologia Classica*, XIV (1906), 113-125, esp. 120-122.

[3] Cf. R. Sabbadini, "Sulla *constructio*," *Rivista di Filologia e d'Istruzione Classica*, XXV (1897), 100-103 and *Storia e critica di testi latini* (Catania, 1914), pp. 83-85, 103-113, as well as *Il Metodo* . . . , pp. 14-15. See *Gasparini Barzizii Bergomatis*

to little more than an undoing of the live qualities of speech and eloquence in action, continued on its way unperturbed, since Cristoforo Barzizza, despite the strictures of his illustrious ancestor, reiterated the medieval norms in his grammar, in terms of *rectus* and *obliquus ordo*.[4] Antonio de Nebrija, who had omitted the topic of *constructio* in his famous grammar of 1481, was then compelled by the insistence of his friends to put it back where it seemed to belong.[5] Indeed, even Jean Pellisson who, as Sabbadini put it, unwittingly pronounced a shrewd verdict of condemnation of *constructio* in the following words, still accepted it under the name of *ordo* (thus returning to the ancient terminology of *ordo dictionum* which the medieval men had replaced with *constructio*, since ancient *constructio* was the rough equivalent of our 'syntax'): " Hanc vocat Alexander constructionem non satis proprie, quia construere proprie est aliquid debite componere. Qui autem orationem pueris declarat non construit, sed ab alio constructam resolvit aut destruit aut ordinat, ut a pueris intelligatur. Quocirca rectius dixeris ordinem aut destructionem aut resolutionem aut declarationem." [6] Indeed, the 'Golden Rule of Construing' was never given up, and was destined to be vigorously revived later on by the eighteenth-century rationalists, above all others by Du Marsais. In the meantime, the method was comprehensively analyzed in John Brinsley's *Ludus literarius* (1612), with reference to such predecessors as Martin Crusius (1526-1607).[7]

---

et Guiniforti filii Opera, ed. G. A. Furietti (2 vols., Romae, 1723), I, 4-6. G. Barzizza's " De compositione, prima elocutionis parte" is the only section of a rhetorical treatise printed in the Furietti ed. (pp. 1-14). Cf. Georg Voigt, *Die Wiederbelebung des classischen Altertums* (first ed. 1893 . . . Berlin, 1960⁴), II, pp. 442-443.

[4] Christophori Barzizii *Grammaticarum institutionum* . . . (Brixiae, 1492): "Rectum ordinem dicimus quum in quovis compositionis genere ab eo verbo quod principale appellatur ordinandae litterae initium semper sumitur. Obliquum vero quum idem fere exponendae litterae ordo est qui fuit contexendae. Et ille quidem aliquanto acutior videtur sed certe difficilior, hic et promptior est et elegantior et eius, cuius est compositio, voluntati accomodatior."

[5] Antonii Nebrissensis *Grammatica* (1530), ff. 136-137. Nebrija objected to the traditional method of construing by pointing out that in parsing *Aen*. I, 108-109, Donatus had placed the object not only before the verb, but even before the subject. Cf. Sabbadini, "Sulla *constructio*," cit., p. 102.

[6] Ioh. Pellisso, *Contextus universae grammatices Despauterianae* (Venetiis, 1585), f. 92. The Preface bears the date 1529. Cf. Sabbadini, *Il Metodo* . . . , pp. 14-15.

[7] Cf. Foster Watson, *The English Grammar Schools to 1660: Their Curriculum and Practice* (Cambridge, Eng., 1908), 349-356. Curiously enough, this method of parsing as a very popular " device of schoolmasters to teach boys to translate Latin," is still occasionally referred to as a sixteenth-century invention. So does,

On the other hand, the 'return to antiquity' which lies at the root of humanism is conspicuous in the area of our investigation.[8] It guides the profound revolution which took place during the Renaissance in the attitudes toward the Latin language. The humanists became aware of the discrepancy between the spoken and current written language of the late Middle Ages, on the one hand, and the ancient usage, on the other. They became also implicitly conscious of the more direct cause of this "corruption" of the noble speech of Rome: the linguistic habits of the vernacular were reflected in the transformed patterns of the mother tongue, in a sort of vicious circle which had commenced with the vernaculars themselves being issued out of Latin at a time when Latin had reached an advanced stage of transformation and popular "corruption." Their main concern, therefore, was for correcting such distortions, as they saw them, and this effort impressed itself on their method of teaching Latin. For this reason they were constantly comparing vernacular forms and expressions with the correct (classical) Latin equivalents.

Such a commitment reflects itself chiefly in a syntactical direction, and we must take it into account when we evaluate the humanistic achievements in the realm of linguistics. True enough, 'syntax' remains a glory of medieval speculation and did not progress dramatically in the early Renaissance. But this was because the interest in speculation had vanished and given way to the empirical observation of facts, historically established—which was a different type of achievement. When, for example, we encounter in Niccolò Perotti's *Rudimenta grammatices* the sentence: "lectio quam a magistro docendi sunt discipuli est difficilis" as the acceptable translation of "la lezione la quale de' essere insegnata dal maestro alli scolari è difficile," accompanied by the warning: "Cave dicas: Lectio docenda . . . ," we sense what kind of task the humanist grammarian had set for himself and why it left him neither time nor taste for the theoretical subtleties of the despised medieval masters.[9]

---

e. g., M. P. Cunningham, "Some Phonetic Aspects of Word Order Patterns in Latin," *Proceedings of the Amer. Philos. Soc.*, CI (1957), 488, who quotes from Watson.

[8] It has been pointed out that Petrarch's appeal to euphony alone to explain his rearrangement of elements in his poems contrasts sharply with the medieval habit of arranging and explaining arrangement strictly by logical divisions, according to the method made canonical by the *summistae*. It was an exemplary and symptomatic case. Cf. E. Panofsky, *Gothic Architecture and Scholasticism* (New York, 1958), pp. 36 f.

[9] I quote from the ed. Brixiae, per Bernardinum Misintam de Papia et Hieronymi

True enough, syntax does progress in the Renaissance in a way that has escaped the attention of some observers. It does so by pervading a larger portion of grammatical treatises at that time than in preceding centuries in the sense that the manner of the treatment is basically syntactical, even when the formal arrangement of subject matter seems to assign only a few brief chapters to *constructio* proper. For one thing, humanistic grammars incorporate a great deal of 'rhetorical' material (*figurae, soloecismi* and *metaplasmi*, etc.), which is treated in a syntactical spirit in that it is intended to display a rich idiomatic use of the language at a stage when the pupil is able to master not only correct forms but genuine Latin sentences and extended passages.

Hence we should not refrain from drawing upon all sorts of grammatical material of the time (starting from the humblest scholastic manuals) in order to solve any problem of this nature. Unfortunately our familiarity with that province of technical literature is still so vague and superficial that any conclusion can only be tentative at this point.[10]

Though relatively late, concentrated attention and original work in the proper area of syntax did come about in the Renaissance. Noticeable emphasis on it appears, for instance—to choose only a couple of rather haphazard cases—, in the early-sixteenth-century grammatical works of William Lily, such as his *Rudimenta* (*G. Lilii Angli Rudimenta*) and specifically his *Libellus de Constructione*.[11] But the major and most authoritative voice that was first heard in this domain within the humanist camp was that of the Flemish Jan van Pauteren of Ninove (Despautère, Despauterius), whose *Syntaxis* was apparently first published in 1510,

---

de Medesano Parmensem Sociorum (sic), 1501. First ed. Sweynheim and Pannartz, 1473.

[10] The best of the early students of humanism had stressed the relevance of the grammatical production. Cf., e. g., G. Voigt, *Wiederbelebung des cl. Alt.* (1960 ed.), II, pp. 373-381, and especially such solid, though pioneering works as Remigio Sabbadini's *Il Metodo degli Umanisti.*

[11] Cf. Vincent J. Flynn, *The Grammatical Writings of William Lily,* ?1468-?1523, Univ. of Chicago Diss. (Bibliographical Society of America, 1943); [W. Lily], *Libellus de Constructione Octo Partium Orationis* (London, Pynson Press, with Colet's Preface, 1513). It was often reprinted under the same title in Erasmus' amended version. On the *Institutio compendiaria totius grammatices* erroneously attributed to William Lily but largely based on his syntax, see, now, C. G. Allen, "The Sources of 'Lily's Latin Grammar': A Review of the Facts and Some Further Suggestions," *The Library,* Ser. V, IX (1954), 85-100. See, also, W. Lily, *A Shorte Introduction of Grammar,* ed. V. J. Flynn (New York, Scholars' Facsimiles and Reprints, 1945).

according to the Preface to the 1537 ed. of his *Commentarii grammatici*.[12] An interesting feature of this work is that the set of rhetorical, or 'pre-rhetorical,' concerns which had traditionally been part of grammatical treatises were now homogeneously incorporated into a coherent system of language theory and specifically absorbed into the grammatical province the author called syntax. Since *congruitas* involves not only *vocem* but also *significationem*, there are two modes of discourse, *grammatice loqui* and *latine*, i. e. *eleganter loqui*. Hence syntax is *praeceptiva, permissiva, prohibitiva*. After treating of the *figurae constructionis*, we find a general theory of *ellipsis* under the heading of *modi subaudiendi*. The first example is that of ellipsis of the *regens*, as in *laus [sit] deo superno*. The problem is that of taking into account and explaining types of clauses and sentences other than the basic, fully articulated ones of propositional statement, command, and desire.

More specifically, even while the borderline between grammar and rhetoric, that is to say linguistics and stylistics, remained vague and unstable, the early sixteenth century witnessed a number of attempts to introduce consideration of composition and word order into the grammatical province of syntax. The example of Despautère points up the fact that Northern humanists (and especially the Germans) were most active in this area, and their syntactic manuals evidently depended on the outstanding example of Alexander of Villedieu, whose *Doctrinale* continued to run strong through the first half of the century in spite of fierce humanistic attacks.[13] Thus word order is treated in Johannes Coclaeus' *Tractatus de constructione et regulis congruitatis*, part of his *Quadrivium grammatices* (Nuremberg, 1511). In the wake of the *Doctrinale*, this work contains *Etymologia, Diasynthetica* (= Alexander's *Diasyntactica*), *Prosodia, Orthographia*. The anonymous *Secunda Pars grammatices sive Synthactica* published in Münster in 1514 was divided into *Constructio* (*transitiva* and *intransitiva*, Word Order, Concord—this whole section conspicuously dependent again on Alexander) and *Regimen*.

Finally, as far as this Northern group is concerned, the very influential

---

[12] See the Étienne ed. of 1537: *Johannis Despauterii Ninivitae Commentarii Grammatici* (Parisiis, R. Stephanus, 1537), p. 24. The *Syntaxis* was widely printed later on: Strassburg, 1515; Köln, 1527 and 1572; Lyon, 1528; Antwerp, 1556; etc. For a critical summary of the contents see J. J. Baebler, *Beiträge . . .* , esp. 156-163.

[13] On these developments see J. Golling, "Einleitung in die Geschichte der lateinischen Syntax," esp. pp. 48-61.

De emendata structura Latini sermonis libri VI (London, 1524) by Thomas Linacer, offers, at the beginning of the third of six Books on syntax, a distinction between the two *genera constructionis,* "alterum, cui nec deest quidquam nec redundat nec loco suo abest nec immutatur, quod non immerito IUSTUM appelletur; alterum, cui deest aliquid vel redundat, vel loco suo abest, vel immutatur [enallage] . . . , quod *figuratum* dici potest." And in the sixth of these Books, which deals with the theory of figures, "De constructionis figuris," and became conveniently tagged *syntaxis figurata,* we find a theory of Ellipsis, Hyperbaton, Synchysis, Enallage, Anacoluthon, and Hellenismus [= Graecismus]. Linacer's way of proceeding established the distinction between *syntaxis regularis* and *figurata,* which was a successful one: we shall find it again, for example, toward the end of the century in a rather influential German philologist, Nicodemus Frischlin of Balingen (1547-1590), whose authorities were Scaliger, Melanchthon, and Linacer.[14]

Attention to questions of order was not exceedingly keen in the Renaissance, but Alexander de Villedieu's teachings in this area remained fruitful well into the sixteenth century. In his Commentary on the *Doctrinale* Josse Bade devoted a whole chapter to construing: "De constructione ac ordine liberali ad eruenda sensa et regimina dignoscenda" (Al. de Vill., *Tertia Pars Doctrinalis,* Paris, 1524-25). As to going beyond the clause, Melanchthon was among the first to indulge in the analysis of the *phrasis* into *kola* and *kommata* (*Grammatica latina,* Basel, 1557², pp. 141-142).[14a]

The key text in the laying of new foundations for the development of our subject is Julius Caesar Scaliger's (1484-1558) *De caussis linguae latinae libri XIII* (1540). In a truly revolutionary spirit, Scaliger showed the way to a new current which runs through the Spaniard Francisco Sánchez de la Brozas (Sanctius, 1523-1601—also known as el Brocense),

---

[14] Frischlin, *Quaestionum grammaticarum libri VIII* (Venice, 1584), reworked in his *Grammatica latina compendiose scripta* (Tübingen, 1585).

[14a] Both texts cited in Jean-Claude Chevalier, *Histoire de la Syntaxe. Naissance de la notion de complément dans la grammaire française (1530-1750)* (Geneva, 1968), pp. 44 and 223. My study was completed when this remarkable and weighty contribution (776 pp.) came to my attention. The scope and purpose of the two surveys are quite distinct, since the complement is one element of the clause, but much of the material treated is common to both. Chevalier's work covers the background of ancient and medieval production only briefly, and concentrates on French speculation. I believe his basic premises and conclusions turn out to be in agreement with mine.

directly down to the authors of Port-Royal. The numerous commentators and followers of Sanctius' *Minerva* (1587), of Lancelot's Port-Royal General and special Grammars, of Arnauld and Nicole's Port-Royal Logic, constitute, together with these capital texts, a tightly-knit current of thought which consistently developed by explicit mutual references down to the middle of the eighteenth century. It was the rationalistic, logically-oriented school which, literally or potentially, was centered on a renewed concern with syntax, thus recalling the heritage of medieval scholastic. Although, in a literal sense, Scaliger himself had omitted whatever related to syntax, as he himself averred, Sanctius focussed upon this latter province as the most necessary, in his work likewise subtitled " On the causes of the Latin tongue " (*Minerva, sive de causis Latinae linguae*). The realization of this concern as common to both works appeared in the very Preface to the Port-Royal Latin Grammar.[15] The medieval doctrines which reached new fruition in the *Minerva* were enriched there with bits of the Arabic grammatical heritage, and with the addition of some personal, valuable notions of Sanctius himself. Above all, the impact of this work was due to a thoroughly original method of organization.

But to understand these complex developments in their proper light one must begin by putting them in a broader historical and theoretical perspective.

A. Pagliaro has aptly distinguished two currents in the history of linguistics, both pertaining to the theory of language:[16] the psychological (concern for the natural relationship between word and object), going from the *Cratylus* to the "harmonic grammars" of 1600-1800 through the development of "etymology"; and the logical (concern for the relationship of word to thought), going from Aristotle through the Stoics down to the Scholastics and the critical grammars of Scaliger, Sanctius, Lancelot and Arnauld. Thirdly we must consider empirical grammar, which without concerning itself with a theoretical foundation offers a practical classification of forms, and shows a normative function and tendency: this current, eminently 'technical,' changes but little (except for such original contributions as those of the Scholastics) after Thrax

[15] See the English trans. by T. Nugent in the London, 1816 ed. (*A New Method of Learning with Facility the Latin Tongue* . . . , trans. T. Nugent, 2 vols., London, 1758; 1803; 1816).
[16] Antonino Pagliaro, *Sommario di linguistica arioeuropea. I: Cenni storici e questioni teoriche* (Rome, 1930), pp. 13-40.

and Dyscolus. We may add, as a close ally of the psychological approach, the emphasis on the affective element in linguistic expression which characterizes the rhetorical method of analysis.

Despauterius and Linacer had transmitted two capital notions destined to exert a far-reaching impact on future elaborations: the assimilation of rhetorical areas into grammar under the heading of *syntaxis figurata;* and the theory of ellipsis, as part of the *figurata* and as principal explanation of all phenomena not immediately reducible to application of the basic, normal patterns. With Sanctius, in whose *Minerva* the theory of ellipsis occupies one third of the whole work (Book IV), this other idea of Despautère and Linacer became a scientific principle of the first order.[17] Furthermore, the explanation of syntactic patterns through ellipsis was made to follow a consistent line of reasoning admitting of no afterthought which would bring the observer back to explicit registration of living usage. Reason has the upper hand over both usage and authority.

In this rationalistically grounded, critical approach Sanctius followed Scaliger. But Scaliger had selected Latin only as a fulcrum for his general theory of grammar as the basic structure of all languages (thus becoming the forerunner of Arnauld and the eighteenth-century general grammarians), while Sanctius sought to prove the inner necessity and logical coherence of the syntax of Latin. Not incorrectly, therefore, Sanctius has been praised for fathering the modern study of Latin grammar as a closed system.[18]

We shall now turn our attention briefly to the formal treatises on rhetoric. In this area, after such a pioneering work as the one, already mentioned, by Barzizza (ca. 1420), and that of George of Trebizond (a paraphrase of Hermogenes composed in the 1430's and first printed ca. 1470), the main Latin texts of the High Renaissance were due to Mancinelli, Guillaume Fichet, Guillaume Tardif, the Florentine Publicius, Melanchthon, Erasmus, Despautère, and Omer Talon.[19]

---

[17] [Francisco Sánchez de las Brozas,] *F. Sanctii Brocensis Minerva, seu de causis linguae latinae* (Salmanticae, Renaut fratres, 1587).

[18] See, on these and the immediately following questions, Golling, pp. 53-61.

[19] Georgius Trapezuntius, *Rhetoricorum libri V* (ca. 1435: ed. princeps Venice, ca. 1470); Antonius Mancinellus, *De figuris opusculum* (Rome, 1489); Guilielmus Fichetus, *Rhetorica* (Paris, 1471); Guillermi Tardivi *Rhetoricae artis ac oratoriae facultatis compendium* (Paris, ca. 1475); Jacobi Publicii Florentini *Oratoriae Artis Epitoma* (Venice, 1485); Joannes Despauterius, *De figuris liber, ex Quintiliano, Donato, Diomede, Valla, Placentino, Mancinello, Nigro pluribusque diligenter*

Bearing in mind the experiences of the medieval controversies, Gas
parino Barzizza's elegant little treatise appears as interesting for what it
says as for what it chooses to overlook. It contains norms on order,
ligatures, rhythm in elocution, after Quintilian and Martianus Capella.
Ordo, iunctura, numerus are given as the three factors on which composition leans. *Elocutio*, in turn, is made up of three parts: *compositio,
elegantia, dignitas.* The humanistic teacher maintains that moments of
high pathos exclude overelaboration in compositive patterns (p. 6). Indeed such moments find more becoming a degree of spontaneous abruptness: in criticizing some traditional examples of awkward composition
in Maecenas (cf. Quint., *Inst.*, IX, iv, 28), he adds: " Non enim quidem
natura ipsa patitur ut, cum gravi aliquo moerore premimur, verborum
compositioni vacare possit animus. Probatur itaque magis illud dicendi
genus quod abruptum est ac simile illis animorum fluctibus, quam ex-
politum ac sedatum." It is, however, evident that judgment here is based
on the achieved impression of naturalness rather than on an objective
pattern of grammatical nature, because Barzizza will approve of a distorted
ordering (*abruptum*) if it is expressive, while he will judge it inappro-
priately artificial if it gives the impression that the writer pays greater
heed to the words than to the actual movements of his mind (" non verba
rebus, sed res ipsas verbis accommodavit "—ibid., p. 6).

There is only one hint at the basic ordering of the subject-verb relationship where he praises the end-positioning of the verb in Cicero's (against

concinnatus (Gandavi, Petrus Caesar, 1520); Erasmus, *De duplici copia verborum
ac rerum* (Strassburg, 1513), *Brevissima maximeque compendiaria conficiendarum
epistolarum formula* (Erfurt, 1520), *Libellus de conscribendis epistolis* (Cambridge,
1521), *De ratione conscribendi epistolas liber* (Basle?, 1535), and other tracts
included in the first tome of Leclerc's ed.; Melanchthon, *De rhetorica libri tres*
(Wittenberg, 1519; Basle, 1519; Leipzig, 1521; Cologne, 1521; Paris, 1527, 1529;
cf. Bretschneider, *Corpus Reformatorum* [Halle, 1834 f.], vol. XIII), *Institutiones
rhetoricae* (Hagenau, 1521; Cologne, 1521; Paris, 1523; Strassburg, 1524), *Ele-
mentorum rhetorices libri II* (Wittenberg, 1531, 1532, 1534, 1536, 1542); Petrus
Mosellanus, *Tabulae de schematibus et tropis* [ca. 1529] (Leipzig, 1532; Paris, 1537);
Joannes Susenbrotus, *Epitome troporum ac schematum* (Tiguri [Zürich], 1540?;
ibid., 1565, 1570 . . .); Audomarus Talaeus, *Institutiones oratoriae* (Paris, 1545),
Rhetorica [1548], editio postrema (Paris, 1562). For a specific treatment of sentence
structure, precisely Ciceronian periodicity, see, as particularly prominent within
the Protestant educational system, the work of Strassburg's Rector Jean Sturm:
Joannis Sturmii de Periodis unus; D. Halicarnassaei de Collocatione verborum alter
(Argentorati, 1550); *I. S. Liber unus de Periodis*, explicatus . . . a Valentino Ery-
thraeo (Argentorati, 1567). On some of these texts see T. W. Baldwin, *Shakspere's
Small Latine* . . . , Index ss. vv.

Antony) "ut tibi necesse esset in conspectu populi romani vomere," because of its effective rendering of *concitatio animorum* (p. 7). Otherwise all his discourse on word order revolves around the less basic and more subtle choices in the arrangement of secondary elements, down to, for instance, the avoidance of a conjunction or preposition at the beginning of a sentence (*Omnes cum honesta facimus; Atticam ad urbem* . . .).

Barzizza's exposition shines, therefore, not for its directness in tackling the linguistic problem of word order, which he avoids altogether, but in giving refined examples of stylistic sensibility in general word arrangement, in the wake of Quintilian. See, for instance, the advice to state first and simply the main point, only to add the qualifications at the end: *Vir fortis omnia pro republica adibit pericula, et quidem impigre*, is declared more 'moving' than *Vir fortis omnia pro republica impigre pericula adibit*. This pattern suits the median style (*mediocris figura*), while the grave style (*gravis figura*) tends to invert it (pp. 4-5).

Somewhat similarly, he limits himself on the subject of sentence structure to the incidental advice to avoid overlong sentences (*nimia verborum suspensio*—p. 9), except in the most solemn parts of the oration. On *numerus* he points out that this most important of all parts of composition has been variously judged by the authors. In particular, Martianus Capella (*De nuptiis Mercurii et Philologiae*, Liber V) brushed aside both Cicero's and Quintilian's precepts, and submitted a doctrine which Barzizza proposes to adopt (p. 11). We cannot follow this interesting exposition because it lies outside the limits we have set to our study. May I only point out the norm that in the rare cases in which the sentence is allowed to end with a monosyllable, it will be best to place before it such a bisyllable that the pattern will alternate vowels according to their length, namely either – ◡, – or ◡ –, ◡ (= trochee + long or iambic + short).

In conclusion Barzizza stresses the principle that any good composition will preserve the *dignitas* of discourse by subordinating form to content: "rebus . . . ars numerorum serviat, et non res arti" (p. 14).

On the level of new, original work it is George of Trebizond's *Rhetoric* that offers to us one of the most elaborate and systematic uses of the category of composition.[20] For Trebizond *compositio* is, together with subject matter and diction (*sententiae, verba*), one of the three elements

[20] First ed. Venice, 1470. See the Basle ed.: Georgii Trapezuntii *Rhetoricorum libri quinque* (Basileae, 1522). I use the ed. Lugduni, ap. Gryphium, 1547. Cf. Voigt, *Wiederbelebung* (1960[4]), II, 442-443.

of any style genus (*figurae orationis*, i. e. high, low, or median) (p. 375). And he regards it as clearly the most important aspect of elocution (384), harder and nobler than diction (425). He separates the periodic from the loose construction, and attempts to distinguish the former into *ambitus* and *circuitus* (this last having more " force "—*vis*). He points out that this forcefulness is signally achieved by ending the *circuitus* variety of period with a short colon, whereas a long one contributes *dignitas* to the *ambitus*. The *ambitus* is more becoming to the exordium, the *circuitus* to all aspects of argumentation (415). In short, he gives examples of all three, namely of *oratio soluta, ambitus,* and *circuitus,* in order (417-418):

Dicendum est enim mihi de Cn. Pompeij singulari eximiaque virtute. Huius autem orationis difficilius est exitum quam principium invenire, ita mihi non tam copia, quam modus in dicendo quaerendus est.

Nam quum dicendum sit mihi de Cn. Pompeij singulari eximiaque virtute, cuius orationis difficilius est exitum quam principium invenire, non tam copia quam modus in dicendo mihi quaerendus est.

Nam cui dicendum est de Cn. Pompeij singulari eximiaque virtute, cuius orationis difficilius est exitum quam principium invenire, ei non tam copia, quam modus in dicendo quaerendus est.

This is one of the earliest attempts to define the rhythmic value of final phrase-lengths in terms of the whole. We shall remember this antecedent when we come across " Beauzée's law."

Trebizond then takes his contemporary Guarino Veronese to task for his inept composition and submits three samples from his Oration in praise of the Carmagnola (1428), now revised in a Ciceronian periodic form. The best of these examples, already quoted by Sabbadini, deserves all our attention for the thoroughness of Trebizond's re-elaboration: [21]

Plerique sunt, comes insignis ductorque magnifice, qui res et facta veterum singulari admiratione consequantur [22] et praecipuis laudibus (in caelum) efferant (et recte sane). Dignissimum enim est eos suis non fraudare praeconiis, qui aut vitam per inventas artes excoluere aut praeclara edidere facinora. Verum enimvero iidem adeo asperi vel fastidiosi potius rerum aestimatores sunt, ut aetatem nostram aspernentur ac damnent, quae tamen

---

[21] Trapezuntius, *Rhetoric*, V, pp. 423-425; Basle ed. V, 140 ff. Cf. R. Sabbadini, *Storia del Ciceronianismo* (Torino, 1886), pp. 17-18.

[22] 1547 ed.: *persequantur*. Phrases in parentheses were dropped in Trebizond's revision.

permultos divino ingenio, excellenti doctrina et imperatoriis artibus nobis instructos ornatosque prodúxerit.

Plerique sunt, comes insignis ductorque magnifice, qui, quoniam dignissimum est eos suis non fraudare praeconiis qui aut praeclara edidere facinora aut vitam per artes excoluere, et res atque facta veterum praecipuis laudibus efferunt singularique admiratione prosequuntur, sic aetatem nostram aspernantur ac damnant; quos ego ideo asperos vel fastidiosos potius rerum aestimatores iudico, quod hanc aetatem permultos divino ingenio, excellenti doctrina atque imperatoriis artibus instructos atque ornatos nobis video produxisse.

Note how the periodic 'roundness' is achieved at some expense of logical development, since the *aspernantur* is not exactly a consequence of the clause introduced by *quoniam*. The stylistic improvement is, however, evident.[23]

Aside from the technical treatises on which our survey must principally rest, the humanistic production is fraught with aperçus on matters of composition. We shall have to limit ourselves to very few examples, and I must quote two passages that impose themselves for their explicit relevance.

Medieval composition of the schematic type (i. e., relying on Gorgian schemata) was kept alive through the Renaissance in several areas which remained largely aloof from humanistic influences. Foremost among these were the sermons written according to the *mos fratrum*, which Coluccio Salutati perceptively criticized in a letter. He was praising a sermon by the bishop of Florence for not yielding to the features of the *mos fratrum*: "It does not trifle with that artificial rhythm; there is none of that equality of syllables, which is not wont to happen without exact counting; there are none of those clausules which end or fall alike. For this is reprehended by our Cicero as nothing else than a puerile thing which is far from decent in serious matters or when used by men of gravity." The sermon at hand "can be read without a tune or an effeminate prattle of consonance" ("sine concentu et effeminata consonantiae cantilena").[24]

Indeed the humanists, exceedingly refined judges of Latin style, were perfectly capable not only of distinguishing between ancient and medieval forms, but also between classical and pre- or post-classical forms within

---

[23] The Gorgian figures are rather unsystematically expounded in the following pages, with the nomenclature of the *Ad Herennium*.

[24] Quoted by Norden, II, 765 fn., transl. by Croll, "Sources . . . ," in Patrick and Evans' ed. p. 269.

antiquity. Erasmus, for example, could discern the peculiar modes of Patristic writing. In his *Ciceronianus* he pointed out how St. Ambrose had a way of writing " rhythmic and measured by virtue of short isocola, so that his style, while original and inimitable, is most un-Ciceronian " ("membris, incisis, comparibus numerosus ac modulatus, suum quoddam dicendi genus habet aliis inimitabile, sed a Tulliano genere diversissimum").[25] Then in his *Ecclesiastae sive de ratione concionandi,* while summarily assessing the stylistic potentialities of composition by different manners of periodic and loose members and *articuli,* he would point out how the suggestion of balance and sound effects had been so persuasive as to have conquered even such austere authors as St. Paul, St. Augustine, and St. Gregory the Pope.[26]

Together with their unprecedented ability to characterize general styles, schools, and style periods, we also find in the humanists a reliable aptitude to define stylistic personalities. In the *Ciceronianus* (1528) Demosthenes is said to have *vis, nervosum quiddam ac naturale,* Seneca sentences, Caesar *joci,* Sallust and Brutus brevity. Cicero is inferior in these respects, and also sins in his lack of measure, the virtue of Spartans and Attics.[27] "Compositio vitiosa, inepta et absurda" is called that in which Cicero uses echoes such as *ne voces referas feras; res mihi invisae visae sunt Brute.*[28] Cicero is imitated by starting off with *si, etsi, quamquam, quum*—devices which create periodic suspension.[29] We must be aware of the dangers inherent both in the elaborate periodicity of Isocrates and in the loose style of Seneca: "Applauditur Isocratis structurae numerisque. Huc qui vehementer annitatur, in periculum veniet, ne superstitione compositionis sit molestus, et artificii jactatione fidem amittat. . . . In Seneca compositionis abruptum et sententiarum immodicam densitatem multae virtutes excusant."[30] Both tend to become exaggerated through imitation: we are prone to fall into vices related to characteristics of our models. Thus if we try to imitate Cicero, however little we may add to his compositional modes we shall turn from orators into singers: "Si compositioni [Ciceronis velis addere], fies pro oratore cantor."[31]

[25] Erasmus, *Opera omnia,* ed. Joannes Clericus (Leyden, 1703-1706), I, col. 1008, reprinted Hildesheim, G. Olms, 10 tomes, 1961-1962, t. I.
[26] Cf. *Opera omnia,* t. V, *Ecclesiastae,* book III, cols. 989 A-D and 1000 C-1001 A.
[27] Ibid., I, cols. 980-981.
[28] Ibid., I, col. 984.
[29] Ibid., I, col. 986.
[30] Ibid., I, col. 990.
[31] Ibid., I, col. 991.

Erasmus artfully introduces a new sense of history in his conception of stylistic character. He is criticizing Ciceronianism in a seeming paradox: " Ciceronianus sit maxime qui Ciceroni sit dissimillimus, hoc est, qui optime aptissimeque dicat, quum diversa ratione dicat; nimirum, rebus jam in diversum commutatis." Thus, if a painter wanted to paint an old man portrayed by Apelles when he was young, he would be " unlike Apelles " if, in order to be " like him," he insisted on painting his subject young. At this very point Erasmus makes his claim that styles must change in time because they must tally with the subject matters. Thus the old humanistic argument of a union of res et verba is brought to final fruition by denying the static nature of models, since we must always be ourselves, different from others and from our forebears (just as the ancients were pagans and we are Christians, with a necessarily different language). " Modo fateris eum Ciceronianum, qui dilucide, copiose, vehementer et apposite dicat pro REI NATURA, proque TEMPORUM ac personarum conditione." [32] A pertinent application, in sum, of the criterion of aptness, within the welcome discovery of the principle of originality versus imitation.

The periodic style may vary from author to author in ways that demand close analysis to be revealed: thus Augustine may sound like Cicero in his use of lengthy periods, but look closely and you will see how they are more markedly scanned into their constituent cola and commata: " Augustinus . . . hoc habet Ciceronis, quod praelongo ambitu circumducit periodum, . . . verum non aeque ac Cicero, prolixum orationis ductum, membris et incisis distinguit." [33]

The sense of history appears once again in the argument against declamationes (while he is criticizing Longolius' orations). Even when we merely exercise ourselves, we must choose real questions (and he gives examples) relevant to contemporary matters and circumstances, social, political, or others; if we choose literary subjects, they must at least be in keeping with the historical circumstances of the times to which they refer.[34]

Chapter xxx of Erasmus' De copia analyzes under compositio asyndeton, polysyndeton, epanalepsis, and syzeugmenon.[35] This last is the

[32] Ibid., I, col. 1001.
[33] Ibid., I, col. 1008.
[34] Ibid., I, col. 1018.
[35] Ibid., I, col. 22.

coupling of several sentences under one verb, and it can be effected by a threefold ordering: the predicate can come first, last, or in the middle. E. g.: *deflorescit forma vel morbo vel aetate; vel morbo vel aetate forma deflorescit; aut aetate forma deflorescit aut morbo.* The chapter on *compositio* in *De conscribendis epistolis* seems to reduce the subject to *numerus*, and disposes of it summarily.[36]

This closer look at the paradigmatic case presented by Erasmus should suffice to satisfy our curiosity. For the authority of the writer and for the detailed character of the exposition I should also single out one more example of humanistic commentaries on ancient rhetorical texts dealing with composition, namely Pier Vettori's Commentary on Demetrius. He followed the original text step by step and expanded it, in a learned and lucid manner, into an original commentary four to five times as long as the original.[37]

All in all, the humanists were fond of reminding themselves that more precious teachings could issue from the great orators than from the theorists of oratory, not excluding Cicero himself.[38] Nevertheless the age produced a plethora of rhetorical manuals. They lean chiefly on Quintilian, Cicero, and Hermogenes. Although on the whole they continued to lay emphasis on style,[39] we can recognize two kinds of them: those of the former deal mainly with invention and disposition, while the others turn almost exclusively to elocution. This latter current, which became most methodically associated with the Ramists, is the one which prevailed in the course of the sixteenth century. We thus witness a far-reaching shift from the exaltation of a ' total rhetoric ' with Valla and Politian, toward a reduction of rhetoric to *elocutio* and *actio* with Agricola, Vives, Sperone Speroni, Nizolio, Ramus, Patrizi.

The trend is exemplified by the early case of Juan Luis Vives, who in Book IV of his *De causis corruptarum artium* (1531), misconstruing the

[36] Ibid., I, col. 349. Of the *Ciceronianus* see, now, the critical ed. with It. trans., intr., and notes, by Angiolo Gambaro: Desiderio Erasmo da Rotterdam, *Il Ciceroniano o dello stile migliore* (Brescia, La Scuola, 1965).

[37] *Petri Victorii Commentarii in librum Demetrii Phalerei de Elocutione* (Florence, Giunta, 1562). Pp. 1-28 deal with general matters. Cf., also, P. *Victorii Commentarii in tres libros Aristotelis de arte dicendi* (Florence, Giunta, 1548 and 1579), esp. pp. 526-543 of 1548 ed.; and P. V. *Commentarii in primum librum Aristotelis de arte poetarum* (Florence, Giunta, 1560; 2ª editio 1573).

[38] Cf. G. Voigt, *Wiederbelebung* (1960⁴), II, p. 442.

[39] Cf. J. A. Symonds, *Renaissance in Italy: The Revival of Learning* (New York, 1888), p. 525.

genuine role of classical *inventio* (originally the discovery or finding of places, the material content of arguments), ruled it out of rhetoric altogether. Whether or not this procedure (together with the important precedent of Rudolph Agricola) can be regarded as the source of Ramus' 'reform,' it ratified the stand of those Renaissance logicians who assigned *inventio* and *dispositio* to logic. In a similar manner the remaining major subdivision absorbed all the attention of medieval rhetoricians (with a resulting formalism which had already characterized the Second Sophistic), while it had become the lot of debate or *dialectica* to monopolize the places and their organization (again, *inventio* and *dispositio*, respectively).[40] Thus the first Book of Vives' *De ratione dicendi* (1532) dealt mainly with sentences (*compositio*), e. g. with dilation and conciseness as in Erasmus' *De copia,* and with the period (Ch. vii).[41] Francesco Patrizi in the ten dialogues *Della Retorica* ventured to go so far as to deny any scientific substance to ancient rhetoric. Eventually Ramus 'saved' rhetoric by reserving for it no other province than that of elocution (*Institutiones dialecticae,* 1543; *Scholae in artes liberales,* 1555), even though he 'rhetoricized' logic precisely by incorporating into it not only all the topics, but the theory of order (disposition), exposition, and 'method' as well. In thus assigning topical rhetoric and arrangement of subject matter to dialectic, Ramus and his collaborator Omer Talon followed a pattern which, in a different historical context, reminds one of the scholastic period (starting perhaps with Abailard's *Sic et Non,* as McKeon has brilliantly demonstrated), and which will be adopted again and again by philosophers directly or indirectly related to the Ramist tradition—and in a signal manner in Arnauld's *Logique.*[42] Since we are about to

---

[40] Text in vol. VI of Vives' *Opera,* ed. Majansius (Bruges, 1532; Valencia, 1745, 8 tomes, reprinted London, 1964). See, also, the Sp. trans. in Vives, *Obras completas,* ed. Lorenzo Riber (Madrid, 1948), vol. II, pp. 453-475. Book IV of *De causis* was entitled "De corrupta rhetorica," and followed B. II "De grammatica" and B. III "De dialectica corrupta."

[41] Vol. II of Vives' *Opera* (1964), pp. 117-129, which comprise *De rat. dic.,* ch. vii on "Periodus" and ch. viii on "Ordinatio verborum." Also in Riber's ed., II, 692-719. Ch. vii is the only relevant section for our purpose, with some interesting examples of periods. Vives thinks a sequence of *incisa* without ligatures can make a period when they "fit together" perfectly. Otherwise, rather than in order as such, he in interested in orderliness for the sake of clarity.

[42] Cf. Talon's Preface (dated Paris, 1544) to *Petri Rami Professoris Regii, et Audomari Talaei Collectaneae Praefationes, Epistolae, Orationes* (Marburg, 1599): "Peter Ramus cleaned up the theory of invention, arrangement, and memory, and

witness the impact of the doctrine of 'plain style' on theory and practice of composition, let me anticipate that the most authoritative specialist on Ramus, Father Walter J. Ong, has recalled that the connection between non-theological Scholasticism, Ramism, and 'plain style' had previously been suggested in one of the first major studies of the influence of Ramism, Perry Miller's well known *The New England Mind: The Seventeenth Century* (New York, 1939).[43]

For M. W. Croll, the clear beginning of the new 'Atticism,' the core part of baroque style, is to be sought in the theory and practice of Marc-Antoine Muret (Muretus, Muret 1526–Rome 1585), who resided in Italy after 1555. Muret appears to have found his definitive 'new' style in a series of orations starting with one of November 1565, followed by the academic discourses of 1567, 1569, and 1571 at the University of Rome, where he had become Professor of Moral Philosophy.[44] The Roman discourses have as their subject the necessary union of science and art in a movement from *sapientia* (private wisdom) through *prudentia* (public wisdom) to *jurisprudentia* (civic virtue). Croll characterizes the oration of 1565 as "pure Baconian positivism in rhetoric," marked by broken periods, every phrase being a thought and the original metaphors, themselves thoughts. Croll identifies Lipsius, Quevedo, Gracián as later examples of phases of this "positivism" in prose style coming to light within the Jesuit Order or under its patronage (p. 277). At any rate, by 1565 Muret had renounced the *genus sublime* and the *genus ornatum* or *medium* of ancient rhetoric. He had adopted the *genus humile*, the 'plain style,' as an 'Atticist'—specifically, the *genus stili concisum* of the *oratio astricta verbis, densa sententiis*. He proposed to correct the barbarism of the (Bartolist) jurists by a style that could boast the three qualities of the Stoic rhetoric: purity of idiom that can be studied in the conversation of cultivated people; terseness; aptness or expressiveness. "The vessels

returned these subjects to logic, where they properly belong. Then, assisted indeed by his lectures and opinions, I recalled rhetoric to style and delivery (since these are the only parts proper to it)." Trans. in Howell, *Logic and Rhetoric in England,* 148-149.

[43] W. J. Ong, "Ramus and the Transit to the Modern Mind," *The Modern Schoolman,* XXXII (1955), 301-311, esp. 305. Miller laid special emphasis on the connection between Ramism and the Puritans' obsession for logic and distaste for symbolism.

[44] See Croll, "Muret and the History of 'Attic Prose,'" 280-281. These orations, not in Muret's *Scripta Selecta*, are found in ed. Leipzig, 1629, I.

need not be golden, they can be earthen, provided the viands are fine and the vessels themselves are well rubbed (*tersa*), clean (*nitida*), trim in appearance." [45]

Muret had learned a taste for Plautus from Budé and especially Cujas: the first step Justus Lipsius took after Muret converted him from Ciceronianism in 1568, was "a public profession of his pleasure in the rustic words and the ingenuous style" of Plautus.[46] Finally, in an oration of 1572, Muret allied himself with Erasmus and Ramus,[47] and after attacking the doctrine of imitation in favor of individualism (his "parrots" remind one, through Erasmus, of Politian's "monkeys"), he lined up the true ancient speakers and teachers of style on the side not of rhetoricians and sophists, but of the *politici*.

In that same programmatic oration of 1572, Muret "placed the study of rhetoric firmly upon the foundation of Aristotle's treatise, where it was to rest during the century of 'Attic' prose which was to follow." This meant "to divorce prose-writing from the customs of epideictic oratory and wed it to philosophy and science." [48] Rhetoric is thus conceived as "something that arises out of a mixture of dialectic and politics": reasoning, feeling, and demonstration are its basic processes. He uses Book I and II and ch. 17 of Book III of Aristotle's treatise to base his wedding of rhetoric to dialectic, and leaves aside, as the 'Attics' later did, the theory of conventional style in the remainder of the work. "As the dialectician, says Muret, uses two instruments of proof, the syllogism and induction; so the orator, the twin and true comparative of the dialectician, . . . has two also . . . : the enthymeme, which corresponds to the syllogism, and the *exemplum*, which corresponds to induction." [49] The reader will only have to recall the two contrasting currents in antiquity, namely the Sophistical and the Peripatetic, in order to realize the full import of Muret's stand on this matter. (See Ch. I, A above.)[50]

---

[45] See Oration 17 in ed. Leipzig, I. Croll 283.

[46] Croll, "Muret," 284. See, also, Croll, "Juste Lipse et le mouvement anti-Cicéronien," *Revue du Seizième Siècle* (July 1914), p. 211. Later, Croll found that this old art. of his needed revision at several points.

[47] Cf. Oration 7 in *Scripta Selecta*, on assuming the new chair of rhetoric in 1572.

[48] Croll, "Muret," p. 286.

[49] Croll, ibid., 287.

[50] It seems to me that the current dispute as to the true meaning of the *declamationes, orationes, invectivae*, and sundry dialogues and epistolary controversies which obtained among the 'civic' humanists of the first Quattrocento generation is improperly defined on account of a lacking realization of the two historical traditions of

At the same time, the placing of elocution at the center of the rhetorician's attention produced in the second half of the sixteenth century a
new art of elocution, a sort of stylistics different from rhetoric as such,
whose peculiar task had been to teach the modes of eloquent reasoning.
The change in emphasis became evident in Francesco Robortello's edition
of the *Sublime*, where it was proclaimed that the true prize of the orator
lay not in " persuasion," but in " striking" the audience " as with a clap
of thunder" by means of the sublime, the marvelous, the extraordinary.
F. Panigarola's posthumous *Il predicatore* (Venice, 1609) adapted this
new view to sacred oratory. The way was open to the aesthetic of conceits,
with Gracián and Tesauro. The attention thus shifted from logic to
psychology, from reasoning per se to its emotional understructures, hence
from substance to ornate form. When, in later times, the rationalism
of the Classicists and of the Enlightenment will bring grammar and
rhetoric back to logic, as with Arnauld, Bouhours, Orsi, Du Marsais and
a host of other theorists, we might view this as a return to a previous
tradition in terms of ideology, although the context of the debate had
changed altogether. By that time, in one way or another the taste for
anti-classical forms which affects our subject had inexorably set in:
periodic structure and harmonic word order had broken down without
possible recourse. This change lay at the root of baroque stylistic, and
continued to bear fruit amidst the movement that followed.

rhetorical debate. Neither side of today's historians engaged in these conflicting
interpretations mentions the distinction pointed out above. For one side, the
Florentine humanists rediscovered the fundamentals of liberty versus tyranny as a
result of their personal involvement in the war against Gian Galeazzo Visconti; for
the other, those same humanists were no more committed to one party than as
rhetorically trained composers of official propaganda pamphlets for the consumption
of a relatively ignorant public. Yet it may well be that the answer lies in the fact
that the rhetoric the humanists were using was once again, after so many centuries
of actual neglect, that of a Demosthenes or a Cicero, who could undoubtedly calculate
the psychological effects of their consciously applied devices, but were far from
personally uncommitted to the issues at stake. The true discovery of the same
humanists was perhaps, we are entitled to assume, that of the genuine, almost
forgotten tradition of the heyday of ancient rhetoric. This polemic has recently
centered on Hans Baron's *The Crisis of the Early Italian Renaissance: Civic Humanism and Republican Liberty in an Age of Classicism and Tyranny* (Princeton, 1955,
1966[2]); see, e. g., Jerrold E. Seigel, *Rhetoric and Philosophy in Renaissance
Humanism: The Union of Eloquence and Wisdom, Petrarch to Valla* (Princeton,
1968).

B. THE TRANSITION TO ANALYSIS OF THE VERNACULAR

1. We have been gradually moving toward the borderline between speculation on Latin and speculation on the spoken languages. In this regard, not only as the direct background of later events, but also for its intrinsic originality within the confines of our subject, France appears to be the place where the ideas on composition in the vernacular were most significant in the late Renaissance. Italy had produced the most advanced and pace-setting grammarians and rhetoricians in the vernacular during the first half of the sixteenth century; but in the field of composition, and thanks to the pervasive success of the Bembine theses, Italy remained too close to the classical models (Latin and fourteenth-century Italian) to allow much theoretical realization of the new needs before the middle of the eighteenth century. Nonetheless one must recognize that precisely in Italy new ideas were brought forward in the rhetorical field through the work of some isolated but influential rebels. As regards Spain, despite the exceptional personality of Nebrija at a pioneeringly early stage, that country offers, in the vernacular, little to compare with Sánchez' work in the area of Latin. Religious concerns and social circumstances, among other factors, were keeping the German lands in a long state of Limbo, not to mention the difficulties of relating to the independent structures of German such problems as had arisen within Latin. Although the very unsettled condition of her language would seem to keep England unripe for any activity of the kind, that country was suddenly to become a productive leader after the turn of the century, and we can see clear signs of things to come even in the latter half of the sixteenth century.

The formation of 'baroque' taste and ideas in the seventeenth century has become one of the most tormented questions in modern cultural history. Within this broader context, the central issue of the imitation of Cicero and the connected attitudes toward styles are of direct concern to us. In the peculiar development of stylistic canons from, roughly, 1500 to 1750, Ciceronianism, periodicity, and grand style were closely related, just as were their opposites: anti-Ciceronianism, loose composition, and plain style. We have seen above (Ch. I, B) that the original Aristotelian distinction between periodic and unperiodic composition can be seen to lie at the origin of the technical definition of the two basic styles. Although plain style does not necessarily demand unperiodic composition nor the grand the periodic, these correspondences were commonly implied.

We are now coming to a time when the theoretical rejection of the yoke of Latin patterns by the modern vernaculars results in the replacing of periodic style with one more appropriate to the spirit of the vernaculars. We shall have to envisage these changes within the framework of a new conscious taste for the plain, unperiodic style—a taste which continued to grow from, roughly, 1575 to as late as 1800.

The process we are about to trace begins with the strengthening of the anti-Ciceronian current within humanism. Such authors as Poggio, Valla, and Politian, had gone on record as dissociating themselves from the generally prevailing tendency toward strict Ciceronian imitation both in a linguistic and in a stylistic sense. Pico, Ermolao Barbaro, and Politian, the remarkable triad who, together with Ficino, dominated the last generation of fifteenth-century humanism, were all averse to imitation of fixed models, though each in a personal way. In his well-publicized polemic with the leading Ciceronian Paolo Cortese, Politian had curtly concluded: " Non exprimis, inquit aliquis, Ciceronem. Quid tum? Non enim sum Cicero; me tamen, ut opinor, exprimo." [1] Erasmus, the most determined and decisive antagonist of the Ciceronians, regarded Barbaro and Politian as heroes for their stand on this matter.

Speaking of Cortese, we cannot afford to pass by a testimony included in his last work, at a time when his former Ciceronianism had become much tempered by a healthy broadening of his historical horizon. Not only was he now prepared to embrace such authors of Late Latinity as Apuleius; he even associated himself, on the plane of the vernacular, with the partisans of the interregional " courtly language," Colocci, Calmeta, and, later, Castiglione. In a somewhat unexpected analysis of vernacular styles which occurs in the chapter " De sermone " of his *De Cardinalatu* (1510), a landmark in the genre of humanistic encyclopaedias, Cortese offered a classification of style genera which he based on methods of composition.[2] Idiosyncratic as this application of the compositional categories may be, the text is a most enlightening one—and not only because

---

[1] See *Prosatori latini del Quattrocento,* ed. Eugenio Garin (Milan-Naples, 1952), p. 902.

[2] A long excerpt of this chapter from Book II of Cortese's *De Cardinalatu* is edited in Carlo Dionisotti, *Gli Umanisti e il Volgare fra Quattro e Cinquecento* (Florence, 1968), pp. 62-72. See p. 66 for the passage in question, and esp. pp. 72-77 for Dionisotti's interpretation. The work was privately printed " in castro Cortesio," that is in the author's house, by Simeone di Niccolò Nardi in 1510, publication being completed shortly after the author's death.

it amounts to " the first and, prior to Bembo's *Prose,* most important document of a rhetoric of the vernacular." We read here that there are two aspects to elocution, namely *structura* and *ornatus.* The former consists of word arrangement, *collocatio,* which is in turn divided into proper use of words and apt manner of speech. The proper use of words is tantamount to the middle style, where nothing is found in excess (as in the high style) nor in defect (as in the subdued style). This style is exemplified by Boccaccio's *Decameron* and Pietro Bembo's *Asolani;* the high style by Boccaccio's *Filocolo;* and the subdued by Giovanni Villani's Chronicle.[3]

We must pause here for an observation on the early grammatical work in Italy. The first Italian grammars, with the isolated exception of Alberti's *Regole,* were not directed to the school.[4] All preceding grammars (i. e. Latin), when short, were so directed, except such para-grammatical tracts as the *de modis significandi,* which were for logicians. This explains both the lack of scholastic method in the presentation (e. g. no paradigms) and the incompleteness of the treatment which generally omits what seems analogous to Latin forms in order to concentrate on apparent anomalies and departures from the parent language.

Even so we witness in the crucial texts of the second quarter of the century an exemplary episode with respect to the constant trend toward the interpenetration of the Trivium arts. To begin with, despite the meritorious efforts of the Schoolmen (terminalists and modists), syntax was still slow in coming into its own. Now, at least according to some inter-

---

[3] Intelligendum est duplex esse locutionis excolendae genus, unum quod in structura, alterum quod in ornatu versatur. Structura enim in verborum collocatione consistit, collocatio autem proprio verborum usu et consentanea loquendi ratione continetur. Proprium genus est quod nec altitudine nec tenuitate constat, sed quod intermedia mediocritate temperatur. Altitudo vero ea nominatur quae pinguium verborum constructione tumet, quale id genus sermonis videri potest, quod est Joannes Boccacius eo exquisito genere commentus, quod a Graecis *philocalon* nominari solet. Tenuitas vero est quae arida et exili ratione constat, quo genere maxime Joannem Villanum in annalibus usum fuisse cernimus, a quo ita multa sunt tenuia collecta minutatim, ut nihil esse posset altiori concinnitati loci. Mediocritas autem ea videri debet, in qua nihil aut defuturum aut redundaturum sit, quo sit in alterutram propensura partem: quo genere maxime est idem J. Boccacius in mythologica centuria usus; quod idem etiam modo Petrus Bembus Venetus sequi in eo maxime libello solet, in quo per antilogiam de amatoria ratione disceptatur. . . . At consentanea loquendi ratio ea videri potest quae maxime a Barbarismi et Soloecismi perversitate abest [i. e., " correctness "].

[4] Cf. Trabalza, *Storie della grammatica italiana* (Milan, 1908), p. 70.

preters, the second book of Bembo's *Prose della volgar lingua* (1525) must be regarded as the central one, and it is the one which covers syntax.[5] This might mean that the main thrust of the whole work is rhetorical and stylistic rather than linguistic. But in particular, syntax as meant there practically coincides with word arrangement, since *de facto* it covers little else.[6]

A somewhat later development will elicit an even broader interest on our part. Bembo had been a true disciple of humanism in playing down the normative approach ("one speaks thus," he would point out, rather than "one must speak thus"). Now G. Gelli went so far as to throw doubt on the very possibility of setting rules for other than dead languages.[7] With a living language, so he thought, one cannot foresee the remainder of the curve of its progress, perfection, and decadence, so as to determine where the peak occurs and fix its conditions as *rules*. Hence rules cannot be written for Tuscan. At any rate, norms and precepts are inconsistent with the nature of languages, whose structures become settled before the rules are established, not after, therefore cannot be regulated. The last part of this reasoning marks an unequivocal revolution from the concepts of the "invention of grammar" and "grammatical" languages which had prevailed before.

Alongside this bold ideological framework, Gelli's dialogue also submitted that syntax must be developed over grammar. And it fell to Giambullari to carry on this proposal; his treatise *Della lingua* contained two books of Grammar (I, Morphology of Declinabilia; II, of Indeclinabilia), and no fewer than six books of Syntax, duly divided into *regularis* (= "*intera*") and *figurata*.[8] The latter included the treatment of ellipsis, pleonasm, and inversion or "permutation." Thus Book III covered the Syntax of Nouns, IV of Verbs, V of Indeclinables, VI Enallage and Antimeria (parts of the Tropi), and, finally, all the Schemata, that is, the Figures of Word in VII, and the Figures of Thought in VIII—200 figures in all! The rhetorical side of traditional grammar preempts the space that

<hr/>

[5] Trabalza, p. 77, claimed against Cian the preeminent position of this Second Book of the *Prose*.

[6] Trabalza, ibid.: "La sintassi, con questi criteri, era tutt'uno con la collocazione e disposizione delle parole."

[7] P. F. Giambullari, *Della lingua che si parla e scrive in Firenze e un Dialogo di G. Gelli sopra la difficultà dell'ordinare detta lingua* (Firenze, Lorenzo Torrentino, 1551).

[8] Op. cit.

should have been made available for true syntax, but, at least, the use of the word and concept of syntax, if not the thing itself, is making headway. Above all, proportions and implications are the more relevant aspect of this treatment of the discipline. Soon enough, composition as style will find its due place both within formal rhetoric and grammar, as well as independently as general literary criticism.

True enough, the first quarter of the Cinquecento witnessed the culmination of the imitative effort, thanks chiefly to the impact of Cardinal Bembo, its staunchest and triumphant supporter. But toward the middle of the century the other trend was, at last, ripe. We can spot the clearest signs of this in the tone of some rather obscure treatises.

In the first book of Bernardino Tomitano's *Ragionamenti della lingua toscana* (Venice, 1545), a rather confused dialogue in three books on the vernacular orator and poet, the protagonist, Sperone Speroni, is made to repeat his contention that the study of language is not the gateway to philosophy. As he epigrammatically puts it: "Things make men wise; words only make them seem so." Tomitano apparently takes him to mean that philosophy feeds style, not viceversa.[9]

Accordingly, Petrarch was perfect in style BECAUSE he was full of philosophy.[10] This last-hour presentation of the humanistic topos of *res et verba* implicitly denies the traditional progression of *artes sermocinales* as late antiquity and the Middle Ages had transmitted it. The sequence language, style, reasoning, or grammar, rhetoric, logic as necessary propedeutics, in that ascending order, to ethical and physical knowledge had finally lost its vitality, though it continued to be echoed long afterwards. The distinction of *verba* and *res* became an opposition in a sense that reverses the traditional, progressive movement from the former to the latter, thus unwittingly preparing the ground for the fundamentalist appeal to the reality of things within the anti-Ciceronian and anti-rhetorical struggle of 'Atticists' and scientists in the following century. The spirit of Cato's polemic against the rhetoricians ("rem tene, verba sequentur") renews itself in a more sophisticated context and for different ends.

Change avails itself of the spirit of revolt without adopting its literalness. Just as Tomitano seems to reject the rhetorical tradition, Bartolomeo Cavalcanti chooses from it what serves the new needs. Through denial, a functional affirmativeness has been reached. Cavalcanti, a Florentine

---

[9] Cf. Baldwin, R. L. T. P., p. 60.
[10] Ibid.

born in 1503 and a member of the republican " Orti Oricellari " group in exile at Padua, distinguishes himself from the Paduan rhetorics, such as that of Tomitano, in his Italian *Retorica* (Venice, Giolito de' Ferrari, 1558/9², 1560³; first ed. 1555, reprinted Pesaro 1574), which draws on all the classical sources it summarizes: Aristotle, Cicero, Quintilian, Hermogenes, Demetrius 'Phalereus,' Themistius, and above all Pier Vettori's Commentary on Aristotle's *Rhetoric*. He draws his examples (all translated) mainly from Cicero and Demosthenes and, all in all, sounds consistently Aristotelian: in a true Aristotelian spirit he devotes to style only one of his seven books, the fifth. Rather exceptionally, Cavalcanti eschews confusing his subject with poetic, is clear and progressive in both plan and manner of exposition, despite his diffuseness (over 550 closely printed pages), and displays a strictly classical character and scope. His anti-Bembine orientation is revealed by his ousting of Petrarch from his position of monopoly as the exemplar of everything imitable. Book V has, besides the usual list of figures, an unusually definite treatment of *compositio* as sentence management. This appears particularly noteworthy if we consider that elocution is reduced to minimal proportions, and arrangement of sequence (*dispositio*) to a meager summary. In discussing periodic structure (p. 279, 1559 ed.) the author depends on the *De elocutione* then attributed to Demetrius of Phalerum. In treating of number or rhythm he warns against the unmanliness of the Gorgian figures characteristic of the elevated style: " le spesse corrispondenze de i pari e de i simili che fanno l'orazione lasciva. . . ." As an antidote, he recommends "una certa mediocrità." [11]

Although M. W. Croll does not mention Tomitano or Cavalcanti, their relevance to the genesis of the phenomena he studies seems clear, especially when one bears in mind that Muret started his courses in the chair of eloquence at Padua in 1554-55.

2. In their effort toward artistic prose, the French had started to experiment in diverse directions after Latin patterns. Alain Chartier (b. 1385-†1430-1440), for example, had adopted Latin movements in a Senecan

---

[11] Cf. Baldwin, *R. L. T. P.*, pp. 63-64, and Christina Roaf, " L'Elocuzione' nella *Retorica* di Bartolomeo Cavalcanti," in *La Critica Stilistica e il Barocco letterario*, Associazione Internazionale per gli Studi di Lingua e Letteratura Italiana (Florence, 1957?), pp. 316-319. The Fifth Book, " Dell'elocutione," of Cavalcanti's *Retorica* occupies pp. 249-362 of the 3ᵈ ed.: *La Retorica di M. Bartolomeo Cavalcanti . . . divisa in 7 libri . . .* , 3ª ed. revista e accresciuta (1560).

mold, marked by conspicuous antitheses and sententiousness: " Vie curiale
. . . c'est une pauvre richesse, une abondance misérable, une hauteur qui
choit, un estat non stable, ainsi comme un pilier tremblant et une mour-
euse vie." [12] " Ilz [les grands] vivent de moy, et je meur par eulx. Ilz
me deussent garder des ennemis, hélas! et ilz me gardent de mengier mon
pain en seureté." [13] But he was also fond of Ciceronian balance. He is an
example of the *grande rhétorique* which produced the elaborately artificial
prose of a Jean Lemaire de Belges.[14] Jacques Amyot's (1513-1593) epochmaking experiments in confronting the potentialities of his language with
the splendor of Greek and Latin masters were paralleled by his refined
theoretical insights into the nature of French periodic style. They are part
of his commitment to formulate a *Projet de l'éloquence royale*: " Les
clauses entières [meaning *phrases*, i. e. ' sentences '] ne doivent point être
plus longues que quatre vers alexandrins," a notion which remained basic
through the age of French classicism, as Curtius has reminded us. This
is justified on grounds of both logic and physiology: " tant pour être
mieux entendues [subj.: les clauses] et la sentence mieux comprise . . . ,
que pour n'accourcir et lasser l'haleine." He draws more heavily upon
Cicero's *Orator* by assigning different sentence lengths to different parts
of the oration: " Il y a plus de montre et de parade ès clauses longues. . . .
Aussi s'en sert on plus en l'exorde et en la péroration, et des entrecoupées,
on en use ès deux autres parties." In quoting these passages A. François
conclusively remarks, with apparent surprise, that with all this *la période*
appears to be as hard to handle as verse, with which it competes.[15] But
the *Orator* had stated just so much (198-199), and we know that the
question had been discussed by the Greeks ever since the time of Isocrates.

Le *Projet de l'éloquence royale* shows the weight of the classical heritage
nowhere more clearly than in the recommended use of ' conjunctions '
for the effect of periodic continuity (a procedure from which the later

[12] Quoted from Le *Curial* by Lanson, *L'Art de la prose*, p. 23. Y. Le Hir,
Rhétorique et stylistique (Paris, 1960), 105-117 contains some notes on 16th-century
French rhetoricians; pp. 83-102 deal with " L'ordre des mots " and " La Phrase "
according to French rhetorical theory at different times. But this study is not very
useful in detail.

[13] *Quadrilogue invectif* (1422): ed. E. Droz, 1923, CFMA. Cf. Delaunay, *Étude
sur Alain Chartier*, pp. 107, 110, 165, 166.

[14] Lanson, op. cit., p. 25.

[15] A. François, *Histoire de la langue fr. cultivée*, I, 218-219, esp. 219. The *Projet*
remained unpublished until 1805: see Jacques Amyot, *Projet de l'él. r., composé
pour Henri III* (Versailles-Paris).

French usage will drastically depart): "Il te faut étudier à joindre, mais aussi à lier les clauses ensemble, et, tant que faire se pourra, diversifier et changer les conjonctions qui les entretiennent, afin que rien n'y soit décousu ni interrompu, ains que tout coule de suite, et toutes les périodes soient assemblées comme les membres d'un même corps." [16]

The sensual approach to phonetic arrangement remains of paramount importance but, understandably, rhythm and harmony (*numerus* and *harmonia* or *euphonia*) are no longer clearly distinguished in the derivative doctrine of *nombre* and *harmonie*. According to Fouquelin (Foclin, *Rhétorique françoise*, 1555), *nombre* is to be defined as "une plaisante modulation et harmonie d'oraison," implying, *inter alia*, as Amyot's *Projet* puts it, "aucune dure rencontre de lettres ni de syllabes," and cadences without rhyme.[17]

Both grammarians and rhetoricians begin to turn their attention to word order, and it behooves the modern observer to pay homage to such early theorists for their incipient independence from the patterns of Latin. This independence both announces and conditions the coming developments in our field, to appear at a later time when the *modernes* will be ready to give battle to the tyranny of ancient authorities and their subservient admirers. In his early study *De la syntaxe française entre Palsgrave et Vaugelas* (1877, pp. 53-54), A. Benoist found that Jean Garnier (*Institutio gallicae linguae*, Geneva, 1558) was the only one who attempted to trace rules for the normal construction of French clauses (noun before verb, verb before adverb, etc.), although he was inclined to accept the most daring and varied inversions. He also analyzed imperative and interrogative clauses, both positive and negative.

Ronsard's categorical pronouncement is well known: "You shall *never* transpose words either in your prose or verse: our language will not tolerate it" (Second Preface to the *Franciade*). In his Treatise on French Grammar (Paris, Chr. Wechel, 1550), Louis Meigret (ca. 1510-1560)

---

[16] François, I, 221.

[17] Cf. François, I, 220. On Fouquelin's original contributions to Ramist rhetoric see R. E. Leake, Jr., "The Relationship of Two Ramist Rhetorics: Omer Talon's *Rhetorica* and Antoine Fouquelin's *Rhetorique françoise*," *Bibliothèque d'Humanisme et Renaissance*, XXX (1968), 85-108.

Fouquelin's was perhaps the best attempt to establish a French rhetoric in the sixteenth century, but one must not forget the earlier Pierre Fabri, *Le Grand et vrai art de pleine rhétorique* (1521, . . . 1544), as well as P. de Courcelle's *Rhétorique* (1557)—not to mention such broader-gauged texts as Du Bellay's *Deffence et illustration de la langue françoise* (1549) and Péletier's *Art poétique* (1555).

points out that French and Latin differ sharply in an essential manner with regard to their behavior toward *l'ordre de nature*. Consequently French must no longer look upon Latin as a model for its own advancement and betterment. The cause of national identification thus allies itself with the medieval theory of *ordo naturalis*, from which Meigret borrows his weightiest, fully articulated argument: A word order which is to be regarded as natural shall follow the sequence imposed *par l'ordre de nature* and *par raison*, namely the sequence: agent, action, passion (*ajant, acçion, passion*), which Latin tends to subvert for the sake of elegance.[18] This was part of an embryonic realization (somewhat akin to Sánchez' approach to Latin) that each language is a relatively closed system with its own grammar. This grammatical structure cannot be violated with impunity, even when the reasons for violating it seem to be of the noblest kind, as were those of the partisans of classicist imitation. The elusive and contentious " Quintil Censeur " is also on record for the attribution of the *facilité* and *clarté* of French to its regular word order, in correspondence to the *droit ordre naturel*.[19] It is important to mark these first cases

---

[18] Meigret, *Le Tretté de la grammere françoeze*, ed. W. Foerster (Heilbronn, 1888), pp. 195 f. The argument is worth quoting *in extenso*. He starts out by decrying the current vogue of imitating a Latin order in French, much to the risk of ensuing obscurity: " Je suys asseuré q'une bone partie de çeus qi s'en melet [viz., d'écrir' en Françoes], sont si fríans de suyure le style Latin, e d'abandoner le notre, qe combien qe leur' parolles soét nayuement Françoezes: la maouez' ordonançe rent toutefoes le sens obscur, aueq vn gran' mecontentement de l'orelle du lecteur, e de l'assistençe. Si nou' consideron' bien le stile de la lange Latin' e çeluy de la notre, nou' le' trouuerons contréres en çe qe comunement nou' fézons la fin de claoz' ou d'un discours, de ce qe le' Latins font leur commençement: e si nou' considerons bien l'ordre de nature, nou' trouuerons qe le stile Françoes s'y ranje beaocoup mieus qe le Latin. Car le' Latins prepozet comunement le souspozé ao verbe, luy donans en suyte le surpozé: par çe moyen le passif qi par l'ordre de nature dút étre le dernier en claoz' et le premier en prolačion: e le surpozé le dernier, qi par rezon dút etre le premier: d'aotant qe l'ajant et par rézon precedant l'acçion, e passíon, come duquel et le començement du mouuement. Le Latin de vrey dira pour parler elegamment, *Gallos vicit Caesar* . . . aosi ne trouue je pas rézonable q'on doeue s'y asseruir, e lesser vne beaocoup plus façil' e ezée maniere de dresser le bátiment de notre lange suyuant l'ordre qe nature tient en ses euures, e qe l'uzaje de parler a voulu suyure." Also cited, in part, by Ricken, " Rationalismus . . . ," 99 and 263-264. Punctuation and Syntax occupy a last, brief chapter of the *Tretté* (pp. 193-196).

[N. B. In the passage above it has been necessary to replace with a plain *e* the *e* with cedilla which occasionally appears in the Foerster ed., because such a font is currently unavailable.]

[19] The anonymous author of *Le Quintil Horatian* (a critique of Du Bellay's *Deffence et illustration*) is sometimes referred to as " Quintil Censeur " and was

in which Quintilian's and Cicero's *rectus ordo* and *directe construere* enter the French language in the form of *droit,* later to be replaced by the more successful *direct.*

Similarly, the *Rhétorique pour Henri III* proscribes inversions from the French language, since they are to be regarded as a cause of obscurity and, more seriously, as a " rude, impropre et désagréable forme de parler." The new self-awareness coming to the French speakers suggests to them that to place Latin on the pedestal of a direct model would practically entail a diminution and betrayal of what is uniquely proper to French.

Just like their Latin counterparts, the vernacular grammars give little room to syntax proper. The earliest modern student of French Renaissance Grammars, Ch.-L. Livet, has already noticed that the only French syntax he could find in the sixteenth century was that of Ramus (2nd Book of his *Grammaire*).[20] And for Ramus, too, syntax was no more than what it was for most of his European contemporaries, and continued to be until the middle of the eighteenth century: a study of concord between single words, rather than a study of word patterns within the clause and clause patterns within the sentence. The only remarks on the ways clauses are bound together seldom extend beyond the mention of the coordinating conjunctions *et, ou, mais, or, donc, car,* familiar to logicians, while realization of the role of subordinating particles or of reciprocal influence between clauses was practically non-existent. Livet was aware of the exceptional role of Perizonius with respect to the beginnings of syntax of the clause. It was an instance of cooperation from philosophy, which had,

---

first identified with Charles Fontaine by Barbier, *Dict. des ouvr. anon.,* but is now thought more likely to have been Barthélemy Aneau (see, e. g., P. Rickard, op. cit. below, p. 48). The first ed. of 1550 is now lost, but it was reprinted in 1551, 1555, 1556, 1557, and 1573, either together with Sébillet's *Art poétique françois* or with Du Bellay's *Deffence.* The main part of this text was also reprinted in the ed. of the *Deffence* by Em. Person (Paris, 1892), but not the passage in question, which appeared in the *Quintil sur l'Olive, Sonnetz Antérotique Odes et Vers Lyriques de I. D. B. A.* (= Du Bellay). I read it in the 1555 ed. of Sébillet's *Art,* p. 117[r]: " duquel [langage françois] la plus grande vertu de facilité et clarté est qu'il suit le droit ordre naturel, sans entremesler les dictions. Mais tu trouues beau de mettre la charue deuant les boeufs." (Du Bellay is being criticized for a bold hyperbaton in verse.) *Quintil Censeur,* ed. 1573, p. 259 is cited in Ferdinand Brunot, *La Doctrine de Malherbe d'après son Commentaire sur Desportes* (Paris, 1891), p. 495.

[20] *Grammaire de P. de la Ramée* (Brunet gives 1562 for first ed.—See 1572 ed., Paris, André Wechel). Cf. Ch.-L. Livet, *La Grammaire fr. et les grammairiens du XVIe siècle* (1859), pp. 234-236.

until then, limited itself to supplying a few definitions, and was not yet ready to come to the aid of grammar for the purpose of analyzing the inner mechanisms of language. This did not happen until the time of the Encyclopaedists.

With Maupas (1607) the notion of natural order appears to depend on grammatical rather than logical categories—at least in his description if not in the label he uses—when he equates, with regard to French, the *ordre naturel de l'entendement* with the precedence of the *diction régissant* over the *diction régie*.[21]

These general points find confirmation in recent studies. Peter Rickard has examined (besides many more handbooks for foreigners) 15 French grammars between 1529 and 1607 (Jacques Dubois, Louis Meigret, Jean Garnier, Th. de Bèze, Maupas . . .) and discovered, *inter alia*, some common traits in a confusion of word order with punctuation and lack of the concept of subordination.[22]

3. Meanwhile in England the application of rhetoric to the vernacular began with Sherry, the English *Auctor ad Herennium*. Richard Sherry's 1550 *Treatise of Schemes and Tropes*[23] had little to say on "composition (sinthesis)" beyond repeating the familiar warnings against "puttynge a weaker word after a stronger, but that it styl go upward and increase," in favor of the "naturall order, as to saye: men and women, daye and nyght. . . ." Again he admonishes his readers against cacophony, ex-

---

[21] Cf. E. Winkler, *La Doctrine grammaticale française d'après Maupas et Oudin* (Halle, 1912), p. 290, and U. Ricken, "Rationalismus . . . ," p. 100. Sahlin, *Du Marsais*, p. 88 cites Ioannes Susenbrotus' *Grammaticae artis institutio*, which appeared in 1529, for mentioning *ordo naturalis*, fol. 204^v f.

[22] Peter Rickard, *La Langue française au seizième siècle: Étude suivie de textes* (Cambridge, U. Press, 1968). See, esp., pp. 29-30 and 55.

[23] The original ed. is now available in facsimile reprint (1961). It was only reprinted once before in the revised ed. of 1555. Regardless of its great historical significance, its success was therefore limited. It can be looked upon as the English *Ad Herennium* in that it introduced its public to the art of speaking and writing by anglicizing the *Ad Herennium*, just as the latter had introduced the Roman public to the Greek art. Of course, it performed the task far less brilliantly and less successfully. Furthermore, Sherry himself tells us that he also relies on Renaissance sources such as Erasmus' *De copia* (1513) and Mosellanus' *Tabulae de schematibus et tropis* (ca. 1529). The reduction of rhetoric to the theory of elocution and, specifically, figures, is a reflection of the medieval tradition—which again, as we have already seen, owed much to the *Ad Herennium*. A remarkable feature of this work is the methodical use of the equivalent Greek, Latin, and English technical terms, case by case.

cessive alliteration and homoioteleuton, and rambling sentences. Sherry has his Quintilian and his *Orator* before him (pp. 38-39). On the other hand, many an observation bearing on our subject appears under other headings, like a section on " figures of construccion "—namely word order—, which, together with those " of diccion," make up the " figures of worde." We cannot dwell on these details, but I shall simply give the list of sub-headings: prolepsis (praesumpcio, a taking before); zeugma (iunctio, ioynyng, " as Linacer sayeth "), divided into presozeugma (?), meso-zeugma, hypozeugma (preiunctio, media iunctio, postiunctio); diazeugma (disiunctio, disiunccion); silepsis (conceptio); epergesis (appositio); hyper-baton (transgressio); anastrophe (reversio, a preposterous order); hystero-logia (prepostera loquutio); tmesis (dissectio); parenthesis (interpositio); eclipsis (defectus); antiptosis (casus pro casu) (pp. 28-32). If one follows the successors of Sherry one will realize how the examples he uses here and elsewhere contributed to the crystallization of the vernacular nomen-clature.

Thomas Wilson's 1553 *Arte of Rhetorique* [24] marked a return to classical rhetoric with a sound plan for its application to the needs of the English language. It presented a simplified scheme of the virtues of elocution by dividing the latter into four parts: plainness, aptness, composition, exorna-tion. While the first two concern diction or choice of words and the first, in particular, somewhat covers the traditional notions of correctness and clarity contiguous with grammar (in Wilson's own *Arte of Logike* a rime on the liberal arts begins thus: " Grammar doeth teach to utter wordes: / to speake both apt and plaine "), observe that composition has been made a full-fledged major category, separate from *ornatus* or theory of figures (pp. 166-169 of Mair ed.). A glance at the chapter on composition will readily show the closeness to Quintilian's heritage, with the accretion of some matters of concern at that time. While " harmonie " for the ear's delight still looms large next to " apt order," " natural order " in the traditional acceptation is amply documented—and with refreshing humor to boot: " Some will set the Cart before the Horse, as thus. My mother and my father are both at home, as though the good man of the house did weare no breches, or that the graie Mare were the better Horse. And what though it often so happeneth (God wot the more pitty) yet

---

[24] I use the Mair ed. based on the 1560 ed., which is the one usually quoted. The first ed., 1553, is now available in facsimile reprint. On the relationship be-tween the two eds. see Howell, *Logic and Rhetoric in England*, pp. 98-99.

in speaking at the least, let us keepe a naturall order, and set the man before the woman for maners sake." Likewise don't order your servant "helpe me of with my bootes and my spurres." He could hardly do it that way. And it is "foolish" to say "the Counsaile and the King, but rather the King and his Counsaile, the Father and the Sonne. . . . The wise therefore talking of divers worthie men together, will first name the worthiest, and keepe a decent order. . . ." Going on to grammatical order, he cautions against excessive separations: "Some overthwartly sette their wordes, placing some one a mile from his fellowes, not contented with a plaine and easie composition," but seeking a "strange composition" that seems "wonderful" to them alone.

The heart of the matter is that Wilson is a partisan of plain style and a critic of Euphuism. He begins by warning against abuse of alliteration: "Some use overmuch repetition of some one letter, as pitifull povertie praieth for a penie" etc. (p. 167). He is equally suspicious of parison, paromoion, and homoioteleuton, in terms which clearly remind us of Salutati's demurrers against the *mos fratrum* in church oratory:

Some end their sentences all alike, making their talke rather to appear rimed Meeter, then to seeme plaine speeche, the which as it much deliteth being measurably used, so it much offendeth when no meane is regarded. I heard a preacher deliting much in this kind of composition, who used so often to ende his sentences with wordes like unto that which went before, that . . . they ended all in Rime for the most parte. Some not best disposed, wished the Preacher a Lute, that with his rimed sermon he might use some pleasant melody, and so the people might take pleasure divers waies, and dance if they list. Certes there is a meane, and no reason to use any one thing at al time, seing nothing deliteth (be it never so good) that is alwaies used. (p. 168)

The anti-Catholic polemic cannot obscure the fact that Wilson's objections start on the level of style and go on from there. I have referred above to the trend toward medieval schematism among the early Fathers and the writers of Silver Latinity. Wilson was equally aware of such a trend:

S. Augustine had a goodly gift in this behalfe, and yet some thinkes he forgot measure, and used overmuch this kind of figure. Notwithstanding, the people were such where he lived that they tooke muche delite in rimed sentences, and in Orations made ballade wise. Yea, thei were so nice and so waiward to please, that except the preacher from time to time could rime out his sermon, they would not long abide the hearing. . . . Tullie was forsaken, with Livie, Caesar, and other: Apuleius, Ausonius, with such

Minstrell makers were altogether followed . . . . I speak thus much of these ii. figures [i. e. " like ending and like falling "], not that I thinke folie to use them . . . but . . . that they should neither onely nor chiefly be used, as I know some in this our time do overmuch use them in their writings. And overmuch . . . was never good yet.[25]

While implicitly alluding here to the schematic style based on parison, paromoion, and homoioteleuton, Wilson was not missing the opportunity to criticize the contemporary analogues of *cultismo* and Euphuism.[26] He also pointed out that such a style was cultivated in preaching, in church liturgy, in courts of law, and in courtly diplomacy or parade.

Ramism was generally unkind to our subject. Ramist rhetoric was first Englished by Dudley Fenner in the second part of his anonymously published *The Artes of Logike and Rhetorike* (Middleburgh, R. Schilders, 1584, 1588[2]), followed at some distance by the similarly successful Latin rendition of Ramist (read: Talaeus') rhetoric in Charles Butler's *Rhetoricae libri duo* (Oxford, 1598).[27] Both were concise treatments of elocution and " pronunciation " (delivery) alone. Composition is completely neglected, and Butler goes only so far as to mention hyperbaton as a device to create cadence.

The student could find considerably more meat in Peacham's *Garden* (1577), which saw its second edition when the century was drawing to a close (1593).[28] But even this was nothing more than a dictionary of figures, dealing with word order mostly under Hyperbaton, Anastrophe, Hysterologia, Hysteron proteron, Tmesis, Parenthesis, Hypallage, Synchisis, and Amphibologia.

[25] Mair ed., p. 203.

[26] Cf. Croll, " The Sources . . ." in Patrick and Evans's ed., esp. pp. 270-271.

[27] On medieval and Renaissance rhetoric, with particular reference to England, see Howell, *Logic and Rhetoric in England*, pp. 64-145, and, specifically, pp. 98-110 on Thomas Wilson, 125-137 on Sherry and Peacham, 219-222 and 276-279 on Fenner, and 262-266 on Butler. Fenner's *Artes* can now be read reprinted in R. D. Pepper, ed., *Four Tudor Books on Education*, " Scholars' Facsimiles and Reprints " (Gainesville, Fla., 1966), pp. 145-180.

[28] Cf. the Introduction in W. G. Crane's ed. of the *Garden* (1954) for the rich bibliography on English Renaissance rhetorical production and its Continental Latin sources.

CHAPTER FOUR: BAROQUE AND ENLIGHTENMENT

A. GENERAL: USE AND MEANING OF COMPOSITIONAL FORMS

1. After 1600 analysis of, and speculation on the structures of the Latin language lost much of their vitality and relevance, even while they gained in sophistication of methods and scientific sureness of results. The classical heritage passed into the handling of the vernaculars, and it is mainly in this area that we shall look henceforth for dynamically new applications and developments.

Nevertheless, the age of the great classical philologists produced a large body of literature bearing on linguistic and grammatical questions applied to the study of Latin—especially, insofar as our subject is concerned, in Germany and Holland.

As we have seen, at the end of the Renaissance the combined approaches of Despauterius, Linacer, Scaliger, and Sanctius had firmly established a new distinction of vital import for the following period, namely that of *syntaxis naturalis*, common to all languages and the future subject of "general grammar," and *syntaxis figurata* or *arbitraria*, the particular property of individual positive languages. Both could be discovered and analyzed rationally, thanks especially to the phenomena of ellipsis in the area of the *arbitraria*. The empirically-minded observer found his more congenial ground in the concrete realities of the *arbitraria*.

Syntax appeared once again divided into *regularis*, *irregularis*, and furthermore, *ornata* in the anonymous *Grammatica latina* [by Caspar Finckius and Christophorus Helvicus] published at Gießen (Giessae) in 1606. It bore, in other respects, a Ramist imprint. Caspar Schoppe (Scioppius, 1576-1649) of Neumarkt in der Pfalz, whose *Grammatica philosophica* appeared in Milan in 1628, inherited Sanctius' doctrine within Linacer's system; after Linacer he distinguished between *syntaxis regularis* and *irregularis* or *figurata*. On the other hand Sanctius' chief commentator, the Dutch Jacob Voorbroek (Perizonius, 1651-1715), stood fully apart from his master in a basic matter of principle. He sought to overcome and refute Sanctius within a context of empirical analysis of the forms.

Empiricism was bravely fighting its battle against the rationalist invaders, as witnessed in the monumental *De arte grammatica libri VII* by the great Ger. Jo. Voss (Vossius, 1577-1649) of Heidelberg.[1] His norm, unlike Sanctius' *ratio*, was *usus,* as with most of the French grammarians of that century, who moved in the wake of their mentor, Vaugelas.

G. H. Ursin of Speier (Ursinus, 1647-1707) upheld Sanctius' doctrine against Perizonius' strictures.[2] Nevertheless, just as Perizonius had shown the role of chance in the formation of language, so did Ursinus assume a *syntaxis arbitraria* for which there is no other *ratio* " quam quod auctoribus linguae, qui ita instituerunt, sic placuit." This approach belonged in the most authentic humanistic tradition: suffice it to mention Guarino Veronese's splendid decision to support his proposal in favor of restoring the ancient Roman *tu* as against *vos,* the medieval polite form of address: " We shall then use the singular, because it is a locution truer to nature, since a single man is not plural; furthermore, thus did the ancients write " (" et quia ita scriptitabant antiqui "). In this magnificently curt simplicity one senses that for Guarino the second argument carried a more decisive weight than the first, or, rather, that ' reason ' and ' nature ' coincided with the actual taste of the ancients almost *a priori.* Similarly Valla had identified linguistic rule with ancient taste or usage: " Ego pro lege accipio quicquid magnis auctoribus placuit" (*El.* III, 17). Now again, Augustinus Maria de Monte [3] fought Scioppius' theories as " metaphysicum figmentum " " in rebus grammaticis, quae aliam rationem non admittunt, quam usum et praxin iuxta illud vulgare adagium: Sic dixere priores." Otherwise de Monte shows the running dry of grammatical views in the eighteenth century, on the whole a rather uneventful century in the domain of Latin grammar.

Thus we have a basically empirical current which ties together such personalities as Vossius, Perizonius, Ursinus, de Monte, as opposed to the rationalistic one which descended from Scaliger to the school of Port-

---

[1] 4 vols. (Amsterdam, 1635), reprinted as *Aristarchus sive de arte grammatica l. VII* (Amsterdam, 1662), then in Vossius' complete works at the end of the century: *Vossii Opera in Sex Tomos divisa* (Amsterdam, 1695-1701), t. II. We now have an incomplete modern ed. by C. Förtsch and F. A. Eckstein (Halle, 1833-1834).

[2] See, esp., Ursinus, *Institutiones plenissimae quibus linguae latinae et praecepta vernacula . . . traduntur et causae . . . eruuntur . . .* (Regensburg, 1701). For this and the following note see, especially, Golling, pp. 57-72.

[3] *Latium restitutum, sive lingua latina in veterem restituta splendorem* (Rome, 1720), 4 vols.

Royal through Sanctius and Scioppius. The division is rather schematic and abstract, for in the actual work of each of these scholars elements of the two contrasting points of view are uniquely combined. Thus, for example, we find in Sanctius an implicit critique of Scaliger's rationalistic movement toward *grammaire générale,* even if Sanctius remains fundamentally a rationalist in his appeal to reason rather than usage and in his effort to reduce an individual language to a consistent logical system, though a self-enclosed one with regard to other languages. I insist on these questions of general method because the evolution in attitudes toward the French language from Vaugelas to Port-Royal will go through the same stages and the same issues, and such orientations will directly affect our subject.

Curiously enough, the doctrine of figures and the *syntaxis ornata* survived in the standard grammars well into the nineteenth century. According to Golling, K. G. Zumpt was the first to brush them aside in his *Lateinische Grammatik* (Berlin, 1818), but only until the third ed. (1823), where they were both reinstated in the form of appendices, next to word order and periodic arrangement (*Periodenbau*). This, after all, is the way many Latin grammars still present these subjects down to our own day.

Similarly, we are about to encounter ample evidence of how constant the presence of the ancient paraphernalia remained on a general theoretical level. Yet, if we accept the three principles identified by E. Norden as remaining firm in the evaluation of art prose from early Greece down to the Renaissance, namely that ornate prose should be 1) figurative, 2) similar to poetry, 3) rhythmical,[4] we must recognize that these views, as a unified system, started to break down in the course of the seventeenth century, and the rationalists of the following century worked hard to bring about their final liquidation, though not without meeting strong resistance.

2. To return now to the combination of style genera and compositional forms as they became applied to the vernaculars, it appears that the contrasting attitudes toward sentence structure came to a head immediately after Bembo's formulation of the Ciceronian stand, owing to the increment of the anti-Ciceronian stylists which go from the French Italianate Muret through Justus Lipsius down to their followers, stoically oriented historians, orators, preachers, essayists, and critics of all sorts throughout

[4] E. Norden, *Antike Kunstprosa*, I, 50-55.

Europe. The forms which resulted from this revolt are part of baroque culture and are typologically akin to some aspects of the Asianic oratorical schools, but what characterizes them is the abandonment of periodic form for the quickness, loose freedom, and intuitive sharpness favored by the Atticists. This justifies Croll's use of the label of "Atticism" for the whole current of sixteenth-, seventeenth-, and early eighteenth-century anti-Ciceronian cultists of plain style, although he may have confused the issue somewhat by failing to specify that this was a narrow aspect of Atticism, the compositional aspect. Seneca and Tacitus, the new models, can be called Attic from the viewpoint of distrust for periodic composition. Otherwise their hermeticism, declamatory orientation, and intended obscurity through curtness, are not always clearly distinguishable from certain aspects of Asianism. Moreover, we may remember that the Stoics (and Montaigne, Justus Lipsius, Malvezzi, Corneille, etc. were stylistically just as Stoic as Seneca and Tacitus) were linguistically, that is "grammatically," partisans of anomaly, roughly an intuitionist theory of language and expression, whereas the Atticists were "analogists," that is, partisans of a logical evaluation of expression for its virtues of clarity and straightforwardness.

The baroque phase of this Attic movement (we might make up another label for it by calling it 'anomalist Atticism') was only part of its story. 'Analogist Atticism,' so to call it, came into its own through the rationalist heritage of Cartesianism in the course of Classicism and Enlightenment.

If it is true that, in a sense, baroque consists of an exasperated complication of the formal elements, it is equally true, on the other hand, that the same phenomena can also be traced to an actual preoccupation with substance. Ramism, for example, did contribute to that aspect of baroque which can be labeled as positive, naturalistic, or 'Attic.' By the shifting to dialectic of traditionally rhetorical material, rhetoric penetrated dialectic: but the perspective became muted, since the aim was now truth rather than effectiveness, and it was now assumed that correct method meant *méthode de nature*. This method stood for a pattern of mental operations conforming to the order of objective outside reality (adaptation of mind to the real). The NATURE OF THINGS became the criterion for the natural order of argumentation and reasoning, which is, on principle, unique, since the order of nature is presumably unique.[5]

[5] Ramus, *Dialecticae libri II* (Paris, 1560), II, 208; on the distinction between rhetoric and dialectic, ibid., I, fn. p. 10, or the different ed. Paris, 1566, I, fn.

This vindication of the dialectical function of persuasive argument, as against the merely literary or artistic notion of *ornatus*, seems to underlie many a text in the evolution of the seventeenth-century revolt against Ciceronianism and, more generally, formalism. To this aspect of the problem Croll was fully alive;[6] yet it seems to deserve even greater emphasis and sharper focussing.

Ostensibly the most valid contributions of Croll's studies lie: a) in the discovery of the 'anti-Ciceronian' layer of the stylistic speculations and practices of seventeenth-century prose, thus adding to our historical understanding of the baroque period by relating it more explicitly to the ancient and humanistic rhetorical tradition; b) in isolating the philosophico-scientific ingredients of the essay style, the Senecan, Tacitean, and Atticist subtlety of *concettismo*, and the metaphorical tension of *cultismo*; c) in contrasting the distinct historical function of the *schemata sententiarum* and *schemata verborum*.

To begin with the last point, the traditional oratorical style was alleg-

---

p. 156, where the point is further developed. Cf. C. Perelman, *Traité de l'argumentation: La Nouvelle Rhétorique* (1958), II, pp. 669 ff. But the difference between rhetorical and dialectical 'places,' that is to say the differential functions of the topics of reasoning and argument in dialectic and rhetoric respectively, did not arise with Muret and Ramism: it was as old as Aristotelianism itself. One of the most influential treatments of it was the fourth Book of Boethius' *De differentiis topicis*, current as a textbook of rhetoric in the 12th and 13th centuries: cf. P. L. LXIV, 1177 (Book I) and 1205-6 (Book IV). " Boethius finds the distinction between dialectic and rhetoric in their matter, use, and end (*materia, officium, finis*): the matter of dialectic is ' theses,' that of rhetoric ' hypotheses,' and theses and hypotheses are related as two kinds of ' questions,' the one universal, the other particularized as to circumstances; dialectic uses interrogation and response, and its arguments are set forth in syllogisms; rhetoric uses continuous speech involving enthymemes; the end of dialectic is to force what one wishes from an adversary, that of rhetoric to persuade a judge," etc.: cf. R. McKeon, " Rhetoric in the Middle Ages," in R. S. Crane, *Critics and Criticism, Ancient and Modern* (Chicago, 1952), p. 271. For Ramus (*Rhetoricae distinctiones in Quintilianum*), the error of Cicero consisted in transferring all the Aristotelian devices of dialectic to rhetoric and of having made one art of two, while Quintilian mixed rhetoric with all the other arts.

[6] See, e. g., Croll, " ' Attic Prose ' in the Seventeenth Century," p. 103, and pp. 76-77 of *Style, Rhetoric, and Rhythm*, cited below. This weighty paper is chiefly concerned with the anti-Ciceronian trend, 1575-1660.

Croll's collected papers have been posthumously reprinted in a recent volume carefully and critically edited by two of the master's former students: J. Max Patrick and Robert O. Evans, *Style, Rhetoric, and Rhythm. Essays by Morris W. Croll* (Princeton, 1966). Every section and article is accompanied by a critical discussion which also brings the reader up to date on subsequent research and bibliography.

edly "distinguished by the use of the *schemata verborum* . . . , which are chiefly similarities or repetitions of sound used as purely sensuous devices to give pleasure or aid the attention. The essay [or plain] style is characterized by the absence of these figures," or their use with subtle variations making them hard to spot . . . , "and, on the other hand, by the use of metaphor, aphorism, antithesis, paradox, and the other figures which, in one classification, are known as the *figurae sententiae,* the figures of wit or thought." [7]

The oratory of Lysias and Demosthenes was on the side of the plain style, *genus humile,* in that it disdained the symmetries and melodious cadences of the Isocratean model, and "professed to make its effect by the direct portrayal of the mind of the speaker and of the circumstances by which he has been aroused to vehement feeling." [8]

Working as it does in depth rather than on surface means of communication, this style shows a striking analogy with the 'metaphysical' literature of 'wit' as well as with the great scientific writers of the same period, such as Galileo (and even, at an earlier period, Machiavelli). This type of *genus humile* "was unmistakably grander than the *genus grande* and had the same uses," [9] in that it could arouse the emotions and produce *pathos,* although through entirely different channels. Even Longinus' 'sublime' was, in this sense, akin to the plain style.

Of the virtues of style which the Stoics inherited from the Greek tradition, namely clearness, purity, brevity, and appropriateness, the first, or CLEARNESS, was not always taken very seriously by them: think of Tacitus, *prince des ténèbres,* and of the Stoic propensity toward the ways of hidden personal illumination to attain the mysteries of higher truth. Thus Tacitus himself, Persius, Tertullian, just like their imitators Donne (in his letters), Gracián, Bacon, Malvezzi (see pp. 286-291 below), are "distinguished by their cult of significant darkness." [10]

The virtue of PURITY of language (as determined by the use of good society, and interchangeable with *Hellenismos* and *Latinitas*) was close to the original notion of Atticism, but it was alien to the universalistic framework of Stoicism, so that when it did appear, as in the Roman Stoics of the second century A. D., it sounded like a virtual equivalent of 'appropriateness.'

---

[7] Croll, "'Attic Prose,'" p. 82 of original ed.
[8] Ibid., 105.
[9] Ibid.
[10] Ibid., 111-113.

BREVITY was closest to Stoic hearts, "for they made greater use than any of the other sects of the art of condensing their experience into 'golden sayings,' *dicta*, maxims, aphorisms, *sententiae*." [11] We might want to add that this heritage remained very much alive among the humanists and the French classicists, if we only think of such texts as Erasmus' *De copia* and *Apophthegms* and of the *maximes* of the French moralists. "Chrysippus, working perhaps on hints received from Pythagoras, gave directions for the manufacture of *sententiae*, and the use of them in moral discipline, directions which are familiar to modern readers through Bacon's reproduction and expansion of them in his *De augmentis*.[12]

APPROPRIATENESS can be to thing or person. The former possibility, strictly speaking, belongs within dialectic and has little to do with rhetoric. For if, as Lipsius defines it, "everything is said for the sake of argument" (or subject), and "the vesture of sentence and phrase exactly fits the body of the thing described," thought and discourse are exactly identical, and there is only one science of both: . . . logic or dialectic. Appropriateness as to person can refer to hearer, which typically produces sophistic oratory, or to speaker, which corresponds to Stoic interests. For the Stoics rather tend to "identify the two phases, the proper and effective mode of impressing one's hearers being, in fact, to render one's own experience in the encounter with reality as exactly, as VIVIDLY, as possible." [13]

Literati, thinkers, scientific writers from all Europe who in the course of the seventeenth century identified themselves in one way or another with Atticism, Stoicism, and the plain style, share among themselves a general aversion to the schemes or figures of sound, while they espouse the figures of wit conveying a substance of thought. ANTITHESIS is foremost among these, but "as a means of expressing striking and unforeseen relations between the objects of thought," [14] not as a merely architectonic device for formal balance (which it frequently was in antiquity), because, as such, it could still qualify as a figure of sound. Connected with the antithesis carrying wit is the study of 'POINTS,' or *argutiae*, which nearly always convey an antithesis, either open or veiled. Of equal importance, and of greater literary value, is the METAPHOR.

[11] Ibid., 114.
[12] Ibid.
[13] Ibid., 115. Emphasis mine.
[14] Ibid., 116.

Cicero himself seemed to confirm such definitory views when he called *genus humile* or *stilus stoicus* the opposite from his. He attributed to it brevity, significant abruptness, tendency to sententiousness, preference for the figures of thought over those of sound. This authorized the Atticists of the baroque age to regard Cicero himself as the master of Asianism, in a polemic simplification which rather forgivably glossed over the precise historical nature of his uniquely personal style, the subtle differences between actual Asianism and his Rhodianism, and the evolution through different forms in the course of the master's rich career.

The seventeenth century saw a significant shift of taste from the models of the first century B. C. to those of the first A. D. It was a century

in which Lucan had a more effective influence on the ideas and the style of poetry than Virgil did; in which Seneca was more loved and much more effectively imitated in prose style than Cicero had been in the previous generations; in which Tacitus almost completely displaced Livy as the model of historical and political writing; in which Martial was preferred to Catullus, and Juvenal and Persius were more useful to the satirists than Horace; in which Tertullian, the Christian representative of the Stoic style of the Empire—*notre Sénèque,* as he was called—exercised a stronger power of attraction over the most representative minds than St. Augustine, who is the Cicero and the Ciceronian of patristic Latin.[15]

It is known that Bacon had, originally enough, moved to assign rhetoric to the Quadrivium or advanced course, rather than to the Trivium. He boldly indicted the whole drift of the preceding century, for " the whole inclination and bent of those times was rather towards copie than weight," when, concurrently, men used to " study words and not matter."[16] Now Croll recalls that, for the Latin translation (1622) of his *Advancement of Learning,*[17] Bacon added a passage to his famous denunciation of Ciceronianism where " he describes another *styli genus,* characterized by conciseness, sententiousness, pointedness, which is likely to follow in time upon a period of oratorical luxury. Such a style is found, he says, in Seneca, Tacitus, and the Younger Pliny, ' and began not so long ago to prove itself adapted to the ears of our own time.' "[18] This, Croll goes on

---

[15] Ibid., 123.

[16] Bacon, *Advancement of Learning,* Book I, ch. iv, § 2; Book II, chs. xviii f. Cf. Sir Thomas Eliot, *The Book of the Governour* (ed. Croft, I, 116).

[17] The *Advancement* was published in 1605, the translation, titled *De Augmentis scientiarum,* in 1622. See *De aug.* I; also Croll, ". . . Lipsius, Montaigne, Bacon," pp. 189-190 in Patrick and Evans' ed.

[18] " ' Attic Prose,' " 126. But on the manifold aspects of Bacon's stylistic experi-

to point out, "is admirably confirmed by what Father Caussin said in France in 1619: he describes the new form of style in the same way, mentions the same ancient models, adding Sallust to the list, and says it is the style that *everyone now covets*." [19] At the end of the century, Shaftesbury complained that " no other movement of style than Seneca's— what he calls the ' Senecan amble '—had been heard in prose for a hundred years past." [20]

Elsewhere, Croll pointed out that as long as such a difficult style as that of Cicero remained the predominant model, " a normal form of French or English prose could not appear"; but from the end of the Renaissance the new models chosen were such as to become truly operative.

Seneca is easy. There is nothing in his syntax that could prove a bar to the expression of the ideas . . . concerning the moral experience of [those] times . . . ; on the contrary, the brevity of his constructions, the resolved and analytic character of his sentences, would provide [the contemporary writer] with a mold exactly adapted to the character of his mind and the state of his language. Tacitus, of course, is harder reading; but the kind of difficulty that he offers would prove to be no more than a welcome stimulus and challenge to the trained wits of rationalists. . . . Ancient Anti-Ciceronianism worked in a *resolved* style, and the perfect success with which its manner was transferred to French, Italian, Spanish, and English style during the early seventeenth century is proof of its fitness to serve as the model on which a standard modern prose could be formed. [21]

One of Croll's last writings, " The Baroque Style in Prose " (1929), marked a ' correction ' of his previous definition of Attic style, which he now identified with baroque prose style. This use of ' baroque' as a blanket designation covering all the phenomena under study was not entirely fortunate, and ultimately served to confuse some of the issues. [22]

---

mentation see, now, Brian Vickers, *F. Bacon and Renaissance Prose* (Cambridge, U. Press, 1968), with a survey of critical reactions to Bacon's style. Vickers challenges the ' Senecan ' interpretation of Bacon's style by underscoring his artful use of symmetrical syntax in a Ciceronian vein.

[19] Nicolaus Caussinus [Nicolas Caussin], *Eloquentiae sacrae et humanae parallela, libri XVI,* II, chs. 14-16, pp. 73-78 of Paris, Chappelet, 1619 ed. First ed. Louvain, 1609. Reprinted Paris, Chappelet, 1619, 1623, 1627; Paris, Henault . . . , 1630³, 1643; Lyon, 1643. Cited by Croll, " Attic Prose,' " 126.

[20] Croll in Patrick and Evans' ed., p. 215.

[21] Croll, ". . . Lipsius, Montaigne, Bacon," p. 186 in Patrick and Evans' ed. On the cult of Tacitus in Italy, see Giuseppe Toffanin, *Machiavelli e il ' Tacitismo '* (Padua, 1921).

[22] Wellek seems to take a more favorable view of this terminological shift, while

That 1929 paper, however, interests us directly because it dealt specifically with "the form of the period," which the author chose as the most

he finds the earlier 'Attic' "a rather obscure and misleading term" for the anti-Ciceronian movement. Cf. René Wellek, *Concepts of Criticism*, S. G. Nichols, Jr., ed. (New Haven and London, 1963), "The Concept of Baroque in Literary Scholarship" (1945, with a 1962 Postscript), pp. 69-127: see p. 87. I am rather inclined to stress that the phenomena to be subsumed under the label of Atticism did not quite coincide with what we currently call 'baroque.' Attic is at the same time more specific and broader than baroque, while the latter term, vague as it turns out to be in actual usage, seems to exclude some typical concerns which come within the former. There is an 'attic' baroque as well as an 'asian' baroque, and then again there is also an Atticism that is not baroque at all. To complicate matters, the individual authors of the period 1600-1750 are not always consistent in their attitudes toward the models. Although the Attic ideal is most frequently found in the first century A. D., at times it is identified with its 'opposite,' namely the taste of the first century B. C. For some, like Bayle and Bouhours, Cicero is common sense and good taste, as opposed to the extravagance of Seneca and Tacitus. Most of the seventeenth-century literary vanguard looked upon Cicero as empty sound for its own sake, but that century had plenty of that too, e. g. in Italy. The underlying thesis of baroque poetics (in a signal manner, that of Tesauro) is that language is not a foundation of LOGIC—a firm axiom of medieval scholastic 'realism,' with its inclusion of logic among the *artes sermocinales,* the linguistic arts or arts of expression—, but an operation of the IMAGINATION. Therefore it is not at all the plain style that such poetics tend to defend, but the poetic style, which, in rhetorical terms, is closer to grand style than to anything else. Metaphors are looked upon as departures from logical truth and realistic description; the further removed they are from these, the more effective they will turn out to be. The general orientation is thus opposite to the classical insistence on measure and common sense, which will come back only with the rationalist part of the Enlightenment as a reaction against baroque. Cf. Camillo Pellegrino, *Del concetto poetico* (1598, unpublished until 1898); Federico Zuccari, *L'Idea de' pittori, scultori, et architetti* (Torino, 1607); Baltazar Gracián, *Agudeza y arte de ingenio* (Madrid, 1642, 1648 . . .); Emmanuele Tesauro, *Il Cannochiale Aristotelico* (Torino, 1654). Also, such typical baroque treatises as Matteo Peregrini, *Delle Acutezze* (Genoa, 1639); Sforza Pallavicino, *Trattato del Dialogo e dello Stile* (Rome, 1646). Peregrini names seven symbolic figures: "the marvellous, the ambiguous, the aberrant, the obscure metaphor, the allusion, the witticism, and the sophism." Tesauro, in turn, defines the poet as a man who "establishes relationships between the most removed objects," and who "can transform anything into anything, a city into an eagle, a man into a lion, and a flatterer into a sun." Croll praises Giovanni Ferri, *De l'Éloquence et des Orateurs anciens et modernes* (Paris, 1789), pp. 228-233 for bringing out the Aristotelian derivation of concettismo. See now *Style, Rhetoric, and Rhythm,* fn. p. 77. Besides, Croll's identification is equivocal since 'baroque' is a modern evaluation, whereas Attic was a concept used at the time to define a current and distinguish it from surrounding rival forces, such as those of Ciceronianism. Just as seriously, the two terms, together or separately, do not apply in the same way to the various countries. On the interpretation of the texts just mentioned as Mannerist theories see now Klaus-Peter Lange, *Theoretiker des literarischen Manierismus. Tesauros und Pellegrinis Lehre von der Acutezza oder von der Macht der Sprache* (Munich, 1968).

functional issue through which the peculiarities of Attic-Baroque style could be exemplarily treated, and precisely as the last of the " elements of prose technique," these being successively articulated into " diction or choice of words, figures, balance or rhythm, form of period or sentence." [23] Croll also elaborated on what I should call the ' internal mental portrait ' characteristic of many a baroque stylist. This stylist avoids quite deliberately such " processes of mental revision " as are implied in the compositive revision postulated by traditional rhetoric. He avoids them " in order to express his idea when it is nearer the point of its origin in his mind." The task he is pursuing is that of portraying " not a thought, but a mind thinking." In Pascal's words, he aims to produce *la peinture de la pensée.*[24] For it was then felt that ideas ceased to have anything but a verbal existence when, in the Ciceronian periods of sixteenth-century Latin rhetoricians, they lost " the ardor of their conception." [25]

A first consequence is that ligatures, such as conjunctions and pronouns, can either be used in a loose and casual manner or eliminated altogether. The former possibility characterizes what was designated as " loose style " or " loose period "; the latter, the *style coupé, période coupée,* " curt style," or " curt period." Croll gives examples of this latter from Montaigne, Pascal, La Bruyère, Burton, Felltham, Browne.[26] The examples are said to begin with a complete factual statement, a sentence, *le dernier point* (Montaigne), followed by separate acts of imaginative realization, in what constitutes, therefore, a ' descending movement.' The members are formally unconnected and, above all, ASYMMETRIC, which makes them ' anti-classical ' and ' modern.'

---

[23] " The Baroque Style in Prose " is reprinted on pp. 207-233 of Patrick and Evans: see, also, the very useful preface by J. M. Wallace.

[24] Patrick and Evans, 209-210.

[25] Cf. A. Arnauld, *Logique,* ed. L. Barré (1874), p. 284: " La principale [partie de l'éloquence] consiste à concevoir fortement les choses, et à les exprimer en sorte qu'on en porte dans l'esprit des auditeurs une image vive et lumineuse, qui ne présente pas seulement le choses toutes nues, mais aussi les mouvements avec lesquels on les conçoit." (Cf. Croll, " ' Attic Prose,' " p. 95 fn., and p. 67 fn. in Patrick and Evans.) Thus the artistic style, containing what Longinus had called ἐνάργεια, is ultimately different from the plain objectivity of scientific exposition. Later on, while similarly justifying his style against contemporary criticism, Marivaux opposed to the closed system of traditional rhetoric an open style which did not presume to exhaust the representation of the object, since our language cannot express all we feel: cf. Marivaux, *Pensées sur la clarté du discours,* from the *Nouveau Mercure* of March 1719, now edited by J. von Stackelberg, " Marivaux novateur," *Studi in o. di I. Siciliano,* II (Florence, 1966), 1155-63.

[26] Patrick and Evans, 211-213.

It appears convincing to associate baroque art forms and some literary implications of *style coupé*: both tend to accomplish the imaginative search for mystery and infinity through means which at the time seemed to run counter to the more immediately 'rational' ways of expression (i. e. the explicit transitional particles designed to establish logical relationships). Indeed we can add that the baroque conceit or *concetto*, a particular product of wit, is generally akin to the *pointe* in a sense indicated by Aristotle in a passage of capital importance for his baroque interpreters: "Those expressions of thought are witty which afford the opportunity of being grasped quickly." [27] By this he meant those cases when the recipient is thrilled by his response to the writer's or speaker's challenge—the challenge consisting of supplying the terms of the argument without the conventional transitions (verbal and logical). The effect plays hard on the emotions, and is heightened by the device of coupling contraries through antitheses. Eugenio Battisti has adroitly invoked these rhetorical considerations as conducive to a proper understanding of such baroque architectural experiences as those of Guarino Guarini (especially in his genial suppression of transitions between light and darkness, dome and walls, in the Sindone and San Lorenzo interiors of Torino).[28]

The systematic implications of the conceit within the Aristotelian context deserve stressing. 'Aστεία (*urbanitates, arguzie,* witticisms) are a type of judgment characterized by a particular syntactic twist which affects the mode of apprehension and the psychological response they elicit. It must be kept in mind that the conceit in all its forms is unfairly impoverished of its deep, serious content if we assess it as mere *ornatus*. It is an *ornatus* which finds its roots in a *iudicium*.[29] The baroque stylist irresistibly

---

[27] Ar., *Rhet.* III, x, 1410 b. Cf. Gracián, *Agudeza y arte de ingenio*: "Quien dice misterio, dice preñez, verdad escondida y recóndita, y toda noticia que cuesta, es más estimada y gustosa. Consiste el artificio desta especie de agudeza en levantar misterio entre la connexión de los extremos, o términos correlatos del sujeto. . . ." *Obras completas*, ed. Arturo del Hoyo (Madrid, 1960), pp. 260-261. The first theorist of mannered living, Castiglione, had remarked in his *Cortegiano* that "if a writer's words carry with them, not exactly difficulty, but at least a degree of concealed wit (*acutezza recondita*), . . . he will acquire more authority for it. The reader will be raised above his own powers and will appreciate all the more the ingenious talent and the learning of the writer." *Cortegiano*, I, xxx.

[28] E. Battisti, *Rinascimento e Barocco* (Torino, 1960), pp. 279-280. He quotes G. Morpurgo Tagliabue, "Aristotelismo e Barocco," in *Retorica e Barocco, Atti del III Congr. Intern. di Studi Umanistici, 1954* (Rome, 1955), pp. 119-195: see pp. 139-140.

[29] Cf. G. Morpurgo Tagliabue, op. cit., p. 138.

brings to the fore all the riches of his training in dialectical analysis, that is the intellectualistic cult of *dispositio* he inherited from the humanistic past. One must therefore " beware of confusing the baroque taste with the triumph of ornate elocution, with a sort of degeneration of Renaissance decorativism." [30] As pointed out by G. Morpurgo Tagliabue from whom I quote the preceding words, the origins of baroque lie in such a process also, but they lie as well in the analytical training just mentioned. This student of the Aristotelian tradition goes on to stress what seems to him the central problem of the baroque mode of expression: a unique blending of didacticism and hedonism, which results from this alliance between the tasks of *dispositio* and those of *elocutio*, between the dialectical ordering of subject matter and its stylistic embellishment, between, as the traditional formula put it, *docere* or *prodesse* on the one hand and, on the other, *delectare*. Thus art shares with philosophy the goal of moral teaching, yet it is characterized and justified in its separate existence by its aptness to reach that goal through pleasure. The agreement between the two emphases was an unstable compromise, but it is essential that we remain aware of its pervasive operativeness, and of its marking a firm advance beyond the Late Renaissance formalization of elocution at the expense of invention and disposition. Invention, however, did fade into the background, and this crisis of the traditional accepted opinions embodied in the *loci communes* accounts for the intellectual and moral restlessness of baroque exposition and, at times, its sophistical garb.[31]

Although the *coupé* style abstractly corresponds to the ancient loose style, the idiosyncratic nature of its modern employment must be defined. On the surface, periodic and coupé composition conspicuously differ by the relative length and brevity of their respective units. Yet this is not in itself a very significant difference. There are times when it hardly amounts to more than a matter of punctuation. Indeed in the age between the Renaissance and Romanticism one could have sequences of respectable proportions, say of five or six members, where these members were rather indifferently separated by period marks or, more commonly, colons or semicolons.[32] Yet if we take these sequences as units equivalent to a

---

[30] Ibid., p. 137.

[31] Ibid.

[32] Croll (Patrick and Evans, 230-231) claims that the modern editorial practice of putting commas or periods in place of seventeenth-century colons or semicolons reflects the bias of the grammatical, non-rhetorically trained analyst.

period and hypothetically compare them to the way a Ciceronian would
have composed them into a true period, we shall find the following difference: the *style coupé* sequences

logically do not move. At the end they are saying exactly what they were
at the beginning. Their advance is wholly in the direction of a more vivid
imaginative realization; a metaphor revolves, as it were displaying its
different facets . . . , a chain of ' points ' and paradoxes reveals the energy
of a single apprehension in the writer's mind.[33]

Indeed, Bouhours will justly criticize this mode of expression on the
ground that, "with all its pretensions to brevity and significance, this
style makes less progress in five or six successive statements than a
Ciceronian period . . ." does in one construction. And Croll to conclude: " The criticism is, of course, sound if the only mode of progression
is the logical one; but in fact there is a progress of imaginative apprehension " . . . " and this spiral movement is characteristic of baroque prose."

To identify styles in such a highly experimenting age is a delicate
matter. A formal ' violation ' of the rules of *style coupé,* for instance, is
found in a characteristic seventeenth-century trick of connecting the two
members (or the last two members) of a period with *and, or,* or *nor;* the
passage remains essentially *coupé* because these particles have " no logical
plus force whatever." [34] We may add that this observation jibes with the
linguists' discovery that the conjunctions generally acquired a conscious
logical force in French (and other modern languages) only at the end of
the same century.[35] Prior to that, they could also be used expressively, to
show a real connection between two ideas or images even when the formal
syntactico-logical connection that would justify a conjunction was properly
lacking.

If Croll's views on the development of the cut style and its relationship
to the periodic are found basically correct, a detailed reassessment of the
accepted notions on seventeenth- and eighteenth-century writing will have
to be made. The analysis and evaluation of English prose has, by and
large, already aligned itself with these ideas, thanks mainly to the American critics who have worked in the wake of Croll's studies, but such
studies have remained widely ignored by the specialists of other European

[33] Ibid., 218-219.
[34] Ibid., 215.
[35] Brunot, e. g., speaks of this ' loose ' *and* (*et*): *H. L. F.,* t. III, 2ᵉ Partie (Paris,
1911), pp. 651-652.

literatures, with the exception of some limited applications to French--
mostly, once again, by American historians.

It is customary among historians of French literature and language to
regard the seventeenth century as dominated by a basically 'classical'
type of periodic composition. This is the impression one gathers, for
instance (to mention one standard authority only), from Brunot's monumental and painstakingly careful analysis of an enormous mass of linguistic and critical material in his *Histoire de la langue française*. Now Guez
de Balzac (to take a master of style widely recognized in his own time)
succeeded in giving the impression of periodic rotundity by adding symmetrical elements at the beginning of his members, which made him much
admired by the classicists. Yet Balzac's immediate source was the style of
the 'Senecan' Montaigne. In a passage quoted by Croll Balzac gave a
shrewd definition of *style coupé* even while he criticized it:

Nous demeurasmes d'accord que l'Autheur qui veut imiter Seneque commence par tout et finit par tout. Son Discours n'est pas un corps entier:
c'est un corps en pieces; ce sont des membres couppez; et quoy que les
parties soient proches les unes des autres, elles ne laissent pas d'estre
separées. Non seulement il n'y a point de nerfs qui les joignent; il n'y
a pas mesmes de cordes ou d'aiguillettes qui les attachent ensemble: tant
cet Autheur est ennemy de toutes sortes de liaisons, soit de la Nature,
soit de l'Art: tant il s'esloigne de ces bons exemples que vous imitez si
parfaitement.[36]

True enough, the Cartesians eventually rejected baroque Atticism even
while they brought to fruition the Atticists' deep postulates of brevity and
clarity. Malebranche said, with telling generalization:

One of the greatest and most remarkable proofs of the power of imagination lies in the ability of some authors to persuade without reason whatever.
Thus the periods of Tertullian, Seneca, Montaigne, and some others, have
so much gracefulness and splendor that they blind the intellects of most
even though they are nothing but a weak painting and, as it were, a shadow
of these authors' imagination.[37]

---

[36] " De Montaigne et de ses escrits " in Balzac, *Œuvres*, ed. L. Moreau (Paris,
1854), II, 402-403, N° XVIII. Cf. Patrick and Evans, p. 217. The passage is
reminiscent of Caligula's 'pointe' against Seneca's style: *arena sine calce*, 'all sand
and no lime.'

[37] " Une des plus grandes et des plus remarquables preuves de la puissance que
les imaginations ont les unes sur les autres, c'est le pouvoir qu'ont certains Auteurs
de persuader sans aucunes raisons. Par exemple, le tour des parolles de Tertullien,
de Seneque, de Montagne, et de quelques autres, a tant de charmes, et tant d'éclat,

Yet the plain style had powerful allies everywhere. For deep in the heart of the Legislator of Parnassus, Boileau himself, there was a special corner, a very sensitive spot for that aspect of the "sublime" which, Longinus had taught him, resides elsewhere than in elegant vocabulary and complicated twists of sentence. Boileau did not have to look very far to find an equivalent to Longinus' biblical example (*Fiat lux, et lux facta est*) in Corneille's *Horace*: *Que vouliez-vous qu'il fist contre trois?— Qu'il mourust.* (Act iii, sc. 6.)[38] And what was this if not plain style, or at least the *sermo humilis* taught by Paul and Augustine?

Note that many a rhetorical manual of the last century was wont to use the term "loose sentence" to denote the DESCENDING construction (with the main clause coming at or near the beginning), as contrasted with the "periodic sentence," which is inherently ASCENDING. The distinction is at least useful to alert us against apparent complexity. Although inherently most un-Ciceronian, many a baroque 'loose' sentence is made deceptively akin to Ciceronian periods by virtue of its mere length. It is based on parataxis, with a fondness for absolute participle (often 'dangling') and conjunctions of a kind that is only apparently subordinating, such as *for, whereas, as . . . so, though . . . yet,* and especially the antithesis with *and, but, nor* (= *and not*). Bureaucratic prose (in its legal or parliamentarian varieties or imitations thereof) is still fond today of interminable sequences of preambles with *whereases* followed by *therefores.* They could serve as a caricature of baroque loose style at its worst. At its best, however, the asymmetrical, sprawling period of the loose style is the style of Montaigne (after he found himself), Bacon, La Mothe Le Vayer, Sir Thomas Browne, Donne (in his letters), Pascal, St.-Évremond, Halifax, Sir William Temple, Fuller, and Jeremy Taylor: it is libertine, anti-Stoic, but usually in writers who have undergone a Stoic education.[39]

The process may or may not be quite conscious. When Montaigne says of himself: "J'ecris volontiers sans project; le premier trait produit le second," he is far from indicating that he writes casually. But he does write "loosely," meaning that he strives to express the train of thought

qu'il éblouit l'esprit de la plûpart des gens, quoi que ce ne soit qu'une foible peinture, et comme l'ombre de l'imagination de ces Auteurs." Malebranche, *De la recherche de la vérité* in *Œuvres complètes*, ed. A. Robinet, t. I (Paris, 1962), p. 341.
[38] Cf. Scaglione, "N. Boileau come fulcro . . ." and "La responsabilità di Boileau . . . ," in *Convivium,* and Brody, *Boileau and Longinus.*
[39] Patrick and Evans, 222.

as it actually unfolds in his mind—which is a conscious artistic method—rather than 'constructing' by logical rearrangement and revision *a posteriori*. Together with the epigrammatic, Senecan terseness, this looseness became a distinctive mark of the seventeenth century.

The distinction between *coupé* and 'loose' remained, however, a problematic one. The major follower of Croll, Professor George Williamson, took it upon himself to test and focus the master's research and eventually came up with a plan for substantive revision. To him the plain style marked the culmination of a process which started with Erasmus' anti-Ciceronianism and led to the assimilation of the demands advanced on style by the members of the Royal Society. The Senecan experiments of the early seventeenth century acted as the essential catalyst in this process. No presentation of Williamson's views could be more comprehensive than J. M. Wallace's, in one of the prefaces to the recent re-edition of Croll's papers:

Croll's own division of styles was basically twofold: on the one hand were the styles which specialized in patterns of sound (*schemata verborum*), and which were distinguished by rigid parallelism, paromoion, and jingles of every kind—even Cicero must be included . . . ; on the other hand were the new expressive writers whose schemes were the figures of thought or wit, and whose styles as a whole were marked by deliberate asymmetry. Williamson returned to the three ancient categories of style, which he defined structurally as the circular (Ciceronian), the antithetic (Euphuistic), and the loose (Senecan), and he has shown conclusively that all these styles share different qualities with each other: that Gorgian patterns are common in Seneca, . . . that terse Asian and Stoic styles are hard to tell from all but the plainest Attic, and that antithetic constructions can be used to display either thought or sound. The use to which the schemes are put, not their mere presence or absence, is to Williamson of primary importance. Croll's division of the anti-Ciceronian style into its curt, loose, and obscure forms Williamson alters so as to make curt the norm, from which writers moved either towards a Tacitean truncatedness . . . or towards the loose, which is not essentially a brief style at all.[40]

Croll was perfectly aware of the close connection between linguistic or stylistic situations and the impact of the new natural sciences. But he

[40] Ibid., 204. Professor Wallace's résumé appears based on Williamson's *The Senecan Amble* (1951), to which one must add the early papers reprinted in his *Seventeenth Century Contexts* (London, 1960; Chicago, 1961), esp. chs. 5, "Strong Lines," and 10, "The Rhetorical Pattern of Neo-Classical Wit," pp. 120-131, 240-271. These two papers are originally dated 1936 and 1935, respectively.

believed that this impact could be viewed as a natural evolution within the literary and rhetorical tradition. Richard F. Jones, however, had a different view of the matter. In a number of important articles and a pair of weighty volumes he offered a detailed analysis of the way scientific concerns grew in England quite independently of literary traditions. Eventually, they operated on the latter by implicitly allying themselves with an antirhetorical current already going strong within the literary circles. The 'plain,' simple style of the later seventeenth century is thus directly attributed to the influence of the new science, whose ideals of clarity and objectivity as recommended by the Royal Society succeeded in ousting the once fashionable loose style.

This raises the important question of the true nature of the anti-Ciceronian reaction in all its basic aspects. Although Croll's picture is so broad as to encompass a great number of different factors, the general impression it generates is that the theory of plain style is essentially part of the rhetorical tradition, within which it grows and thrives through the process of electing one conventional style, the *humile,* against its opposite, the *grande.* This way of putting the problem may not do full justice to extra-rhetorical factors. To begin with, the demands for purity of language, though close to the ancient rhetorical notions of *puritas, Latinitas, Hellenismus,* in the transition between Renaissance and baroque came *de facto* from the grammatical milieu in reaction against rhetorical training—at least in England. This will become apparent in the course of our exposition. For the time being, it is sufficient to call attention to a general phenomenon which developed between 1600 and 1750, especially in France and England, namely a growing distrust for the 'rhetorically' oriented language of poetry in favor of a grammatically correct and logically sound prose-directed plain style to be respected and imitated even by the poets.

Ben Jonson gives a very early indication of this incipient trend, as pithily indicated by M. A. Shaaber:

Ben Jonson is impatient of the elaborate formalism of much Renaissance poetry; he dislikes sonnets and stanzas and he has gone far beyond the trumpery of the poetical rhetoric of his day. "Pure and neat language I love, yet plaine and customary. . . . The chiefe vertue of a style is perspicuitie." Not a word about its being poetical; to Jonson, in fact, "the forme and soule of any Poeticall worke" is the fable or fiction, i. e., the plot. By the end of the century the style of poetry had been restricted within the bounds of the rational, and even lyric poetry had contracted sensuousness to smoothness. The result was, as Drummond put it, "denuding her [i. e., poetry] of her own habits, and those Ornaments with which she hath amused [= held the attention of] the World some thousand Years." [41]

In his comprehensive anthology of representative seventeenth century English prose texts, Shaaber underlines that most of the pre-Restoration writers selected exemplify one or another form of Senecan style (Bacon leaned toward Tacitus), even though the more traditional forms—more or less assimilable to the grand style—were far from becoming extinct: "There are a few holdouts; Milton with all his ruggedness, Jeremy Taylor in some of his moods, and Sir Thomas Urquhart leaned toward what the last called a style 'periodically contexed (sic) with isocoly of members.'" [42]

True enough, the geographic scope of Croll's definitions seems too broad, while his examples are almost exclusively limited to French and English. Even those two literatures cannot perhaps bear the same historiographic schemas for the period. Granted, for example, that Puritan preaching [43] and, even more, the influence of scientists (Royal Society, Sprat, etc.) were chief factors in the establishment of plain style in the last 40 years (1660-1700) in England: this picture is, of course, inapplicable to France or the rest of Europe, even though Galileo's school was, for one, very influential in Italy (but not at the same time).

The manifold questions raised by Croll's thesis have perhaps reached their fruition in a recent study by an Australian scholar, K. G. Hamilton.[44] Starting from England, he proposes to envisage, "at the risk of some oversimplification," three periods in the stylistic development that goes from approximately 1575 to the end of the following century.[45]

[41] M. A. Shaaber, ed., *Seventeenth Century English Prose* (New York, 1957), p. 29. For a detailed treatment of Jonson's rhetoric see now Jonas A. Barish, *Ben Jonson and the Language of Prose Comedy* (Cambridge, Mass., 1960), and Wesley Trimpi, *Ben Jonson's Poems: A Study of the Plain Style* (Stanford, Ca., 1962); Id., "Jonson and the Neo-Latin Authorities for the Plain Style," *PMLA*, LXXII (1962), 21-26.

[42] Op. cit., p. 2. On Milton's possible use of different style levels to contrast moral values (evil speaking a rhetorically 'ornate' style), see Peter Berek, "'Plain' and 'Ornate' Styles and the Structure of *Paradise Lost*," *PMLA*, LXXXV (1970), 237-246.

[43] Cf. H. Fisch, "The Puritans and the Reform of Prose Style," *E. L. H.*, XIX (1952), 229-248, an account somewhat similar to Jones's *Triumph of the English Language*, with emphasis on the effect of Puritanism on style in the earlier seventeenth century. Further complication of the issue is found in Ruth C. Wallerstein, *Studies in Seventeenth-Century Poetic* (Madison, University of Wisconsin Press, 1950).

[44] K. G. Hamilton, *The Two Harmonies* (Oxford, 1963).

[45] Ibid., pp. 6-7.

i. In prose, Ciceronian imitation and Euphuism, differing in structure but alike in the emphasis on VERBAL qualities.[46]

In poetry, the elaborate, florid harmonies and ornamentation associated with Spenser, and like its contemporary prose, prompted by a desire to make English a fit vehicle for literary expression.

ii. In prose, the various forms of Senecan style (curt, obscure, loose, etc.) which cultivate wit but primarily for the sake of thought or 'point.'

In poetry, first metaphysical and later antithetic wit, where again the poetry resembles the prose in seeming to have been partly dictated by a desire to make words a more direct expression of thought.

iii. In both poetry and prose, an emphasis on simplicity, clarity, intelligibility, propriety, naturalness, refinement, ease, etc.

These changes—according to Hamilton—may be seen as successive stages in a cyclical process of action and reaction, in which the Romantic movement was to be the next stage: the metaphysicals and Senecans revolted against Elizabethan verbalism, the neo-classicists against metaphysical extravagance, the Romantics against neo-classic aridity, the reaction in each case being against the tag end of the former stage which has lost its initial inspiration. This at least is the conventional explanation accepted by literary historians.

Furthermore, the effects of these movements within prose are understood to have been largely indiscriminate: they affected prose "in almost all its forms and uses, except perhaps the most unselfconscious and non-literary." [47]

Hamilton's schema is attractive for its very neatness and undogmatic articulateness. It has the great advantage of starting from the narrow boundaries of English literature, without losing the appeal of Croll's original, more ambitiously continental scope, for it shows an obvious analogy with the schemas which every other national literature would call for with due regard to its own peculiarities. More importantly, we have here a historically-viewed breakdown of a flux into logically fitted phases whose reciprocal relationships are both factually convincing and ideally intelligible. Should the reader feel inclined to keep this schema in mind, he will probably find more meaningful and orderly the analytical review of texts in the following sections.

The inclusion of Euphuism in the first phase is particularly noteworthy. In his first important study, Croll had demonstrated that the striking

---

[46] I. e., sound figures—remember Williamson's characterization of antithesis, which can also be used as a figure of words.

[47] *The Two Harmonies*, 6-7.

'baroque-like' qualities of *Euphues* were based on *schemata verborum* and had their origin in medieval Latin prose.[48] Lyly had nothing whatever to do with anti-Ciceronian Atticism.[49]

Hamilton's results in trying to refine prior investigations into the impact of science also appear convincing. He starts out by recalling how William-son linked the scientific style with the older philosophic style without separating the former from the anti-Ciceronian movement that had re-placed the extravagant floridity of the sixteenth century with the curt 'Senecan' style particularly associated with Bacon. But he concludes that "this linking may serve to blur a real difference in attitude." [50] To begin with, "Erasmus, with whom as Bacon (and following him William-son) suggests the study of anti-Ciceronianism must begin, was first and foremost a humanist, with the humanists' rhetorical approach to life," that is a conception of the word as the central fact of human reality and of culture itself (*humanitas*). Indeed, we might add, Erasmus' anti-Ciceronianism was so much part of his humanism that it harked back to a quite articulate current among the earlier Italian humanists, from Poggio to Politian. For, as with Erasmus, anti-Ciceronianism as a whole was not a movement against rhetoric. "The various forms of anti-Ciceronian style remain essentially rhetorical forms of style closely related to classical forms, a point to which Williamson himself devotes a complete chapter. (*The Senecan Amble*, pp. 32 ff.) " [51] Anti-Ciceronianism was not anti-Cicero-ism: its affiliates respected Cicero as much as they despised his "apish" imitators, as Politian put it.

Indeed, the English plain style owes a good deal to attitudes of very different origin. Thomas Sprat (1667) put it unequivocally and radically: "Eloquence ought to be banish'd out of all civil Societies, as a thing fatal to Peace and good Manners." [52] Thus the style sought by the

[48] Cf. Croll, Introduction to J. Lyly's *Euphues*, ed. H. Clemons.

[49] R. Wellek, "The Concept of Baroque," op. cit., pp. 101-102. On the 'rebirth' of Gorgianic patterns in some vernacular prose of the Late Renaissance see, also, Norden, *Kunstprosa*, pp. 786 ff., 1923 ed. (4th); T. K. Whipple, "Isocrates and Euphuism," *Modern Language Review*, XI (1916), 15-27 and 129-135; Theodor Gomperz, *Greek Thinkers*, trans. L. Magnus (London, 1920), pp. 478 ff.; Gilbert Highet, *The Classical Tradition* (New York, 1949), pp. 322 ff.

[50] Hamilton, op. cit., p. 105.

[51] Cf. Hamilton, p. 106, where he adds that Croll, " 'Attic Prose,' " p. 80, made a similar point.

[52] Sprat, *The History of the Royal Society* . . . (London, 1667), p. 111, cited by Hamilton, p. 106. Bishop Sprat says: "They have extracted from all their mem-

scientists may have had something in common with that of the anti-
Ciceronians, but not the attitude toward words that lay behind it.[53] As
to Croll's highly suggestive insight into the psychic mechanism of baroque
style as "the moment in which truth is still IMAGINED," Hamilton
demurs: "This may be to read Senecan prose with the same twentieth-
century expectations as have been attributed to Eliot in his reading of
the poetry of Donne."[54] Furthermore, just as with the schools of the first
century A. D., modern Atticism could be mainly polemical, antirhetorical
from the philosophical point of view (Seneca), even while the Asianic
experiences remained profoundly alive with the very same Stoics who
occasionally proclaimed themselves Attic.

As an episodic example of the complication and absence of linearity
in the development of these stylistic manners and notions, I shall adduce
Hugo Friedrich's recent reminder that Cicero, Quintilian, Persius, and
other critics of the *genus asiaticae dictionis* coined such terms as *ingenium,
argute dicere* (cf. Italian *arguzie*), *sententiae, cultus, lepidum, acutum*
(cf. Sp. *agudeza*), all applied to the *stilus atticus*. Such terms reemerged
in the baroque poetics of the seventeenth century, and especially in those
of Gracián and Tesauro, without derogatory connotations.[55]

The main drift of all the preceding analysis lies in the upsetting of some
widespread views. As early as 1909, in a didactic manual much celebrated
at its time, Antoine Albalat[56] used the term *atticisme* to designate the
'spontaneous,' simple, natural, and clear ways of the French classics. But
his reference to Voltaire as the one "qui résume ce genre de style sans
rhétorique" unequivocally showed how the qualities he had in mind

---

bers a close, naked [= figureless], natural way of speaking; positive expressions,
clear senses; a native easiness; bringing all things as near the mathematical plainness, as they can: and preferring the language of Artizans, Countrymen, and
Merchants, before that of Wits or Scholars." See the text of this whole, fundamental passage on the Society's ideal of plain English reprinted in J. E. Spingarn,
Critical Essays of the Seventeenth Century (Oxford, 1908), vol. II, pp. 116-119.

[53] Hamilton, op. cit., p. 107.

[54] Ibid., p. 6. As for these "expectations" attributed to Eliot, reference is here
made to Frank Kermode, "Dissociation of Sensibility," *K. R.*, XIX (1957), 169-194.

[55] Similarly, *ekphrasis* and *epideixis* characterize manneristic style, as after Seneca
the Elder. Cf. H. Friedrich, "Über die *Silvae* des Statius . . . und die Frage des
literarischen Manierismus," *Wort und Text, Festschrift für Fritz Schalk* (Frankfurt am Main, 1963), 34-56, and Id., *Epochen der italienischen Lyrik* (Frankfurt
am Main, 1964), esp. pp. 604-608.

[56] Albalat, *La Formation du style par l'assimilation des auteurs* (Paris, 1909),
pp. 295-296.

were the 'un-baroque' ones of the later rationalism, even though common
to both the centuries of Port-Royal and the Encyclopaedia. Voltaire's ideal
appeared pithily stated in a letter of advice to a young lady of June 20,
1756:

Les bons auteurs n'ont de l'esprit qu'autant qu'il en faut, ne le recherchent
jamais, pensent avec bon sens, et s'expriment avec clarté. Il semble qu'on
n'écrive plus qu'en énigmes.

Now, whether or not we approve of Croll's final association of Atticism
and baroque, it should remain firm that Albalat's French Atticism, which
would correspond to Hamilton's third stage of style, can be shown in
the light of the aforementioned studies to have naturally issued from
those very experiments in wit, antithesis, metaphysical effort to the point
of obscurity (though often with an antirhetorical orientation), of which
on the surface it appears to be little more than a direct denial.

In the evolution (roughly between 1500 and 1800) from a prevalence
of grand style modes to a general orientation toward plain style, there is a
transitory phase characterized by indulgence in the intense, pregnant
obscurity of Stoic imprint. This transition was not accidental, and it
repeated the stylistic process which had obtained in the experience of the
ancients. The Stoics' obscurity had been a sort of substitute for the grand,
elegant, overstated *ornatus* they officially rejected. In this sense, while
they reacted against rhetoric they still moved within it. For, obviously,
it is clarity and naturalness, rather than 'obscurity,' that runs counter to
ornamentation. But "rhetoric tended to teach the Roman to write finely
before he could write simply and clearly." [57] This heritage was hard
to brush aside, and it could actually amount to a deliberate loss of intelligibility. Quintilian told the story of a teacher from at least as early as
the Augustan age, who used to say, when his pupil's compositions seemed
too clear: "Σκότισον, Darken it." [58] Many in the days of Quintilian
deemed it impossible to write elegantly unless the writing required interpretation. [59] When the Senecan and Tacitean baroque fashions were on
the wane and the ideal of *clarté* shone brightest, Bouhours could look back
on such defeated modes and express his condemnation by recalling Quintilian's anecdote with an added twist of amused irony: "ce pédant dont

---

[57] M. L. Clarke, *Rhetoric at Rome* (New York, 1963), p. 159.
[58] Quint., *Inst.* VIII, ii, 18, recorded on the authority of Livy.
[59] Cf. Clarke, op. cit., ibid.

parle Quintilien, qui enseignoit l'obscurité à ses écoliers, et qui leur disoit: 'Cela est excellent, je ne l'entends pas moy-mesme.'"[60]

I have hinted earlier that the identification of Atticism and baroque did a disservice to a good cause, for we do want to include in our acceptation of the term 'baroque' not only some criteria other than stylistic (and therefore also the type of imagery and the mental attitudes toward specific contents), but also some types of excessive emphases on sound patterns. We can, for instance, neither exclude Petrarchism, which is mainly a matter of imagery, nor the sophisticated verbalizations and obsessive musicality of much of 'Secentismo,' since we cannot accept a view of baroque which would do without Marino and Marinismo, without Lohenstein and Hofmannswaldau, without so many bombastic preachers and orators in Italy, Austria, Spain, and other countries. We may well end up, perforce, with a more workable notion of baroque by encompassing in it, in a burst of generosity, Euphuism itself, along with Sidney's *Arcadia* and the later Shakespeare, Cervantes, Lope, Calderón. . . .

Indeed, among the most provocative contributions of recent scholarship on stylistic structures are the studies by Dámaso Alonso on *plurimembrismo* in Petrarchist poetry, a methodically symmetrical approach to structural patterns which from the rhetorical viewpoint is clearly to be classed within the sound figures.[61] Since Alonso turned his attention mainly toward such poets as Góngora, the English metaphysicals, and the European Marinists, this is obviously part of baroque even though some of the poets involved might, in other respects, be both anti-Ciceronians and anti-Petrarchists.

Alonso's analysis directly invests the area of compositional structures, yet I must refrain from dealing with it extensively because it is chiefly confined to the realm of poetry. I believe a simple comparison of textual examples, without further comment, will illustrate the point sufficiently

[60] Bouhours, *Manière de bien penser* (1715 ed.), p. 487.

[61] See D. Alonso, "Un aspecto del Petrarquismo: La Correlación poética" in Alonso and Carlos Bousoño, *Seis calas en la expresión literaria española* (Madrid, 1951), 79-111; also "Sintagmas . . . pluralidades," ibid., 2d ed. (Madrid, 1956), 25-45; *Estudios y Ensayos Gongorinos* (Madrid, 1955), Part II, pp. 117-247; "La poesia del Petrarca e il Petrarchismo (Mondo estetico della Pluralità)," *Studi Petrarcheschi*, VII (1961), 73-120.

On the abuse of hyperbata in Spanish *culteranismo* as distinct from, and even opposed to *conceptismo*, as well as on the differences between Italian and Spanish baroque, see now W. Theodor Elwert, *La Poesia lirica italiana del Seicento: Studio sullo stile barocco* (Florence, 1967), esp. pp. 168-173.

well, and I shall take these examples from Gorgias and from the Petrarchist literature in order to stress the similarity between Sophistic or Asianic symmetry and certain cases of baroque.

The following passage from Gorgias' *Encomium of Helen* is translated by Larue Van Hook with a view to reproducing " in English the effect of the original Greek ":

Embellishment to a city is the valor of its citizens; to a person, comeliness; to a soul, wisdom; to a deed, virtue; to a discourse; truth. But the opposite to these is lack of embellishment. Now a man, woman, discourse, work, city, deed, if deserving of praise, must be honored with praise, but if undeserving must be censured. For it is alike aberration and stultification to censure the commendable and commend the censurable.[62]

See, now, Petrarch's Sonnet 133:

> Amor m'ha posto come *segno* a *strale*,
> com'al *sol* neve, come *cera* al *foco*,
> e come *nebbia* al *vento*; e son già roco,
> donna, mercé chiamando, e voi non cale.
>
> Dagli occhi vostri uscio 'l *colpo* mortale,
> contra cui non mi val tempo né loco;
> da voi sola procede (e parvi un gioco)
> il *sole* e 'l *foco* e 'l *vento*, ond'io son tale.
>
> I pensier son *saette*, e 'l viso un *sole*,
> e 'l desir *foco*; e 'nsieme con quest'arme
> mi *punge* Amor, *m'abbaglia* e mi *distrugge*.
>
> E l'angelico canto, e le parole,
> col dolce spirto, ond'io non posso aitarme,
> son l'aura innanzi a cui mia vita fugge.

Finally, sonnet 56 from Edmund Spenser's *Amoretti*:

> *Fayre ye be sure, but* cruell *and* unkind
> *as* is a *tygre*, that with greedinesse

[62] Isocrates, III, ed. Larue Van Hook (London, Eng. and Cambridge, Mass., 1945, . . . 1954 . . .), p. 55. Cited by Clark, *Rh. in G.-R. Ed.*, p. 93. C. N. Smiley has stressed the point that the Gorgian figures are as permanent as oratory itself: he has showed that Lincoln (apparently one of the most unrhetorical minded among great modern orators) used freely all sorts of antithesis, anaphora, alliteration, assonance, balanced clauses, similar endings: see "Lincoln and Gorgias," *Classical Journal*, XIII, 2 (Nov. 1917), 124-128.

hunts after bloud, when he by chance doth find
a feeble *beast*, doth felly him *oppresse.*
Fayre be ye sure, but proud *and* pittilesse,
as is a *storme*, that all things doth prostrate,
finding a *tree* alone all comfortlesse,
beats on it strongly, it to *ruinate.*
Fayre be ye sure, but hard *and* obstinate,
as is a *rocke* amidst the raging floods,
gaynst which a *ship*, of succour desolate,
doth suffer *wreck* both of her selfe and goods.
That ship, that tree, and *that same beast* am I
whom ye doe *wreck*, doe *ruine*, and *destroy*.[63]

But prose texts will be more fitting for our purpose, and here again
Alonso himself will provide for us a most appropriate example of the
return of 'Asianic' symmetries in the baroque age, in the form of correlative pluralistic patterns. When we read this passage in the *Quixote*, Part
II, ch. viii:

. . . allí tomaré la *bendición* y *buena licencia* de la sin par Dulcinea, con
la cual licencia *pienso* y *tengo por cierto* de *acabar* y *dar felice cima* a
toda peligrosa aventura,

we cannot fail to perceive the methodic binary pattern of the italicized
paratactic terms. They are even more remarkable because they are " practically tautological." [64] Nor is this an exceptional case: indeed,

esa bimembración, aproximadamente tautológica, es característica de casi
toda la prosa del período áureo de nuestras letras. Se corresponde con la
compostura, la gravedad, aún en los usos sociales; evoca una falta de prisa,
una necesidad de hacer con majestad, con nobleza. . . . Poco o nada se gana
así en lo pictórico, muy poco (y sólo a veces) en lo conceptual . . . . Son,
pues, necesidades rítmicas . . . (poso, gravedad, equilibrio). . . .[65]

In other words, we have a case of grand style based on the eloquence of
sound figures at the expense of thought figures. And the critic shrewdly
points out that this is Quixote's style, not Sancho's. Sancho is all the

[63] Cf. Alonso, SP (1961), pp. 101 ff. and 115.
[64] Alonso, *Seis calas* (1951 ed.), p. 30. This analysis occurs in a precious foray,
so to say, by Alonso into prose patterns: " Sintagmas no progresivos y pluralidades:
tres calillas en la prosa castellana," ibid., pp. 23-42.
[65] Ibid., pp. 30-31.

opposite, a master of plain style—as in the typical dialogue that follows the passage just cited.

In all fairness to Croll, it behooves us to give him credit for being aware of these complicating factors.

We think of the tumor,—he noted—the exaggerated emphasis, the monstrous abuse of metaphor in the preaching of the first half of the century in all the European countries; or of qualities dangerously related to these in the non-oratorical prose writings of Donne, Gracián, Malvezzi, and other masters of the ' conceit '; or even of tendencies of the same kind that we may observe in writers so normal as Lipsius, Bacon, Balzac, and Browne. There is a kind of Asianism, in short, that arises from a constant effort to speak with point and significance, as well as from an excessive use of the ornate figures of sound, from too much love of expressiveness as well as from the cult of form; and inasmuch as this vice was more familiar to the reformers at the end of the century than the other, and was the one that was in immediate need of correction at that time, it has taken its place in our traditions as typical Asianism.[66]

In other words, he found that the anti-Ciceronians fell into these errors through an excess of their own qualities: they dubbed themselves ' Attic ' " because they avoided certain traits they disliked, and did not observe that they sometimes ceased to be Attic through avoiding and disliking them too much." [67] For even the ancients recognized two ways of becoming Asian: *aut nimio cultu aut nimio tumore*; the first way is that of Bembo, Lyly, and many in the sixteenth century; the second (exaggerating the *sententiarum venustas*) is that of Montaigne, Lipsius, and Browne in the seventeenth.[68] Yet once we have paid homage to Croll's unfailing information, we must conclude that what his qualifications really point out is the difficulty of a clear-cut distinction among the manifold and somewhat contradictory ingredients which went into the making of the major stylistic trends of the seventeenth century.[69]

[66] Patrick and Evans, p. 69.
[67] Ibid.
[68] Croll, " ' Attic Prose,' " 96-97, and Patrick and Evans, p. 69 fn.
The factual foundation of Croll's position, with particular regard to England, has been recently put into question by Earl Miner, " Patterns of Stoicism in Thought and Prose Styles, 1530-1700," *PMLA*, LXXXV (1970), 1023-1034, on the ground that the frequency of publication of Stoic and Ciceronian writings between 1530 and 1700 does not bear out the claim that anti-Ciceronian Stoicism reached its peak in the period 1580-1630. But see J. Freehafer and F. B. Williams, Jr. in *PMLA*, LXXXVI (1971), 1028-30, challenging Miner's data and method.
[69] An outspoken attack against stylistic typology, in favor of a direct study of individual styles without reference to collective categories, can be read in Louis T.

On the more positive side our critic's thesis has the incomparable merit of having coalesced the basic threads of the extraordinarily complex stylistic situation obtaining at the beginning of the modern era. For the purpose at hand, it provides a unitary perspective through which to investigate the problems of composition at a time when they became more fashionable than at any other, by viewing them not simply as a technical chapter in grammatical or rhetorical casuistry, but as a vital knot at the very center of a heightened concern for style which, at the time, seemed to hold the answer to a number of questions of intense intellectual, moral, and even religious value. The uncertainty that will invest a good deal of the necessary details is likely to be due to the temporary lack of extensive and detailed interpretive studies of the area. In particular, Croll's orientation will reveal its usefulness for us through the distinction between 'loose' and *coupé* composition as successive forms of anti-Ciceronian style in the transition from the apparent periodicity of the seventeenth century to the open anti-periodicity of the eighteenth. We shall then beware of accepting the evaluations by contemporaneous theorists in that they will often continue, especially on the Continent, to analyze what was in reality a 'loose' form as if it were still a 'periodic' structure. What we are about to witness is another case of theoretical lag as against the dynamic innovations of compositional practices. Whether or not we feel prepared to accept a consistent, continuous current clearly defined between the Greek Attics, through the Stoics, to the baroque, one fact remains firm: a conspiring of Stoicism, 'Atticism,' and 'baroque,' as well as anti-baroque classicism and scientism (both of these last movements demanding clarity, pithiness, directness, although in different ways) in the course of the seventeenth century, with particularly conspicuous developments in England.

It is also imperative to bear in mind that even the basic terminology for this period remains in a conspicuous state of flux. The most recent case of a proposed drastic revision of the whole terminology is that of Arnold Hauser, who in a provocative study of Mannerism has argued for a sharp distinction between phenomena subsumed under that term (roughly 1520-1650) and Baroque proper, which in his mind seems to become

Milic, "Against the Typology of Styles," in S. Chatman and S. R. Levin, eds., *Essays on the Language of Literature* (Boston, 1967), 442-450. Milic uses James R. Sutherland, "Restoration Prose," in *Restoration and Augustan Prose* (Los Angeles, U. C. Press, 1956), 1-18, as an example of what he considers unproductive attempts to apply generic categories to groups of writers.

a rather secondary, more limited movement than traditionally postulated.[70]

By his definition, Mannerism (which would typically include all of Petrarchism, Euphuism, and anti-classical drives) is predominantly an intellectual, introverted, and socially exclusive attitude which gives birth to a sophisticated, reflective, broken style, thoroughly paradoxical, culturally saturated, and yet unmindful of overall structure in favor of an "atomized," episodic one. In baroque works, on the contrary, a unifying principle always prevails, the total effect is uniform and subjected to a dominant accent but, more importantly, the general attitude is strongly emotional and open to a larger audience, and the style is spontaneous and simple by comparison, thus representing "a return to the natural and instinctual, and in that sense to the normal, after the extravagances and exaggerations" of the preceding period.

Hauser's somewhat intemperate method of approach is only a particularly comprehensive example of a broad reassessment of the relationship between Renaissance and Baroque which already boasts an impressive body of critical literature. Such names as Georg Weise, Wylie Sypher, René Hocke, and most recently John Shearman are becoming or have become familiar to all students of Cinquecento culture. But we have already strayed far enough from the primary purpose of this study, which is to analyze the theory rather than the practice of style. It did seem to be in order to point out that the importation of the notion of Mannerism from art to literature may well turn out to be a fruitful method of solving some thorny, central difficulties. But it also seems clear that the evolution of stylistic modes from, roughly, 1500 to 1750, particularly with regard to compositional formulae, cannot be properly understood by using the broad categories of Renaissance Classicism, Mannerism, Baroque, and Rococò. These categories are not such as to explain some of the crucial aspects of our subject.

Stylistic typology is fraught with the dangers of generalization on the level of literary practices. The typology we are concerned with is legitimate because it is that of the doctrines of style, and theorists work by abstraction and broad categories. No movement has a monopoly of any

---

[70] Arnold Hauser, *Mannerism. The Crisis of the Renaissance and the Origin of Modern Art* (London, 1965, 2 vols.—from 1964 German original), pp. 274-275. Following the above definitions, a list of authors seems to exemplify the two trends, namely Góngora, Marino, Donne, and Marvell as distinct from Guarini, Chiabrera, Dryden, Milton, Racine, and Bossuet (p. 275). It is clearly pointed out that the two movements are often combined in complex and unique ways in the same work.

particular compositional formula, because compositional forms can be used for different ends within different schools. They are primarily techniques, and as such they, too, have their own history.

B. THE THEORY OF COMPOSITION IN FRANCE: 1600–1800
I) PERIODICITY AND COUPÉ STYLE

1. The peculiar evolution of French literary taste in the course of the seventeenth century was such that in the last third of that century the gradual shifting away from every form of indulgence in verbalisms as well as witticisms, from every *préciosité* toward the severe ideals of classicism, made France the least hospitable place to all the 'Asianist' orientations which characterized much of European baroque. The French critics were by and large hostile to the very notion of eloquence as oratory. Their respect for rhetoric implicitly demanded a reform of this discipline which would turn it from its overwhelming concern with auditive gratifications to a prevalent interest in the intellectual contents of speech, in other words a shift from a delivery-oriented approach to one centered on writing and reading. Muret in Italy, Bacon in England, and finally Pascal and Arnauld in France echo the Aristotelian statement (beginning of the *Rhetoric*) that the justification of oratory is to be found in the weakness of judgment of an uneducated public, incapable of the ways of reason.[1] For France, the "libertine" La Mothe Le Vayer reveals the earliest symptoms of the change to come. In 1638, at the beginning of his *Considérations sur l'éloquence françoise de ce temps*[2] he professes to treat of written style alone, *l'éloquence muette* or *éloquence des livres,* a style to be read, not heard. All that has to do with speaking he repudiates. Also, he explicitly refers what he calls *style coupé* to the plain style of the old rhetoric, specifically for its use of *pointes,* allusions, *sententiae,* even while he imputes it to Virgilio Malvezzi, Italian author of discourses on Tacitus. Although he makes these identifications with the intent of condemning, not proposing, the "cut" style, it is clear that within the framework of his general orientation he cannot truly espouse the periodic style of old. The only conclusion we are entitled to draw for the moment

[1] Cf. Croll, " 'Attic Prose,' " 92-93.
[2] François de La Mothe Le Vayer, *Œuvres* (Paris, 1662³, 2 tomes), I, p. 435, or the later ed. of his *Œuvres* (Paris, 1684), IV, 4-7. Cf. Croll, " 'Attic Prose,' " 95.

is that the 'periodic' style thus professed will have to carry a different type of periodicity than the ancient one. At the turn of the century Belthasar Gibert drew upon La Mothe's exposition when he advanced his sharp and unequivocal distinction: "L'opposé du style périodique est le style coupé." [3] Williamson informs us that Hugh Blair imported these French terms of *style périodique* and *style coupé* into English.[4]

There was in this discussion an echo of the polemic which some Italians (such as Agostino Mascardi [1591-1640] in his *Dell'arte istorica*, 1636) had opened in blaming the French historian Mathieu for having corrupted their own manner of writing; but we know, now, that in Mascardi's attack Mathieu was little more than a straw man, while his true target was no other than Malvezzi himself.[5] In return La Mothe implies just that when after citing Mascardi's charges he singles out Malvezzi, but only in order to gloss over those of his own nation who do worse than he: "[pour] se taire de ceux de notre nation, qui font pis que luy." Meanwhile Malvezzi, for one, has given his style the "allure des petits enfans qui ne vont que par secousses," and "une faiblesse comme au vol des oiseaux qui n'ont pas l'aisle assez forte et qui n'osent encore se hazarder que de branche en branche." He is, accordingly, the chief exponent of that "style trop concis," "trop entrecoupé" which resembles "le parler d'un asthmatique," with its characteristic "contrepointes dont la pluspart sont fondées sur un jeu de paroles qui n'a rien de serieux." It reminds one of what the Latins called "scopae dissolutae." [6] And Brunot, after

---

[3] See Belthasar Gibert's (1662-1741) summary of La Mothe's *Considérations* in his *Jugemens des Sçavants* published as continuation of Adrien Baillet's *Jugemens des Sçavans* (Amsterdam, 1725), VIII, 278.

[4] G. Williamson, *The Senecan Amble*, pp. 56 and 354. On Blair's *Lectures on Rhetoric* (cf. Lect. XI for the key passage), see the English Section later on in this Chapter.

[5] Ferdinand Brunot, *Histoire de la langue française des origines à 1900*, Tome III, 2e Partie: "La Formation de la langue classique (1600-1660)" (Paris, 1911), ch. xi, "La Phrase," pp. 684-711. See p. 697.

Cf. Agostino Mascardi, *Dell'arte historica Trattati Cinque* (Roma, 1636; Venetia, 1646; Venetia, Baba, 1655; new ed. Venetia, 1674). Reprinted Florence 1859, ed. A. Bartoli (title *Dell'arte istorica*). See pp. 431-432 and 441-448 for the severe judgment on Pierre Mathieu. The 4th Treatise deals entirely with style and elocution, and so does ch. viii of the 5th Treatise. On this polemic see my ch. IV, C below and, in particular, Raimondi, *Letteratura barocca*, p. 185, and B. Croce, *Storia dell'età barocca in Italia* (Bari, 1929), pp. 142-144 (on Mathieu).

[6] La Mothe Le Vayer, *Œuvres* (Paris, 1662³), I, 451-452. In these *Considérations* composition is treated on pp. 447-455. Also *Œuvres* (1684), IV, esp. pp. 40-42. See, also, 1662 ed., II (1), p. 648 on Seneca's style.

noting with regard to La Mothe that " il est, lui, le théoricien de l'éloquence française, tout à fait hostile à cette sorte de phrases," rather hastily
concludes: " Je ne vois personne qui ait déclaré sa préférence pour la
phrase courte, alerte, à la française," that is for the plain style or, more
specifically, the *style coupé*. " On en use sans doute, mais les théoriciens
ne s'en occupent point." [7]

Even for the classic period (1660-1715) Brunot again found that " le
style coupé " made, indeed, headway, "mais nulle part on n'en trouve
la théorie: elle était trop simple apparemment. Les maîtres du style y ont
pourvu [in their practice]." [8] He gave an example from La Bruyère, II,
185, De quelqu. us. 43: " Le devoir des juges est de rendre la justice;
leur métier de la différer. Quelques uns savent leur devoir, et font leur
métier." [9]

Perhaps a bit uneasy about the simplicity of his conclusions, Brunot had
incidentally remarked on the absence of satisfactory studies of the way a
French rhetorical system came into being. This research, he noted,
promised to be hard but interesting, while the influence of the
Italians and the ancients would have appeared for what it really was, that
is, first tyrannical and misleading, then beneficent, once it had become
adapted to the character of the language to which one wanted to apply it. [10]
This kind of study has been recently re-attempted by an American literary
historian, Hugh M. Davidson; [11] but more seems to be needed in order
to see clearly the significance of relevant works against their complex
historical background.

Erycius Puteanus (Eerryk de Putte, 1574-1646), Lipsius' successor in
the chair of rhetoric at Louvain and evidently his follower, had produced
a rhetoric of 'Laconism' as extreme development of the Stoic *brevitas*

---

[7] Brunot, *H. L. F.*, III, 2, p. 697.

[8] Brunot, *H. L. F.*, IV, 2 (1924), p. 1181.

[9] Further on in this manual (t. VI, P. 2, Fasc. 2, pp. 1980-1981), A. François
will suggest that Father Buffier (*Grammaire françoise sur un plan nouveau*, Paris,
1709, 1714) may have been the " discoverer" of *style coupé*, while nowhere else
does one find the equivalent of his brilliant analysis, even at that late date.

[10] Brunot, III, 2, p. 695. Brunot adds: " On est tout étonné de voir des règles
de ce genre entrer dans un livre aussi élémentaire que celui de Cl. Irson." See
Claude Irson, *Nouvelle méthode pour apprendre facilement les principes et la pureté
de la langue françoise* (Paris, 1656, 1660, 1662, 1667). Cf. pp. 89 ff. of 1656 ed.

[11] *Audience, Words, and Art* . . . (1965). B. Munteano, *Constantes dialectiques*
. . . (1967), pp. 139-185 deals with broad principles of the French rhetorical
tradition between Renaissance and Romanticism.

(*De Laconismo Syntagma*, Louvain, 1609). Thinking that there was too much *copia* in Demosthenes [12] and other Attic orators, he marshaled "an array of 'brief' ancient writers, Thucydides, Cato, the Gracchi, Sallust, Tacitus, especially, who are properly called Attics, he says, because they are so reticent, so incisive, so significant." But he preferred to call them Spartans.[18] Guez de Balzac in the preface to his *Socrate Chrétien* (1652) made the same distinction: If it becomes necessary to let our heart enter our speech, let it be in a Spartan style . . . or at least Attic: "qu'il ne déborde pas par ces harangues Asiatiques, où il faut prendre trois fois haleine pour arriver à la fin d'une période." Modern lungs begin to give signs of weariness when challenged by the manly sweep of antique periods. He then refers to the "Attiques de Rome, qui contrefaisoient Brutus, et n'imitèrent pas Ciceron," meaning Seneca and his school.

The leading ideas in Vaugelas' *Remarques* appear in the traditional order, running from correctness through elegance to rhythm. The great grammarian began by praising French as the most *pur, net, propre* ("pour toute sorte de styles"), *élégant*, and, ultimately, for "le nombre et la cadence dans ses périodes, . . . en quoy consiste la véritable marque de la perfection des langues." [14] He then reverted to the classical sources for such standards: "Un language pur, est ce que Quintilien appelle *emendata oratio* et un language net, ce qu'il appelle *dilucida oratio* . . . ; nettement, c'est-à-dire clairement et intelligiblement. . . ." [15] *Netteté* or clarity can also be had without purity. He concluded his original Remarks with the reminder that "*A la pureté et à la netteté du stile*, il y a encore d'autres parties à ajouster, *la proprieté des mots et des phrases, l'elegance,*

---

[12] The reader will recall that, in a polemical thrust against the Latin Atticists of his time, Cicero had also singled out Demosthenes for the splendor of his rhythms. Demosthenes was Attic, but the more extreme Atticists despised rhythm—essentially a *schema verborum*—: cf. *Orator*, 234. Nevertheless, Demosthenes' rhythms were not exactly in line with Isocratean and Gorgian cadences and symmetries.

[18] Croll, "'Attic Prose,'" 98-99. Cf. Puteanus, *De Laconismo Syntagma* (1609), esp. pp. 27 and 78-79. See, also, Id., *Laconismi Encomium* and *Laconismi Patrocinium: Dialogus quo Breviloquentia firmatur*, both Milan, P. and M.-T. Malatesta, 1606. Cf. *Bibliotheca Belgica*, IV (1964); and Th. Simar, *Étude sur E. Puteanus* . . . (Louvain, 1909), esp. pp. 79-83.

[14] Claude Favre de Vaugelas, *Remarques sur la langue française* . . . , ed. Jeanne Streicher (Paris, 1934) [Facsimile of the first ed., Paris, 1647], last section (xv, 3) of the "Préface."

[15] Vaugelas, *Remarques*, Streicher, p. 578. Quintilian, *I. O.*, Book VIII, also used the term *perspicuitas*.

. . . et . . . *le ie ne sçay quoy, où le nombre, la briefueté et la naïfueté de l'expression*, ont encore beaucoup de part."[16]

Indeed, under the fateful term of *netteté* Vaugelas boldly subsumes both major aspects of composition. In a passage marked by F. Brunot as one of the "most unjust" in his *Remarques*,[17] Vaugelas maintained that Malherbe had had little or no part in the movement toward the reform of the sentence, *la perfection de la phrase*, including both major aspects of composition—sentence structure and word order:

> Vn des plus celebres Autheurs de nostre temps que l'on consultoit comme l'Oracle de la pureté du language, et qui sans doute y a extremement contribué, n'a pourtant iamais connu la NETTETÉ DU STILE, soit en la SITUATION DES PAROLES, soit en la FORME et en la MESURE des PERIODES, pechant d'ordinaire en toutes ces parties, et ne pouuant seulement comprendre ce que c'estoit que d'auoir le STILE FORMÉ, qui en effet n'est autre chose que de bien arranger ses paroles, et de bien former et lier ses periodes. Sans doute cela luy venoit de ce qu'il n'estoit né qu'à exceller dans la Poësie, et de ce tour incomparable de vers, qui pour auoir fait tort à sa prose, ne laisseront pas de le rendre immortel.[18]

And he went on to offer a long list of examples of Malherbe's objectionable *transpositions* (ed. Chassang, II, 361-364).

However that might be, the new code to which Vaugelas adhered demanded a "constructed" (*construite*) type of sentence, specifically of the periodic variety. This was to be more than a strict application of grammatical correctness. Even an anacoluthon can be felicitous, if it is

---

[16] *Remarques*, Streicher 593. See, also, the ed. by A. Chassang (2 vols., Versailles-Paris, 1880), II, p. 372.

[17] Brunot, *H.L.F.*, tome III, 2e partie, p. 688.

[18] *Remarques*, Streicher, 579; Chassang, II, 361 (emphases mine). See also, for the contrastive definitions of *pureté* and *netteté*, ed. Chassang, II, 567: "La pureté du langage et du style consiste aux mots, aux phrases, aux particules et en la syntaxe. Et la netteté ne regarde que l'arrangement, la structure ou la situation des mots et tout ce qui contribue à la clarté de l'expression." Since clarity is the opposite of both obscurity and a confusing diffuseness, *netteté* forbids both opposite excesses in the length of the periods. In particular, "*La longueur des periodes* est encore fort ennemie de la netteté du stile. I'entens celles qui suffoquent par leur grandeur excessiue ceux qui les prononcent, comme parle Denis d'Halicarnasse, . . . surtout si elles sont embarrassées et qu'elles n'ayent pas des reposoirs, comme en ont celles de ces deux grands Maistres de nostre langue, Amyot et Coëffeteau; Il seroit importun et superflu d'en donner des exemples, qui ne sont que trop frequens dans nos mauuais Escriuains. *Les longues et frequentes parentheses* y sont contraires aussi." Streicher 592; Chassang, II, 371-372. In his *Nouvelles Remarques* Vaugelas again criticized Malherbe for an overlong period (Chassang, II, 381-382).

functional, whereas Malherbe could see in that nothing but a flaw, a phrase "sans construction."[19] As far as he is concerned Vaugelas shows no taste for the *style coupé*. On the contrary, in the characteristic vein of his time, he tends to favor the heaping of ligatures with a horror for leaving any syntactical or logical transition unexplicit, and with the prejudice of increasing the periodic tightness. The results are those famous sentences top-heavy with *qui*'s and *que*'s, which are characteristic of the "Louis XIII style"; by becoming redundant and rambling, they sin against true periodicity by excess. In analyzing phrases Vaugelas approves of such relatives and conjunctives freely and abundantly distributed: he even tends to add some *qui* or *que* of his own for clarity's sake.[20]

It was Lanson who shrewdly called attention to this *style Louis XIII,* which witnessed for the French sentence the highest degree of complication.[21] The abuse of conjunctions and relatives, *qui, quoique, si,* and especially *que,* weights down those prolonged and suspended sentences in which belligerent characters vigorously attempt to canvass their strong emotions within the logical frame of a rigorous thought.

Les mots sont serrés dans le cadre logique que construisent les relatifs, conjonctions et participes présents, comme la pierre de taille encadre la brique dans les hôtels de la Place Royale. On sent un esprit robuste qui se contraint à une discipline nouvelle, à une marche posée et régulière: il se crée une forme un peu lourde, claire et régulière.

A form, to sum up, which is ample and long-winded—more precisely, long-tailed, as Lanson put it.[22]

It fell to Louis XIV's generation to bring that opulence under control. And it fell to Balzac to teach his public *la juste mesure des périodes,* in Boileau's words. Both Vaugelas' 'rambling' and Balzac's 'tight' brands of periodicity evolved under the aegis of an intended imitation of Latin movement, methodically approached in both cases even though with different results.

---

[19] Malherbe, *Commentaire sur Desportes,* in Malherbe, *Œuvres complètes,* ed. Lud. Lalanne (Paris, 1862, 4 tomes), IV, p. 269. This t. IV contains Malherbe's *Commentaire sur Desportes,* where one finds the example in question. Cf. Ferdinand Brunot, *La Doctrine de Malherbe* (Paris, 1891), pp. 507-508. Pp. 495-516 deal with Malherbe's ideas on word order and sentence structure.

[20] Cf. Brunot, III, 2, p. 699. Also, on the sentence of Vaugelas, Charles Bruneau, *Petite Histoire,* I (1955), pp. 167-169.

[21] Gustave Lanson, *L'Art de la prose* (Paris, 1908), pp. 56 ff., esp. 65.

[22] Ibid.

The process of acclimatization of rhetoric to the needs of the French language had gotten under way under the official aegis of Louis XIII and Richelieu, and through the Academy founded in 1635. Indeed, Richelieu opined that the tasks of the Academy could not start any better than by " the noblest of all arts, viz. eloquence." [23] After the first, somewhat timid attempts such as the *Tableau de l'éloquence françoise* by Charles Vialart de Saint–Paul (1632, 1633², both now rare, followed by the more often mentioned ed. *Tableau de la rhétorique françoise,* 1657) and Fr. de La Mothe Le Vayer's *La Rhétorique du Prince* (Paris, 1651; not to mention his *Considérations sur l'éloquence,* 1638), the treatises began to roll off the presses in quick succession, from *La Rhétorique françoise* by René Bary (1659; limited first ed. 1653?) [24] on to those of N. de Hauteville and G. Guéret (both 1666), Jean de la Sourdière sieur de Richesource and François Hédelin abbé d'Aubignac (both 1668), Michel-Antoine sieur Le Gras (1671), Bernard Lamy (1675), and J. Carel de Sainte-Garde (1676).

I have pointed out above that only in recent years has this technical production begun to be surveyed in detail and in a comprehensive manner, as in the study by H. Davidson. In turn, its pervasive impact on the major writers of the century, obvious though it should have been to any attentive student of the cultural background of the time, is now being carefully analyzed, often for the first time, as by Roger Lathuillère for the *précieux,* Patricia Topliss for Pascal, Peter France for Racine. Similarly, Malherbe's dependence on Stoic ideas even in his linguistic theory is the object of a recent study by Manfred Lentzen.[25]

[23] Cf. Pellisson's vol. I, p. 41 of Pellisson and d'Olivet, *Histoire de l'Académie française* (Paris, 1743³).

[24] R. Bary, *La Rhétorique françoise . . . où l'on trouve de nouveaux exemples sur les passions et sur les figures* (Paris, P. le Petit, 1653; nouvelle éd. augmentée, Paris, Le Petit, 1659); *La Rhét. fr., où pour principale augmentation l'on trouve les secrets de notre langue* (Paris, 1665; Amsterdam, 1669; nouv. éd. Paris, 1673; Lyon, 1676 . . .). The first ed. is very rare and variously dated at 1653 or 1655. Saint-Paul's 1657 ed. is often mentioned by modern historians but unavailable in the Bibl. Nat. of Paris, Br. Mus., or Libr. of Congress.

[25] Cf. H. Davidson, op. cit.; M. Lentzen, " Malherbes aüsseres und inneres Verhältnis zur stoischen Philosophie," *Die Neueren Sprachen,* LXVI, 2–XVI N. F. (1967), 66-84; R. Lathuillère, *La Préciosité. Étude historique et linguistique.* Tome I: *Position du Problème. Les Origines* (Geneva, 1966); P. France, *Racine's Rhetoric* (Oxford, 1965); P. Topliss, *The Rhetoric of Pascal. A Study of his Art of Persuasion in the ' Provinciales ' and the ' Pensées '* (Leicester U. Press, 1966). It is to be hoped that studies such as these will tend to correct the traditional disre-

Indeed, the triumph of the art was so complete that, despite its central insistence on correctness and clarity (the grammatical phase within the rhetorical system), Vaugelas' ' grammar ' was, all told, rhetorically oriented. But Descartes' followers were anxious to make their voice heard. Their moment came with the *Logique* of Port-Royal (1662, 1664²). Here Arnauld, in his quiet but formidable manner, replaced the grammatical and rhetorical slant with the logical in all judgments of style. Even in the preceding *Grammaire générale et raisonnée* (1660) [26] the parts of speech were analyzed and defined by reference to mental acts which are, as we find out later in the Logic, none other than "conception" and "judgment." The grammar of Port-Royal leads to logic and not to rhetoric as in the ancient plan. Nor did Arnauld and his collaborator Nicole see any need for adding an art of expression, the effect of which was simply, in their view, to encourage false and hyperbolic thoughts and forced figures.[27]

The debt toward Scaliger and Sánchez, the authoritative upholders of a rational method of linguistic analysis, was gratefully acknowledged by the masters of Port-Royal as early as in their first important scholastic manual, Lancelot's *Méthode . . . latine* (see the Preface to the 5th ed., 1656). The impact of the Port-Royal *Grammar* was also enormous, even though it appeared the very year when the Petites Écoles, for which it was composed, were closed down. It marked the triumph of the new ' objective ' principle, *la raison,* against the tyranny of usage, already under attack as inconclusive, contradictory, subjective.

Port-Royal's logical exclusivism, however, needs qualification. For it was the result, not of inability to perceive the inherent complexity and the irrational elements in mental and linguistic functions, but of a conscious struggle toward a selective and hierarchic view of all the factors involved

gard implicit in this statement by Brunot (*H. L. F.,* IV, 2, p. 1093): "On était en droit de croire aussi que l'Académie, fidèle à ses statuts, donnerait la rhétorique, à laquelle Fénelon la conviait encore à travailler. Il n'en fut rien. L'art fut abandonné à des grimauds, qu'on ne peut en aucune façon considérer comme les créateurs de la phrase française. Le rôle d'un Bary n'est nullement comparable à celui d'un Bouhours, leur authorité n'a jamais été semblable." At any rate, grammarians were about to claim equal rights with rhetoricians over the French sentence.

[26] See A. Arnauld and Claude Lancelot's *Grammaire générale et raisonnée* now critically reproduced in facsimile from the 3ᵈ ed., 1676, by Brekle (Stuttgart, 1966, 2 vols.), and from the 1660 ed. in the Scolar Press series (Menston, Eng., 1967).

[27] See *Logique,* 2ᵈ ed. (1664), p. 28. I shall quote from this 2ᵈ ed., which also contained, at its beginning, two important *Discours.*

in the thinking process. It was a rigorous attempt to assign due priorities, and putting first things first meant to put reason on the throne. Nicole himself had authored as early as 1659 a *Traité de la beauté des ouvrages d'esprit* translated from Latin: it was, indeed, a sort of ' art of expression ' where he discovered, under the sovereign principle of *nature*, what later came to be called the *langage affectif*, as against the *langage raisonné* of ancient rhetoric. This language of the emotions reappeared in the *Logique* (I, xiv) as the *sens accessoire*, an added dimension to the meaning of words beyond their objective and literal *signification*: this happens when supplementary ideas are *excitées* by the word in its vivid, total reality. Even while this view of mental functions inserted the pathos of expressive rhetoric directly into the body of logical analysis, it also amounted to an upsetting of the traditional rhetoric of *ornatus*. In this sense the *Logique* left its mark in the successive developments of formal rhetoric, since in dealing with "natural rhetoric" the Oratorian Father Bernard Lamy (who borrowed almost everything from Port-Royal) took up again and elaborated on the principle of *idées accessoires*.[28]

The complex attitude of the Port-Royal theorists vis-à-vis the traditional categories of rhetoric must be understood within their Cartesian distrust, not only of rhetoric itself, but even of formal dialectic, since they viewed the latter as a ' theoretical rhetoric ' and the former as a ' practical dialectic.' This distrust centered on the critique of the method of commonplaces or topics, regarded as a mental aberration, which hindered and corrupted the operations of our natural powers by supplying ready-made sets of arguments to be adapted to any given question. The habit of reasoning through commonplaces thus blunted the need to evolve our arguments directly out of the concrete, circumstantial nature of the question at hand and, ultimately, discouraged our willingness to concentrate on accurate thought.[29] This radical change of approach could go so

[28] Lamy, *L'art de parler* (Paris, Du Puis, 1701[4], last and most complete edition): see I, v; II, i. Cf. A. François, *Histoire de la langue française cultivée,* vol. I (Geneva, 1959), 326-328; Sainte-Beuve, *Port-Royal,* Livre IV; Istvan Söter, *La doctrine stylistique des Rhétoriques du XVIIe siècle* (Budapest, 1937); A. François, "Précurseurs français de la grammaire affective," *Mélanges de linguistique offerts à Charles Bally* (Geneva, 1939), 369-377.
[29] *Logique*, pp. 291-296. "L'esprit s'accoutume à cette facilité, et ne fait plus l'effort pour trouver les raisons propres, particulières et naturelles, qui ne se découvrent que dans la considération attentive de son sujet" (p. 295). The art of finding encourages a readiness "à discourir de tout à perte de vue" (p. 296). Mark the title of ch. xvi of Part 3 (*Du Raisonnement*): "Des lieux ou de la méthode

far as to affect the whole notion of mimesis of the real. Just as the topics, hence the whole of "invention," were discredited in the eyes of these authors, they also cut out, "in everything except sacred oratory, most of the third link in the rhetorical chain of invention, arrangement, and elocution." [30] The condemnation of the established approach to elocution as *ornatus* was unequivocal. Ornate language and expecially the copious eloquent style which Cicero called *abundantem sonantibus verbis uberibusque sententiis* tend to conceal falsities (*Logique*, p. 358). We must be persuaded of the "excellente règle, qu'il n'y a rien de beau, que ce qui est vrai: ce qui retrancherait des discours une infinité de vains ornements et de pensées fausses" (*Logique*, 360). Points, rhyme, verbal jingles are all sources of error, just like the pagan allusions the Ciceronians regarded as *de rigueur* for correct and elegant Latinity. The Port-Royalists thus echo Erasmus (in the famous passage of his *Ciceronianus*) when they ridicule Cardinal Bembo for announcing that a pope had been elected *deorum immortalium beneficiis*, 'with the favors of the immortal gods.' [31]

Yet, the road to the rationalism of Classicism and Enlightenment was long and far from straight.[32] Vaugelas, for one, *distrusted* reason. A consistent empiricist, he would place reason last in the sequence of criteria ruling over the literary language. The normal order of authority would go for him from *bon usage,* supreme ruler, through the example of the writers (like the *auctores* of medieval and Renaissance memory), down to *raison.* But he could disregard this order if the case required it: *l'usage de toute la cour,* where one said *Je va,* contradicted the authority of the writers and the learned, who say *Je vais, tu vas, il va.* If this, in turn, also contradicts *la raison,* that is the criterion of analogy, it shall yet stand.[33] He could go as far as giving a perverse twist to his preferences by his way of putting the problem; or so he struck the sensitive logicians of

de trouver des arguments. Combien cette méthode est de peu d'usage" (p. 290). Cf. Davidson, op. cit., esp. pp. 57-69. But see the Foreword and the Introduction to the recent English trans., A. Arnauld, *The Art of Thinking* (1964), where the Port-Royal *Logic* is praised for the reintroduction of the topical tradition in formal logic in a different sense than the above.

[30] Davidson, p. 62. Davidson does not mention Ramus, but it is with him that lies the main historical responsibility for this trend.

[31] Davidson, p. 78.

[32] On the linguistic significance of Arnauld's *Logic* see H. E. Brekle, "Semiotik und linguistische Semantik in Port-Royal," *Indog. Forsch.,* 69 (1964), 103-121.

[33] Cf. François, *H. L. F. cultivée,* pp. 321-324.

Port-Royal, who in the *Grammaire* of 1660 took offense at his holding
the view that "les façons de parler sont d'autant plus belles qu'elles sont
contraires à la grammaire, c'est-à-dire à la raison." [34]

No such contradictions were conceivable for the good *solitaires* of Port-
Royal. The human mind, God's noblest work, could not be thought to
operate so awkwardly. The result was, at least on principle, a complete
denial of the method sponsored by Vaugelas. The rigor of logic was
called in to replace the uncontrollable fancies of the courtiers, and usage
was dethroned. Yet paradoxically enough, one could be disappointed in
the expectation that this method of reducing all linguistic phenomena to
reasonable ends might have actually balanced the more radical consequences of the doctrine of absolute usage based on the sometimes whimsi-
cal fashions of the court. It is not, or not yet, in the *Grammaire générale*
that one could find practical examples of defense of reasonableness
against habits sanctioned by Vaugelas. [35]

This preamble on the broader theoretical foundations leads us to understand the Jansenists' disinclination to overstress the value of sentence
structure, as of any sort of 'ornamentation.' This was part of their vigorous reaction against the formalistic concerns of the time, which dated at
least as far back as the generation of Vaugelas. Who else than Vaugelas
had pointed out such formalism when, without necessarily approving of it,
he gave it apparently as a *de facto* situation: "On appelle . . . un prédicateur éloquent lorsque ses périodes sont bien justes, et qu'il ne dit
point de mauvais mots; et sur ce fondement M. de Vaugelas dit en un
endroit qu'un mauvais mot fait plus de tort à un prédicateur ou un avocat
qu'un mauvais raisonnement." [36]

Even if only indirectly, this attitude typically contributed to the disso-
lution of the periodic style, both in its 'Ciceronian' or 'Isocratic' forms
and in the baroque forms of the *pointes* as well. The Jesuits (and,
signally, their spokesman, Father Bouhours) had an easy time mocking
the Port-Royalists for their rambling periods. Their nonchalance in this
regard reflected an interest in other virtues than periodicity, for they prized
"une manière d'écrire simple, naturelle et judicieuse" (*Logique*, pp. 28-
29), and, furthermore, preciseness: "Il est vrai que cette exactitude rend

[34] François, op. cit., p. 325.
[35] Cf. F. Brunot, *H. L. F.*, t. IV: La langue classique (1660-1715), 1ère partie
(Paris, 1913), p. 58.
[36] *Logique*, p. 556, cited by Davidson, p. 76.

le style plus sec et moins pompeux; mais elle le rend aussi plus vif,
plus sérieux, plus clair, et plus digne d'un honnête homme: l'impression
en est bien plus forte, et bien plus durable; au lieu que celle qui naît
simplement de ces périodes si ajustées, est tellement superficielle, qu'elle
s'évanouit presque aussitôt qu'on les a entendues" (*Logique*, 360).

One might conclude that the movement which started out with anti-
Ciceronianism thus eventually came to fruition by dissolving rhetoric
itself from within. Logic filled the vacuum left in the rhetorical theory
of composition and *ornatus*. The shift of emphasis from rhetoric to logic
displaced—in spite of Ramus' and Port-Royal's assimilation, hence rescue,
of dialectical rhetoric within logic itself—the traditionally rhetorical treatment of rhythm and harmony (euphony), as well as of the phrase and
the period as part of general stylistic composition. These areas could thus
fall, for the first time, into the discipline of GRAMMAR seen in a logical
context.

On the other hand, together with this technical shift went a broad
change of aesthetic sensibility which deeply affected the critical attitudes
toward literary values. Dionysius of Halicarnassus (*De comp. verb.* xxv-
xxvi) had suggested that the best prose is that which resembles poetry
though not entirely in meter, and the best poetry is that which resembles
beautiful prose. Much as the attitudes of the age of Fontenelle may
remind us of that ancient dictum, there remains the difference that
Dionysius' way of putting the matter placed the emphasis on poetic qualities, while the new rationalism (within both Classicism and Enlightenment) was clearly oriented away from poetry toward a 'prosaic' *forma
mentis*. For Aristotle, let us recall, the primary virtue of elocution was
clearness. But clearness is not everything; style must have distinction.
Only thus does it become artistic. Clearness is therefore the more elementary level of virtue, the 'grammatical'—together with the even more rudimentary virtues of correctness. In their moving away from lyricism toward
prosaic excellence the eighteenth-century grammarians-rhetoricians-critics
placed clearness, correctness, and preciseness (*le mot juste*) on such a high
pedestal that these tended to incorporate and subsume all other possible
qualities of style. The French classicists and rationalists fastened on
them with enthusiastic exclusiveness. True enough, 'Longinus' exerted a
powerful influence through Boileau, especially in France and England,
through the eighteenth century, and can be said to have laid the foundations of modern, " individualizing " literary criticism by virtue of his appeal
to the enthusiastic effect produced by the great artist through his unique,

personal, super-human gifts. Nevertheless, when Boileau discovered 'Longinus,' he could not but concentrate his attention on those chapters which condemned bad taste in matters of rhetorical detail. Thus again Pope, who also pondered Boileau's *Réflexions* on 'Longinus,' was all for correctness.[37]

The changed viewpoint under the direct impact of the Port-Royal manuals invaded both rhetorical and grammatical treatises: suffice it to mention the new rhetoric by Bernard Lamy and the grammatical works by L. Mauger, Grimarest, Regnier-Desmarais, and Buffier.[38]

Lamy boldly undertook to move Arnauld's theoretical logic toward practical logic, from principle to rule: " Les langues ne se polissent que lorsqu'on commence à raisonner, qu'on bannit du langage les expressions qu'un usage corrompu y a introduites, qui ne s'apperçoivent que par des gens sçavants, et par une connoissance exacte de l'Art que nous traitons " (*Rhétorique*, 1688[3], pp. 73-74).

It was the beginning of the new thrust toward practical metaphysics and the discarding of the empirical method for the deductive one. As Brunot put it, " bientôt toutes les recherches tourneront de l'observation à la speculation philosophique déductive. L'école historique de Ménage et de Du Cange, vaincue, cédera à l'école rationaliste." Accordingly, his assessment of eighteenth-century philosophical grammar was negative:

[37] Cf. Scaglione, "Boileau come fulcro . . ." and "La Responsabilità di Boileau . . ." in *Convivium* (1950, 1952) and, briefly, J. A. K. Thomson, *Classical Influences on English Prose* (1956; New York, 1962), p. 273 of 1962 ed.

[38] *La Rhétorique ou l'art de parler* par le R. P. Bernard Lamy (Paris, 1675, 1676, 1681, 1688[3]. . . , 1701[4]); Laurent Mauger, *Nouvelle Grammaire françoise* . . . (Rouen, J. Besongne, 1705); Jean-Léonor Le Gallois sieur de Grimarest, *Commerce de lettres curieuses et savantes* (Paris, 1700); Id., *Discours sur l'usage dans la langue françoise*, bound together with, and after, his *Traité sur le commerce des lettres et sur le cérémonial* (Paris, J. Estienne, 1708); Id., *Traité sur la manière d'écrire des lettres et sur le cérémonial, avec un Discours sur ce qu'on appelle usage dans la langue françoise* (Paris, J. Estienne, 1709); Id., *Éclaircissemens sur les principes de la langue françoise* (Paris, Flor. Delaulne, 1712); François-Séraphin Regnier-Desmarais, Secrét. perpétuel de l'Acad. fr., *Traité de la grammaire françoise* (Paris, 1705, 1706[2], . . . 1760[7]); Claude Buffier, *Grammaire françoise sur un plan nouveau* (Paris, N. Le Clerc, 1709); Id., *Suite de la Grammaire françoise sur un plan nouveau, ou traité philosophique et pratique d'éloquence* (Paris, N. Le Clerc, 1728, 1732).

The title given above for the work of the Oratorian father Lamy appeared only with the third ed. (1688). The work had previously been published without name of the author and under the title *De l'art de parler*, which caused the three English editions (*Art of Speaking*, 1676, 1696, 1708) to be advertised as the "Port-Royal Rhetoric." See Howell, *Logic and Rhetoric in England*, pp. 378-382.

"Ce cartésianisme linguistique a été certainement une cause de retard pour le développement de la science." [39] He went even farther:

Avec Vaugelas et les siens la fantaisie grammaticale, ne dépendant que de l'usage, restait sujette au changement. Bientôt on la raisonnera, et sans en rien retrancher là où elle paraîtra contraire à la raison, on la fondera en raison partout où on le pourra, par des subtilités plus ou moins spécieuses; de sorte que l'instrument qui eût pu arracher la langue à de sottes tyrannies, manié par l'école grammatico-philosophique, servira dans le siècle qui suivra à l'asservir tout à fait.[40]

This rather typical critique rests chiefly on matters of vocabulary, morphology, and traditional syntax. In the area of composition, however, on both sentence structure and word order, 'reason' will turn out to be a stimulating and creative factor by imposing new standards and new emphases (*style coupé, ordre naturel*). True enough, the new taste and the 'logical' theoretical postulates will go hand in hand toward a radical, far-reaching reform of attitudes and modes of expression. Furthermore, on the positive side of the ledger, the Port-Royal grammar must be credited with a basic new slant in the understanding of the mechanism of sentences. Because of its distinctly 'scientific' nature, it is not the place here to expand at length on this remarkable contribution, which was due to an evident Cartesian background. Transformational and other linguists have recently focussed on it with a considerable amount of attention. Chomsky has rediscovered in the *Grammaire générale* the principles underlying the generative grammarians' distinction between deep structure and surface structure, as analyzed by Arnauld through his example *Dieu invisible a créé le monde visible,* a linguistic transformation from the 'original' thought *Dieu qui est invisible a créé le monde qui est visible,* a complex of logical judgments.[41]

Meanwhile, the new feeling for the unity of the sentence makes headway. If one could still find anacolutha in the *Princesse de Clèves* ("de

[39] Brunot, *H.L.F.*, IV, 1, p. 58.
[40] Ibid., p. 59.
[41] Cf. Chomsky, *Cart. Ling.*, esp. pp. 33-42: see *Gr. gén.*, pp. 68-69. Also cf. Chomsky, "De quelques constantes de la théorie linguistique," in *Problèmes du Langage* (Paris, 1966), pp. 14-21, on the Port-Royal *Grammar* viewed from the vantage point of modern generative grammar. Karl D. Uitti, *Linguistics and Literary Theory* (Englewood Cliffs, 1969), pp. 62-92, proposes an original interpretation of French linguistic speculation from 1500 to 1800. See also, for a reëlaboration of some points made in *Cart. Ling.*, Chomsky's *Language and Mind* (New York, 1968), ch. i, pp. 1-20.

vous dire des détails qui me font honte à moi-même de les avoir re-
marqués "),[42] soon such lack of logical coherence between the parts will
no longer be tolerated. The sensitivity of the critics will go so far as to
rule out even a harmless change of subject as offensive to this need for
logical continuity: Father Bouhours feels uneasy about the following
sentence in Port-Royal's translation of *L'Imitation de Jésus-Christ*: "Je
me trouve assiégé d'une foule de pensées et de grandes frayeurs se sont
élevées en moi." [43] Along somewhat similar lines, Jobard hypercritically
censures "Alexandre vainquit Darius, et son armée fit un prodigieux
butin," on the ground that the conjunction *et* seems to link *Darius* and
armée as two accusatives! [44] This even in spite of the punctuation. Again,
Richesource blames the phrase "ils y camperent . . . et on leur envoya"
because the conjunction links two predicates with different accidence. "La
nécessité de cette rectification," the critic elaborates, "est marquée par la
copulative, *et*, dont l'office est de ne joindre jamais que des choses sem-
blables, soit noms, soit verbes. . . ." [45] With this exaggerated sense of
logic in conjunctives, the concern for unity risks turning into an obsession.

All these matters are made to fall under the categories of *netteté,
clarté, simplicité*. Another interesting application of these same criteria
affects the use of pleonasms. The 'Asiatic' taste had, within the copiousness of the eloquent or grand style, expressly justified the introduction
of synonymous and redundant elements into the phrase as fill-ins required
to achieve roundness and rhythm. The apologist of La Bruyère could
still advance the claim that "la rondeur de la période et la propreté du
discours demandent quelque fois ces additions; elles sont nécessaires dés

[42] *Œuvres de Madame de La Fayette*, ed. Robert Lejeune, II (Paris, 1928), 235.
[43] Cf. Th. Rosset, "Le P. B. critique de la langue des écrivains jansénistes,"
Annales de l'Univ. de Grenoble, XX (Paris-Grenoble, 1908), 55-125; "Le P. B.
continuateur de Vaugelas," ibid., 193-284; "Le P. B. théoricien du style classique,"
ibid., 401-497. See p. 266 for passage quoted. The critique was in Bouhours' *Doutes
sur la langue françoise* (Paris, 1674), p. 208.
[44] Jean-Baptiste Jobard, *Exercices de l'esprit* (Paris, 1675), p. 200.
[45] Jean de la Sourdière, sieur de Richesource, *La Relation de la Prise de Fribourg
du Bureau des Gazettes*, Mise en Partition selon les regles de la Critique par . . . Sr.
de Riche-Source (Paris, 1677), pp. 82-83. For the preceding examples, see Brunot,
IV, 2, pp. 1095-1097. Further on (p. 1112) Brunot remarks that " l'analyse d'Andry
l'a mené fort loin dans l'examen du role des propositions relatives, et que peu de
théories montrent mieux l'union qui était en train de se faire entre la grammaire et
la logique." Cf. [Andry de Boisregard,] *Réflexions sur l'usage présent de la langue
françoise* (Paris, 1689), 208-209, etc.

qu'elles contribuent à la grace d'une élocution nombreuse." [46] But that
defense sounded unconvincing, for the taste of the public was no longer
inclined to accept this approach, however sanctioned by a long tradition.
Words not strictly required by a direct, sober, logically coherent expression
of the subject matter were now rejected as ' useless words.' [47] The new
rationalistic framework supersedes the hedonistic sensualism of old.
Writers become accustomed to the idea that everything has its correct
way to be expressed, and one only, *une expression unique* (La Bruyère
I, 145)—which excludes variation and choice. This crystallization of
expression has a linguistic (grammatical) as well as a stylistic (rhetorical)
side. On the one hand, the vocabulary has firmed up and become fixed
in its definitions, so that hesitation and groping are no longer tolerable:
" On pouvait s'exprimer d'un coup, et représenter d'un trait sur. L'accumulation de touches différentes n'est plus un signe de richesse, comme
au temps de Rabelais ou d'Estienne, mais une marque de faiblesse, l'essai
d'un apprenti qui tâtonne." [48] On the other hand, the rejection of frills
and semantically unjustified variants or fill-ins moves hand in hand with
the assertion of plain style, which demanded just that.

Another difficulty was presented by ellipsis, of which Sánchez had
made so much as his basic law to explain the derivation and departure
of actual language from a hypothetic, original, rational speech. The
desideratum of the rationalists was now to divest the language of its ano-
malous figures and bring it back, as much as possible, to a state of grammatical purity. This need for regularity and clarity was bound to come
into conflict with the ideal of brevity and sobriety; these latter were, all
in all, rather readily sacrificed. Some ellipses could, of course, be tolerated,
but they were more and more looked upon as ' figures,' to be, like all
figures, distrusted. This assimilation of rhetorical modes into grammatical
procedures implies reaction against rhetoric, sometimes in the name of
stylistic plainness and directness. The figures were tendentially eliminated
from prose—and sharply reduced even in verse, since the best poetry was,
after Fontenelle, one that looks like prose. The ancient enemy of the Stoic
ideal of the laconic style, marked by ellipsis and curtness, was the need

[46] *Apologie de M. de la Bruyère ou Réponse à la Critique des Caractères de Théophraste* [par Brillon] (Paris, 1701), p. 13.
[47] Cf. Brunot, IV, 2, pp. 1119-1122.
[48] Brunot, IV, 2, p. 1124. To realize the significance of this change of attitudes it will suffice to recall D. Alonso's examples of Don Quijote's way of rounding out his periods through a methodic use of pleonasms (see above, Ch. IV, A, p. 184).

for *concinnitas* and roundness. The new enemy was now grammatico-
logical regularity. The new standards were simplicity, directness, faithfulness to truth and fact.

Meanwhile, the French sentence was undergoing profound changes.
One of the most revealing elements is the use of conjunctive particles.
The abuse of them which characterized the *style à la Louis XIII* could
reflect an effort toward a tighter, more 'logical' construction. But on a
less artistic level it could also be a sign of nonchalant neglectfulness.
Brunot has remarked that Saint-Simon "use des conjonctions comme
un homme du peuple"; "sans souci du rapport logique, il se contente
d'établir un lien quelconque." Here is an example: "Plus de dix ans
avant qu'il fut maréchal de France, et que [= quand] sa fortune n'étoit
pas commencée" (XVIII, 205).[49] But note the difference when the
intuitive use of conjunctions is introduced through the variety of incipient
style coupé characteristic of libertine literature: Bussy-Rabutin writes:
"Quand tout le monde les aurait voulu servir, ils auraient tout detruit par
leur imprudence, et tout le monde leur voulait nuire" (*et = alors que,
au contraire*).[50] As we shall see, such theorists as Le Gras, Bary, and
Grimarest underline the new awareness of the right value of conjunctions,
to be used sparingly and functionally.

The impact of the plain style even on the classic phrase of Louis
XIV's age is evident in such a paradigmatic master of narrative libertine prose as Bussy-Rabutin, if only we heed Lanson's persuasive assessment of his merits: "La phrase se compose parfois d'une proposition,

---

[49] Brunot uses the Boislisle ed. of St.-Simon's *Œuvres* (Paris, 1880 . . .). Cf. F.
Brunot, *H.L.F.*, t. IV, 2e ptie (1660-1715) (Paris, 1924), p. 1078. Livre VI in
this vol. deals with the "syntaxe" of the Classic period, and ch. xxxi with "Les
Conjonctions," ch. xxxiii with "La Phrase."

[50] Bussy-Rabutin, *Histoire amoureuse des Gaules* (Liège, 1665), "Histoire
d'Ardélise" (p. 35 of J. Orieux ed., Paris, 1966). This is not to imply that Bussy-
Rabutin had consistently overcome the awkwardness of the *phrase à la Louis XIII*,
witness the following: "Angélie . . . fut fort embarrassée de la manière dont on
venait de traiter Baurin *qu'*elle voyait bien qu'il n'en pouvait soupçonner d'autres
qu'elle." "Toute mon étude est à présent de me conduire de façon que . . . je
demeure toute ma vie persuadée de l'affront que l'on m'a fait qui me touche si
sensiblement qu'il m'est impossible de ne m'en point ressentir." *Hist. amour.*, "Hist.
d'Angélie," pp. 107 and 110. *Quandoque bonus dormitat Homerus*. . . . The
achievement of clarity and *netteté* was not without frequent relapses, and one can
see that Lanson's generalization (quoted below) on this writer's syntactic linearity
deserves some qualification. See, also, Bussy-Rabutin, *Hist. amour. des Gaules*,
ed. A. Adam (Paris, 1967). For the complex history of the text see Christian
Garaud, "Problèmes concernant la composition de l'*H. A. des G.*," *Romance Notes*,
XI (1969), 121-126.

souvent de deux, dont l'une est subordonnée; on va rarement au delà de trois, à moins que ce ne soit par coordination, en soudant au moyen d'un *et* des phrases d'ailleurs parfaitement distinctes." [51]

While the new compositional patterns are being hatched, the more traditional forms still remain closer to the hearts of the classicists, at least on the higher levels of 'serious' literature. According to Lanson, "Le suprême effort de l'art de la prose, c'est la création de la grande phrase oratoire, plus sonore que colorée, phrase d'apparat, non de combat, dérivé un peu froid de la péroraison cicéronienne." [52] In the way of exemplification Lanson admiringly cited a passage from Bossuet's *Sermon sur l'unité de l'Église*. In his judgment that sentence marked the most astonishing effort of Bossuet's oratorical genius, without parallel in the French language.[53] But the Abbé Quillacq gave that same sentence as an example of *période libre*:[54] even in the most exceptional master of French oratory the true type of classical periodicity could not be duplicated, since the different spirit of the language did not allow it. Furthermore, even though Bossuet has gained the first place among the preachers of his century, we must be aware that his 'Isocratean' position made him rather isolated or, at least, placed him at the opposite end from the taste of many a critic. In his firm stance as the harshest opponent of Isocrates and his school, Fénelon was conscious that his condemnation invested, last and yet first, the great Bossuet.[55]

To turn now to the more specific comments on sentence structure as

---

[51] Lanson, *L'Art de la prose*, pp. 90-91.

[52] Lanson, op. cit., p. 94. Brunot, IV, 2, p. 1195 (also p. 1178), agreed with this analysis of the classic age.

[53] Lanson, *Bossuet* (Paris, 1891, 1894³), p. 91. On the style of the classic masters see the precious analyses in Ch. Bruneau, *Petite histoire de la langue française*, vol. I (Paris, 1955), pp. 178-240. Bruneau points out that Bossuet could also produce *coupé* sentences, of which he gives examples (p. 203). On the other hand, he cites (ibid.) a shrewd passage in which " Valéry, jugeant Bossuet, s'est amusé à fabriquer une phrase à la Bossuet ":
Il spécule sur l'attente qu'il crée, tandis que les modernes spéculent sur la surprise. Il part puissamment du silence, anime peu à peu, enfle, élève, organise sa phrase, qui parfois s'édifie en voûte, se soutient de propositions latérales, distribuées a merveille autour de l'instant, se déclare et repousse ses incidentes qu'elle surmonte pour toucher enfin à sa clé, et redescendre après des prodiges de subordination et d'équilibre jusqu'au terme certain et à la résolution complète de ses forces.

[54] J.-A. Quillacq, *La Langue et la syntaxe de Bossuet* (Tours, 1903), p. 782.

[55] See Fénelon, *Dialogues sur l'Éloquence* (1692), beginning of I and end of II. Cf. the interesting ch. on Fénelon and the French sentence in Marcel Cohen, *Grammaire et Style, 1450-1950* (Paris, 1954).

we encounter them in technical treatises, we shall first note how close
the rhetoricians remain to their tradition, at least on the surface. The
Rethorique (sic) *françoise* by Le Gras (Paris, 1671, 1674²), for one, still
echoes Quintilian's distinction of *ordo, iunctura, numerus* (IX, iv, 22),
which he renders as *ordre, liaison, nombre.* Order has to do typically with
gradation or climax, or priority in a sequence of ideas (e. g. day and night,
man and woman).⁵⁶ After the Greek ῥυθμός he speaks of *rime* meaning
rhythm and measure, and adds that this metrical discussion leads to a
short section on periods, since the oratorical period is composed of members
having some resemblance to verses. But this nomenclature and the frame
of reference it reflects was beginning to face the reality of new patterns
of sensibility.

We read in Le Gras that periods must be enclosed " dans un certain
tour où elles soient soûtenuës, jusques à ce que le sens soit achevé; et en
ce rencontre il faut user des liaisons qui servent à ce soûtien, et à partager
les périodes, afin de les racourcir, et empescher qu'elles ne donnent de
l'impatience à l'Auditeur par leur longueur." Examples of such *liaisons*
are *d'une part, d'autre part, de sorte que, ainsi que, au lieu que,* etc.⁵⁷
But we soon begin to hear about the art of economizing such ligatures:
it is one of the secrets of effective style. Bary gives a telling example where
the expression is tightened up and made more direct simply by dropping
the conjunction. " *Il a raison de blâmer en son fils la passion des dames,
parce qu'un sot ne s'en défait pas facilement. Il ne faloit point user du
mot de parce, le mot de sot, qui le suit, porte sa raison.*" ⁵⁸ At the threshold
of the eighteenth century Grimarest proclaims the principle that conjunctions must not be abused: valuable they are, but only when used
functionally.⁵⁹

The Latin sense of weight at the end has been replaced, in a general
way, by the 'logical' order which assigns the end-position to the least
important elements. But the old principle returns in a new form within
a strictly compositional framework through the rule against the *hors-*

---

⁵⁶ Le Gras, *Rethorique*, 1671 ed., pp. 225-229. Le Gras deals with matters of
composition on pp. 177-184 (*arrangements des paroles*, and esp. S → V, and adjective + noun) and 224-239 (sentence structure).

⁵⁷ Le Gras, *Rethorique* (1671), p. 232. On this and the following see also
Brunot, IV, 2, pp. 1145-1182, who cites from Le Gras' 2ᵈ ed.

⁵⁸ René Bary, *Les secrets de notre langue* (= *Rhétorique françoise*), cited by
Brunot, IV, 2, p. 1146 from the ed. Lyon, 1776, p. 85.

⁵⁹ Cf. J. Léonor Le Gallois, sieur de Grimarest, *Commerce de lettres curieuses
et savantes* (Paris, 1700).

d'œuvre which endangers the balance of the sentence: "We have an *hors-d'œuvre* every time any element of the phrase arrives a bit too late, when it is no longer expected as a necessary adjunct; every time the reader risks the temptation of stopping before the actual end." [60]

The Father of Saint-Paul had recalled, after the ancients, the four basic sentence lengths:

La periode simple, n'est autre chose qu'vne seule et simple proposition, qui n'est diuisée, ny par virgule, ny par deux points. La grande periode est celle qui a plus de quatre parties; la petite en a moins de quatre; et celle qui est appellée mediocre en a quatre precisement: et c'est elle que l'on appelle quarrée, par ce qu'elle est composée de quatre parties qui sont égales, ainsi que les quatre angles d'vn quarré.

And he went on analyzing the effect of masculine and feminine endings to these members: the former abound in the *grave* style, the latter in the *délicieux*, otherwise one should alternate them. Of course the square period is the most excellent, as Demetrius, Cicero, and Quintilian agreed. Saint–Paul's phrasing is echoed by R. Bary, not without irony for this sort of *rafinement*: "On dit que la grande période a cinq ou six parties, que la petite en a deux ou trois; et que la médiocre en a quatre." But as we approach the turn of the century, the taste for sustained complex sentences begins to suffer a decline. La Touche, *L'Art de bien parler françois* (1696), reports that

Les personnes qui entendent le mieux la langue, prétendent que les belles périodes ne doivent avoir que trois membres, et que le nombre des sylabes ne doit pas aller au-delà de soixante et dix, ou de soixante-quinze.

More drastic still, Buffier will reduce this optimum span to no more than 20-25 syllables for each *phrase*, so that the longest periods by the good authors have no more than 60-70 syllables distributed into three *phrases* or members. [61]

Nevertheless, at least on the abstract level, the *période tétragonale* or

----

[60] Brunot, IV, 2, p. 1148.
[61] Père Ch. de Saint-Paul, *Tableau de l'Éloquence françoise* (Paris, 1632 and 1633² eds.), 58-59. Brunot, III, 2, p. 695 cites part of this passage from the 1632 ed. The statements by Bary (*Rhét. fr.*, 1673 ed., I, p. 266), de La Touche (*L'Art . . .*, Amsterdam, 1747⁶, 2 tomes, I, Book III, ch. viii, p. 335), and Buffier (*Gr.*, 1709 ed., § 783, p. 343), are also quoted, but imprecisely, in Y. Le Hir, *Rhétorique et stylistique de la Pléiade au Parnasse* (Paris, 1960), pp. 92-94, who, e. g., makes Buffier assign 20-25 syllables to the whole sentence.

période à quatre membres remained the supreme ideal. Le Gras offered this example:

Si l'impudence avoit autant de crédit dans le Barreau, et parmy les Iugemens,// que l'audace a de pouvoir dans une campagne deserte, et dans les lieux solitaires;// Cecinna (sic) ne cederoit pas moins icy à l'impudence de Sextius Albutius,// qu'il a cedé à son audace, dans la violence qu'il luy a faite.[62]

The reader will promptly recognize this as a translation of Quintilian's example from Cicero's *Pro Caecina*:

Si, quantum in agro locisque desertis audacia potest,// tantum in foro atque iudiciis impudentia valeret,// non minus in causa cederet Aulus Caecina Sexti Aebutii impudentiae// quam tum in vi facienda cessit audaciae.

Only note that the members have been shifted around: the sequence baAB has been turned to abAB. In other words, the chiastic arrangement has been eliminated. This is a case of *période arrondie*, since the four members correspond so neatly that they can be turned around in more than one way; it is a variation of the plain *période carrée*, where the members hang together simply in virtue of their practical isocolon quality.[63]

Such examples betray the persistence of the ancient fondness for symmetry, which indeed remains very strong, as witnessed by some excesses found in Bary and Richesource. Bary, for instance, corrects "Nous eussions esté plûtost delivrez, si nous nous fussions plûtost confiez à votre expérience" as follows: "Nous eussions esté plus promtement guéris, si nous eussions esté plus promtement crédules." [64]

As we have already noted in passing, Father Bouhours would yield first place to no one among those who criticized the Port-Royal writers for their unstructured sentences. "[Les Solitaires] ne peuvent, dit Ariste,

---

[62] Le Gras, *Reth.*, p. 231.

[63] Cf. Rev. P. Joseph Jouvency, *L'élève de rhétorique . . . au Collège Louis le Grand de la Sociét⁴ de Jésus . . .* , trans. H. Ferté (Paris, 1892), pp. 52-53. Ferté also translated as *De la manière d'apprendre et d'enseigner* the original *Christianis litterarum magistris de ratione discendi et docendi* (Paris, 1692 . . . ; Frankfurt, 1706 . . .) by Father J. Jouvancy (so spelled in the Latin eds.). This work was officially adopted as the new *ratio studiorum* in the Jesuit schools of the Paris area and approved by Father Tamburini, General of the Society of Jesus, at the turn of the century.

[64] Bary, *Secrets*, 1776 ed., pp. 124-125. In this work about 150 pages are committed to the correction of unsatisfactory periods, and about 300 to show all alphabetical variations, from A to Z, for starting a sentence.

estre accusez de laconisme; ils aiment naturellement les discours vastes;
les longues parenthèses leur plaisent beaucoup, les grandes périodes . . . ,"
to the extent of leaving the speaker breathless and the listener at a loss
to grasp the whole.[65] This vice—alleges the illustrious critic—comes from
the oratorical habits of which the *solitaires* will probably never rid themselves. Indeed, not satisfied with their overlong periods and unable to
part with them, these good fellows would append to them a participial
phrase such as *étant certain que, rien n'étant plus avantageux que* (p. 131).
The high lesson of Balzac is thus lost, since his heritage of effective word
arrangement and beautiful cadences is squandered and betrayed—" nous
devons à ce grand homme le bel arrangement de nos mots et la belle
cadence de nos périodes" (*Entretiens*, p. 116).

In a capital passage (*Entretiens*, pp. 58-61) Bouhours, after returning
to the question of *transpositions* (" un étrange embarras dans les autres
langues"), brought together all the issues concerning composition. French
happily combines the advantage of direct order with compactness of
sentence structure in the use of short periods and *style coupé*: " les autres
langues ne s'accomodent guère d'un style coupé" (p. 61). This is the
foundation for the excellence of that language in all virtues of style,
namely *netteté* (correctness) and *clarté*, to which he now adds the (Stoic
and Attic) *brièveté*, even while he also specifically condemns *le style
asiatique* for its diffuseness (p. 59). Modern French is thus superior to all
languages, including not only the effeminate Italian and pompous Spanish,
but even Latin and Greek.[66] It is superior in that it uniquely combines
the purity of Caesar and Livy and the compactness of *coupé* style char-

---

[65] Bouhours, *Entretiens d'Ariste et d'Eugène*, ed. R. Radouant (Paris, 1920),
pp. 129 f. This ed. is based on the 1st ed. of 1671 (1672²). Sainte-Peuve, *Port-
Royal* (Paris, 1860², 5 vols.), II, 547 f. had also registered Father Vavassor's
remark (ca. 1652) that Port-Royal writers did not know the art of " une
phrase courte et coupée": " Quid caesim sit, quid membratim dicere." Cf. Brunot,
IV, 2, p. 1150, and the Index (vol. VII) under " Style" in C.-A. Sainte-Beuve,
Port-Royal (7 vols., Paris, 1900-1901⁶). Also, on the question of the " Jansenist
style," ch. i, pp. 3-21 in vol. IV (Paris, 1920) of Henri Bremond, *Histoire littéraire
du sentiment religieux en France*. Even Racine criticized Port-Royal's " longues et
doctes périodes": see P. France, *Racine's Rhetoric*, cit., p. 143. The whole ch. iv of
this study (pp. 114-163) is concerned with the seventeenth-century theory and
practice of " pattern rhetoric," i. e. compositional balance, including periodic construction. The author realizes that " the long period is frequently accompanied by
inversion, about which—he curiously adds—I shall say nothing as it is not a rhetorical
figure" (p. 145).

[66] These remarks are traced back to Pasquier's *Recherches* by Barbier d'Aucour,

acteristic of Seneca and Tacitus (while in Latin those two patterns were *de facto* mutually exclusive), and it does so without falling into the obscurity of a Tacitus. The Italians can boast a sententious conciseness with Malvezzi, but the Academy of the Crusca will have none of that. Obscurity, on the other hand, is, in other languages, a consequence not only of an excessive conciseness, but also of their awkward tolerance of transpositions. Furthermore, Greek is inclined toward overlong periods, too generously sprinkled with " de particules superflues," while, together with Latin, it yields too much to cadence and rhythm in order to "chatouiller l'oreille" rather than "contenter l'esprit," this last being the supreme law of French.

Despite his sensitivity to the charms of *style coupé*, the influential Jesuit critic equates Seneca with the baroque taste of his century and allows his preference to go to Cicero. His *Manière de bien penser dans les ouvrages de l'esprit* (1687) [67] makes this point vividly and dramatically through the encounter between the two interlocutors of the dialogues. "De tous les écrivains ingénieux, celuy qui sçait le moins réduire ses pensées à la mesure que demande le bon sens, c'est Sénèque" (*Manière . . . ,* Dial. 3, p. 399). To make sure that his thoughts will not fail to strike the reader, Seneca repeats them and turns them on all sides, thus spoiling them. Pallavicino also agreed with this judgment. "Le style de Cicéron a plus de tour et plus d'étenduë que n'en a celuy de Sénèque, qui est un style rompu, sans nombre, et sans liaison. Mais les pensées de Sénèque sont bien plus diffuses que celles de Cicéron: celuy-là semble dire plus de choses, et celuy-ci en dit plus effectivement" (p. 401).

Eudoxe (Bouhours' and the classicists' mouthpiece) is likewise uneasy with Tacitus (pp. 422-423) and his imitators such as Malvezzi, Ceriziers, etc., "faiseurs de réflexions politiques ou morales . . . un peur visionnaires, . . . qui sophistiquent leurs pensées" (p. 425). Their fault is an excess of wit and "refinement" (*ils raffinent*). At the end of this dialogue Philanthe, the admirer of Tasso, avows that he is about to "change his tastes" and to prefer Virgil to Lucan, Cicero to Seneca.

It is not enough for a thought to be proportioned to its subject and to be noble, agreeable, and delicate without falling into corresponding

the Jansenist who promptly counterattacked the Jesuit Father in the *Sentiments de Cléanthe sur les Entretiens d'Ariste et d'Eugène* (Paris, 1671). Radouant's ed. of the *Entretiens* also contains extracts from this interesting rebuttal.

[67] I quote Bouhours' *Manière de bien penser* in the nouv. éd., Paris, F. Delaulne, 1715.

excesses; it must also be clear: *net, clair, et intelligible* (Dial. 4, p. 462).
Clarity is the first virtue of style. Bouhours exemplifies his distinction
between *phébus,* an acceptable though objectionable kind of obscurity,
and *galimatias,* obscurity without hope of solution, through a long,
humorous analysis of some of Saint-Cyran's letters (pp. 472-481). He
quotes Maynard's references to Muret and Lipsius as keys to the interpretation of baroque obscurities (p. 481). As to Gracián, "il n'est pas clair,
et son stile est coupé, concis, et énigmatique" (p. 487). This section,
which is perhaps the wittiest and most inspired of the whole work, continues the Jesuit's campaign against the literary enemies of the Order by
censuring Lipsius for his commentary on Tacitus, more obscure than the
original.

Further on we find out once again that classicism rejects ellipses:
brevity is a virtue but the elimination of necessary elements creates obscurity, a defect that both Seneca and Quintilian reproach to Sallust when
the former attributes to this historian a habit for "pensées coupées et
un peu obscures," the latter warns "qu'il faut éviter cette brieveté de
Salluste et ce genre d'écrire concis et rompu qu'il affecte quelquefois." [68]

In conclusion, as forecast at the end of the third dialogue, Eudoxe
congratulates Philanthe "que vous ne soyez plus capable de préférer les
pointes de Sénèque au bon sens de Cicéron, et le clinquant du Tasse à
l'or de Virgile" (p. 532). We might add that the taste for the coupé
style makes a very noticeable appearance in Bouhours' criticism, but without compromise between classicism and the 'baroque' models of the plain
style. Through an apparent eclecticism of methods, Bouhours holds to a
classicist balance which seeks the best of both worlds without ever indulg-
ing in radical choices.

Longish periods become the target of a number of rhetoricians. Port-
Royal held no monopoly in that sphere, since the most careful stylists,
including Balzac, could not avoid that pitfall. But now that sentences
made rambling by lack of surveillance or by slackness of construction and
syntactic articulation are definitely ruled out, the critics can concentrate
on the overlong period, no less faulty than "un discours décousu et sans
liaison" (Le Gras, *Reth.,* 1671 or 1674 ed., pp. 237-238). True enough,
we may find inadequate the traditional reasons offered by Le Gras (*Reth.,*

[68] "Sallustio vigente amputatae sententiae et obscura veritas fuere pro cultu."
Sen., *Ep.* 114. "Vitanda illa Sallustiana brevitas et abruptum sermonis genus."
Quint. IV, ii, 45. Cf. *Manière . . . ,* p. 519.

238) and Lamy (*Rhét.*, 1688³ ed., 181), who make appeal to the breathing span.[69] Such vaguely conceived physiological considerations were less pertinent than the logical and psychological ones we would have a right to expect from such critics, but they were the ones they read in their classical sources.

While the coupé style was making bold appearances among many and the best writers of the time, critics still limited themselves to recognizing it without studying it in depth and detail. Le Gras and Lamy do not go beyond recommending the wise mixing of styles by juxtaposition of diverse compositional forms to achieve elegant variation—a familiar traditional precept. In particular Le Gras submits that "il faut encore faire en sorte que le discours soit varié par le mélange des périodes, avec les membres et les coupures," that is, by alternating periods and single clauses and phrases.[70] Richesource goes further. He teaches how to disassemble a long, *asiatique* period into a sequence of clauses; above all, he praises the succinct or laconic variety of *style coupé* provided it is well cut: he even finds it preferable for narrative prose.[71]

In his Dictionary Bayle, while analyzing the taste of the French historian Benjamin Priolo for the anti-Ciceronians of the first century A. D., enlarges his theme into a discussion opposing Cicero, Livy, and Virgil, who, he maintains, display the same general sort of eloquence, to Seneca, Tacitus, Pliny, and Lucan, whose style he severely censures. He then adds that "the French begin to be sick of the same distemper."[72] We may add, in turn, that they were 'sick' from earlier generations, as Bayle himself may have been aware. Indeed, it might suffice to recall that as early as 1619 Father Caussin had remarked that "everyone now covets" a basically Senecan and Tacitean style (see Ch. IV, A, p. 167). Pascal notes, likewise, that "la manière d'écrire d'Epictète, de Montaigne et

[69] Cf. Brunot, IV, 2, 1156.
[70] Le Gras, *Rethorique* (1671 or 1674 ed.), p. 237.
[71] *Prise de Fribourg* (1677), 13, 53-54, and 157. Also 163, where Richesource criticizes an overlong sentence by an author otherwise adept at the chopped-up manner, "tant il aime les discours décousus, brisez et demanchez, pour ainsi dire à la façon des Annales, à la Tacite, ou à la Suétone." Cf. Brunot, IV, 2, 1180-1181.
[72] Cf. Croll, "'Attic Prose,'" p. 125; p. 98 in Patrick and Evans. Croll was quoting from one of the two contemporary English translations, viz. *Mr. Bayle's Historical and Critical Dictionary*, 2ᵈ ed. (London, 1734-38, 5 tomes), t. IV (1737), p. 778 note L. But see the definitive French ed. (5ᵗʰ): *Dictionnaire Historique et Critique de M. P. Bayle* (Amsterdam, 1740, 4 tomes), t. III, art. "Priolo," pp. 813-817: p. 817 fn. L for passage in question: ". . . Les François commencent à se sentir de la même maladie. . . ."

de Salomon de Tultie [= Louis de Montalte = Pascal himself in the *Lettres*] est le plus d'usage." [73] At any rate Bayle in exile was unsympathetic toward the cut style: he even found it diffuse. It is, he avers, less exposed to the danger of ambiguity; yet "vous et moi, Monsieur, qui nous sommes accoûtumez au STILE LIÉ . . . , nous sommes en effet plus courts que ceux qui se servent du STILE COUPÉ, et néanmoins les mauvais juges s'imaginent que nous emploions plus de paroles." [74] Indeed, he went on, there is hardly a writer more given to verbiage than Seneca. These ideas are not new to us: Bouhours had already acquainted us with such a critical twist.

2. To apprehend how the phrase of the eighteenth century has evolved out of that of the *grand siècle* it may suffice to observe that, as it were, what was then on top fell to the bottom and vice versa. That is to say, the grand manner of a Balzac, a Bossuet, even a Pascal became lost in the irrelevance of preaching and panegyric, neglected and despised genres in the century of the Encyclopaedists, whereas the *langage spirituel* of the court and of the world, Racine's historical prose, Bussy-Rabutin's and Sévigné's epistolary or satyrical manners, Bouhours' critical prose, and, last but not least, La Bruyère's stress on visual rather than auditive qualities, on sensibility rather than straight intellect, became the original elements of the new style. From Hamilton and Fontenelle we thus reach the accomplished masters of this nervous, *haché* manner with Montesquieu and Voltaire.[75]

---

[73] Pascal, *Pensées*, I, 18, ed. Brunschvicg, p. 327.

[74] Pierre Bayle, *Œuvres diverses* (Hildesheim, 1964-68, 4 vols.), IV, p. 719, Lettre 179 à M. Rou (2-II-1696). This is a reprint of *Œuvres diverses de M. Pierre Bayle, contenant . . . , excepté son Dictionnaire . . .* (La Haye, 1727-31, 4 tomes), t. IV (1731). Brunot, IV, 2, p. 1182, cites this letter from the 1737 ed. (The Hague), t. IV, p. 723. In a letter of 21-IX-1706 to Des Maizeaux, Bayle confirmed Le Clerc's judgment which postulated a resemblance between Seneca's and Saint–Évremond's styles: cf. Bayle, *Œuvres diverses*, IV (1968), 881; Saint–Évremond, *Jugement sur Sénèque, Plutarque et Pétrone* in his *Œuvres* (Amsterdam, 1726), II; and, for Le Clerc, *Bibliothèque Universelle*, t. XII, art. xiv, § 2, p. 561 and *Bibliothèque Choisie*, t. IX, art. viii, p. 327.
Just the same, even without espousing the cut style the critics were definitely in a mood to favor shorter sentences. Cf. Thomas Corneille's note to Vaugelas' critique of overlong periods: "Pour les longues périodes, il n'y en a presque point qui n'embarrassent l'esprit. Plus elles sont courtes, plus elles contentent le Lecteur ou l'Auditeur. Il faut qu'elles aient des reposoirs, comme dit M. de Vaugelas. . . ." Vaugelas, *Remarques*, ed. Chassang, II, 373.

[75] Cf. Lanson, *L'Art de la prose*, pp. 140-141.

Speculation on syntactic structures (periodic and clausal) has never
been more lively than in the later Middle Ages (1200-1400) and in the
eighteenth century. It so happens that these are also the periods in
which the coupé style was most widely cultivated, both in Latin and in
the vernaculars. Was it mere coincidence, or were there some common
elements underlying the particular brands of intellectuality and sensibility characteristic of both these ages? However that may have been,
in both periods the profound stylistic changes which were taking place
aroused critical reflection.

A particular use of conjunctions is, we have seen, a basic feature of
cut style. The classical languages were generously endowed with a wealth
of purely decorative or euphonic particles (μέν . . . δέ, γάρ, ἀλλά, καί,
αὐτάρ, nam, -que, igitur, quidem, equidem, atque, vero, enim, tum-cum,
. . . relative pronouns at times). In the Middle Ages some conjunctions
had become technified (quare, quia . . .), others, coveralls (quod). The
Renaissance and baroque age had yielded to the classical examples and
imported into the vernaculars a number of conjunctions used merely to
achieve a rather perfunctory feeling of periodicity. The eighteenth century
witnessed a severe effort to define the meaning and function of conjunctions, now at last used to denote precise, limited relationships, not just
vague liaisons du discours. Otherwise, one felt inclined to eliminate
formal ligatures between phrases, such as c'est pourquoi, vu que, car,
puisque, etc. (the very kind that still survived so tenaciously in other
languages, cf. the famous It. conciofossecosaché). For the same reasons
one tended to curtail the use of relatives and participles.[76]

The new appeal to logic in terms of a necessary correspondence between
arrangement of words into sentences and the logical sequence of our
thinking processes was put in the broadest possible context by Father
Buffier. The study of language is important, he says,

puisque l'art d'aranger les mots a une connexion essentielle avec la maniére
d'aranger les pensées. C'est par là qu'il sert de base aux plus hautes

---

[76] Cf. A. François, Hist. de la l. fr. cultivée, p. 68: "cette 'période en style
coupé' se caractérisait par l'élimination de toute ligature formelle: conjonctions,
relatif, participe."

John Locke (1632-1704) dedicated a chapter of his Essay Concerning Human
Understanding (1690) to the use of particles, i.e. prepositions, adverbs, and
conjunctions, and did not hesitate to assert that "it is in the right use of these that
more particularly consists the clearness and beauty of a good style." See Essay,
Book III, Ch. vii "Of Particles," vol. II, p. 98 of ed. A. C. Fraser (2 vols., New
York, 1959).

siences, et sur-tout à la logique; et qu'il fournit des régles, où la Théologie même est quelque fois obligée d'avoir recours.[77]

But one must not fail to note that this correspondence tends to rely on mere sequence and to exclude formal ligatures. The nature of the period as then understood is discovered by Buffier to be "logical" also in the sense that it is metagrammatical:

Quelques-uns peut-être ne voudront pas apeler périodes cet amas de diverses phrases qui sont sans liaison grammaticale. A eux permis. . . .

He gives an example of the kind of *périodes* in question (that is, *périodes du style coupé*):

Il vient une nouvelle; on en raporte les circonstances les plus marquées; elle passe dans la bouche de tout le monde; ceux qui en doivent être les mieux instruits la croient, la disent, la répandent; j'agis sur cela; je ne crois pas être blamable.[78]

He regards the last as the main clause. If we attempt to reconstrue this *période* in the traditional, classical manner, we shall have something like the following:

Je ne crois pas être blamable SI j'agis sur une nouvelle QUI vient, ALORS QU'on raporte . . . ET QUE . . . ET QUE. . . .

For Buffier, the essence of the sentence is in the contents, not in the form:

Dans les narrations, les particularitez de la chose qu'on veut raconter forment la période: comme, *les ennemis avoient fait une marche secrette* (1709: later eds. = *forcée*); *quelques cavaliers avancent pour les reconnoître; toute notre armée fuit lentement.* . . . (1709 ed. § 997)

---

[77] Buffier, S. J., *Grammaire françoise sur un plan nouveau, pour en rendre les principes plus clairs* . . . (Paris, N. Le Clerc, 1709; Bruxelles, 1711; Paris, 1714²; 1723, 1726, 1732, 1741). The passage in question is cited from the 1741 ed., p. xiv in the recent monograph on Buffier (1661-1737): Kathleen Sonia Wilkins, *A Study of the Works of Claude Buffier*, "Studies on Voltaire and the Eighteenth Century, nᵣ 66" (Geneva, Institut et Musée Voltaire, 1969), p. 38. Cf. pp. 31-45 on the grammar; 146-166 on the rhetorical and aesthetic ideas. See, also, my fn. 38 above.
  Buffier remains celebrated for his theory of punctuation, of which he attributed the invention to modern grammarians: cf. G. Harnois, *Les Théories du langage*, p. 36. He also deserves praise for a firm stand on the uniqueness of each language's grammatical system, which has been perilously misunderstood by applying Latin patterns, e. g., to French: see *Grammaire*, 1709 ed., p. 8.
[78] Buffier, *Gr. fr.*, 1709 ed., §§ 996-998, pp. 430-432, also quoted from 1714 ed., nᵣ 995 by François in Brunot, VI, 2², p. 1980.

We must observe that the trend we are considering was potentially
conducive to a reduction of hypotactic to paratactic forms through the
aid of ellipsis. Instead of saying: "Your friend did not mention you to
me, although he had an opportunity to do so when I saw him yesterday,"
the speaker affecting the modes of cut style might say: "I saw your
friend yesterday; he did not mention you to me." The outcome is undoubtedly a gain in vividness and rapidity. A most effective example of
this mode being turned into a veritable formula (somewhat approximat-
ing the classic asyndeton *veni, vidi, vici*) is one by Louvet: *Il m'avoit
salué, il s'en alloit, il est revenu.*[79] This again can be translated into
periodic style at the expense of speed, and in a glossator's vein: *Après
m'avoir salué, il était déjà en train de s'en aller, quand, soudainement, il
décida de revenir.* In the original one admires not only the dramatic
effectiveness and conciseness, but also the rigorous economy of the tenses.

Thus Condillac (who marks the high point in the linguistic and
stylistic speculation of his century) prescribes that "quand une proposition principale se lie naturellement à d'autres, il faut bien se garder d'en
faire une phrase subordonnée; car, si les conjonctions n'embarrassent pas
le discours, elles le rendent au moins languissant."[80] Similarly, Étienne-
Simon de Gamaches (1672-1756) defined the underlying principle of this
norm, that is the appeal to an intuitive perception of relationships swifter
than in the slow process of the other method—an insult to the listener's
intelligence: "C'est à ceux à qui nous parlons à sentir les rapports . . . ,
nous ne devons point paroître nous défier de leur intelligence. . . ."[81]

The heart of the matter is that for Condillac the sequence of statements
is an *explication des idées* in their logical and psychological succession;
as to their relationships with one another, the *phrases principales* are tied
together (*liées*) chiefly by the fact of the succession itself, aided and
implemented by *gradation* and *opposition*. Condillac is speaking of

[79] Louvet, *Varmont*, I, 17, cited in Brunot, VI, 2², p. 1983.
[80] Condillac, *Cours d'études*, III: *Art d'écrire*, Book I, ch. vii. See Condillac,
Œuvres philosophiques, ed. G. Le Roy (1947), vol. I, p. 531. Cf. Brunot, H. L. F.,
t. VI, 2ᵉ pᵗⁱᵉ, fasc. 2 (by A. François) (Paris, 1933), pp. 1979-1981.
[81] É.-S. de Gamaches, *Dissertation sur les agrémens du langage réduits à leurs
principes* (Paris, 1718), 81-84. Also his *Dissertations littéraires et philosophiques*
(Paris, 1755), and the "nouvelle éd." under the title *Les Agrémens du langage*
etc. (Paris, 1757). Cf. Charles Bordes, *Réflexions sur les langues vivantes* (1749),
II, 573: the *coupé* style is "moins un innovation dans le langage, qu'un progrès
dans l'art du raisonnement, une facilité, une rapidité de pensées, perfectionnées par
l'exercice." Brunot, VI, 2², p. 1981.

sequence of words, phrases, *and* clauses. Therefore what he calls *construction* is essentially an extension of word order (both within and beyond single clauses), since the relationships will result from succession rather than from specific tie-words. In this manner Condillac completes Father Buffier's intuition of a style (the *coupé*) in which the logical progression of thought is merely a consequence of syntactic suggestion, without explicit morphological transitions. It is then pertinent to recall that the traditional *constructio* or syntax was, as far as sentence structure was concerned, essentially geared to the use of subordinating elements (conjunctions, adverbs). Beyond that, the medieval grammarians had limited the theory of word order to the clause (with some few exceptions which have been pointed out above), and only to the effect of identifying the logical units and sequences of subject and predicate.

Du Marsais gave the *style coupé* the canonic blessing of the *Encyclopédie* by discussing it in his famous article "Construction." He defined it as being made up of phrases: "composé d'incises, c'est-à-dire de phrases courtes par opposition aux membres de la période, qui ont une certaine étendue." E. g.: "*Turenne est mort; la victoire s'arrête; la fortune chancelle; tout le camp demeure immobile* (Fléchier). Voilà quatre propositions qui ne sont regardées que comme des incises, parce qu'elles sont courtes; le style périodique emploie des phrases plus longues." As one can see, the distinction is rather superficial; it is based merely on physical length.

By that time the Abbé Noël Antoine Pluche, one of the *mécaniciens* (in sharp opposition to the *logiciens* represented by Du Marsais), could already complain that this *coupé* style was applied to all genres: "Il n'y a plus proprement qu'un style par lequel toutes les compositions se ressemblent, comme grand nombre de dames de tout âge et de tout état se ressemblent par le fard." [82] Batteux, the leader of the *mécaniciens,* yielded this fashionable style to narration and argumentation, but invoked a return to the periodic for all other prose forms. He explained Dionysius' passage on Isocrates (ch. xxiii) by quoting Fléchier's moral portrait of Turenne, which allegedly showed the same qualities of suspended balance through symmetry and multiple correlations exemplified by Isocrates:

"Soit qu'il fallût préparer les affaires ou les décider; chercher la victoire avec ardeur, ou l'attendre avec patience; soit qu'il fallût prévenir les des-

[82] Pluche, *La Mécanique des langues et l'art de les enseigner* (Paris, 1751), p. 333. Brunot, VI, 2², p. 1983.

seins des ennemis par la hardiesse, ou dissiper les craintes et les jalousies des alliés par la prudence; soit qu'il fallût se modérer dans les prosperités, ou se soutenir dans les malheurs de la guerre, son âme fut toujours égale. . . . Si la licence fut réprimée; si les haines . . . ; si les lois . . . ; si l'ordre . . . ; si les membres . . . ; c'est à lui, France, que tu le dois." [83]

Similarly Crevier echoed d'Olivet's critique of the style décousu, haché, and déchiqueté: [84] he spoke of "style brusque, sautillant, haché, . . . un ciment sans chaux" (cf. arena sine calce). [85] This reaction was to be expected. The distinction between coupé and haché became established: thus Hérissant accepted the former while he warned against the excesses of the latter. [86]

Le Gras' Rethorique françoise had displayed a sharp awareness of the potentialities contained in a methodic use of antithesis. He commended periods dramatized by a closing antithesis: "mettre plus près qu'on pourra de la fin de chaque période deux mots qui fassent entre eux antithèse ou opposition," as in Il n'y a rien de si INCROYABLE que l'éloquence ne fasse CROIRE rather than Il n'y a rien de si incroyable qu'on ne puisse rendre croyable par le discours (p. 233). He even advised the use of "double antitheses," namely in the middle and end of the sentence, in order to achieve both balance and emphasis: "La période est encore plus élégante, lorsque l'opposition est double et qu'elle se rencontre au milieu et sur la fin de la période" (ibid.).

Indeed the favorite structure of the new style, in whichever variety, is binary, and the antithesis, which the seventeenth century had brought to the heights of the most consummate refinement, lends itself magnificently to this pattern. Voltaire is the master of the binary cut style as a vehicle for antithetic paradox. Starobinski has recently shown how this stylistic pattern was the center of a system which embraced Voltaire's

[83] Batteux, "Traité des genres en prose," 1ère partie, sect. 3, ch. ix, in Principes de la littérature (Paris, 1774), t. IV, pp. 196-197 and 201.

[84] Abbé d'Olivet (Pierre Joseph Thoulier d'Olivet), Traité de la prosodie françoise, avec une diss. de M. Durand sur le même sujet (Geneva, 1760), V, ii (1st ed. 1736); Remarques de grammaire sur Racine (Paris, 1738), 137. The Prosodie françoise and the Remarques sur Racine were then reprinted together with the same author's Essais de Grammaire (1732) under the general title: Remarques sur la langue françoise par M. l'Abbé d'Olivet (Paris, 1771), now again available as a Slatkine reprint (Geneva, 1968): see pp. 116-124.

[85] J.-B.-L. Crevier, Rhétorique françoise (Paris, 1765, 2 vols.), II, 48 of 1770 ed.

[86] L. Théod. Hérissant, Principes de Style, ou observations sur l'art d'écrire, receuillies des meilleurs auteurs (Paris, 1779), 15. On these documents see Brunot, VI, 2², pp. 1983-1984.

whole conception: in *L'Ingénu* he worked, composed, and conceived by a *doppietta* law or binary method expanding from the antithetic structure of the sentence through the arrangement of chapters, all the way to the very organization of the tale as a whole. One can also demonstrate that the *style coupé* could rigorously lean for entirely new effects on the time-tested devices of isocolon and jingle-like endings, in other words, on a newly felt sense of formal symmetry.[87] I might add that Voltaire's shrewdest paradox lay perhaps in this stylistic achievement: bending the devices of the grand style to serve the most uncompromising plain style.

Even the *style haché* could be handled advantageously by the best writers. The characters of some of Diderot's works, such as *Le Père de famille, Le Fils naturel, Les Bijoux indiscrets*, regularly speak by syncopated phrases, isolated words, monosyllables, exclamations, all sorts of elliptic twists. It was the farthest point one had yet gone along the path of the loose style! When reflecting on style, Diderot did not hesitate to take Seneca's defense: "le reprendre d'une affectation de briller, c'est reprocher à l'hirondelle la légèreté de son vol." [88] He even gave us a curious insight into the contemporary musicians' point of view when he made the "neveu de Rameau" speak on their behalf as follows: "C'est au cri animal de la passion à dicter la ligne qui nous convient. Il faut que ces expressions soient pressées les unes sur les autres; il faut que la phrase soit courte, que le sens en soit coupé, suspendu. . . . Il nous faut des exclamations, des interjections, des suspensions, des interruptions, des affirmations, des négations." [89]

Although Beauzée's *Grammaire générale* (1767) clearly inserted the treatment of word order within Syntax, as we shall see, the 'period' still remained with him outside grammar as a rhetorical matter, since he carried his syntax little further than the clause: "Toutes les vues de la syntaxe . . . se rapportent à la Proposition." [90] He does give us a theory of parts of the period (subordinate clauses), but it is quite brief.[91] Furthermore, it is conducted within a logical context, just as the clause

[87] J. Starobinski, "La doppietta di Voltaire. La Filosofia di uno stile e lo stile di una filosofia," *Strumenti Critici*, 1 (Oct. 1966), 13-32.
[88] Diderot thus defends Seneca's style in the 2d ed. of his *Vie de Sénèque*: see Douglas A. Bonneville, *Diderot's Vie de Sénèque: A Swan Song Revised* (Gainesville, Fla., Un. of Fl. Press, 1966).
[89] *Le Neveu de Rameau*, p. 487 in Diderot, *Œuvres*, ed. A. Billy (Paris, "Bibl. de la Pléiade," 1951).
[90] N. Beauzée, *Gr. gén.*, 1819 ed., p. 388.
[91] Ibid., pp. 401-415.

is identified with the logical proposition.[92] It specifically refers to the Port-Royal *Art de penser*. In detail, this treatment is a good witness of the still primitive conditions of this province of syntax, which had advanced little from the rather disorganic and partial observations transmitted by Priscian, and was now enriched only with a few definitions carried over from logic. A truly grammatical definition is attempted for the period, to be opposed to the rhetorical treatment of it, but it ends up with an awkwardly unconvincing distinction between sentence and clause (pp. 410-415), or, rather, between the members of a full-fledged period and the incidental clauses (*propositions incidentes, incises*, viz. classical *incisa*) of a complex *proposition détachée*. Yet, the extraordinary development of the syntactical part of grammar (meaning word order and the clause) is indicated by the sheer bulk of this section—a full half of a ponderous treatise.

The last section of Beauzée's *Grammaire générale* (Book III, ch. v, pp. 768-806) deals with Punctuation, with direct bearing on sentence structure. It is worthwhile pausing briefly once again on this particular aspect of our subject, whose long tradition we have been unable to follow in a continuous manner. After noticing that the ancients had a merely physiological notion of punctuation ("les besoins naturels de la respiration . . . les besoins des poumons"), Beauzée adds two new, truly 'analytical' principles: "la distinction des sens partiels, les différents degrés de subordination" (776).

He repeatedly mentions the *style coupé* (cf. 783-785, 795, 797), which he defines as follows: "Un sens total est énoncé par plusieurs propositions qui se succèdent rapidement, et dont chacune a un sens fini et qui semble complet" (783). He once praises it for its rapidity due to the lack of conjunctions: "Si elles [viz. *les propositions*, united by the logical context, but grammatically isolated] ne sont unies sensiblement par aucune conjonction expresse, c'est pour arrêter moins la marche de l'esprit par l'attirail traînant des mots superflus, et pour donner au style plus de feu et de vivacité" (784). As against the majority of the writers and a great number of grammarians who, Beauzée tells us, still recommend semicolons or even colons (the heavy pauses once so popular with Tacitus' and Seneca's followers, like Malvezzi), he proposes to separate these clauses by commas: "Ce seroit donc aller directement contre l'esprit du style coupé, et détruire sans besoin la vérité et l'unité de la pensée totale, que

<hr />

[92] Ibid., pp. 389 ff.

d'en assujettir l'expression a une prononciation appesantie par les inter-
valles trop grands" (ibid.).

We are then offered an interesting example of a sentence written in
the two styles, periodic and coupé. He takes it from the Abbé Girard,[93]
and proposes a method of punctuation designed to show the logical relationships and degrees of subordination in a finer way than in Girard, who
was closer to the seventeenth-century Senecan taste in that he chopped
up the whole into every constituent clause-statement.

L'amour est une passion de pur caprice, qui attribue du mérite à l'objet
aimé, mais qui ne fait pas aimer le mérite: à qui la reconnaissance est
inconnue; parce que chez lui tout se rapporte à la volupté, et que rien n'y
est lumière ni ne tend à la vertu.

L'amour . . . caprice. Il attribue du mérite à l'objet dont on est touché,
il ne fait pourtant pas aimer le mérite: jamais il ne se conduit par reconnaissance; tout est chez lui goût ou sensation, rien n'y est lumière ni vertu.

All in all, the conservative point of view remained, of course, opposed
on principle to the new forms of curt and cut styles in favor of the more
relaxed periodizing of the age of Louis XIV, which with its noble gravity
began to be looked upon as 'classic.' Bossuet could appear as the perfect
model of French eloquence to these somewhat *rétardataire* admirers of
things past. They never spoke more plausibly than through the voice of
Buffon (*Discours sur le style,* the acceptance speech on taking his seat
at the Académie Française on the 25th of August, 1753), whose implicit
targets were some of the most significant writers of the century, such as
Montesquieu, Voltaire, and Marivaux. Buffon gently but firmly blamed
them for the abuse of antitheses, *pointes, traits saillants,* and those patterns
of *pensées fines* and *idées légères, déliées, sans consistance* which, in his
mind, betrayed a lack of mental discipline, careful planning, and general
orderliness. "Le style n'est que l'ordre et le mouvement qu'on met dans
ses pensées," and its foundation is a severe planning: "ce plan n'est pas
encore le style, mais il en est la base." Thus "ceux qui écrivent comme
ils parlent [in a way the ideal of the plain style], quoiqu'ils parlent très-
bien, écrivent mal." They write "des morceaux détachés, ... tant
d'ouvrages faits de pièces de rapports," even without due subordinations
and transitions. The style he advocated was, however, the "classic" style
made of purity and clarity, not the copious, nor the pompous and florid,
nor the pathetic one: "il ne suffit pas de frapper l'oreille et d'occuper les

---

[93] Girard, *Vrais Principes,* tom. II, Dis. xvi, p. 461.

yeux [with jingles and rhetorical colors], il faut agir sur l'âme et toucher le coeur en parlant à l'esprit." The *Discours* was extraordinarily success-ful, but, all in all, more so in the schools than in the practice of the writers.[94]

The cut style could be satisfying as long as it drew force and richness from those ingredients inherited from the baroque which could be put to advantage by curtness of exposition, namely wit, sententiousness, and paradox, all served by the versatile device of antithesis. Once these sources of inspiration had started to slacken and dry up, the style began to show its limitations and sound arid. Hence Buffon's and Rousseau's reaction, or rather progression toward a new kind of intellectual com-plexity and musical sweep—some new kind of ' period.'

II) DIRECT ORDER AND INVERSION

1. Word order became a fashionable and most lively issue in France between 1600 and 1800, reaching a climax around 1750. The stylistic consciousness of the age fastened on it as a testing ground for some of its most original ideas, in a unique convergence of grammatical, rhetorical, and logical criteria. In the grammatical treatises and, to a lesser extent, in the rhetorical ones, we find a striking contrast between the inspiring sections devoted to such matters and the frequently drab and pedantic remainder of the treatment. Even outside the technical treatises the debate on word order was a powerful catalyst in the ripening of a modern ap-proach to stylistic values as a key aspect of literary criticism.

The progressive stages in this prolonged debate typically correspond to the evolution of the main cultural movements of the age. After a first stage exemplified by the empiricism of Vaugelas, placing usage above reason, the Cartesian position, chiefly through Port-Royal, proposed reason to explain the apparent arbitrariness and whims of usage. Rationalism provoked its own reaction in the form of sensationalism. The ensuing battle between these two schools of thought temporarily ended in a victory for the rationalists, but the sensualist position eventually ripened into the Romantic approach. Condillac is the authority who ushered in this final assimilation.

[94] Buffon, *Discours sur le style* (both versions) and, also, *De l'art d'écrire*, in *Œuvres philosophiques de Buffon*, ed. Jean Piveteau (Paris, 1954), pp. 500-511. See Charles Bruneau's Introduction to these writings, ibid., pp. 491-499.

Many of the documents of this fascinating question are mentioned in Brunot's monumental history of the French language; they have been recently surveyed by Ulrich Ricken, a *dix-huitièmiste* from Leipzig; and they have been used again, from a special point of view, by Noam Chomsky.[1] But the issues and the texts that bear them out have never been placed in the broader context of the traditional speculation on composition, and even for their own time word order and sentence structure have not been studied together as related parts of composition theory.

To begin with, we have seen how *rectus ordo* and 'natural order' started to be speculated about with modern implications rather early in the Middle Ages. The French exploitation of the matter in a nationalistic sense also began rather early. The vernacular grammarian Louis Meigret (ca. 1510-1560) maintained that one should put an end to the imitation of Latin because the *ordre de nature*, which is characteristic of French, established a barrier between the two languages. Thus "Quintil Censeur" attributed the *facilité* and *clarté* of French to its regular word order in correspondence to the *droit ordre naturel*. We have also seen how Maupas founded the French 'natural order' on the *ordre naturel de l'entendement*.[2]

For his part, Vaugelas had come upon the realization that the arrangement of words is one of the great secrets of style, and was praised for it by later critics.[3] In detail, he limited himself to contrasting *la construction naturelle* or *situation naturelle des paroles* with the *situation forcée*, and could go so far as to declare inversions to be virtues in poetry (especially that of Malherbe), but vices in prose, although without excluding them altogether.[4] For his part Nicolas Mercier maintained that the subversion

[1] F. Brunot, *H.L.F.*, t. II, pp. 497 ff. on fixation of word order in the 16th century; t. III, 2e Ptle (Paris, 1911), ch. x, pp. 657-683 on "L'Ordre des Mots," and ch. xi, pp. 684-711 on "La Phrase" for the period 1600-1660. Subsequent sections on theoretical statements will be quoted below. U. Ricken, "Rationalismus und Sensualismus in der Diskussion uber die Wortstellung" (1961); Id., "Condillacs *liaison des idées* und die *clarté* des Französischen" (1964); N. Chomsky, *Cartesian Linguistics* (1966). Also A. François, *Hist. de la l. fr. cultivée* (1959), I, 218-219; II, 21-30, 63-73, 153-158.
[2] See above, pp. 152-155 in Ch. III, B.
[3] Cf., e.g., Beauzée, *Gr. gén.*, 1819 ed., p. 438. See, also, p. 192 above, with fn. 18.
[4] Vaugelas, *Remarques sur la l. fr.*, ed. A. Chassang (2 vols., Versailles-Paris, 1880), II, pp. 215-219, 235, 361-367, 401 f., 471 f.; ed. Streicher (Paris, 1934), pp. 376-377, 481-483. On the *usage-raison* binomium in Vaugelas see, now, H.

of *ordre naturel* by *inversion* exacted a high price in the form of the ensuing *confusion*.[5] On a more practical level, critical readers began to show a keen sensitivity to inversion.

OF had established the "rejet du sujet," viz. the verb + subject—inversion when the clause began with a complement, a relative, an adverb, or even a conjunction. This habit persisted through the Renaissance. But Malherbe began to censure such constructs as: *Sitôt que m'apparut ce chef-d'oeuvre des Cieux* (t. IV, p. 328) and *Là fut-il assailly* (IV, 416).[6] It would appear that Vaugelas accepted the inversion of the subject after the verb only when the clause begins with the relative *que: l'avis que lui donna son ami* (*Rem.* II, 28). Thomas Corneille was categorical on this rule, which on the other hand the grammarians seemed to accept implicitly.[7]

Similarly for Le Gras "l'hyperbate," good in Latin, is bad in French, whose " génie consiste à s'exprimer dans un order naturel." [8] Matters such as these were particularly close to the hearts of practical critics, whose name is legion in this and the following century. Their most eloquent representative is probably Richesource, who will carry into the midst of the classic age his battle against transpositions—the 'figure' he did his best to discredit by using the term *synchise* of medieval memory, or, even more vividly, *sauteuse*. He did admit, of course, the one exception of the object relative *que*, as in *Aux trouppes que commandoit le Baron de* etc. He even praised such turns as elegant: "Ce déplacement, dans de certaines occasions, que demandent la matière, le temps, le lieu et les autres conjonctures . . . est l'un des plus agréables ornemens de l'Éloquence françoise." [9] Given the phrase *Que le duc d'Enghien gagna* he would

---

Weinrich, "Vaugelas und die Lehre vom guten Sprachgebrauch," *ZRP,* 76 (1960), 1 ff.; in later authors see A. Pizzorusso, "La Poetica di La Bruyère," *Studi Francesi,* I, 1 (1957), 43-57 and I, 2 (1957), 198-212.

[5] N. Mercier, *Manuel des grammairiens* (Paris, 1657), p. 162.

[6] Malherbe, *Œuvres,* ed. Lud. Lalanne (Paris, 1862, 4 tomes). T. IV contains the *Commentaire sur Desportes,* where one finds the criticism just quoted. Cf. Brunot, *H. L. F.,* t. III, 2, pp. 663-664.

[7] Brunot, *H. L. F.,* t. IV, 2ᵉ Partie (Paris, 1924), pp. 1086-1087. See, in this vol., the whole of Livre VI, ch. xxxii on word order (ch. xxxiii on the sentence).

[8] Le Gras, *La Rethorique françoise* (Paris, 1671, 1674²), p. 197, also quoted by Brunot, IV, 2, pp. 1106-1107.

[9] *La Relation de la Prise de Fribourg du Bureau des Gazettes,* Mise en Partition selon les regles de la Critique par . . . Sr. de Riche-Source (Paris, 1677), p. 67. Cf. Brunot, *H. L. F.,* IV, 2, 1084, 1087 fn., 1108.

rule that "cette expression est moins élégante que celle-ci, *que gagna le Duc* . . . , parce que la transposition du Nominatif ou du Verbe lui donne beaucoup de grace." [10] Otherwise he was uncompromising, especially when one separates what goes logically and semantically together: in *Eschappé, en passant le Rhin, aux Trouppes,* "l'interruption . . . broüille la construction ou l'ordonnance . . . à l'exemple de la figure Synchise des Grecs et des Latins, qui pour trouver leur Rythme, leur cadence ou leur harmonie, mettent toutes les phrases en désordre et en confusion." [11] A correct arrangement based on syntactic priorities will avoid synchysis, as in *Donner de bons cartiers, à plusieurs Regimens de son armée, avant la fin de la campagne* (V + dOb + iOb + iCC). [12]

Progress on a more theoretical level came rather slowly. Yet the ground was being prepared for momentous developments. The Port-Royal Latin grammar, by Claude Lancelot (1650), started out the great debate to come by a rather simple, yet pregnant statement: "L'hyperbate est le meslange et la confusion qui se trouve dans les mots contre l'ordre naturel de la construction, qui devroit estre commun à toutes les langues comme nous le voyons en la nostre." (In the 1655 ed. "comme nous . . ." was replaced by "selon l'idée naturelle que nous avons de la construction.") [13] It was not, one must admit, a very unprejudiced way to introduce the pupils of the Petites Écoles to the peculiarities of Latin construction. [14]

Considering the eminently 'syntactic' approach entailed in the definitory and logical method of philosophical grammar, one is perhaps surprised to find that little space is given in the *Grammaire générale et raisonnée* to a syntactical section proper. Indeed we read there that a grammar has little to say on rules of sentence construction, if one excepts the figurative use of language (one type of which is the *hyperbate ou renversement*). [15] Furthermore Arnauld and Lancelot pointed out that

[10] *Prise de Fribourg,* p. 134.
[11] Ibid., p. 67.
[12] Ibid., p. 101.
[13] Cl. Lancelot, *Nouvelle Méthode . . . Latine,* 1650 ed. p. 402, 1655 ed. p. 602, ch. vi "Des figures de construction." The text went on as follows: "Mais les Romains ont tellement affecté le discours figuré, qu'ils ne parlent presque jamais autrement."
[14] Cf. Guy Harnois, *Les Théories du langage en France de 1660 à 1821* (1928), pp. 13 ff. on the Port-Royal grammars.
[15] *Gr. gén.,* 1660 ed., pp. 145-147. While dealing with "figures de construction" in this section, the authors tells us that there are four manners of speaking

French uses such "figures de construction" less than any other language, "parce qu'elle aime particulièrement la netteté, et à exprimer les choses autant qu'il se peut dans l'ordre le plus naturel et le plus désembarrassé, quoy qu'en mesme-temps elle ne cède à aucune en beauté ni en élégance."[16] Likewise Lamy, in his *De l'art de parler* of 1676 (p. 25), justified his omission of any discussion concerning "l'ordre des mots et les règles qu'il faut garder dans l'arrangement du discours" by the simple suggestion that "la lumière naturelle montre si vivement ce qu'il faut faire," that no more is needed.[17] Chomsky has shrewdly remarked that "the failure to formulate rules of sentence construction in a precise way was not simply an oversight of Cartesian linguistics. To some extent it was a consequence of the express assumption that the sequence of words in a sentence corresponds directly to the flow of thought, at least in a 'well-designed' language, and is therefore not properly studied as part of grammar." He added that "this notion seems to have developed in connection with the controversy over use of the vernacular to replace Latin."[18] And yet, the *Grammaire générale* did pay attention to at least one particular aspect of word order, which came within the province of Sánchez' notion of ellipsis. In observing (1660 ed., pp. 69-70) that *video canem currentem* is translated as *je voy un chien qui court*, the authors somehow began to realize what some modern linguists refer to as the emerging of particular 'surface structures' out of the common substratum of 'deep structures' through grammatical and syntactic 'transformations'; they accordingly formulated the rule that the relative comes first even when it takes the place of the object, which should come last; only a governing preposition shall precede it.[19] Cf. *Dieu que j'ayme; Dieu par qui le monde a esté créé.* In other words, the authors of the *Grammaire* looked upon the actual sentence as arising on the logical level from an

---

called *figures*, all being "irregularities" of sorts, and all derived from our tendency to think about our thoughts rather than our words while we speak: (1) *syllepse* or *conception* (cf. medieval *conceptio*), when we follow the sense of our words rather than the words' grammatical ties (e. g., *il est six heures* instead of *ils sont six heures*); (2) *ellipse* or *défaut*; (3) *pléonasme* or *abondance*; (4) *hyperbate* or *renversement*.

[16] *Gr. gén.*, 1660 ed. p. 147; 1768 ed. pp. 236 ff.

[17] N. Chomsky, *Cartesian Linguistics*, p. 28, has pointed out the parallel of Bishop Wilkins's position on the matter (1668): see the English section below.

[18] Chomsky, *Cart. Ling.*, p. 28 and fn. 53 pp. 93-94.

[19] Ibid., p. 34: "The position of the rel. pronoun in the *proposition incidente* is determined by a rule that converts deep structure to surface structure. . . ."

underlying system of elementary propositions which would undergo 'grammatical transformations' by certain rules being applied to them.[20] Word order could be part of this process. Somewhat similarly, chapter vi of the *Grammaire* considers the structure of the proposition by pointing out that the relationships between the terms can be expressed either through a case system, by internal modifications (as in the Hebrew construct case), by particles, or more simply by a fixed word order.

The argument that the French language was superior to Latin by virtue of its adhering to natural order had been part of the "Querelle des anciens et des modernes." In his important *Discours physique de la parole* (1666) Géraud de Cordemoy, a Cartesian metaphysician and theorist of language, boldly proclaimed that language to be more perfect whose word order follows the order in which little children, in learning the language, appropriate the particular word-types: first they grasp the signs for things, then those for their qualities, then those for actions, and finally the objects of such actions.[21]

The Jesuit Father Le Laboureur three years later added arguments to this doctrine of natural order and turned it into something systematic, offering it again as proof of the superiority of French over Latin and perhaps *all* other languages, since French seemed to him almost alone in its degree of faithfulness to the order of nature *and logic*.[22] Nor did he stop here. In Latin, he maintained, *conception* and *expression* did not correspond: the latter was not a *véritable image de leur pensée*. He therefore felt free to advance the bold paradox that "Cicéron et tous les Romains pensoient en François devant que de parler en Latin."[23] This

---

[20] Ibid., p. 35. When the substantive is recalled by a relative which replaces it, this latter finds its place at the closest point to the noun it replaces, regardless of its function in its own clause. See my p. 201 above.

[21] Cordemoy, *Discours physique* . . . (1666, English trans. 1668): see pp. 45 ff. of 2ᵈ ed. (Paris, 1677).

[22] [Louis] Le Laboureur, *Avantages de la langue françoise sur la l. latine* (Paris, 1669), 2ᵉ dissertation, pp. 148-174. The author leans on Cordemoy to uphold the French phrase as "plus juste, plus naturelle à l'esprit et plus convenable au bon sens que n'est l'autre" (viz. the Latin). He deems that "la transposition des mots qui se rencontre sans cesse dans le Latin fait dans l'esprit un embarras qui ne se trouve guère dans notre langue." Cited by Barbier d'Aucour, *Sentimens de Cléanthe* (1671), p. 59. Cf. H. Rigault, *La Querelle des anciens* . . . (1856), pp. 101-102 fn. The first Dissertation of the *Avantages* had also been published Paris, 1667.

[23] See Le Laboureur, *Avantages*, p. 156, and cf. G. Sahlin, *César Chesnau Du Marsais* . . . (Paris, 1928), pp. 88-89.

disparity between verbal sequence and flow of thought entails a betrayal of the goal of language, the immediate and clear communication of thought. Hence inversion represents a " désordre contraire à l'institution de la parole, en tant qu'il suspend et qu'il trouble même quelque fois l'intelligence du discours" (p. 149 of 1669 ed.). This not only in the order of words within the clause, but even in the ordering of clauses in a sentence, particularly the parenthetic ones. And he reiterated: " J'ay dit que les Latins pensoient ainsi que nous autres François" (1669 ed., p. 166) because word order mirrors the order of perceptions and thoughts: these follow *raison* and *logique,* which are eternal, universal, and common to all peoples. Consequently, it is to be assumed that in speaking the Romans avoided those inversions and long periods which characterized their written language.[24]

The ' normal ' order, meaning the most frequent, seemed ' natural ' and ' rational ' to the philosophically inclined because of its apparent correspondence to a succession of parts based on their logical function (i. e. their function when regarded as ingredients of logical propositions), and because of the traditional view of inversion as an artifice to achieve special, ' artistic ' effects. Accordingly, the critics became increasingly sensitive to word position and its expressive value. Boileau attributed this incipient awareness to Malherbe, and adroitly expressed himself on the matter through an inversion which tacitly illustrated the principle involved: *D'un mot mis en sa place enseigna le pouvoir.*[25]

The impact of rationalism in this area is nowhere more evident than in Bouhours, if we only pay attention to the characteristic fact that this moderate follower of the *modernes,* above all a follower of Vaugelas and his doctrine of *usage* above *raison,* did acknowledge the unqualified rule of *raison* in the particular domain of word order, where, according to him, usage has no authority. The domain of custom remains thus restricted to lexical choice and semantics. Reason rules over the binding of words into clauses and sentence, i. e. syntax. " L'usage qui est le maître absolu des mots ne l'est pas tant de l'union des mots. Il les forme comme il veut et les attache sans raisonner à des sens et à des idées; mais après cela c'est la raison qui les unit les uns avec les autres . . . pour en faire des images et des expressions de ses conceptions et de ses raisonnements."

[24] See, also, Le Laboureur, *Avantages,* pp. 157, 167, 174. Cf. Ricken, " Rationalismus und Sensualismus," pp. 104-105.
[25] Boileau, *Art poétique,* i, 133.

"Une des choses qui contribuë davantage à la netteté du stile, est de suivre cet ordre de la nature que notre langue aime tant, et qui est si conforme à la raison." [26]

In line with this way of reasoning, in his successful *Entretiens* Bouhours came out squarely in favor of direct order, which he upheld as a decisive advantage of French, "perhaps alone" in this among all languages. He acknowledged that this remark, which he had made before, he said, had been made by others before him—an allusion to the *Avantages de la langue françoise* by his Jesuit *confrère* Le Laboureur (duly identified in the second edition, 1672, of the *Entretiens,* after Barbier d'Aucour's charge that Bouhours had been amiss in giving credit to this chief source of his). In his words, "la langue françoise est peut-être la seule qui suive exactement l'ordre naturel, et qui exprime les pensées en la manière qu'elles naissent dans l'esprit." [27] Bouhours thus stresses the adherence of language to thought, as he does methodically in his more conclusive *De la manière de bien penser,* a work, as he pointed out, "concerning the right thinking processes as applied to literature," chiefly to art prose.

Ricken has appropriately suggested that Bouhours' position on this matter implies a realization of aesthetic value as independent of, and possibly conflicting with, the laws of reason and clarity in the use of language (other than French).[28] But, of course, this inference was consistently implied in the centuried speculation on style. What does emerge in Bouhours is the notion that French enjoys a unique advantage in combining the aesthetic and the logical, the emotional and the rational, harmony and clarity, since it does not need inversion to achieve elegance. "Le premier soin de notre langue est de contenter l'esprit, et non pas de chatouiller l'oreille. Elle a plus d'égard au bon sens qu'à la belle cadence." [29] Italians and Spaniards are about as "disorderly" as the Latins for the sake of beauty: "L'élégance de ces langues consiste en partie dans cet arrangement bizarre, ou plutost, dans ce désordre et cette

[26] Bouhours, *Doutes sur la langue françoise* (1674), 353, in Rosset, p. 114. Cf. *Commentaires sur les Remarques de Vaugelas,* ed. Jeanne Streicher (Paris, 1936, 2 tomes), t. II, p. 802, citing the last passage in our text from the original ed. of the *Doutes* (Paris, 1674), p. 204, also used by Rosset. See Streicher, op. cit., pp. 801-804 for other comments by Ménage, Bouhours, Patru, T. Corneille, and the Academy on word order after Vaugelas.

[27] Bouhours, *Entretiens* (first ed.), ed. Radouant, pp. 55-56.

[28] Ricken, "Rationalismus," pp. 106-107.

[29] Bouhours, *Entretiens,* ed. Radouant, p. 59.

transposition étrange de mots. Il n'y a que la langue françoise qui suive la nature pas à pas . . . ; et elle n'a qu'à la suivre fidèlement pour trouver le nombre et l'harmonie que les autres langues ne rencontrent que dans le renversement de l'ordre naturel." [30] Instead of saying *César a vaincu Pompée dans la bataille de Pharsale,* the Greeks and Romans would have said in their tongues: *de Pharsale dans la bataille a vaincu Pompée César.*

The ruthless charge of ' disorderliness' leveled against Latin became a trademark of the "modern" party in the famous *Querelle.* Desmarets de St.- Sorlin spoke of that ancestral tongue as "embarrassée, obscure, . . . qui montre toûjours son désordre étranger." [31] The arguments of the *modernes* were summarized by Charpentier, another champion of their cause.[32] The question of *construction directe,* a central part of his argumentation, occupies a whole chapter in his 2-tome work.[33] He may have derived this term from Quintilian's *rectus ordo,* and brings in authorities from Plato through Aristotle and Cicero to Quintilian to support the preference for ORDRE DIRECT. This term, carrying with it the new logistical emphasis, will tend to replace the previous *ordre naturel.* The chapter reaches its climax with the statement that Quintilian's idea of the accomplished type of eloquence is properly a representation of the characteristics of the French language (II, 681). What he fails to note is that such a conclusion can only be based on the preliminary phases in the ancient way of putting the matter, since Quintilian eventually said the opposite under that heading (see the often quoted passage *nimia quorundam fuit observatio, ut . . . ,* discussed above).[34] Charpentier reveals the ideological undertone of such a position by expressly linking the much-heralded *clarté* to Descartes' *évidence.*

[30] Ibid., p. 56.

[31] Desmarets de Saint-Sorlin, *La Défense de la langue et de la poésie françoise* adressée à M. Perrault (Paris, 1675), p. 29.

[32] François Charpentier, *De l'excellence de la langue françoise* (Paris, 1683): vol. II, pp. 639-682 for what follows. And cf. H. Gillot, *La Querelle des anciens et des modernes* (Nancy, 1914), pp. 435 f.

[33] The title of this chapter xxx is peremptory: "Que la construction directe comme est celle de la langue françoise est incomparablement plus estimable que la construction renversée de la langue latine, et que les Grecs et les Latins mesmes en ont jugé de la sorte." *De l'excellence,* II, 639. See esp. pp. 651 and 672-678. As to the term *direct* may I recall that Quintilian's *rectus ordo* was already echoed in "Quintil Censeur"'s interestingly comprehensive *droit ordre naturel* (see p. 469 above).

[34] Ricken, p. 108, also fails to point out this violence done to the ancient texts.

Another of Le Laboureur's ideas is taken up again by Charpentier where he maintains that every departure from the right construction involves an increased effort on the part of the hearer, with two operations being needed instead of one, since the direct order must be mentally restored to attain intelligibility (651 f.). And Bouhours' argument on the coupling of the logical and the aesthetic is presented anew in a most original and significant fashion when we are told that "il n'y a que la langue françoise qui puisse exprimer les grandes émotions, et conserver la politesse d'un discours estudié parce que dans cette langue la Nature et l'Art sont presque tousjours d'accord" (II, 650). Indeed, how can an orator arouse genuine wrath or sorrow if he must worry over the number of syllables and the ordering of words [while the hearer is distracted by these same questions]? Our reader will remember that the same demurrer had been entered by Cicero against the formalistic excesses of Isocratean Asianism. In retrospect, that is to say in the light of the sensualist reaction which followed, it may seem paradoxical that Charpentier could so effectively use for his own rationalist purpose the argument of passions being part of the expressive content of language.

Bayle adroitly summarizes this argument and lays stress on the unique ability of French to achieve harmony and vigor without having to sacrifice direct order, while the Romans' recourse to inversion was justified by the unfortunate ineptitude of their language to combine these two basic desiderata of effective expression:

M. Charpentier . . . tire un grand avantage de la construction directe. C'est un argument que M. le Laboureur a poussé avec beaucoup de force, et qui est assurément fort bon, quoi qu'il semble que M. l'Abbé Danet ait voulu prouver, dans la Préface de son second Dictionnaire, que les transpositions font bien de l'honneur à la langue des Latins. M. Charpentier au contraire prouve, par le propre témoignage des meilleurs critiques de l'Antiquité, que c'est une perfection que de ranger les paroles selon l'ordre de la nature. Il croit avec beaucoup de raison que les Latins n'ont quitté cet ordre, qu'à cause qu'en le suivant leur discours étoit trop rude, et trop raboteux, ou bien trop lâche. . . . Voici une période qui à cause de ce renversement, peut avoir quatre sens également bons: *Sub idem tempus nunciatum fuit Turcas captivos Polonos trucidasse.*[35]

[35] *Œuvres diverses de M. Pierre Bayle . . . excepté son Dictionnaire . . .* (La Haye, 1727-31, 4 vols., repr. Hildesheim, 1964-68), I (1727, 1964), 122. Cf. Brunot, *H. L. F.,* IV, 2 (1924), 1105-1106. Somewhat similarly, Joseph Leven de Templery, *Entretiens sur la langue françoise à Madonte* (Aix, 1698), p. 298, submitted a

I have remarked above that the rationalism of Port-Royal deserves qualifications. A keen interest in the mental processes leading to linguistic expression had compelled Arnauld and his collaborators to fill, in part, the gap left by Descartes in this area. Generally speaking, for the Cartesians the pure level of thinking takes place in a mind divorced from the body. It consists of a process of abstraction which is necessary to correct the distortion and corruption suffered by our perceptions in travelling from the corporeal senses through the imagination and the passions. The objects act through the senses, and by stimulating them cause sensorial *impressions* which are then carried over the nerves to the brain in the form of images. The mind now takes over, but before they reach the nobler level of pure thinking the impressions-images enter the antechamber of the *passions* and *imagination*, where they are renewed, interpreted, and also distorted. It falls, at last, to reason to filter and purify them.[36] The mechanistic nature of Descartes' physiology, as documented in his treatise on *Les passions de l'âme*, seemed to his early followers to conflict with the metaphysical side of his system. Some of them were inclined to lay the stress on the former, so that this inner contradiction between Cartesian physics and metaphysics fostered, somewhat paradoxically, a naturalistic orientation which in due course fed the most consistent adherence to empirical sensationalism and even outright materialism. Thus La Mettrie eventually concluded that the theory of the two substances, mind and matter, was only a trick which thinly veiled Descartes' true view of a feeling and thinking matter.

For what concerns us here, this conflict first clearly emerged in Géraud de Cordemoy's *Discours physique de la parole* of 1668. Here the imagination is attributed an essential role in the formation of language. The coupling of sign and impression takes place in the brain in a purely mechanical process.[37] This pronouncement of that early follower and interpreter of the master started a polemic on imagination in which basically Cartesian thinkers took a position in defence of imagination, as Arnauld did. La Bruyère[38] and Fénelon carried this defence to the

humorous example of equivocal phrasal arrangement: " Un homme . . . , étant interrogé si une petite chienne étoit à luy, répondit fort-naïvement, C'est la chienne de ma femme, que je ne caresse jamais." Brunot, IV, 2, 1110.

[36] Cf. J. H. Roy, *L'imagination selon Descartes* (Paris, 1944).

[37] Cf. Ricken, " Condillacs *liaison des idées*," 556 ff.

[38] Both Vigneul-Marville and P. Coste (and the dictionaries of the time, such

realm of *ordre naturel,* as did the Abbé Du Bos from the vantage point of his sensualistic aesthetics.[39]

As early as 1676 Lamy's *Art de parler* for the first time presented the opposition to the *ordre naturel* in a theoretically grounded context involving the doctrine of *imagination.* He drew the analogy of the "painting" to describe the mental events leading to speech, whose foundation thus became psychological rather than rational. The Latin phrase was said to show the unity of a picture giving simultaneously all its elements, whereas the French breaks them up through a descending succession: the spatial totality of the former contrasts with the time-fragmentation of the latter.[40] Similarly the Chanoine de Gamaches, *Les agrémens du langage réduits à leurs principes* (Paris, 1718), opposed to *ordre naturel* a higher principle of *enchaînement des mots* which is at times achieved through inversion.[41]

Thus, even though leaning on the Port-Royal Logic, Lamy's Rhetoric opened the way to a lively current which was referred to as *rhétorique naturiste,* and was also represented by Du Marsais, Louis Racine, Batteux, Condillac (*Art d'écrire*), and J.-J. Rousseau (*Essai sur l'origine des langues*). More on this later.[42]

The group of generally 'Cartesian' statements roughly enclosed between 1650 and 1680 was followed by a phase of consolidation during

as Richelet's) interpreted La Bruyère's *termes transposés* as nothing but inversions, whereas modern readers tend to take them as "metaphors." See Pierre Coste, *Défense de M. de La Bruyère et de ses Caractères contre les accusations . . . de M. de Vigneul-Marville,* in L. B., *Les Caractères . . .* (Amsterdam, t. II, 1739), pp. 250 ff. Pizzorusso, *Teorie letterarie in Francia,* p. 100, concedes the ambiguity of the passage.

[39] Jean Baptiste Du Bos, *Réflexions critiques sur la poésie et sur la peinture* (first ed. Paris, 1719, 2 vols.), ed. Paris, Pissot, vol. II, sect. 22 and 23, pp. 339-371 on the primacy of *sentiment* (then the current term for 'imagination') in the judgment of works of art; vol. I, sect. 35, pp. 312 ff., esp. 327-332 on construction. See below on this matter.

For a broad, up-to-date study of Du Bos' rhetoric, see B. Munteano, *Constantes dialectiques* (1967), pp. 297-374: "Un rhéteur esthéticien. L'Abbé du Bos."

[40] Lamy, *Rhétorique,* 1701 ed., p. 67. Also cf. Paris, 1688³ ed., p. 179.

[41] E.-S. de Gamaches, *Agrémens . . . ,* pp. 1-43. We find there a remarkable doctrine of *transformations* which, under the headings of *répétition, regroupement, réduction des termes,* seems to hark back to the medieval rhetoric of *abbreviatio* and Sánchez' notion of ellipsis. Cf. A. François, *Hist. de la l. fr. cultivée,* p. 66.

[42] Cf. A. François, *Hist. de la l. fr. cultivée,* pp. 79-87. See on p. 80 a valuable bibliographic digest of the impact of the *rhétorique naturiste.*

which the positions we have just witnessed are often reiterated more or less mechanically as if the issues could be taken for granted. The ground was thus being prepared for the great polemic of the mid-eighteenth century.[43] Meanwhile, the speculation of the classic age received a sort of official seal when the Preface to the *Dictionnaire de l'Académie* of 1694 placed at the highest rank among the virtues of the French language "cette construction directe, qui, sans s'eloigner de l'ordre naturel des pensées, ne laisse pas de rencontrer toutes les délicatesses dont l'art est capable." [44]

2. True enough, the Academy was and continued to be the target of those who felt dissatisfied with the rigidity of the prevailing regulatory trend, of which the Academy itself appeared as the conspicuous and official embodiment. Foremost among the critics were the classical philologists like Anne Dacier, who lamented the growing inflexibility of the French language with regard to both the form of the sentence (which had begun to exclude all floridity) and the arrangement of words (which was being forced into fixed, regular patterns): "Mais cette composition melée [which partakes of the austere and of the florid—*l'austère* and *le fleuri*], source de ces grâces, est inconnue à notre langue; elle n'a ni ces particules nombreuses, dont elle puisse soutenir ses termes, ni cette dif-

---

[43] The principal texts besides those already cited are indicated by Ricken (p. 265 fn. 52): B. Lamy, *De l'art de parler* (Paris, 1676), p. 33; (Paris, 1688), pp. 47 f.; D. Vairasse, *Grammaire méthodique* . . . (Paris, 1681), p. 438; Fr.-P. Gillet, *Discours sur le génie de la l. fr.* in *Plaidoyers et autres œuvres* (Paris, 1696), pp. 55 ff. of 1718 ed.; Jean Frain du Tremblay, *Traité des langues* . . . (Paris, 1703), pp. 128 ff.; J. Morvan de Bellegarde, *Réflexions sur l'élégance et la politesse du style* (Amsterdam, 1706), p. 238. Also interesting the dictionaries by Richelet (1728 ed.), s. vv. *arrangement, construction, inversion, transposition,* and by Furetière (1727 ed.), s. vv. *construction, inversion.*

One should add that many a new insight affecting language and literary style can be gleaned outside the technical production on rhetoric, grammar, or literary criticism. This is, indeed, a characteristic of the age, when practically everybody becomes interested in *grammaire.* I shall only mention here the idiosyncratic position of the Abbé Girard, who classified the languages on the basis of word order as *analogues* [= analytical], *transpositives* [= flectional], and *mixtes* or *amphibologiques,* and extended this characterization to the point of denying the filiation of French, Spanish, and Italian from Latin: *Vrais Principes,* Disc. I, tom. I, pp. 23 ff.

[44] Brunot, *H. L. F.,* t. VI, 2e partie, fasc. 2e (by A. François) (Paris, 1933), p. 1936. See, in this fasc., esp. pp. 1933-1942, 1967-1980, 1994-1999, 2013-2025, 2055-2060, 2115-2120 for this portion of our subject.

férente harmonie qui nait du différent arrangement des mots. . . ." All of which made it awkward for modern French to attempt an adequate translation of Homer, in Mme Dacier's judgment.[45]

Such positions had begun to sound like a lost cause. Yet the partisans of the Ancients could find comfort on this matter in at least one impressive authority toward the end of Louis XIV's life. In his celebrated Letter to the Academy (composed in 1714 but published posthumously in 1716), Fénelon, in a rather isolated position among the leading literati, complained that, what with the desire to correct the excessive liberties the writers of the Pléiade had taken with the language, one had fallen into the opposite extreme:

On a appauvri, desséché, et gêné notre langue. Elle n'ose jamais procéder que suivant la méthode la plus scrupuleuse et la plus uniforme de la grammaire. On voit toujours venir d'abord un nominatif substantif qui mène son adjectif comme par la main; son verbe ne manque pas de marcher derrière, suivi d'un adverbe qui ne souffre rien entre deux; et le régime appelle aussitôt un accusatif, qui ne peut jamais se déplacer. C'est ce qui exclut toute suspension de l'esprit, toute attention, toute surprise, toute variété, et souvent toute magnifique cadence." [46]

It was to be expected that the party of the Moderns would take issue with Fénelon. The Abbé de Pons, for one, countered that there is no justification for separating an adjective from its noun because " no inter-

---

[45] *L'Iliade* d'Homère traduite en François par Madame Dacier . . . (Amsterdam, Wetsteins and Smith, 1731, 3 tomes), " Préface," t. i, p. 42.

[46] *Lettre à l'Académie* in Fénelon, *Œuvres complètes* (10 vols., Paris, Leroux, 1851-52), t. VI, p. 627. We now have a critical ed. by Ernesta Caldarini: F., *Lettre à l'Académie, avec les versions primitives* (Geneva, 1970). Cf. Brunot, H. L. F., IV, 2, p. 1107. See an essay on the French sentence at the time of Fénelon in Marcel Cohen, *Grammaire et style, 1450-1950* (Paris, 1954), pp. 65-72. Arnaldo Pizzorusso, *La Poetica di Fénelon* (Milan, 1959) contains a detailed study of the *Lettre à l'Académie*. See, esp., pp. 88-91. Also W. S. Howell, " Oratory and Poetry in Fénelon's Literary Theory," QJS, XXXVII (1951), 1-10.

Du Cerceau could soon echo this passage closely, finding in it a confirmation of his own theory (even though, as Pizzorusso points out, Fénelon was not referring to the language of French prose as contrasted with that of poetry): " c'est par cette heureuse hardiesse . . . qu'ils [= les poètes] se sont mis en état de produire cette suspension d'esprit, cette attente, cette surprise, cette variété et ces magnifiques cadences, où selon M. de Cambray, la prose ne peut atteindre." Du Cerceau, " Deffense de la poésie françoise," pp. 35-38, quoted by Pizzorusso, op. cit., p. 91.

mediary idea intervenes in our mind between those two ideas," and so on concerning other kinds of illogical disjunctions.[47]

Bouhours' statements soon transcended the boundaries of his country to give rise to a prolonged polemic started by the Bolognese Marquis G. G. Orsi in 1703, and amounting to an invidious comparison of the respective natures and merits of the French and Italian tradition. (See the following Section.) It will suffice here to say that the organ of the "modern party," the influential *Mémoires de Trévoux,* understandably took the side of Bouhours and that the members and associates of the Italian Academy of Arcadia rose practically to one man (there were only scattered dissents or qualifications) to denounce the French position. The polemic centered mainly on the contrast between the French rationalistic aptitude for prose, with consequent lack of a "poetic language," and, on the other hand, the Italian absolute appreciation for poetry, with its special language.

A. Pizzorusso has analyzed the writings of Du Cerceau, an important author overlooked by all those who had so far surveyed our subject.[48] He has expertly situated this author within the main trends of French debates on literary theory. It is a pity that he has not placed him squarely and with detailed cross references within the terms of the Orsi-Bouhours polemic, where he seems rightfully to belong by the very nature of the arguments he chose to develop.

J.-A. Du Cerceau undertook a defence of poetry in a series of articles in the *Nouveau Mercure* between 1717 and 1718.[49] He distinguished between elocution and invention in the sense of style of poetry and content of poetry, and insisted that, just as there can be poetic treatment without poetic form (as in Fénelon), so can there be poetic style without

---

[47] Abbé J.-F. de Pons, "Dissertation sur les langues en général, et sur la langue françoise en particulier," *Le Nouveau Mercure* (March, 1717), pp. 22-25. Cf. Pizzorusso, op. cit., p. 90.

[48] A. Pizzorusso, *Teorie letterarie in Francia* (1968), ch. x: "Jean-Antoine Du Cerceau e la teoria delle inversioni poetiche," 401-429.

[49] Du Cerceau, "Réflexions sur la poésie françoise, où l'on examine en quoy consiste ce qui fait le caractère propre du vers françois, et ce qui le distingue essentiellement de la prose," *Nouveau Mercure* (nov. 1717), 5 ff.; "Examen des transpositions permises ou défendues dans le style poétique"; "Examen des transpositions du nominatif et de l'accusatif"; "Examen de la transposition des verbes" etc., 5 more articles after the first, published between dec. 1717 and april 1718 in the *Nouveau Mercure,* then all reprinted in J.-A. Du Cerceau, *Réflexions sur la poésie françoise* [. . .] avec les *Réflexions sur l'églogue et sur la poésie pastorale* par l'Abbé Genest et quelques autres pièces (Amsterdam, 1730). Cf. Pizzorusso (1968), p. 404 fn.

poetic content. The style of poetry or of verse consists essentially not of rhyme and rhythm, but of word order.

C'est à dire qu'il y a un tour de Phrase qui est Poétique et un qui est Prosaïque; que ce dernier, avec la Mesure la plus exacte et la Rime la plus riche, est toujours dans le fond véritablement Prose; au lieu que l'autre, sans Rime même et sans Mesure, est toujours réellement Poésie.[50]

The obvious corollary to this way of seeing the matter is that French offers the greatest difficulties in determining this possible difference between poetic order and prosaic order. This corollary was clearly drawn by Louis Racine.[51] Du Cerceau saw the arrangement of words as the "internal form" of poetic style, and rhyme, rhythm, and caesura as its "mechanical form." The former thus becomes the "objective criterion" one seeks in order to identify the difference of poetic diction, and consists typically of the use of inversion.

C'est uniquement le Tour qui met de la suspension dans la Phrase, par le moyen des inversions ou transpositions reçues dans la Langue, et qui n'en forcent point la construction.[52]

Therefore only the *inversions reçues* (assimilated by the current language) will be acceptable. The value of this stratagem lies in the creation of suspense: "Je regarde donc la suspension comme l'âme du Vers. . . ."[53] This effective challenge to the reader is due to a tension between the order of words and the order of things represented.

Yet inversions, we have been told, must be rigidly controlled: the *transpositions trop hardies* must be excluded, and, furthermore, the relative boldness of admissible inversions depends on the literary genre involved, the epic being the one that admits the boldest kind. Du Cerceau defends Ronsard (although otherwise his practical taste as a poet and critic remains delimited within the taste and schemes of Boileau's classicism) for having introduced a truly "poetic elocution" on the pattern of the freedom which characterized Greek and Latin. True enough, he exaggerated and thus sinned against the *génie* of the French language.[54]

---

[50] *Réfl. sur la poésie*, p. 13. Cf. Pizzorusso (1968), p. 409.

[51] Louis Racine, *Réflexions sur la poésie* in *Œuvres* . . . , 6th ed. (Amsterdam, 1750, 3 vols.), vol. III, Part v, pp. 87-88. Cf. Pizzorusso (1968), p. 409.

[52] Du Cerceau, *Réfl. sur la poésie*, p. 18. Cf. Pizzorusso (1968), pp. 410-411.

[53] Du Cerceau, *Réfl. sur la poésie*, pp. 18-19.

[54] Cf. Pizzorusso (1968), pp. 412-413.

Above all, the criterion to be used is to avoid all ambiguity and equivocation. The genius of French remains absolute clarity and rational directness.

Our author had to defend himself against his critics in the *Réponse générale à la principale objection qu'on forme contre mon opinion.*[55] Desfontaines had objected that Du Cerceau's system could be upset simply by observing that there are beautiful lines without any shadow of inversions. In return, Du Cerceau insists that he has supplied a complete and coherent theory of the objective nature of poetic elocution. Batteux also tried to confute him because he understood his basic allegiance to a rationalistic, "modern" view of expression. For Batteux inversion does not distinguish poetry but all effective expression, in prose as well as in verse.[56]

The seeds of further developments to come were clearly contained in Gamaches' *Agrémens du langage.* The modest appearance of this little treatise concealed a good deal of originality, to which Condillac and Beauzée, in particular, were duly sensitive. For Gamaches was the first to analyze the facts of word order on a comprehensive and extensive scale, over and above the basic elements of the logical proposition. He pointed out the importance of phrases and complements beyond the nucleus of subject-predicate. It is with him that there began a methodical substitution of logical order and clarity for the ancient (and in fact quite different) principle of sensuous number. He even suggested that considerations of rhythm and harmony could evasively cover up the lack of realization of the way our thoughts strike us as beautifully expressed when they are expressed effectively, that is 'clearly.' And in moving within a grammatical rather than rhetorical context he began the shift that was to be consummated by the *métaphysiciens.* "Il y a long-temps qu'on cherche ce que c'est que le nombre en matière de langage; mais il est facile de le découvrir en suivant nos principes. Le nombre est le rapport sensible des parties du discours rangées selon l'ordre que demande la netteté du style." [57] Beauzée will exploit these principles fully, not without duly quoting his worthy predecessor.

---

[55] *Réfl. sur la poésie,* pp. 247 ff.

[56] Batteux, "Lettres sur la phrase françoise comparée avec la phrase latine, à M. l'Abbé d'Olivet," in *Cours de belles-lettres* . . . (Paris, t. II, 1748), pp. 105 ff., esp. 112.

[57] Étienne-Simon de Gamaches, *Les Agrémens du langage* (1718), Part I, p. 31.

Departing from a passage by Boileau, Gamaches proposed to offer a "new art" of style which would transcend Grammar and Rhetoric. An early reviewer praised this bold attempt even while expressing reservations as to its final results.[58] In this "espèce de logique" (a "logique du goût," to use Diderot's expression) elocution was divided according to three kinds of *agréments: style net, style vif, élocution brillante.* These are the headlines to the three Parts of the work. In harmony with Bouhours, Gamaches so defines the *ordre direct,* essential element of the clear style, *style net:*

> Pour s'exprimer clairement, il faut que le sujet aille à la teste de la phrase, suivi de ses modificatifs, et que le verbe vienne ensuite suivi pareillement des siens. Il faut encore que les modificatifs subalternes paroissent immédiatement après ceux auxquels ils servent de modification.[59]

As for inversions, we may recall that Du Cerceau's discrimination between prose and poetry on this ground found a precedent in Vaugelas, who looked upon inversions as virtues in poetry, but vices in prose—without, however, excluding them altogether.[60] Yet Gamaches reminds us even more closely of Du Cerceau's terms of discrimination when, although he accepts only those inversions which serve the supreme goal of clarity, he specifically admits the *transpositions hazardées* in poetry and only the *communes* in prose (that is, those authorized by logic and usage).

In this approach clarity tends to subordinate to itself every other value. Gamaches, it bears repeating, went so far as to view even harmony as part of clarity, and offered his famous rule of the longer segments at the end in the light of this conception:

> Je viens de dire que quand les deux phrases partialles [sic] d'une proposition composée étoient inégalles, la plus courte devoit être mise la première; et en parlant de l'arrangement des mots dans une phrase simple, j'ay dit, que quand un mot avoit plusieurs modificatifs, les plus longs ne devoient se trouver qu'à la suite des plus courts.[61]

Cf. Pizzorusso (1968), 352-399: ch. 9: "Il 'Sistema' di E.-S. de Gamaches: Lo Stile e la *Science du Coeur,*" esp. (on the *Agrémens*) pp. 374-395.

[58] *Europe Savante* (April 1719), pp. 190 ff. Cf. Pizzorusso (1968), 374-376.

[59] *Agrémens* (1718), pp. 4-5. Cf. Bouhours, *Doutes sur la langue françoise, proposez à Messieurs de l'Académie Françoise par un gentilhomme de province* (Paris, 1674), pp. 183-184, 204, cit. by Pizzorusso (1968), p. 379 fn.

[60] See fn. 4 above: cf. Pizzorusso (1968), p. 380 fn.

[61] *Agrémens* (1718), pp. 31-32. Cf. Pizzorusso (1968), p. 382.

The *style vif*, in turn, is based on parallelisms and symmetries (and could obviously remind us of the Asian style); the *brillant* has to do with the *tours de pensée*, including the objectionable *pointes* and conceits (roughly, the "Senecan" style).

After such interventions as we have just seen, the specific contribution of the Abbé Du Bos, long celebrated as a 'precursor of Romantic criticism' in other respects, may sound rather old-fashioned. In line with the 'Party of the Ancients,' Du Bos devoted a long chapter of his *Réflexions critiques sur la poésie et sur la peinture* (1719) to a review of the arguments in favor of Latin superiority over French, placing syntax, specifically construction, among them.[62] This meant to him that Latin could arrange itself in any order for the sake of harmony, which French cannot do because the lack of inflection would harm intelligibility. Yet French would seem to need inversion even more than Latin, owing to its lesser phonetic harmony and to the great frequency of hiatus, since final stressed vowels in French cannot be elided in pronunciation. Some *inversion*, though on a limited basis, does remain available to French, but no *transposition* of modifier and modified.

The leading exponent of the 'logistic' position in the new and decisive phase of the ensuing polemic was César Chesnau Du Marsais (1676-1756), who again, somewhat like Bouhours, remained a determined rationalist on word order even though he borrowed much from Locke's empiricism on other linguistic matters, and indeed could, on the general level, even be taken as an exponent of the inductive-sensationalist method. This apparent contradiction must be kept in mind when trying to assess the complex (and now rather controversial) historical position of this leading grammarian.[63] Du Marsais began early by entering the argument through a side issue. His 1722 *Exposition d'une méthode raisonnée pour apprendre la langue latine* proposed recasting into *ordre naturel* the Latin texts used for instruction: "Vous dites que je francise le latin; je le nie, je le réduis seulement à l'ordre naturel, qui est de tout pays; et comme

---

[62] Du Bos, *Réflexions critiques*, ed. 1770 and 1967 reprint, vol. I, Section 35, pp. 312 ff., esp. 327-332.

[63] The empirical orientation of Du Marsais and of the whole grammatical part of the *Encyclopédie* is much emphasized by Rosiello, *Linguistica illuminista* (1967), esp. pp. 92-104 and 132-150, in polemic against the more traditional interpretation of Du Marsais as a leading Cartesian rationalist. See, e. g., for this latter interpretation, F. Venturi, *Le Origini dell'Enciclopedia* (Torino, 1963), esp. p. 62.

je conserve les propres termes de l'original, je conduis plus aisément le disciple à l'intelligence du texte pur " [sic].[64] He recalled that he was merely practicing in writing what had long been done orally by the method of parsing, *faire la construction,* for purposes of sentence and clause analysis. But note the intrepid consequentiality with which our grammarian would present the pupils with the 'logically' recast texts *first,* to be followed by their original form only at a later moment. Horace served as guinea pig with his *Carmen saeculare,* as an example. What was meant by the *texte pur* was the 'rational,' intellectual and factual part of the text itself, deprived of the *passions* and *imagination* which had led the author to introduce all his 'inversions.'

Du Marsais was aware that inversion was made possible in Latin by the flectional system, which essentially weakened the grammatical basis for word order, but shrewdly submitted that this same argument demonstrated his main point: The speaker always starts out from the direct order, otherwise how could he place the complements in the right case if he were not thinking first of the verb which textually follows them? [65] On the other hand, Du Marsais was prepared to concede to the adversary camp a major point, namely the legitimacy of the *langage affectif.* As early as 1724, in a defence of his *Exposition* he distinguished between a " simple and necessary syntax, which follows the order of thought," and a " figurative syntax, which follows the order of passions and affections," dependent on imagination. He who speaks with passion does not follow the natural order.[66] Linacer's dichotomy of *syntaxis regularis* and *syntaxis*

[64] Du Marsais, *Œuvres* (Paris, 1797, 7 tomes), I, 159-160. Cf. Ricken, 110-112 and A. François, *Hist. de la l. fr. cultivée,* II, 26-27. The reading of the texts in direct construction was achieved by the method of interlinear translation. Rosiello, p. 137, claims that Du Marsais was the first to adopt this idea from Locke. But the idea of interlinear translation was an old one: it was practiced in the early Italian humanistic schools (such as that of Vittorino da Feltre in Mantua)—although presumably it did not include construing, which the humanists so firmly abhorred.

[65] These ideas are best elaborated in Du Marsais' posthumous treatment of inversions: *Œuvres,* III, 346 ff., 358 ff. His *Les véritables principes de la grammaire, ou nouvelle grammaire raisonnée pour apprendre la langue latine* (1729, then in *Œuvres,* I, 183-279), more " general " than the 1722 *Exposition d'une méthode* . . . , was the Preface to a " new grammar " of which the only other part published, the *Traité des tropes* (1730, then in *Œuvres,* III, 170 ff.), was to be the seventh part. See, also, Dumarsais—Fontanier, *Les Tropes,* Intr. G. Genette (2 tomes, Geneva, Slatkine Reprints, 1967).

[66] Du Marsais, *Lettre à Mr.**** . . . *touchant le livre intitulé: Exposition d'une*

figurata could still rescue a *grammairien-philosophe* from an embarrassing impasse.

This way of *raisonner les langues* on both the theoretical and the prac-tical level was not long in eliciting a vigorous reaction from the sensualists. The first treatment of inversion from this new vantage point came in 1746, in Condillac's *Essai sur l'origine des connaissances humaines.*[67] Chomsky has recently called our attention to the principle of innate ideas which lay at the foundation of the linguistic approach brought about by Cartesianism. He has also illustrated the distance between the Cartesian view of all languages having the same intellectual foundations and Humboldt's views on the relative multiplicity of language systems. But the contrast between these two stands goes back to the antirationalist reaction of the self-styled *mécaniciens* and their mentor in this field, to wit Condillac. To begin with, one aspect of Condillac's conception of semantic processes relates him to Humboldt's ideas in a way that Chomsky has not illustrated. Instead of conceiving words as mere signs for thoughts, which to the rationalists are the true mental reality, Condillac strove to reveal their influence on thinking itself. Cognition arises out of the two stages of *sensation* and *réflexion*. He carried this Lockean position further by studying the reciprocal conditioning of language and the thinking processes in their historically evolving interrelationship. Furthermore, Condillac anticipated an aspect of Humboldt's system by denying the

méthode raisonnée pour apprendre la langue latine, first published in *Journal des Sçavans,* march 1724, pp. 175 ff., then in Du M., *Œuvres,* t. I (1797), p. 157. See also, for the preceding assertions, *Œuvres,* t. V (1797), p. 31: *Mélanges de gram-maire, de philosophie . . . tirés de l'Encyclopédie,* art. " Construction." Also *Œuvres,* t. III, pp. 170 ff.: *Des Tropes, ou des différens sens dans lesquels on peut prendre une même langue . . . ;* and *Fragment sur les causes de la parole,* in *Œuvres,* III, p. 397, as well as the art. " Inversion," ibid., pp. 339-375, esp. 375. Cf. Pizzorusso, *Teorie letterarie,* pp. 425-426.

Besides the *Exposition* (Paris, 1722, 1795, then in *Œuvres,* I, 1-41, followed by the application of the method to the *Carmen saeculare* of Horace, I, 45-79), the *Véritables principes,* and the art. " Inversion," the 1797 *Œuvres* also reprinted D'Alembert's *Éloge de Du Marsais* (I, xxxi-xcii), the *Remarques sur les articles 52 et 53 des Mémoires de Trévoux . . . 1723,* a follow-up to the *Exposition* (I, 83-146), the articles from the *Encyclopédie* down to " Grammairien " (*Œuvres,* IV and V), and the *Logique* (V, 303-386).

[67] Condillac, *Œuvres philosophiques,* ed. Le Roy, I, pp. 1 ff. Condillac's later *Traité des sensations* (1754) developed these ideas even more explicitly, as part of his theory of knowledge.

possibility of a hierarchy of logical categories binding on all men at all times, just as he rejected the innate principles of thinking.

The key statement that ties the linguistic to the stylistic level has a surprising ring that, even in its thoroughly empirical context, reminds one immediately of Vico: "Le style, dans son origine, a été poétique, puisqu'il a commencé par peindre les idées avec les IMAGES les plus SENSIBLES." [68] This *langage d'action* vanished gradually in giving way to expository prose. The celebrated chapter " Des Inversions " (II, I, xii) followed up these premises. Condillac had seemed to play into the rationalists' hands by formulating his well-known principle of the *liaison des idées* as the basic rule of both sentence structure and word order. Sequences of words do and must reflect sequences of thoughts by placing contiguously in the linguistic expression what is linked together in the process of thinking. But now he was coming out with a rather surprising justification for the occasional disjoining of the ideally connected: such disjoining can be thoroughly functional if required by expressive needs:

Ainsi le foible obstacle qui vient de leur éloignement [= construction où les termes s'écartent de la liaison des idées = inversion] ne paroît fait que pour exciter l'imagination; et les idées ne sont dispersées qu'afin que l'esprit, obligé de les rapprocher lui-même, en sente la liaison ou le contraste avec plus de vivacité. Par cet artifice, toute la force d'une phrase se réunit quelquefois dans le mot qui la termine. [69]

He took his example from Horace, Book I, Ode 28: *Nec quicquam tibi prodest / aërias tentasse domos animoque rotundum / percurrisse polum, morituro,* thus illustrating once again the un-Romance principle, which

---

[68] Condillac, *Essai*, II, I, viii, in O. P., ed. Le Roy, I, p. 80, § 67. On Condillac's historical thought as related to his historical view of linguistic evolution see, now, Roberto Parenti, " Il pensiero storico di Condillac," *Rivista critica di storia della filosofia*, XVII (1962), 167-179, 309-320; XVIII (1963), 32-43. Also Pasquale Salvucci, *Linguaggio e mondo umano in Condillac* (Urbino, 1957); Id., *Condillac filosofo della comunità umana* (Milan, 1961). But the most competent examination of Condillac's role in the evolution of linguistics from Bacon's empiricism to modern structuralism is L. Rosiello, *Linguistica illuminista* (1967), esp. pp. 60-85; also ibid. for ideal points of contact between Condillac and Vico. Karl D. Uitti, *Linguistics and Literary Theory* . . . (1969), pp. 77-92, offers a broad assessment of Condillac's thought from a modern linguistic vantage point.

[69] *Essai*, p. 93, § 121. The ch. xii on inversions on pp. 92-94, §§ 117-126. Condillac's position cannot be assimilated to that of the logicians like Du Marsais in that he recognizes the NECESSITY of the figures (inversions, ellipses, transpositions).

he had just stated, of weight at the end, characteristic of ancient theory and practice.

Yet this theory of inversion was not a departure from the 'logical' order which a rationalist would have seen implied in the principle of the *liaison des idées*. The poetic nature of primitive language made it essentially a gesture-language: the original order, we are told, was *fruit vouloir Pierre* for *Pierre veut du fruit* (*Essai*, p. 84). The regimen came *before* the verb because what strikes the imagination as the most important element of the phrase demands to be expressed first.[70] It is not the order according to logic that makes sentences intelligible, but according to the *liaison des idées* AS THEY OCCUR to the mind. Conversely, key words and objects may naturally come at the end for suspense and emphasis, as in Virgil, *Ecl.* 5, v. 20: "Extinctum Nymphae crudeli funere Daphnim | Flebant." This leads our philosopher to formulate his theory of the *tableau peint* (reminiscent of Lamy's physiological explanation of the simultaneity of the thinking process): The natural arrangement of terms in a sentence is not the narrative, logical, or chronological, but that in which our mental image is formed and retained, essential elements having their due priority over the others.[71]

This does not mean that the *ordre analytique* is not without its special merits. It has led away from the primitive naturalness, but it has brought us the "progrès de l'esprit philosophique," for which French must be praised, thanks to its *netteté, simplicité,* and *justesse*.[72] François has claimed that Condillac resumes the two schools of thought, the rationalist and the empirical or sensationalist, by acknowledging the "natural" character of both constructions, the direct and the inverted, on the general ground of the *liaison des idées*.[73] But it must be added that, formally speaking, this was rather the position of the sensationalist *mécaniciens* in their more temperate moods, as we are about to see.

---

[70] *Essai*, p. 84. Also *Œuvres*, I, 577 ff.

[71] *Essai*, p. 94, § 122.

[72] Cf. *Essai*, ch. xv "Du génie des langues" in the same Sect. I of the Second Part of the *Essai*.

[73] Cf. A. François, *Hist. de la l. fr. cultivée*, II, 65. François goes on to comment that "Nul sujet n'a plus occupé la grammaire philosophique. Dans aucune partie de la grammaire et du style, elle n'a introduit plus d'ordre et de méthode. Deux 'principes' interviennent à cette occasion: celui du régime et celui de la subordination. Selon Dumarsais (sic), le regime est déterminé par la place des mots: sujet, verbe, attribut ou complement, construction type." (*Ibid.*)

The misunderstanding caused by abuse of the term 'natural' is shown deftly and definitively by Condillac in his *Grammaire,* part of the *Cours d'études*:

Le mot *naturel* n'est pris ici [en parlant de ' construction '] qu'improprement. Il ne signifie pas ce que nous faisons en conséquence de la conformation que la nature nous donne; mais seulement ce que nous faisons en conséquence des habitudes que nous avons contractées. . . .
A parler vrai, il n'y a dans l'esprit ni ordre direct, ni ordre renversé, puisqu'il aperçoit à-la-fois toutes les idées dont il juge. . . .[74]

The mind perceives in the same way as the eye sees (a sort of Gestalt-psychologism *avant-la-lettre*).

Condillac promises details on the use of inversion in his next treatise, the rhetoric (= *Art d'écrire*, strongly reminiscent of Gamaches' *Agrémens*). In the meantime we must note that he is speaking of *ordre renversé* not only within the clause but within the sentence as well, at least by implication, since he offers the following example of a complement coming at the beginning of a sentence, before its term of reference: *Avec des procédés comme les vôtres.* Such a phrase could easily become a subordinate clause. Condillac's subsuming of the order of sentence parts under the general heading of word arrangement becomes more evident as he moves on to introduce the following distinction: " Il y a dans le discours deux choses: la liaison des idées et l'ensemble": direct order gives us the former by breaking up the unity of complex thought (for instance, when we must repeat the main idea); periodic style gives us the *ensemble* at the expense of direct order. It necessarily demands inversion: " Pour peu qu'une pensée soit composée, l'ensemble ne peut se trouver que dans l'ordre renversé. Il est donc absolument nécessaire de faire usage des inversions; et si elles sont nécessaires, il faut bien qu'elles deviennent naturelles." [75] In his rare use of the term inversion to designate the placing of subordinate and incidental clauses before the main clause Condillac gives a beautiful and definitive statement of the case for inversion in its broadest and most meaningful terms, all future rationalists' protestations notwithstanding. Generally speaking, while he prefers the term *construction renversée* for inversion, he designates by *construction directe* the cases in which the subordinating and determined (quali-

[74] Condillac, *Œuvres*, ed. Le Roy, I, pp. 502 end–503, ch. xxvii, 2^d p.
[75] Ibid., p. 504.

fied) precedes the subordinate and determinant (qualifier).[76] Word order then pertains not simply to the arrangement of subject, verb, object, but to all aspects of the phrase and sentence, including the distribution of complements as well as clauses.

Starting from this broad point of view, we are shown how even the French, when good stylists, know how to transgress *l'ordre naturel*: Fléchier, instead of saying:

cet aigle dont le vol hardi avait d'abord effrayé nos provinces, prenait déjà l'essor pour se sauver vers les montagnes,

said, so much more dramatically:

déjà prenait l'essor, pour se sauver vers les montagnes, cet aigle dont le vol . . . .

Condillac calls "dont le vol . . . provinces" *la partie fuyante*, which psychologically acquires weight by concluding the inverted sentence.

Again, Fléchier, instead of

La nature se trouve saisie à la vue de tant d'objets funèbres; . . . tous les coeurs sont émus par horreur, par compassion ou par faiblesse,

chose the following order:

A la vue de tant d'objets funèbres, la nature se trouve saisie; . . . soit horreur, soit compassion, soit faiblesse, tous les coeurs sont émus.[77]

Condillac is consequentially sensualistic in his position, which is grounded on a historico-genetic approach.[78] Against the rationalistic (and still, in a way, Lockean) positing of an a priori thinking faculty which preexists language and dictates to it forms and laws, he begins by con-

---

[76] Condillac, *Grammaire* and *Art d'écrire* in *Œuvres*, I, 502, 520 ff. Note the national conditioning of this scheme, in which the notion of the modified naturally preceding the modifier is akin to the medieval notion of noun preceding the adjective on the ground of a logico-natural succession substance → accident. The scheme clearly does not apply to English in these terms, and rigorously speaking, not even to French. Cf. Ricken, "Condillacs *liaison des idées*," pp. 552-553.

[77] *Œuvres*, I, p. 576. The first example from Fléchier is borrowed from Gamaches, *Agrémens*, 1718, p. 28.

[78] The best treatment of Condillac's doctrine of word order within his general system and the preceding tradition is U. Ricken, "Condillacs *liaison des idées*." For the influence of Warburton on C.'s linguistic theories see now Clifton Cherpack, "Warburton and Some Aspects of the Search for the Primitive in Eighteenth-Century France," *Philological Quarterly*, XXXVI (1957), 221-233.

ceiving thought as a *sensation transformée*. Against the Cartesian placing of the linguistic processes after the purifying abstraction operated by the rational faculty, for Condillac sensations and linguistic signs move on parallel tracks and condition each other, as language and thinking consequently do, in a process of increasing abstraction from gesture language.

Latin is seen to have belonged to a stage prior to that of French. The problem of word order can thus be put for the first time on a historical basis, since the logical categories, previously regarded as absolute, eternal, and universal, are brushed aside for the sake of the new principle of organic development postulated by the *liaison des idées*. It is important to understand that this position derives directly not from Locke, but from the seventeenth-century opposition to Descartes' psychophysiology.

Now with his definition of thought as *sensation transformée*, Condillac eliminates the contradiction implicit in the Cartesian dualistic separation between the rational and the emotional, logic and actual language use. Consequently, under the common denominator of the *liaison des idées*, he succeeds in bridging the traditional boundaries between Grammar and Rhetoric, which were still clear in Du Marsais' and, again, Beauzée's treatment of inversion. It is important to realize how bold and far-reaching this unification was, since the impact of Cartesian dualism continued to be felt for sometime, even in such theorists as Batteux and Diderot, with all their sensualistic inclinations. Against Descartes' effort to postulate a level of communication uncontaminated by the psychic perturbations which detract from the purity and clarity of reason, Condillac uncompromisingly holds that the very nature of language involves the expression of *sensations, sentiments, impressions,* and all movements of the observer affected by perception. For him, ideas in a state of complete calm do not exist and are no part of the language process.[79] "Tout en lui [l'homme] est l'expression des sentiments." The only difference between calm and perturbed reflection is one of degree. To the abstract categories of the *ordre naturel* he opposes the individual concreteness of experience and the type of expression which truly adheres to it. He continually refers to the *manières différentes de voir*, the *variété dans les choses*, the particular circumstances of experience.[80] He was the first who undertook a methodical study of the "tours propres au sentiment." For

---

[79] Condillac, *Œuvres*, I, p. 578.
[80] Cf. Ricken, "Condillacs *liaison des idées*," pp. 563-565.

him usage establishes itself "d'après ce qu'on sent, et le sentiment est bien plus sûr que les règles des grammairiens." [81] Condillac, Batteux, and Diderot distinguish themselves for harking back to the origins of speech, like Vico before them. There is perhaps a difference to be noted here, in that Vico's stress is on sense and imagination rather than sheer emotion; yet Condillac was clearly aware of the sensorial factors, at least in the visual direction. And if the reader will recall that (as pointed out by way of Croll's analysis) the effort to portray the mind in action, in all the heat of the thinking processes, was peculiarly distinctive of baroque plain style, Condillac will appear as the true theoretical heir of this deep revolution, even at such a seemingly late date.

In conclusion, for Condillac the only valid criterion of analysis is that of *liaison*. Neither type of construction is more 'natural': both are equally so, as long as the *liaison* obtains. Ultimately, the principle of expression is one of evidence (sensorial and emotional), and one can say that word order in the phrase is like the distribution of light and shadow in a painting.

Exceptionally enough, Condillac had an influence on French prose, which indeed moved in the direction pointed out by him: he legitimized the emotional and 'pictorial' style of a Diderot, a Rousseau, a Chateaubriand. Recent research has, more generally, pointed out the progress of inversion in modern French prose—without loss of *clarté*! For this, Le Bidois, to mention one researcher, has given credit to Condillac's theory (See Section on Modern Theory).

Despite the course the polemic continued to follow during the remainder of the century, what Condillac achieved looks somehow like Machiavelli's revolution in political thought—if I may be forgiven this rather preposterous *rapprochement*. For he replaced the deontologic approach (the postulate of what language should be if it is to satisfy the philosopher's aspiration toward the noblest exercise of man, the exercise of reason) with an empirical observation and interpretation of the *realtà effettuale* of language practice.

Condillac's more direct followers in the sensationalist approach to the primitive origins of language include Maupertuis (*Réflexions philosophiques sur l'origine des langues et la signification des mots*, 1755), De Brosses (*Traité de la formation méchanique des langues*, 1765), A. Court

---

[81] Condillac, II, pp. 10 and 75; *Art d'écrire*, I, i and x. Cf. François in Brunot, VI, 2², 2056-2057.

de Gébelin (*Monde primitif analysé et comparé avec le monde moderne, considéré dans l'histoire naturelle de la parole; ou Grammaire universelle et comparative*, 1772, 1776, nouv. éd. Paris, 1787, 2 tomes), and, finally, A. Destutt de Tracy (*Éléments d'Idéologie*, 1801-1815, 4 vols.).

When seen in historical perspective, the "logicians"' or *métaphysiciens'* theses answered the desiderata of the more organized sectors of the contemporary intelligentsia, as we shall presently witness, while the *mécaniciens'* message was destined to a greater impact among the Romanticists. As to the possible modern uses of these experiences, we have seen how the generative grammarians have sought some corroboration in the Cartesian camp. Even more recently another linguist, L. Rosiello, has opposed to that of Chomsky a view of eighteenth-century linguistics as equally dependent on both the empirical current and the rationalistic one of Descartes–Port-Royal. The interpretation may seem in part tendentious, at least to the extent that it does some injustice to the rationalistic background inherent in both adversary positions, and that it disregards the greater popularity of the Cartesian position. Yet the point is well taken to the effect that the empirical milieu (especially Condillac, underplayed by Chomsky) was no less creative than that of its opponents, and generally closer to later developments. There, more than elsewhere, lay the foundations of a historical, expressive view of language as communication of the whole thought, not just the rational part of it, and as a psychological rather than eminently logical event.[82]

Two years after Condillac's *Essai*, Charles Batteux made himself the leader of the radical wing among the adversaries of direct order through his "Lettres sur la phrase françoise comparée avec la phrase latine" (appeared in his *Cours de belles-lettres*, Paris, 1747-48, vol. II). The paradoxical position he dared to take was that Latin, rather than French, had a natural word order; consequently, French is all textured with inversion. He was obviously taking a 'rhetorical' position versus a 'grammatical' one, but he chose to label the distinction as being one between *ordre moral ou pratique* and *ordre spéculatif ou métaphysique*. Although the background of the two liberal arts was evident, this terminology fell neatly in line with the contemporary context of the division between the two sides of Cartesianism, and with the imminent crystallization of two neatly divided camps: *mécaniciens* versus *métaphysiciens*, the up-

---

[82] L. Rosiello, *Linguistica illuminista*, loc. cit. (see fn. 68 above). Also Uitti, 77-92.

holders of expressiveness versus the partisans of logic, in other words, inversion versus direct order.[83]

Batteux boldly aimed at the very foundations of Cartesianism as he retorted that *esprit* is not innate, not common to all men: it cannot, therefore, be the basis for a natural sequence of thoughts and words. The true masters of the language are the people, and the people do not think in logical categories. How could they possess such categories, since there is nothing in the intellect that has not come to it through the senses? (Cf. Aristotle's *nihil est in intellectu quin prius fuerit in sensu.*) Conception in the people arises, then, from sensation, the impressions of the environment upon the senses. Given such utterances as *rotundus est sol; serpentem fuge; panem praebe mihi*, how could we achieve a more 'natural' ordering by withdrawing from first place what has actually struck first? (One feels tempted to lend Batteux a couple of French examples, such as *qu'il m'enrage, ton ami; ils m'enragent, ces gens-là.*)[84]

According to a contemporary reviewer,[85] the true aim of Diderot's celebrated *Lettre sur les sourds et muets* (1751, addressed to Batteux) was to propose a genetic theory of inversion: "Le but propre et unique qu'il s'est proposé, c'est de rendre raison de l'origine des inversions." Most relevant for us is his criticism of Batteux for abandoning the historical perspective.[86]

[83] Ricken, "Rationalismus . . . ," fn. 85 pp. 267-268, holds that Eugen Lerch, *Hist. fr. Syntax*, esp. pp. 252 ff. in vol. III, ch. on Word Order, offers a distinction which essentially echoes that of the 18th century: his *impulsive* and *nicht-impulsive* word order somewhat correspond to Batteux' *o. pratique* and *o. métaphysique*. Lerch also calls the latter order *pädagogisch*, thus echoing Diderot's *ordre didactique* and Batteux' *ordre d'exposition*, another term for *o. métaphysique*.

[84] Batteux, *Cours*, II, 13-14. The more metaphysical considerations appeared in explicit form in the later *Traité de la construction oratoire*, published in the *Principes de la littérature* (Paris, 1764), t. V: see pp. 8 ff.

[85] *Bibliothèque impartiale*, May-June 1751, pp. 410 ff. Cf. Ricken, "Rationalismus," pp. 97 and 117-119.

[86] The *Lettre* is in Diderot, *Œuvres*, ed. Assézat-Tourneux, I, 349-392. Cf. F. Venturi, *La Jeunesse de Diderot* (Paris, 1939), pp. 237 ff. concerning the position of the *Lettre* in the debates on inversion. For a general view of D.'s ideas on style, see A. Boutet de Monvel, "Diderot et la notion de style," *Revue d'Hist. litt. de la France*, LI (1951), 288-305; also Marlou Switten, "Diderot's Theory of Language as the Medium of Literature," *Romanic Review*, XLIV (1953), 185-196. Jean Mourot, "Sur la ponctuation de Diderot," *Le Français Moderne*, 20 (1952), pp. 287-294, relates D.'s punctuation, on the one hand, to Grimarest's ideas and to the art. on this subject in the *Encyclopédie*; on the other, to the general 18th-

According to Diderot, the impressions from the environment strike our senses in a given order, the 'natural' order, according to the intensity of their impact. Objects strike through their qualities, which are the first elements of reality: hence "l'adjectif est tout" (p. 350). The rational abstraction of the noun follows. (One will note that this 'English' ordering of modifier before the modified has no bearing on French word order.) It was the need for clarity that created the syntactic norms, namely the *ordre d'institution, grammatical* or *didactique*. 'Natural order' is thus subverted into the opposite of what that term meant in the rationalist view. French would thus result to be, of all languages, the most suited for the expression of conceptual thinking, while free-order languages are better suited for the expression of emotions (370 f.). Diderot went so far as judging modern French, for these reasons, as the aptest medium for science, just as other European languages were, by virtue of their freer and more impressionistic word order, more suitable for literary expression:

J'ajouterais volontiers que la marche didactique et réglée à laquelle notre langue est assujettie, la rend plus propre aux sciences; et que pour les tours et les inversions que le grec, le latin, l'italien, l'anglais se permettent, ces langues sont beaucoup plus avantageuses pour les lettres. Que nous pouvons mieux qu'un autre peuple faire parler l'esprit, et que le bon sens choisirait la langue française; mais que l'imagination et les passions donnent la préférence aux langues anciennes et à celles de nos voisins.

French is the language of truth, the others " de la fable et du mensonge," "le francais est fait pour instruire, éclairer et convaincre; le grec, le latin, l'italien, l'anglais pour persuader, émouvoir et tromper; parlez grec, italien au peuple; mais parlez français au sage." Note that, interesting as it was in its new context, this was not a new distinction. Diderot had found it in Pier Jacopo Martello's *Il vero parigino italiano* (1710), where French was characterized as a "philosophical" language, Italian an "oratorical" one, more suited to express emotions and oriented toward the task of persuading.[87] Two years later J.-J. Rousseau will turn this same argu-

---

century usage, of which he regards D.'s practice as typical. More specifically on the *Lettre*, see Jean Pommier, "Autour de la *Lettre sur les sourds et muets*," *Revue d'Hist. litt. de la France*, LI (1951), 261-272, and Paul H. Meyer, "The *Lettre sur les sourds et muets* and Diderot's Emerging Concept of the Critic," *Diderot Studies*, VI (1964), 133-155. More general, Jacques Proust, "Diderot et le problème du langage," *Romanische Forschungen*, LXXIX (1967), 1-27.

[87] See fn. 38 in Ch. IV, C, below.

ment against the French language, praising Italian as better suited to poetry and music.[88] Even this was not new, for Charles de Brosses had similarly attributed an alleged advantage of Italian verse over the French to a more "sonorous harmony" and to less uniformity thanks to a more liberal use of inversions. French, he concluded, can boast no more than a greater clarity—which makes it better suited for historiography, the drama, and didactic writing, even while it handicaps it in the epic. De Brosses wrote:

> La poésie italienne a de grands avantages sur la nôtre: celui de la langue préférable à la nôtre, quoi qu'on veuille dire, plus coulante, plus sonore, plus harmonieuse, également propre au style majestueux et aux grâces badines outre qu'elle se permet un peu plus d'inversion, ce qui rend ses constructions moins uniformes. Notre langue n'est que claire; par là propre à l'histoire, à la dissertation, au poëme dramatique. Pour l'épique il nous est plus difficile d'atteindre. . . .[89]

De Brosses' and Diderot's equation of the 'genius' of the French language with the didactic genres and of that of Italian with the lyrical ones or, in Diderot's more appropriate and precise evaluation, the pathetic-rhetorical ones, could once again find an echo in the following passage by Voltaire on the obstacles to a French epic (but with the difference that Voltaire found the difficulties in the 'genius' of the nation rather than that of the language):

> De toutes les nations polies, la nôtre est la moins poétique. Les ouvrages en vers qui sont le plus à la mode en France sont les pièces de théâtre: ces pièces peuvent être écrites dans un style naturel, qui approche assez de celui de la conversation. Despréaux n'a jamais traité que des sujets didactiques, qui demandent de la simplicité; on sait que l'exactitude et l'élégance

<hr/>

[88] Cf. A. François, *Hist. de la l. fr. cultivée*, II, 86. Chomsky, *Cart. Ling.*, fn. 53 p. 93, deduces from the *Lettre* that "Diderot is so convinced of the 'naturalness' of French that he regards it as more suitable for science than for literature, the other European languages, 'unnatural' in their word order, being more suited for literary expression." But the term 'natural' cannot be given these connotations with regard to Diderot. Indeed, if pressed with the question, he would have probably put it the other way, since the *ordre d'institution* is conventional, acquired, in this sense 'unnatural.' Chomsky goes on to quote Bentham and Huarte (late 16th c.) as upholding the universal rational excellence of English and Latin, respectively.

[89] Ch. de Brosses, *Lettres familières écrites d'Italie . . . en 1739 et 1740* (Paris, 1858, 2 vols.), II, p. 233.

font le mérite de ses vers comme de ceux de Racine; et lorsque Despréaux
a voulu s'élever dans une ode, il n'a pas été Despréaux. Ces exemples ont
en partie accoutumé la poésie française a une marche trop uniforme:
l'esprit géométrique, qui de nos jours s'est emparé des belles lettres, a encore
été un nouveau frein à la poésie. Notre nation . . . est de toutes les
nations la plus sage la plume à la main. La méthode est la qualité dominante
de nos écrivains. On cherche le vrai en tout. . . .[90]

The traditional question of 'naturalness' in word order thus loses its
meaning, since Condillac, upon whom Diderot evidently draws, had
shown that any language at any of its stages is just as 'natural' as any
other with respect to word order. Even more importantly, Diderot derives
from Condillac the view of a historical process which moves both language and the thinking activity (in a common development) away from
the primeval language of gesture and direct impressions. Genially enough,
Diderot attributes the cause of this evolution, insofar as modern French
is concerned, to the impact of the Aristotelian categories even as recently
as under Louis XIII and XIV: it was thus that French lost the *inversions*
it had before, as Latin had them.[91]

By the time of Diderot's *Lettre* the two camps became clearly defined,
and in the same year 1751 the sensationalists found for themselves a

---

[90] "Essai sur la poésie épique," in Voltaire, *Œuvres complètes*, ed. Moland
(Paris, Garnier, 1877), t. VIII, p. 362. See M. Fubini, *Dal Muratori al Baretti*
(Bari, 1954²), p. 148, where the two texts by De Brosses and Voltaire are placed
side by side to show how they echo the position taken by Eustachio Manfredi within
the polemic Orsi-Bouhours.

[91] *Lettre*, p. 351. Ricken, "Rationalismus," pp. 266-267 fn. 74 recalls that Eugen
Lerch, *Französische Sprache und Wesensart* (1933), 4 ff.; *Historische französische
Syntax*, III, 252 ff., has shown how the loss of the 2-case-system of OF did not
necessarily bring about the regular word order of modern French. Indeed, I should
add, the loss of cases did not prevent Italian from remaining remarkably more
flexible than French in that respect. Lerch's view is now shared by many linguistic historians. It is particularly interesting that he found the reasons for this
fixation of French word order as subject + verb + object in the grammarians' con-
tempt (around 1600) for the *impulsive* anteposition of the object, and in the 17th-
century search for rational rules (the habit of *construere* was undoubtedly an
influence). Yet Ricken adroitly points out that there may be a deeper element
of truth in Diderot's stressing of the Aristotelian categories than in such explanations as Lerch's. On the theoretical level the Cartesian influences upon the concern
for a reasoned and general grammar were somewhat analogous to the impact of the
newly discovered Aristotelian concept of rational science upon the speculative
grammars of the thirteenth century. Cf. Chomsky, *Cart Ling.*, p. 106.

label in the very title of the Abbé Pluche's *Mécanique des langues*.[92] The *mécaniciens* thus opposed themselves to the logicians, who ambitiously styled themselves *métaphysiciens*. Pluche reiterated that languages are not learned by reasoning, but through the ear and through usage. He insisted that Latin construction was as 'natural' as the French analytic construction. If this still sounded like an intolerable paradox to 'metaphysician' ears, in spite of Condillac's and Diderot's interventions, it was not nearly as shocking as Batteux coming out squarely in favor of Latin as natural, accusing French of being all artificially 'inverted.'

In the *mécaniciens* one finds hints of that approach to language which is implied in what we now call the "direct method"; they also displayed clear elements of Vico's philosophy, even though, as one could note in Turgot, the *métaphysiciens* could also ring Vichian bells. Turgot, about the same year, 1751, as Pluche's *Mécanique*, masterfully revealed the more ambitious reaches of the *grammairiens philosophes* in his *Réflexions sur les langues*: "L'étude des langues bien faite serait peut-être la meilleure des logiques," he asserted. "Cette espèce de *métaphysique expérimentale* serait en même temps l'histoire de l'esprit du genre humain et du progrès de ses pensées, toujours proportionné au besoin qui les a fait naître." [93] One could hardly find in such a different climate a more conspicuous summary of some of Vico's leading ideas, including the merger of philosophy and philology (*verum et factum*), and the treatment of linguistic and literary development as the key to man's historical evolution on the spiritual level, to be paralleled by the institutional level.

It may be hard for us to understand the pervasive impact of these debates on their time and the true measure of involvement on all sides. Almost everybody thought he had something at stake in these debates. Every *philosophe* was somewhat of a grammarian, and every grammarian thought of himself as a metaphysician.[94]

---

[92] The term appears again in another important contribution to this school of thought, Ch. de Brosses, *Traité de la formation méchanique des langues* (Paris, 1765).

[93] "Réflexions sur les Langues" in Turgot, *Œuvres*, ed. Gustave Schelle (5 vols., Paris, 1913-1923), I, p. 347. The ed. Daire (Paris, 1844), II, 753 is cited in Brunot, *H. L. F.*, t. VI, 2e partie (by A. François), fasc. 1er (Paris, 1932), pp. 912-913 fn. I do not find in the art. "Analogie" of the *Encyclopédie*, by Du Marsais and the abbé Yvon, "an illustration of these principles," as claimed in Brunot, ibid.

[94] A. François' summary of the situation at mid-century is worth quoting *in extenso*: "Finies le 'bagatelles' dont se contentait la modestie de l'âge précédent!

DIRECT ORDER   255

The important grammatical section in the *Encyclopédie* was assigned to Du Marsais, who authored for it such acclaimed articles as that on *Construction*, among a total of over 150. Upon his death his task was taken over by Beauzée, who, together with Douchet, authored such leading voices as *Grammaire, Inversion, Langage, Langue, Mot,* etc.[95]

Du Marsais' major treatise, with the telling title *Logique et Principes de Grammaire* (published posthumously in 1769), represented in definitive form the nomenclature proposed by the master. The term *construction* should be applied to "l'arrangement des mots dans le discours," and

'Peu de gens,' dit Moncrif, 'connoissent quel éloge est attaché au titre d'excellent grammairien.' Cela signifie 'avoir saisi une infinité de principes, qui pour être apperçus dès leurs sources, demandent et beaucoup d'étendue d'esprit et l'esprit philosophique.' Ainsi la tâche du grammairien dépasse-t-elle plus que jamais l'observation et l'enregistrement de l'usage. Elle s'élève jusqu'aux sommets de la spéculation philosophique. Tout grammairien se sent 'métaphysicien.' Tout philosophe s'honore d'être peu ou prou grammairien. Certains noms reçoivent de la grammaire un lustre inouï. L'Europe honore ces génies d'un nouveau genre; les souverains les choient; les académies les réclament. Il semble que la gloire même du dix-huitième siècle soit attachée au progrès de la grammaire générale." Brunot, *H. L. F.*, VI, 2¹ (by A. François), pp. 899-900. Cf. Harnois, *Les Théories du langage en France*; Sahlin, *Du Marsais*. See Paradis de Moncrif, *Œuvres* (Paris, 1768, 4 vols.), II, 63. This text goes back to 1742.

[95] See a fairly complete list of Du Marsais' articles and a discussion of the grammatical section of the *Encyclopédie* in Rosiello, *Linguistica illuminista*, pp. 92-104. The replacement of Du Marsais by Douchet and Beauzée, both professors of grammar at the École Royale Militaire, was announced at the end of the celebrated "Éloge de M. Du Marsais" in the *Encyclopédie*, t. VII, pp. i-xiii.

Pierre Juliard, *Philosophies of Language in Eighteenth-Century France* (The Hague, 1970), fn. p. 23, quotes the author of the linguistic articles in the *Encyclopédie* after t. VI as "B. E. R. M." or "E. R. M." and declares him to be further unidentifiable. This seems like unnecessary caution since the siglum can mean nothing else than "Beauzée, École Royale Militaire" (= "B. E. R. M.") or Douchet and Beauzée as joint authors (= "E. R. M."), as indicated in the key. Juliard cites Maurice Piron, ed., Turgot, *Étymologie* (Bruges, 1961), as also holding that the author "B. E. R. M." is unknown. Aside from this detail Juliard's study, a doctoral dissertation, is based on the valuable contention that eighteenth-century linguistic doctrines must be perceived, and can only be understood, as an aspect of the sociologically-oriented thought of the *philosophes*. The treatment is uneven, bibliographically inadequate, and naïvely argued. The polemic on inversion is disposed of in one page (51-52) as marginal and even "ridiculous," but the author misrepresents his sources, simplifies their reasoning, and ignores their precedents and context. He ends up presenting as his conclusion, like a fresh observation, the thesis of the *mécanicien* party, which he had neglected to report as such.

syntaxe to "la connoissance des signes" which determine "les rapports successifs que les mots ont entr'eux." Thus the three sentences *accepi litteras tuas, tuas accepi litteras,* and *litteras accepi tuas* exhibit three separate constructions but one syntactic pattern.[96] To put it differently, syntax has to do with thought-relations, word order with linguistic, formal patterns (respectively deep and surface structure, as a 'transformationist' would now have it). This is precisely what the *mécaniciens* would have rejected as an injustice to the wholeness of expression. In fact, Du Marsais claimed that each of those three sentences "excite dans l'esprit le même sens, *J'ai reçu votre lettre*," which is correct only up to a point, that is only when the variation is merely one of rhythm or harmony, as it is in Du Marsais' example. But he typically chose to overlook that the different arrangements could have expressive value, as in *pater filium amat, filium pater amat, pater amat filium, amat filium pater,* where the stress can be alternately placed on *amare, filium, pater,* or nothing in particular. Likewise, he insists (as in his proposal on the 'construed classics') that the natural order is necessary to understanding and, when lacking in the surface structure, must be reconstructed mentally. The *constructions figurées* "ne sont entendues, que parce que l'esprit en rectifie l'irrégularité . . . comme si le sens étoit énoncé dans l'ordre de la construction simple." [97] Of course we might object that the order is relative: e. g. whether the modifier must precede or follow the modified is relative to each language (cf. Saxon and German genitive, position of

---

[96] Du Marsais, *Logique,* pp. 229-231, and articles "Concordance" in *Œuvres,* IV and "Construction," *Œuvres,* V, pp. 1-3. This ch. "De la construction grammaticale" is drawn from the celebrated article "Construction" of the *Encyclopédie:* see tome IV (1754), pp. 73-92 (p. 73 for the statements in question).

[97] Du Marsais, *Logique,* p. 292; also p. 196. Cf. Chomsky, *Cart. Ling.,* pp. 47-51. Chomsky looks with favor upon the notion of 'natural order' as a "hypothesis of some significance regarding language structure" and, as such, better than the behavioristic descriptions of language in terms of "habits," "patterns," etc. See p. 94, fn. 56.

Just as he separates *construction* from *syntaxe,* Du Marsais distinguishes the *construction pleine* from the *elliptique.* But this latter is an aspect of the *construction figurée:* "la vivacité de l'imagination, l'empressement à faire connoître ce que l'on pense, le concours des idées accessoires, l'harmonie . . ." are the factors which cause ellipsis and change the order. Thus ellipsis and inversion are placed among the "figures," like hyperbaton. And to construe, "faire la construction," means to reestablish "l'ordre que la vivacité et l'empressement de l'imagination, l'élégance et l'harmonie avoient renversé."

adjectives and possessive complements in Germanic and Romance languages, etc.).

Yet, to do Du Marsais full justice, one must acknowledge the positive originality of his distinction between construction and syntax, which enjoyed a wide following: signally, besides Beauzée and even Condillac (*Grammaire*), Court de Gébelin (*Monde primitif* . . . , 1772, nouv. éd. Paris, t. II, 1787), and Antoine-Isaac Silvestre de Sacy, *Principes de Grammaire générale* (Paris, 1799). Du Marsais had started out from a critique of the "méthode ordinaire" of conceiving and teaching grammar, which first drew up deductive categories and only later presented the facts of real languages. He wanted to begin, rather, with the observation and assimilation of actual texts, simple or didactically simplified, and then inductively proceed to abstracting general categories. This latter part, grammar proper, should begin with "la connoissance de la proposition et de la période," not in a rhetorical sense, but only "en tant qu'elles sont composées de mots." He was thus taking leave of the Aristotelian-Cartesian-Port-Royalist identification of language structure with the basic logical proposition, and at the same time was insisting on studying words as semantic parts of whole sentential contexts. The last part of grammar would then, completing a full circle, revert to syntax. Here, without really developing the promise of studying the *période*, which became somehow excluded as rhetorical matter, he would begin by rejecting the traditional convention of syntax of concord and of regimen. This because he found it hopelessly entangled in the Aristotelian realism that conceived words as representations of real substances and accidents in things; whereas in his empirical approach to language as pure convention Du Marsais wanted the words to be felt as elements related to one another only for the sake of translating between THOUGHTS in our mind (not between THINGS). These relationships between words are the only way for us to see their true function, since words taken in isolation lose full meaning and become abstract. They can be expressed in two ways: by position (= Construction) or by the use of formal accidents, i. e. morphological signs, *terminaisons et autres signes* (what we would call "morphemes"), like cases and prepositions (= Syntax). In this theory we have both a welcome emphasis on the wholeness of the sentence and on the true role of word order. For Du Marsais saw word order as *rapport de détermination* (perhaps related to Leibniz's "sufficient reason"), as against the more properly syntactic *rapport ou raison d'identité* (Leibniz's "principle of identity"), which consists mainly of concord. Sahlin found this distinction partly unsatisfactory in that it placed *construction* outside *syntaxe*, of which, at least for French, it should be an integral part (since order may designate function as the equivalent of cases); but we may be more interested in Du Marsais' further distinction of *construction* into *simple* and *figurée*, this latter being such as to transcend syntax and grammar in a complete sense, since it belongs to stylistics.[98] (See p. 241 above.)

The most elaborate and systematic presentation of the *mécaniciens'* case came with Batteux' *Traité de la construction oratoire* (1763).[99] It is divided into two *Parties*: (1) 1ère Section, De l'arrangement naturel des mots par rapport à l'esprit; 2e Section, . . . par rapport à l'oreille; (2) De la construction particulière à la langue française. There follows a translation of Dionysius of Halicarnassus' *De compositione*.[100] The polemic with Du Marsais is explicit. "Quand les *Lettres sur l'Inversion* parurent pour la première fois,[101] il me revint que M. du Marsais n'étoit nullement de mon avis. Je l'avois prévû. Ce qu'il a écrit dans sa *Méthode pour apprendre la langue latine* est précisément le contraire de ce que j'avois tâché d'établir dans ces *Lettres*."[102] He hears that Du Marsais had treated the subject of the origin of the French *construction directe*—which allegedly caused the dropping of the cases. But since that has remained unpublished, he must rely on the article "Construction" in the *Encyclopédie* (1754).

The polemic as it actually unfolded was reduced to a rather narrow area in which a basic value judgment was brought forward. For the remainder, both parties implicitly agreed, with remarkably solid information, on a string of observed facts. We get to the core of the problem at

---

[98] Sahlin, *Du Marsais*, pp. 57-58. In this excellent monograph see, esp., chs. iii ("La Construction," pp. 80-96) and iv ("La Proposition," pp. 97-139). For the interpretation of this whole aspect of Du Marsais' system, cf. also Rosiello, pp. 132-150.

[99] Batteux, *Principes de la littérature*, nouv. éd. tome V. I cite from the ed. Avignon, Chambeau, 1809, adding the pagination of the Paris, 1774 ed. The *Traité de la construction* occupies all of this t. V.

[100] The trans. of Dionysius occupies tome VI of the *Principes*, ed. 1809, but it was not included in the 1774 ed.

[101] Cf. Batteux, *Cours de belles-lettres* (1747-48), II (1748). The "Lettres sur l'inversion" are four of the six "Lettres sur la phrase françoise comparée avec la phrase latine" (the other two dealing with "La traduction"), published at the end of t. II of the *Cours* with renewed pagination 1-139.

[102] *Principes*, t. V, p. 189 (p. 234 of 1774 ed.): *Traité*, 2e partie, ch. iii.

the precise moment when Du Marsais defines hyperbaton as a deviation from *l'ordre successif de la construction simple* EVEN FOR LATIN, whereas Batteux retorts that the Latins could not be aware of doing anything unusual in placing, say, the verb last. Hence—and here lies Batteux' paradox so irritating to his opponents—they were really using hyperbaton when they followed *la construction simple*.[103]

Batteux had pointed out earlier that the correct rendering of ideas in their appropriate order will force French into inversion even where we cannot properly speak of inversion in Latin: *Non bene conveniunt, nec in una sede morantur majestas et amor* (Ovid) will be rendered as: *Difficilement habitent ensemble la dignité et l'amour,* where the initial position of a circumstantial complement due to necessary emphasis brings about an inversion (as it regularly did in OF—contemporary French would tend to use the construction *C'est avec difficulté que la dignité . . . habitent . . .*).[104] The matter threatened to become one of mere semantics: What was 'natural' for Batteux was not so for Du Marsais. (Condillac and Diderot had tried in vain to brush aside that misleading term.) Yet both practically agreed on one thing—the one that mattered, incidentally, within the sphere of the Italian *questione della lingua*—to wit: In a general way inversion is unnatural, artificial, or outright alien to such modern languages as French and English.

Finally, Du Marsais touched the most sensitive point in Batteux' system: he charged him " d'extravaguer par principes " in that the criterion of interest or of emotion is so vague and uncertain that it is impossible to base a theory on it.[105] It is at this very point that Batteux reached what strikes me as the peak of his polemic eloquence—however right or wrong we may choose to judge him. He retorted that if the 'metaphysical' or 'speculative' approach was susceptible of clear definition, so perforce was the other, its exact opposite. When Du Marsais found that the 'speculative' order was *not* followed (and he would then speak of inversion), Batteux replied that it was really a question of another kind of order—and it must be so for some good reason, even though Du Marsais might be inclined to disregard it. Where, then, is all that uncertainty and lack of objective precision? We only have to give the speaker the benefit of the doubt as to his having some reason for speaking

---

[103] Ibid., p. 191 (pp. 236-237 of 1774 ed.).
[104] Ibid., p. 24 (28 of 1774 ed.).
[105] Ibid., pp. 204-205 (254-255 of 1774 ed.).

as he does—especially if he is a great poet or orator. Does he use the
direct order? He is being expository and logical. Whenever he does not,
he is expressing something else: emotion, interest, even harmony. Let
us look for this other end, whatever it may be. Batteux was pleading,
as it were, for a bit of tolerance and liberalism. Enough with that
prejudice of the French way being the only sensible way!

Batteux declared that he had become interested in this problem while
searching for objective guiding rules for translators.[106] He proposed some
very interesting points of method as 'rules': e. g., not to change the order
of ideas (with an excellent example from Fléchier); not to CUT periods;
in particular, not to omit any CONJUNCTIONS: "On doit conserver
toutes les conjonctions. Elles sont comme les articulations des membres
[de périodes]."[107] Clearly, the *mécaniciens* were for periodic style. In
essence, his advice is tantamount to an unqualified insistence on greater
faithfulness than usually practiced up to his time (we might say, at any
time) on the formal, stylistic level.

We are then offered an application of criteria for translation to specific
genres: history, oratory, poetry (lyrical?).[108] Batteux appears to favor the
'ascending' syntactic construction, and in this respect he seems to regard
the case of subordinate clause preceding main clause as a *transposition*
(inversion).[109] Inversion in French prose (or verse) is said to be
justified by *clarté, énergie, harmonie.* The *style simple* has only recourse
to the first of these reasons, the *élevé* to all three, and poetry relies on the
third more than prose does. It is false that inversion is what makes
verse—and this takes care of Du Cerceau.[110]

The free exposition of Batteux' own theory comes in the first Part
of his treatise. He recognizes three *ordres*: the *grammatical*, the *métaphysique*, the *oratoire*.[111] The last, as he will again and more specifically
state when dealing with harmony,[112] can be ruled by *l'esprit* or by
l'oreille in determining *l'arrangement des mots*.[113] *Arrangement naturel*

---

[106] Ibid., ch. iv, pp. 208 ff. (258 ff. of 1774 ed.).
[107] Ibid., p. 220 (273-274 of 1774 ed.).
[108] Ibid., ch. v, pp. 230 ff. (286 ff. of 1774 ed.).
[109] Ibid., p. 252 (314-315 of 1774 ed.).
[110] Ibid., p. 256 (318-319 of 1774 ed.).
[111] Ibid., p. 8.
[112] Ibid., p. 32.
[113] Under *oreille* Batteux broadly subsumes *mélodie, nombre,* and **harmonie**
oratoire.

is the oratorical one, "point de vue de celui qui parle." To *esprit* and *oreille* he will later add *le coeur (sentiment, passion)*.[114]

Then he summarizes the mental itinerary followed by Dionysius in arriving at his classic stand (ch. v). Having found no treatment of word arrangement before him, he started to reflect on it, searching for a law of nature. It was at the end of a process of elimination that he seized upon harmony as the supreme rule of composition. Batteux appropriately criticizes him [115] for having passed from the possibility of an analytical order, which he rejected, directly to his explanation on the mere ground of harmony—a complementary and peripheral factor—, thus missing the truly correct stand, that of *la construction ou arrangement des idées*.[116] The justness of this position (which clearly embodies Condillac's lesson) results from the peculiarly French experience of *l'esprit*, the intellectual element in language within the broader stressing of that element by the baroque theorists and practitioners of style. Coupled with a keen appreciation of the sensorial dimension of language, the resulting 'idea and sound' position corrected the unilaterality of ancient 'hedonism.' At the same time, Batteux attributed to Dionysius the realization that "autre est la construction dans le sang froid, autre dans la passion." [117]

Less comprehensively, Batteux tends to explain all figures of speech on the ground of emphasis of the more important elements.[118] Just as ellipsis is effective in that it drops the inessential elements and consequently enhances the essential ones it picks up, so does position in the phrase stress and enhance by its very nature. In other words, priority from 'interest' affects internal groups as well: *neque TURPIS mors FORTI viro, nec immatura consulari, nec misera sapienti* (no death can be shameful for the man of valor . . .): *mors* and *vir* are secondary.[119] True enough, Batteux' inclination to recognize initial position alone as carrying stress is less realistic than Condillac's integrating principle of secondary emphasis

---

[114] *Traité de la construction*, e. g. p. 65.

[115] See, e. g., p. 65 (77 of 1774 ed.).

[116] This is precisely Weil's criticism, but when this linguist advanced his remarkable systematic study on word order (see Modern Theory below) he did not explicitly defer to Batteux for the invention of his thesis. Weil's stand on the matter was directly issued from Steinthal's psychologism, but had been anticipated by the psychologism of Condillac and Batteux.

[117] *Traité*, p. 78 of 1774 ed.

[118] *Ibid.*, p. 31 of 1809 ed., 35 of 1774 ed.

[119] *Ibid.*, p. 25 (28 of 1774 ed.).

in end position.[120] Nevertheless, just as the exclamations *au feu!*, *au meurtre!* (which elliptically drop subject and predicate) carry emotional impact by expressing the important part of the idea immediately, or the predominant idea alone,[121] likewise initial position brings forth what should be placed at the center of our attention.

As with Condillac, the principle that "l'ordre naturel est que l'objet important soit en tête" is equally applicable to the composition of the clause and to that of the sentence as a whole.[122] Moreover—and this is an important, original development with Batteux—, once stated, the true 'subject' of our thought must remain at the center until exhausted. The *liaison des idées* demands that the 'first' element continue to dominate until we shift to a different matter. This brings in the difficult art of 'transitions' between leading subjects: the statements must follow one another in a natural chain of thought.[123]

While the supreme virtues of style, as our author defines them, retain a conspicuously French ring, he aims to do justice to the most time-honored characteristics of ancient writing. *Naïveté* (defined on p. 42) reigns supreme—encompassing *vérité, justesse, clarté* and meaning *franchise, liberté, simplicité.* We might observe that all these traits conspicuously fall within the ideal of the plain style. This *style naïf* is eminently characterized by the *ordre naturel des mots.* At the same time Batteux will go to great length to explain the beauty of typical ancient twists. In Cicero's *Quem ad finem sese effrenata jactabit audacia?* (*Cat.* I) note, he warns us, the anteposition of *effrenata*, and *audacia* separated from its heightened attribute for the sake of harmony (clausula). But here again Condillac went one step further with his theory of the suspense created by separation of linked parts—which is, after all, what Geoffrey of Vinsauf had pointed out long before ("gravitas quaedam quando quae jungit constructio separat ordo").[124]

---

[120] Cf. ibid., pp. 29-30 and 55. See the example from Cicero, . . . *vomere postridie*, pp. 29-30 (34 of 1774 ed.—cf. Cic., *Phil.* II, 25, 63), which Batteux tries to explain by the principle of stress in initial position. It became more meaningful when explained through end position, as originally in Quintilian, *Inst.*, IX, iv, 29-31.

[121] Ibid., p. 52 (61 of 1774 ed.).

[122] Ibid., p. 55 (62-65 of 1774 ed.).

[123] Ibid., pp. 56-58 (65-68 of 1774 ed.).

[124] This t. V of the *Principes* contains, after the *Traité*, a *Nouvel éclaircisse-*

D'Alembert touched upon our subject in three separate essays (*Éclair-cissement sur l'inversion, Réflexions sur l'élocution,* and *Sur l'harmonie des langues*).[125] In the first of these he made a useful, though rather unusual, distinction between *ordre métaphysique* and *ordre grammatical*. By the former any order, except placing the verb first, appears natural, since there is no objective way of establishing the order in which the ideas occur to our mind. Often several ideas are simultaneous, therefore no order is 'logically' an inversion. By the *ordre grammatical*, however, we conclude that it is not natural to place first a morpheme which is determined by an element which follows it, as in *Darium vicit Alexander,* since *Darium* owes its form to *vicit* and *vicit* to *Alexander*.[126] Hence, only the *ordre grammatical* is a legitimate ground for establishing cases of inversion. It also determines the general rule whereby, in a cogently 'descending' order, the sentence must so proceed that its elements always lean on the preceding, never on the following: " en sorte que les mots, à mesure qu'on les prononce, soient des modificatifs des mots qui les précè-dent, et par conséquent supposent l'idée que les mots précédens expriment,

---

ment sur l'inversion pour servir de réponse aux objections de M. Beauzée (ed. Paris, 1774 and later eds.). Also see the original ed. of this note by Batteux concern-ing Beauzée's remarks on the subject in his *Grammaire générale* of 1767: *Nouvel examen du préjugé sur l'inversion, pour servir de réponse à M. Beauzée* ([Paris], 1767).
   [125] D'Alembert, *Œuvres complètes,* t. I (Paris, 1821), pp. 246-260: " Éclaircisse-ment sur l'inversion, et à cette occasion sur ce qu'on appelle le génie des langues " (this study is part of his *Essai sur les éléments de philosophie;* it was also published in his *Œuvres philosophiques, hist. et litt.,* II, Paris, 1805, 264 ff.); *Œuvres com-plètes,* t. IV (Paris, 1822), 274-290: " Réflexions sur l'Élocution oratoire et sur le style en général " (also in *Mélanges,* t. II, 1773); *Œuvres complètes,* t. IV, 11-28: " Sur l'harmonie des langues " etc. The art. " Élocution " (ibid., 517-535) is essen-tially a digest of the *Réflexions.* In both he declares, among other points, that the ancient proscription against lines inserted within prose does not hold so well for French, and quotes as an example a prose passage from Molière almost entirely built with *octosyllabes.* Further on (p. 532) he quotes Cicero's *Orator* to show that the plain style is relatively free from concern for harmony: " En effet, le plus ou moins d'harmonie est peut-être ce qui distingue le plus réellement les différentes espèces de style." In the essay " Sur l'harmonie des langues " we find the appropriate suggestion that one should speak of the 'melody' of a language rather than 'harmony,' since the sounds of a language are successive, not simul-taneous (p. 12). D'Alembert was fond of Tacitus' and Bacon's styles, and trans-lated from the works of both.
   [126] *Œuvres complètes,* t. I, p. 252.

sans que ces mots précédens supposent nécessairement l'idée que les modificatifs y ajoutent."[127]

In the *Réflexions sur l'élocution* he took a rather unprecedented negative stand apropos the current opinion that French excelled by the natural clarity bestowed upon it by virtue of direct order and other qualities. To him French was the least clear by nature.[128]

The most detailed presentation of the *métaphysiciens'* case appeared in the ponderous *Grammaire générale* (1767) by Nicolas Beauzée (1717-1789), Professeur de Grammaire à l'École Royale Militaire. Here again, as is true of a large portion of this kind of literature, the topics of concern to us stand out as the liveliest spot within the whole work.

Beauzée begins by laying the keystone to his rationalistic philosophy of language: "C'est par le langage qu'elle [la raison] transmet l'image de la pensée. C'est le but de toutes les langues" (p. iii).[129] He distinguishes implicitly between *la pensée* (one and indivisible) and *les idées*, its singular, divisible components which Logic abstracts through the method of analysis. These elements or ideas make up the "thought" (assumedly equivalent to a complete sentence) by being arranged in a certain FIXED order according to their mutual relationships. "Je donne à cette succession le nom d'*ordre analytique*, parce qu'elle est tout-à-la-fois le résultat de l'analyse du discours dans toutes les langues." This analysis is based on the eternal Reason which guides human reason and is ever identical with itself (p. iv).

Grammar has as its object the enunciation of thought by means of words. It divides itself into: General Grammar, a deductive science ("la science raisonnée des principes immuables et généraux du langage") whose principles coincide with those guiding human reason in its intellectual operations and, as such, ANTECEDES all existing languages; and Particular Grammar, an inductive art which applies the "principles" to the arbitrary, conventional institutions of actual usage in a given

[127] Ibid., p. 253.

[128] *Œuvres complètes*, t. IV, p. 282 and *Mélanges* (1773), II, 336.

[129] Beauzée, *Grammaire générale ou exposition raisonnée des éléments nécessaires du langage, pour servir de fondement à l'étude de toutes les langues* (Paris, J. Barbou, 1767, 2 tomes), pp. xlviii + 619 + 664. I shall refer to this first ed. only occasionally, and normally quote from the following: Beauzée, *Gr. gén.*, nouv. éd. revue et corrigée avec soin (Paris, A. Delalain, 1819), pp. xxvi + 835. On Beauzée's contributions to linguistics see, now, Rosiello, *Linguistica illuminista* (1967), pp. 150-166.

language. The latter, of course, comes into existence AFTER the particular languages (pp. v-vi). Beauzée seems to postulate the universality of linguistic principles on the ground of the natural origin of all languages (p. vi), and this implies a UNIVERSAL NATURE, identical for all peoples.

His precursors in demonstrating the kinship between *science de la parole* and *science de la pensée* are, as he singles them out, Sanctius, Wallis, Arnauld, Du Marsais (p. x); to these he adds later on Duclos, Girard, Vaugelas, and Bouhours (p. xvi). To find his "system of grammatical metaphysics" he has employed, he avers, Descartes' method. The principles have not entered language through reflection, but reflection brings them out and shows the nature of linguistic phenomena. This justifies the need for philosophical grammar (pp. xiv-xv). The *finesses métaphysiques* have been put into languages, without the speakers' knowledge, by that *raison éternelle* which "nous dirige à notre insu" (almost like Hegel's *Vernunft*, or Vico's Providence). It is thanks to this "logique naturelle qui dirige secrétement, mais irrésistiblement, les esprits droits" that the better speakers speak better (ibid.).

Finally, he trusts that his treatise (which is addressed to specialists and teachers) will be a guide toward the accomplishment of more practical school manuals, where the cumbersome strings of autocratic rules will be replaced by a reasoned ensemble of a few, simple principles. Among these the questions of direct order, inversion, and ellipsis will have to loom large.

The Introduction (pp. 387-388) to the "Syntax" (Book III) is important. After repeating the logical definitions from pp. iii and iv of the Preface, he recalls the distinction between *syntaxe* and *construction* as expressed first by Du Marsais in his art. "Construction" for the *Encyclopédie*. Construction or the theory of (direct) word order is the fundamental rule of syntax, and somehow precedes the latter taken in its narrow sense, which is that of theory of accidence divided into concord (*concordance*, when the relationship between words is one of identity) and regimen (*régime*, when the relationship is one of *détermination*, modification). Such relationships depend on and follow from the *construction* inasmuch as the latter, in its 'natural' aspect, "est l'image de la succession analytique des idées et l'exposition fidèle de la pensée" (388). This radical assimilation of *construction*, previously a rhetorical matter, into the broader realm of syntax, with its well defined and distinct role, is a fundamental step forward in the history of grammar, and it occurs in the wake of the nomenclature established by Du Marsais (note, also, the repetition of the Leibnizian binomium of identity and determination, from Du Marsais).

The paramount criteria of *netteté* and *clarté* (cf. Quint. I, iv: "summa virtus est perspicuitas") require the complement to be as close as possible to its term of reference—especially in the languages which cannot show such relationships by flectional endings (429). This renders more tangible the logical relationships, the ties between the elements of the phrase. This simple principle is, however, complicated by a rule now known as "Beauzée's law" after H. Weil so referred to it. Beauzée, in turn, drew it from Gamaches. He approvingly quoted this critic's now famous examples: *parer le vice des dehors de la vertu* and *parer des dehors de la vertu les vices les plus honteux et les plus décriés*, and repeated the rule: [130] In a series of complements all referred to the same term, the right progression will go from the shortest to the longest. Should any difficulties arise because the last complement is too far removed for clarity, this can be placed before its term of reference: *c'est un des rois qui ont,* APRÈS UN SIÈGE DE DIX ANS, *renversé la fameuse Troie.* At times a need to avoid amphiboly will suggest a break from the basic rule, as in Father Buffier's example: *L'Evangile inspire aux personnes qui veulent être sincèrement à Dieu une piété qui n'a rien de suspect,* to avoid the ambiguous sequence *suspect aux personnes.*[131]

Clearly, this famous 'rule' is not linguistic but stylistic: it pertains less conspicuously to logical relationships than to the rhythmic equilibrium of the sentence. Yet at one point the basic shift that had occurred from the classical type of preoccupation with sensuous qualities to the enlightened intellectualism of the *métaphysiciens* is brought home to us. Thomas Corneille ("Note sur la Remarque 454 de Vaugelas") had insisted that one must both avoid ambiguity and satisfy the ear. Echoing Gamaches and, after him, Batteux, Beauzée subtly objects that where one used to find faults in the musical aspect, the sound pattern of a phrase, the real trouble often had another, and deeper, cause. It is not possible to

---

[130] Cf. Gamaches, *Dissertation sur les agrémens du langage*, Part I, ed. 1718, pp. 10 and 33-34. This "quatrième règle" is so phrased by Gamaches: "Pour la netteté du style il est encore nécessaire que, quand un mot a plusieurs modificatifs, les plus courts soient placez les premiers; par ce moyen ceux qu'on met aux dernières places ne se trouvent éloignez du terme modifié que le moins qu'il est possible; ainsi l'on diroit *parer le vice.* . . ."

[131] Buffier, *Grammaire françoise* . . . , § 774, pp. 337-338 of 1709 ed.

"satisfaire l'oreille sans contenter l'esprit" (432), "il faut consulter un autre guide que l'oreille, c'est l'esprit." Thus, since Beauzée's rule is allegedly dictated by clarity, or at least subjected to it, it shall not be mechanically applied when it might result in a violation of clarity itself. It may therefore become necessary, under given conditions, to place the circumstantial or indirect complement before the direct object (precisely as in Buffier's example just quoted). The above exceptions are, therefore, only apparent.

The rule will equally apply to the parts of a complement: we shall say *Dieu agit avec justice et par des lois ineffables,* but *Dieu agit par des lois ineffables et avec une justice que nous devons adorer en tremblant.* As one can see, one close unit must be made of a complement and, so to say, its sub-complements, as *avec une justice que nous devons adorer en tremblant,* even if these latter are made of subordinate clauses, as long as the whole phrase is uttered as an indivisible entity. This, once again, is rather to be determined on a rhetorical than a grammatico-logical plane, since it refers directly to the manner of delivery.

But what if the complements are equal, or practically so, in length? The arrangement shall then be determined solely by logical priorities. Beauzée introduces here a very original and shrewd justification of inversion (the type of which we now know the medieval Germanic origin). Since it is of paramount interest to show the rapport of the complement to its term, if for any reason the complement must precede the rest, it will be better to invert the subject after the verb, especially when that subject is so long that it would unduly suspend the union of modifier and modified, complement and term of reference. Thus *c'est ce que Minos, le plus sage et le meilleur de tous les rois, avoit compris* (*Télémaque,* V) is less good than *c'est ce qu'avoit compris Minos, le plus sage et le meilleur de tous les rois.* We could hardly disagree, with all respect due to the great shadow of Fénelon. On the other hand we have no right to undue squeamishness whenever the unity of complex complements, or even sentences, with their antecedents and incidental clauses, may have to be broken: instead of *Il y a un air de vanité et d'affectation dans Pline le jeune, qui gâte ses lettres,* one ought to have said *Il y a, dans Pline le jeune, un air* etc.

To conclude this discussion, "Il n'y a peut-être pas un point de syntaxe plus important . . . que celui qui concerne l'arrangement des divers compléments d'un même mot" (437). He gives credit to Gamaches for realizing this fundamental aspect of style, and for explaining its secret

by recasting the traditional notion of rhythm in the more pertinent terms
of a logically fluent word order, as we have seen above. Among all the
French grammarians only Gamaches and Father Buffier had been aware
of this question of ordering the complements, although the Jesuit failed
to perceive the full import of such a discovery. Restaut and Fromant, for
example, did not even mention it (438). Incidentally, it was Du Marsais
who (in his article "Article" for the *Encyclopédie*) introduced the term
complément in place of *régime* (Lat. *regimen*)—an instance of his commendable independence toward the ways of Latin grammar (439).[132]

Even more central for our purpose is the lengthy section on "Ordre de
la Phrase" and "Inversion" (698-767; II, 464-566 of 1767 ed.).[133]
Beauzée begins with Batteux' subversion of the more established view
and Condillac's adoption of his system in his own *Essai sur l'origine des
connaissances humaines* (but we will remember that Batteux' *Lettres*
were published two years after the *Essai*). Pluche and Chompré followed
suit, respectively in the *Mécanique des langues* and the *Introduction à
la langue latine par la voie de la traduction*, while Diderot proposed a view
of his own (a sort of 'third party') in the *Lettre sur les sourds et muets*.
Then Beauzée opens the discussion by repeating his definitions of the
unity of thought and the analytic abstraction of separate but ordered
thought-components (700—See *Préface*). Languages have two alternative choices: they can reflect the universal order of thought in the actual
word order of the sentence, or they can show the relationships implied in
that order by means of flectional endings and "abandonner ensuite l'arrangement dans l'élocution à l'influence de l'harmonie, au feu de l'imagination, à l'intérêt, si l'on veut, des passions." This would be the basis for
Girard's distinction of languages into *analogues* and *transpositives*. Once
put this way, we might say that analytical languages are viewed as tending
to give priority to logical relationships, while flectional languages pre-
ferentially lean on distinct values of harmony, imagination, and emotion.
Which brings us back to Beauzée's reduction of harmony to a dimension

[132] On Du Marsais as the one who introduced the term 'complement' see Sahlin,
Du Marsais, p. 124. This praise of Du Marsais by Beauzée echoes the campaign
newly inaugurated by Wallis in favor of a 'national' approach to the study of a
modern language. Beauzée commends de Wailly's *Grammaire françoise* as the best
to date (439).

[133] These sections are derived from the art. "Inversion" in the *Encyclopédie*, t.
VIII (1765), pp. 852-862.

of logical clarity rather than a separate value, as far as French is concerned.

Analogy, relying on logical order, imposes not only a progression sub-ject → verb → complement (rather, a regression from substance to acci-dent), but also from main clause to incidental clause (subordinate clause), since the modifier must follow its modified in order as it does in import-ance (702). "*Prius est esse quam sic esse.*" Of course Beauzée is here partly wrong, because although he brings in English and professes else-where to have kept Chinese in mind (but not Turkic), all these languages do not quite respond to his definition as given here.

To prove his point he cites Latin examples of *constructionem facere.* They presumably testify to the Latins' consciousness of a logical order showing the connection of parts in the most natural and intelligible way.[134]

Batteux had maintained that "nous ne cherchons pas l'ordre dans lequel les idées arrivent chez nous; mais celui dans lequel elles en sortent," since we aim to understand how to effect persuasion in the audience.[135] This order must be the one in which the event presents itself: "Cet ordre doit être dans les récits le même que celui de la chose dont on fait le récit"—to wit, most important things first. This 'physiology of expression,' as it were (or rather 'communication'), is most pertinent in the light of the correspondence of style to the dynamics of perception and mental experience we discussed above as part of the baroque stylistic sensibility. To Batteux' sensationalism, Beauzée opposes a rationalistic, Cartesian objectivism. To exemplify, Batteux had taken the anecdote of Domitian skilfully throwing arrows through the open fingers of a slave placed at a distance, without hurting him (719). This is the way the

[134] Here (pp. 708-712), as before on pp. 856-857 of the art. "Inversion" in *Enc.* VIII, Beauzée countered the reasoning of the *mécaniciens* Batteux, Pluche, Chompré, and De Brosses by recalling the ancient precedents of *constructionem facere*, namely: Isidore (*Orig.* I, 36, examples of synchysis) and his models Servius (construing *Aen.* II, 348 ff.), Donatus on Terence, and Priscian on *Arma virumque* etc. He then quoted Quintilian, IX, iv, 708-710 and esp. VIII, vi, where hyperbaton was defined as *verbi transgressio* called for by a *ratio compositionis* which sometimes must change the *necessitas ordinis* (= direct construction) into an *ordinis mutatio* (= inversion) for the sake of *sermo numerosus* and avoidance of *oratio aspera et dura et dissoluta et hians.* An even more persuasive confirmation he found in Cicero's *De partitione oratoria* VII, alit. 23 and Dionysius of Halicarnassus, ch. v. Cf. Viscardi in *Paideia*, p. 206. Beauzée's articles, including "Inversion," were gathered in J.-F. Marmontel and N. Beauzée, *Dictionnaire de grammaire et de littérature* (Liège, 1789, 6 vols.).
[135] Beauzée quotes Batteux' *Cours de belles-lettres* (1753), tom. IV, p. 306.

modern speaker would tell the story. But this order corresponds NEITHER to the unfolding of the event NOR to that of its conception in Domitian's mind. It is their exact opposite. Only in Suetonius' way of telling it do we find a faithful correspondence between *l'ordre du dessein, l'ordre de l'exécution,* and *l'ordre du récit:*

In pueri procul stantis, praebentisque pro scopulo dispansam dextrae manus palmam sagittas tanta arte direxit, ut omnes per intervalla digitorum innocue evaderent.

Similarly, when Scaevola wanted to tell Porsenna that he was a Roman, he said *Romanus sum civis;* whereas Gavius, wanting to stress his being a citizen undeservedly hanging from a cross, said *Civis romanus sum.* These classic examples made canonical in the course of the polemic were purported to show the functionality of inverted order from the point of view either of assigning first places to the more 'interesting' elements of the statement, or of narrating the event as it unfolds itself before the mind that perceives it.

Beauzée's rebuttal is elegant in its curt, peremptory finality: "Je demande donc d'abord, si les décisions de l'intérêt sont assez constantes, assez uniformes, assez invariables, pour servir de fondement à une disposition technique? Chacun sait que tels doivent être les principes des sciences et des arts; et il seroit, ce me semble, bien difficile de démontrer cette invariabilité dans le principe de l'intérêt" (720). He supports his objection through a further argument which contradicts those of Batteux even while it starts from the same principle. "Nous aimons à présenter d'abord les idées qui nous intéressent d'avantage; mais cet arrangement dicté par l'amour propre est bien différent de celui que prescrit l'art de plaire."[136] He thus places himself on the rhetorical plane, like Batteux, but he turns his own criterion against him by opposing the vantage point of the audience to that of the speaker. The argument of Beauzée (and

[136] Beauzée avowedly draws here upon Louis-Jean L'Évêque (Lévesque) de Pouilly, *Théorie des sentimens agréables,* "Éclaircissement sur l'harmonie du style," p. 197. He adopts the point of view expressed in this passage, which he supposedly quotes *verbatim.* Of this work's numerous editions (Brussels, 1736; Paris, 1736; then expanded in some of the later eds.: Geneva, 1747, 239 pp.; ibid., 1748, 195 pp.; 1749, 191 pp.; 1774, 355 pp.) I should assume B. used that of 1747, in which the pagination does not correspond to the quote. See, in this 1747 ed., ch. vii, "De l'harmonie du style," pp. 87-110, esp. 103. Let us recall that this objection of the principle of interest being too vague and variable is taken over from Du Marsais, to whom Batteux had already replied (see p. 259 *supra*).

of his source, L'Évêque de Pouilly) proceeds further in a way which, at first, might seem neither clearly nor too conclusively relevant. The gist of it is to correct the unilaterality of the "main thing first" criterion. The interest and pleasure of the audience, he goes on, quickly fade away as soon as they begin to decline. Hence the most interesting ideas, as well as the best-sounding phrases (*les expressions les plus sonores*), must, as far as possible, come at the end. The rhetoricians recommend that, when one musters a weaker argument together with more decisive ones, one shall not begin by what might prejudge the weakness of the case. The first argument, then, must win favor; the weakest one must be played down by burying it in the middle; and the last must be the most striking. "Il convient quelquefois d'avoir une pareille attention dans l'arrangement des idées d'une période." In thus applying to composition the principle of rhetorical 'disposition,' he aims to deny the validity of the 'main thing first'-rule by denying its very effectiveness.

To put it in a nutshell, we are here confronted with a seeming paradox. The *métaphysicien* is arguing for an 'ascending' order, traditionally the favorite cause of the rhetorically inclined (doctrine of end position), while the *mécanicien* appeared to insist on a 'descending' order (initial position), traditionally the 'logical' or analytical type of sentence structure and word order.

The real barrier between the two viewpoints lay in the notion of nature as a principle necessarily simple, eternal, immutable, and universal (and therefore abstract), while Beauzée regarded *l'intérêt* as something so variable, individual, and relative as to be worthless for the purpose of defining what is natural in word order. Each school of thought was thus ultimately close-minded toward the other. Batteux set up the classical free order as the opportunity to express natural interest; therefore he could not really justify the modern languages, which only exceptionally can function along those lines. On the other hand, his opponent could not justify the role of freedom in the non-analytical languages of antiquity.

Beauzée accepted the classical viewpoint as concerns the ancient languages, but with the stricture that the effective criterion was that of harmony rather than interest or pathos—harmony being "la première et peut-être l'unique cause qui a déterminé le génie de vos deux langues [Greek and Latin] à autoriser les variations des cas, afin de faciliter les inversions de l'ordre grammatical, plus propres à flatter l'oreille par la variété, par la mélodie, par le nombre, que la marche inflexible et monotone de la construction naturelle et analytique" (724). Of course, we can disregard the aberration of postulating the search for harmony as the CAUSE of a supposed shift from an original analytical stage to the formation of cases—a linguistic absurdity which once again betrays the basic intellectualism of this approach. The main drift of the argument was to strengthen the case against the *ordre d'intérêt* by pointing out that the ancients were unable to explain their word order on any other ground than harmony, with no mention of anything ever approaching Batteux' principle.[187] Curiously enough, we have thus gone full circle back to Dionysius' thesis.

The *Lettre sur les sourds et muets* (p. 3) had entered another possible approach, namely the order of perception. Diderot's *muet* will not say, in seeing a body for the first time, that it is *une substance étendue, impénétrable, figurée, colorée et mobile* (from the abstract and the general to the particular), but that it is *une colorée, figurée, étendue, impénétrable, mobile substance,* in this order (727). Hence the 'natural order' is, for him, "l'ordre dans lequel les idées arrivent chez nous," whereas for Batteux it is that in which "elles en sortent." For Beauzée both approaches are mistaken, because they are both subjective. He submits, once again, that "le seul ordre fondamental et naturel dans les langues est donc l'ordre analytique des rapports qu'ont entre elles les idées partielles de nos pensées" (728). We might object that, in the end, this a posteriori order is what is given *de facto* without any 'natural right' to being so. The logical order can change just as much as the others can, for, what is the subject if not what grammar makes it be? Change the sentence to the passive form and you will have another subject.

Diderot's *Lettre* further suggested (p. 135) that inversions are relics of the primitive, pre-logical surging of ideas in the *balbutie* of primeval man. Beauzée retorts by expounding a historical view of language which includes a theory of its origin (729-730). The original order was the analytical: "les inversions sont des effets de l'art," introduced at a much later time, just as the ensuing flectional systems. We might consequently infer that French is more akin to the original language than, say, Latin was—an implication of Beauzée's context which, aside from its paradoxical

---

[187] For this Beauzée quotes Cicero, *De or.,* III, xliv, alit. 174; *Orator,* xlix, alit. 162; Dionysius of Hal., ch. xii ex interpret. sim. Bircovii. He finds no trace in them of Batteux' *construction pathétique*—but then again, we should interject, 'interest' is rather psychological than plainly emotional, as nineteenth-century linguistics will reveal.

aspect, may not turn out to be too remote from actual fact, as far as inversion is concerned, on the ground of the little we know of early spoken Latin. Yet this notion of inversion as an *effet de l'art,* correct as it may be on the literary level, really misses the main point. For the need that produces inversion is basic in the psychology of the speaker, quite separately from the conscious, artistic bend of the sophisticated orator seeking for ornate elegance.

Despite his previous acceptance of the ancient inversion on the sole ground of harmony, our author now accepts the *mécaniciens'* discovery of the expressive, *pathétique* and emphatic value of special position for key words, as in Horace, I, ode 28:

. . . nec quicquam tibi prodest aërias tentasse domos animoque rotundum percurrisse polum MORITURO. (731)

Nevertheless he remains convinced of the universality of the analytic construction, and proudly attributes to himself the priority in having asserted it. Batteux had charged Du Marsais with having only intimated it without daring to spell it out—allegedly because he dimly realized its absurdity. Beauzée is unmoved by Batteux' scorn for a style dominated by direct order ("Cette Construction est donc l'ordre contraire à la vivacité, à l'empressement de l'imagination, à l'élégance et à l'harmonie; c'est donc l'ordre contraire à la nature"). He nonchalantly dismisses the indictment by countering with the traditional conception of eloquence as an artifice taught by an art. A well-planned language can do without it: "l'éloquence n'est qu'un accessoire artificiel" (742-743). On the contrary, "la nature du langage consiste uniquement ou du moins elle consiste essentiellement et principalement dans la manifestation des pensées, par l'exposition fidèle de l'analyse qu'en fait l'esprit" (742). This sharp separation of the grammatical and logical use of language from the rhetorical use of it ("Mais M. Batteux veut étendre ses vues sur l'élocution oratoire jusqu'à l'élocution grammaticale"—743) marks a stage in the history of *ars grammatica* as distinct from the *ars rhetorica* according to the ancient, and not yet extinct, Trivium system, the system of the sciences of speech. The distinction between the *artes sermocinales* will be finally abolished only by the Romantics (clearly preceded in this by Vico, and thanks to their view of the organic unity of expression).

Beauzée then enters a most timely distinction between hyperbaton, as separation of terms linked by meaning or morphological function, and inversion, change of order without separation (755-756). Hyperbaton in particular and all figures of construction are, like figures of speech in general, a departure from direct order. This departure is acceptable only when it conforms with established usage (745). Our critic thus implicitly sanctions the classical French language, which was characterized by a 'prosaic' style welcoming more figures than it would seem on first approach, but only on condition that they were based on collective usage (at least of the court in-groups). At the same time, he implies a reaction against the personal, uniquely individual metaphor of baroque lyricism. As to determining what constitutes the normal linking violated by hyperbaton, Condillac's *liaison des idées* is here found wanting as vague, in that it did not specify, as Priscian's *coniunctio sequentium* so clearly did, the question of order (priority or posteriority) in the linked elements (745-747).

Rivarol's celebrated *Discours de l'Universalité de la langue française* (1784) is undoubtedly the best-known offspring of the polemic we have been following. Its main theme is characteristic of this new phase. French had become the universal language; direct order was said, chiefly by Beauzée, to be universal. Putting two and two together, the step that remained to be taken was to declare that French was universal BECAUSE of its identification with direct order. This is precisely what Rivarol did, categorically and without a moment's hesitation.[138]

The story of the "Concours" proclaimed by the Berlin Academy in 1782 is too well-known to need retelling. The results, made public in 1784, gave the prizes to Rivarol and to Jean-Christ. Schwab. Both entries deserve our close attention for different reasons.

The second of the three questions submitted by the "Concours" was: "Par où la langue française mérite-t-elle d'être la langue universelle en Europe?"[139] Addressing himself to that question in the second part of

---

[138] See of Rivarol's *Discours* the 1964 reprinting of the second ed. (1785) by M. Lob and, above all, the critical eds. by M. Hervier (1929) and Th. Suran (1930). Also useful the eds. by P.-H. Simon: R., *Maximes, Pensées et Paradoxes* . . . (Paris, 1962) and Jean Dutourd: *Les plus belles pages de R.* (Paris, 1963).

[139] The reasons for the universality of French had often been examined before. See, e. g., Voltaire, *Dict. philos.*, "Langues," sect. i, § "Génie des langues" (ed. Moland, vol. 19, p. 558), where he tackled the question of direct order in answer to De Brosses' *Traité de la formation méchanique des langues* (1765); "François [Français]" (ed. Moland, 19, 184-185); and *Siècle de Louis XIV*, ch. 32 end. Also D'Alembert, *Réfl. sur l'éloc. orat.* in *Œuvres*, t. IV, p. 282 (where political and literary reasons are recognized, not linguistic ones).

his *Discours,* Rivarol undertakes to demonstrate that " Si la langue française a conquis l'empire par les livres, . . . elle le conserve par son propre génie." [140]

For Rivarol the excellence of the French language is due to its rationality and consequent clarity, both eminently based on its strict adherence to the direct order of subject + verb + object.[141] He brilliantly—if tendentiously—distinguishes French, as a language founded on *raison* on account of its "logical" direct order, from all languages founded on the more natural movement of *passions* (= "tout phénomène affectif ou passif"), and therefore regularly allowing inversion. Similarly, these other languages respond to the stimuli of *sensations* (a psychological dimension of speech which, in them, produces similar effects to the rhetorical concern for "l'harmonie des mots"), so that they "nomment le premier l'objet qui frappe le premier," while direct order is "presque toujours contraire aux sensations." [142]

"Le français, par un privilège unique, est seul resté fidèle à l'ordre direct, comme s'il était toute raison," Rivarol asserts, stating the case for French in the trenchant manner that gave his pamphlet a cachet of conclusiveness. He feels bold enough to mortgage even the future: That condition must last forever, the syntax of direct order is bound to the incomparable *clarté* of the 'universal language' in an unshakeable equation: " Il faut toujours qu'il existe . . . , la syntaxe française est incorruptible. C'est de là que résulte cette admirable clarté, base éternelle de notre langue: CE QUI N'EST PAS CLAIR N'EST PAS FRANÇAIS; ce qui n'est pas clair est encore anglais, italien, grec ou latin." [143] Feeling sure enough of himself, he spares no words to make his point

---

[140] The question is treated in §§ 64-79 of the Suran text (Hervier pp. 88-100); §§ 65-74 are concerned with *ordre direct* and *inversion.*

[141] This evoked the first of Garat's objections: See *Mercure,* 6 août 1785, pp. 33-34.

[142] Rivarol, *Discours,* Suran § 65; Hervier pp. 88-89. Rivarol follows Batteux against Voltaire when he clarifies his views by admitting two causes for inversion: *sensations* and *harmonie:* § 65 D. Fn. 27 in this § 65, however (Hervier p. 126), moderates the impact of the pronouncement above, when Rivarol compares the effectiveness of Batteux' ex. *serpentem fuge* to *Monsieur, prenez garde à un serpent qui s'approche:* the snake would be there before the sentence is completed, he remarks with appropriate irony.

[143] Ibid., Suran § 66; Hervier 89-90.

as categorically as possible, without managing the feelings of his international audience.

Clarity derives from direct order thanks to the latter's impersonality and universality, but such a precious advantage exacts a price in the relative loss of *souplesse*—that *souplesse* which allows inverted languages to follow the subjective, variable order of *sensations* for the benefit of both music and poetry. French is the language of prose par excellence or, conversely, prose is the form par excellence of the French language.[144] He concedes that Racine and La Fontaine have regularly named first the object that struck first "sans jamais blesser le génie de la langue." Nevertheless, "On ne dit rien en vers qu'on ne puisse aussi bien exprimer dans notre prose," since a fine prose "poursuit le vers dans toutes ses hauteurs, et ne laisse entr'elle et lui que la rime" (and "la mesure," he adds later). As Dionysius put it, there is

une prose qui vaut mieux que les meilleurs vers, et c'est elle qui fait lire les ouvrages de longue haleine; parce que la variété de ses périodes lasse moins que le charme continu de la rime et de la mesure.[145]

Rivarol does not underplay the momentous import of his subject, indeed he rises to a sort of epic tone: "Un des plus grands problèmes qu'on puisse proposer aux hommes, est cette constance de l'ordre régulier dans notre langue."[146] He consummates the trajectory of philosophical gram-

[144] Ibid., Suran §§ 65-68. The reference to music is perhaps an indirect answer to Lulli's and Rousseau's contention that music could not use French as advantageously as it could Italian. See J.-J. Rousseau, *Lettre sur la musique française* (nov. 1753), which raised a storm of 'patriotic' indignation in France with the thesis that the French language lacks musical accent, and that "the French have no music and can have none." This and Grimm's *Le petit prophète de Boehmischbroda* (jan. 1753) are among the outstanding products of the polemic concerning the differences between Italian and French music, especially opera, occasioned by the performance of Italian *opere buffe* at Paris around 1750. Some of these ideas derive from Charles Pinot de Duclos, whose notion that French lacks musicality was also echoed in Rousseau's *Essai sur l'origine des langues*, ch. 7. Also cf. Suran, § 73 A; Rousseau, *Confessions*, ed. Jacques Voisine (Paris, Classiques Garnier, 1964), p. 455 fn.; and L. Richebourg, *Contribution à l'histoire de la querelle des Bouffons* (Paris, 1937).
On explicit strictures against the language of poetry it will suffice to refer to the long tradition which included A. Houdar de la Motte, Fontenelle, Marivaux, Duclos, Montesquieu, Buffon.
[145] Ibid., Suran §§ 70-73; Hervier 96-98. Cf. Brunot, *H. L. F.*, t. VIII, 2e et 3e parties (1935), pp. 860-861.
[146] Ibid., Suran § 69 A; Hervier 93.

mar by identifying with direct order that deep, immanent 'nature' of languages which speculative linguists had always sought for, from the medieval *modistae* through the Renaissance rationalists like Scaliger and Sanctius down to Port-Royal.[147] This is, explicitly or implicitly, the common element of all well-ordered languages, the syntactic pivot of 'natural,' 'rational,' 'philosophical,' or 'universal' grammar. The degrees of adherence to or departure from this standard belong to the 'particular,' positive grammars of individual languages, among which French excells because it remains the closest and most faithful to that sort of Platonic idea of what a language really is and should be.

Because all people prize clarity, " je ne croirai jamais que dans Athènes et dans Rome les gens du peuple aient usé d'inversions." [148] As a matter of fact, the ancient theorists themselves showed their awareness of a virtue so often violated by their writers: " Quand on lit Démétrius de Phalère, on est frappé des éloges qu'il donne à Thucydide, pour avoir débuté dans son histoire par une phrase de construction toute française." [149]

Latin word order was less clear because it unduly and problematically taxed the mind of the listener, who had to proceed through a double operation of analysis and consequent synthesis to understand what was being said—in other words, he had to construe just as we do when we read that dead language. His " esprit, qui n'a cessé de décomposer pour

---

[147] In his *Lettre au Père Mersenne* on a universal, Esperanto-type of language, Descartes had similarly distinguished two levels of operation for language, the absolute and the relative (historical languages belonging to the latter).

[148] *Discours*, Suran § 70 A; Hervier 94. The 1784 ed. had: "usé de fortes inversions."

[149] Ibid., Suran § 70 C; Hervier 94. We have seen before this rather distorted representation of ancient theory. Demetrius, *On Elocution*, § 44, referred to the passage in question anent sentence structure (articulation of members). He cited Herodotus' first sentence as well. He did, however, recommend a 'natural' word order as part of the plain style (§ 199), referring to Thucydides I, ch. 24: "Epidamnus is a town situated on the right hand side when one enters the Ionian gulf." By this mode of presentation, he remarked, we first introduce the object of our thought, then we define this object as a town, and so forth. He then concluded (§ 200): "Of course one could change this construction and say: *There is a town, Ephyra* [Homer, *Il.*, vi, 152]; but we neither unconditionally approve the former order nor condemn the latter. We are merely setting forth the natural method of arrangement." Cf. my pp. 80-81 above, and Hervier's fn. p. 94. Suran also cites this passage, without comment. One doubts that Rivarol had acceded directly to Demetrius' text, while he confidently relied on Charpentier, *De l'excellence*, t. II, pp. 652-656 of 1683 ed.

composer encore, résout enfin le sens de la phrase, comme un problème."[150]
It is this puzzle-like aspect of the language (as literarily used) that
typically lent itself to the ambiguities exploited by oracles—thanks to
inversions and hyperbata.[151]

More than any of his predecessors, Rivarol establishes a rapport of
cause and effect between direct order and *clarté*, although the formula had
already made a first appearance in Le Laboureur's *Avantages* (where
Bouhours had picked it up); then again Charpentier had proposed *clarté*
as the chief advantage resulting from direct order. But for Rivarol faithfulness to direct order is also caused, in turn, or rather stimulated and
strengthened in a sort of circular movement, by the need for clarity which
is a mainspring of the French spirit.[152]

It was to be expected that a writer so keenly appreciative of the
linguistic elements of style could not fail to write well himself. Indeed
it has been remarked that the greatest glory of Rivarol's style is his
sentence. As a stylist, he was even above his prejudices, and one notes
with a smile that he could not refrain from an inversion even while
singing the praises of direct order (" C'est de là que résulte cette admirable
clarté . . ."").

His sentence fits his time, but it remains one of the last monuments to
the spirit he expressed so well through his ideas. Even while he was
writing, one was beginning to grow tired of Montesquieu's and Voltaire's
ton spirituel;[153] such masters of style as Buffon and Rousseau were eman-
cipating themselves from the *style coupé* and with their language satisfied the need for a more broadly based poetical or oratorical prose rhythm.[154]

Rivarol, of course, did not remain unchallenged. In two celebrated
articles which appeared in the Parisian *Mercure de France* of the 6th and

---

[150] *Discours,* Suran 72 A.

[151] Ibid., Suran 66 E. This draws upon Charpentier, *Excell. l. fr.* (1683), II,
672-678: classic would be the case of acc. + infin. followed or preceded by object.

[152] Ibid., Suran §§ 70-71. Cf. Suran's fn. 8, p. 255. This manner of tight
association was criticized by Garat, *Mercure,* 6 août 1785. See, also, in Suran's ed.,
Rivarol's *Notes* at the end of the vol. and the Appendix on *Ordre Direct,* pp.
363-364.

[153] " On désire une phrase moins leste et plus étoffée, une harmonie plus grave
et plus large, et autre chose que le perpétuel accompagnement de malice et de
persiflage." Lanson, *L'Art de la prose,* p. 195; see, also, p. 141. Cf. K.-E. Gass,
Rivarol . . . (1938), p. 55.

[154] Gass, ibid.; Brunot, *H. L. F.,* VI, 2², pp. 2109-2114.

13th of August 1785 (pp. 10-34 and 63-73), Garat moved some well adjusted censures, even though his severity caused Grimm to qualify him as *fielleux.* After praising the method of the " grammaire philosophique " (pp. 25-27), he protested that " l'ordre direct n'est pas la seule source de clarté. Des idées bien déterminées, bien ordonnées, rendues ou avec le mot propre ou avec le mot qui fait une image juste, seront claires dans toutes les langues " (p. 31). Hence he denied Rivarol's singling out of French and his suggested foundation of the French *clarté* as well. Spanish, Italian, English are just as dedicated to direct order as French is (not a very meaningful statement except for English), yet they are less ' clear.' This quality, then, must be traced to matters of vocabulary and semantics rather than word order.

The other prize-winning *Mémoire* of the 1782 " Concours " was due to the pen of Jean-Christ. Schwab (1743-1821) from Ilsfeld, Württenberg.[155] Interestingly enough, it displays the rather different vantage point of the ' foreigner' using the language for communication, not for artistic, literary purposes. Schwab disapproves of certain recent *grammairiens philosophes* who have " considéré comme naturelle toute construction qui peint fidèlement les sentiments et les pensées "—a reference to the *mécaniciens.* What is truly " natural " for him is to " placer les fondements avant l'édifice," meaning " le sujet avant l'objet et le but. . . ." [156] This natural construction as posited by the ' metaphysicians' in no way hinders the special processes which are particular to the " genres pathétique, pittoresque, euphonique." [157] These latter, however, are not the ones which matter to people (including ' foreigners' and non-natives) who " désirent uniquement un instrument commode de COMMUNI-CATION." [158]

Thus in analysing the reasons for the diffusion of French—which to an ' impartial ' outsider may not appear directly caused by its intrinsic merits— he singles out " la facilité de l'apprendre, qui a sa source dans la régularité de la construction." [159] This is what puts a language like German at a disadvantage: " La construction s'éloigne en partie de l'ordre naturel,

---

[155] Schwab's *Mémoire* was only published in 1803 in the French translation prepared by the Dijon " chanoine " Denis Robelot in 1796.
[156] Schwab, *Mémoire* . . . , Robelot ed., p. 44. Cf. fn. 4. See Brunot, *H. L. F.,* VIII, 2ᵉ et 3ᵉ parties, pp. 866 and, esp., 882-887.
[157] Schwab, pp. 45-46.
[158] Ibid., p. 47.
[159] Ibid., p. 134.

le verbe est très souvent rejeté à la fin "; " la construction éprouve un changement suivant que la phrase commence avec telle ou telle particule." " Nos grammairiens ont découvert les règles de cette construction; mais c'est de leur multitude précisément que résulte l'irrégularité de notre langue." [160]

Of the remaining lot of participants to the " concours," Brunot regards Jean Auguste Eberhard's (1739-1809) Dissertation as the best.[161] The attractiveness of his approach lies in his freedom from dogmatism. He fully realizes, and honestly expounds, how problematic the handling of word order has become. The term 'natural' has been used indiscriminately in this connection, and critics have felt inclined to regard Greek and Latin as removed from naturalness. Perhaps we could restrict the term to designate a flow of discourse in which every word appears to contribute something to the word immediately preceding. Latin often departs from such a standard, and yet before passing judgment we should make sure that perfectly tenable causes do not govern the different type of order—which is normally the case. The fact is that there are several kinds of natural order. It is only to abstract subject matters that direct order seems to pertain *de rigueur*; even French all too frequently departs from it.

Eberhard's analysis reveals the full extent of the danger implicit in the potentially confusing association of nature and reason which most 'classicists' had taken for granted. Much difficulty might have been avoided had direct order been referred to as 'rational' rather than 'natural,' in the sense that when a word follows the one it completes, the rule for their being so ordered would appear to be based on the way the mind orders them when understanding is the only purpose. In that sense Latin order could be said to be other than characteristically 'rational.' But more on this later. Eberhard, for one, remains convinced that French syntax aims at clarity in its general organization. The price it pays to attain this goal is that of sacrificing some degree of harmony, picturesqueness, expressiveness, vigor, and, of course, freedom of arrangement.[162]

---

[160] Ibid., pp. 157-159.

[161] Cf. Brunot, *H. L. F.*, VIII, 2e partie, p. 903 and 952-958. Also Suran, p. 91. Eberhard's Dissertation was in German, and is extant in a Ms. (Ms. A or No. 1 in the file of the papers from the Berlin " concours ") which Brunot ascertained as the one published by the author in his *Vermischte Schriften*, t. I, pp. 29 ff.

[162] Eberhard, *Diss.*, pp. 47-49 of printed ed., f.os 196r–197r of Ms.

Another dissertation in the collection establishes an interesting comparison. Starting from the standard example of *filium pater amat*, which was offered to demonstrate the functionality of variation, we hear that in order to translate *Den Sohn liebt der Vater* one must say *C'est le fils qu'aime le père*, since *le père aime le fils* would, in homage to 'natural' order, miss the nuance altogether.[163]

It seems appropriate to close this part of our survey with Urbain Domergue. At the same time that he closed his century he opened the way to Romantic and modern speculation, since he genially reaped the fruits of both conflicting schools, the sensualist and the rationalist. Properly speaking Domergue was a sensualist. In the programmatic opening of his *Grammaire générale analytique* (1799) one reads that " L'homme sent et pense," where *pensée* is understood as Locke's " reflexion," following sensation as the latter of two steps of understanding. Indeed it is not opposed to sensation (as the Cartesians were inclined to view it), but is defined as a *sensation transformée*, in a nomenclature reminiscent of Condillac.[164] Domergue consequently asks: How can a conflict arise between rational word order and the order suggested by the sequence of our sensations? A most pertinent question indeed, and one which underscores Domergue's sensationalist slant in Condillac's direction. Would there be something 'unnatural' in the operations of our senses, if it is true that, as Condillac demonstrated, the analytical order is arrived at by natural evolution of the language? His answer lies in separating *ordre direct* and *ordre grammatical*, which almost everybody had confused together. The former governs most languages, and consists of placing signs according to the rank held in our mind by the ideas they stand for. The latter, very rare because very dry and cold, orders the proposition according to the sequence Subject + Verb + Attribute (and Complements), to wit *judicande + judicateur + judicat*. Disengaging linguistic speculation from chauvinistic overtones he concludes that the French *clarté* is the result not of regulated word order, but of a univocal lexicon.[165] If Rivarol had his way, *Un serpent, fuyez!* should be replaced by that masterpiece of expressive ineptitude: *Monsieur, prenez garde, voilà un serpent qui*

---

[163] Cf. Ms. S, f. 29ʳ, cited by Brunot, VIII, 2, p. 958.
[164] Cf. Ricken, " Sensualismus," pp. 120-121.
[165] Domergue, *Gr. gén. anal.* (Paris, an VII [1799]), pp. 71-75, esp. 72. I must note here Domergue's vigorous pointer toward a better syntactical awareness: " Le grammairien vulgaire ne parle pas de la proposition; il traite seulement des parties du discours " (ibid., p. 32).

s'approche. Domergue ironizes on this absurdity and adds more elaborate examples. (We recall, however, that Rivarol had bent over backward to justify that particular type of inversion.)[166] But in sum, a truly effective mode of expression must be whole and complete, including both *raison* or *sens commun* and *les passions*, since the former demands and stimulates the latter. How could a speech by Mirabeau not have been clear, since it aroused the patriots?

The parabola of the polemic is appropriately concluded: in the course of a linguistic debate, an originally rhetorical matter has been brought back to the rhetorical roots of the tradition, in its fullest and deepest sense. The rightness of the theory and the effectiveness of the practice are to be tested in the forum. Domergue, son of the Revolution, understands and gives us as sound linguistic theory what made for effective speech in the Revolution. But he does not stop there. While he attacks and ridicules Rivarol's rationalism in grammar, he exposes the traitor and *émigré* who as a man and as a scholar belonged to the *ancien régime.* Domergue was more than the last eminent representative of philosophical grammar. He was its hero—*grammairien-patriote,* as his age saw him. As the century closes, the two schools of thought symbolically come to coincide with the spirit that moved two opposite ideologies on the sociopolitical as well as on the cultural level. And the defense of passion against reason moves on toward an entirely new context, that of the Romantic Revolt, where it will bear fruit of a new and unexpected kind.[167]

C. THE THEORY OF COMPOSITION IN ITALY: 1600–1800

1. The position of Italy within the evolution undergone by European prose forms in the baroque age is admittedly an idiosyncratic one, for this country seemed to pursue a basically Asianic course, apparently immune from the trends which loomed so large elsewhere. This fact accounts for her increasing isolation at that time, and for the consequent hostility her dominant forms began to encounter abroad, starting with France. It was also a reason for the decisive revolt that took place in Italy at the end

---

[166] Cf. fn. 142 above.

[167] D. Thiébault's *Grammaire philosophique* (1802) contains an interesting summary of grammatical speculation from the Greeks through the eighteenth century, conducted from the vantage point of philosophical grammar. See the "Lettre à M. Pinglin sur l'histoire de la science grammaticale," t. II, pp. 161-214.

of the century against the "bad taste" and "empty bombast" which the
Arcadia Academy came to identify with baroque, in an attempt to replace
it with a new "simplicity," "clarity," and "reasonable truth." Yet, Italy
was no true exception to the trends which asserted themselves more per-
vasively in France and England—and not only on account of the scientific
style of Galileo and his school. Important as it is to establish such a
European perspective on the basis of the so-called "baroque Atticism,"
only recently has this become the subject of a comprehensive study,
namely a brief but brilliant paper by Ezio Raimondi. This scholar draws
explicitly on G. Williamson's *The Senecan Amble*, even though he does
not refer to Croll's studies which laid the foundations of that book.[1]

Italian Seicento writing, it bears repeating, is not consistently affected
by the systematic features of the new Atticism. Yet in Italy the new
movement made remarkable inroads, even if we hesitate to apply the
term 'plain' writing to any aspect of Italian baroque—except for much
of Tuscan prose, particularly of the scientific variety eminently represented by Galileo (usually regarded as an 'exception' to the prevailing
trends).

Some theorists could still echo the traditional formulae, as when
Francesco Panigarola's *Il Predicatore* (Venice, 1609) submitted that "the
composition will be deemed magnificent whenever it displays long members, whenever it is periodic, . . . whenever, in short, one has taken pains
to arrange every word, however unimportant, like pawns on a chess-
board."[2] But the critical mind of Traiano Boccalini (1556-1613) was
more responsive to the changing tastes. In an allusion to Lipsius' *Commentary* on Velleius Paterculus (an author in whom Gracián found a
store-house of his favorite *agudezas*), Boccalini's *Ragguagli di Parnaso*
(1612) staged an emblematic scene: Paterculus leading Lipsius into the

---

[1] Raimondi, *Letteratura barocca: Studi sul Seicento italiano* (Florence, 1961),
pp. 175-248: "Polemica intorno alla prosa barocca" (hereafter cited simply as:
Raimondi). On the speculative side of Seicento letters in general see, especially,
L. Anceschi, "Le poetiche del Barocco letterario in Europa," in *Momenti e
problemi di storia dell'estetica* (4 Parts in 3 vols., Milan, 1959-1962), Part I, ch. 7.
[2] "Magnifica sarà la composizione quando . . . avrà membri longhi, quando sarà
periodica, . . . quando insomma si devano mettere e togliere tutte le parole grandi
e piccole, come i pezzi sulla scacchiera." *Il Predicatore*, II, p. 113. Cf. G. Zonta,
"Rinascimento, Aristotelismo e Barocco," *G. S. L. I.*, CIV (1934), 1-63 and 185-
240: see pp. 197-198; G. Morpurgo Tagliabue, "Aristotelismo e Barocco," p. 140.
See Aristotle, *Rhet.* 1409A on the compact style (κατεστραμμένη λέξις).

presence of Apollo between Seneca the Moralist and Tacitus the Politician, while Lipsius' works were offered to the god to document the petition for immortality.[3]

The most articulate indictment of the advancing vogue of coupé style we can perhaps find in the whole century is Agostino Mascardi's (1591-1640) *Dell'arte istorica* (1636).[4] Note the early date at which this partisan of a moderate Ciceronianism attempts to stem a trend he despises and fears as equally unpalatable to him and popular among so many. Mascardi begins by investigating the very nature of style, and his conclusion (see esp. p. 288) is that style is individual. In this respect it resembles *maniera* in painting, while the "characters" (= style genera) are only three, and common to whole groups of writers.[5] The study is the result of a very thorough and learned review of all the relevant literature from antiquity, and especially Aristotle, Cicero, Dionysius, Demetrius, Hermogenes, Seneca, and Quintilian. Mascardi opines that Quintilian must have learned from Dionysius the overwhelming significance of word arrangement, and that Cicero himself might well have been the source of this realization for both (pp. 251-252). All three of them affirm the principle and exemplify it by garbling. Cicero garbled one of his own sentences and followed this up by ordering another one by someone else, which he found unsatisfying to him: "Quantum autem sit apte dicere experiri licet, si aut compositi oratoris bene structam collocationem dissolvat permutatione verborum; corrumpitur enim tota res: ut haec nostra in Corneliana, Et deinceps omnia etc." (p. 252). Most authors tend to regard composition as one of the three or so most significant factors in good writing: "Cornificius" lists them as "elegantia, compositio, dignitas"; Quintilian, more typical in his terminology, lists them as "emendata,

---

[3] Cf. Croll, "'Attic Prose' . . . ," p. 123 fn. (p. 96 of Patrick and Evans' ed.). Cf. Boccalini, *I Ragguagli di Parnaso e Pietra del Paragone politico*, ed. G. Rua (Bari, 1910), pp. 67-75 (I, 23). The dates for the *Ragguagli* are 1612 (1st centuria) and 1613 (2d centuria).

[4] Mascardi, op. cit., 1859 ed. See, esp., pp. 234-288 and 419-454. On the historical use of Tacitus among political theorists and historians after Machiavelli, a standard work is Giuseppe Toffanin, *Machiavelli e il 'Tacitismo'* (Padua, 1921).

[5] This "individualizing" approach to the notion of style remained fertile in Italy, as exemplified later on by the critical methods of Father Tommaso Ceva: see his *Memorie di alcune virtù del Sig. Conte F. de Lemene con alcune riflessioni su le sue poesie* (1706¹, Milan, Bellegatta, 1718). And cf. M. Fubini, *Dal Muratori al Baretti* (Bari, 1954²), p. 162.

collocata, figurata," meaning that elocution needs, with respect to words taken in groups, correctness, composition, ornatus (p. 253). In particular, Mascardi gives much credit to Hermogenes' notion of style "ideas" or "forms" (ἰδέαι, expounded in his 2 books with this title), which are here interpreted as equivalent to a new classification of style genera. There are seven of these principal forms, subdivided into thirteen secondary ones, namely: clear (pure, lucid), grand (serious, rough, vehement, splendid, vigorous, twisted), beautiful, quick, moral or ἦθος (simple, sweet, acute, moderate, βαρύτης or 'resented'), truthful, forceful (p. 278).

Of more pertinent concern to us remains a long chapter toward the end of Mascardi's treatise, where, in order to defend his ideal of a moderate and flexible form of elevated style as the most appropriate for the historian, the theorist vigorously attacks the chopped-up style which some, as he avers, attributed to imitation of Pierre Mathieu, a "most unworthy" French historian. The vogue, he points out, is not entirely recent. Seneca had already attributed it to the generation of Sallust, when, as he put it, "amputatae sententiae, verba ante exspectatum cadentia, et obscura brevitas fuere pro cultu" (p. 425). But Seneca himself was censured for a similar vice by Quintilian, who strove to "corruptum et omnibus vitiis fractum dicendi genus revocare ad severiora iudicia" (p. 426). Now the ancients had cautiously acknowledged that some degree of roughness in composition may contribute to sublimity of style (Demetrius: ποιεῖ δὲ καὶ δυσφωνία συνθέσεος ἐν πολλοῖς μέγεθος—p. 424): but the method was so easily overdone that even Thucydides incurred a just blame for it.[6] His authority was lightheartedly invoked by any cheap writer who, because he chopped up his sentences, considered himself a brother to Thucydides, to express it in the words of Cicero: "Quum mutila quaedam et hiantia locuti sunt, . . . germanos se putant esse Thucydidis" (p. 425).[7]

Now all ancient demurrers on this score would most pertinently apply to our own time, Mascardi continues, "poiché o in latino, o in italiano

---

[6] Cf. Hermogenes: "At videtur hoc excedere, praesertim in dictione, magis vergens ad asperitatem et duritiem, quam ob causam vergit etiam ad obscuritatem, ita etiam in structura dictionum." Cited by Mascardi, p. 425.

[7] Similarly Quintilian: "Qui, praecisis conclusionibus obscuri, Sallustium atque Thucydidem superant"—Mascardi, p. 435. Further, extensive information on Mascardi and his circle is now available in Raimondi, *Anatomie secentesche* (Pisa, 1966), esp. chs. 2 and 3.

si scriva, lasciate le bellezze ch'adornavano virilmente una sensata favella, oggi si rivolgon le penne degli ingegnosi alle acutezze; e con minuzzoli di sentenze e di sensi s'impoverisce la maestà dell'antica eloquenza." Today's eloquence reminds one of a lady who goes abroad clad in rags: "con un centone di pezzuole diverse, più tosto mal cucito che ben tessuto . . . , non piú con passo magnifico e fermo passeggia . . . , ma tutta mobile e ondeggiante a capriole saltella." "Non ha respiro ne' suoi viaggi entro a camere agiate di ben disposto periodo, ma vien cacciata nell'angustie di quattro parole malamente intrecciate; discinta per difetto di legatura, sconcertata per mancamento di numero, fosca per la spezzatura della favella, rotta, anelante . . ." (p. 426). Indeed "one has seen for some time a sort of books which bear the imprint of oversubtle and bizarre intellects"; "hanno dicitura sì saltellante e minuta . . . , ad ogni terza, o quarta parola, s'urta incautamente in un punto; e in vece d'un periodo, o d'un spirito, altri s'avviene in un corto motto d'impresa . . ." (p. 430). By "spirit" he refers to the breath length which naturally measures a well-cut clause. This new gait is worthy of locusts, not men (p. 431).

In short, the *style coupé* or *haché*, which Mascardi calls *dicitura spezzata,* has three faults: it is "caliginosa per accorciamento di clausole; disciolta per mancamento di concatenazione; molesta per troncamento di numero" (p. 432). That is to say: the clauses are too curt for clarity, the conjunctions too scarce for proper linkage, the rhythm too truncated for satisfaction of the ear. To be sure obscurity has many causes, but this manner of brevity is the most obnoxious, as Horace pointed out: *Brevis esse laboro,/ Obscurus fio.* Just as bad as the *spezzatura* of members is their accumulation without proper links, namely the *scatenatura,* as he picturesquely calls it. Demetrius had already underlined this vice, in Pier Vettori's rendering of his text: "Quod autem caret coniunctionibus, et dissolutum est totum, obscurum est omne" (p. 435). The outcome sounds like a ladies' game popular in some parts of Italy: according to the *giuoco degli spropositi* or game of mal-à-propos, each participant whispers a word in his neighbor's ear. When the circle is completed and all words are put together, those who have contributed a word which does not fit in with the preceding one pay a fine. By this rule Pierre Mathieu would have to be fined almost as many times as he has words, since they are all so "scatenate," that "ogni tre parole fanno casa da sé, né soffrono di contrattare o con quelle che le precedono, o con l'altre che da vicino le seguono" (p. 436). According to Mascardi, Aristotle betrayed his low esteem for such brevity when he forbad the cola "without tail" (δεῖ δὲ καὶ τὰ κῶλα καὶ τὰς περιόδους μήτε μειούρους εἶναι—p. 438). But brevity is really an unfair misnomer for this now fashionable abuse. Mascardi insists that what is actually taking place is that necessary linguistic elements are dropped even while an unbearable mass of irrelevant material is heaped together in the form of sententious abstractions (imprese). Prolixity rather than conciseness results. He proves his point by editing in a satisfactory style the first, longish pages of Mathieu's History of France. He reduces their length to approximately one sixth of the original; he feels certain that nothing necessary to the story has been sacrificed (pp. 441-448).

Whether it would yield a more concise outcome or the very opposite, the "Tacitean" style found its radical hero in Virgilio Malvezzi (Bologna 1595-1654). This political moralist and historian, now neglected, was in his days a recognized master of the sententious expression, much acclaimed and discussed even outside his country. Indeed this standard-bearer of the curt style was the "secret target" of Mascardi's eloquent demurrers, as Raimondi has recently stressed, just as he was to become again a whipping post in Daniello Bartoli's L'uomo di lettere difeso ed emendato (1645).[8] We have also seen how La Mothe Le Vayer singled him out as the chief exponent of a "style trop concis, trop entrecoupé" which resembled "le parler d'un asthmatique," with its characteristic "contrepointes dont la pluspart sont fondées sur un jeu de paroles qui n'a rien de sérieux." Similarly Bouhours censured his leading role among the moralists "qui sophistiquent leurs pensées." But in Italy Lancellotti had praised him as early as 1636 as "perhaps" the inventor of a new mode of "Senecan compositive texture."[9] Among modern critics Croce has

[8] Cf. Raimondi, pp. 175 ff., where a letter by the baroque theorist Sforza Pallavicino published in this author's Lettere inedite in 1848 is adduced to show how Malvezzi was displeased at discovering in Bartoli's Uomo di lettere a covert rebuke of his own maniera (Raimondi, p. 183).

[9] Secondo Lancellotti, L'Oggidì, II (Venice, 1658), p. 265: "Parmi . . . di vedere da poco tempo in qua sorgere un modo di tessere alla senechista molto raro e d'importanza. Non so se 'l signor marchese V. Malvezzi sia stato il primo e l'inventore; so bene c'hassi acquistato luogo molto sublime fra gli scrittori." Lancellotti contrasted Malvezzi and Mascardi as the "two modern champions" of opposite styles, to wit the Tacitean or Senecan and the Ciceronian. Cf. Raimondi, pp. 185-186 fns. In L'Hoggidì overo gl'Ingegni non inferiori a' passati (Venice, 1636), first ed. of the Second Part of L'Hoggidì (the First Part first appeared Venice, 1623), pp. 170-171, I find not only Mascardi and Malvezzi extravagantly singled out as two diverging wonders of modern style, but also Boccaccio dis-

spoken of his works as, indeed, epigrammatic strings of *sententiae* ("collane di sentenze—'collane di perle' egli le avrebbe chiamate ").[10]

More than a style, the procedure was an obsessive mannerism to the extent that the author remained incapable of a continuous, organically structured discourse. Yet his very excesses were symptomatic of a trend. The painstaking search for the "quintessence" of the object at hand, to be rendered through the mode of expression, similarly inspired such devotees of conciseness and of the laconic conceit as Manzini and Peregrini or, on a higher level of achievement, Gracián and Quevedo.[11]

Malvezzi's anti-Ciceronianism could not be made more evident than by his defense of "obscurity" in Tacitus, if his veritable horror for redundance in form did not suffice.[12] More generally, he regarded Tacitus as the loftiest master of the "laconic style," no less superior to the "asiatic than pure wine is to watered wine." Its very obscurity imparts to the reader the same pleasure deriving from the metaphor inasmuch as it challenges him to integrate the apparent gaps in the sentence by intervening with his own wit. In his writing Malvezzi buttressed the sustained tension caused by *coups de théâtre* in the form of antitheses, through the use of simple and immediate ligatures, which, rather than reducing the impact of the sentence, made it more "internal," more surprising. Thus he could even utilize the coordinating conjunction *e* in an essentially adversative connotation: such a subverting of the nature of grammatical

paragingly referred to in the same breath: "ancorché già fosse tenuto per idolo della lingua, pare che quasi se ne ridano gl'Ingegni de' nostri tempi, . . . e Paolo Beni fra gli altri l'ha scopato ben bene." On p. 206 those praises are repeated and Pierre Mathieu is quoted "ancorché alcuno l'habbia per un poco troppo affettato imitatore di Tacito."

[10] Croce, *Storia dell'età barocca in Italia* (Bari, 1929), pp. 149-150. Croce also touched upon Pierre Mathieu, Malvezzi, the Quevedo of *Marco Bruto*, and Senechism in his *Nuovi saggi sulla letteratura italiana del Seicento* (Bari, 1931), ch. viii, "V. Malvezzi," pp. 96-105.

[11] Cf. Rodolfo Brändli, *Virgilio Malvezzi politico e moralista* (Basel, 1964), pp. 48-49. This lone monograph on Malvezzi is but marginally concerned with the stylistic aspect. But see Ezio Raimondi's penetrating study in *Letteratura barocca*, cit., 175-248. As to the "quintessence" cf. Gracián: "más valen quintas esencias que fárragos," cited by Anceschi and then Raimondi, p. 201 fn. It must be remembered that Quevedo deigned to translate Malvezzi's *Romulo*, which he prefaced as a laconic masterpiece, "libro donde es immensa la escritura y corta la lección." Raimondi, p. 183.

[12] See the defence of obscurity in Malvezzi's Address to the Reader at the head of his *Discorsi sopra Cornelio Tacito* (Bologna, 1622), on which his fame principally rested.

functors which we have witnessed in other languages, like French and
English (but in later authors), achieved the end proposed by surprising
the reader, who intuitively reconstructed a disguised relationship.[13]

Famiano Strada, the teacher of Bartoli and Pallavicino, professed to
have followed Sallust's and Tacitus' examples as a historian. In a shrewd
analogy with musical practices of the time, he critically underlined the
new vogue of *pointes*, sharply worded sentences, asymmetrically arranged.[14]
Pallavicino, in turn, singled out Sallust as the "master of loose style,"
dir disciolto, opposed to Virgil's and Horace's *dir legato*. He then defined
his search for an "open style, not inane and languid in subject matter,
but full of substance, wit, and energy. The one who selects his topics with
polished care and then treats them in the plainest manner available,
writes plainly and well (*cum laude planus*)." Elsewhere he supported
this by explicit references to ellipsis as the grammatical foundation of
significant brevity.[15] In Raimondi's judgment, Pallavicino marked the
transition—parallel to that of English prose—"from the Senechism of

[13] Cf. Raimondi, pp. 199 and 229. Raimondi adds (pp. 229-230): "Se per
l'occasione adottassimo la terminologia del Tesauro" (cf. *Cannocchiale aristotelico*,
ed. Venice, 1688, pp. 77 ff., and *L'Arte delle lettere missive*, ed. Venice, 1681, pp.
281-290), "il periodo del Malvezzi dovrebbe essere definito di tipo fortemente
'conciso,' a struttura antitetica per 'clausolette' e per 'termini corrispondenti,' con
qualche ritorno di gusto eclettico alle 'pause' e ai 'respiri' del periodo 'rotondo.'"

[14] Strada, *Prolusiones academicae* (Venice, 1684), p. 307: "In musicis . . .
fastidit haec aetas nostra . . . concentum stabilem et gravem, . . . modulos nescio
quos amamus et frequentamenta quibus concidatur minutim cantus fractusque
dissiliat ac plena illa et sonora vocum vis ac potestas enervetur; revocati praecisique
ex insperato numeri, collisi durius soni, suspensa illico vox et ubi minime expectes
amputata, artis hodie medulla sunt plausumque multitudinis consequuntur. An non
haec eadem in poesi perversitas? Satietas iam nos solidae suavitatis cepit: delicias
e fuco quaerimus. Vibratae aliquot sententiolae, dicta punctim aculeata, inaequalium
morsiunculae numerorum hae languentem plerumque gustum irritant oscitantique
huius saeculi palati apprime sapiunt." Cf. Raimondi, pp. 203 fn. and 246-247 fn.
Raimondi, p. 203, compares this passage (which he finds "of great intelligence") to
Malvezzi's similar allusion to the "substantial identity of evolution between music
and literature at the time," where he speaks of "dotti contrapunti, peregrine deli-
catezze, grazie, gruppi, trilli, accenti e spiriti."

[15] Cf. Raimondi, pp. 246 and 246-247 fn. The texts are in Sforza Pallavicino's
Vindicationes societatis Jesu (Rome, 1649), p. 174 and *Trattato sulla Provvidenza*,
p. 284 (posthumous, cf. his *Opere edite ed inedite* [Rome, 1844], t. I): "Apertam
quaerimus dictionem, at non rebus inanem atque elanguidam, sed succi plenam, sed
argutam, vibrantem. Ille cum laude planus est in scribendo, qui cum lectissime

conceit to the philosophical discourse, from curt to plain style, from the prose of wit to that of the method."[16]

The theoretical recognition of the new taste was thus gradually gaining ground. P. F. Minozzi, a follower of the *acuto* style quoted by Raimondi, in his *Delle libidini dell'ingegno* (Venice, 1636, p. 261) referred disapprovingly to what he called, at such an early date, *la dicitura SPEZZATA, massimamente congionta con rotti numeri* (a broken style with broken rhythms—which he found to be an emasculated type of eloquence). But G. B. Manzini (cf. *Dalle lettere del sign. comm. d. Gio. Battista Manzini*, Bologna, 1646, I, pp. 38-39) seemed to defend that very style against Minozzi by judging it "robust by grace of its dishevelled efficacy. . . ."[17] The most brilliant theorist of baroque writing, Emmanuele Tesauro, took his turn at facing the problem squarely by acknowledging two distinct kinds of syntax, the "sweet and continuous" (*soave, continuata*) and the "sharp and segmented" (*acuta, trinciata*).[18] Tesauro often (and especially in his *Capricorno scornato*) ridiculed the rigor of 'grammar' as falling short of style or 'rhetoric,' where grammatical rules can be happily, if consciously, broken. His *Cannocchiale aristotelico* also dealt with the violation of grammatical regularity in the composition of effective periods, which, in his taste, should conscientiously and diligently drop the conventional balances of old and seek instead an ingenious and controlled disorder. This superficial appearance of "discord" will ingeniously conceal a deep, essential "concord," a "disconcerted concert."[19] Shortly

scribat et conditissime, cum his maximam quae sociari potest planitatem coniungit." [Ellipsis] "brevitati atque acumini serviens, multa verba tacite intellecta computat, quo cuspidata et vibrans locutio micet" (*Vindicationes*, pp. 162-163). "Ha le sue breviature ancor la gramatica, chiamate ellipsi, o vogliam dire tralasciamenti: halle il parlar familiare, e molto più halle la filosofia, come quella che ricide volontieri tutto il superfluo . . ." (*Trattato*, p. 284). It is abundantly clear how Sanctius' theory of ellipsis can be tied in with what modern generative grammarians refer to as "elision transformations," in the light of all the linguistic and rhetorical speculation from 1600 to 1800, and not only in France. In the *Vindicationes* Lipsius is praised as the greatest Neo-Latin prosewriter (ed. Rome, 1649, p. 164).

[16] Raimondi, p. 247.

[17] Cf. Raimondi, p. 204 fn. Elsewhere (p. 209 fn.) this scholar recalls that Manzini was one of the earliest Senecan stylists, starting with his *Furori di gioventù* (1629). May I point out that Minozzi's term *spezzata* is identical and contemporaneous with Mascardi's (see above).

[18] Cf. fn. 13 above for Tesauro's texts indicated by Raimondi.

[19] *Cannocchiale Aristotelico*, ed. Venice, 1688, esp. p. 113. Cf. on this question Raimondi, *Letteratura barocca*, "Grammatica e retorica nel pensiero del Tesauro," pp. 33-49.

after the middle of the century the fashion of once unorthodox writers had clearly imposed itself. Pallavicino could then note that "the more obscure authors, such as Tacitus, Persius, and Dante, are read more than others with a special enjoyment, at least by those who can understand them." [20] The inclusion of Dante within the new canon is exemplary: indeed Dante could appear to the baroque reader as an unequalled master of the curt plain style.

Baroque taste carried along with it, as part of an anticlassical campaign, an implied hostility to Bembo's rhetorical orientation. Dante, whom Bembo had placed on the margin of the recommended models since he lacked a sufficient degree of polish, now lent himself to the polemic of the anti-rhetoricians. Similarly the philosopher Tommaso Campanella (1563-1639), who placed the book of nature above all academic authorities, exalted Dante because he scorned the frivolities of elegant language. When studied for itself, *politissima oratio*, overrefined speech, corrupts the republic and is, therefore, disdained by the true sage. (This was also Bartolomeo Cavalcanti's view in his *Retorica* of 1559.) Admittedly it is in the state of tyranny that the art of speech attracts immoderate attention and leans toward an elegance designed to flatter the ear (*conditur sermo et elegans placensque redditur*). Consequently Campanella gave precedence to Seneca over Cicero because the latter spoke more to the ear than to the heart. He eventually came to identify *res et verba*, subject matter and style, because he despised rhetoric as a separable study of superficial phenomena.

Campanella's *Philosophia rationalis* (published in 1638) was articulated into a *Grammatica*, a *Rhetorica*, a *Poëtica*, and a *Dialectica*.[21] The *Rhetorica* dealt with *collocatio verborum* and *periodi* in Ch. xiii.[22] Contrary to the logico-analytical implications found in the *Grammatica*, the

[20] " Gli scrittori più oscuri come Tacito, Persio e Dante leggonsi più che altri con ispecial godimento, da chi gli intende." *Trattato dello stile e del dialogo* (Rome, 1662, 3ᵈ and definitive ed., revised), p. 161. Cf. Morpurgo Tagliabue, p. 143.
[21] See T. Campanella, *Tutte le Opere*, ed. Luigi Firpo, vol. I (Milan, 1954). In the *Grammatica*, even though C. devotes only a passing remark to the right precedence of nominative over verb and complements (p. 614), all examples of *constructio* tend to arrange the logical elements of the clause in analytic order, as in the didactic language of medieval schoolmen (pp. 610-664). The discourse is more extended on periodic structures, which are presented under the heading of punctuation (pp. 694-698).
[22] See pp. 896-902 in Firpo ed.

line followed here is that of Quintilian (the language referred to is, of
course, Latin). *Ordo naturae* is that which requires, e. g., that day be
mentioned before night. We are then advised to close the sentence with
the verb, "quod in vulgari lingua etiam Boccaccius servat" (p. 896),
except when contrarily required by *iunctura*. On *periodi*, we hear that
the *membrum* differs from the *incisum* since it is *numeris conclusus*, while
the latter is *non expleto numero*. We can speak *circumscripte* (*per
circumscriptionem* = full-fledged, suspended period), like Bernardino Te-
lesio (but his periods are too lengthy), or *membratim* like Plato, or even
with sentences of one *membrum*, like Pliny and Seneca, which suits
narration and praise. Finally the author considered the *numeri,* and
advised freedom from the bonds of *ornatus,* figures and rhythms in the
acutus sermo, which proves and teaches and contains sharpness of argumentation, whereas we do need amplification and grave rhythms in the
vehemens sermo, based on periods. The *mediocris,* lastly, will lie in
between. But we must never affect rhythm and rules: it is better to be
carried away by nature than to speak ostentatiously through art, which
appears always useless and offensive: "melius est dissolute utque natura
fert, quam affectate, quod semper inutile et noxie fit, loqui per artem"
(p. 902).

2. All the preceding details appear very promising to the person who
wishes to investigate further. Whatever happened in Italy before 1700
provided a suitable backdrop for the developments of the following
century, when questions of composition were brought to the fore even
more explicitly and systematically. The focus of attention, however,
shifted from matters of sentence structure to problems of word order.

As against a negative *romantico-risorgimentale* interpretation, which had
prevailed heretofore, a more positive view of the Arcadia now regards
it as a response to solicitations issuing from the new philosophical rationalism of English and French imprint.[23] In particular, that school is
reputed to have valiantly contributed to the modernization of the language. Muratori, as Folena has pointed out, introduced a whole new
language, a fact that has been totally missed through the traditional

---

[23] This positive view of Italian Arcadia (roughly 1690-1750) was proposed by
Croce, who is followed in this respect by such recent analysts as Fubini and Folena:
see Folena, "Le Origini . . ." in Elwert, *Problemi* . . . , and Ettore Mazzali,
"L'Arcadia nella critica," *Cultura e Scuola,* IV (1965), 13-24.

judgment of flatness and slackness charged against his style. We are directly interested in his new way of writing which displays, according to Folena's description, "a firmly and surely rational structure as to vocabulary, a direct, analytic syntax, a predominance of nominal constructions, the abolition of subordinating features, and finally, the dual articulation of the sentence into coordinate members." Next to him Scipione Maffei appears notable for "the quick gait of his syntax, the tying of sentences through the logical structure of the discourse, . . . and the presence of new patterns bearing a French stamp." [24] So much for the early manifestations of the new manners. Further examples of modern inquiries into the linguistic nature of such phenomena will be mentioned in the last section of this book.

To do justice to the local conditions of the debate, one must recognize that the problem of the Italian language and literary style, which came to be couched in terms comparable with those of the French critics under the direct impact of the latter, was however differently oriented. "Reason" was constantly invoked in the course of the prolonged debates. But it is good to remember that this key term chiefly meant for the Italians the correction, through the reasonableness and common sense of the speakers or the people, of the exaggerated influence of some great writers as interpreted by a certain scholarship, such as the Crusca.

It is sufficient to recall the terms of the polemic with Batteux in Beauzée's *Grammaire générale* to realize the real nature of the French controversy, which became theoretical and abstract. The markedly different character of the Italian dispute on the same topic was due to the diverse context of the local tradition. The basic issue for the Italians

---

[24] "Nel saldo e sicuro impianto razionale del lessico, nella sintassi diretta e analitica, col predominio delle locuzioni nominali, con l'abolizione dei nessi subordinativi, con la bipartizione della frase in membri coordinati. . . ." "L'andamento spedito della sintassi, . . . il collegamento dei periodi affidato alla struttura logica del discorso, . . . la presenza di nuovi moduli di impronta francese. . . ." Folena, "Le Origini . . . ," pp. 399-406. Muratori distinguished three degrees of eloquence: the "necessary," the "voluptuous," and the "full" (*necessaria, voluttuosa, piena*), and praised the clarity, brevity, and fitness of Descartes' style as the best example of the first, while he exemplified the second through Sforza Pallavicino and the third through Cicero, Quintilian, St. Augustine, Erasmus, and, were it not because he leaned toward Seneca, the Latin Petrarch. Cf. his *Riflessioni sopra il buon gusto* (part I, Venice, 1708; II, 1713; Venice, 1717; 1723 . . .). See M. Fubini, *Dal Muratori al Baretti* (1954[2]), p. 24, and *La Cultura ill. in It.* (1964[2]), p. 72.

concerned not what was right or wrong in a general conception of linguistic theory, but what they should actually do, in practice, as literary
writers. Direct order appeared to them, generally speaking, as something
to be opposed to a rhetorical tradition which they had acquired in their
literary habits. It appeared desirable, to them, because it was more
natural, while their prevailing habits were artificial. Yet the objection
was heard that actual expression does need inversion for its psychological,
pathetic, and aesthetic value. When everything has been duly taken into
account, the visual angle of the Italian polemicists appears such as had
never been really contemplated in France, where it was less a question
of advising writers—though much of the remainder of the theory (e. g.
style coupé, order of complements) was indeed so directed. In Italy the
critique of periodicity and of inverted order became the supporting argument for a broader attack on the Latinized patterns of the linguistic and
stylistic tradition. This attack, together with the rejection of purism and
of the Florentine intransigence vested in the Crusca, constituted the rally-
ing point for the partisans of modernity.

A number of Italian literati arose to dispute the merits of Bouhours'
position and to defend their own stand against his critiques. On the
surface, the notorious polemic inaugurated by the Marquis G. G. Orsi
was a conservative and nationalistic demonstration of resentment for the
French Jesuit's disparagement of Italian bad taste and intemperance (the
'Asian baroque ').[25] On a deeper level, it was a sign of unwillingness
to yield to the rationalistic solicitations coming out of France; it was a
movement of resistance which *de facto* corresponded to the upholding of
the rights of the imagination that was also taking place within the
sensualist school.

---

[25] Gian Giuseppe Orsi, *Considerazioni sopra un famoso libro franzese intitolato La
Manière de bien penser dans les ouvrages d'esprit* (Bologna, 1703). The later ed.
*Considerazioni del Marchese Giovan-Gioseffo Orsi bolognese sopra "La Maniera di
ben pensare ne' componimenti"* . . . P. D. Bouhours (2 vols., Modena, Soliani,
1735) contains the contributions by other polemicists, among them Anton-Maria
Salvini, L. A. Muratori, Giusto Fontanini, Scipione Maffei, and Eustachio Manfredi. Fontanini, notes G. Folena ("Le Origini . . . ," in Elwert, *Problemi* . . . ,
p. 395), pointed out two sectors of the French impact on the Italian language,
vocabulary and syntax, and thus spoke of the new French-oriented prose of some
secentisti, in *style coupé* fraught with *pointes*. Of the extensive literature on the
subject I shall only mention G. Toffanin, *L'Arcadia* (1946; Bologna, 1958³), a
spirited apology for the Arcadia movement which is chiefly centered around the
Orsi-Bouhours polemic and its implications.

The most genial Italian analyst of language, Vico, opposed with determination all forms of rationalistic and intellectualistic interpretation of
linguistic phenomena. This stance caused him to fight Cartesianism in
the light of his far-reaching discovery of the intuitive, imaginative, sensualistic and emotional foundations of language as expression. He specifically criticized Sánchez' *ars supplendi* and doctrine of ellipsis.[26] It is noteworthy that Vico had started out by participating in the rhetorical polemics
of his time when in his *De nostri temporis studiorum ratione* he sided
with the Italian critics who rose up against Bouhours in defense of the
Italian tradition and of "poetry." [27] On balance, in his mature thought
Vico was virtually on the side of the *mécaniciens*. Yet, French literati of
all denominations had to address themselves to a public which generally
moved within a context of alienation from poetry toward prose. Vico
identified poetry with expression and language itself at its most creative
stages. He also conceived of eloquence as a natural product, primeval
and coeval with the origin of language, thus producing a different kind of
poetic elegance from that cultivated by later "art." It is nevertheless
fitting to stress (as has been recently done by a linguist) the closeness
between Vico's basic linguistic assumptions and those of Condillac. Both
men, moving within an essentially nominalist and sensationalist framework (despite Vico's idealistic orientation in other respects, which has
overshadowed the empirical framework in the mind of his Crocean inter-
pretors), firmly assert: (1) a rejection of Descartes' innate universal ideas;
(2) the necessity of understanding genetically the nature of language,
i. e. by tracing it historically back to the conditions of its first formation;
(3) the original causation of language signs and images by the psychological impact of natural phenomena through the senses on the imagina-

---

[26] Cf. C. Trabalza, *Storia della Grammatica Italiana* (1963[2]), pp. 368-376 for
an excellent analysis of Vico's critique of Sánchez. See B. Croce—F. Nicolini,
Bibliografia vichiana, I (Naples, 1947), pp. 89-90, and Vico, *Scritti vari e pagine
sparse*, ed. F. Nicolini (Bari, 1940), pp. 43-44: "Idea d'una grammatica filosofica:
a proposito della *Grammatica* di Antonio d'Aronne."
[27] Cf. M. Fubini, *Stile e umanità di G. B. Vico* (Bari, 1946): "Vico e Bouhours." One of the most competent examinations of Vico's linguistic thinking
is offered by A. Pagliaro, *Altri Saggi di critica semantica* (Messina-Florence, 1961),
"Lingua e poesia secondo G. B. Vico," pp. 299-444. For a discussion of Vico as
the inheritor of the Renaissance tradition see R. A. Hall, jr., *Idealism in Romance
Linguistics* (Ithaca-New York, 1963), pp. 21 ff., in opposition to Croce's idealistic
interpretation.

tion; (4) the necessity of the "figures of speech" as the essential part of a language based on sensation, the "poetic" "early" language.[28]

Vico's exceptional isolation notwithstanding, his circumscribed censure of the French language for resisting inversion and for being able to master little more than *membri di periodo*—rather than full-fledged periods—, was to be echoed again and again during his century.[29]

As on the rest of the Continent, so in Italy grammatical speculation was then affected by the gradual displacement of traditional empiricism under the impact of the new rationalistic approach first inaugurated by Scaliger in 1540 and vigorously carried on by Sánchez, Scioppius, and Vossius, in a linear movement destined to bear its conclusive results at Port-Royal. Such developments within Latin grammar directly influenced linguistic matters in all languages. Whatever had been new in Buommattei, for example (to cite only one of the most successful authors of Italian grammars in the baroque age), clearly derived from the Latin grammarians just mentioned.[30]

In the 'philosophical' century it was not surprising that Muratori, himself a master of the new, didactic loose style, would recommend philosophy as the necessary propedeutic to grammar, language, poetic, rhetoric, and all arts and sciences.[31] Thus the speculative or philosophical grammar proposed by Port-Royal did not fail to be popular also in Italy. An outstanding specimen of this current is Giovanni Barba's *Dell'arte e del metodo delle lingue* (Rome, 1734).[32] Here the study of language is again offered, as in the familiar medieval schemes of the *artes sermocinales*, as the first in the sequence of the contiguous arts of speech (*arti confinanti*), to wit grammar, rhetoric, poetics, logic, and dialectic. Gram-

---

[28] Cf. Rosiello, "Le Teorie linguistiche di Vico e Condillac" (1968); Id., *Linguistica illuminista* (1967), esp. p. 75; A. Corsano, *G. B. Vico* (Bari, 1965), esp. p. 187. Also pertinent Tullio De Mauro, "G. B. Vico dalla retorica allo storicismo linguistico," *Cultura* (Milan), VI (1968), 167-183; trans. in G. Tagliacozzo and H. V. White, eds., *G. B. V.: An International Symposium* (Baltimore, 1969), 279-296.

[29] Cf. Vico's *De studiorum ratione*, ch. vii. See B. Croce, *La Filosofia di G. Vico* (Bari, 1922²), pp. 254 f. and 281.

[30] B. Buommattei, *Della lingua toscana* (first complete ed. Florence, 1643). Cf. Trabalza, 365, where Buommattei's finality appears, however, exaggerated.

[31] Muratori, *Delle riflessioni sopra il buon gusto* (Venice, 1717), Part II, p. 296.

[32] See the ed. Rome, Zempel, 1734, in 3 vols. Trabalza, p. 377, having seen only vol. I at the Marciana, praised it for its "ample and solid construction," and as a "magnificent exception" in its time.

mar and logic are singled out as the two arts that are "organ and instrument" to the others. Logic is asserted to depart from grammar by only one step, just as it is by a single step that reasoning differs from speaking.[33] It was chiefly against the background of this new rationalism that the subject of composition came to the fore.

The main thrust of Pier Jacopo Martello's *Comentario* (1710) was an attempt to strike a judicious balance between the renewed enthusiasm for Trecento and Cinquecento writing, inaugurated by the Arcadia Academy, and the now rejected baroque tradition: specifically, a wistful reconciliation of Petrarch and Marino. In a show of balanced criticism involving the restored sacred masters of the Trecento, Martello turned momentarily to matters of prose style. He remarked that even the Latins, for example Cicero, used periodic turns only when a display of eloquence was in order, as in the introductions to Cicero's dialogues, but not in the "natural" discourse required in the body of the dialogues. Boccaccio followed his natural bent, since at that time the closeness of Latin as the mother language was still deeply felt, yet he might have chosen a plainer style had he turned to Latin models other than Cicero. This remark is made against the followers of Boccaccio, who consider that any good style must be based on end-shifting of the verb and complex periodic roundness (*il verbo in ultimo* and *ritondità d'intrecciato periodo*).[34]

In his dialogue *Il vero parigino italiano*, published in the 1718 *Prose* of the Arcadia group, Martello contrasted the French tradition with the Italian by praising the French for "portraying their thoughts in the very order in which they perceive them within themselves, so that they adopt in this the teachings of nature, whereas you [the Italians] follow those of Homer, Cicero, Boccaccio, and Casa."[35] A good third (the

[33] "Due sono le arti che dire si possono organo e istrumento di tutte le altre: la grammatica e la logica." "Per un sol grado dalla grammatica la logica si discosta, come per un sol grado il ragionare dal parlare si allontana." Barba, *Dell'arte* . . . , pp. 89 and 73 (cited by Trabalza, loc. cit.). The best known among the Italian "philosophical" grammars of the eighteenth century is the *Grammatica ragionata della lingua italiana* by Francesco Soave (Parma, 1770). See Trabalza, pp. 407-416 on Soave, and pp. 361-363 on Barba's anticipation of philosophical grammar.

[34] See the *Comentario* in P. J. M., *Scritti critici e satirici*, ed. H. S. Noce (Bari, 1963), esp. pp. 147-148.

[35] "I Franzesi dipingono il loro concetto in quella stessa positura in cui lo sentono dentro di se medesimi, e però più si uniformano agl'insegnamenti della natura, mentre voi vi uniformate a quelli di Omero, di Cicerone, del Boccaccio e del Casa."

whole "Second Act") of this charming dialogue is taken up by a discussion of word order, and in it more indications can be singled out of Martello's awareness of the new syntactic developments.[36] He harmonized his Arcadian taste for a graceful, *précieux* simplicity with the didactic straightforwardness of the incipient Enlightenment. Thus he proposed that transpositions and prolonged periods be banned from Italian prose: "Via dunque dalle nostre lettere questa vana pompa oratoria, e cara sieci la semplicità di uno stile grazioso, agile e naturale, tanto nemico delle trasposizioni quanto amico della brevità ne' periodi." [37]

Interestingly enough he distinguished French, a "dialectical" language ever on the move, from Italian, a language eminently "oratorical," backward looking, adapted to persuasion and the expression of emotions through oratory and historiography.[38] Diderot will remember this shrewd distinction in his *Lettre sur les sourds et muets*. As to the quarrels concerning word order, Martello, somewhat in line with the *Weltbild* theory we shall mention below, maintained the sensible position that the differences among languages in this respect are more than merely formal or, worse still, arbitrary departures from a universal norm, since they mirror the nations' varied traditions in the art of communication. An established habit can therefore become second nature, so that at any given point one no longer knows whether the figures of construction are the effect of passion or of art.[39] Yet this is little more than a passing remark. Much weightier appears the fact that Martello figured among the very first who attempted to place the question of word order within a broad historical framework. Not content to derive the Italian taste for transpositions from Latin (both grammatically and rhetorically, that is, both through the

---

See the dialogue in M., *Scritti critici e satirici*, ed. Noce, p. 354 for passage quoted. The dialogue was first published in *Prose degli Arcadi* (Rome, A. de' Rossi, 1718), II.

[36] Folena, "Le origini . . ." in Elwert, *Problemi* . . . , pp. 396-397.

[37] Martello, *Il vero parigino*, ed. Noce, p. 366. Also p. 361: "Io non intendo . . . che l'una piuttosto che l'altra collocazione debbasi eleggere, né che la ritondità periodica platoniana e tulliana per noi si debba mimicamente affettare, siccome alcuni antichi e certi fra' moderni Italiani si sono dati superstiziosamente ad intendere."

[38] Martello, ibid., pp. 346-349.

[39] In Italy "gli animi, già dal lungo uso dimesticati ad ammettere, come naturali, le artificiose collocazioni, più agevolmente reputano quasi effetti di ripulita natura quelle figure che sono figlie, non si sa allora, se della passion di chi parla o dell'arte." *Il vero parigino*, p. 348.

spoken language and an imitation of literary models), he also took into consideration the medieval impact of alien linguistic patterns, two of which he singled out as working in opposite directions, the Provençal for directness and the "Gothic" for inversion. He then went on to compare the 'naturalness' of transpositions in Italian and in German—even though he overlooked the basic differences between the syntactic necessity of the latter and the more frequently stylistic choice involved in the former. He also showed his discriminating judgment when he maintained in considerable detail that any meaningful assessment of usages concerning sentence construction must be qualified by reference to the specific genre being studied. Not until the birth of Romance philology was such a method destined to enjoy more skillful developments.

The moderate enlightened position was again represented by Count Francesco Algarotti, who in a letter of 15 May 1747 assimilated the current grammatical and rhetorical allegiance toward Bembo and his school to the past idolatry of Aristotle in philosophy.[40] This critical stand toward the academic tradition in Italian writing, nevertheless, was tempered by a declared unwillingness to foresake the peculiar merits of Italian and sacrifice them to the fashionable French standards. Thus Algarotti's *Saggio sopra la rima* of 1752 gave priority to Italian over French on the ground of the former's aptitude for inversion (though limited, he added, by the absence of cases, which rendered Greek and Latin more flexible in this respect). That essay referred to poetry, but the same preferences were applied to prose in the still earlier *Saggio sopra la lingua francese* (1750), where, echoing Fénelon, French was blamed for its strict adherence to direct order: "To deprive a language of all transposition is to render it cold and mellowed to the point of nausea (*stucchevole*). It is to deprive it of the best means of raising expression above the simplest common speech."[41] Luckily, Italian is relatively free from these shackles

---

[40] "Quella divozione che era una volta nelle classi di filosofia verso Aristotele, pare che sia presentemente passata nelle classi di grammatica e di retorica verso il Bembo e quella scuola." Cf. B. Migliorini, *Storia della lingua italiana* (Florence, 1960), p. 511. See, also, Algarotti's *Lettere sull'Eneide del Caro* (1744) in A., *Opere* (Venice, Palese, 1791-94), VII, 336, for the same thought. Algarotti's attitudes toward language and style are analyzed in detail in Scaglione, "Algarotti e la crisi . . . ," *Convivium* (1956) and "F. A.," *Letteratura Italiana: I Minori*, III (Milan, 1963), 1959-1971.

[41] ". . . il privarla di ogni trasposizione è un renderla fredda e stucchevole, è un privarla del miglior mezzo di allontanare le espressioni le più semplici dal comune

of "grammatical order," just as old French used to be freer and stronger (ibid.). These perspicuous, though somewhat summary, remarks will be better understood in their historical perspective if we take notice of the organic correlation Algarotti was asserting between "genius of the language" and "genius of the nation," and his consequent extolling of a spontaneous and natural manner of expression in line with his comparative interpretation of the Italian tradition (Crusca notwithstanding).[42]

It is equally noteworthy that these contrastive statements on the respective merits of Italian and French were already, by the time of Algarotti, an established theme in the Italians' effort to reassess the status of their tradition within a European context. Despite the Arcadia's sharp revolt against the "bad taste" and empty sonority of Italian baroque verse, such Arcadia-oriented authors as Muratori, C. M. Maggi, and A. M. Salvini could not forsake the heritage of baroque altogether in that they continued to demand of verse a high degree of sonority (*numero, armonia, musica, rotondità*), for which they found the Cinquecento lyric and Petrarch's poems somewhat wanting. Along this line the Italians remained proud of their unique tradition, which set the language of poetry apart from that of prose. They pointed out that the excellence and separateness of the former relied heavily on the liberal use of transpositions. These ideas were clearly advanced by Scipione Maffei and Algarotti's teacher and early mentor, Eustachio Manfredi, who was thus contributing his share to the Orsi-Bouhours polemic.[43] Nor was Manfredi

---

parlare, è un tagliarle la via di sostenersi sicché non dia nel basso." See now these essays in the critical ed. by Giovanni Da Pozzo: F. A., *Saggi* (Bari, 1963), pp. 253 and 281-282 for the passages just quoted. The Essay on the French Language draws heavily on Fénelon's *Lettre à l'Académie*, which it quotes extensively. Cf., in particular, M. Vitale, *La Questione della Lingua* (1960), p. 133. Also H. Bédarida, *Parme et la France de 1748 à 1789* (Paris, 1927), ch. xiv, 1, "La Question de la langue," pp. 577-581, on Algarotti's defense of Italian against French; and most recently M. Fubini, *La Cultura illuministica in Italia* (Torino, 1957), "Dall'Arcadia all'Illuminismo: F. Algarotti," pp. 69-86. It is interesting that these remarks found a sympathetic echo in Leopardi, who agreed with Algarotti's censure of French for the excessive regularity of its construction. See *Zibaldone*, ed. F. Flora (Milan, 1957⁵), t. I, pp. 136 and 706.

[42] Cf. esp. Puppo, *Discussioni linguistiche del Settecento* (1957), pp. 32-36, and Da Pozzo's observations in the Critico-bibliographic Note, *passim* (see, e. g., pp. 529, 532, 539), to his ed. of the *Saggi*, cit.

[43] Cf. S. Maffei, *Rime e Prose* (Venice, Cleti, 1719); E. Manfredi, Letter to the Marchese Orsi in G. G. Orsi, *Considerazioni . . . sopra la Maniera di ben*

simply moved by a desire to contrast one national tradition with another, but, rather, two different conceptions of what makes true poetry (as Fubini has aptly stressed), since he was criticizing contemporary French poetry but extolling, by contrast, the past achievements of Ronsard. He was doing so in a context which clearly reminds us of Fénelon or Du Bos, with their demurrers as to the damage done to French verse by the newly-found repugnance for inversion and all types of bold constructions.[44]

On the conservative side, the Crusca Academy carried the banner of resistance to change. Thus the Academician Gerolamo Rosasco rejected the notion that there is contradiction between naturalness and artistic transposition: rather he erected the latter to the status of a sign of *atticità* and *urbanità linguistica*, a goal which, to be attained, requires a language subjected to artistic elaboration.[45] Last among the notable conservatives in his century, the Piedmontese Gianfrancesco Galeani Napione Count of Cocconato stubbornly maintained the superiority of Italian as capable of many styles, more articulate and lively thanks to transpositions (*trasporto di frasi*) than French, which is condemned to a rigid uniformity.[46]

Yet, even conservative quarters began to reflect the irresistible force of the new trends: the language now sought was to be "natural" and therefore simplified, especially in syntax. Thus, in a *Dialogo della lingua toscana* (1759), the Barnabite Onofrio Branda from Milan rebuked the longish Boccaccesque periods and proposed to choose for imitation, among the Cinquecentisti, Casa and Caro as closer to *uso vivo*; the uncomplicated models of the latter, in particular, seemed far preferable to Bembo's Trecentista models, or the "avvolgimenti e rigiri" of a Salviati, whose "sperticati periodi, . . . intricatissimi giri e stravolgimenti di membri e membretti," in other words, overelaborate periods fraught with transpositions of cola and commata, deplorably and inevitably ended in high-

---

pensare ne' componimenti . . . Padre D. Bouhours (Modena, 1735), vol. I. See a detailed discussion of these texts in M. Fubini, *Dal Muratori al Baretti* (Bari, 1954[2]), pp. 131-150.

[44] Fubini, op. cit., p. 147.

[45] Rosasco, 7 dialogues *Della lingua toscana* (Torino, 1777), Dialogue vii, ch. xvii. Cf. Vitale, p. 152.

[46] Francesco Galeani Napione di Cocconato, *Dell'uso e dei pregi della lingua italiana* (Torino, 1791; definitive ed. Florence, 1813, 2 vols.), I, 134 and 158; II, 72 of 1813 ed. Cf. Vitale, pp. 152-155, esp. 154. On the important polemic with Cesarotti see, now, Gianni Grana, "Lingua it. e lingua francese . . ." in Elwert, *Problemi . . .*, 338-353.

sounding and long-winded cadences, "vi conducono alla cadenza . . . sesquipedale." A polemic arose, with Parini participating.[47]

Meanwhile, the innovators were active. Their standard-bearer, the indomitable Baretti, had declared open war on the Italian academic tradition which, in his unhesitating militancy, he viewed as having stood in the way of all progress and modernity. His radical attack aimed beyond the Cinquecento to the Trecento established models, beyond Bembo to Boccaccio. A letter of 19 April 1758 to C. A. Tanzi contained an interesting aside in which Crusca, Bembism, and the imitation of Boccaccio appeared pooled together: "Non senti tu que' loro vocaboli cruscantissimi? quelle loro frasi cinquecentesche? que' loro bei periodi alla certaldese?"[48] The direct attack started only in 1763. In a review of a legal treatise by G. A. di Gennaro (Frusta letteraria, n° 4, 15 November 1763)[49] Baretti plainly rejected the inverted construction, as he did again in the "Risposta d'Aristarco ad Aristofilo," in the "Lettera al Signor filologo etrusco," and in the "Diceria di Aristarco Scannabue" (Frusta, n° 13, 1 April 1764; n° 18, 15 June 1764; and n° 25, 15 January 1765).[50] In the Gennaro review, his groundbreaking piece, Baretti, with a sweeping indictment of the Italian academic tradition, advanced the dubious yet singularly effective thesis that the good style (natural, plain, and modern— naturale e piano e corrente) is easiest to find. The Italians have become incapable of it precisely because they try so hard to select the most striking one among the infinite possible ways of saying something. He therefore offered, as a replacement for the established models of Boccaccio, Casa, and Firenzuola, the admirably "simple, clear, quick, and lively" manner of Cellini, which he placed on a level with Machiavelli, Caro, Bellini, and Redi (and he added that he could find very few others to propose). Cellini is the most exemplary, "il meglio maestro di stile che s'abbia l'Italia," because, although "ignorante e plebeo," he always devoutly invoked nature, who taught him to write 'just as it came,' "quel che vien viene," and especially to place "il nominativo innanzi al verbo, e dietro al verbo

[47] Branda, Della lingua toscana (Milan, 1759), pp. 6, 11. Cf. G. B. Salinari, "Una polemica linguistica a Milano nel sec. XVIII," Cultura neolatina, IV-V (1944-45), 61-92.

[48] Baretti, Epistolario, ed. L. Piccioni (Bari, 1936, 2 vols.), I, 111-115.

[49] See Baretti's Frusta in the Luigi Piccioni ed. (Bari, 1932, 2 vols.). Cf. I, 85-102, esp. 85-95.

[50] See the "Risposta" in Frusta, ed. cit., I, 342-343, the "Diceria" ibid., II, 252-262, esp. 259-262, and the "Lettera" ibid., II, pp. 57-66: passage in question on p. 60.

l'accusativo," and so forth, every other part of speech falling where it
naturally belonged. Aside from the apparent oddity of identifying this
artistic master of Cinquecento Mannerism as the paragon of unsophistica-
tion, the choice was eminently felicitous in its very radicalism. To the
unique virtues of Cellini's autobiography Baretti turned once again in a
review of Antonio Cocchi's *Dei discorsi toscani* (*Frusta*, n° 8, 15 Jan.
1764), this time with a calm, spirited assessment of the peculiar psychological ingenuity to which the formal qualities of Cellini's self-portrait
appeared so eminently becoming.[51]

Baretti assigned various causes to the historic fact that Boccaccio and
other old writers did not follow " the natural order of ideas in their respective styles" (p. 88). He blamed this on the nature of the Tuscan language, and also, more correctly, he attributed the phenomenon to the
influence of Latin. Of course he could not account for the inversions
which are really derived from Germanic patterns or from medieval
Romance innovations.[52] For Baretti, Boccaccio's language is generally excellent, even while his style (meaning his syntax, concretely) is very bad:
" lingua . . . per lo più ottima, e il suo stile per lo più pessimo."[53] More
conclusively in the " Diceria di Aristarco" one read the categorical assessment of Boccaccio's style as having been (but without *his* fault) the
" ruin " of the Italian language.[54]

It would be amazing if the " barbarous century" in which Boccaccio
was born could have produced an author capable of bringing the language
to its perfection. At any rate Boccaccio's success was due to the prejudice
of legions of Latinists who admired in him that " pedestrian and servile

---

[51] *Frusta*, I, 199-211 (203-204 on Cellini's *Vita*). On the central position of
these notions of anti-Boccaccesque, " natural" word order within Baretti's critical
work see M. Fubini, *Dal Muratori al Baretti* (Bari, 1954²), esp. pp. 252-253.

[52] Cf. Migliorini, *Storia*, pp. 513 and 544-545; A. Schiaffini, " Aspetti della crisi
linguistica italiana del Settecento," *Momenti di Storia della lingua italiana* (Rome,
1953²), 91-132: see p. 99 on Baretti.

[53] Cf. *Frusta*, ed. cit., I, 342.

[54] " Il B., senza sua colpa però, è stato la rovina della lingua d'Italia, anzi è
stato la cagione primaria che l'Italia non ha ancora una lingua buona ed universale,
perché alcuni scrittori, che gli succedettero da vicino, e poi gli accademici della
Crusca, invaghiti del suo scrivere, che a ragione trovarono il migliore . . . ,
l'andarono d'anno in anno e di età in età celebrando tanto, che finalmente si stabilí
l'opinione universale, o per dir meglio, l'universale errore che il B. in fatto di lingua
e di stile sia impeccabile impeccabilissimo, e per conseguenza che chi vuole scriver
bene in italiano deve scrivere come il B." (p. 260).

imitator of the transpositions characteristic of a dead language." The Crusca Academicians made a rational canon of this prejudice and turned Boccaccio into the absolute model for Italian prose. "Thus the rage became universal of never putting the slightest part of a sentence where the natural order of ideas would want it." Worse still, this divergence of every written sentence from a spoken sentence, regularly underlined by the relegation of the verb to the end, gave Italy an artificial language for literature that is indigestible to the common reader—which cannot be said of French and English. Boccaccio remains thus ultimately responsible for the unique unpopularity of Italian literature.

The attack against Boccaccio's sintactic patterns was not exactly a novelty. Toward the end of the Seicento some followers of Lionardo di Capua had opposed themselves to Marinismo and baroque prose by imitating the great Trecentisti. Now another fierce adversary of baroque, Basilio Giannelli (1662-1716), chided these archaizing "Capuisti" for presuming to follow Boccaccio's example merely because they placed the verb at the end of their interminable sentences ("in ogni periodo il verbo in fine . . ."), instead of using the direct construction for which the French and Spanish writers were to be praised.[55] But Baretti went further than anyone would have ever dared. He boldly set before his readers the examples of Cellini's ungrammatical autobiography side by side with the *Decameron,* and unhesitatingly gave the prize to the former because it was natural and correct in the spirit of the Italian tongue, whereas Boccaccio led the whole Italian tradition astray by teaching how to do violence to the language for the sake of a distorted, unfunctional ornamentation according to artificial Latin and rhetorical formulae.

The critical consistency of the Piedmontese polemicist is obvious. His explicit position on word order and his less explicit advocacy of free, lightly-built sentence forms are tied together in his ideal of the *stile naturale e piano e corrente.* It is nevertheless correct to state that, just as the conservative Carlo Gozzi could not suffer the coupé style, *stile interrotto* or *a singhiozzi,* likewise Baretti was much less sympathetic toward what he called *periodetti spezzati* than he was in favor of direct order.[56] If, moreover, his own actual practice was not as 'Attic' as he may have believed, in harmony with his theories, this is due to the fact that his ideas sprang from an impulsive personality: they ran well ahead of his

---

[55] Cf. Fausto Nicolini, *La giovinezza di G. Vico* (Bari, 1932), 150-160, esp. 156.
[56] Migliorini, *Storia* (1960), p. 545.

acquired habits which, like much of his literary taste, were still, in good part, those of his adversaries. Indeed in his writings we often find direct order violated without necessity. For in his idiosyncratic personality one can observe a fascinating mixture of reformist and conservative, of progressive and reactionary, on various levels and in separable contexts. After all he was, like a Galeani Napione and an Alfieri after him, a true Piedmontese.

Baretti's cause was forcefully advanced by the group of the *Caffè* (a militant journal which appeared briefly between 1764 and 1766), the Verri brothers and Cesare Beccaria leading the way, sometimes without any regard for moderation. In the *Caffè* of July 1764 Alessandro Verri's famous "Rinunzia avanti notajo" saw the light of day.[57] The author made public his solemn, or rather mock-heroic renunciation of any pretence of keeping in line with the Tuscan, *Cruscante*, academic establishment. He later declared that it would be far better for Italians to imitate the syntax of Montesquieu, Addison, Swift, and Hume ("Dei difetti della letteratura, etc.").[58] This affirmation referred specifically to a manly, business-like style that would brush aside all unnecessary conjunctions and awkward subordinations, both for a long time pedantic features of Italian formal writing.[59]

Beccaria supported the "Rinunzia" in the form of an ironic protest ("Risposta alla Rinunzia"), where he satirized the notorious "Ciceronian" periods adopted by hosts of pedantic writers: he condemned them because they diluted the most trivial thoughts into rows of gigantic "cakes" which could hardly stand up despite the laborious but tenuous links of minute particles.[60]

---

[57] Besides the two older selections: *Il Caffè*, ed. L. Collino (Torino, 1930), and *Antologia de 'Il Caffè,'* ed. Ezio Colombo (Milan, 1945), see now the complete, critical ed. *Il Caffè*, ed. Sergio Romagnoli (Milan, Feltrinelli, 1960), with the "Rinunzia" on pp. 39-41; Cesare Beccaria's "Risposta alla Rinunzia," pp. 78-79; Pietro Verri's "Pensieri sullo spirito della letteratura d'Italia" (t. I, foglio xix), pp. 152-159; C. Beccaria's "Frammento sullo stile" (t. I, foglio xxv), pp. 197-202; P. Verri's "Su i parolai" (t. II, foglio vi), pp. 332-334; and A. Verri's "Dei difetti della letteratura, e di alcune loro cagioni" (t. II, foglio xiii), pp. 377-384. It is interesting that *nodaro* in the title of the "Rinunzia" was changed to the more Tuscan *notajo* in the *errata corrige*.

[58] *Caffè*, ed. Romagnoli, p. 380.

[59] Ibid., p. 378. Cf. Schiaffini, "Aspetti . . . ," 103 with bibliography.

[60] "Avete voi acquistata l'arte soprafina di stemprare un pensiero, anche comune, con qualche centinaio di parole, e poi impastarne tutto il composto in un bel

In his highly lauded essay "On the Spirit of Italian Literature," Pietro
Verri, after condemning the sterile academic tradition of Italian writing,
which consisted of empty words without substance, singled out for his
century two recently deceased authors, Antonio Cocchi and F. Algarotti,
who "with different style but with the same philosophic spirit have enriched our language with their works." The style of Algarotti, we must
admit, still pleasantly impresses us with its didactic sincerity and subdued
elegance. More specifically for our subject, Verri emphatically cited two
appropriate utterances from Seneca in his programmatic article "Su i
parolai" ('Against verbiage'). One was from *Ep.* 115: "Oratio vultus
animi est, si circumtonsa et fucata est et manufacta, ostendit illum quoque
non esse sincerum, et habere aliquid fracti; non est ornamentum virile
concinnitas." With the aid of the Stoic master of ancient and modern
Atticism, Verri thus changed, with a telling severity, the aesthetic aspects
into moral substance: *le style c'est l'homme même*, he could have added
with Buffon, and an overelaborate, overelegant and artificially 'balanced'
construction betrays insincerity of character (*Caffè*, Romagnoli ed., p.
334). He concluded by warning against separating the art of composition
from the nature of the message at hand, whose value should fill the mind
of the speaker and dictate its own form: "Nimis anxium esse te circa
verba et compositionem, mi Lucili, nolo: habeo maiora quae cures; quaere
quid scribas, non quemadmodum" (*Ad Luc.*, ibid.).

The *Caffé* was chiefly oriented toward practical purposes, and its
literary interventions seem scanty when compared with the political, social,
and economic statements. This group of radical social scientists could
hide potentially far-reaching allusions to linguistic matters, however, even
in remote contexts, as, for instance, the following remark in Pietro Verri's
essay entitled "Meditations on Political Economics" (not published in
the *Caffé*):

Everywhere . . . the lawmakers . . . have attempted to embridle those spontaneous movements of society, whose laws . . . can never be prescribed
in advance. Likewise it has happened that the grammarians have never
been able to organize the languages at their will but only to examine them,
after they had been formed by the masses of speakers with their own free

periodone di mole gigantesca, e tutto cascante di vezzi, e sostenuto da tante
minutissime particelle, che fanno poi il segreto dell'arte; il di cui gran capo, le
di cui gran braccia, il gran busto, le grandi gambe si legassero con sottilissime fila?"
(p. 79).

choices; later on the philosophers have analyzed them and compared their analogies.[61]

The acute feeling for the civic values of human liberty, which P. Verri most frequently applied to political and social orders, granted him an implicit appreciation of a 'mechanistic' standpoint, which he couched in a vocabulary reminiscent of the modern distinction between the legitimately descriptive and the illusorily normative approaches in the study of language.

The Mantuan Saverio Bettinelli, one of the most fearless proponents of reform in linguistic and literary taste, became another harsh judge of the style, not only of Boccaccio's academic imitators, but of Boccaccio himself, about whom he said: "Affettata è la sua rotondità di periodo, faticosa la costruzione, dure e spiacevoli le trasposizioni." What could one find to be praised in this classic writer, after saying that his construction was laborious and affected, and his inversions unpleasantly top-heavy?[62] His Latinizing example shackled and "spoiled" the whole of the Italian tradition. Nor was this merely a matter of style: Boccaccio "hindered the progress of all knowledge because it is impossible to say new things with conventional and slavish phrases."[63] Yet, although Bettinelli praised French as "naturally constructed," he refrained from commending it for imitation: he pointedly discouraged Italians from following that particular example.[64]

When the polemic attained to the ripeness of constructive meditation on the multiple principles at stake, one had to reckon with the presence

---

[61] Cf. "P. Verri e il Caffé" in Fubini, La Cultura illuministica in Italia, p. 117.

[62] Bettinelli, Il Risorgimento d'Italia (1773). See the ed. Del Risorgimento d'Italia negli studi, nelle arti, e ne' costumi dopo il Mille (Venice or Bassano, 1775), I, 181-183, or in S. B., Opere edite e inedite, tomes VII-X (Venice, A. Cesare, 1799), t. VIII, p. 7.

[63] Boccaccio "guastò lo stile di tutti," therefore "venne tardando con quel della lingua il progresso d'ogni sapere, essendo impossibile il dir cose nuove con frasi copiate e servili." Bettinelli, Risorgimento (1799 ed.), t. VIII, p. 8. Boccaccio's impact is said here to have remained steady down to Bettinelli's own days ("fu . . . mirabilmente tiranno dell'italiano stile sin presso a noi"), but through the Decameron alone (his other works retaining authority only in Crusca, p. 9), and with the exception of the Seicento, which neglected him ("trattone solo il Seicento, che lo trascurò").

[64] See, beside the Risorgimento, also Bettinelli's classically-slanted Saggio sull'eloquenza (1782). See, for example, p. 225 in ed. cited of Opere edite e inedite, t. XXIII (1801).

of Condillac in Italy, particularly close to some of the most representative participants. We should remember, for example, that Francesco Soave, already cited as author of the best known Italian "philosophical grammar," had been called to Parma by Dutillot to teach first at the Pagerie, then at the University. He personally knew Condillac and was in contact with him during a few months, remaining in Parma until Dutillot's fall. The impact of this friendship proved more durable than the political fortunes of the French circles, since he remained imbued with the new philosophy of sensationalism.[65]

More important is the close relationship between Condillac's thought and Beccaria's and Cesarotti's ideas on language. In his *Ricerche intorno alla natura dello stile* (Milan, G. Galeazzi, 1770) Beccaria reelaborated a *Caffé* article of five years earlier ("Frammento sullo stile," in t. I, foglio xxv) where he had applied Condillac's psychological method to stylistic laws.[66] Now the two most conspicuous features of sensationalist grammatical doctrine (both bearing on language use and style) concerned: (1) the function and use of "particles," mainly conjunctions; (2) word order. Speaking to the first point Beccaria submitted in his *Ricerche* (ch. viii, pp. 93-98 or 261-266) that all the *parole grammaticali*, namely *particole, congiunzioni*, as well as concrete words which do not actually represent objects, impressions, affections, or sensations, should be omitted— unless the logical ties embodied in them remain strictly necessary to the clarity of speech. His words betray a departure from the preceding rationalism and logicism: "le parole grammaticali nulla significanti"— as though 'signification' were properly becoming only to signs directly pointing to things. And yet one senses a continuity between his attitude and Sanctius' theory of ellipsis, through the intermediary of the Port-Royal grammar. Indeed Beccaria developed Sanctius' ellipsis on a stylistic plane, when he explained *leves stipulas crepitantibus urere flammis* by adding the missing 'service words' or grammatical functors: *stipulas, quae sunt leves, urere flammis, quae sunt crepitantes* (p. 96 or 265). The

[65] Cf. Vincenzo Lozito, F. *Soave e il Sensismo* (Voghera, 1914); G. Capone-Braga, *La Filosofia francese e italiana del Settecento* (2 vols., Arezzo, 1920), t. II; Bédarida, *Parme et la France de 1748 à 1789* (Paris, 1927), p. 423.

[66] This 1770 ed. comprised only the First Part. The Second Part, not completed, is now ch. xvi, and was only found in manuscript in 1809. See now the complete *Ricerche* in Beccaria, *Opere*, ed. S. Romagnoli (Florence, 1958), I, 193-336. For my quotations I shall give first the page numbers in the 1770 ed., followed by those in this ed.

reconstruction of this 'transformation' is directly reminiscent of Arnauld's *Dieu qui est invisible a créé le monde qui est visible.*

Beccaria is equally a sensationalist when he borrows from his master Condillac (*Essai sur l'origine des connaissances humaines*, tom. II, § 121, 122) the Virgilian example of inversion (*inversione*) and analyzes it, likewise, in a context of guided *sensazioni*: *Extinctum Nymphae crudeli funere Daphnim flebant* is, he avers, more effective than the 'logical' *Nymphae flebant Daphnim extinctum funere crudeli,* because it presents a *quadro riunito* (= *un tableau achevé*) instead of a succession of sensations. Thus the imagination is compelled to consider contemporaneously the two objects.[67]. The SIMULTANEITY is achieved by mixing the elements instead of giving them separately in chronological or logical succession.[68]

When Melchiorre Cesarotti's celebrated *Essay on the Philosophy of Language* is contrasted with the rationalist or *métaphysicien* positions that had prevailed up to his time, it appears, at first, as a brilliant document of the Romantic reaction to the intellectualism of the Enlightenment. But when viewed in the light of the sensationalist critiques which immediately preceded it (and especially Beccaria's), that impression soon reveals itself as rather deceptive and historically out of focus. And yet, even though all his arguments can be textually traced back to Condillac's and Batteux' encounter with their triumphant adversaries, Cesarotti's balanced presentation does transcend the limitations of earlier debates. We find here a new ring, a renewed spirit, and a sweep of broader horizons; the "sentiment" so dear to later Romanticists gushes forth, and is both more encompassing and deeper than the feeling and emotion cherished by eighteenth-century polemicists. The entire context can serve as an adequate demonstration of the way Romantic attitudes and ideas emerged from eighteenth-century sensationalism.

A good portion of the philosophical *Saggio* is methodically technical.[69]

---

[67] "È dunque sforzata l'immaginazione a considerare contemporaneamente i due oggetti." For all this see Beccaria's *Ricerche*, end of ch. i, pp. 38-40 of 1770 ed., p. 222 of 1958 ed.

[68] Of course, the defense of inversion did not mean outright defense of the academic tradition which had made of Latinized transpositions a second nature in the use of literary Italian, especially in poetry. Condillac, for one, had judged the language of Italian poetry alien to the spirit of the time: cf. *Art d'écrire* (t. II of *Cours d'études*), l. IV, ch. v.

[69] Cesarotti's *Saggio sulla filosofia della lingue applicato alla lingua italiana* of

Syntax appears divided into inflection, concord, regimen, and construction (*desinenze, concordanza, reggimento, costruzione*).[70] Construction concerns: (1) the number of parts of a sentence; (2) their order (*ordine della loro disposizione*). With respect to the former, the construction may be full or defective (*piena o difettiva*—cf. Sanctius' doctrine of ellipsis); with respect to order, it may be direct or inverted (*la costruzione, rispetto all'ordine, è di due specie: diretta e inversa*). It is direct when it reflects the analytic order of ideas; indirect when it reflects their degree of importance or interest to the speaker. The direct therefore serves the intellect, the indirect *l'affetto,* the expression of emotion.[71]

We read, then, a clear restatement of the *mécaniciens'* thesis: "It has been generally thought heretofore that the direct construction belonged to nature, the indirect, to art. The *philosophers* of our century have shrewdly observed that the matter stands the other way around, and that the syntax of inversion is a spontaneous filiation of nature, while it is the direct one which is born out of meditation and art." [72]

This unequivocal stand does not, however, *per se* do justice to the method of the author. For what characterizes Cesarotti's analysis and accounted for the immediate success of his *Saggio,* is the firm desire to envisage the good side of every position, without sacrificing common sense to the merits of a system. This basically conciliatory and eclectic approach does not exist without peril. Not only do we lack here the daring vigor that marked both the earlier polemicists and the later Romantics; we are also left with an uneasy feeling that this brilliant exposition owes its comprehensiveness to disregard for apparent contradictions—unless we are prepared to accept some captious qualifications to the statements we have

---

1800 was a revision of the earlier *Saggio sopra la lingua italiana* of 1785. See it now in M. C., *Opere scelte,* ed. G. Ortolani, I (Florence, 1945), from which I quote. See, also, the ed. by R. Spongano (Florence, 1943) of the *Saggio* alone.

[70] See, for these divisions of Syntax, *Saggio,* Parte II, cap. xviii, pp. 58-64 in vol. I of Ortolani ed.

[71] *Saggio,* II, xviii, § 4, 60-64.

[72] " Si è creduto generalmente sino a questi giorni che la costruzione diretta fosse quella della natura, quella dell'arte l'inversa. I ragionatori di questo secolo osservarono sagacemente che la cosa è tutta all'opposto, e che la sintassi inversa è figlia spontanea della natura, la diretta è frutto della meditazions e dell'arte " (p. 62). Viscardi (*Paideia,* p. 209) attributes to the circle of Cesarotti the early Italian translation of Batteux' *De la construction oratoire* (Venice, Francesco di Nicolò Pezzana, Padua licence 1772), which appeared anonymously.

read. One conclusion, for instance, is that Boccaccio did (as Baretti charged) violence to the nature of the Italian language, but not because he spoke through transpositions and elaborate periods (since transpositions *are natural*). He did so because inverted order is natural in Latin, but not in a Romance language. "Boccaccio, followed in this by Bembo and all the *Cinquecentisti* with the sole exception of Davanzati, attempted to subvert the nature of the Italian language (*snaturarla*) by adopting a Latin manner of inversion and the periodic flow (*ondeggiamento periodico*)." [73] Thus Cesarotti charges the Italian contemporary style with empty periodic sonority, forced inversions, and an accompanying dearth of ideas, all in deference to the Crusca Academy. [74] These habits are particularly out of place during an epoch when public taste demands more substance than copiousness, and above all a sentence "which pierces like an arrow through its forceful brevity." [75]

As Cesarotti had explained above, inversion was natural to the ancient inflected languages, but the lack of cases makes the direct construction necessary in our languages. [76] Yet—and we begin to wonder where exactly the author intends to lead us—, for "rhetorical" purposes of variation and embellishment, it will be considered permissible to use judiciously, sparingly, and effortlessly, the inverse order alongside the direct (pp. 63-64). Furthermore the *langage affectif* falls within this rhetorical purvue: "The defective or elliptical construction will be prized when it serves to render the haste, the quickness, the tumult, the perturbation of our emotions

---

[73] "Boccaccio, seguito dal Bembo e da tutti i cinquecentisti, trattone il Davanzati, cercò di snaturarla [la lingua], effettuando l'inversione alla latina e l'ondeggiamento periodico" (p. 63). An echo of this lingering critique of Boccaccio's impact on the language is still felt in Leopardi: Boccaccio erred by depriving Italian prose of "il diretto e naturale andamento della sintassi, e con intricate e penose trasposizioni infelicemente tentando di darle il processo della latina": *Zibaldone*, ed. F. Flora (Milan, 1957⁵), t. I, p. 928: this was a direct quote of Monti, *Proposta*, t. I, p. 231, where Boccaccio was blamed for not following Dante's example in this matter of word order.

[74] ". . . la servile deferenza alla Crusca, . . . la vuota sonorità periodica, le inversioni sforzate, il fraseggiamento ozioso, la lentezza, la pesantezza" (p. 181: *Rischiaramenti apologetici*, II: "Sul francesismo," § 9, published in appendix to the *Saggio*).

[75] "Altro è quello che al presente sembra aver fissato il gusto dell'Europa. Ella è da qualche tempo avvezza ad esigere che i sentimenti abbiano più sostanza che diffusione, che la sentenza sia vibrata a guisa di strale da un'energica brevità."

[76] ". . . la sintassi diretta [è] . . . necessaria alle nostre lingue per la sola mancanza dei casi" (p. 62).

(*affetti*), or to fasten our mind upon a dominant idea, or to add vigor to a phrase" (p. 61). In other words, Cesarotti eventually rejects both the rationalistic priority of direct construction because it renders a language "excessively precise and logical" (*soverchiamente precisa e logica*— p. 63), and the opposite notion of the absolute preeminence of inverted construction, which is alien to the nature of modern languages and was imposed, or superimposed, on Italian by Latin and Boccaccian imitation.[77]

Note how, through a complex back and forth movement, we have witnessed the redemption of inversion on the philosophical ground, next its banishment from the Romance area on a historical level, and finally its readmission through the window of rhetoric, after it had been chased through the door of grammar. Thus, not only does the notion of 'naturalness' betray its inner ambiguity through the two juxtaposed acceptations here at hand (inversion is synchronically natural to express emotion, it is diachronically natural only to inflected languages); more seriously, the two levels of grammar and rhetoric do not quite jibe, since their distinction is not immediately clear. Syntactic order constitutes at the same time a grammatical and rhetorical matter, both linguistic and stylistic, but one does not fully comprehend the possibility of distinguishing when inversion is 'natural' (rhetorical), since this distinction cannot merely be based on the languages, as if it were always one way in Latin and another in Italian.

Later we discover a passage where the author elaborates more clearly than elsewhere on his distinction between 'language,' made essentially of morphological structures with a logical function, and 'style' (which he calls the rhetorical element), more individual, changeable, and relative than the former. It is where he assigns two meanings to the eighteenth-century term, "genius of a language": "The elements of a language are of two kinds: rhetorical ones and logical ones—or, should we say, grammatical. It necessarily follows therefrom that the genius of a language . . . is also of a double kind, to wit the grammatical one and the rhetorical."[78] Now syntax falls mainly under the former, while the expressive, emotive elements are essentially 'rhetorical.' In this way

---

[77] Cf. Vitale, p. 145.

[78] "Le parti della lingua sono di due classi, rettoriche e logiche, o vogliam dire grammaticali. Quindi ne fluisce necessariamente che il genio della lingua . . . è anch'esso di due specie, vale a dire grammaticale e rettorico." *Saggio*, Parte III, cap. xix, p. 108 of Ortolani ed. *Genio rettorico* is further defined on p. 109.

the departure from the rationalistic notion of *construction directe* as normal and natural is made not suddenly but gradually; for the questions of order and inversion properly fall within the variable and relative class of phenomena (the rhetorical), where 'naturalness' ceases to be a categorical notion. That the higher degree of changeability be assigned to the rhetorical level doubtless makes sense, even though Cesarotti may seem too peremptory in advising, by contrast, that one should refrain from changes on the mechanics of the grammatical level. This is the only blemish in his splendid, common sense liberalism.

The view of grammar as the logical part of language (the logico-grammatical parallelism once again), therefore inherently inflexible and unchangeable, as contrasted with the extreme flexibility of style, lies at the bottom of Cesarotti's least felicitous idea: the possibility, which he advocated at the end of the *Saggio*, of compiling two comparative Italian dictionaries—a scientific one and a practical one—, including a systematic scrutiny of all dialects and related languages.[79] He promised many advantages from such an undertaking. Finally, in a sort of post-script he confirmed that he had tried to reconcile the innovators and conservatives by granting something to each: " Let us conserve the grammatical genius intact, provided we do not deny the rhetorical genius its right to improve and perfect itself, or to assume any form at will." [80]

In the light of the above propositions it is interesting to recall that the editor of the *Saggio* stressed the essentially linguistic character of the text. The Abbé Juan Andrés, a Spanish Jesuit migrated to Italy, had praised Cesarotti's Essay in t. V of his *Dell'origine, de' progressi e dello stato attuale d'ogni letteratura*.[81] The " Avvertimento degli Editori " re-

---

[79] *Saggio*, Parte IV, cap. xvi, pp. 140-147. G. Marzot, *Il gran Cesarotti* (1949), p. 191, defines the proposal " fantastic."

[80] " Del resto conservisi pure intatto il genio grammaticale . . . ma non si tolga al genio rettorico il diritto di migliorarsi e perfezionarsi, o di prender a suo grado tutte le facce." This occurs in the appendices to Cesarotti's *Saggio: Rischiaramenti apologetici* II, " Sul francesismo," § 9, p. 179 of Ortolani ed. He also contrasts the richness of the Italian poetic language to the inadequacy of Italian prose, especially vis-à-vis the French style, which is now demanded in all Europe (pp. 180-183). Cf. Schiaffini, *Momenti*, p. 107; Vitale, p. 144.

[81] " L'Italia gode . . . nel *Saggio sulla lingua italiana* del Cesarotti d'un'opera grammaticale, quale non l'aveva veduta sinora, e per la quale solo la Francia potea fornirgliene pochi esempi." Giovanni Andrés's work was first published at Parma, 1782-1822, 8 tomes in 6 vols., with the slightly different title: *Dell'origine, progressi e stato attuale d'ogni letteratura*; then at Venice, 1783-1808, 22 tomes in 11 vols.

plied to Andrés's strictures as follows: "The theories of style could find
no place here except occasionally, since this is a study not in rhetoric,
but in philosophy of grammar (*filosofia grammaticale*) considered in its
relationship to rhetoric." [82]

True enough, in such a complex summary of the trends of the century,
and such a brilliant attempt to resolve all the issues raised, it ought not
to surprise us if we find the thought of the theorist to oscillate somewhat.
After all, even Baretti could induce some hesitation in the reader when,
in seeming contradiction, he first accused Boccaccio of having done
violence to the nature of the language, then tried to separate the imitators from the master by maintaining that Boccaccio himself did, after
all, follow what he felt to be "i suggerimenti della natura." The contradiction was, once again, more apparent than real: Baretti affirmed that
good and original writers (including Boccaccio and Baretti) follow their
own inspiration according to the spirit and the needs of their time, which
is not the accomplishment of the imitators of past models.

Contemporary readers of the *Saggio* were impressed with the richness
of insights and the comprehensiveness of the approach, which appealed
to the 'moderns' without necessarily alienating the conservatives. Cesarotti favored the simplification of the sentence and of syntactic processes.
He believed that familiarity with the vernacular, with modern foreign
languages, and with the thought and style of philosophers and scientists
would have achieved his purpose.[83] The most stubborn prejudice in
favor of a traditional affection toward redundant and overstructured syntax
derived from the assumption that it was the sign of a sophisticated cultural maturity. Cesarotti denied this assumption, which Herder proved
wrong by analyzing the 'primitive' languages. Furthermore, he declared
that the most intricate refinements in syntactic patterns, such as elaborate
ellipses, were "a spontaneous filiation of nature," rather than typical
literary artifacts.[84]

Modern linguists, in turn, have highly esteemed the *Essay,* whose
author was considered by Croce "in some respect almost an Italian
Herder." [85] Karl Jaberg is reputed to have once remarked that in Cesarotti

[82] Ortolani ed., p. 148. The "Avvertimento" appeared in Cesarotti's *Opere*, I
(Pisa, 1800).

[83] Cf. G. Marzot, *Il gran Cesarotti* (1949), p. 181. Ch. ix, pp. 173-195 of this
monographic study deals with the *Saggio*.

[84] Marzot, 182.

[85] Croce, *Problemi di Estetica* (Bari, 1954⁵), p. 383.

cne could already find the "convergence des langues" postulated by A. Meillet, as well as the distinction, rediscovered by twentieth-century linguistics, between intellectual and 'affective' expression.[86] One must add, however, that the background for this latter distinction had been amply prepared by earlier French analysts, as we have seen.[87] It should be clear that his concepts derived directly from the linguistic speculations of the masters of the Enlightenment—both the rationalists and those, mostly within the sensationalist camp, who now stand as forerunners of Romanticism. These include, especially, Locke, Condillac, Du Marsais, Batteux, and Beauzée, rather than the remote Vico, with whom Cesarotti has a lot in common but not necessarily by straight contact. Nor does this fact detract from his originality, but there results a continuity of thought within the culture of the Enlightenment and even between the Enlightenment and Romanticism. We should also pay attention to a particular idea recently shown to underlie much of the thinking of the century before it appeared in a deep and ripened form in Herder and Wilhelm von Humboldt and then again in modern linguistics under the heading of Leo Weisgerber's *Weltbild* and, independently, the so-called Sapir-Whorf theory. Christmann has shown how the theory that our thoughts are conditioned by linguistic forms and structures, including vocabulary and syntax, even before they exert their own influence, finds its roots in the Enlightenment at least as far back as the Göttingen philosopher Johann David Michaelis, whose " Dissertation on the reciprocal influence of language on our opinions and of the latter on language" won the 1759 competition of the Berlin Academy. This essay was published in 1760 in German, in 1762 in French (*De l'influence des opinions sur le langage et du langage sur les opinions*, with notes and additions), had two English editions, and was heeded by D'Alembert and in a conspicu-

---

[86] Jaberg's remark is said to be contained in a letter of May 31, 1937 to Schiaffini: see Schiaffini, "Aspetti . . . ," p. 132, where the following are also adduced: B. Migliorini, "Convergences linguistiques en Europe," *Synthèses*, IV, n. 47 (April 1950), 185-191, and G. Nencioni, *Quidquid nostri praedecessores . . .* , in *Atti e Memorie dell'Arcadia*, s. III, vol. II (1950), 3-36; see pp. 15-28.

[87] Thus, for example, one cannot fail to ask whether Trabalza, p. 419, had temporarily forgotten the whole current of the *mécaniciens* when he concluded on Cesarotti as follows: "The rights of imagination (*fantasia*) so sharply asserted as against those of the intellect are undoubtedly a novelty vis-à-vis the *raisonnée* grammar of the Encyclopaedists, which recognized in speech no other function than the logical."

ous manner by both Cesarotti and Galeani Napione.[88] The question interests us too, inasmuch as the problem of the relationship between expression and impression, language and thought lay at the basis of the whole speculation on the correct principles of composition, and particularly of the 'myth' of the greater nobility of an order which adheres to the natural and logical flow of ideas. Now in the *Saggio* Cesarotti assumed a symbolic position which, if carried to its consequences, could subvert the traditional (basically Cartesian) concept of a process going unilaterally from the object to the word through: sensation, imagination, association, thinking. He claimed that "words are like a transversal chain which links the chain of objects to that of the ideas." The intuition of a linguistic *Weltbild* could be similarly found *in nuce*, according to Christmann, in such disparate authors as Diderot, Charles de Brosses, Cesare Beccaria and Francesco Soave, all similarly indebted to Michaelis.[89] I would add to this list the master of them all, Condillac. (See p. 242 above.)

D. ENGLAND: 1600–1800

1. The studies referred to at the beginning of this Chapter have revealed in English literature a very fruitful ground for exploration along our line of interest. This is so, thanks to a prolonged concern among English writers for specific aspects of stylistic composition both on the theoretical and on the practical level. Because modern scholarship has been consistently aware of the relevance of such matters in the English area, as witnessed by so many masterful studies which remain easily

---

[88] The French version of Michaelis's thesis, *De l'influence* . . . (Bremen, 1762), is now reprinted in facsimile, with an Introd. by H. E. Brekle, in the "Grammatica Universalis" Series (Stuttgart, Frommann-Holzboog, 1970).

[89] Cf. Hans Helmut Christmann, "Un Aspetto del concetto Humboldtiano della lingua e i suoi precursori italiani," in Elwert, *Problemi* (1965), 328-333; *Beiträge zur Geschichte der These vom Weltbild der Sprache*, Akad. der Wissen. und der Literatur Mainz: Abhandlungen der Geistes- und Sozialwiss. Kl., Jahrg. 1966, Nr. 7, 31 pp. (Mainz-Wiesbaden, [1967]).

I should add here a recent, broad study of intellectual backgrounds to our subject and period: Guido Morpurgo Tagliabue, *Il concetto del gusto nell'Italia del Settecento* (Florence, 1962). For the transition from Enlightenment to Romanticism, see, in particular, *Leopardi e il Settecento*, Atti del I Convegno intern. di studi leopardiani, 1962 (Florence, 1964): Salvatore Battaglia, "La dottrina linguistica del Leopardi," 11-47; Giulio Herczeg, "Premesse teoriche per un'interpretazione stilistica della frase leopardiana," 321-365.

accessible, I will not have to linger on the texts already brought out by Croll and his successors, and can limit myself to add some supporting material from the more technical literature. Within this literature, the agreements between British and continental pronouncements will stand out even more significantly when we consider the peculiar literary climate of England in those centuries.

To begin with, the context of the baroque speculation on style was subject to important geographical variations. When, for example, Hobbes defined wit in this manner: " Celerity of Imagining [that is, swift succession of one thought to another]; and steddy direction to some approved end"; "Good Wit; by which, in this occasion, is meant a Good Fancy" (*Leviathan*, 1651, I, viii), he was underlining the imaginative element in the artistic process.[1] Hobbes further specified that "the Fancy must be more predominant" than judgment in all kinds of poems and in most orations. And, finally, the difference of wits "proceeds . . . from the passions; which are different, not only from the difference of men's complexions; but also from their difference of customs, and education."[2] In other words, as a modern observer has put it, whereas the Italian and Spanish theorists were striving to explain wit (*acutezza, agudeza*)

as, on the formal level, an artifice, a rhetorical syllogism [or enthymeme], an ' act of understanding,' the contemporary English theorists were explaining it as an effect of our feeling on our memory. . . . What distinguished English ' wit' was the recognized influence of ' feeling ' or, as one then put it, ' the passions.' And passions proceed from physiological and sociological conditions.[3]

The other difference I wish to underline is that the high degree of detailed and sophisticated speculation on matters of composition was developed in England on a predominantly stylistic level, since it took place

---

[1] Hobbes, *Leviathan*, Part I, ch. viii. See the ed. by H. W. Schneider (Indianapolis–New York, 1958), pp. 65-66, or the Oxford ed. (1909, 1929), pp. 53-54.

[2] *Leviathan*, ibid., p. 56 in 1958 ed.

[3] Cf. Morpurgo Tagliabue, "Aristotelismo e Barocco," in *Retorica e Barocco* (Rome, 1955), cit., p. 160. The trans. is mine. Let us note, however, that M.-T. does not follow Hobbes' reasoning to the end, where there appears a contradictory use of the notion of *wit* according to the evolution this term was undergoing in the course of the century, namely from denoting ' imagination ' to denoting the distinct and even opposite ' judgment,' from synthesis to analysis. See the comprehensive and lucid account in William K. Wimsatt, Jr. and Cleanth Brooks, *Literary Criticism: A Short History* (New York, 1966[2]), 229-232.

against the background of a singular absence of grammatical regulations. "The Elizabethans became eloquent before they became grammatical." [4] They had numerous rhetorics and only two elementary grammars: William Bullokar's *Bref Grammar of English* (1586), which remained unsuccessful, and Paul Greaves's *Grammatica Anglicana* (1594).[5] Historians have discovered a socio-politico-religious pattern to this situation. The democratic humility of the earlier Protestants, implicitly prone to handle the English vernacular as "honest and uneloquent," gave way to the aristocratic self-assuredness of the Elizabethan poets, who overlaid their language with all sorts of figures of speech, in a mood of supreme faith in the potentialities of a medium that was still as free and flexible as they could ever wish it to be.

The pendulum was soon to swing back to a new sobriety; this was partly due to the pressure of the new science, which had its impact on the theorists of style even to the extent of encouraging the grammatical effort. Thus the Puritan John Wallis (1616-1703), enthusiastic promoter of experimental science, coherently made himself the spokesman of the new method not only by espousing the cause of regulating the language, but by opposing, as a true "modern" that he was, the Renaissance-honored way of legitimizing the forms of the vernacular through the process of assimilating them to the 'authoritative' forms of Latin.[6] Beauzée thought highly of Wallis, and protested against his having been neglected on the continent, even by Arnauld. One could see here faint yet eloquent traces of a connection between the French rationalists and the English scientific-minded theorists of the plain style. It was more than a connection of sympathy, even though Beauzée could distort the picture

---

[4] R. Foster Jones, *The Triumph of the English Language* (1953), p. 213.

[5] See the end of my Ch. III for English rhetorics of the Renaissance. P. Greaves's work is edited by Otto Funke, *Grammatica Anglicana von P. Gr.* (1594) (Vienna and Leipzig, 1938), with a learned Introduction on its Ramist background.

[6] Wallis, *Grammatica linguae anglicanae* (Oxford, 1653 and 1664, Hamburg 1671, Oxford 1674, 1688, 1699, 1727, 1731, 1740, 1745). See the Preface to the 1674 ed.: "All bring our English language too much to the Latin norm (because of which almost all who treat of modern languages are in error), and so introduce many useless principles concerning the cases, genders, and declensions of nouns, and the tenses, moods, and conjugation of verbs. . . ." Cf. Otto Funke, *Die Frühzeit* . . . , and R. F. Jones, *The Triumph* . . . , pp. 288-292. The whole passage is also translated from the *Praefatio* of the 1653 ed. in S. I. Tucker, *English Examined*, p. 36.

slightly when he insisted on Wallis's role as a "fondateur de la grammaire générale."

A symptomatic case of the aptitude to face the phenomena of a language independently of Latin schemes is revealed by Christopher Cooper's (d. 1698) *Grammatica linguae anglicanae* (1685).[7] Modern linguists have often related free word order to inflected systems and fixed word order, conversely, to the loss or absence of flectional endings. Now in Cooper the criterion of word order replaced the criterion of logical function previously determined by flection. In a revealing display of drastic mental shift from (flectional) case-determined nexus to word-order-determined nexus, he defined the difference between nominative and oblique case of pronouns on the ground of their position rather than for their function as subject or object (or complement): "I, thou, he, she, we, ye, they, verbis anteponuntur, me, thee, him, her, us, you, them, postponuntur verbis et praepositionibus." And Jespersen observes: "However naïve the modern grammarian may find this definition, it contains a good deal of truth: this is the popular perception which often overrides the older rule according to which the use of *I* and *me* was independent of position."[8]

If wit and plainness were the two, not always converging, mottoes in the seventeenth century, that of the eighteenth was 'correctness.' Yet the task of achieving purity or correctness demanded as a prerequisite the solution of some theoretical questions. The ancient opposition of anomaly and analogy first came back with the French grammarians' concern with custom and/or reason. This problem did not explicitly bother the still earlier Italian grammarians, who were chiefly committed to establishing as norm either a Latin pattern or that of an Italian authoritative model. But Meigret and Ramus were both tempted to have their cake and eat it too when they tried to reconcile the somewhat conflicting principles of *usage* and *raison*. True enough, the main stress, at least for the time being, remained on usage.[9] Many in England felt also torn, although

---

[7] P. 121, quoted by O. Jespersen, *A Modern English Grammar*, Part VIII, 6.45 (p. 241).

[8] Jespersen, ibid.

[9] Meigret: "Il n'y a point d'autre regle du langage que l'usage" (in his grammar), but (in his treatises on logic) usage must be "joint à la rezon." Ramus, in turn, held that "the people is sovereign lord in language," and that good French shall be learned not from teachers of Hebrew, Greek, or Latin, but "au Louvre,

their stronger empirical thrust generally kept them from pushing rationalistic positions too far. Finally, however, A. Lane, otherwise a good
Lockean, maintained "the true end and use of Grammar" to be "according to the unalterable Rules of right Reason" (*A Key to the Art of
Letters: or English a Learned Language, Full of Art, Elegancy, and
Variety*, 1700).[10] It was he, he claimed, who transferred to grammar the
logical terms of subject, object, and predicate, thus giving the first Art
her due since, he somewhat rashly concluded without checking his sources
too closely, "If I have borrowed these terms from Logick, I am persuaded
that Aristotle borrowed them first from Grammar, which was in being
long before his Logick."[11]

Reason was unequivocally enthroned by William Ward, Schoolmaster
in Yorkshire: Custom is not the "Effect of Chance," but "a consistent
Plan of communicating the Conceptions and rational discursive Operations
of one Man to another." Consequently "it is the business of Speculative
or Rational Grammar to explain the Nature of the means," meaning that
"the most simple of the elements of Logic will become familiar to those
who engage in a course of Grammar, and Reason will go hand in hand
with Practice." Yet the empirical method was to have the last word
against this (explicitly or implicitly) normative "Universal Grammar,"
and it spoke through no lesser an authority than Joseph Priestley, the
discoverer of oxygen: "The general prevailing custom . . . can be the only
standard for the time . . ." (*Course of Lectures on the English Language*,
1762). John Fell agreed: "It is certainly the business of a grammarian
to find out, and not to make, the laws of a language." "It matters not
what causes these customs . . . owe their birth to; the moment they become
general, they are laws . . ." (*Essay towards an English Grammar*, 1784).[12]

Yet, much as the professional *artigraphi* could strive toward the progress
of syntax, this remained the Cinderella of linguistic concerns among the
Lords of the cultural élite. In *A Grammar of the English Language*

au Palais, aux Halles, en Greve, à la place Maubert." Cf. G. H. McKnight, *Modern
English in the Making* (1930), pp. 221-222.

[10] Cf. McKnight, op. cit., pp. 291-293, and the whole ch. xv: "Eighteenth-
Century Grammarians," pp. 377-399.

[11] McKnight, p. 293.

[12] McKnight, p. 388 on Ward, 390 on Priestley and Fell. See now this Rhetoric
(also containing remarks on word order) reprinted from the 1777 ed. in Joseph
Priestley, *A Course of Lectures on Oratory and Criticism*, eds. Vincent M. Bevilacqua
and Richard Murphy (Carbondale, Ill., 1965).

prefixed to his *Dictionary* (1755), Samuel Johnson "comprised the whole syntax in ten lines," as Bishop Lowth complained in his own *English Grammar* (1762). The reason for that miserly treatment was, in Johnson's words, that "our language has so little inflection, that its Construction neither requires nor admits many rules."[13]

The imperative standard of correctness was signally applied to sentence structure and word arrangement, both on the level of explicit norms and of actually 'correcting' the authors.[14] James Buchanan not only took pains to supply the nation with *A Regular English Syntax, Wherein is exhibited the whole variety of English construction, . . . the elegant manner of arranging words, and members of sentences . . .* (London, 1767, 1st American ed. Philadelphia, 1780), but did not hesitate to follow it up with an exemplary application: *The First Six Books of Milton's Paradise Lost Rendered into Grammatical Construction* (Edinburgh, 1773), where he duly solved the ellipses and righted the inversions at the foot of the page, for the sake of a prose version "more easily understood." England had now her Du Marsais, shifting his efforts from Latin to more basic English.[15]

Buchanan was far from isolated in his distaste for Milton's inversions and disjunctions. The same feeling of uneasiness before such an effort to use English as a language endowed with a free construction had prompted the young Adam Smith (in 1761) to contrast Milton's version with Horace's original, the former being, in his opinion, unintelligible without the latter. English is hopelessly limited in this respect and, comparing ancient freedom with modern constraint in word order, Smith

---

[13] McKnight, 377-385 on Johnson, Lowth, and Harris. For further documentation, see A. C. Baugh, *A History of the English Language* (1957²); S. I. Tucker, ed., *English Examined: Two Centuries of Comment on the Mother Tongue* (1961); W. F. Bolton, ed., *The English Language: Essays by English and American Men of Letters, 1490-1839* (1966). Also still precious the older anthologies by Joel E. Spingarn, *Critical Essays of the Seventeenth Century* (Oxford, 1908) and W. H. Durham, *Critical Essays of the Eighteenth Century* (New Haven, Conn., 1915). May I also mention, as rich with insights and information, Otto Funke, *Studien zur Geschichte der Sprachphilosophie* (1927) and *Englische Sprachphilosophie im späteren 18. Jahrhundert* (1934).

[14] Cf. St. A. Leonard, *The Doctrine of Correctness in English Usage, 1700-1800.*

[15] For Buchanan's *Syntax* I use the ed. Philadelphia, 1783. Despite the promising title there is nothing of interest for us in [Philip Withers,] *Aristarchus, or the Principles of Composition . . .* (London, 1788). I have seen only the London, 1822 ed.

was induced to take the position of a partisan of the ancients. He attributed the loss of ease (and consequently, effectiveness) in modern languages to the "simplification" brought about by the dropping of inflection, and saw little gain in that.[16]

Buchanan, for one, was unequivocally affiliated with the rationalistic side of Sánchez and Du Marsais. His *Syntax* gave much room to parsing, which he called "resolution" (p. xvi of 1783 ed.), and which he practiced by rigorously resolving all the ellipses and recasting the sentences according to the "natural order" of "plain style." He admitted the transpositions of the "artificial order" only if they can show beauties denied to the natural. But the latter is the firm point of departure and constitutes the true general and universal grammar, since it is the same in all languages, which vary only in their different uses of transpositions. By exercizing himself extensively in parsing, the student of language will cease to be surprised by "the more violent Inversion of the learned [= classical] Languages, but will soon perceive, that though the inverted or artificial construction differs more or less according to the Genius of every Language, yet that the True or Natural is much the same in all Languages, i. e. according to the Conceptions of the Mind" (p. 139). A corollary of this naïve faith in the universal correspondence of the natural order to the modus operandi of the human mind, that is the order of ideas, is that Buchanan denied the value of classical education as propedeutical to all studies. The pupil should always learn the syntax of his own language first, since it is fundamentally the same for all languages, instead of learning his language after studying Latin grammar, as the humanistic tradition wanted it (pp. xv-xvi).[17]

2. Within the framework of these general orientations, we may now linger on the specific analyses contained in a few, representative rhetorical treatises.[18]

[16] Adam Smith, "Considerations concerning the First Formation of Languages," *The Philological Miscellany*, vol. I (1761): see it now reprinted in J. Ralph Lindgren, ed., *The Early Writings of Adam Smith* ([New York,] 1967): cf. pp. 250-251 for passage discussed.

[17] For the opposite viewpoint, upholding the superiority of the synthetic languages on account of their expressive freedom in word order, see James Burnett, Lord Monboddo (1714-1799), *The Origin and Progress of Language* (Edinburgh, 1773-92), vol. II, Part II, Book 3, chs. 1 and 2.

[18] For a systematic discussion of rhetorical texts not included in the following

Bishop Wilkins (1614-1672) echoed the pure logician's (and Port-Royal's) unconcern for formal questions of syntax by maintaining that those constructions which follow the "natural sense and order of the words" need no special discussion, since it is little more than a question of arranging the sequence S + V + Ob or S + copula + adjective, or the ordering of "grammatical" and "transcendental" particles relative to the items they govern, etc. This is the teaching of "Natural Grammar." [19] On the other hand he did set aside the idiomatic constructions whose characteristic is that of being merely "customary," such as *to take one's heels and fly away, to hedge a debt, to be brought to heel*, etc. These belong to "Instituted Grammar." Wilkins was the most famous proponent of a "universal language," the sort of project which ambiguously wavered between a practical esperanto and a notational system of formal logic—this latter being destined to a more deserving success in the form of Leibniz's *characteristica universalis*.[20] Both Cartesian rationalism and Baconian empiricism were at work in Wilkins's mind, and this is not the place to discuss which one had the upper hand.

John Lawson's 1759 *Lectures concerning Oratory* were rather conservative on the whole. "Harsh transpositions" he condemned as a fault against "clearness": "to this fault the writers of the Roman language seem peculiarly liable" (p. 188). The Attic style of the Greeks was "pure, terse, and properly concise"; the Asianic occurs when "the thought becomes darkened by a multitude of words." But excess in shortness is a "principal cause of obscurity": "*brevis esse laboro, / obscurus fio* (Horace, *Ars poet.*)" (189). These remarks appear in Lecture 12 "of Elocution or Style." In Lecture 14 Lawson treats "of Composition." Although his definition is comprehensive (Composition is "the

sampling, may I refer to Howell, *Logic and Rhetoric in England*, especially pp. 321-323 on Thomas Farnaby, *Index Rhetoricus et Oratorius* (London, 1625); 324-325 on Obadiah Walker, *Some Instructions Concerning the Art of Oratory* (London, 1659, 1682², enlarged); and 392-397 on Joseph Glanvill, *An Essay Concerning Preaching, Written for the Direction of a Young Divine* (London, 1678). Under Elocution Walker dealt with 1) Words, 2) "Periods and the Artificial Placing of the Words in them," 3) Figures, 4) Styles.

[19] John Wilkins, *An Essay towards a Real Character and a Philosophical Language* (London, 1668), p. 354.

[20] Leibniz, *De arte combinatoria*, 1665. The other better known work in line with Wilkins's attempt was Georgius Dalgarnus, *Ars signorum, vulgo character universalis et lingua philosophica* (London, 1661).

due arrangement of words with regard to signification and sound"—227),
he covered under this title only harmony ("sound"), having relegated
the structural and intellectual aspects of the subject ("signification")
among the figures and virtues of style. He found that, while writers of
the preceding centuries sinned by overlong periods, present-day writers
sinned by the opposite excess, which "causes obscurity by cramping the
expression" (234-235). He attributed this change in taste partly to
the influence of poetry which passed from overlong stanzas like the
Spenserian to the couplet. For the French, too, the heroic verse "went
attended by prose of the like narrow gait" (236). One precept he
offered was to alternate periods with short sentences. The former contribute "numbers and harmony," the latter "vigour and vivacity." He
then announced 'Beauzée's law' as an alternative to dividing the sentence into equal periodic members, which he otherwise found unobjection-
able (237).

In his celebrated *Elements of Criticism* (1762) Henry Home (Lord
Kames) offered a rather diffuse but circumspect discussion of both sentence structure and word order, which he treated continuously (ch. xviii,
Sec. 2, esp. pp. 49-83 in vol. II), and which contains at least one passage
that elicits our curiosity.[21] Of all the texts that had prepared the ground
for him, the eminent theoretical critic chose to single out one for his
explicit perusal—and consequent disapproval—: in his *Réflexions sur la
poësie françoise*, we are told (pp. 81-82),

[Du] Cerceau ascribes so much power to inversion, as to make it the
characteristic of French verse, and the single circumstance which in that
language distinguishes verse from prose: and yet he pretends not to say,
that it hath any other effect but to raise surprise; he must mean curiosity,
which is done by suspending the thought during the period, and bringing
it out entire at the close. This indeed is one effect of inversion; but neither
its sole effect, nor even that which is the most remarkable . . . [The other
effects being "the force, the elevation, the harmony, the cadence" . . .].

George Campbell's *Philosophy of Rhetoric* (1776),[22] judged by Saints-

---

[21] I quote from the 7th ed., "with the author's last corrections and additions,"
2 vols. (Edinburgh, 1788). See, now, Arthur E. McGuinness, *Henry Home, Lord
Kames* (New York, Twayne Publishers, 1969).

[22] It went through numerous editions in the nineteenth century. I quote from
L. F. Bitzer's (Carbondale, Ill., 1963) photo-offset reprint of the London, 1850 ed.
The editor's competent Introduction does not go into the historical background of

bury as "the most important treatise on the New Rhetoric that the eighteenth century produced,"[23] can be regarded by us as the most conclusive treatise for our period, in spite of its relatively early date. It was only gradually superseded by the works of Richard Whately, John Bascom, and Henry Day, who often comfortably rested on it as a classic source.

The empiricism of Humean imprint as transcribed by Priestley led Campbell to the sensible position that grammar receives its laws from language, it does not give them to it: in other words, the "reason" of rules rests on custom (p. 139). He thus resolved such a centuries-long controversy, ultimately descended from the battle between analogy and anomaly, by resting his case on Quintilian's neat formula: "non ratione nititur [=analogia], sed exemplo, nec lex est loquendi, sed observatio, ut ipsam analogiam nulla res alia fecerit quam consuetudo." [24]

Two thirds of the work formally deal with "elocution" or style, to which are attributed "five simple and original qualities, . . . considered as an object to the understanding, the imagination, the passions, and the ear . . . , i. e. *perspicuity, vivacity, elegance, animation,* and *music.*" All of them follow next upon purity, which is "a quality entirely grammatical" (p. 216). Note how this scheme eclectically yet aptly summarizes all the basic postulates advanced since the Renaissance, namely the rationalist (which stressed understanding), the baroque (imagination and/or passions), the classical-hedonistic (the ear). In practice, however, the whole discussion revolves around the three categories of purity, perspicuity, and vivacity (something which reminds one of Longinus' *enargheia,* much discussed in that century). Composition is included within this last category. It is particularly relevant for us that in this originally revamped scheme of the traditional 'virtues of style,' music, that is all that traditionally came under the broad headings of harmony, euphony, and rhythm, though recognized, is left practically untreated. This is perhaps the most decisive concession to the rationalistic and logistic thrust of the age and, from the viewpoint of the progress of our subject, it was a positive omission.

French and other stylistic debates. Hume's influence on the work has been studied by Bitzer in his unpublished Ph. D. Dissertation, State University of Iowa, 1962. On its impact on subsequent English treatises of the art, see Warren Guthrie, "The Development of Rhetorical Theory in America, 1635-1850," *Speech Monographs,* XV (1948), 61-71.

[23] George Saintsbury, *History of Criticism,* II, 470.

[24] Quint. I, vi, 16; Campbell, p. 141, fn.

Indeed the very elaborate treatise intended to bring to fruition, as the title clearly implies, the speculative effort of the century. To this effect another noteworthy feature of our work is the bold introduction of grammatical material. In the area of composition, this affects both the shift from concern with delivery to criteria of logical analysis and, in particular, the ample discussion of conjunctions and "connectives." Earlier in the book (p. 35) we read: "The grammatical art has its completion in syntax; the oratorical, as far as the body or expression is concerned, in style. Syntax regards only the composition of many words into one sentence; style, at the same time that it attends to this, regards further the composition of many sentences into one discourse." (Also cf. 1776 ed., vol. I, p. 101.)

Composition narrowly understood occupies the last section of the work (Book III, chs. iii-v, pp. 353-415). It begins with word order, which is said to center on the principle of "emphasis." The decision as to what place in the sentence is the most emphatic is, however, not a simple one. Generally speaking, the beginning and the end carry most weight. This is, then, a law of 'general grammar' (though Campbell does not use the expression here—but see p. 34), but when we turn to real languages we must conclude that, on that ground, modern languages are at a disadvantage vis-à-vis the ancient, since this comparative lack of flexibility does not allow to exploit the force of EPo to the fullest. One begins to gather that Campbell is placing himself in the camp of the *mécaniciens*. Indeed, since his position is a moderate one, and one which allows him to reap the full harvest from both schools, we could look upon him as a sort of English Cesarotti. Yet he does not hesitate to assert that his "sentiments" on the subject of word order "are entirely coincident with" those of the author of the *Traité de la formation mécanique des langues,* which he claims to have seen while he was writing this chapter (p. 364, fn.). He has not seen Batteux on Inversion, but from the references to it in the *Traité* he approvingly quotes a long passage which includes the following: "ceux qui l'auront lu, verront que . . . les mots étant plus faits pour l'homme que pour les choses, l'ordre essentiel à suivre, dans le discours représentatif de l'idée des objets, n'est pas tant la marche commune des choses dans la nature que la succession véritable des pensées, la rapidité des sentimens ou de l'intérêt du coeur, la fidélité de l'image dans le tableau de l'action; que le Latin en préférant ces points capitaux procède plus naturellement que le Français," etc. (ibid.). The logical and metaphysical dimensions of this statement appropriately jibe with Campbell's fundamental phenomenalism, which modifies and refines his allegiance to his time's sensationalist school of thought (I, v). Incidentally, Campbell agrees heartily with his quotation in the criticism of French, and finds the English language better off than the French in that its analytic word order is less rigid. Once the question has been put in the foregoing terms, one must conclude that what is heard here implies a misunderstanding of actual Latin word order, which was perhaps more conditioned by harmony than the *mécaniciens* were prepared to admit, though less than the Latin rhetors thought. Overdo it as they might, the *mécaniciens* were nonetheless right in stressing the element of pathetic and psychological emphasis in inversion, and Campbell raised that criterion of order to a pre-eminent position.

Turning now to "English syntax," as he puts it, our author finds "no more general law" of order than this: "the nominative has the first place, the verb the second, and the accusative . . . the third" (p. 355). The choice of terms is unfortunate, since what he means are subject, predicate, and object (and A. Lane had shown the way three quarters of a century earlier), but the sense is clear. "Yet this order," he hastens to add, "to the great advantage of the expression, is often inverted." The lengthy and detailed discussion of inversions which ensues is studded with well chosen examples chiefly drawn from the Scriptures, and he aptly elicits shrewd comparisons of the Hebrew and Greek forms side by side with their Latin, French, Italian, and English renderings. Thus Μεγάλη ἡ Ἄρτεμις Ἐφεσίων of Acts xix, 28 and 34 (the cry of general uproar among the people of Ephesus on the occasion of Paul's preaching there against idolatry) is paralleled by Erasmus' Vulg. *Magna Diana Ephesiorum,* Castal. Beza's *Magna est Diana Ephesiorum,* Diodati's *Grande è la Diana degli Efesii,* and Engl. *Great is Diana of the Ephesians;* and it contrasts with the inept French of Le Clerc, *La Diane des Ephésiens est une grande déesse!* or, worse, Beausobre's *La grande Diane des Ephésiens!* or Saci's *Vive la grande Diane des Ephésiens!* (Campbell, pp. 355 and 358).

Consequently, Campbell objects to the dubbing of "the customary arrangement" as "natural order," and of inversion as a violation of it (p. 356). Aside from realizing that "custom becomes a second nature," it is clear that what is "accounted natural in one language, is unnatural in another. In Latin, for example, the negative particle is commonly put before the verb, in English it is put after it; in French one negative is put before and another after." For his argument, he uses the case of Hebrew, a language in which, if anywhere, "one would expect to find an arrangement purely natural," on account of its basic simplicity. Yet its "most usual," i. e. its "grammatical" word order for the narrative style is V + S + CC: *In principio creavit Deus coelum et terram*. In conclusion, "the only principle in which we can safely rest is, that whatever most strongly fixes the attention, or operates on the passion of the speaker, will first seek utterance. . . . Nearest the heart, nearest the mouth" (pp. 357-358). This, once again, was the position of Batteux. One might sense here a contradiction with the previous statement that every language is nothing but custom (therefore has its own nature), since, if different languages place different elements first in expressing the same thought, which one of the elements can be regarded as the most important? For the most emphatic place is not quite the same in all languages. Yet Campbell is speaking, not of statistical patterns within each language, not of the grammatical or 'normal' order for each, but of the rhetorical or 'pathetic' order, which was Batteux' meaning too. Again, *Benedictus qui venit in nomine domini*, literally equivalent to the Greek original, must be rendered, as it has been, as *Blessed is he that cometh* etc., *Benedetto colui* etc. Likewise, Peter said to the cripple: "Silver and gold have I none, but such as I have, give I thee," where the 'grammatical' order seems entirely subverted, bit by bit. The *none* at the end, in particular, is witness to the principle that, even in English, "the next place to the first, in respect of emphasis, is the last" (p. 359). And how can we render Ἔπεσεν, ἔπεσε Βαβυλὼν ἡ πόλις ἡ μεγάλη, which matches the Hebrew of Is. xxi, 9? With something like *Cecidit, cecidit Babylon, urbs illa magna*, of course; therefore not with the inept *Babylone est tombée, elle est tombée, cette grande ville* (Le Clerc and Saci), or *Babylon is fallen, is fallen, that great city*, but with *Elle est tombée, elle est tombée, Babylone la grande ville* (Beausobre) or, even better, *Caduta, caduta è Babilonia, la gran città* (Diodati). No English translation has done the job, and Campbell suggests: *Fallen, fallen is Babylon, the great city* (pp. 360-361). (We might perhaps find it less awkward to make use of the typically English and French device of the anaphoric pronoun, and say, after Beausobre's example, *It has fallen: Babylon, the great city, has fallen!*)

Even particles can carry weight, cf. *Up goes my grave impudence to the maid* (p. 361), or oblique pronouns: *There was no king like Solomon . . . : nevertheless even HIM did outlandish women cause to sin* (p. 363).

To sum up, Campbell protests that the position of hypostatizing the "artificial or conventional arrangement" as "sacred and inviolable, by representing every deviation as a trespass against the laws of composition" (which was the position of the *logiciens*), "is one of the most effectual ways of stinting the powers of elocution and even of damping the vigour both of the imagination and of passion." And with this 'pre-romantic' *prise de position*, he replies to the French rationalists that "no man is more sensible of the excellence of purity and perspicuity," but not to the extent of giving up the third virtue, *vivacity*, for their sake: "I would not hastily give up some not inconsiderable advantages of the English tongue, in respect both of eloquence and of poetry, merely in exchange for the French *netteté*" (p. 365). Forthright words indeed, and clear too.

Passing now to sentence structure, we first hear something on the conjunctions, "of all the parts of speech . . . the most unfriendly to vivacity; the next to them the relative pronouns, as partaking of the nature of conjunction" (ibid.). The matter is so close to our author's heart, that he returns to it in greater detail in the last two chapters of the book (esp. pp. 384-399, 403-415). The sage of Ferney would have smiled with delight on reading these pages, and all the partisans of the *style coupé* with him. Campbell ascribes to asyndeton "a wonderful efficacy," and since the rhetors also saw virtues in its opposite, the polysyndeton, he solves the apparent contradiction in the following manner: "The conjunctions and relatives excluded by the asyndeton are such as connect clauses and members; those repeated by the polysyndeton are such as connect single words only. All connectives alike are set aside by the former; the latter is confined to copulatives and disjunctives" (p. 368). The deep reason for distrusting connectives is philosophical. Sensation suggests to the mind "the notion of power, agency, or causation." But this notion of cause and effect is intuitive rather than rational, "suggested and not perceived." To put it differently, "it is *conceived* by the understanding, and not *perceived* by the senses" (pp. 366-367). If, therefore, you use connectives, whose function is the formal establishment of relations, "you will present us with a piece of reasoning or declamation." But if you don't, you "give to reasoning itself the force and vivacity of painting"; "you will thus convert a piece of abstruse reflection . . . into the most affecting and instructive imagery." You will cater to the "fancy" according to the way of the senses in their "perception of the things themselves"; briefly, you will do a work of poetry (p. 367).

Campbell sees progress in the elimination or reduction of overlong and composite conjunctions: the *che, que,* or *that* of such monsters as *concio-*

fossecosaché, encore bien que, although that has been dropped at long last, when the whole nexus has not fallen into desuetude. This particle had been added " in order to distinguish the conjunction from the preposition or the adverb," but experience has shown that " this expedient is quite superfluous" (p. 386). Supplying all the 'logical' transitions is an insult to intelligence and detracts from the imagination.

Complex sentences are divided into " periods" and " loose sentences." " A period is a complex sentence, wherein the meaning remains suspended, till the whole is finished. The connexion, consequently is so close between the beginning and the end, as to give rise to the name *period,* which signifies circuit" (p. 369). " Most modern critics," Campbell complains, " seem to have mistaken totally the impact of the word *period,* confounding it with the complex sentence in general, and sometimes even with the simple but circumstantiated sentence" (369 fn.). Even the ancients gave inadequate analyses of it, though they clearly meant something like the above definition. But the most serious blame is deserved by such *logiciens* as Du Marsais, trapped by the very nature of their 'logical' approach: to maintain that " la période est un assemblage de propositions liées entr'elles par des conjonctions, et qui toutes ensemble font un sens fini," [25] misses the main point of suspense and circularity, since it stops at complexity and formalization of transitions through connectives (ibid.). What Campbell means in the ensuing analysis seems, once again, entirely apropos. What the moderns have usually called a period was very often not a period at all but only a complex sentence with expressed transitions. For the most ordinary way to keep the sense suspended was by reserving the verb, on which the sense entirely hangs, for the end. This was within the reach of the ancient languages, but it is something that " in most cases the structure of modern languages will not permit us to imitate " (70).

The real difference between the modern imperfect period and the true period of the ancients lies in the ' descending movement' of the former as against the ' ascending movement' of the latter. Campbell does not use these terms, but his analysis is to the point and reaches that goal by a different route: In a modern complex sentence, he says, we have unity in one direction only, in that each member leans on and needs the preceding ones, not viceversa. He gives an example of such " loose sentences" often mistakenly regarded as periods:

---

[25] Du Marsais, *Principes de Grammaire,* " La Période."

One party hath given their whole attention . . . to the project of enriching *themselves*, and impoverishing the rest of the *nation*; and by these and other means, of establishing their *dominion* under the government and with the favour of a family who were *foreigners*, and therefore might believe that they were established on the throne by the good will and strength of this party alone.

One could stop, he tells us, at any of the words in italics and we would always have a complete sentence. What keeps the whole together is simply the fact that,

though the preceding words, when you have reached any of the stops above mentioned, will make sense, and may be construed separately, the same cannot be said of the words which follow. In a period, the dependence of the members is reciprocal; in a loose sentence the former members have not a necessary dependence on the latter, whereas the latter depend entirely on the former.

Let us now go one step further, and we shall find that " if both former and latter members are, in respect of construction, alike independent on one another, they do not constitute one sentence, but two or more" (p. 370). One consequence of this clever insight into what keeps propositions together is that punctuation, even the most apt possible, is a relative thing in determining the type of construction we are confronted with (ibid.). A style can be loose even though complex, and when its members are independent, as it were, ' backward and forward,' even though such members are not separated by full stops (or " points," as Campbell called them, " periods," as we now call them).

After remarking that the innumerable observations by both ancient and modern critics " on the formation and turn of periods " have been " chiefly calculated with a view to harmony " (p. 372), our author continues his syntactico-stylistic analysis by pointing out that " antithesis in the members " of the period contributes powerfully to vivacity. This too can be overdone, as by Seneca, who so " stuffed his writings with antithesis " that " they abound with pleasant faults," to say it with Quintilian (X, i, 129: " eo perniciosissima, quod abundant dulcibus vitiis "). " Hence Seneca is justly considered as one of the earliest corrupters of the Roman eloquence " (380). " Such a style, compared with the more manly elocution of Cicero, we call effeminate, as betraying a sort of feminine fondness for glitter and ornament. There is some danger that both French and English will be corrupted in the same manner." Mr. Campbell can rest in peace; we are now happily in a position to let him know that the danger lay more in the past than in the future. The cult of Seneca had, in its way, served the cause of the plain style, essentially Mr. Campbell's cause, and any excesses were, by his time, already discounted. One of the last points considered by our rhetor contributes once again to the excellence of the classical languages. It concerns "sentences" in the narrow sense (*sententiae* or maxims), especially in the form of devices or emblems for inscriptions and other purposes. The reason why Latin is still so popular in this respect is not its universality—a disputable claim in the 'French century'—but rather its incomparable superiority "in respect of vivacity, elegance, animation, and variety of harmony," even though clarity or perspicuity may be less easy to attain in it than in modern languages (399). Take the following mottoes: *Non mille quod absens* and *Conantia frangere frangit*, meaning "A thousand cannot equal one that is absent" and "I break the things which attempt to break me." Try as you may, you will never render them satisfactorily in modern languages (400 fn.).[26]

In his *Lectures on Rhetoric and Belles Lettres* (1783) Hugh Blair offered one of the most diffuse treatments of "the proper composition and structure of sentences" (in three of the Lectures, the last one covering "harmony" and the second including word order and inversion).[27] He wasted no time before entering the distinction of *style périodique* and *style coupé*, the terms he is credited with importing from French (p. 260 or 146). And he pronounced as "properties most essential to a perfect sentence": Clearness and Precision, Unity, Strength, and Harmony. Without bothering to follow the details of his exposition, we are particularly interested in his notion that the climactic progression is forceful and elegant, and demands that we place longer members last, as well as that we avoid particles or circumstantial phrases at the end (pp. 300-306 and 169-172). This also responds to reasons of rhythm, for sense and sound show a mutual influence (pp. 314 and 183-184). But Blair denies that the modern languages are as susceptible of harmonious arrangement as the ancient, so that we should not grant such a large role to sound as the ancients did.

[26] These illustrations are from Bouhours' *Entretiens d'Ariste et d'Eugène*, vi, "Les Devises."
[27] I use the 3d ed. (London, 1787), in 3 vols. and the 3d American ed. (Boston, 1802), in 2 vols. See the three Lectures (11-13) on pp. 258-342, vol. I, and pp. 145-191, vol. I, respectively.

In England the Romantic age saw a resurgence of the *mécanicien* position in a more unequivocal manner than represented in France, for example, by Domergue. Accordingly, it is interesting to note a similar trend in the United States. John Quincy Adams, for one, was a moderate epigone of the *mécaniciens*. After Lecture 25 on "Elocution. Purity" and 26 on "Perspicuity," namely the first two virtues of style, Lecture 27 of his *Lectures on Rhetoric and Oratory* (2 vols., Cambridge, Mass., 1810), vol. II, turned to "Composition" and began by dealing with "Order," since he had divided composition into order, juncture, number, and period (pp. 187-188).

He pointedly distinguished the natural order (which he defined as what we could call the 'pathetic'), the grammatical, the metaphysical (= 'logical,' i. e. that of the *métaphysiciens*), and the musical (= harmony). Classical languages adhered mostly to the first and last, the modern to the second and third (p. 190). Take, as examples, the phrases *amor patriae* and *patriae amor*. The former is grammatical (nominative before genitive) and musical (it avoids the encounter of vowels of the latter); the latter, metaphysical (cause before effect—but we must note that by this standard the analytical languages are not "metaphysically" ordered on this score). Both are natural, depending on the emphasis desired (p. 191). In all languages the style of ordinary usage tends to adhere to the grammatical order, formal discourse to the metaphysical if speculative, to the natural if oratorical, and, finally, the poetical style to harmony. Moving closer to the earlier *mécaniciens*, Adams shows the untranslatable advantages of natural order in Latin through the canonical examples of *Romanus sum civis* (Scaevola stressing his being a Roman when discovered in his attempt to kill the foreign enemy Porsenna—Livy II, 12) as against *civis Romanus sum* (when Gavius protests the indignity of his own crucifixion by Verres' order as unbecoming to a citizen—Cic., *Verr.* II, v, 65, 66). Similarly, in *pro Roscio Amerino* Cicero marvelously stressed the contrast between the unseemly roles of the unjust accusers and the defendant, their true victim, both by placing these words first and by calling attention to them through parallel repetitions.[28]

In concluding, Adams claims that classical order could be imitated more

---

[28] "Accusant ii, quibus occidi patrem Sexti Roscii bono fuit; causam dicit is, cui non modo luctum mors patris attulit, verum etiam egestatem. Accusant ii, qui hunc ipsum jugulare summe cupierunt; causam dicit is, qui etiam ad hoc ipsum judicium cum praesidio venit, ne hic ibidem ante oculos vestros trucidetur." J. Q. Adams, pp. 199-200.

successfully in English (as by Milton) than in French (as by Ronsard) (p. 202). And so on with observations on inversion, emphasis, front-position and end-position.

After Lecture 28 on "Juncture and Number," we turn to "Sentence" with Lecture 29. Following a treatment of (logical) propositions, we hear at length on the "complex loose sentence" (it "may be compared to a mathematical triangle or square, enclosing a given space within three or four distinct lines, connected together by junctions at particular points"—p. 233) and the period (a circle with suspended meaning). The drift of the exposition is reminiscent of Campbell. Adams then speaks of "ascending progress" in the period (p. 245) and also of the "descending progress" which often accompanies it typically in the "decussated period," when it is composed of two upward moving members and two downward ones. This type of square period lends itself to antithesis, while the other combinations (e. g. 3 up + 1 down) can develop climax. Of climax and antithesis he speaks at greater length within the next branch of elocution, i. e. ornamentation or "dignity."

Archbishop Richard Whately's *Elements of Rhetoric* (1828) was the last substantial treatise of the art to be published in England.[29] Here composition comes within the discussion of "style," while "elocution" is made a synonym of "delivery." First we find the "Construction of Sentences" treated under "perspicuity" (pp. 263-264). It is perhaps a sign of the times that the precept taught there is such as to threaten the very principle of suspenceful circularity on which periodic style was based. The precept, enunciated in the name of perspicuity, is: Let the sentence be such as "to be understood clause by clause, as it proceeds" (repeated on p. 319). Composition is treated once again under "energy" (avowedly the same as Campbell's "vivacity" and Aristotle's ἐνέργεια—p. 275) (pp. 312-327). An interesting variation in Whately's arguments is the claim that "in a majority of instances, the most emphatic word will be the predicate" (315): in fact most of Campbell's examples, which are repeated here, lend themselves to such a conclusion. The device of the anticipatory impersonal *it is* (like French *c'est*) is recommended for expressing an emphasis which Latin could have rendered through position alone, as in *it was Cicero that praised Caesar* or *it was Caesar that Cicero praised.*

[29] See the reproduction of the 7th ed. (London, 1846), ed. Douglas Ehninger (Carbondale, Ill., 1963).

Everything is a loose sentence that is not a period. For the latter Campbell's definition is adopted (317), but without excluding simple sentences. The example is very apt: *We came to our journey's end—at last—with no small difficulty—after much fatigue—through deep roads—and bad weather* is a "very loose sentence" (and yet an effective one) which will become a period by a process of reversal: *At last, after much fatigue, through deep roads, and bad weather, we came, with no small difficulty, to our journey's end* (ibid.).

Whately also adopts Campbell's test for distinguishing the loose from the periodic, the test that we could label as of the RETRODEPENDENCE of members. He claims that the tendency toward periodicity is evident in all languages in that they all contain particles having "no other use or signification but to suspend the sense," such as Greek μέν, δέ, τέ, English *neither* in *neither . . . nor* (instead of simply *not . . . nor*), *both* in *both . . . and* (instead of simply *. . . and*), and even many a subordinating conjunction (318). Curiously, he recommends that, "if one clause be long and another short, the shorter should, if possible, be put last" (320). We might assume that this could be reconciled with Beauzée's law by understanding the latter as confined to complements within clauses, yet Whately's examples do not sound very cogent. Abuse of periods must be discouraged because "the display of art is to be guarded against" (322); but in another significant reversal of the ancient point of view, the period is declared to suit the composition to be read rather than the one to be delivered. In applying his criteria and critical taste, our author finds the style of Bolingbroke "one of the most periodic," those of Swift and Addison "among the most loose" (322). Antithesis is looked upon as conducive to "energy" of expression because of the gratification resulting from learning quickly and easily (Aristotle's dictum), and is not relegated to the period (323-324). An acute remark follows to the effect that "an antithesis may be ever more happily expressed by the sacrifice of the period" (326)—which, one may add, was one of the secrets of eighteenth-century *coupé* style.[30]

---

[30] William Minto, "Professor of Logic and Literature" at the University of Aberdeen, wrote one of the last classic manuals of composition. Quoting extensively his authoritative predecessors from Lord Kames and Campbell to Whately, he critically reviewed all the relevant literature and added the important remark that the rhetoricians had never been able to rise beyond the sentence toward an understanding of the way paragraphs are formed by a close interrelation among successive sentences

We had agreed to stop around 1800, following the suggestion of Ernst R. Curtius (and E. K. Rand long before him) that the remarkable continuity of the classical tradition, signally in the form of the rhetorical approach to the values of communication and of literary expression, suffered a major break in the course of the Romantic experience. I have crossed that boundary with just a couple of examples of rhetorical manuals from the English area only. These turned out to be the kind of " exception that confirms the rule": they were among the last cases of true vitality in an art which had fulfilled its historical role—all appearances of survival in the schools down to our own age notwithstanding, since the context of modern references to rhetoric has been thoroughly transformed by the Romantic conception of "organic" criticism. Besides the impact of the organic approach, the true death of rhetoric was also due to the Romantic notion of art, poetry, and expression itself as a direct effusion of the soul. The change was already clearly announced in Home's *Elements of Criticism* (1762), where the figures were seen as originating not in a rational principle, but in the emotional urge, which can neither be regulated nor controlled, with the result that the hallowed " rules " of rhetoric become external, inadequate, and finally irrelevant as nothing but a posteriori constructions, mere afterthoughts.

Furthermore, there would be little point in following up with the rhetorical literature down to the present also because the more recent evolution of our subject entails its assimilation into the modern child of the other " art," the *ars grammatica*, namely linguistics. The following chapter will indeed cover a good portion of the nineteenth century by showing how the linguists took over these problems in a changed context.

(see p. 11 of 1901 ed.): W. Minto, *A Manual of English Prose Literature, Biographical and Critical, designed mainly to show characteristics of style* (1872, 1881[2], 1886[3]). I quote from the Amer. ed. (Boston, 1901). The historical section is remarkable for several masterly discussions of the styles of individual writers conducted along the lines of classic compositional rhetoric.

CHAPTER FIVE: MODERN THEORY: LINGUISTIC APPROACHES TO THE PROBLEM *

Contrary to what had taken place in antiquity, modern speculation (especially linguistic) has seized upon word order as a more provoking question than sentence structure, which it has preferred to leave to the school textbooks of rhetoric or composition. The former could become crucial enough even to lay the ground principles for the latter, as it happened, for example, with the philosopher Herbert Spencer.

Spencer's *The Philosophy of Style* (oct. 1852),[1] which shows a psychological approach within a positivistic framework, is immediately reminiscent of the empirical orientation of the *mécaniciens*,[2] even though his solutions appear thoroughly original. We are told that, as the modifier must come before the modified, so the qualifier, the abstract, the less important, the circumstantial, the subordinate, must come before the qualified concrete, the principal thought or event, *both* in the phrase or clause *and* in the sentence. So the object must precede the verb, the complement everything else, the predicate the subject. This implies, of course, a drastic 'inversion' of the normal English order, at least with regard to the basic elements of the affirmative proposition (S, V, C), but Spencer curiously chooses to call it the *direct* style (as distinct from the *natural* style—see p. 19–, and as opposed to the *indirect* style), because it leads from the referring to the referred, from the vague quality to the precise substance, from the preliminary to the essential. The direct order would " convey each thought step by step with little liability to error," while the indirect " conveys each thought by a series of approximations which successively correct the erroneous preconceptions that have been raised " (p. 17). The question once put in this way, little doubt remains of the superiority of

* The discussion will be generally limited to sentences of the propositional or affirmative type, with some reference to exclamatory constructs, since inversion and word order in the interrogative constructs are not normally subject to a similar degree of stylistic choice.
[1] See it reprinted in H. Spencer, *Literary Style and Music* (New York, 1951), and cf., in particular, pp. 8-21, 27-28.
[2] See, e. g., pp. 30-31.

337

the 'inverted' order: for a description fitting such an ideal we would
have to look toward something resembling Turkish rather than English,
let alone French.

All this is based on the principle of economy of mental energies, and
amounts to a statement of preference for the 'ascending' order in composition. It also contradicts the principles of Aristotelian logic whereby the
mind is said to proceed from the known to the unknown, from the general
to the particular, and from the genus to the species. But Spencer is not
talking about ordinary, enunciatory speech. As a matter of fact, he conclusively extols poetic language as the acme of expression, true " style."
" Force of Expression " was, indeed, the original title of this essay, and
Spencer tells us that he meant to deal not with language as it is, but
with its particular, " forceful " use which can be called style. So in commending the *direct* (= inverted) style, he understood what is obvious to
all, namely that it is unusual, rare, and " poetic." [3]

But by the time of Spencer's pointed essay a fresh new start had been
made thanks to a young classical philologist, Henri Weil, whose brilliant
1844 study of word order went through three successful editions and has
remained much quoted to our own day.[4]

Weil admired the way Herling and Becker had investigated the German
modes of construction as determined by the syntactic relationships between
the parts of the sentence rather than by the analytical order.[5] He admitted he had learned from them (p. 12); still he proposed to depart

---

[3] P. 28. The text is studded with many rich, though not always felicitous,
examples. See the example on top of p. 15: Spencer uses "subordinate" and
"principal" in a different way from ours (that is, logical rather than formal).

[4] Weil, *De l'ordre des mots dans les langues anciennes comparées aux langues
modernes: Question de grammaire générale,* "Recueil de travaux . . . philologie
et . . . histoire littéraire . . . M. Bréal," 3e fasc. (Paris, A. Franck, 1869²). I shall
quote from this 2ᵈ ed. The Preface to the 3ᵈ ed. (Preface dated 1879) says it
is a reproduction of the 2ᵈ, which was the same as the 1ˢᵗ (1844) except for a few
modifications and additions. The English trans. by Ch. W. Super (Boston, 1887)
was based on the 3ᵈ ed. Translations in the text will be mine. It elicits more
than mere curiosity that Weil (1818-1909) produced this learned and penetrating
study at the age of 26.

[5] S. H. A. Herling, *Die Syntax der deutschen Sprache* (2 vols., Frankfurt am
Main, 1830); Karl Ferdinand Becker, *Ausführliche deutsche Grammatik* (3 tomes,
Frankfurt a. Main, 1836-39: see t. 2, 1837). On the German theory of word order,
as applied to the German language, see M. H. Jellinek, *Geschichte der neuhochdeutschen Grammatik* (2 vols., Heidelberg, 1913-1914), II, §§ 563-615.

from this doctrine and search for a principle of word order that is independent of both syntax and logic.

The Introduction (pp. 5-13) succinctly covers the history of the problem. Weil takes issue with Dionysius' concentration on euphony and number, and finds that the ancients had a fine ear for something on which they were unable to theorize adequately (p. 6). One of Cicero's examples would suffice to belie Dionysius' and Cicero's own theories (pp. 7-8). *Orator* lxiii (§ 214) vouchsafed the success of the tribunus C. Carbo in a passage ending in a double trochee (dichoreus): *temeritas filii cōmprŏbāvĭt*. Weil shrewdly rebuts that *comprobavit filii temeritas* would have been no less "numerous": it would have ended in a paeon, a foot which Cicero elsewhere recommends, as Aristotle did. He infers that the preference for the former arrangement was due, instead, to "la succession des idées," mainly to the encounter *Patris dictum SAPIENS ↔ TEMERITAS filii comprobavit*. The survey concludes by praising Batteux and Beauzée for the best statements of the terms of the eighteenth-century polemic.

The essay is neatly articulated into three chapters. Ch. 1 deals with the basic "Principle," which is stated right at the outset: The order of words can be and should be no other than the order of ideas, the train of thought. It is not in this respect that languages differ from one another, but in their ways of combining word order and syntactic order, and this is another matter altogether. In some languages (as in French) the syntactic cast and the "march of ideas" tend to coincide, but, rather than this, the main point is that all languages will follow the march of ideas in their word order. Which means that a skillful translator will be truly "faithful" by taking liberties vis-à-vis the syntactic arrangement of the original in order to preserve what really matters, its train of thought, hence the order of its words. On principle, every statement should begin from what has been made known by the preceding statement. Thus in announcing that Romulus founded Rome we shall choose the sequence *Idem Romulus Romam condidit* if we have just told the story of the birth of Romulus; *Hanc urbem condidit Romulus* if we have been showing the city to a traveller; *condidit Romam Romulus* if we have been mentioning the founding of famous cities. Condillac's associationist doctrine of the *liaison des idées* is originally applied here, as one can see, by placing, at long last, the question of word order in the context of the whole discourse. We cannot understand the arrangement of a clause unless we know its total meaning, that is, what preceded it. In a natural and elegant arrangement the ensemble of the sentences forms a *continu-*

ous whole. Weil uses a fitting simile to contrast modern and ancient
languages in this respect. Greek and Latin sentences, he avers, form a
chain of which the parts interlink; French sentences are comparable to
a necklace of pearls, joined only by the thread of the thought. The
advantage lies clearly with the ancients.[6] Nor is our author merely
speaking of connecting particles and pronouns, but of the basic terms of
the proposition (p. 35). He points out two typical manners of linkage. If
the beginning of a clause or sentence corresponds to the beginning of the
preceding one (*reprise de la notion initiale*), the remainder of the statement also tends to take the gait of a "parallel march" (either through
similarity or opposition); if it is related to the "goal" (*le but*) of the
preceding, we have a "progressive march." The celebrated chiasmus is
a particularly neat case of progressive march. Weil offered some examples,
but his 'rules' can be empirically proved or disproved, and it would be
of considerable interest if someone would put them to a broad statistical
test.

At this point Weil introduces the notion of inverted or pathetic order:
The normal sequence of ideas may be subverted (in all languages) when
we are deeply moved, and this is the only true inversion. Obviously his
use of this term is completely independent of the tradition, since it has
nothing to do with syntactic order. Traditionally, everything that departed
from the analytic or syntactic order was called inversion; Weil speaks of
inversion when, and only when, the sentence begins with its "goal" or
end, rather than with its "initial notion," *even if* this happens to give
an analytic arrangement. Thus, Lucretia's saying *Vestigia viri alieni in
lecto sunt tuo* is both "inverted" and analytical, since the unemotional,
"normal" order would have been the (syntactically "inverted") *In lecto
tuo, Collatine, vestigia sunt viri alieni.* The example may not be very
convincing, but Weil's meaning is clear.

We have seen, then, that the principle of "general grammar" to be
held firm is that word order comes before syntax (the latter being sub-

---

[6] This analysis of classical habit was an important discovery, acknowledged by
later linguists and now a firmly acquired feature of standard manuals. Cf. A.
Meillet and J. Vendryes, *Traité de grammaire comparée des langues classiques*
(Paris, 1924, 1948[2] . . . , 1963[3]), § 849, p. 579: "Le premier mot est d'ordinaire
celui qui permet à la pensée de rattacher le plus commodément la phrase à celle
qui précède." I must also add that the first realization of this principle can be traced
back to Batteux, once again not specifically acknowledged by Weil as his source
(see my p. 262 above).

ordinate to the former), not after, as grammarians were consistently in clined to put it. This is why Δαρείου καὶ Παρυσάτιδος γίγνονται παῖδες δύο is correctly translated, following the order of ideas, as " Darius and Parysatis had two sons," not as " Two sons wcrc born to D. and P.," which is strongly tempting for the insensitive translator who proceeds in terms of grammatical subject (παῖδες).

By thus insisting on a phenomenon other than, and eventually contrasting with syntax, Weil, an idealist of Kantian denomination, meant that word order is an expression of the real operations of the speaker's mind, hence is founded on the psyche rather than on 'logic.' Syntax is related to the external world of things, as it were, word order to the speaking subject. Consequently we have in the clause or sentence two different movements: an objective movement, expressed through syntactic relationships, and a subjective one, word order itself. In this manner he thought to resolve the dilemma of the *mécanicien—métaphysicien* polemic; perhaps more importantly, he was among the first to do away with the secular impasse created by the tendential equalization of linguistic and logical categories.

One of the most persistent myths among didactic grammarians was that of the logical nature of Latin syntax. Weil found the ancient movement of discourse indeed more logical, but in the sense of the linking of ideas, not of the nature of the forms. It proceeded, as the syllogism does, from the known to the unknown, whereas modern languages are often compelled to reverse the train of thought and shift us about while new, unconnected, unprepared-for concepts come to the surface in the form of new subjects. Plato, after having spoken of medicine, would say: Ὑπὸ μὲν οὖν τὴν ἰατρικήν ἡ ὀψοποιικὴ δέδυκεν, but his translator (Cousin) says: "La cuisine s'est glissée sous la médecine," thus breaking the continuity of thought (p. 35). Old French was more flexible and smoother in its logical transitions, not hesitating to use functional inversions for the purpose.

Ch. 2, on " The Relation between Word Order and Syntactical Form," begins by classifying languages according to their behavior on order. Latin and Greek are in the class of free order. Fixed order, on the other hand, can be broken down into two basic possibilities with four resulting variations. The sequence: French, English, German, Chinese, Turkic is progressively arranged from the more relative to the more absolute in rigidity. All the languages of the Turkish and Tartar groups display an immovable order of a syntactically ascending type: the adjective is always placed before its noun, the governed before the governing element, and the complement before the verb (the ideal order postulated by H. Spencer). E. g., their arrangement for the sentence: " We have seen that one finds consolation for many ills in devout prayer " would be: " In devout prayer for many ills consolations to be found we have seen." The Tartar languages and Latin have in common a marked preference for the end-positioned verb (and for the effect of dignity and picturesqueness of the Turkish construction Weil refers to the Turkish Grammar of Arthur Lumley Davids and the papers of Sir W. Jones); while English and Chinese share the habit of placing the modifier before the modified (as German does) at the same time that they place the subject, the predicate, the direct object, and the indirect object in this order (as French does).

To sum up, there are two basic types of construction, " ascend'ng " and " descending," according to whether we move consistently from the governed to the governing or vice versa. The character of the ascending construction lies in enhancing the unity of the thought, that of the descending construction in distinctly showing all its parts.

The descending construction is more appropriate to analysis, and the ancients could adopt it when the occasion so demanded. In Greek the closest example to the French construction is indeed the analytic definitory style created by Aristotle: Ἔστιν οὖν τραγῳδία μίμησις πράξεως σπουδαίας καὶ τελείας (the tragedy is the imitation of an action both serious and complete), to be compared with the non-analytical repetition, once the breakdown into parts is no longer needed: κεῖται δ' ἡμῖν τὴν τραγῳδίαν τελείας καὶ ὅλης πράξεως εἶναι μίμησιν. Plato, on the contrary, was truly ' classical ' in his avoidance of analytical, descending sequence because he sought the roundness of the total impression: ἡ ἐκ τοῦ μὴ ὄντος εἰς τὸ ὂν ἰόντι ὁτῳοῦν αἰτία πᾶσά ἐστι ποίησις (poetry is all cause which makes anything pass from non-being to being—Symposium, 205B).

In a way the sentence can be looked upon as an extended clause (subordinate clauses being equivalent to weightier complements). A direct, analytical arrangement would be of the descending type, having the main statement first and the secondary ones (subordinate clauses) next, in due order. Now, interestingly enough, French, strict as it may be about direct order within the clause, finds no objection to an ascending arrangement within the sentence. While the descending sentence tends to show a certain looseness, the ' inverted ' or ascending sentence (of which the period is only a special kind) does tend to show a tighter whole, a more accomplished unity between the parts. But it also demands greater effort on the part of the audience. This realization had clearly dawned upon Hermogenes, who called the indirect order in the period πλαγιασμός, and warned against its difficulty: ταραχὴ γάρ τις εὐθὺς ἐγγίνεται (one feels a certain uneasiness from the very beginning of this sort of sentences).[7] Weil gives this "ascending" example (Cic., *Pro lege Manil.*, ch. 22): *Tamen etiamsi qui sunt pudore ac temperantia moderatiores, tamen eos esse tales, propter multitudinem cupidorum hominum, nemo arbitratur.*

Ch. 3 turns to "The Relation between Word Order and Rhetorical Emphasis." Weil introduces here the principle of "accentuation or emphasis," which can likewise be ascending or descending. The most conspicuous application of the former are the *versus rhopalici* ('club-shaped lines'), where each word is one syllable longer than the preceding, as in the hexameter *Rem tibi concessi, doctissime, dulcisonoram* (p. 82—See, also, the arrangement by increasing members in *Friends, Romans, Countrymen*). To this pattern is akin the reasoning behind Beauzée's law, with which, however, Weil feels a little uneasy. He would prefer to express it as follows: "Of several related complements give the most concise form to that which is closest to the modified term, and so on, the farthest one becoming the longest," rather than: "We should put the shortest first and the longest last." The difference lies in stressing the notion that the order must not be pampered with if it is right, while the length of the complements, in itself a flexible matter, can be easily modified at the speaker's choice. Moreover, the rule can always be reversed for rhetorical emphasis. At any rate, most languages may use both types of accentuation, although, e. g., French strongly inclines toward the ascending.

In conclusion, Weil agrees with the ancient analogy between *dispositio* and *compositio*, that is, between the three levels of rhetorical ordering: composition of the whole speech, distribution of the parts of the sentence, word arrangement within the clause. "We have then (he comments on Quintilian) the same principle applied to the composition of a discourse and the ordering of a sentence. The most important places are the beginning and the end; they are, as it were, the places of honor both in the order of arguments and in the order of words."[8] A passage from Bossuet, cited by Weil (p. 82), provides an eloquent example:

[7] Hermogenes, *De formis orationis*, I, 3 in Walz, *Rhetores Graeci*, vol. III, p. 205. See also Walz, III, 588 and 708.
[8] Cf. Quintilian, *Inst.*, VII, i, 3.

Vous avez exposé [au milieu des plus grands hazards de la guerre] [une vie aussi précieuse et aussi nécessaire que la vôtre.]

The object has been placed at the end for greater emphasis, and after the indirect complement against the rules of analytical order. But the way this has been done illustrates Beauzée's law. Had it been placed where it normally belongs, "une vie si précieuse" would have sufficed for the object; once put at the end, it had to be lengthened to balance the sentence.

Now we may want to linger on a few basic points in Weil's theory. To begin with, it seems possible to carry further one question which he left incomplete. It would appear that in the analytical languages (French foremost among them) there is a potential tension between descending construction and ascending accentuation, that is, between logical (or, rather, syntactical) rhythm and oratorical rhythm, no absolute prediction being possible on the final outcome. Thus the example from Bossuet agrees with Weil's principle of word order in terms of correspondence to thought emphasis, whereas it seems to run counter to logical order (since the direct complement follows the indirect): the direct object acquires all the weight it deserves, from its end position, according to the principle of first and last stress. And Beauzée was right (or, if we prefer, Weil in his rephrasing of the "law") in the sense that placing the accusative last necessitated lengthening it. Yet the lengthening will not be necessary when emphasis at the end carries a high degree of pathos, as in Weil's reverse of Beauzée's law (p. 80): *parer le vice des dehors de la vertu* can become *Grand Dieu! vous osez parer des dehors de la vertu, le vice.* *Vice* then becomes the key word, as it is placed in position of stress.

Weil remained justly famous for the cogency of his clear, pithily stated presentation. Taken one by one, the parts of his theory were closely reminiscent of the tradition, and especially of the Condillac–Batteux–Beauzée polemic. He shrewdly organized their findings—not always acknowledging his debts—, but did so within an original speculative framework. As we are about to see, Jespersen played down the principle of emphasis, without disproving its usefulness; Marouzeau criticized Weil's notion of front- and end-position, yet by and large the classicists stood firm on it. In particular, Weil sanctioned the modern trend to qualify and play down the ancient over-reliance on sound-patterns (harmony). In explaining many cases of apparent hyperbata not on a basis of *ornatus* but of oratorical rhythm, he clearly distinguished between this essential, thought-bearing rhythm and a purely phonetic, musical rhythm residing in prosodic quantity and metric feet arrangement: *idque quod numerosum in oratione dicitur non semper numero fit*, as Cicero (*Orat.*, lix) had intuited without being able to specify the *other* factor. This also corresponded to Karl Reisig's distinction between "thought-rhythm" and "word-rhythm." [9] Furthermore, Weil's broad notion of the psychological subject, as distinct from the narrower grammatical subject, was echoed again and again by later scholars. It even helped them to overcome the traditional tendency to identify the logical subject with the noun.[10]

Weil's noble effort in the quest of a "general grammar" was carried on, especially for the definition of the strategic places in the sentence (first and last place, complicating factors, etc.) by the philosophers of language, first and foremost W. Wundt (*Völkerpsychologie*, I, 2, Leipzig, 1900 and *Sprachgeschichte und Sprachpsychologie*, Leipzig, 1901; also Sütterlin, *Das Wesen der sprachlichen Gebilde*, 1902),[11] but also by some leading

[9] Chr. Karl Reisig, *Vorlesungen über lateinische Sprachwissenschaft*, ed. Fr. Haase (Leipzig, 1839), p. 817. In objecting to Weil's maxim that the order of words is the order of ideas, M. P. Cunningham, "Phonetic Aspects of Latin Word Order," *Proc. Amer. Philos. Soc.*, CI (1957), 487, has brought out Quintilian's "express statement that such an order is to be avoided," and that for the composition as a whole "the first thing that comes to mind is practically always to be put last" (*Inst.*, VII, i, 25, and esp. VIII, vi, 62-64). But Weil was speaking of hyperbaton as a figure of thought, not as a figure of words (merely to produce rhythm)—this latter being Quintilian's meaning.

[10] Cf. Albert Sechehaye, *Essai sur la structure logique de la phrase* (Paris, 1926), pp. 45, 128-130. Also, on the distinction between psychological and grammatical subject, Hermann Paul, *Prinzipien der Sprachgeschichte* (Halle a. S., 1880, . . . 1909⁴; Tübingen, 1960), §§ 87-88, pp. 124-127 of 4th ed.

[11] Wundt returned to his ideas on the subject in more summary form in *Elemente der Völkerpsychologie* (1912: see Schaub's trans., *Elements of Folk Psychology*, London-New York, 1916, 1921, ch. i, 5-6, pp. 53-74). He drew his generalizations from studies of gesture-language used by deaf-mutes and by American Indian tribes as well as of "primitive-stage" languages such as Ewe (Sudan) and Bushman. Adhering to the root-agglutination theory, he maintained that primitive languages had no grammatical categories and their syntax or word order strictly followed the sequence of perceptions (lacking abstract thoughts), i. e., basically, the construction SAOV (Subject + Attribute—Adjective + Object + Verb) or, exceptionally, when the action is more closely related to the subject than to the object, SAVO (the sequence in "our language" being, instead, ASVO). Cf. p. 67: Gesture-language syntax "follows the principle of immediate and perceptual intelligibility," and the diachronic changes in ways of thinking are directly mirrored in "word-formations and the position of the words within the sentence" in early-

Indo-Europeanists, like Delbrück (*Vergleichende Syntax*, 1900: also K. Brugmann). Nevertheless, even though recently we have been witnessing a renewed interest in the idea of general grammar (among the transformational linguists), it is elsewhere that we shall have to turn for most of the specific progress achieved in our field of inquiry, namely to the method of dealing with the structure of each language as an *unicum*.

I shall, then, briefly present some typical results of modern linguistic and philological research distributed according to the languages covered in this study, i. e., in order, Greek and Latin, French, Italian, and English.

Since we will be dealing mainly with syntactic studies (which also tend to include some stylistic matters of concern to us), it may be good to preface our excursus with a summary view of the way this part of the linguistic discipline reorganized itself in modern times, so as to know what sort of material a work of syntax can be expected to embody.

The standard meaning of syntax as the theory of the relationship between words in sequence is probably due to the Stoics. At any rate syntax may be said to begin with Apollonius Dyscolus, followed by Priscian who rendered σύνταξις with *constructio*. Their example imposed for a long while the view of the syntactic domain as somewhat like the doctrine of the proposition-clause (what German scholars call *Satzlehre*). Modern developments, on the other hand, have been conditioned by the contributions of the following German linguists, who methodically sought for a more appropriate definition.

Chr. Karl Reisig (*Vorlesungen über lateinische Sprachwissenschaft*, ed. Fr. Haase, Leipzig, 1839) assigned three parts to Grammar: *Etymologie* (= *Formenlehre*, morphology); *Semasiologie* (= *Bedeutungslehre*, meaning of forms); *Syntax* (= *Lehre der Verbindung der Wörter*, theory of word sequence). C. W. Krüger (*Griechische Sprachlehre*, 1852-

---

stage languages. Interestingly enough, the anteposition of the object to the verb (the classic *rejet*, a type of inversion ") could thus appear as eminently 'natural' to Wundt (but in the Ewe language the verb generally precedes the object, pp. 71-72). A VOS construction, not infrequent in Latin and German, "would be absolutely impossible in gesture-language " (p. 65).

On the root-agglutination theory see Wundt's response to Jespersen's reverse solution of the question (*Progress in Language*, 1894: free word order is more primitive, fixed order more advanced—see below) in *Sprachgeschichte und Sprachpsychologie* (Leipzig, 1901), pp. 83 ff., and similarly Delbrück's response in *Grundfragen der Sprachforschung* (Strassburg, 1901), pp. 85 ff. and 119 ff.

56³) [12] submitted a broader view of Syntax, which he divided into Analysis (roughly corresponding to Reisig's semasiology) and Synthesis (roughly Reisig's syntax, but defined as Linking of Logical Elements, Construction of Clauses, Concord, and Word Order: *Satzgefüge*). Franz Miklosich, on the other hand (*Syntax der slavischen Sprachen*, 1868, 1883², 4th vol. of his *Vergleichende Grammatik der slavischen Sprachen*), both restricted and displaced the realm of Syntax in the direction of Reisig's semasiology, by defining it as nothing else than "the theory of the meaning of word-classes and word-forms."

In an essay that won much attention (*Was ist Syntax?*, Marburg, 1894), John Ries reviewed the preceding, and argued for the view that syntax must concern itself only with what Krüger called synthesis, while the semantic of forms (including cases, moods, etc.) should be directly integrated with the treatment of forms. This desideratum exerted much impact, and was followed especially by the leading comparatist Brugmann. Most linguists, however, had begun to mix syntax (conceived as both theory of meaning and word order) together with morphology, with a result that Wackernagel regretted as unfortunate disorderliness.

Jacob Wackernagel (*Vorlesungen über Syntax*, I, 1910, 1926²), though maintaining the basic correctness of Ries's viewpoint on principle, accepted the prevailing distinction and separation of semasiology from morphology, and followed a notion of syntax as including both the theory of meaning and function and the theory of sequential organization (on clause- and sentence-level), *provided* the two are handled distinctly. Allowing for individual variations, this is roughly the definition that has prevailed ever since.

It must be mentioned in passing that the autonomy of syntax has apparently been threatened by some implications contained in the teachings of the school of Geneva. In Vendryes' terminology, if we divide the words in the sentence into *semantemes* and *morphemes* (like the Chinese 'full' and 'empty words'), we can consider word order itself as a *morphème*

---

[12] Cf. Wackernagel, *Vorlesungen über Syntax, mit besonderer Berücksichtigung von Griechisch, Lateinisch und Deutsch*, Erste Reihe (Basel, 1926²). See a survey of the question on pp. 1-3. I follow Wackernagel's reconstruction and interpretation of the background to Ries, which does not literally correspond to Ries's own exposition of the matter. In particular, Ries does not specifically discuss Krüger's contribution. See Carl Wilhelm Krüger, *Griechische Sprachlehre für Schulen* (3ᵈ ed., 3 vols., Berlin, 1852-56; 4th enlarged ed., ibid., 1861-62; the first ed., 2 vols., was dated 1845-55).

complémentaire. This view is approvingly referred to by Le Bidois in the most comprehensive *Syntaxe du français moderne.*[13] Thus Jespersen at one moment went so far as placing word order within Morphology. This may be seen as somewhat parallel to Sechehaye's position on conjunctions when, moving from de Saussure and Bally, he perceptively placed them on the same plane with prepositions, as " prépositions de propositions." [14] Under the category of morpheme one could, then, see as contiguous the structure of the clause and that of the complex sentence, at least insofar as explicit (conjunctions) or implicit (word order) morphemes are involved. It is, seemingly, in reaction against this type of structuralist orientation that the generative grammarians have recently reëmphasized the role of syntax.

On the other hand Saussure had pointed out how, in keeping with the linear nature of language (which excludes the simultaneous uttering of two sounds), words in speech contract relationships in virtue of their being linked together consecutively. Every term draws part of its value from its dynamic contrast with what precedes it or what follows it or both.[15] Consequently, a word sequential pattern which has become customary has *ipso facto* acquired the status of morpheme, to wit, of a grammatical category.[16] These truths seal the relevance of word order as part of grammar or syntax from a linguistic point of view, at the same time that they neatly define by omission the stylistic aspect of word order and ' inversion ' whenever such phenomena are the result of a choice on the part of the individual speaker or writer.

Before we take our leave of General Grammar we must give its due, at least in token form, to something rather akin to it though certainly not identical with it, namely Philosophy of Grammar, which rightfully enters our discourse through the contribution of one of its outstanding representatives. It was perhaps Otto Jespersen who realized first and most clearly the importance of studying word order within the framework of

[13] Vendryes, *Le langage,* p. 93; Jespersen, *Philosophy of Grammar,* p. 44. Cf. G. and R. Le Bidois, *Syntaxe du français moderne* (1967²), vol. I, p. 19 and vol. II, p. 3.

[14] A. Sechehaye, *Essai sur la structure logique de la phrase* (1926): see the whole, interesting chapter on conjunctions, pp. 205-209.

[15] F. de Saussure, *Cours de linguistique générale* (Paris, 1955), pp. 170-171.

[16] A. Meillet, *Linguistique historique et linguistique générale* (Paris, 1921), p. 147. This is again in keeping with Vendryes' terminology accepted by Le Bidois (see fn. 13 above).

the newer linguistic theories—word order still remaining "the Cinderella of linguistic science," as he put it in a brilliant chapter of his provocative work (originally derived from his dissertation), *Progress in Language* (London, 1894: see p. 90).

That chapter was entitled "The History of Chinese and of Word-Order" (pp. 80-111), and it started out by arguing against the older theory (that of the Schlegels, as modified by Franz Bopp) whereby the primeval state of language was to be represented as one of isolated monosyllabic roots arranged according to a fixed pattern of word order, which later would have given way to agglutination and finally a flectional system with free word order, showing relationships by endings instead of by arrangement of sequence—a transition from a prevalently syntactic system to a prevalently morphologic one. The modern languages with their minimal case system and relatively fixed word order would, in this view, represent a decadent regression, a relative state of corruption rather than an improvement. Jespersen held, instead, that the real progress of language lies in its having evolved in precisely the opposite way: Chinese is not an example of primordial, but of highly advanced language, very similar, in this sense, to English or even French, whereas German must be regarded as a less 'advanced' language than these, and Latin as an 'early' linguistic stage. The two aspects, flection and fixed order, are apparently related, probably in the sense that a natural development toward fixed arrangement has made useless, and eventually eliminated, the case-endings.

One could add here that the majority of Romance philologists have been inclined to assign a decisive (though not exclusive) role to the loss of cases for the establishment of analytic order in Romance. They have, however, tended to posit the latter as a consequence of the former, so that the relationship of cause and effect between the two phenomena has usually been seen as the reverse of Jespersen's perspective.

A. CLASSICAL LANGUAGES

In the light of the historical perspective one acquires by following the controversies on "naturalness" and "logic" in composition, it may seem surprising that students would be taught (until very recently) that they should study Latin for its "logical" merits. It is hard to see how this state of affairs could subsist alongside the displays of national pride, as it were, in the unique "logic" of analytical word order (especially French). Yet the prejudice has long remained deeply rooted and, curiously enough, it was based precisely on criteria of composition. It is already half a century since Wilhelm Kroll (1869-1939) first pleaded for a scientific approach in the classroom when he decried the inveterate habit of stressing the "logical rigor" of Latin sentence structure and even word order.[17] He remarked that "any notion endowing Latin with a logical structure much stronger than that of German, and possibly of any other language of the earth, is based on the unilateral concern with the writers selected for the classroom, and above all, Cicero" (p. 5 of 1962 ed.). Even in as scientific a *Syntax* as Ziemer's (1893), Kroll pointed out to exemplify, one would read: "The Latin language, rigorously bound by the laws of logic (think of the *consecutio temporum*), generally also follows the same in its word order" (p. 88, cf. Ziemer, § 357). True enough, the facts of the language eventually compelled Ziemer to add a serious qualification: "There are at work in the psyche of the speaker manifold influences which force him to deviate from the current order. Word order then follows psychological rules; it is a circumstantial matter, motivated by some particular cause" (88).

Yet the prejudice in question did contain an element of truth, and to dismiss it out of hand would be an oversimplification. For, it is not a prejudice but a well established fact that comprehension of the Latin period in its classical, oratorical form does require a lively use of logical faculties. On the other hand, spoken Latin, as well as much of pre-Ciceronian and non-Ciceronian literary Latin, differed to a much lesser extent from the psychological make-up of modern Western languages.

In detail, however, the behavior of synthetic languages in the domain of word order varies so greatly from that of analytic languages that it is hard to see how any broad conclusion concerning one of them can apply to any other in a different group. In non-flectional languages the limited flexibility with respect to inversion demands structural changes to achieve the emphases required by the 'real' meaning of a statement. "Socrates was put to death by the Athenians in 399 B. C." is a strait, narrative-descriptive statement, which must be subjected to drastic modifications if we propose to enhance a focal point in it: "It was in 399 B. C. that . . ."; "Death was the verdict that Athenians passed against Socrates . . ."; "The

---

[17] Kroll, *Die wissenschaftliche Syntax im lateinischen Unterricht* (Berlin, 1925³, 1962⁴, originally based on 1917 lectures). I shall quote and translate from the 1962 ed. See ch. v, pp. 88-100 on Word Order. See, also, the trans. of the 3ᵈ ed.: *La Sintaxis científica en la enseñanza del Latín* (Madrid, 1935).

Athenians themselves put their own citizen and greatest philosopher. . . ."
In flectional languages all this can be achieved by inversion (word order
in simple form).

Once we have realized the extent of these differences it will come as
no surprise that, in the most extensive and authoritative treatment of
Latin word order, J. Marouzeau decided that further progress with regard
to the classical languages could not be achieved without discarding the
traditional approach down to, and including, Weil, in favor of an entirely new method.[18] He identified this new method with the theory of
syntactic units or groups, first applied to word order by the Indo-European-
ist A. Bergaigne.[19] Marouzeau denied the possibility of reaching any
scientific conclusions by referring to the clause as a whole, and stressed
the priority of word arrangement inside small groups of words that
directly determine one another and can be rigorously defined—"des groupes
élémentaires rigoureusement définis." In a phrase such as *Novi ego tuum,
Attice, animum, sicut tu meum,* the eminent classicist observed, what interests us is not the relationship (and reciprocal position) between *ego* and
tuum or *tu* and *meum*, but that between *ego* and *novi* or *tuum* and
animum.[20] He maintained that Weil's acknowledgment, even though
marginal, of this fact, completely voided all other principles stated by him,
as even the "first and last place" principle is voided by admitting possible internal stress positions.[21] In other words, in Marouzeau's view
Weil's original principle of psychological order was contradicted and
gradually displaced by his admission of the pathetic order, first, and then
the *repos d'accent* and *l'hyperbate*—all of which de facto led him to the
realization of the *groupe syntaxique*, "la considération qui rend inutiles
toutes les précédentes." [22]

Of course our willingness to accept this criticism of Weil will depend
on our readiness to adopt fully and exclusively the method of syntactic
units. It seems to me that such a clash of opposite vantage points (that
of Marouzeau amounting to a rejection of the whole tradition, that of

[18] Marouzeau, *L'ordre des mots dans la phrase latine* (3 vols., Paris, 1922-1949).
[19] Bergaigne, "Essai sur la construction grammaticale . . ." (1878); also Id.,
"La place de l'adjectif épithète en vieux français et en latin," *Mélanges Graux*
(Paris, 1884), 533-543. Marouzeau, I, p. 6.
[20] Marouzeau, ibid., I, 6.
[21] Ibid., I, 3-6.
[22] Ibid., I, 4-5. Cf. Weil, 1869 ed., pp. 15, 52, 63, 95.

Weil to a bold yet balanced revision of it) cannot be assumed to invest
the matter in a general, "interlingual" way. Marouzeau's great merit
lies in having proved that each language has its own fairly closed system,
and its own set policies on word order. Marouzeau's principles apply much
more cogently to the classical languages than to the modern ones, while
Weil's work better on the modern.

The net result of Marouzeau's extensive venture into our province (a
commitment which stretched over a period of roughly 30 years) amounts
to the following major points.[23] Latin word order is free, but not indifferent. Likewise, just as only few of its constructions are indifferent, only
few are compulsory. Latin has inherited from Indo-European the tendency
to assign the second spot from the beginning of the clause to enclitics and
accessory words.[24] One cannot speak of 'places of honor' in the clause:
a term can be placed first because it is felt as crucial, but position alone
will not confer special status upon it. The verb is the only part of
speech which has a locative preference (for the end). Note that Marouzeau does not deny that 'places of honor in the clause' can obtain in some
other languages, as they certainly do in the Romance languages: more
broadly, we can see here a distinction between classical and analytical
languages.

Before belonging to the clause, the word belongs to a group (preposition
or adjective to its noun, complement to its verb, etc.). It is only within
the group that the notion of inversion becomes meaningful and legitimate,
whenever the normal order is subverted for the sake of some special effect.
But normal orders are always quite specific: the qualitative adjective, for
example, precedes (*bonus hospes*), the determinative adjective follows
(*homo romanus*). Even here extreme caution is called for. The instance
given, *homo romanus*, is a good case in point: it so happens that with
this particular adjective the inverted order, *romanus homo*, is statistically
dominant because the high opinion the Romans had of themselves made

---

[23] See the author's general conclusions in the excellent summary he appended
to the 3[d] volume, pp. 191-197 (also *Lingua*, I, 1948, 155-161).

[24] Wackernagel, "Über ein Gesetz der indogermanischen Wortstellung," *Indogermanische Forschungen*, I (1892), 333-436, esp. 406-430, confirmed by W. Kroll,
Die wissenschaftliche Syntax (1962), p. 92, related this law of enclitic words to
their preference for tonically low places (i. e., second places) within the tonic inflection which dominates the melody of the sentence. See my fn. 27 below.
Wackernagel's essay was reprinted in his *Kleine Schriften*, I (Göttingen, 1953),
1-104.

them use this adjective in expressive position, whereas the " inexpressive " position (" ordre banal ") was in fact rare (therefore " normal " for the adjectival class to which *romanus* belongs, but not for this particular adjective itself).

Disjunction has a similar effect of emphasis, but on the first disjoined term alone. I should interject here that, at least in the example offered by Marouzeau: *magnae sunt saepe parvis ex causis consecutae irae*, we may feel that not only *magnae* and *parvis*, but also *irae* becomes stressed. Furthermore, if we consider the following felicitous case of disjoined apposition (Caesar, B. c. I, 57, 3): *neque multum Albici nostris virtute cedebant, homines asperi et montani et exercitati in armis*, we find that not only the SECOND term receives stress from the delay, but, in a manner rather peculiar to Latin, the modifier is detached from the modified chiefly for the sake of CLARITY, as against the non-flectional languages' way of achieving clarity through positional *liaison des idées*, i. e. the strict closeness of modifier and modified. As to other languages, think of the following separation of the object from its verb: *Avez-vous vu, au fond de ce bois, là-bas, cet homme?* The detached element attracts both because it has been delayed and because it ends the clause. This is so effective that we accept it even in the face of " Beauzée's law." In fact, compare these two sentences, one made smooth by following " Beauzée's law," the other suspenseful by separation of verb and object: *Have you seen that lonely old woman, standing at the street corner in the cold?—Have you seen, standing at the street corner in the cold, that lonely old woman?*

The mechanism of both inversion and disjunction, Marouzeau further submits, can be psychologically explained by the expectation of surprise induced in the recipient. Further attempts along a psychological analysis of arrangement are futile. The notion of logical order is illusory. Likewise for the " grammatical order," since, in a free-order language, grammar dictates order only exceptionally, and one finds no principle involved in such rare cases. The third conventionally recognized " order," the psychological, is equally elusive. Is one supposed to move naturally from the datum, the known, toward the new element, the true object of communication? But it is impossible to determine which elements are present in the speaker's mind at a given stage during the process of expression, since the conceptual components of a thought occupy the mind almost simultaneously. The speaking process is not primarily concerned with the contents of the speaker's mind, but rather with the manner of transferring them to the audience. Marouzeau's implications on the nature of the logos, we might interject, seem to be that communication has priority over expression. Speech, as it were, is not a copy of thought, it is a translation of it: we do not follow its order, we interpret it. This critique of the traditional "orders" is radical enough; but here again, lest we be misled into undue generalizations, these conclusions appear tailored specifically for the classical languages. Marouzeau's statements are repeatedly qualified by his limitation: "in a free-order language" (*dans une langue à construction libre*—which was, incidentally, Weil's expression). At any rate, he has not been followed in this respect by his colleagues on other languages: cf. Le Bidois, *Syntaxe du français*, where the three orders, precisely as the logical, psychological, and aesthetic, prominently reappear (see below).

Marouzeau goes on to list seven main *facteurs de variation*, among which I should single out the following. (1) We tend to express first what emotionally, therefore urgently, affects our consciousness, followed next by factors of intellectual order, which demand some effort of calculation. (This is a felicitous phrasing of what amounts to a fundamental psychological discovery concerning order; it can be found with other modern linguists as well.) (2) Literary writers are particularly fond of elegant variation. Our author closes on the note that "the study of word order is one of the hardest and least advanced in the area of stylistics."

We cannot take our leave of this leading classicist without mentioning his picturesque comparisons between Latin and French sentence structure. The French sentence, he says in his *Traité de stylistique appliquée au Latin* (1935), "is a sequence of statements each of which satisfies the mind; the Latin sentence puts a series of questions almost none of which is answered until the very end." Again, "the Latin sentence is a charade, . . . the French sentence is a series of explanations, each one of them being concluded before the next one is broached." [25]

[25] Marouzeau, *Traité*, p. 225. See also, in particular, pp. 291-302.

For an example of the role historians of the Latin language assign to our questions and of their mode of treating them, one can consult Giacomo Devoto, *Storia della lingua di Roma* (Bologna, 1944²), pp. 95-97, 118 ff., 165 f., 220-223, 351 ff. on word order and sentence structure. Essentially, Devoto underlines that transpositions came about either for expressive or for decorative reasons, the latter including mainly the search for variety and rhythm. P. Berrettoni, "Ricerche sulla posizione delle parole nella frase italica," *A. S. N. S. P.* (1967), carrying on after Rosen-

As for Greek, the most recent student of the problem, K. J. Dover,[26] lists ten theoretically possible "determinants" of word order: (1) phonological (e. g. the longer word precedes), (2) morphological (nouns precede verbs), (3) syntactic (subject precedes), (4) semantic (words of motion precede), (5) lexical (certain types of words precede), (6) logical (the term least expected precedes—'logical' being used here as an adjective corresponding to the noun 'thought'), (7) emotive, (8) social or ceremonial (precedence by rank), (9) individual history of the speaker (habit of repeating previous patterns), (10) stylistic or aesthetic (mainly variation).

Dover is dealing with Greek, but the list of categories is general enough to be applicable to any language. Of course such a diversification marks a notable refinement over the traditional recourse to such simpler and inclusive notions as 'rational' and 'emotional,' but the possibilities it offers are not as numerous as they seem to be. For one thing, several of those categories are purely hypothetical and do not appear to obtain in the reality of most languages one attempts to describe. Once we reduce them to the real determinants we find, furthermore, that some distinctions are not as functional as promised. Dover takes exception to the traditional notion of 'emphasis,' for example. The term does not appear in his list, and it would correspond to (6) and (7) according to the manner in which it has been traditionally used (pp. 32-33). This indeterminacy of the term is precisely the reason for his objection, for the distinction between 'emotive' and 'emphasis for the sake of clarity' is, in his view, vital. And so it may well be, although 'emphasis' still seems useful enough at least to the extent that it covers what the ancients chose to designate, vaguely yet effectively, with the term 'force or importance' (vis). At any rate the more positive element in Dover's approach, it seems to me, lies in focussing upon the distinction (ultimately derived from Weil) between syntactic and logical categories, or, more precisely, between syntactic subject and predicate on the one hand, and logical subject and predicate on the other. He finds the latter categories (here again called

kranz, claims that in Osco-Umbrian the genitive determinant, habitually anteposed to its determinand, could be postponed to it to enhance its relative importance, as in the case of predicative value, although Oscan and Umbrian do not behave identically in this respect.

[26] Dover, *Greek Word Order* (Cambridge, Eng., 1960), pp. 3-4. Also, see the end of my Ch. I on Dover's theoretical conclusions.

'logical' by reference to 'thought,' not to 'logical analysis') practically
equivalent to other linguists' 'psychological' and 'cognitional' subject
and predicate, or 'determinand' and 'determinant,' or 'thema' and
'rhema' (pp. 34-38). He explains his meaning by the example *dogs bite*,
a statement syntactically fixed and invariable in its constituents, but 'logically' manifold according to whether it answers one or the other of the
following questions summarizing the context of an actual discourse: What
do dogs do? Which animals bite? In answer to the latter question the
statement would have *bite* as its logical subject, *dogs* as its logical predicate, and vice versa. "In each case the utterance would be reduced to
the logical predicate alone; it would be laconic, but it would be intelligible; the logical subject is the element which is common to question
and answer" (35). The relevant consequence for us is that if it is true
that "in English the syntactical categories determine the order of words,
the logical categories the volume of the voice" (34), other languages
operate differently. Greek and Latin, for instance, could express the
logical relations through word order and the syntactical relations through
inflection—which raises the question of using such grammatical devices as
it is I who . . . , *as for* . . . ("as for John, they caught him," p. 38),
c'est lui que . . . , as Weil had shrewdly pointed out in investigating the
secrets of true translation.[27]

B. FROM LATIN TO ROMANCE

Latin had carried to its most radical consequences the preference of part
of the Indo-European group for a sentence structure characterized by the
end-position of the verb—a preference demonstrated through the Sanskrit
studies of the leading glottologist Delbrück (*Die altindische Wortfolge*,
1878; also *Altindische Syntax* in Delbrück, *Syntaktische Forschungen*, V,

---

[27] The position of enclitics could come under Dover's determinants (1) and
(5): Greek preserved particularly well the Indo-European tendency to reserve the
second place in the phrase to accessory words, often enclitic. Cf. A. Meillet and
J. Vendryes, *Traité de Grammaire comparée des langues classiques* (Paris, 1924,
1948[2], . . . 1963[3]), § 850. This now standard manual deals briefly with word
order (§§ 848-852, pp. 578-583), and essentially points out that in Greek the verb
tended to place itself in the middle of the clause, in Latin at the end (§ 851).
It also calls attention to the importance of some cases of relatively fixed order in
'idiomatic' phrases (§ 852).

1888). The task of explaining how this Latin pattern could give way to the clearly antagonistic systems of all Neo-Latin languages was assumed by a capable Romance philologist, Elise Richter, in her widely discussed *Zur Entwicklung der romanischen Wortstellung aus der Lateinischen* (1903; followed later on by "Grundlinien der Wortstellungslehre," 1919).

Assuming, according to E. Richter's reasoning, that the mind proceeds from the known to the unknown,[28] the speaker will go from the subject to the remainder of the sentence, since the grammatical subject is usually the point of departure, and will therefore start the sentence, or at least precede the predicate. On this basis the Romance sequence, Subject + Verb + Object + Complements, is naturally the clearer one (p. 7), because it makes each modifier IMMEDIATELY FOLLOW its (known) term of reference, to which it adds something yet unknown. The prevalent Latin order was, instead, Subject + Complements + Object + Verb, where, after starting with the main modified member, each member is PRECEDED by its modifier. But E. Richter believed that both types of construction coexisted in Latin from the earliest times, and she deduced this from numerous examples of early- and late-ancient Latin. Nevertheless one must at least admit, if I am not mistaken, that the anteposition of direct and indirect objects to the verb was generally natural to Latin on all levels, which would tend to reduce the 'Romance' type of order in Latin to the anteposition of the verb to the secondary complements only, and, above all, to the avoidance of disjunctions. The 'Romance' construction was essentially popular, the 'classical' essentially learned, and the tension between the two was finally resolved in favor of the 'Romance' type in the course of the fourth century, since the *Acta Apostolorum Apocrypha*, the Vulgate, and the *Peregrinationes Hierosolymitanae* display a thoroughly 'Romance' style within otherwise perfectly correct Latin forms.

The idealistic school of thought submitted some interesting philosophical insights into the enduring questions underlying the transition from Latin to Romance. Vossler proposed a psychological theory whereby one could see in the classical (S+)CC + V–O a "prëeminence of the speaker," and in the vulgar–L. (S+)V + CC–O a "prëeminence of the listener."[29] He described the transition from the former to the latter as

[28] Same principle also previously stated by Meyer-Lübke, *Grammaire des langues romanes*, III (Paris, 1900), p. 792.

[29] K. Vossler, "Neue Denkformen" (1922).

a change of thinking processes away from a "naïve egocentric anthropo-morphism" toward a "movement to the other," involving a setting in of 'symbolic' thought processes as against the ancient 'mythical' processes.

Vossler's disciple Alfons Schmidl also adopted a typically *geistesge-schichtlich* method to explain this polarity between EPo and MPo of the verb. In his view, the former was essentially the expression of an "impres-sionistic-phenomenologic" view of the world, in which the single elements of thought were aligned one after the other in a relatively 'isolating' manner. The MPo, instead (the verb being placed between the subject and the remaining parts of the clause), is representative of the modern, "synthetic" way of thinking, which heavily relies on factual causality. The verb thus acquires the function of tying together the subject, which plays a 'causal' role in the statement, and the complements, which, after a fashion, correspond to the goal, end, or operational 'effects' of the event. In this sense, the VEPo in German sCls, e. g., can be regarded as a relic of that ancient, 'primitive,' impressionistic-phenomenologic way of seeing things.[30] This corresponds to Malblanc's[31] view of the verb as synthetic element of the phrase, so that, in this philologist's terms, the French $S + V + CC–O$ bends in the direction of a priori judgment, while German displays an aptitude to a posteriori judgment in its tendency to send the finite verb to the end of sCls and the indefinite elements of the verb to the end of mCls (participles, indefinite mood, separable par-ticles). For, in general terms, "le verbe est l'organe principal du juge-ment en même temps que l'organe de liaison entre les différents éléments de la proposition."

Taking his cue from Vossler and Schmidl, and similarly concentrating on the question of the position of the verb in the clause (an aspect only of our problem, but the crucial one in the realm of Latin word order), H.-G. Koll has focussed his positive corrections of E. Richter's views on such *geistesgeschichtlich* hypotheses, thus offering a conjecture which would combine the statistical facts of the positivistic method with the causal explanations of the idealistic method. For if the fact remains of a shift from classical order to Romance order as, basically, a shift from $(S+)CC + V$ to $S + V + CC$, even when we refine E. Richter's con-

---

[30] Schmidl, *Vulgärlateinische Wortstellung*, p. 18. However, the late appearance of this phenomenon in the evolution of the German language may present an obstacle to the adoption of the above schema.

[31] A. Malblanc, *Stylistique* (1961), p. 153.

clusions through the results of later research, the problem remains open
as to the more or less 'ultimate' cause of that shift.[32] Most remarkable
about the change, even if we postpone the basic dating from Richter's ca.
400 A. D. to Koll's ca. 700 A. D., is that it coincides with the victory of
Christianity over paganism. In fact, Christianity introduces a sense of
'causality' in the *modi cogitandi*—as one can infer, e. g., from a basic
innovation over ancient mythological religion, namely the conception of
God as Creator and the World as His Creation. Koll only points out a
complicating difficulty here, in that Greek word order, essentially different
in behavior from the Latin, showed a strong tendency toward VMPo
several centuries *before* the advent of Christianity, so that we must hesitate
to identify VEPo as 'ancient' and VMPo as 'Christian.' Yet an answer
to such an objection can be found in the simple observation that Greek
thought started to witness since the sixth century B. C. a shift from myth
to Logos, this latter clearly embodying a recognizable, 'scientific' sense of
causality, as in the early physicists' and Aristotle's striving after the " first
causes." This aspect of the Greek *forma mentis* was inherited and expanded by Christianity, which assimilated it as part of its Eastern-Mediter-
ranean heritage and carried it on into the logicism of Scholastic, where
it reached, in a sense, a peculiar moment of exasperated fruition. Thus
the VMPo does remain part of Christian linguistic culture because it
never became the norm in any epoch of Greek culture. Furthermore, as
Koll phrases it, we have a diachronic polarity between VEPo and VMPo
(from antique impressionistic phenomenology to Christian causality), but
also a synchronic one (between the practically-oriented, mythic *mos
maiorum* of the Romans and the Logos of the Greeks). Indeed, we can
add that the Greek sentence normally experienced a relatively perfect
'analytic' order (expressing what Schmidl styled as the 'synthetic' line
of thought) in the definitory passages of Aristotle's didactic language (as
indicated by Weil).

Our knowledge of medieval Latin sentence structure is still too far from
adequate both in general terms and in studies of detail. Yet, to enjoy
our *geistesgeschichtlich* mood a little longer, we might wonder whether it
is not appropriate to conjecture a rapport between stylistic expression and
basic mental attitudes as they come to the surface of literary practices and

[32] Cf. Koll, "Zur Stellung des Verbs" (1965), pp. 270-272.

even doctrines. We might then perceive a suggestive analogy between the medieval rhetorical doctrine of *amplificatio* through *diversio* (='digression')[33] and the rather rambling character of much of medieval sentence movement (longish and complex syntactic subordination, yet inherently loose), still visible in the Italian periods of a Boccaccio: more apparently than actually Ciceronian, his peculiar type of sentence is neither ancient nor modern. The notion of *diversio* underlies or at least partly reflects (not to commit ourselves to criteria of cause and effect) the literary habit of composing by juxtaposition and loose subordination of incidents—a method whose nature and relative value has been shown at play in such exemplary works as the *Roman de la Rose*.[34] This way of composing, both on the stylistic level and in the structural organization of the works, is somewhat like the digressive 'plan' of Gothic architecture and ornamentation, for which C. S. Lewis has spoken of "love of the labyrinthine" and "ramifying energy of a strong tree, glorious with plenitude." [35]

The literary style of the time may (but quite misleadingly) appear to be akin to the classic periodic style; hidden below its façade lie the seeds of the later *coupé* style with the actual 'fragmentation' inherent in it. Despite the long stretch of its ten centuries of development, it seems a fair generalization that medieval style, specifically from the viewpoint of composition, has an entirely different ring from the ancient, even when the humanistically inclined and philologically trained among those writers more or less consciously strove to restore the modes of classical prose. Often we witness a type of rhythm which can be described as essentially "segmented" or "fragmented." [36] At other times, perhaps less often, the flow of discourse is remarkably smooth, but this smoothness is somewhat more spontaneous and facile than that of ancient 'Atticism.' Both possibilities were also clearly reflected in the prose of the vernacular languages, and we undoubtedly have a phenomenon of reciprocal influence, at least after such a time when the vernaculars first became literarily established.

---

[33] Cf. Geoffrey of Vinsauf, *Poetria nova*, III, A, 527-553 in Faral, *Les Arts poétiques du XIIᵉ et du XIIIᵉ siècle* (1923), p. 213. See C. S. Lewis, *The Discarded Image* (Cambridge, Eng., 1964), pp. 192-194.

[34] Cf. A. M. F. Gunn, *The Mirror of Love* (Lubbock, Tex., 1952).

[35] Lewis, op. cit., p. 194.

[36] 'Segmentation' and 'fragmentation' are terms systematically used by Luigi Malagoli in his numerous works dealing with characteristic aspects of medieval Latin style.

My purpose above (in the Medieval Section) has been to record, whenever they sound loud and clear enough to warrant registering, any signs of theoretical awareness of such phenomena which appear to us as changes and relative differences from the ancient patterns.

As another aspect of fragmented movement, this time on the stylistic level, I have briefly illustrated above the parallelisms inherent in Isidorian and Ilarian patterns (see Medieval Section). But to return to more directly syntactical aspects, the more striking characteristics of medieval sentence structure, both in Latin and in the vernaculars, lie perhaps in the widespread tendency to conceive by coordination or clumsy and only apparent subordination. About this, however, it is difficult to generalize. A recent linguistic study of Old French brilliantly argues the point that the ratio of parataxis and hypotaxis is more a matter of literary style and formal traditions (genres) than of historical linguistic transition from a more primitive to a more advanced stage.[37] Thus it would be incorrect to infer that French was syntactically less developed at the time of the *Chanson de Roland* than at that of the *Roman de Thèbes* BECAUSE the percentage of subordinate clauses jumps from 20 in the former to 30 in the latter, since one finds 30% to be the case in the earlier *Alexis* and even 75% in the *Serments de Strasbourg*. In other words, we can only legitimately conclude from that comparison that the language of the epic differs from that of the courtly romance. Indeed, one is bound to infer—on the ground of that kind of evidence—that OF is not inherently more paratactic than Classical Latin, if one remains within the sphere of the epic, since 20% also happens to be the rate of incidence of hypotaxis in the *Aeneid*.

Basic devices and forms of sentence structure appear at different times and places in the function, as it were, of eternal constants. This makes it difficult to characterize individual styles on those terms and to identify specific influences and sources. Yet whenever these constants come to the surface, they acquire unique complections which are conditioned by particular historical circumstances. This is also true with the medieval

---

[37] W.-D. Stempel, . . . *Satzverknüpfung* . . . (1964), esp. pp. 32-96.

Using the statistical approach in a rather summary and abstract way, B. B. Marcou, "Two Points in French Style," *American Journal of Philology*, VI, 23 (1885), 344-348, exemplified the progressive simplification of the French sentence by revealing that the mean sentence had 6.02 verbs in Montaigne, 4.48 in Fénelon, 3.89 in Voltaire, and 3.38 in Daudet.

sentence, both Latin and vernacular. If we consider it legitimate, as we
well might, to refer to the three characters of periodicity, symmetry, and
looseness, and attribute circularity to the first, schematism to the second
(in the sense of relying on the verbal schemes), tropicality to the third (if
we can identify the tropes with the thought schemes, as many do), we
shall find the following. The use of symmetrical sound schemes (essentially isocolon, parison, and paromoion) is rare in antiquity outside the
period; even within the period, it is always kept in check, especially in
the good authors (like Isocrates), by the sober constraint of good taste
and tempered by a sustained study of variety in both form and rhythm.
This variety also graces the cola within the period, which, as in Cicero,
where it is the normal unit, is circular and cumulative. On the other
hand the medieval sentence has, by and large, no true periodicity and
can be either loose (with or without tropes) or symmetrical (schematic).
In the latter case it tends to use the schemes without preoccupation for
any sense of measure and with rather exacting uniformity, heightened
by the sharpness of its short cola. This last pattern begins to be found
among the Fathers of the Church of the Silver Age and, as Croll has
demonstrated,[38] survives from the churchly literature of the Middle Ages
well into the Renaissance and the early seventeenth century in the
various forms of *estilo culto* (as in Antonio de Guevara, John Lyly, and
some courtly literature). Whereas in the classical prose the schemes had
the function of underscoring the rhythm, in the medieval writers they
become the chief source of a new, 'schematic' rhythm, which occasionally
achieves a repetitive sing-song of magic incantation. The fountainhead
of the schematic style were the imperial and papal courts, the *aula* and
the *curia,* where the direct child of the *ars dictandi,* the *oratio aulica*
emanating from the official chanceries or secretarial bureaux, pervaded
even the more mundane and literary productions gravitating around them.
To the *aulici* the humanists opposed themselves as *eruditi,* starting as early
as with Petrarch, in an attack which eventually brought the humanists
to take control of the courts and change their style. This triumph was
gradual, and while in Italy, where it began with Petrarch's successor
Coluccio Salutati, it became widespread in the fifteenth century, it never
proceeded very far afield in some more peripheral countries, such as

[38] Croll, " The Sources of the Euphuistic Rhetoric."

England.[39] Again, what the Middle Ages cultivated as 'the grand style' was essentially schematic composition, while the 'humble style' was little else than the loose. Dante theorized a language as well as a style which were meant to be illustrious (noble), courtly (aulico-aristocratic), and artificial (*curiale* like the language of the ecclesiastical bureaucracy); Boccaccio tried to rediscover the ancient circularity. But both remain essentially in the medieval tradition, in the senses just indicated, regardless of the unique features of their individual genius.

The contrast between Latin and Romance word order still raises a number of questions. Since the latter derived from a natural evolution within the former, at what time did the major transition occur? What was the cause, hence, the meaning of it? As to the documentary evidence of the change, principally the literary texts, we wonder: What role did the literary language play as distinct from the spoken language (Vulgar Latin)? What factors influenced a particular text with regard to its word order? Was it the classical or late-ancient Latinity, the language of the Bible, or the spoken language? Furthermore, to what extent have artistic or rhetorical considerations determined or co-determined the choice of word-order type?

It is along these lines that the theses of E. Richter's 1903 book (still to this date the broadest study available on the subject) have been carried on, corrected and improved by such scholars as Linde, Haida, Stempel, and Koll.

Fundamentally correct though it was, E. Richter's position has been shown by later studies to be an extreme simplification of a much more varied picture. Firstly, the types that coexisted in Latin were more than two (S...V and SV...), and at least three are basic ones, counting VIPo. Secondly, the evolution from 'classical' to 'Romance' Latin order was not quite so linear. P. Linde, e. g., has drawn up some statistics which show how VEPo is found in 84% of the main clauses in Caesar's *De bello gallico* II, and in 93% of the dependent clauses, whereas Victor Vitensis (ca. A. D. 486) has only 37 and 63% respectively. On the other hand, before Caesar we find in Cato's (234-149 B. C.) *De agricultura* a VEPo ratio of 70% in mCls, 86% in sCls. This can be related to his known antiliterary and antirhetorical stand, austerely refraining from the 'frivolity' of *variatio*. Even his archaic imperatives in *-to* (*facito* etc.) stand

---

[39] Ibid., esp. fns. on pp. 272 and 284 of Patrick and Evans's ed.

after the Ob with monotonous regularity, and mostly in EPo. But the surprise is that Cicero, another classical exponent of *pura latinitas,* and what a one!, appears even less classical than Victor by such standards, since the figures for his *De republica* show 35 and 61%![40]

In Linde's computation, the percentages of VEPo appear as follows:

	mCls	sCls	
Cato *De agricultura*	70	86	
Caesar *De b. g.*	84	93	
approximate average of Cato, Cicero, Sallust	60+	75	
Cicero *De republica*	35	61	
Livy	63	79	
Tacitus	64	86	A
Gaius	64	80	
Seneca	58	66	
Petronius	51	67	
Pliny the Younger	50.5	68	B
Apuleius	58	62	
Firmicus Maternus (4th c.)	56	64	
Peregrinatio Aegeriae (ca. A. D. 400)	25	37	
Victor Vitensis *Historia*			C
persecutionum (ca. A. D. 486)	37	63	

As Koll pointed out,[41] group A falls somewhat above the classical average, group B below it BUT above Cicero, and only group C (for reasons suggested below) falls noticeably below Cicero himself.

The frequency of VEPo decreases, generally speaking, slowly but continually from the end of the Republic to the end of the Empire, but one must allow for striking individual variations within that long process. R. Haida has shown how even within a particular text the choice of different orders is dependent on types of verbs, types and lengths of sentences, and other factors.[42]

---

[40] P. Linde, "Die Stellung des Verbs in der lateinischen Prosa," *Glotta,* XII (1923), 153-178. Cf. H.-G. Koll, "Zur Stellung . . ." (1965), 243, 249 fn. 30, 262.

[41] Koll, "Zur Stellung," 263.

[42] R. Haida, *Die Wortstellung in der 'Peregrinatio ad loca sancta,'* Diss. (Breslau, 1928), cited in Koll, "Zur Stellung," 243.

Linguists may feel tempted to organize questions concerning word order schematically, for instance by reducing the possible types of construction according to such simplified formulas as S + V + Ob, V + S + Ob, S + Ob + V etc., with as many additional subdivisions and refinements as convenient. When everything is considered, however, this method must be resisted as misleading and ultimately inconclusive. First of all, a given scheme acquires entirely different meanings from language to language: *amo patriam* has the verb in initial position but is not like a case of initial verb in a language requiring the express subject pronoun.[43] More importantly, a language like Latin enjoys such an extreme mobility of parts and members that all sorts of hyperbatic disjunctions can make a scheme unrecognizable. E. g., what can one do with *matrem diligit suam?* Essentially the type here would have to be (S) + Ob + V, yet one cannot quite attribute an EPo to this verb.

Of the particular studies on individual medieval texts one of the most interesting, from the point of view of an application of modern methods in syntactical investigation, is F. Müller-Marquardt's work on the *Vita Wandregiseli* (1912). The author separately distinguishes the reciprocal positions of S and V, V and Ob (nominal and pronominal), auxiliary V and nominal predicate, participle, infinitive, attribute, and S, whether in mCls or sCls, distinctly (see esp. pp. 235-240).

But the most solid contribution is the very recent one by H.-G. Koll.[44] One only wishes it had been based on more extensive scrutiny of the texts chosen, instead of a few paragraphs or pages in most cases. Koll tabulated a statistical analysis of Latin texts going from Cicero to the ninth century, with results which correct Richter's rather summary conclusions and introduce a new, in its way quite startling interpretation of the dramatic change of order from Latin to Romance. To point out the more significant trends shown by Koll's analysis, I extract a few data from his complex tables. The respective percentages are, on a select basis, as follows: [45]

[43] A similar warning against division of the problem into schematic relative position of the verb (or other parts of the sentence) is also found in Koll, " Zur Stellung," 243-244.

[44] Koll, " Zur Stellung."

[45] The post-classical texts are examined on the chrestomathy by Rohlfs, *Sermo vulgaris latinus* (1956²).

	mCls Ob+V/V+Ob	sCls Ob+V/V+Ob
Cicero I Catilin. 20-26	66.7/33.3	88/12
Cicero De legibus II, 1-2	81.8/18.2	90.9/9.1
Varro Rerum rusticarum III, 13-15 Keil	63.6/36.4	64.7/35.3
Tacitus Annales II, 18-23	76.5/23.5	83.3/16.7
Bible: Itala/Vulgata (3rd-4th c.), Matth. 13, 1-9; 24-30 ed. Rohlfs	17.6/82.4	11.1/88.9
Peregrinatio Aegeriae (ca. A. D. 400) ed. Rohlfs	32.1/67.9	47.6/52.4
Compositiones Lucenses (6th c.) ed. Rohlfs	15.4/84.6	100/0
Vitae Patrum (middle 6th c.) ed. Rohlfs	19.2/80.8	33.3/66.7
Gregory of Tours (fl. 550-573) ed. Rohlfs	82.9/17.1	100/0
Chronicae Fredegarii (A. D. 613- 768) ed. Rohlfs	90.3/9.7	75/25
Vita Dagoberti III (after 843) ed. Krusch (MGH merow. II, 215- 328), chs. 4-6	46.8/53.2	50/50

One can easily observe how conservative the Latin language remained, in its written and relatively 'literary' form, with respect to word order, contrary to what one might expect and to Richter's explicit assumptions. It is also easily noticed that for the whole period covered, in the clear majority of cases the sCls display greater conservativeness than the mCls in preserving the classical VEPo, more specifically, the Ob + V–O rather than the V + Ob–O typical of Romance. Furthermore, one is more likely to find extreme cases of rigidity in VEPo at the end of this period than in the golden age of the first century B. C.–if one excludes Caesar. But Caesar, an extreme exponent indeed of the Atticist current, had, in this respect at least, one thing in common with the late imitators of the classic pattern, in that they both 'had something to prove' and in their relative militancy were being rather 'rhetorical' than merely 'natural.'

As a matter of fact, Caesar, an Atticist and analogist, militantly adhered to a strict linguistic and stylistic ideal of maximum simplicity, regularity, and logical clarity, in conscious opposition to the fullness and variety of expression propounded by the Asianists, to whom, in this regard, Cicero belonged.[46] To these observations must be added that, in the vast majority of the texts analyzed, the Ob + V–O is relatively more frequent when the Ob is a pronoun—a phenomenon of particular relevance in the light of the fact that the pre-verbal position of the atonous (proclitic) pronoun Ob became one of the basic norms in the Romance languages. Koll also reminds us that the temporary tendency to relatively greater frequency of VEPo in sCls than in mCls in Spanish and Italian must be regarded as a regressive feature rather than a remnant of Latin habits. We might add that even in German the rule of VEPo in sCls in its modern, highly rigid form, is a late development, not shared by other Germanic languages.

In the majority of the texts examined by Koll the proportion of classical word order (at least within the rather narrow confines of Koll's inquiry, namely that of VPo vis-à-vis the Ob) remains at least as high as in Cicero's and Varro's chosen texts until the Carolingian 'Renaissance.' Indeed, among the linguistically most corrupt Merovingian texts there are some which are not much less rigorous and consistent in classical word order than Caesar himself and the Cicero of such 'learned' prose as that of his *De legibus*. Of particular interest are such cases as that of the popular preacher Caesarius of Arles (†542), who consciously refrained from the mannerisms of traditional rhetoric in order to reach the people with unequivocal directness; nevertheless, in his speeches delivered in court or in the Senate, he respected the 'classical' order more consistently than Cicero. Koll (p. 264) appropriately asks himself whether one must assume that Caesarius shunned this last concession to 'literature' in his actual, oral delivery—a question we are unable to answer.

On the other hand—and this is Koll's rather surprising finding—, the only texts which for the whole period show a significant prevalence of Romance-type word order are, aside from some technical, mostly didascalic texts, those that lean on the syntactic patterns of Greek models, either as direct translations or reelaborations thereof, or also as works linguistically and stylistically under the influence of the Bible, which in turn borrowed its characteristic order from the Greek original. The *Peregrinatio Aegeriae* and perhaps some hagiographic literature of the early Middle Ages (and even such authors as Victor Vitensis) would seem to belong to this last

[46] Koll, " Zur Stellung," 262 fn. 67.

group.[47] Koll thus finds himself in a position to modify both Richter's conclusions (which placed the incipient triumph of 'Romance' order over classical order as early as the 4th century A. D.) and Linde's perspective, according to which the period from Caesar's death to the end of the Empire saw a steady process of erosion of VEPo. He finds Linde's line of argument self-contradictory in that, on the one hand, he makes Caesar, the "fanatical partisan of VEPo," the point of departure for his chronological schema, yet he admits that not only many of his contemporaries (such as Cicero, Sallust, Varro), but even the strict conservative Cato the Censor, one full century earlier, displayed a markedly lower incidence of VEPo than Caesar.

In conclusion, for the nine-century-long period as a whole, the only group of texts which clearly stands out as showing a noticeably lower incidence of VEPo and (S+)Ob + V–O than average seems to coincide with a direct or indirect influence of Christian texts through Bible-translations. To put it differently, Koll feels entitled to conjecture that the Latin Bible was a major influence in bringing about the Romance-type order, directly in Latin, indirectly in the Romance languages. This was due, he assumes, to the patterns surfacing in the Greek Bible, which coincided with the trend of Vulgar Latin. This trend, however, did surface to the level of written Latin thanks primarily to the Christian religious, non-literary writers' need to adhere to the ways of the common man in their style, whereas the rhetorical, literary milieus continued to resist this pressure from popular strata at least until the ninth century.[48]

In this exposition of Koll's hypothesis I believe I have somewhat moderated its terms, since Koll carries it to the point of asserting that even in the language as actually spoken by the people the change of order may have been conditioned by biblical and liturgical modes (p. 270). This position sounds exceedingly radical and unrealistic, although it will appear not entirely implausible if we only think of the undeniably decisive impact the language of the Church must have exerted in the linguistic evolution of the West in the High Middle Ages. This is not to deny the validity of the traditional explanations of the change, Koll appropriately warns. After all, the change in word order, like so many other major linguistic processes, may well have had *several* causes, such as, also, the

---

[47] Ibid., p. 262.
[48] Ibid., 269-272.

fall of the case-system, the changed rhythm of the phrase, and so forth.[49]
A rather obvious caveat might also be in order, to dispel any danger of a
naïve misunderstanding. Whereas E. Richter was basically concerned
with discovering, through documentary evidence, what was happening on
the unrecorded level of actual speech, Koll is always speaking of literary
usage, no matter how democratically inclined at times.

C. FRENCH

Meanwhile, historical linguists had started to turn their attention to
more circumscribed areas, and the first to receive an expert comprehensive
treatment was French. In his pioneering *Petite Syntaxe de l'ancien
français* (1919, 1930[3]) Lucien Foulet approached our subject in a brilliantly systematic manner, revolving around an original principle he introduced. He called it " le principe du moindre effort," and equated it with
" a desire for logic which for more than three centuries has operated
within the French language " (p. 268 ed. 1919, p. 340 ed. 1930 and 1963).
It is this *besoin de logique* that is chiefly responsible for the choice of
the direct order, $S + V + CC$, over the other three orders possible and
standard in Old and Middle French. For in the Middle Ages not only
was the construction more flexible, but the logical ties were easily
neglected. In saying *Li chevaliers le feri / de sa lance e fist grant anui*
(for *et LI fist*), Chrétien cavalierly overlooked the lack of concord, since

---

[49] I should add here that there is a monographic study of the impact of Gospel
Greek on the word order of translations into Gothic, Armenian, and Old Slavonic:
Georges Cuendet, *L'Ordre des Mots dans le texte grec, et dans les versions gotique,
arménienne et vieux slave des Évangiles:* 1ère partie, *Les Groupes Nominaux* (Paris,
1929).
On the *sermo humilis*, 'humble style' derived from the early translation of the
Bible (*Vetus latina*), and its lasting impact on subsequent Christian literature,
cf. such standard investigations as Josef Schrijnen, *Charakteristik des altchristlichen
Latein.* "Latinitas Christianorum Primaeva: Studia ad sermonem Latinum Christi-
anum pertinentia, I" (Nijmegen, 1932); Wilhelm Süss, "Das Problem der lateinischen Bibelsprache," *Historische Vierteljahrsschrift*, XXVII (1932), 1-39; Id.,
Studien zur lateinischen Bibel, I: *Augustins Locutiones und das Problem der lateinischen Bibelsprache.* "Acta et Commentationes Universitatis Tartuensis [Dor-
patensis]," Ser. B: Humaniora, XXIX, 4 (Tartu, 1932); Erich Auerbach, *Literary
Language and its Public* . . . (1965 ed.), pp. 45-52; Albert Blaise, *Manuel du
latin chrétien* (Strasbourg, 1955); Christine Mohrmann, *Études sur le latin des
Chrétiens* (3 vols., Rome, 1958-61-65).

le indicated an accusative and the following dative should have been marked with an additional *li*.[50]

Given the six possible arrangements of the sequence Subject–Verb–Complement, Foulet found that the following four were standard in medieval French:

$$
\begin{aligned}
&\text{a) } S + V + C \quad (I)\\
&\text{b) } S + C + V \quad (II)\\
&\text{c) } V + S + C \quad (IV)\\
&\text{d) } C + V + S \quad (VI)
\end{aligned}
$$

the first two having in common the position of the subject before the predicate, while in the last two the predicate precedes the subject. Order VI (d) is produced by the rule whereby whenever the DIRECT OR INDIRECT OBJECT comes at the outset of the sentence or clause, it calls for the INVERSION of the subject. This form is very common in poetry, much less in prose and in spoken French. But this rule is further extended by the consideration that, whenever ANY TYPE OF INDIRECT COMPLEMENT comes at the start of a clause, it determines inversion. Thus a secondary complement placed at the beginning, to wit a circumstantial complement of any kind, especially adverbs or adverbial phrases (but not conjunctions, to be carefully screened out), will produce type IV (c). As Foulet put it: *régime direct ou indirect* for VI, *un régime quelconque* for IV. This form IV is, on equal footing with I, the most common in Old French, and is respected both in verse and in the spoken language. Foulet's schema would have been even clearer had he used the term Object in the place of Complement (with the variant [C+]V + S + Ob for constr. IV), so that his fundamental rule of inversion for OF ("chaque fois que le régime direct ou indirect est placé en tête de la phrase, il y a inversion [constr. VI]"–p. 242 ed. 1919, 307 ed. 1930 and 1963: § 450) would have covered both type IV and VI without need of further explanation, instead of covering VI directly, and IV by extension. It would have sufficed to add: "(indirect) ou un complément circonstanciel." At any rate, this rule is "one of the most firmly established in the syntax of OF" (ibid.); it was only violated in the non-standard Construction III ("Complément–Sujet–Verbe"), of which Foulet discovered no more than two cases.

[50] Chrétien de Troyes, *Li Contes del Graal [Perceval]*, ed. Baist, based on Ms. B. N. fr. 794, 1210-1211.

The subsequent, and gradual, loss of the cases contributed to the fixation of type I, but its triumph was also powerfully aided by the historical fact that the classicists and the Encyclopaedists wanted the direct order because it was more *logique* (although they overstepped their rights in claiming it was also " natural "). This, I should add, is an obvious realization to whoever will only think that Italian also lost its cases, even while it remained remarkably more flexible than French in its word order. Foulet shrewdly underlines that modern French is clear not because it is logical, since medieval French could be quite clear even while it could be quite " illogical." It is clear because it WANTS to be logical.[51] The seventeenth-century equation of *clarté* and *raison* was, in this sense, a *non sequitur*: the stress was no more on clarity than it was on logic.[52] And, we may add, the other equation of nature and reason or logic was, in this strict sense, equally for domestic use. The effect of Latin on Romance (through Humanism) was, we may also add, to make it " logic-conscious"; if not " clearer," at least more " regular," and Latin conspired with scholastic logic toward a converging effort whose primary effect was to discriminate in practice between what is definitely not defensible in logical terms—and this was gradually rejected—and what was logically irrelevant (like the inversion) but sentimentally expressive—and this was further cultivated and refined.

Foulet's presentation was remarkable above all for the methodical clarity of its phrasing and the psychological slant of its explanatory framework. Otherwise the basic facts had already been prospected by a host of predecessors (starting perhaps with R. Thurneysen) and ably codified by Meyer-Lübke, who had also inserted an additional variant: When the adverbial complement comes at the head of the clause, the order can be either " A. V. S." or " A. V. S. R." (to put it in our own code: $C + V + S$ or $C + V + S + Ob$).[53]

---

[51] " Le français moderne n'est pas logique parce qu'il veut être clair, il est clair parce qu'il veut être logique" (p. 271). See pp. 36-44 and 306-344 (1930 and 1963 ed.) on construction and word order (§§ 49-58 and esp. 446-480).

[52] L. Foulet also published relevant articles on particular aspects of word order (mostly French) in *Romania*, XLVII (1921), 243-248; XLIX (1923), 118-126; L (1924), 54-93; LII (1926), 445-459; LIII (1927), 301-324. See Foulet's complete bibliography in *Romance Philology*, XXII (1969), 373-383.

[53] W. Meyer-Lübke, *Grammaire des langues romanes*, t. III (Paris, 1900), p. 832. See the whole ch. vi, pp. 792-850 on word order (§§ 712-762), which is treated concomitantly with the principles of accentuation. Cf. esp. p. 794 for bibliography

The focus of attention turned from diachronic to synchronic investigation, from medieval to modern French with the extensive monograph on *L'Ordre des mots en français moderne* by the Danish linguist Andreas Blinkenberg (in two parts, Copenhagen, 1928 and 1933). Without naming his predecessor, Blinkenberg made a careful screening of the assets offered by Weil's distinction between psychological subject and grammatical subject (or predicate)—a distinction which he received from a long line of more recent philosophers (like Wundt) and linguists.[54] In the end he recognized it as "indispensable," though not general enough to cover all possible types of sentences (Part I, p. 27). Weil's heritage is, however, clear in the use made of some stylistic twists. For example, the following colloquial phrases, 'natural' because 'popular': *La faim, je n'y pense plus; Mon stylo, je ne le vois plus; Cet homme, je le connais,* are said to be equivalent to these others: *La faim est oubliée; Mon stylo a disparu; Cet homme m'est connu* (therefore, implicitly, not to *Je ne pense plus à la faim,* etc.); which contains precisely Weil's message.

The examples just seen are cases of "dislocation," Charles Bally's term (*Traité de stylistique française,* 2 vols., Heidelberg, 1909) which Blinkenberg found irreplaceable (I, 22). Dislocation indicates a movement from an organized state of the sentence either toward a truly disorganized one (e. g. when one answers the statement *Tu es riche!* by *Riche! Moi!*) or a simply unorganized one (as in the three examples above).

The treatise is methodically articulated on the basis of the "syntaxic groups," from the major ones (subject–predicate, verb–object, etc.) to the minor ones (noun–adjective, preposition–noun, etc.). Students of OF had by that time firmly established that medieval 'inversions' were not, by and large, a rhetorical exercise in the classical, conscious or 'artificial' sense, but largely cases of Germanic influence—namely influence from an "impressive" language, concentration of attention being the basic criterion in Germanic word order. Such patterns in German developed further and became fixed over the centuries, whereas in French

---

of previous studies on medieval word order in French. Meyer-Lübke found the other Romance languages often conspiring with French on word order, but with less regularity. Ch. iv (§§ 530-690, pp. 595-770) deals with "Le Groupe de Propositions."

Also cf. Rosalyn Gardner and Marion A. Greene, *A Brief Description of Middle French Syntax* (Chapel Hill, N. C., 1958), esp. ch. vi: "Word Order," pp. 142-148.

[54] Blinkenberg even repeats Weil's phrase "notion initiale et but de l'énoncé" (I, 27).

they suffered an implacable regression. (In other Romance areas, as the Italian, Germanic syntax had practically no influence.) Without any display of diachronic interest, it is precisely the upshot of this progressive "degermanization" of French since the Middle Ages that Blinkenberg covered. The degermanization was fortunately incomplete, as shown by some cases of recrudescence of inversion in today's French.

W. von Wartburg, *Évolution et structure de la langue française* (Leipzig, 1934, 1937²; Bern, 1946³, 1949⁴, . . . 1958) repeated the six possible constructions of OF, with the necessary qualifications, and followed with attention their gradual reduction to the only one acceptable to Malherbe's generation (pp. 104-105 and 133-134 of 3ᵈ ed.). The result was, he pointed out, that the verb which in OF had enjoyed the dominant position (second place in the clause), thus expressing the "activism" of the medieval speaker ("La vision immédiate de l'action comme émanation de la personne et s'identifiant avec la personne, est ce qui domine l'esprit et la langue "), yielded that position to the subject: people were now more given to reflection and calculation ("plus adonnée à la réflexion et au calcul "). In the twelfth century one would have said *maintenant s'agenoillent li six message* (Constr. IV), but Joinville already writes *maintenant li six message s'agenoillent*. On the other hand, Constr. VI survived well into the fifteenth century, as in the phrase *Un autre parlement assembla ce duc*.

As to the structure of the sentence, medieval activism allows no more than mere justaposition of the clauses (even though von Wartburg decries Vossler's excessive claims). All the prosewriters cultivate a "style coupé," even "haché," but from the fourteenth century on the transitions become more sophisticated, the number of available, diverse conjunctions increases, and the phrasing starts to become periodic (pp. 105-106 and 137).

We have noticed, ever since the Middle Ages, a gradual erosion of the classical stress on harmony in the efforts to define both sentence structure and word order. Logical, intellectual, or psychological considerations became more and more decisive and appeared to afford the more convincing explanations. Yet the old theory never lost its appeal altogether. Eugen Lerch, for one, wrote an authoritative paper on "the essence of the clause and the importance of melody for the definition of the clause" ("Vom Wesen des Satzes und von der Bedeutung der Stimmführung für die Satzdefinition," 1938). He rejected the definitions of the phrase available to that date and, in particular, denied the possibility of a psychological definition. He proposed, instead, that melody be taken as the point of departure toward such definitions—adding, however, that a proposition cannot subsist without meaning.

In two widely acclaimed general manuals, *Histoire de la langue française* (1930) and *Le Génie de la langue française* (1943, 1947²), Albert Dauzat assimilated Blinkenberg's data and the many more that had started to come in from both historical and general descriptive linguists.[55] Since Dauzat's two works are complementary we will take them together.

Word order ("l'aspect le plus important de la syntaxe"—*Génie*, p. 230), which in Latin was pre-eminently expressive, has gradually acquired a logical value in French, replacing the syntactic function of the cases. The maximum degree of crystallization has been reached in present-day popular speech, "which adds to the poverty of its phraseology a great monotony of construction." Literary language, and especially that of poetry, has remained more conservative and has thus preserved some of the old agility. The spoken language of the educated class remains, as usual, in between the two (*Histoire*, p. 425).

The *rejet*, rejection of the verb to the end, after the object, according to the schema $S + C + V$, was particularly popular in Latin both in main clauses (*rex populum amat*) and in subordinate clauses (but the ancients could already scoff at the abuse of *esse videatur* for cadence in Ciceronian periods, a conspicuous case of *rejet*). Vulgar Latin, on the other hand, already showed a strong inclination toward placing the verb before its object, as well as placing the subject first. Then a reaction took place when the Frankish conquest brought to France a Germanic influence which became conspicuous through a recrudescence of inversion (of the subject after the verb) and *rejet* (*Histoire*, 432-433; *Génie*, 237). Yet, OF seldom used the *rejet* in main clauses (*li rois le peuple aime*) outside the more ancient texts (esp. *Saint Léger*), while the relative frequency of it in subordinates is due to Germanic influence. Take the *Serments de Strasbourg*, whose syntax is altogether German:

In quant Deus savir et podir me dunat . . . . Si Lodhuwigs sagrement, que suon fradre Karlo jurat, conservat . . . .

---

[55] See *Histoire*, pp. 425-439 on word order, 462-467 on "L'expressivité (Syntaxe affective)"; *Génie*, pp. 228-254 on definition of syntax and word order, 279-285 on "Syntaxe affective." See also, for its exemplary didactic clarity in the exposition of the issues at stake, A. Dauzat's *Les Étapes de la langue française* (Paris, Presses Univ. de Fr., Coll. "Que sais-je?", 1944, 1948), pp. 25-26, 46-47, 65-66.

Similarly in the *Eulalie*, out of the first four lines, three offer some kind of inversion. But the *rejet* begins to make itself scarce at an early date: this is part of a general trend toward the type of construction S + V + C, which is already present in two clauses out of three in the *Chanson de Roland*, three out of four in Joinville. (Yet these statistics appear to be contradicted by those of von Wartburg, who assigns 42% of the clauses in the *Chanson de Roland* and 11% in Joinville to the construction C + V + S.)[56] The other constructions are eliminated little by little, and our everyday speech allows no more than a few scattered relics to survive, mostly stereotypes and proverbial phrases (*honni soit qui mal y pense; geler à pierre fendre*) (ibid.). A special case, also of Germanic origin, is the *rejet* of the past participle in main clauses: Villehardouin, *Les Grecs avoient le pont coupé*. This survived at least until La Fontaine, who could still write *J'ai maints chapitres vus* ("Le conseil tenu par les rats," *Fables*, II, 2) (*Histoire*, 434).

German is "an impressive language, that can place at the head of the sentence any word toward which it wants to call the attention"; French eventually abandoned the impressionistic movements brought to it by German because, besides having lost the cases which made such flexibility possible, it had to reflect the genius of the French people, which were becoming rationalistic and imbued with logic (Lerch) (*Histoire*, 432; *Génie*, 229). Dauzat echoes here an argument so often repeated that no one will feel inclined to take issue with it, provided this relationship of logic-mindedness and direct order is not taken as one of cause and effect. Direct order cannot be *ipso facto* a sign of rationalism, for in this case it would be found only by mistake in the language of the English, who are not "rationalists" and yet could claim the order S + V + C as their own with a title at least as good, if not better, than that of the French, as Jespersen has shown (see below).

Traditionally, normal order and inversion were traced to calm reasoning and emotional impetus (or "impressionism"), respectively, and on this basis they were assigned one to grammar, the other to rhetoric. The distinction reappears in modern linguistics through the substitution of stylistics for rhetoric. For Charles Bally the role of emotion in the *parole* looms so large that it covers almost the entire province of "style." He insisted on the significant structural divergence between a mode of logical

---

[56] Cf. von Wartburg, *Évolution et structure* . . . , p. 133 ed. 1946.

communication, which produces such phrases as *Vous ne pouvez pas songer sérieusement à une chose pareille*, and the "segmented," emotive phrase: *Une chose pareille! Voyons! sérieusement, y songez-vous?* [57] This latter mode, as we know, does not only belong to colloquial speech: the eighteenth-century French prosewriters were fond of it (think of Diderot), and Batteux thought it equally significant (remember his examples *au feu!, au voleur!, Un serpent, fuyez!*) as Bally did.

In his *Linguistique générale et linguistique française*, Bally produced a most articulate analysis of the far-reaching implications contained in a methodic study of compositional forms.[58] He pointed out how a sentence (and its order) can be constructed in three essentially autonomous ways. Since the complete statement includes at least two elements, a theme and a purpose, *thème* and *propos* (this being a *dirème*, beyond the elliptical *monorème*, such as *Magnifique!, A la porte!, My kingdom for a horse!, Les aristocrates à la lanterne!*), the way to tie the two can be either coordinate (*Il y a là un oiseau et [cet oiseau] s'envole*), segmented (*Cet oiseau, il s'envole*), or continuous (*Cet oiseau s'envole*). His own terminology was *phrase coordonnée, segmentée, liée* (§§ 61 ff.).

More generally still, we can tie our words together according to the principle of analysis or that of synthesis, respectively corresponding to linearity and non-linearity (*dystaxie*) (§§ 213 ff.). The former is characteristic of French, the latter of German. Again, the former is eminently progressive (in the logical and grammatical sense, not in the melodic sense—§§ 313 ff.) in that every element depends on the preceding and adds something to it. It is listener-oriented, and it is parallel, on the phonetic-melodic level, to the oxytonous rhythm, characteristic of French: in *La terre* TOURNE the stress is, typically, on the last element, the predicate AND determinant, just as in the single words the accent falls at the end (§ 436). Dystaxic arrangement, on the other hand, is parallel to barytonous rhythm. It is speaker-oriented, and it includes such typical features as disjunction (also possible, as a complicating element, in French: *ne* PARLE *pas; tu* M'abandonnes; *j'ai* BEAUCOUP *souffert*, but a favorite of German) and anticipation (whenever the determinant precedes: *Grand fut mon étonnement; meines Vaters Haus*—§§ 265-272).

To his continuing comparison of French and German, Bally also added

[57] Bally, *Traité de stylistique française* (Heidelberg, 1909), I, p. 312.
[58] See the 4th ed. (Bern, 1964), esp. §§ 61-109, 265-272, 308-461, 593-594.

a final *geistesgeschichtlich* touch where he defined French as "clear" and German as "precise"; more exactly, "if French loves clarity, German has a passion for precision." Clarity simplifies, precision goes in depth; clarity works by antitheses, dichotomy, classification; precision wants to see things through, tends to penetrate them even to the risk of getting lost in them (§§ 593-594).

The *Syntaxe du français moderne* by G. and R. Le Bidois (2 vols., 1935-38, 1967²) leans on Bally for his "capital opposition": "Le français ordonne les termes de l'énoncé par détermination croissante, . . . l'allemand par détermination décroissante." French shows a "séquence progressive" as against the "séquence anticipatrice ou synthétique" of German (2ᵈ ed., vol. II, p. 2). Furthermore, the authors go back to Weil's distinction between ascending construction (again exemplified, as first by Weil, with Turkish and, to some extent, German) and the descending one (as in French and English) (ibid.). They recognize three types of word order: logical, affective or psychological, and aesthetic or stylistic, this last aiming at such effects as variety, emphasis, suspense, surprise, etc. (II, 2 ff.). Most of the second volume goes on to analyze inversion of the subject after the verb in main and in secondary clauses, the place of the direct object and of the adjective and adverb, and, finally, the types and functions of subordinate clauses.

The study of subordination has been, even more than word order, the Cinderella of linguistic science. But it has begun to elicit the attention it seems to deserve. Petar Guberina has subjected French clauses to systematic analysis on the basis of their logical form, as expressed through formal subordinating conjunctions, or their affective form, either expressed through generic conjunctions or centered on the semantic value of the parts as well as their ordering.[59] And, to mention just one more example, Alexandre Lorian has begun a series of studies of the places occupied by secondary clauses in the French complex sentence.[60]

It is well known that in France, as well as in England and the United States, the rhetorical tradition has continued stronger than elsewhere on the scholastic level. We can hardly close our survey without sampling

---

[59] Guberina, *Valeur logique et valeur stylistique des propositions complexes* (Zagreb, 1954²).

[60] Lorian, *L'ordre des propositions . . . : La cause* (Paris, 1966). See, also, Kr. Sandfeld, *Syntaxe du français contemporain: Les propositions subordonnées*, nouv. éd. (Geneva, 1955).

this sort of production. For France I will choose a rather recent and particularly lucid manual: Émile Loubet, *La Technique de la composition française.*[61] The author distinguishes three manners of sentences. "La phrase brève," exemplified by Voltaire, is eminently analytical and aims to give a particularly clear presentation for the benefit of a large public. The "phrase longue inorganisée" produces a style which shines by neither purity nor character, yielding as it often does to the music of the words; Lamartine is a good case in point. The "phrase longue organisée" obviates the deficiencies of the preceding, as in Bossuet. It is and must be "tight" (*liée*); that is to say, it admits, on principle, neither parentheses nor "hors-d'œuvres." It also must have a definite rhythm graced with alternation of high and low tone-levels (*silences—sonorités*) (pp. 115-119). One will easily recognize here the traditional categories of the cut, loose, and periodic styles. In conclusion (p. 121), we hear the same advice of the rhetorical tradition: variation is always commendable, no single style should be used exclusively. It was Cicero's advice, too.

Writers can also show a marked preference for the binary arrangement of their sentences, and this is usually antithetic (Voltaire), or a ternary one (Proust, we can also add), which is usually progressive ("valeur croissante"), sometimes regressive ("valeur décroissante").

Contemporary manuals tend to avoid the term "natural order," but they do still speak of logical order, which they will distinguish from the sentimental and the aesthetic. In dealing with the inversion of the subject Loubet intends to show how the ancient exploitation of the "emphatic" frontal position of a complement is still alive (pp. 99-101):

Ainsi se tenait, devant ces bourgeois épanouis, ce demi-siècle de servitude (Flaubert)

Là se montrent ingénuement la grossièreté et la franchise; ici se cache une sève maligne (La Bruyère)

Peu de temps après parurent les casques des municipaux (Flaubert)

Fière est cette forêt dans sa beauté tranquille, et fier aussi mon coeur (Musset)

Heureux sont les hommes libres!

Terrible était la menace qui pesait sur notre armée.

[61] (Paris, 1954): see, esp., pp. 99-101, 115-121.

To these we could add the examples of inversion surviving in bureaucratic style (*inversion administrative*), such as: *Ont été arrêtés pour vol
les nommés X, Y, Z* (Ferdinand Brunot, *La pensée et la langue*, p. 5);
Ont comparu . . . ; Sera passible de. . . .[62]

D. ITALIAN

A detailed and intensive study of word order in individual writers of
modern literatures—a subject still largely untapped—promises to yield very
interesting results. For Italian, the recent investigations by a Yugoslav
linguist, Domenico Cernecca, on Dante's *Vita Nuova* (1965) and Manzoni's *Promessi Sposi* (1963) have been as fruitful as they are rare.[63]
I believe it is fair to say that this scholar tends to simplify the matter
by offering all departures from the normal $S + P + Ob$–O as stylistic
variants, after the suggestion of B. Pottier.[64] The question is that Pottier

---

[62] "Statements with Inversion" are treated from the vantage point of transforma-
tional grammar in Ch. iv of the new French grammar by Th. Mueller, E. N.
Mayer, and H. Niedzielski, *Handbook of French Structure: A Systematic Review*
(New York, 1968).

Y. Le Hir, *Rhétorique et stylistique* (1960), pp. 83-89 assembles, in a rather
cavalier pot-pourri, a number of testimonies from various authors and critics. Nevertheless he justly brings out some less than central yet important aspects of order.
I will glean some of his typical cases. Take the "phrases optatives véhémentes"
with a personal pronoun singled out by Maupas (1607), such as *puissè-je*. Or the
placing of the *adjectif épithète*: "Vous êtes un trompeur insigne ou un insigne
trompeur. Je dis l'un et l'autre pour contenter deux grammairiens de mes amis qui
ne sont pas d'accord sur la préséance de l'adjectif." (Balzac, *Lettre à M. de Girard*,
1647, 160.) In this regard (apropos of Fénelon's *de riantes images*) it is curious
to note that Napoléon Landais, *Grammaire générale ou résumé de toutes les gram-
maires françaises* (1833) could use *style coupé* apparently as synonymous with
'informal': "Dans le style coupé, il peut être indifférent de dire riantes images
ou images riantes, . . . mais dans le style périodique, leur place peut influer de
bien des manières sur la beauté des phrases." The placing of the *pronom régime*
in different positions in the same phrase could represent an elegant variation in the
18th century: *Voyez-le et le consolez* (Lévizac), although de Musset's *Poète,
prends ton luth et me donne un baiser* could be due to other reasons, such as rhythm
and the discreet avoidance of the strong *moi*. Most interestingly, order could have
a morphological impact when a postponed participle was affected by concord:
Aucun étonnement n'a leur gloire flétrie (Corneille, *Horace*); *avoir toute honte bue*.

[63] Cf. D. Cernecca in Bibliography.

[64] Pottier, *Systématique des éléments de relation* (Paris, 1962), p. 66: "Lorsque

speaks of "choices," whereas several cases of inversion submitted by Cernecca are not free stylistic choices of the author, but compulsory grammatical patterns. At any rate, one observes that Italian, like all modern vernaculars, followed the pattern already introduced by Vulgar Latin and ecclesiastical Latin and soon tended to adopt the progressive descending order of subject—predicate—complement as the preferred norm. Other patterns were allowed, especially in secondary clauses, either for expressive (stylistic) reasons, in which case they remained optional, or, but perhaps less frequently, as variations due to particular syntactic circumstances. The Tobler-Mussafia law, e. g., is neither stylistic nor semantic, but phonetico-syntactic, and it subverts the direct order. Similarly, interrogative, optative, hortatory, and exclamatory sentences bring about a relatively compulsory kind of inversion.

The first "decidedly vernacular sentence in the Italian area" that has been preserved, the *Placito Capuano* of A. D. 960, contains a clear case of typically Romance inversion (Ob + P + S), leaning on another typically Romance feature, the repetition of the object in the pronoun form *le* (*ripresa*), which did not appear in the equivalent Latin formula of this document's Latin counterpart, dated 954: *Sao ko kelle terre, per kelle fini que ki kontene, trenta anni LE possette parte Sancti Benedicti.* 'I know that the order of St. Benedict had possession of those lands within the boundaries indicated here for 30 years.' [65]

Cernecca identified 231 cases of inversion of the subject in the prose sections of the *Vita Nuova*, 90 of them in main clauses, 141 in subordinate clauses. In the *Promessi Sposi*, instead, the proportion favors the main clauses, and the overall count is 1900. The researcher feels entitled to conclude that OIt, at least as witnessed in the *Vita Nuova*, was more inclined to use inversions than modern It., since the resulting ratio is of 5 to 3 between Dante's and Manzoni's prose narratives.

---

la structure de la langue présente deux ou plusieurs constructions, sans que la signification en soit fondamentalement changée, il s'agit de variations stylistiques."

See, on this matter, Cernecca, SRAZ, 19-20 (1965), but also 15-16 (1963), 59 with fn. 47.

[65] Cf. A. Schiaffini, *I mille anni della lingua italiana* (Milan, 1960), pp. 15-20; P. Meriggi, "La ripresa dell'oggetto in Italiano," *Volkstum und Kultur der Romanen*, XI (1938), 1-30; D. Cernecca, "Struttura della frase . . . ," p. 143. The corresponding Latin formula of 954, preserved in the 11th-century *Chronicon vulturnense,* read: "Scio quia ille terre, per illos fines . . . , per triginta annos possedit pars Sancti. . . ." Note *ille terre* in the nominative as subject, not object, and see the explanation offered by G. Contini, cited in Schiaffini, op. cit., p. 53.

It is, however, important to note that, even while the syntactic organization of the sentence definitely owed a great deal to imitation of Latin, word order did not—not, at least, until much later times, as in the Boccaccian habit, sanctioned by the Bembian school of the sixteenth century, of placing verbs at the end. Most types of inversion, in particular, except again for the "learned" imitative patterns of later times—perhaps as negative in their true artistic import as the back-shifting of verbs—, owed nothing to the impact of Latin, but were Romance in spirit, even if one includes the influence of Germanic patterns so ably illustrated by Foulet for French. Such typical cases as: *QUELLE PAROLE che tu n'hai dette in notificando la tua condizione, AVRESTÚ operate con altro intendimento* (*Vita Nuova* xviii, 8); *e però che la battaglia de' pensieri vinceano coloro che per lei parlavano* (xxxvii, 4), displaying the order: Ob + P + S, are purely Romance.

In offering his contribution on the *Promessi Sposi*, Cernecca begins by surveying the sparse literature on the subject (Vockeradt, Fornaciari, Rohlfs, Richter, Colagrosso, Schiaffini, Terracini, Segre, Gossen, Kollross, Herczeg, F. Čale, and a few others), with the expected conclusion that the question of Italian word order is in dire need of more basic and extensive study. He claims that his detailed statistics do not bear out Wartburg's contention (typical of the generic attitudes of linguists vis-à-vis Italian order) that, in contrast with the "absolute rigidity" of French as used by many of the classics, Italian enjoys an almost unlimited freedom in its word order and sentence structure. This exaggerated expectation has been, true enough, damaged in its contrastive nature by Le Bidois' studies showing that contemporary French is far from immune to inversion and, actually, "à l'heure actuelle le français écrit est de plus en plus enclin à l'inversion" (*L'inversion . . . contemporaine*, p. 411), which corresponds to the literary historians' remarks on Condillac's influence on Romantic prose and later developments (see above).

The original six variant constructions for the OF elementary clause hinging on Subject, Verb, and Complement gave way to four and, lastly, only two, one (direct) in spoken speech, the other (C + V + S) in literary use.[66] C. Segre (*La sintassi del periodo*, now in *Lingua, Stile e Società*: see esp. pp. 161-174) has shown the same six in OIt: (1) S + V + Ob; (2) S + Ob + V; (3) Ob + S + V; (4) V + S + Ob; (5) V + Ob + S; (6) Ob + V + S. (The order corresponds to that

[66] Foulet, 3d ed., § 447; Le Bidois, II, 6.

established by Foulet for OF.) Cernecca shows that they are all still extant in Manzoni, but with very different weight. (1) and (2) have become purely grammatical, since (2) is only used with objects in the form of atonous pronouns (so that Manzoni ridded literary Italian of the Latinizing postponement of the verb). (3) has similarly become, according to Cernecca, "grammatically normal" (but with a 'spoken' flavor, one must add: *le sue parole io l'ho sentite*). Cernecca characterizes (4) and (5) as affective-stylistic (p. 58). I would rate (5) as rather bordering on the colloquial: *ha ragione quel giovine*. As to (6), I would not find it simply affective-stylistic: *approvava ogni cosa che dicesse un commensale* [67] is practically 'grammatical' (attraction of the inevitable prolepsis inherent in the accusative relative pronoun); *la legge non l'ho fatta io* (28) is 'colloquial,' from the spoken language, typified here by the very common use of the proleptic object with *ripresa* in the atonous pronoun which historically evolved into a proclitic and therefore precedes the verb. *Un qualche demonio ha costei dalla sua* (341) is emphatic (stress on first element, here the object), similar but not grammatically analogous to the preceding because of the remaining close bonds between the three elements (in the preceding *la legge* has an 'absolute' position, practically loose from grammatical ties), and is of the kind which modern languages have generally crystallized in the neo-formation *è . . . che* or equivalent: *è un demonio che costei ha dalla sua; c'est un diable que cette femme a de son côté; it is a devil that.* . . . Once again, *di belle chiacchiere faranno questi mascalzoni* (187) is in tune with the movements of speech.

On the other hand, the reason or effect of the inversion in pattern (6) can only be established case by case. Contrary to *un qualche demonio ha costei dalla sua*, where the front-shifted object is emphasized, in *la legge non l'ho fatta io* the anticipated and then 'recalled' element (It. *ripresa*, F. *rappel* in the pronoun *l'* repeating or recalling *la legge*) is not the one to receive emphasis, but the inverted subject *io*, the meaning being *non ho fatto IO la legge; non sono io che.* . . . In an exemplary study of the *ripresa* Meriggi pointed out that this phrase is of the type where the *ripresa* has the function of balancing the construct melodically and structurally by placing subject and object at opposite, and abnormal, ends.[68]

<hr/>

[67] *I Promessi Sposi*, Caramella ed., 1933, p. 76.
[68] The *ripresa* can also have a semantic impact: in *il giardino L'ho visto, ma la*

As to type (4), one must note that, together with (6), this is the basic form of inversion, and that in modern Italian, just as in modern French and, much more frequently, in OF and OIt, it is regularly triggered by the anteposition of complements or complementary syntagms, including temporal and circumstantial locutions of all sorts, adverbial locutions, and some conjunctions. Only in modern Italian the inversion is no longer automatically triggered (in French it is only in limited cases: *Aussi croit-il . . .*).

It would seem that any further classification of such statistical facts demands a clearer definition of the role of *ripresa* (with the complicating factors of the proclitics, which do not follow laws of word order), and should separate all cases of prolepsis. The example given above for construction (3), *le sue parole io l'ho sentite*, is not correctly represented by the schema Ob + S + V, but by something like the following: Ob, S + ob + V. Such refinements seem imperative when we study authors who, like Manzoni, kept themselves methodically close to the spoken language. (Even for OIt Segre never included proclitics in his paradigms.)

If one adopted the terminology "objective–subjective" or "impulsive–non-impulsive" respectively proposed by Blinkenberg and Lerch to replace the traditional "direct–inverted," it might be fair to characterize those of the above examples which play on emphasis as "subjective," those others which echo colloquial modes as "impulsive," though the terms are distinguishable only in subtle ways and are practically equivalent.

To sum up, Cernecca has counted circa 1,900 cases of inversion in the *Betrothed*, that is an average of 3 per page, of which 1,100 are in declarative main clauses, 800 in subordinate clauses. He has not counted, as less relevant, interrogative, optative, imperative, and exclamatory clauses, nor, because the inversion is here *de rigueur*, declarative incidental clauses (*—disse don Rodrigo—*). Quite relevant is Cernecca's tentative answer to the question raised by G. Herczeg: [69] "The section on word order in the various grammars—last of them, the historical grammar by Rohlfs—sin, in our opinion, by not clearly separating the compulsory from the optional usages of inversion." Cernecca notes that this question has never been solved for Italian by any linguist. He, then, offers the following con-

---

casa no "giardino" is more important; in *il giardino ho visto, non la casa* "casa" is more important. Cf. Meriggi, "La ripresa dell'oggetto," *Volkstum und Kultur der Romanen*, XI (1938), 1-30, cited.

[69] See *Lingua Nostra*, XVI, 4 (1955), p. 119.

clusions based on the single and isolated example of the *Betrothed* (although his later analysis of the *Vita Nuova* yielded similar results). Inversion is compulsory in: incidental phrases with *verba declarandi*; main or secondary clauses in which the verb *essere* 'to be' is preceded by the particles *ci, vi* (as in *there is* . . .); implicit (infinitive) secondary clauses—modal, causal, consecutive, final, temporal, but especially objective—; gerundive and participial absolute phrases. Nine cases, then, in which the normal construction demands inversion (viz. *voltata la stradetta, drizzando lo sguardo, gridavano esser lui il capo,* etc.—but some of the examples are wrong: *la stradetta* is the object: [*avendo*] *voltato la s.*; the second is equally incorrect: there would be inversion only if the subject were explicit: *drizzando egli lo sguardo*).

Aspects of Italian sentence structure have received much greater attention, especially thanks to exploratory investigations by linguists and philologists with particular interest in stylistic phenomena (e. g. Luigi Sorrento, Leo Spitzer, Alfredo Schiaffini, Benvenuto Terracini, Giacomo Devoto, Cesare Segre . . .). This is not, however, the place to survey such contributions because, by and large, they have seldom assumed the form of a comprehensive formulation of general theories. A few scattered examples should suffice to remind us of the type of problems that have been more consistently raised.

Giuseppe Lisio's pioneering work on Dante and his early contemporaries (1902) elicited only limited response, perhaps chiefly on account of its mechanical, positivistic method, until the recent studies by Cesare Segre, just as Schiaffini's analyses of medieval Latin and early Italian prose down to Boccaccio have been widely praised and quoted, but without the active follow-up the subject deserved.[70] I have attempted elsewhere to show how pertinent would be a thorough study of Dante's poetic sentence structures, still largely lacking.[71]

An intriguing Romance innovation is the prolepsis—most typically, anticipation of object at head of clause, often in absolute position followed by *ripresa* in the form of proclitic pronoun, as in *questo dubbio io lo intendo solvere*. Terracini has found it to be characteristic of the prose of the *Vita Nuova*, so that inversion itself often appears as little more than a case of prolepsis. Similarly, Dante pays great attention to the conclusive

[70] See my Bibliography, Medieval Section, for these titles.
[71] See my "Periodic Syntax . . . in the *Divina Commedia*," RPh, XXI (1967), I-22.

part of his clauses, often consisting of a carefully and expressively chosen
adverb in -mente or an absolute adjective equivalent to a gerundive or
adverb. This resembles the *cursus* in rhythmic effect, but without slavishly
clinging to its fixed patterns.[72]

A stimulating essay of structuralist analysis of composition among the
Stilnuovo poets, and particularly Dante, has been recently due to the
combined efforts of Roman Jakobson and Paolo Valesio.[73] "Composition" is here understood in another sense than the one with which we
have been concerned: it refers to inner patterns of numerically based
regularities in grammar and thought, somewhat along the lines of Dámaso
Alonso's epochmaking studies of semantic and formal symmetries in
Petrarch's and the Petrarchists' sonnets.[74] Still, something here is pertinent
to us, in that the researchers have not only attempted to discover patterns
in the creative works, but have grounded these patterns in the conscious
theories of the authors.[75]

Italian scholars have been much intrigued by a peculiar lack of logical
sense in sentence structure often found among medieval and Renaissance
authors, and speak of para-hypotaxis when the writer treats as coordinate,
clauses which would appear to demand subordination.[76] The phenomenon is, of course, far from limited to Italian. A splendid example, especially interesting for its relatively late date, would be the following from
Leonardo da Vinci:

Uno volendo provare coll'alturità [= authority] di Pittagora come altre
volte lui era stato al mondo, *e* uno non li lasciava finire il suo ragionamento,
allor costui disse.

---

[72] Terracini, "Analisi dello 'stile legato' della *Vita Nuova,*" *Pagine e appunti
di linguistica storica* (1957), 247-263, esp. 254-263.

[73] "Vocabulorum constructio in Dante's Sonnet *Se vedi li occhi miei,*" *Studi
Danteschi,* XLIII (1966), 7-33. Also the rejoinder to a critic in P. Valesio,
"Vocabulorum Constructio," *SD,* XLV (1968), 167-177.

[74] For Alonso's studies see my Ch. IV, A, and fn. 61 in that section.

[75] For some time, analogies have been drawn, along such criteria of multiple
symmetries, between literature, or rather poetry, and the visual arts: cf. August
Schmarsow, *Kompositionsgesetze in der Kunst des Mittelalters* (4 vols., Leipzig-
Berlin, 1920-1921).

[76] Cf., typically, L. Sorrento, "Il fenomeno di paraipotassi nelle lingue neolatine,"
Sintassi romanza: ricerche e prospettive (Milan, 1950), ch. ii. See, also, S. Skerlj,
Syntaxe du participe présent et du gérondif en vieil italien (Paris, 1926), esp.
Part II, ch. vii.

Allor postulates coordination between *lasciava* and *disse*, and yet *lasciava* is in a tactical twilight between its grammatical nature of finite mood, which would situate it as an independent clause, and the link through the conjunction *e* with the gerundive *volendo*, by which it should rank as a coordinate secondary clause.[77]

Concerning modern Italian, I should not pass without mention a subtle but potentially far-reaching re-orientation which has begun on the question of what happened to this language in the course of the crucial experiences of the eighteenth century. G. Herczeg[78] has, convincingly enough, associated himself to Migliorini's approach and censured Isidoro del Lungo (and even Schiaffini) for perpetuating the classicistic and puristic prejudice of Italian having been thrown into a serious "crisis" by the impact of French in the Settecento. He maintains that what happened then was a true *rinnovamento* rather than a crisis, since the influence of French was less important than the inner needs of adaptation to the requirements of practical expository prose. Furthermore, we can add, the linguistic manners which were being discarded were, more often than not, far from "pure" and "natural" to the language. Again, Herczeg[79] has identified as originating in the eighteenth century the "modern" reduction of complex periodicity to juxtaposed sequences of nominal complements, preferably appended to the subject rather than to the verb, in the form of nominal appositions (e. g., introduced by the preposition *con*) or, in other cases, of nominal predicates. He has also revealed the presence of inversion whenever such appositional syntagmas are anteposed to their subject, with notable effect of modernity and efficacy: *Avvezzi a gemere . . . , immersi nell'ozio . . . , i Turchi trascuran gli studi . . .* (Casti, *Viaggio a Costantinopoli*),[80] rather than *I Turchi, che sono avvezzi . . . e immersi. . . .* It is especially the qualitative adjectives (*avvezzi, immersi*)

---

[77] Augusto Marinoni has put it well: "We are left unsure as to whether we should regard *lasciava* as a principal verb para-hypotactically tied with the subordinate *volendo*, or *volendo* and *lasciava* as two subordinates, the latter of which implies a missing conjunction (*e POICHÉ uno*), thus reserving to *costui disse* the function of main clause." See Leonardo, *Scritti letterari*, ed. Marinoni (Milan, B. U. R., 1952), "Facezia 11," pp. 42-43.

[78] Herczeg, "La struttura del periodo," in *Problemi . . .* (1965).

[79] Herczeg, art. cit. and "Le enumerazioni appositive nella prosa moderna," *Lingua Nostra*, XXIV (1963), 49-56. Also Id., "Stile nominale nella prosa italiana contemporanea," *Acta linguistica Hung.*, IV (1954), 171-192.

[80] Cf., Herczeg, "Struttura del periodo," p. 367. See Casti, *Opere* (Brussels, 1838), Part I, p. 437.

that lent themselves to such 'inversion' (rather, hyperbaton) by being disjoined from and anteposed to their qualified.

Continuing studies by M.-L. Müller-Hauser, Max Mangold, and Hans Oster on the same problems in French and Spanish, Carl Theodor Gossen has studied unusual cases of word order and syntactic fragmentation for stylistic-affective purposes in modern Italian (prominence and emphasis).[81] As early as 1948 Mario Puppo had made some keen observations on the persistence of Gorgianic figures in modern prose by isolating symmetric patterns in the members of the sentence and especially the use of two- and three-cola groups (*dicoli* and *tricoli*) in the prose of such disparate authors as Tommaseo, Carducci, and D'Annunzio.[82] Mate Zorič has picked up this clue and carried it into an analysis of binary rhythm in the contemporary narrator Bonaventura Tecchi.[83]

E. ENGLISH

1. The relevant literature in English is too vast to be methodically summarized in little space. We will limit ourselves, once again, to a few samples. The study of English with modern linguistic methods can be thought to have started with the American scholar W. D. Whitney (1827-1894) and the British Henry Sweet (1845-1912). Sweet's influential *A New English Grammar, Logical and Historical* (Oxford, 1892-1898, 2 vols., often reprinted) is also remarkable for its detailed treatment of both sentences and order with modern perspectives and terminology.[84]

We need not linger on this work because, on the one hand, Sweet's analysis of sentence structure introduces material which is not directly related to the issues raised within the rhetorical tradition (our primary concern still remaining the transmission of the ancient compositional

---

[81] Gossen, *Studien zur syntaktischen und stilistischen Hervorhebung im modernen Italienisch* (Berlin, Akademie Verlag, 1954). Ch. ii, pp. 63-111, deals with Word Order, distributed according to: 1) front-shifting (of subject, of predicate, of complements); 2) back-shifting of subject (in affirmative sentences, in interrogation); 3) fragmentation with 'pleonastic' pronouns (= repetition of complement by means of a pronoun, usually proleptic).

[82] Mario Puppo, *Tommaseo prosatore* (Rome, 1948), esp. pp. 67, 69-74, 149-153.

[83] Mate Zorič, "Il ritmo binario nella prosa narrativa di Bonaventura Tecchi," *Studia romanica et anglica zagrabiensia*, 27-28 (1969), 153-162.

[84] See, esp., vol. I, §§ 446-510 and vol. II, §§ 1759-1952.

theory), and, on the other hand, whatever Sweet said on word order was fully inherited by subsequent linguists, signally Jespersen.

The first subdivision of our subject was chiefly carried on in composition manuals, the 'practical rhetorics' of our day. Let us look at one of these.

A long-time best seller among composition manuals, William Strunk, Jr.'s *Elements of Style* (the "little book" at Cornell since 1918) [85] clung, for one, to the classic formulas. With characteristic, peremptory pithiness, it announced to all college freshmen that "The proper place in the sentence for the word or group of words that the writer desires to make most prominent is usually the end." Next to that, "The other prominent position in the sentence is the beginning." Generally, the EPo belongs, therefore, to the "logical predicate, that is, the *new* element in the sentence," while the IPo bestows relevance to anything unexpectedly found there: "Any element in the sentence, other than the subject, becomes emphatic when placed first." Therefore, the S will acquire emphasis by inversion: *Through the middle of the valley flowed a winding stream.* These rules go further than the clause, even further than the sentence: "The principle that the proper place for what is to be made most prominent is the end applies equally to the words of a sentence, to the sentences of a paragraph, and to the paragraphs of a composition" (pp. 26-27).

The examples are equally perspicuous as the rules. On EPo:

Humanity has hardly advanced in fortitude since that time, though it has advanced in many other ways.
Humanity, since that time, has advanced in many other ways, but it has hardly advanced in fortitude.

The revised form is a rudimentary case of periodic style, commended by Strunk when it effectively holds off the main statement till the very end. And on IPo:

Deceit or treachery he could never forgive.

I will lend Professor Strunk one further example of EPo, of a somewhat more eloquent nature. Instead of saying: "I believe the half slave and half free government cannot permanently endure," Lincoln put it better in his speech of June 17, 1858:

---

[85] See the new ed. revised by E. B. White (New York, 1959). Quotes refer by page to this ed.

I believe the government cannot endure permanently, half slave and half free.

Finally, we are given a good example of the continuing vitality of periodic sentence even in today's English, at least on a somewhat formal level. Consider this sentence (p. 27):

Four centuries ago, Ch. Columbus, one of the Italian mariners whom the decline of their own republics had put at the service of the world and of adventure, seeking for Spain a westward passage to the Indies as a set-off against the achievements of Portuguese discoverers, lighted on America.

Try to change it or break it up, you will not improve it. It is periodic because it is tight, suspenseful, progressive, and climaxed.

We have seen above how Weil had methodically postulated a relationship between inversion and periodicity. The matter may bear further illustration. A current manual of English composition gives an example of "periodic sentence" by first offering the following normal construct: "Henry James began the writing of his novels by finding a central idea, letting it develop in his mind, and then working it out in extensive written notes." It then proposes a more effectively emphatic rephrasing in which an inversion of the whole AND of the subject would hold the reader in suspense until the very end: "Only after finding a central idea, letting it develop in his mind, and working it out in extensive written notes, would H. J. begin a novel." [86]

2. For an early example of structuralist description within general linguistics I will choose L. Bloomfield's *Language* (1933).[87]

Bloomfield had little to say on sentence structure as we understand it (but he originally proposed that coordinating and subordinating conjunctions be regarded as distinct parts of speech in English—p. 198), more on word order, especially to stress its unpredictable adaptation to the peculiar structures of individual languages. In his determination

[86] Edwin T. Bowden, *An Introduction to Prose Style* (New York, 1955, 1956 . . .), p. 24.
[87] See, esp., pp. 197-201. See, also, Bloomfield's *An Introduction to the Study of Language* (New York, s. a.), esp. pp. 113-114, 171, 174-175, 186-188. Bloomfield denied validity to the opposition of psychological to logical subject (114 fn.). Considering the author's ideal closeness to Bloomfield's school of thought, it may seem curious that Charles F. Hockett's *A Course in Modern Linguistics* (New York, 1958) gives practically no specific room to either complex sentence structure or word order.

never to denote something through a traditional formula, he offered his highly idiosyncratic terminology in exchange. He began by contrasting the "taxemes [= features of grammatical arrangement] of order" in familiar languages: thus, e. g., "standard German differs from English in allowing only one attribute (word or phrase) of the verb to precede a finite verb: *heute spielen wir Ball*" etc. (p. 197). A neat, economic way to summarize the basic principles of German inversion. There follows a detailed explanation of the complicated, rigid French system for arranging pronominal particles around verbs (e. g., *il ne me le donne pas*).

But only languages without inflection and without diversified parts of speech could operate exclusively by word order: "Viewed from the standpoint of economy, taxemes of order are a gain, since the forms are bound to be spoken in some succession; nevertheless, few languages allow features of order to work alone: almost always they merely supplement taxemes of selection" (i. e., patterns of construction consisting of selection of words by classes and sub-classes, along with their flectional morphemes) (p. 198). The major portion of space is then given to Chinese and Tagalog, languages relying most heavily on word order because they have only two basic parts of speech ("full words" and "particles" or "markers").

Not surprisingly, the task of providing the most exhaustive modern treatment of English word order has been shouldered by Otto Jespersen in Part VII (Syntax) of his monumental work, *A Modern English Grammar on Historical Principles* (1949).[88] I shall extract from this volume what I should consider the most relevant points, with a few examples and a few remarks added of my own.

Jespersen organizes his material around a number of formal principles, the first of which being what he calls the Principle of ACTUALITY; this is to say that "What is at the moment uppermost in the speaker's mind tends to be first expressed" (p. 54). The term marks a refinement of the traditional criterion of "importance"; it appropriately lays stress on the psychological or subjective factors, and gives one of the reasons why the subject is generally assigned a front position. "But it may also be the object, or the predicative, or any other element that is drawn forward in this way." The extreme consequences of this "principle of

[88] See chs. ii and iii, pp. 53-125 of this Part VII. Part III, ch. x (10.1-10.5) deals with the position of relative pronouns; chs. xi-xviii with "nexus" (relationship between subject, verb, and object). Only 11.16 in this Part deals with word order, and only as an anticipation of Part VII.

actuality or interest" can be seen in "the jumble often heard in the speech of small children and sometimes in the careless speech of undeveloped minds," where it is carried through to the point of chaos.

Second, the Principle of COHESION: Ideas that are closely connected tend to be placed together (remember Condillac's *liaison des idées*). This is why the subject, object, and predicate tend to cling to the verb, which is the center of the sentence (56).

Emphasis may be achieved, as Sweet says (II, § 1766), by putting the word in any abnormal, that is, unexpected, position, especially front- and end-position. Thus longer phrases or, in complex sentences, whole secondary clauses are generally placed in such outer positions, which can be called "extraposition" (57). All this is related to Behaghel's 'Gesetz der wachsenden Glieder,' the Law of the Growing Members, for which Jespersen's term is: Principle of Relative WEIGHT. This goes beyond word order, but to some extent determines it: "Lighter elements can be placed near the center, while heavier ones are relegated to more peripheral places." See *take it off* versus *take off your hat*. We must add, however, that this principle operates in different ways in different languages and, to be properly understood, it demands a clear distinction between position of emphasis and position of importance. In Latin, e. g., first and last are most important; in English, first and central are most important, while first and last are emphatic for secondary elements.

On the whole, the development has been, in English, towards a fixed word order as a simple consequence of the loss of cases (59).

English appears to hold a privileged position with respect to simple direct order (S V Ob in sentences containing a subject, a verb, and an object):

"Even if I concede that our statistics did not embrace a sufficient number of extracts to give fully reliable results, still it is indisputable that English shows more regularity and less caprice in this respect than most or probably all cognate languages, without, however, attaining the rigidity found in Chinese, where the percentage in question would be 100 (or very near it). English has not deprived itself of the expedient of inverting the ordinary order of the members of a sentence when required, e. g. for the sake of emphasis or poetic expression, but it makes a more sparing use of it than German and the Scandinavian languages" (61).

The percentages in question would be: Goethe (poetry) 30, modern German prose (Tovote) 31, Anatole France 66, G. D'Annunzio 49, Bible 94, Kipling Thackeray Wells 95, Darwin 99.1, Shaw 99.8, Chaucer 84,

Shakespeare 93 prose—86 poetry, Milton 88 prose—71 poetry, Pope 68, Gothic prose 41, Beowulf 16, etc. It is not quite clear how far Jespersen might have meant to carry his comparisons vis-à-vis French, since he does speak of languages cognate to English, but he includes authors from French and Italian.

Going on to more specific reasons for inversion and transposition, the Danish linguist states a modified version of the Germanic law of inversion which Foulet had found valid in OF: "The same word-order V S occurs, but is not glottic,[89] in cases where a sentence begins with some word other than the subject; the front-position may be due to something in a preceding sentence. As remarked above (p. 59) . . . , this order agrees with a custom found extensively in all the cognate languages, but has largely been given up in Present English. Very frequently we have a lesser verb so that the order is v S V, or, in some v V S: *Here will be your place* (Thackeray) " (67-68).

In fact, as stated before by Jesperson (59), TRADITION can be another determinant of order, namely when fixed patterns due to linguistic laws are now mechanically reproduced in the manner of stereotypes, as in such expressions as *up went the flag, well might he say* (59). This formula now sounds stilted and is, on the whole, dying but within it one can observe the general flexibility of the language. For example, the formula can be strengthened (along the line of the Germanic law of inversion, C + V + S) when an additional adverb appears in front: *now off you go*. In other cases, the front-position of the tertiary element can produce inversion: *off went the car, up rose the other fellow, then came in the ambassador,* but the inversion can be invalidated by the principle of Relative Weight: *off he went* (80). And, we can add, the formula is still alive, especially in formal style, when the anteposed element is a weightier complement than just a conjunction or adverb: *for them are all our praises; to them goes our blame; in Peru is the second Japanese colony on the continent; that morning arrived the first ambassadors.*

ANAPHORIC REPETITION (76) refers to what some scholars (French, Danish, Dutch) call an 'anaphoric' pronoun, e. g. *that* or a relative pronoun at the beginning of a clause. This back-reference explains the front-position of such words as *so* (which may or may not cause

---

[89] By 'glottic' J. means that which serves to distinguish one kind of sentence from another (p. 62).

inversion: *so am I, so long a time,* but also *so I am*) and *neither* (which always does: *neither am I*). The above appear to be cases of grammatical attraction, in that the pronominal particle moves to the head of the clause by attraction toward the antecedent for which it acts as a substitute. But then we may have stylistic attraction when the anaphora is a free option of the writer, as follows: " By a stylistic trick, which for more than a century has been gaining ground in literature, a word is repeated and for EMPHASIS given front-position: *Where every one feels a difference, a difference there must be* " (76). Note here the vitality of chiastic arrangement, as old as speech itself—at least artistic speech. This stratagem is particularly interesting in clauses with *if,* more rarely *where: as for your soul,—if soul you have* . . . (Eden Phillpotts, *The Three Knaves,* 1912) (77). Indeed one remembers President Lyndon Johnson occasionally using such rhetorical devices, as when he said: *It is now time to act, and act we should and act we must.* A double anaphora with inversion.

The natural place of the object is after the verb. Exceptionally (archaically and poetically), it will be placed before the full verb: *Hamlet, thou hast thy father much offended.—Mother, you have my father much offended.* This is, of course, poetic, but aside from the possible impact of Latin construction on Elizabethan English, this inversion is functional in terms of emphasis.

Jespersen also speaks of Stress and Rhythm influencing order, of the " empty there " (*there is nothing wrong*), and many more secondary factors, but this sampling may suffice to show his method and his most typical achievements.[90]

Of course Fowler and Fowler's classic *The King's English* is, as usual, studded with smart examples, some of which can supplement the above.[91] The authors talk of BALANCE INVERSION, as in the following: *On these two commandments hang all the laws and prophets.* Balance is used here not in the classical sense, which was rhetorical, meaning symmetry in structure and sound, *concinnitas,* but in a grammatico-logical sense, equivalent to placing some terms in a prominent position " to protect them from being virtually annihilated, as they would have been

---

[90] The empty *there* can produce inversions with full verbs as well: *There has never been known a tribe that.* . . .

[91] Cf. pp. 189-203 on word order in the 3ᵈ ed. (Oxford, 1931). Perhaps the authors overstress the distinction between prominence and emphasis (p. 191).

if left at the end" (see p. 191). We also read here about NEGATIVE INVERSION (*nowhere is this so noticeable*), INVERTED CONDITIONALS (*Should I, Had I* = *If I should, had* . . .), and EXCLAMATORY INVERSION, when the particle *How* is omitted, as in *Bitterly did I regret that folly.*

Speaking of exclamations, may I note that, once again, English is not very rigid in these sequences, including the so current inversion Predicate or Adverb + S + V or Copula, especially when beginning with *How* (*How good he was! How well it sounds!*). See the successful alternation of inverted and non-inverted patterns in Browning's lyrically mocking: *How sad and bad and mad it was—But then, how it was sweet! Sweet* acquires emphasis from the unexpected chiasm.

A modern grammatical device that has often elicited comments is the reduction of a main clause to a relative in function of the impersonal construct *It is* . . . *that*, F *C'est* . . . *qui* (*que*), It *È* . . . *che* (Jespersen's "Cleft Sentences," VII, 147-149). It is often a way of attracting attention to an element which cannot easily be stressed in the modern languages simply by inversion, and it amounts to transforming into a grammatical subject the syntactically secondary element of the clause which Weil would have called the psychological subject. Thus, to avoid the emphatic transposition of the object by front-shifting in *Persistence in the pursuit of an aim he valued above everything*, the sentence can be restructured into something like *It was persistence that he valued* . . . , or *Persistence was that which he valued* . . . , *C'était surtout la persistence qu'il appréciait.* The formula has proliferated with extraordinary vitality, especially in current speech, and one can even hear something like *If it is go you must* for *If you must really go*—if *to go* was felt as the true subject.

Cleaving the sentence in this manner, to use Jespersen's term, has practically become the easiest way for English and French to enhance an element—aside from the purely phonetic emphasis expressed through delivery alone. Italian and Spanish have kept inversion more freely available to them for such purposes. Take the current television and radio advertisement: *We don't know, but we must be doing SOMETHING right.* The alternative would be . . . *but THERE IS SOMETHING we must be doing right.* A Sp. translation could render the emphasis in the 'phonetic' way: *No sabemos, pero tenemos que hacer ALGO bien*, or with the cleft sentence (*pero hay algo* . . .); but the translation actually heard over a Sp. radio program had chosen inversion: *No sabemos, pero ALGO debemos estar haciendo bien.*

The danger in present-day English is not so much that inversions are being dropped, but that they are becoming abused or, rather, misused through a weakened sense of their function. The inversion in *I'm not discussing her personal life. Merely do I compare occupations* is incorrect, since *merely* does not bear emphasis.[92] Otherwise the stylistic potential inherent in the device still remains unlimited: take the humorous Biblical reminiscence heard in a recent harangue, *C. I. A. people move in mysterious ways their wonders to perform.*

"Beauzée's law" remains equally relevant today; we should be as respectful of it as our ancestors were. Compare Hamilton's and Washington's draft of Washington's Farewell Address. Hamilton's: "'Tis our true policy as a general principle to avoid permanent or close alliances." Washington's: "'Tis our true policy to steer clear of permanent alliances with any portion of the foreign world." Both respect the "law": indeed, the two complements *as a general principle* and *with any portion* . . . are not strictly necessary for the thought, and seem placed there simply to balance the sentence in line with the "law." But Hamilton's version suffered from the disjoining position of that weak complement. Today's writing is fraught with examples of our weakening sense of rhythm, and it is especially intriguing when a minimum of attention to the principle inherent in Beauzée's hallowed rule could have preserved BOTH rhythm AND logic or clarity. Whoever drafted the Trustees' current policy for the University of North Carolina should agree on second thought that, instead of writing:

Permissible grounds for suspension or discharge are misconduct of such a nature as to indicate that the faculty member is unfit to continue as a member of the faculty, incompetence, and neglect of duty,

he would have better written: ". . . discharge are incompetence, neglect of duty, and misconduct of such . . . faculty."

Similarly, the strong temptation to place the object immediately next to the verb can disrupt the better rhythm of the sentence and endanger clarity to boot. Consider this case of journalese:

Today's issue of *Der Stern* carries a picture of the Stalin family picknicking, reportedly a few months before the suicide of Svetlana's mother on its cover.[93]

[92] "Count Marco" in the *San Francisco Chronicle.*
[93] *San Francisco Chronicle,* 8-7-1967.

Obviously a minor inversion would have done the trick: "carries on its cover a picture. . . ." The opposite sin is found in a speech by President Nixon, where an uncalled-for inversion of the indirect complement removes the object without need for emphasis:

Once we end this war, we can remove from hanging over our young people the draft.[94]

Both my lack of competence and the merely descriptive-historical character of this study forbid my going into the particular contributions of the more modern schools of linguistics. Without any attempt at an evaluation of results, however, it will be relevant to point out the growing interest among linguists for the understanding of all the complex mechanisms of sentence structure in the broadest sense. Considering the date when the author started working on it (the first draft is said to have been ready in 1939), I believe that the first systematic attempt to produce a comprehensive study of all such mechanisms within a general syntax along structuralist principles is the *Éléments de syntaxe structurale* by Lucien Tesnière (Paris, 1959). It is an impressive achievement, and an interesting pointer of possible further developments.

Within the recent evolution of structuralist approaches we have witnessed a remarkable effort on the part of both linguists and literary critics to bridge the widening gap between their respective disciplines by stressing the role of syntax as a central concern in the making and interpreting of poetic speech. We have thus heard such direct statements as the following: "Syntax . . . is the groundwork of the poet's art" (W. Nowottny); "the significant differences in literature lie in an author's syntactical maneuverings" (H. R. Warfel); and, most authoritative of all, "the poetic resources concealed in the morphological and syntactic structure of language, briefly the poetry of grammar, and its literary product, the grammar of poetry, have been seldom known to critics and mostly disregarded by linguists but skillfully mastered by creative writers" (R. Jakobson).[95] What interests us directly is that this new Linguistics or

---

[94] For an example of didactic, detailed exposition of possible causes for inversion of subject after the verb, see G. Scheurweghs, *Present-Day English Syntax* (London, 1959), pp. 3-11. The most recent historical syntax of verb-centered English constructs is the monumental *An Historical Syntax of the English Language* by F. Th. Visser (Leiden, 1963-1968, 3 vols.).

[95] Cf. Roman Jakobson, "Linguistics and Poetics," in Thomas A. Sebeok, ed., *Style in Language* (Cambridge, Mass., 1960), p. 375, repr. in Seymour Chatman

ENGLISH   397

Linguistic Stylistics presents anew, with all the sophistication of modern
tools of research, the traditional notions of periodic and loose sentences
(which Sinclair will call "arrested" and "released structures"), main
and subordinate clauses ("free and bound clauses" by the same linguist),
balance symmetry and parallelism (which S. R. Levin chooses to designate
as "conventional couplings" as distinct from the "syntagmatic couplings"
according to whether they consist of rhyme, alliteration, and metrical
equivalences, on the one hand, or of grammatically equivalent forms, on
the other—all of them being effective functors of "systemic pressure"),
and, of course, word order.

and Samuel R. Levin, *Essays on the Language of Literature* (Boston, 1967), pp.
269-322: cf. p. 319; Harry R. Warfel, "Syntax Makes Literature," *CE*, XXI
(1960), 251-255; Winifred Nowottny, *The Language Poets Use* (London, 1962),
p. 10. Also see, for grammatical and syntactic analyses of literary language, Donald
Davie, *Articulate Energy* (London, 1955); Francis Berry, *Poets' Grammar* (London,
1958); Roger Fowler, ed., *Essays on Style and Language* (London, 1966), esp.
Fowler, "Linguistic Theory and the Study of Literature," pp. 1-28; Allan Rodway,
"By Algebra to Augustanism," ibid., 53-67; J. McH. Sinclair, "Taking a Poem
to Pieces," ibid., 68-81; and other essays by R. Fowler and Geoffrey N. Leech,
ibid.; S. R. Levin, *Linguistic Structures in Poetry* (The Hague, 1962); M. A. K.
Halliday, "The Linguistic Study of Literary Texts," in *Proceedings of the Ninth
Intern. Congress of Linguists* (The Hague, 1964), pp. 302-307; S. R. Levin,
"Poetry and Grammaticalness," ibid., pp. 308-314 (both Halliday and Levin repr.
in Chatman and Levin, op. cit., pp. 217-223 and 224-230); G. Leech, "'This
bread I break'—Language and Interpretation," *REL*, VI (1965), 66-75; A. A.
Hill, "An Analysis of *The Windhover*: An Experiment in Structural Method,"
PMLA, LXX (1955), 968-978; Nicolas Ruwet, "L'Analyse structurale de la
poésie," *Linguistics*, II (1963), 38-59; J. P. Thorne, "Stylistics and Generative
Grammars," *Journal of Linguistics*, I (1965), 49-59. Most of these and some more
contributions are listed and discussed in the informed essay by Stanley B. Green-
field, "Grammar and Meaning in Poetry," *PMLA*, LXXXII (1967), 377-387. See,
also, Glen A. Love and Michael Payne, eds., *Contemporary Essays on Style* (Chicago, 1969) and Donald C. Freeman, ed., *Linguistics and Literary Style* (New
York, 1970).
   May I conclusively stress the point that the evolution of our subject has had logic
in it, as once expressed in a definitory way by Lerch: "Soweit in der Wortstellung
einer Sprache Freiheit herrscht, gehört die Wortstellung in das Gebiet der Stilistik
[or rhetoric, as was the case in antiquity]; soweit sie geregelt worden ist, gehört sie in
der Syntax." Eugen Lerch, *Historische französische Syntax*, III. Band (Leipzig,
1934), p. 250.

CONCLUSION

1. The chief purpose of this study has been the descriptive analysis of a large body of literature, mainly technical, which at different times and places attempted to explain the structure of sentences and ordering of their elements, both on the linguistic and artistic levels. Given the extensive proportions of this literature as well as its inherent repetitiveness, it should not be surprising if some criteria of selectivity have been applied. The author can only hope that these criteria have appeared neither too arbitrary nor inconsistent. After 1600 the geographical areas and languages covered have been the English, the French, and the Italian. Once again, in attempting to strike a balance between the goal of exhaustiveness and the requirement of manageability, the two crucial stages in our history, i. e. antiquity and the French eighteenth century, have been handled with a mind to reasonable completeness, while the others are mostly based on representative sampling.

The reader may now welcome the opportunity of seeing brought together some of the main threads of our survey.

2. The original motivations that determined the outcome of the ancient rhetorical system apparently have to do with the impact of the musical element of poetic discourse, which became spontaneously applied to prose. In a manner as excessive for him as it was characteristic of that ancient predicament, Quintilian equated composition with the art of versification: "Composition holds in prose the same place that versification holds in poetry" (IX, iv, 116). The ideal period was the square one with four cola, physiologically and aesthetically akin to the lyrical quatrain, and it was scanned according to emotional tension, acoustic needs, and physiological possibilities (breath), rather than with regard to logical divisions, since it was, in its whole and parts as well, fairly independent of logic or syntax (it might not contain the subject or predicate of the sentence, nor end with a full stop).

The notion of 'natural' or 'right' order goes back to some viewpoints established by such Stoic linguists as Chrysippus, who responded to logical or dialectical postulates. It is mentioned, with more or less explicit reference to Stoicism, by Dionysius, Quintilian, Demetrius, Apollonius, and especially Priscian, with an increasing degree of approval (Dionysius cited it only to reject it as an aberration). It is precisely with Priscian that, in the light of this important grammatico-logical orientation, matters of composition first entered with full right the domain of grammar, without forcing the rhetoricians to give them up. And it was also Priscian who established the view that the 'right' order is the 'natural,' right because natural, and natural because 'logical.' With this we witness, for better or worse, both the birth of 'syntax' and, more specifically, of the understanding of sentence structure and word order as part of it within a general logical orientation. Until then, grammarians, rhetoricians, and stylistic analysts had remained content with the identification of the first and last places in the sentence as the most important because of their weight on the hearer (*vis*)—ostensibly a psychological approach to the matter.

3. One of the most striking transformations that took place in the medieval sentence is the shift toward a logical awareness of pauses and divisions, which underlines the tendency to replace periodicity with sequences of propositions set off by *cursus* serving as punctuation. Another fundamental step forward in the direction of linguistic syntax coming into its own can be seen in the fact that the main places for discussion of word order are now the *artes grammaticae*. The rules on order set down in such treatises are a conspicuous codification of what was later to become a distinctive feature of Scholastic Latin, to wit its unashamedly analytic arrangement. The doctrine of 'natural' or 'right' order, which became so crucial with the medieval speculative grammarians, significantly corresponds to the peculiar arrangement of both the medieval Latin clause and that of the Romance languages.

4. Soon enough, composition understood as style found its due place both within formal rhetoric and grammar, as well as independently within general literary criticism. Such a process clearly began to take place in the sixteenth century, Italian literati leading the way. All in all, the humanistic experience of the Renaissance was marked by a determined shift away from logic, with grammar and rhetoric becoming again the central ones of the Trivium arts—a shift of emphasis which affected our subject in a most direct way.

5. The seventeenth century witnessed a division of trends between the empirical (fastening on the arbitrariness of linguistic phenomena) and the rationalistic (differently issued from Scaliger, who insisted on general or universal grammar, and Sanctius, who focussed on the self-enclosed grammatical system of an individual language). This alternative of 'usage'

or 'reason' is carried on from Latin to the vernaculars, and becomes most conspicuous in the opposing schools of Vaugelas and, finally, Port-Royal.

The label of 'Atticism' attached by some critics to the current in favor of plain style in the course of the baroque period is especially justified from the narrow vantage point of compositional forms, with specific reference to a systematic abandonment of true periodicity. In this sense the Atticism of baroque writers reminds us of the ancient grammatical anomalists, with their basic intuitionism vis-à-vis the crucial aspects of language, just as the later Atticism of the eighteenth century will recall, instead, the basic rationalism of ancient analogists.

6. It is also important to keep in mind, as broader background to our subject, the traditional theory of the 'virtues of style.' Originally, purity and clarity, the first two virtues of elocution, were regarded as essentially a part of the grammatical curriculum, while brevity, appropriateness, and distinction (*ornatus*) were characteristically rhetorical in nature. This distinction practically disappeared only in the eighteenth century in an important process of absorption of all these criteria into the rationalist analysis of style which in that century attained to the dignity of a fine art.

In the formation of French classicist doctrine rhetoric was at first so overwhelming as to penetrate and guide even works most explicitly grammatical (e. g. Vaugelas'). Its subsequent displacement by logic under the aegis of Port-Royal had the after-effect of allowing grammar to take the upper hand, signally in the area of composition theory. Thus the rhetorical (and 'poetical') virtues of *ornatus* were replaced in emphasis by those of clearness, correctness, and preciseness (inherently 'prosaic') as the supreme qualities of good style. This rationalist criticism informs most of late-seventeenth- and eighteenth-century reflection on literary writing, and replaced the basic hedonistic sensualism of antiquity. More particularly, the taste for copiousness and roundness of expression gave way first to a taste for brevity (akin to the laconic style of ancient Stoics), this latter to be later replaced in its turn by a stronger need for grammatical regularity.

Despite the important ancient background and the antecedents of Priscian and the *modistae*, syntax, in a specifically modern sense (as J.-C. Chevalier has demonstrated), was truly born at the hands of Arnauld and Du Marsais as a transition from the notion of regimen to that of complement, to wit, by going beyond the conception of word sequences as governed by no more than a relation between a governing word and a governed one. Only then was the clause effectively grasped as a whole,

a 'logical' structure, *proposition;* and only then was the ordering of
its parts comprehended as an overall system of interrelationships rather
than a simple question of relative position between two single elements,
the subject or attribute and the verb or noun. Furthermore, whole clauses
could be perceived as complements to others, thus relating the structure
of the sentence to that of the proposition, and thus understanding the
complex nature of subordination.

Cut style (*coupé*, a variety of loose style, carried to extreme in the *haché*
style) is the outstanding achievement of the period 1600-1800. At the
same time the question of word order generated a lively and all-pervasive
polemic, the two opposite camps being labeled as *métaphysiciens* (the
logically-oriented) and *mécaniciens* (the empirical intuitionists or expres-
sivists, partisans of *sentiment* or emotion and imagination). A deeper
insight into the contrastive nature of modern and ancient modes of expression is afforded by the distinction of 'descending order of construction'
(initial position for main things—upheld by the *métaphysiciens*) and
'ascending' one (end position for main things—favored by Batteux, leader
of the *mécaniciens*).

7. Echoes of Mascardi's criticism of Malvezzi, first major European
cultist of the chopped-up style, were heard as far as France; but he
was also praised by Lancellotti as early as 1636 as perhaps the inventor
of a new manner of Senecan compositive texture. The extreme curtness
of expression and the elimination of grammatical ligatures, typically the
conjunctions, served the purpose of eliciting an intuitive response from
the reader, who had to supply the missing links of the discourse with his
own imagination, thus actively reconstructing the rational framework of
the argument. The polemic reveals the chronological priority of Italy both
in experimenting with extreme forms of curtness and looseness (Malvezzi,
G. B. Manzini, 1629) and in bringing the opposition between periodicity
and cut style out into the open.

The seventeenth century was much concerned with the form of sentences as an outstanding aspect of style. In the following century critics
chose to fasten upon problems of word order. Within the general reorient-
ation represented by the Arcadian school, for Italians direct order became
symbolic of a natural way to be opposed to the academic artificiality of
their acquired literary habits. The partisans of modernity rallied under
this banner while organizing their attacks against purism, the academicism
of the Crusca, the Latinizing patterns long established in language and
style, and the spiritual stagnation inherent in a literariness divorced from

vital issues. In this way Italy was aligning itself with the rationalistic solicitations coming out of France. The French current which upheld the rights of imagination through the defense of inversions and the affective or expressive aspects of language was also well represented in Italy, both in the form of a conservative and nationalistic reaction against Bouhours' 'classical' stand and in the form of a forward-looking, Condillac–oriented critique of a narrowly intellectualistic view of language. Baretti and the Verri brothers stand as the foremost advocates of direct order; Cesarotti synthesizes the two major trends of the century by espousing modernity even while he justifies inversions within a comprehensive view of language and style.

8. The history of our topic in England is one of progressive triumph of the 'plain style.' Critics and technographers uphold this style and abet its triumph. The definitive analysis of the nature of periodic and loose structure can be found in George Campbell (1776), who not only discovered the impossibility of true periodicity in modern languages—at least if we define it in classical terms—, but clearly distinguished the period as made of members all interdependent 'backward and forward,' that is, on both preceding and subsequent members, whereas a loose sentence looks only backward. When the members of a sentence do not even lean on their antecedents to form a complete statement, we have, as it were, wrong punctuation: the sentence should be broken up into several units. Richard Whately was soon to adopt this test of the Retrodependence of Members.

9. I have stopped around 1800 because the technical tradition suffered a break in continuity about that time. But I am far from implying thereby that the issues suddenly and permanently lost importance or vitality. To prove the contrary it would suffice to point out, e. g., Coleridge's stressing of "the resemblances between that state into which the reader's mind is thrown by the pleasurable confusion of thought from an unaccustomed train of words and images, and that state which is induced by the natural language of impassioned feeling." For the realization of such parallels he praised Wordsworth's theory of diction, and both Coleridge and Wordsworth were hereby transferring an ancient thought into the very midst of the Romantic preoccupation with the centrality of emotion and that rendering of it which makes poetry.[1]

---

[1] Coleridge, *Biographia literaria* (1817), ch. xvii.

Indeed, rhetoric proper lost much of its vitality, though not without producing a most original 'final' system with Herbert Spencer (1852). This positivist philosopher postulated a mode of arrangement which identifies poetic speech, true 'style,' as the acme of expressive economy and efficiency, to be understood as based on a thorough subversion of the eminently 'prosaic' principles of Aristotelian discourse. Just as this latter posited a movement from the known to the unknown, Spencer suggested that economy of vital energies would require an ascending order going from the referent to the referred, from vague quality to precise substance, and from the modifier to the modified. Instead of conveying each thought by a series of approximations successively correcting the erroneous pre-conceptions that have been raised—which is what happens in the analytical movement—, the ascending order manages to convey each thought step by step without liability to errors, thus going, in practice, from complement to verb to subject.

10. Meanwhile, modern linguistic speculation on our subject was ushered in by Henri Weil's brilliant study (1844), in which he grounded the principles of word arrangement on psychological factors within the framework of Kantian idealism. He covered word order broadly, to include sentence construction and the whole train of discourse.

The modern period has seen the theory of composition reduced to aspects of linguistics or stylistics, depending on whether one is dealing with necessary sequences or optional variations. Charles Bally most typically shows the end of this process—a process which leads from the traditional to the modern division of disciplines. Traditionally normal order and inversion were traced to calm reasoning and to emotive impetus, respectively. On this basis they were assigned one to grammar, the other to rhetoric. The distinction reappears in modern linguistics through the substitution of stylistics for rhetoric. Bally, for one, does not hesitate to attribute such a large role to emotion as to subsume under this faculty almost the entire province of 'style' (1909). Likewise we have seen how the homogeneity of the two issues of word order and sentence structure, posited *de facto* by the ancient theory of composition, is demonstrated by modern linguistic speculation, in this an unwitting heir to the tradition we have surveyed.

11. Looking back for a moment, we now realize that we have observed *in fieri* a sort of loose correspondence, which constitutes a historical constant, between style genera, compositional forms, and particular uses of

the figures of speech. If we take the middle term, namely compositional forms, as our point of departure, we may find that: (1) periodicity tends to correspond to the high style and is characterized by circularity; (2) balanced or symmetrical arrangement belongs to ornate styles and is characterized by schematism, i. e. dependence on verbal or sound figures; (3) loose structures, in turn, are most commonly associated with the plain style and are often characterized by reliance on tropes, i. e. thought figures. We can now conclude that (1) belongs most properly in antiquity; (2) in the Middle Ages (especially in the modes dependent on bureaucratic examples) as well as in the *estilo culto* and Euphuistic experiments of the late Renaissance and early baroque; (3), finally, is most typical of the Christian *sermo humilis* and emerges triumphantly again in the ages of baroque and Enlightenment.

Sooner or later one may be further tempted to wonder about the multiple relationships—which are left to the cultural historian to test and determine—between the technical assertions and their broader implications on the aesthetic, psychological, and other spiritual levels. Fénelon, for instance, could enter specific statements on word order in a context clearly reminiscent of comprehensive ideas about the overall structure of the artifact and even its religious import: "Il faut avoir tout vu, tout pénétré et tout embrassé, pour savoir la place précise de chaque mot: c'est ce qu'un déclamateur, livré à son imagination et sans science, ne peut discerner."[2] This was meant to clarify the precise and full meaning of Horace's term *ordo* as applied to both sentence structure and the deep unity of a well-knit work, in which no part can be transposed or omitted without adversely affecting the whole.[3]

In conclusion, I dare hope that the present study has helped to document the relevance of technical material for the proper historical understanding of creative literature by focussing on the factors which conditioned at an early stage the particular *forma mentis* of authors and critics. More essentially, however, it has been a study in the history of syntax and its development out of independent yet allied 'arts.'

[2] *Lettre à l'Académie*, p. 623 in t. VI of Fénelon's *Œuvres complètes* (10 vols., Paris, Leroux, 1851-52), cited in Pizzorusso, *La poetica di Fénelon* (Milan, 1959), p. 9.

[3]
Ordinis haec virtus erit et venus, aut ego fallor,
Ut jam nunc dicat jam nunc debentia dici,
Pleraque differat et praesens in tempus omittat.
Horace, *Ars poetica*, vv. 42-44

BASIC BIBLIOGRAPHY

This Bibliography is not meant to be exhaustive. It includes only works found to be of direct usefulness to the investigation at hand, and its chief purpose is to integrate the footnotes and facilitate their use.

Titles are generally assembled on a historical basis by sections as follows: Ancient, Medieval, Renaissance, Baroque—Enlightenment, and Modern Theory. The last section includes both works of modern theory and studies of language history. Some titles have been placed in the section corresponding to the part of the text where they have been most extensively used or quoted, even though they might also apply to other sections. Primary and secondary sources are not separated. References to these works are usually abridged in the text and footnotes. Titles are given in full in the footnotes when they are not included in this bibliography because they do not represent contributions pertaining to the main subjects of our study, or because, as is the case with most primary sources, the choice of edition did not seem to warrant particular stress.

When several editions are listed, the last one was used, unless otherwise indicated.

ANCIENT THEORY

Ammon, Georg: *De Dionysii Halicarnassensis librorum rhetoricorum fontibus* (Monachii, 1889)

Anonimo: *Del Sublime* [*Anonimi de Sublimitate*], ed. Augusto Rostagni (Milan, 1947)

Apollonius Dyscolus: *De constructione libri IV*, ed. G. Uhlig: *Apollonii Dyscoli Quae Supersunt*, II (Leipzig, 1910)

Arbusow, Leonid: *Colores rhetorici*, ed. H. Peter (Göttingen, 1948, 1963²)

Aristides: *Libri rhetorici II*, ed. Wilhelm Schmid: *Rhetores Graeci* V (Leipzig, 1926)

Aristotle: *Problems II*, ed. and trans. W. S. Hett; *Rhetorica ad Alexandrum*, ed. and trans. H. Rackham (London, Eng.—Cambridge, Mass., 1937)

Atkins, John W. H.: *Literary Criticism in Antiquity* (2 vols., Cambridge, 1934, reprinted London, 1952)

Augustyniak, Katarzyna: *De tribus et quattuor dicendi generibus quid docuerint antiqui* (Warsaw, 1957)

Baldwin, Charles S.: *Ancient Rhetoric and Poetic* (New York, 1924)

Barwick, Karl: " Die Gliederung der rhetorischen TEXNH und die Horazische Epistula ad Pisones," *Hermes*, LVII (1952), 1-62

———: *Probleme der Stoischen Sprachlehre und Rhetorik* (Berlin, 1957)

———: *Martial und die zeitgenössische Rhetorik* (Berlin, 1959)

Bonner, Stanley Frederick: *The Literary Treatises of Dionysius of Halicarnassus* (Cambridge, 1939)

———: " Roman Oratory," *Fifty Years of Classical Scholarship*, ed. M. Platnauer (Oxford, 1954), 363-368

Bornecque, Henri: *Les clausules métriques latines* (Lille, 1907)

Both, Ph.: *De Antiphontis et Thucydidis genere dicendi*, Diss. (Marburg, 1875)

Boulanger, André: *Aelius Aristide et la sophistique dans la province d'Asie au deuxième siècle de notre ère* (Paris, 1923)

Brink, Charles Oscar: *Horace on Poetry: Prolegomena to the Literary Epistles* (Cambridge, Eng., 1963)

Buchheit, Vinzenz: *Untersuchungen zur Theorie des Genos epideiktikon von Gorgias bis Aristoteles* (Munich, 1960)

[Cicero]: *Ad C. Herennium de ratione dicendi (Rhetorica ad Herennium)*, ed. Harry Caplan (Loeb Classical Libr.) (Cambridge, Mass.—London, Eng., 1954)

Cicero, M. Tullius: *Brutus, Orator,* eds. G. L. Hendrickson and H. M. Hubbell (Loeb Classical Libr.) (Cambridge, Mass.—London, Eng., 1939)

(Cicéron): *Divisions de l'Art oratoire. Topiques,* ed. Henri Bornecque (Paris, 1924)

Clark, Albert C.: *Fontes Prosae numerosae* (Oxford, 1909)

Clark, Donald L.: *Rhetoric in Greco-Roman Education* (New York, 1957)

Clarke, Martin Lowther: *Rhetoric at Rome: A Historical Survey* (London, 1953; New York, 1963)

Clavel, Victor: *De M. T. Cicerone Graecorum interprete; accedunt etiam loci Graecorum auctorum cum M. T. Ciceronis interpretationibus et Ciceronianum lexicon Graeco-Latinum* (Paris, 1868)

[Cornificius]: *Rhetorica ad C. Herennium,* ed. Gualtiero Calboli (Bologna, 1969)

Cunningham, Maurice P.: " Latin Word Order: The *Status quaestionis*," *Year Book of the American Philosophical Society, 1954* (1955), 360-370

———: " Some Phonetic Aspects of Word Order Patterns in Latin," *Proceedings of the Am. Philos. Soc.*, CI, 5 (1957), 481-505

D'Alton, John Francis: *Roman Literary Theory and Criticism* (London, 1931; New York, 1962)

Darpe, Franz: *De verborum apud Thucydidem collocatione,* Diss. philol. inauguralis (Warendorpii, 1865)

Denniston, John Dewar: *Greek Prose Style* (Oxford, 1952)

Diogenes Laertius: *Lives of Eminent Philosophers,* ed. and trans. R. D. Hicks (2 vols., Cambridge, Mass.—London, Eng., 1925, . . . 1959)

Dionysius of Halicarnassus: *On Literary Composition,* ed. and trans. W. Rhys Roberts (London, 1910)

———: *The Three Literary Letters,* ed. and trans. W. Rhys Roberts (Cambridge, 1901)

Du Mesnil, A.: "Begriff der drei Kunstformen der Rede: Komma, Kolon, Periode, nach der Lehre der Alten," *Zum zweihundertjährigen Jubiläum des königl. Friedrichs-Gymnas.* (Frankfurt a. O., 1894), 32-121

Ebeling, Herman: "Some Statistics on the Order of Words in Greek," *Studies in Honour of Basil Lanneau Gildersleeve* (Baltimore, 1902), 229-240

Fiske, G. C. and Mary L. Grant: "Cicero's *Orator* and the *Ars Poetica,*" *HSCP,* XXXV (1924), 1-75

———: *Cicero's 'De Oratore' and Horace's 'Ars Poetica'* (Madison, 1929)

Fritz, K. von: "Aufbau und Absicht des *Dialogus de Oratoribus,*" *Reinisches Museum,* LXXXI (1932), 275-300

Fuhrmann, Manfred: *Das systematische Lehrbuch. Ein Beitrag zur Geschichte der Wissenschaften in der Antike* (Göttingen, 1960)

Giuffrida, Pasquale: "Significati e limiti del Neo-Atticismo," *Maia,* VII (1955), 83-124

Gomoll, Heinz: "Herakleodoros und die Kritikoi bei Philodem," *Philologus,* XCI (1936), 373-384

Goodell, Thomas D.: "The Order of Words in Greek," *Transactions of the Am. Philol. Assoc.,* XXI (1890), 5-48

Groot, Albert Willem de: *Handbook of Antique Prose Rhythm,* I (Groningen, 1918)

———: *Der antike Prosarhythmus,* I (Groningen, 1921)

———: *La Prose métrique des anciens* (Paris, 1926)

Grube, Georges M. A.: *The Greek and Roman Critics* (Toronto, 1965)

———, ed. and trans.: *A Greek Critic: Demetrius on Style* (Toronto, 1961)

Guillén, José: "Cicerón y el genuino Aticismo," *Arbor,* XXXI (1955), 427-457

Gwynn, Aubrey O., S. J.: *Roman Education from Cicero to Quintilian* (Oxford, 1926)

Hale, William G., and Carl D. Buck: *A Latin Grammar* (Boston and London, 1903; reprinted by University of Alabama Press, University, Ala., 1966)

Halm, Carolus, ed.: *Rhetores Latini Minores* (Leipzig, Teubner, 1863)

Hendrickson, G. L.: "The Peripatetic Mean of Style and the Three Stylistic Characters," *American Journal of Philology*, XXV (1904), 125-146

———: "The Origin and Meaning of the Ancient Characters of Style," *AJP*, XXVI (1905), 249-290

———: "Cicero de Optimo Genere Oratorum," *AJP*, XLVII (1926), 109-123

———: "Cicero's Correspondence with Brutus and Calvus on Oratorical Style," *AJP*, XLVII (1926), 234-258

Hinks, D. A. G.: "Tisias and Corax and the Invention of Rhetorik," *Classical Quarterly*, XXXIV (1940), 61-69

Hollingsworth, John E.: *Antithesis in the Attic Orators from Antiphon to Isaeus* (Menasha, Wis., 1915)

Kennedy, B. H.: *The Public School Latin Grammar*, 7th ed. (London and New York, 1890)

Kennedy, George A.: *The Art of Persuasion in Greece* (Princeton, 1963)

———: "Aristotle on the Period," *Harvard Studies in Classical Philology*, LXIII (1958), 283-288

Kenyan, Grover C.: *Antithesis in the Speeches of the Greek Historians* (Chicago, 1941)

Kroll, Wilhelm: "Rhetorik," *Paulys Real-Encyclopädie der class. Altertumswiss.*, Supplementband VII, 1039-1138 (Stuttgart, 1940)

Landgraf, Gustav, ed.: *Historische Grammatik der lateinischen Sprache* (Leipzig, 1894-1908) III. Band, 1. Heft (1903): J. Golling, "Einleitung in die Geschichte der lateinischen Syntax," pp. 1-96

Laurand, Louis: *Études sur le style des discours de Cicéron, avec une esquisse de l'histoire du "Cursus"* (Paris, 1907)

Lausberg, Heinrich: *Elemente der literarischen Rhetorik. Eine Einführung für Studierende der klassischen, romanischen, englischen und deutschen Philologie* (Munich, 1949; zweite, wesentlich erweiterte Auflage 1963)

———: *Handbuch der literarischen Rhetorik, Eine Grundlegung der Literaturwissenschaft* (2 vols., Munich, 1960)

Leeman, A. D.: "Le Genre et le style historique à Rome: Théorie et pratique," *REL*, XXXIII (1955), 183-208

———: *Orationis Ratio. The Stylistic Theories and Practice of the Roman Orators Historians and Philosophers* (2 vols., Amsterdam, 1963)

Lemmermann, Heinz: *Lehrbuch der Rhetorik* (Munich, 1962)

Lieberg, Godo: "Der Begriff *structura* in her lateinischen Literatur," *Hermes*, LXXXIV (1957), 455-477

Lücke, Johannes: *Beiträge zur Entwicklung der genera dicendi und genera compositionis*, Phil. Diss. (Hamburg, 1952)

Madyda, Władisław: "Über die Voraussetzungen der Hermogenischen Stillehre," *Aus der altertumswiss. Arbeit Volkspolens*, eds. J. Irmscher and K. Kumaniecki: Deutsche Ak. der Wiss. Berlin, Skt. f. Altertumswiss., XIII (1959), 44-51

Marache, René: *La critique littéraire de langue latine et le développement du goût archaïsant au IIe siècle de notre ère* (Rennes, 1952)

Marrou, Henri-Irénée: *A History of Education in Antiquity*, trans. G. Lamb (London, 1956; New York, 1964)

Michel, Alain: *Rhétorique et philosophie chez Cicéron* (Paris, 1960)

Morpurgo Tagliabue, Guido: *Linguistica e stilistica di Aristotele* (Rome, Edizioni dell'Ateneo, 1967)

Norden, Eduard, ed.: P. Vergilius Maro, *Aeneis VI* (Leipzig, 1903; repr. Stuttgart, 1965): Anhänge II-IV, pp. 369-398, on periodic structure, word order, and some cadences

————: *Die antike Kunstprosa* (Leipzig, 1890; Leipzig and Berlin, 1909; Darmstadt, 1958[5], 2 vols.)

Pagliaro, Antonino: *Sommario di linguistica arioeuropea. I: Cenni storici e questioni teoriche* (Rome, 1930)

Patterson, William M.: *The Rhythm of Prose* (New York, 1916)

Pfeiffer, Rudolf: *History of Classical Scholarship, from the Beginnings to the End of the Hellenistic Age* (Oxford, 1968)

[Philodemus]: *Philodemi volumina rhetorica*, ed. Siegfried Sudhaus (2 vols. and Supplement, Leipzig, Teubner, 1892-96; 1902-06[2])

————: *Philodemus über die Gedichte, fünftes Buch*, ed. Christian Jensen (Berlin, 1923)

————: "The Rhetorica of Philodemus," trans. Harry M. Hubbell, *Transactions of the Connecticut Acad. of Arts and Sciences*, XXIII (New Haven, Conn., 1920), 247-382

Polheim, Karl: *Die lateinische Reimprosa* (Berlin, 1925)

Quadlbauer, Franz: "Die *Genera dicendi* bis auf Plinius," *Wiener Studien*, LXXI (1958), 55-111

Quintilianus, M. Fabius: *Institutionis oratoriae libri XII*, ed. Ludwig Radermacher, revised by V. Buchheit (2 vols., Leipzig, Teubner, reprint 1959, 1965, 1971)

Rabe, Hugo, et al.: *Rhetores Graeci*, 9 vols. (V-VI, X-XVI) (Leipzig, 1913—incomplete)

Rackham, H., ed.: *Rhetorica ad Alexandrum* (Cambridge, Mass.—London, Eng., 1937, reprinted 1957)

Radermacher, Ludwig: *Artium Scriptores* (Vienna, 1954)

———— and H. Usener, eds.: *Dionysii Halicarnassei Opuscula* (2 vols., Leipzig, Teubner, 1909)

Riddell, James: "Order of Words and Clauses in Plato," in Riddell's ed. of Plato's *Apology*, pp. 236-246 (Oxford, 1877)

Rist, J. M.: "Demetrius the Stylist and Artemon the Compiler," *Phoenix*, XVIII (1964), 2-3

Roberts, W. Rhys: *Greek Rhetoric and Literary Criticism* (repr. New York, 1963)

Robins, Robert Henry: *Ancient and Medieval Grammatical Theory in Europe with particular reference to modern linguistic doctrine* (London, 1951)

————: *A Short History of Linguistics* (Bloomington and London, 1968)

Rönsch, Willy: *Cur et Quomodo librarii verborum collocationem in Ciceronis orationibus commutauerint*, Diss. (Leipzig, 1914)

Rostagni, Augusto: "Filodemo contro l'Estetica classica," in *Scritti Minori*, I, 394-446 (3 vols., Torino, 1955) [vol. I deals entirely with ancient literary aesthetics]

Russell, D. A., ed.: '*Longinus*' *on the Sublime* (Oxford, 1964)

Schenkeveld, D. M.: *Studies in Demetrius 'On Style,'* Diss. (Amsterdam, 1964 and Chicago, 1967)

Schmid, Wilhelm: *Über die klassische Theorie und Praxis des antiken Prosarhythmus* (Wiesbaden, 1959)

Short, Charles: "The Order of Words in Attic Greek Prose," in C. D. Yonge, *An English-Greek Lexicon*, ed. H. Drisler (New York, 1890), pp. i-cxv

Solmsen, Friedrich: "The Aristotelian Tradition in Ancient Rhetoric," *AJP*, LXII (1941), 35-50

Spengel, Leonhard von, ed.: *Rhetores Graeci*, 3 vols. (Leipzig, Teubner, I 1853, II 1854, III 1856) (vol. I re-edited by C. Hammer, ibid., 1894: this is the ed. used for this vol.)

Spratt, A. W.: "Order of Words in Thucydides," in Spratt's ed. of Thucydides, Book VI (Cambridge University Press, 1912)

Stanford, William Bedell: *The Sound of Greek. Studies in the Greek Theory and Practice of Euphony* (Berkeley and Los Angeles, 1967)

Sullivan, Sister Thérèse: *S. Aureli Augustini De Doctrina Christiana Liber Quartus*, Catholic Un. of Am. Patristic Studies, 23 (Washington, D. C., 1930)

Untersteiner, Mario: *The Sophists*, trans. K. Freeman (Oxford, 1954)

Voit, Ludwig: DEINOTHΣ, *Ein antiker Stilbegriff* (Leipzig, 1934)

Volkmann, Richard Emil: *Die Rhetorik der Griechen und Römer in systematischer Übersicht* (Leipzig, 1885²; reprint Hildesheim, G. Olms, 1963)

Wackernagel, Jacob: *Vorlesungen über Syntax mit besonderer Berück-sichtigung von Griechisch, Lateinisch und Deutsch*, 1. Reihe (Basel, 1910, 1926²), pp. 1-69; 2. Reihe (Basel, 1924)

Wehrli, Fritz Robert: "Der Erhabene und der schlichte Stil in der poetisch-rhetorischen Theorie der Antike," *Phyllobolia für Peter von der Mühll*, ed. Olof Gigon *et al.* (Basel, 1946), pp. 9-34

Wilamowitz-Möllendorf, U. von: "Asianismus und Atticismus," *Hermes*, XXXV (1900), 1-52

Wilkinson, L. P.: *Golden Latin Artistry* (Cambridge—Toronto, 1963)

Zehetmeier, Joseph: "Die Periodenlehre des Aristoteles," *Philologus*, LXXXV (1929), 192-208, 255-284, 414-436; also published as Inaug.-Diss. Munich (Leipzig, 1930)

Zieliński, Tadeusz (Zielīnskii, Faddeĭ Frantŝevīch): *Cicero im Wandel der Jahrhunderte* (Leipzig & Berlin, 1897, 1908², 1912³; Darmstadt, 1967⁵)

————: *Das Klauselgesetz in Ciceros Reden. Philologus*, Supplementband IX, 4. Heft (Leipzig, 1904)

————: *Der constructive Rhythmus in Ciceros Reden. Philologus*, Supplementbd. XIII, 1. Heft (Leipzig, 1920)

MIDDLE AGES

Arts libéraux et philosophie au Moyen Âge: Actes du 4ᵉ Congrès International de Philosophie Médiévale. Université de Montréal, 27 August-2 September 1967 (Montréal, Institut d'Études Médiévales— Paris, J. Vrin, 1969)

Abelson, Paul: *The Seven Liberal Arts. A Study in Medieval Culture*, Diss. (New York, 1906)

Atkins, John W. H.: *English Literary Criticism: The Medieval Phase* (Cambridge—New York, 1943)

Auerbach, Erich: *Mimesis: The Representation of Reality in Western Literature*, trans. W. Trask (Garden City, 1957) [orig. German ed. Bern, 1946, orig. Engl. ed. Princeton, 1953]

————: *Literatursprache und Publikum in der lateinischen Spätantike und im Mittelalter* (Bern, 1958)

————: *Literary Language and its Public in Late Latin Antiquity and in the Middle Ages*, trans. R. Manheim (New York, 1965)

Baldwin, Charles S.: *Medieval Rhetoric and Poetic (to 1400)* (New York, 1928)

Baron, Roger, ed.: *Hugonis de Sancto Victore Opera Propaedeutica: Prac-tica geometriae, De Grammatica, Epitome Dindimi in Philosophiam*, University of Notre Dame Publications in Mediaeval Studies, XX (Notre Dame, Ind., 1966)

Berchem, Denis van: "Poètes et grammairiens. Recherche sur la tradition scolaire d'explication des auteurs," *Museum Helveticum*, IX (1952), 79-87

Bertolucci Pizzorusso, Valeria: "Un trattato di *Ars dictandi* dedicato ad Alfonso X," *Studi Mediolatini e Volgari*, XV-XVI (1968), 9-88, esp. 32-36

Bonnet, Max: *La Latinité de Grégoire de Tours* (Paris, 1890)

Charland, Th.-M.: *Artes praedicandi. Contribution à l'histoire de la rhétorique au Moyen Âge* (Paris—Ottawa, 1936)

Curtius, Ernst Robert: *European Literature and the Latin Middle Ages,* trans. W. R. Trask (New York, 1963)

Di Capua, Francesco: *Il Ritmo prosaico nelle lettere dei Papi e nei documenti della Cancelleria romana dal IV al XIV secolo*: "Lateranum, Nova Series," III, 2-3; V, 2-4; XI-XII, 1-4 (3 vols., Rome, Fac. Theol. Pont. Athenaei Sem. Rom., 1937-39-46)

————: *Sentenze e proverbi nella tecnica oratoria e loro influenza sull'arte del periodare. Studi sulla letteratura latina medievale* (Naples, 1946)

————: *Scritti minori* (2 vols., Rome, Desclée, 1959)

Faba, Guido: *Summa dictaminis*, ed. A. Gaudenzi, *Il Propugnatore*, XXIII or n. s. III (1890), 287-338 and 345-393

Faral, Edmond: *Les Arts poétiques du XIIᵉ et du XIIIᵉ siècles* (Paris, 1924, reprinted 1958)

Gaudenzi, Augusto, ed.: "Boncompagni Rhetorica novissima," in *Bibliotheca Iuridica Medii Aevi* (3 vols., Bologna, 1888-1901), II (1892)

Golling, Joseph: "Einleitung in die Geschichte der lateinischen Syntax," in Gustav Landgraf, ed., *Historische Grammatik der lateinischen Sprache,* III. Bd., 1. Heft (Leipzig, 1903), 1-96 (See under Landgraf in Ancient Section)

Haag, Otto: "Die Latinität Fredegars," *Romanische Forschungen,* X (1899), 835-932, esp. 925 ff.

Howell, Wilbur S.: "English Backgrounds of Rhetoric," in *History of Speech Education in America,* 3-47 (New York, 1954)

Jauss, Hans Robert, and Jürgen Beyer, eds.: *La littérature didactique, allégorique et satirique (Partie historique)*: Grundriss der romanischen Literaturen des Mittelalters, VI, 1 (Heidelberg, Carl Winter, 1968): Cesare Segre, "Arti liberali," pp. 116-123 on grammar and rhetoric

Jellinek, Max Hermann: *Geschichte der neuhochdeutschen Grammatik, von den Anfängen bis auf Adelung* (2 vols., Heidelberg, 1913-14)

Kennedy, Arthur G.: *A Bibliography of Writings on the English Language, from the beginning of printing to the end of 1922* (Cambridge, Mass., and New Haven, Conn., 1927)

Koch, Joseph, ed.: *Artes liberales. Von der antiken Bildung zur Wissenschaft des Mittelalters* (Leiden—Köln, 1959)

Koll, Hans Georg: "Zur Stellung des Verbs im spätantiken und frühmittelalterlichen Latein," *Mittellateinisches Jahrbuch*, II (Festschrift für K. Langosch) (Köln, 1965), 241-272

Kronbichler, Walter, ed.: *Die Summa de arte prosandi des Konrad von Mure*: Geist und Werk der Zeiten, Heft 17 (Zürich, 1968)

Langlois, Charles Victor: *Formulaires de lettres du XIIe, du XIIIe et du XIVe siècle* (Paris, 1890)

Lindholm, Gudrun: *Studien zum mittellateinischen Prosarhythmus: Seine Entwicklung und sein Abklingen in der Briefliteratur Italiens* (Acta Univ. Stockholmiensis, Stockholm, 1963)

Lisio, Giuseppe: *L'Arte del periodo nelle opere volgari di Dante Alighieri e del sec. XIII: Saggio di critica e di storia letteraria* (Bologna, 1902)

McKeon, Richard: "Rhetoric in the Middle Ages," *Speculum*, XVII (1942), 1-32; repr. in Joseph Schwartz and J. A. Rycenga, *The Province of Rhetoric*, 172-212 (New York, 1965)

Meyer, Paul: "Traités catalans de grammaire et de poétique," *Romania*, VI (1877), 341-358; VIII (1879), 181-210; IX (1880), 51-70

Müller-Marquardt, Fritz: *Die Sprache der alten Vita Wandregiseli* (Halle a. S., 1912)

Ong, Walter J., S. J.: "Historical Backgrounds of Elizabethan and Jacobean Punctuation Theory," *PMLA*, LIX, 2 (1944), 349-360

Pazzaglia, Mario: *Il verso e l'arte della canzone nel De vulgari eloquentia* (Florence, 1967)

Pei, Mario: *The Language of Eighth-Century Texts in Northern France* (New York, 1932)

Piper, Paul: *Die Schriften Notkers und seiner Schule* (3 vols., Freiburg i. B., Tübingen, and Leipzig, 1883-1895)

Reisig, Karl: *Vorlesungen über lateinische Sprachwissenschaft*, ed. Fr. Haase (Leipzig, 1839)

Rijk, Lambertus Marie de: *Logica Modernorum: A Contribution to the History of Early Terminist Logic* (2 vols. in 3 tomes, Assen, 1962-67)

Rockinger, Ludwig, ed.: *Briefsteller und Formelbücher des elften bis vierzehnten Jahrhunderts*: Quellen und Erörterungen zur bayerischen und deutschen Geschichte, IX, 1-2 (2 vols., Munich, 1863-64; reprinted by Burt Franklin, 2 vols., New York, 1961)

Rohlfs, Gerhard, ed.: *Sermo vulgaris latinus; vulgärlateinisches Lesebuch* (Tübingen, 1956²)

Rychner, Jean: *Formes et structures de la prose médiévale: L'articulation des phrases narratives dans la ' Mort Artu '* (Geneva, 1970)

Schiaffini, Alfredo: *Tradizione e poesia nella prosa d'arte italiana dalla latinità medievale a G. Boccaccio* (Rome, 1943[2])

Segre, Cesare: *La sintassi del periodo nei primi prosatori italiani (Guittone, Brunetto, Dante)*: Atti dell'Acc. Naz. dei Lincei, Sc. morali . . . IV, 2 (Rome, 1952); reprinted in *Lingua, Stile e Società: Studi sulla storia della prosa italiana* (Milan, 1963)

Stengel, Edmund, ed.: *Die beiden ältesten provenzalischen Grammatiken* [by H. Faidit and R. Vidal] (Marburg, 1878)

Sutter, Carl: *Aus Leben und Schriften des Magisters Boncompagno* (Freiburg i. B.—Leipzig, 1894; also published ibid., 1894, as Habilitationsschrift)

Terracini, Benvenuto: *Pagine e appunti di linguistica storica* (Florence, 1957)

Thurot, Charles: "Notices et extraits de divers manuscrits latins pour servir à l'histoire des doctrines grammaticales au Moyen Age," *Notices et extraits des manuscrits de la Bibliothèque Impériale et autres Bibliothèques,* XXII, 2 (Paris, 1868)

Tognelli, Iole: *Introduzione all' ' Ars punctandi '* (Rome, 1963)

RENAISSANCE

Bahner, Werner: *Beitrag zum Sprachbewusstsein in der spanischen Literatur des 16. und 17. Jahrhunderts* (Berlin, Rütten und Loening, 1956)

Baldwin, Charles S. (D. L. Clark, ed.): *Renaissance Literary Theory and Practice* (New York, 1939; Gloucester, Mass., 1959)

Baldwin, Thomas W.: *William Shakspere's Small Latine and Lesse Greeke* (2 vols., Urbana, Ill., 1944; reprinted 1966)

[Barzizza, Gasparino]: *Gasparini Barzizii Bergomatis et Guiniforti filii Opera . . .* (2 vols., Romae, Maria Salvioni, 1723)

Benoist, Antoine: *De la syntaxe française entre Palsgrave et Vaugelas* (Paris, 1877; Geneva, Slatkine Reprints, 1968)

Blench, J. W.: *Preaching in England in the Late Fifteenth and Sixteenth Centuries* (Oxford, 1964)

Castor, Grahame: *Pléiade Poetics: A Study in Sixteenth-Century Thought and Terminology* (Cambridge, 1964)

Clark, Donald L.: *Rhetoric and Poetry in the Renaissance* (New York, 1922)

———: "Ancient Rhetoric and English Renaissance Literature," *Shakespeare Quarterly,* II (1951), 195-204

Cohen, Marcel: *Grammaire et Style* (Paris, 1954), pp. 19-47: " Comment Rabelais a écrit "

Cox, Leonard: *The Arte or Craft of Rhetoryke* [London, ca. 1530, 1532²], ed. Frederic I. Carpenter: The University of Chicago English Studies, V (Chicago, 1899)

Crane, William Garrett: *Wit and Rhetoric in the Renaissance* (New York, 1937; 1946; Gloucester, Mass., 1964)

Du Vair, Guillaume: *De l'éloquence françoise* [1594], critical ed. René Radouant (Paris, 1907; Geneva, Slatkine Reprints, 1970)

Fabri, Pierre (Abbé Pierre Le Fèvre): *Le Grand et vrai art de pleine rhétorique*, ed. A. Héron (3 vols., Rouen, 1889-1890; original ed. Rouen, 1521)

Hale, E. E., Jr.: "Ideas on Rhetoric in the Sixteenth Century," *PMLA*, XVIII (1903), 424-444

Howell, Wilbur Samuel: *Logic and Rhetoric in England, 1500-1700* (Princeton, N. J., 1956)

Huarte de San Juan, Juan: *Exámen de ingenios* (Baeza, 1575); Eng. trans. Bellamy (London, 1698)

Kennedy, Arthur G.: *A Bibliography of Writings on the English Language . . .* (Cambridge, Mass., and New Haven, Conn., 1927)

King, Walter N.: "John Lyly and Elizabethan Rhetoric," *SP*, LII (1955), 149-161

Kukenheim, Louis: *Contributions à l'histoire de la grammaire italienne, espagnole et française à l'époque de la Renaissance* (Amsterdam, 1932)

————: *Contributions à l'histoire de la grammaire grecque, latine et hébraïque à l'époque de la Renaissance* (Leiden, 1951)

Livet, Ch.-L.: *La Grammaire française et les grammairiens du XVIe siècle* (Paris, 1859)

Mead, H. R.: "Fifteenth-Century Schoolbooks," *Huntington Library Quarterly*, III (1939-40), 37-42

Meier, Harri: "Personenhandlung und Geschehen in Cervantes' *Gitanilla*," *Romanische Forschungen*, LI (1937), 125-186

Monnier, Philippe: *Le Quattrocento* (2 vols., Paris, 1901, . . . 1924⁹), I, 211-234: "Le beau style latin"

Ong, Walter J., S. J.: *Ramus, Method, and the Decay of Dialogue* (Cambridge, Mass., 1958)

————: "Tudor Writings on Rhetoric," *Studies in the Renaissance*, XV (1968), 39-69

Patterson, Annabel M.: *Hermogenes and the Renaissance: Seven Ideas of Style* (Princeton, N. J., 1970)

Patterson, W. F.: *Three Centuries of French Poetical Theory* (Ann Arbor, 1935)

Peacham, Henry: *The Garden of Eloquence Conteyning the Figures of Grammer and Rhetorick . . .* [1577], 1593 revision, ed. W. G.

Crane, in the Scholars' Facsimiles and Reprints Series (Gainesville, Fla., 1954)

Pope, Mildred K.: *From Latin to Modern French* (Manchester, 1934)

Radouant, René Ch.: *Guillaume Du Vair: L'homme et l'orateur jusqu'à la fin des troubles de la Ligue (1556-1596)* (Paris, 1907; Geneva, Slatkine Reprints, 1970)

Rickard, Peter: *La Langue française au seizième siècle: Étude suivie de textes* (Cambridge, Eng., 1968)

Sabbadini, Remigio: *Storia del Ciceronianismo e di altre questioni letterarie nell'età della Rinascenza* (Torino, 1886)

Scaglione, Aldo D.: " The Humanist as Scholar and Politian's Conception of the *Grammaticus,*" *Studies in the Renaissance,* VIII (1961), 49-70

Schwarts, Joseph, and John A. Rycenga, eds.: *The Province of Rhetoric and Poetic* (New York, 1965)

Segre, Cesare: " Edonismo linguistico nel Cinquecento," *Giornale Storico d. Lett. It.,* CXXX (1953), 145-177

Sherry, Richard: *A Treatise of Schemes and Tropes . . .* (London, John Day, 1550; 1552²); 1550 text, ed. H. W. Hildebrand, in the Scholars' Facsimiles and Reprints Series (Gainesville, Fla., 1961)

———: *A Treatise of the Figures of Grammar and Rhetoric* (London, Richard Tottell, 1555)

Sonnino, Lee A.: *A Handbook to Sixteenth-Century Rhetoric* (New York, 1968)

Stengel, Edmund: *Chronologisches Verzeichnis französischer Grammatiken vom Ende des 14. bis zum Ausgange des 18. Jahrhunderts* (Oppeln, 1890)

Talaeus, Audomarus: *Rhetorica* (Paris, 1548 . . .). See W. J. Ong, *Ramus and Talon Inventory* (Cambridge, Mass., 1958), pp. 82-146 for the numerous eds.

Trabalza, Ciro: *La Critica Letteraria (dai primordi dell'Umanesimo all'età nostra)* (Milan, 1915)

Treip, Mindele: *Milton's Punctuation and Changing English Usage, 1582-1676* (London, 1970)

[Vives, Juan Luis]: *Joannis Ludovici Vivis Opera Omnia,* ed. G. Majansius (Bruges, 1532; Valencia, 1745, repr. London, 1964, 8 vols.)

Vossler, Karl: *Poetische Theorien der italienischen Frührenaissance* (Berlin, 1900)

Weinberg, Bernard: *A History of Literary Criticism in the Italian Renaissance* (2 vols., Chicago, 1961)

Whipple, T. H.: " Isocrates and Euphuism," *MLR,* XI (1916), 15-27, 129-135

Wilson, Thomas: *The Arte of Rhetorique, 1560,* ed. G. H. Mair (Oxford,

1909); 1553 text, ed. Robert Hood Bowers, in the Scholars' Facsimiles and Reprints Series (Gainesville, Fla., 1962)

BAROQUE–ENLIGHTENMENT

Açarq, Jean-Pierre d': *Grammaire françoise philosophique, ou Traité complet sur la physique, sur la métaphysique, et sur la rhétorique, du langage qui regne parmi nous dans la société* (Geneva and Paris, 1760-61)

Algarotti, Francesco: *Opere scelte*, vols. I-II (Milan, 1823)

Arnauld, Antoine: *Réflexions sur l'éloquence des prédicateurs*, in Arnauld, Brulart de Sillery, Bernard Lamy, *Réflexions sur l'éloquence* (Paris, 1700)

————: *The Art of Thinking—Port-Royal Logic*, trans. with an Intr. by J. Dickoff and P. James, Foreword by Ch. W. Hendel (Indianapolis—New York—Kansas City, 1964)

[———— et Claude Lancelot]: *Grammaire générale et raisonnée ou la Grammaire de Port-Royal*, éd. critique Herbert Ernst Brekle: I. Facsimile of the 3d ed. (1676); II. Variants and Annotations (2 vols., Stuttgart—Bad Cannstatt, 1966)

———— et Pierre Nicole: *La Logique ou l'art de penser*, éd. critique par Pierre Clair et Fr. Girbal: Coll. Le Mouvement des Idées au XVIIe siècle (Paris, P. U. F., 1965). Original ed. Paris, 1662, 1664²; other important eds. the 6th (Amsterdam, 1685) and that, with collation of earlier ones, in the *Œuvres de Messire Arnauld*, ed. Gabriel Du Pac de Bellegarde and J. Hautefage, 43 vols. (Paris-Lausanne, 1775-83); photoscopic repr. *Logique de Port-Royal*, Intr. P. Roubinet (Lille, 1964): the text is: *La Logique ou l'art de penser*, 5th ed. (Paris, G. Desprez, 1683)

Atkins, John W. H.: *English Literary Criticism: Seventeenth and Eighteenth Centuries* (London, 1951; New York, 1967)

Bahner, Werner: *Beitrag zum Sprachbewusstsein in der spanischen Literatur des 16. und 17. Jahrhunderts* (Berlin, 1956)

————, ed.: See Ricken, Ulrich

Baldensperger, Fernand: *Études d'histoire littéraire*, t. I: " Comment le dix-huitième siècle expliquait l'universalité de la langue française," pp. 1-54 (Paris, 1907)

Baretti, Giuseppe: *La Frusta letteraria*, ed. Leone Piccioni (Bari, 1932)

————: *Prefazioni e Polemiche*, ed. L. Piccioni (Bari, 1911)

————: *Scelta delle lettere familiari*, ed. L. Piccioni (Bari, 1912)

Bartoli, Daniello: *Dell'uomo di lettere*, ch. " Dello Stile," in *Opere*, III, 101 (Venice, 1716; also Rome, 1645; Bologna, Dozza, 1655)

————: *Opere morali* (Rome, Varese, 1684)

Battaglia, Salvatore: *Il Problema della lingua dal Baretti al Manzoni* (Naples, 1965)

Batteux, Abbé Charles: *Cours de belles-lettres* (2 tomes, Paris, 1747-48), I: "Lettres sur la phrase françoise comparée avec la phrase latine"

————: *Nouvel Examen du préjugé sur l'inversion pour servir de réponse à M. Beauzée* (Paris, 1767)

————: *Principes de la littérature,* nouv. éd., tome V (this tome contains the *Traité de la construction oratoire* and, on pp. 321-388, the *Nouvel éclaircissement sur l'inversion*) (Paris, 1774[5], 5 tomes; . . . Avignon, Chambeau, 1809, 6 tomes)

Beauzée, Nicolas: *Grammaire générale ou Exposition raisonnée des éléments nécessaires du langage, pour servir de fondement à l'étude de toutes les langues* (1st ed. Paris, 1767); nouv. éd. revue et corrigée avec soin, pp. xxvi, 835 (Paris, Auguste Delalain, 1819) [Facsimile of 1819 ed., with Introd. by H. E. Brekle, in "Grammatica Universalis" Series (Stuttgart, Frommann-Holzboog, 1971)]

Beccaria, Cesare: *Ricerche intorno alla natura dello stile* (Milan, Galeazzi, 1770)

Bédarida, Henri: *Parme et la France de 1748 à 1789* (Paris, 1927)

Bellegarde, J. Morvan de: *Réflexions sur l'élégance et la politesse du style* (Amsterdam, 1706)

Beni, Paolo: *L'Anticrusca overo Il Paragone dell'italiana lingua* (Padova, 1612)

Bettinelli, Saverio: *Del Risorgimento d'Italia negli studi, nelle arti, nei costumi dopo il Mille,* Part II, ch. i: "Lingua" (1773, . . . Venezia, Remondini, 1786)

————: *Lettere virgiliane e inglesi e altri scritti critici,* ed. V. E. Alfieri (Bari, 1930)

————: *Opere,* II: *L' Entusiasmo delle Belle Arti* (Venezia, 1780)

Blair, Hugh: *Lectures on Rhetoric and Belles Lettres* (2 vols., 1783; . . . London, T. Cadell, Jr., and W. Davies in the Strand, and W. Greech, Edinburgh, 1801[8]); repr. ed. Marold F. Harding (2 vols., Carbondale, Ill., 1965)

Bolton, Whitney French, ed.: *The English Language: Essays by English and American Men of Letters, 1490-1839* (London, 1966)

Brekle, H. E.: "Semiotik und linguistische Semantik in Port Royal," *Indogermanische Forschungen,* LIX (1964), 103-121

Brody, Jules: *Boileau and Longinus* (Geneva, 1958)

Brosses, Charles de: *Traité de la formation méchanique des langues et des principes physiques de l'étymologie* (2 vols., Paris, 1765; . . . Paris, Terrelonge, an IX [1801])

Bruneau, Charles: *Petite histoire de la langue française* (2 vols., Paris, 1955-58), I

Brunot, Ferdinand: *Histoire de la langue française des origines à 1900* (Paris, tome I 1905, . . . 1933⁴; IV 1ᵉ partie 1913, 2ᵉ partie 1924; V 1917; VI 2ᵉ partie fasc. 1ᵉʳ (par A. François) 1932, fasc. 2ᵉ (par A. François) 1933)

Campbell, George: *The Philosophy of Rhetoric (1776)*, ed. Lloyd F. Bitzer (Carbondale, Ill., 1963)

Capone-Braga, Gaetano: *La Filosofia francese e italiana del Settecento* (2 vols., Arezzo, 1920)

Carreter, Fernando Lázaro: *Las ideas lingüísticas en España durante el siglo XVIII* (Madrid, 1949)

Cesarotti, Melchiorre: *Saggio sulla filosofia delle lingue*, in *Opere scelte*, ed. Giuseppe Ortolani, I (Florence, 1945)

Charpentier, François: *De l'excellence de la langue française* (Paris, 1683)

Chevalier, Jean-Claude: *Histoire de la Syntaxe. Naissance de la notion de complément dans la grammaire françoise (1530-1750)*, Public. romanes et françaises, 100 (Geneva, 1968)

Cohen, Marcel: *Grammaire et Style, 1450-1950* (Paris, 1954)

Condillac, Étienne Bonnot de: *Cours d'Études pour l'instruction du Prince de Parme*, in *Œuvres Philosophiques*, ed. Georges Le Roy (3 vols., Paris, 1947-51), vol. I, pp. 397-776 (" II. Grammaire " pp. 427-513; " III. De l'art d'écrire " pp. 517-615; " IV. L'art de raisonner " pp. 619-714; " V. L'art de penser " pp. 717-776); vol. II, pp. 371-414 ("Logique," 1755 ed. with longer title)

————: *Essai sur l'origine des connoissances humaines* (Amsterdam, 1746)

————: *Traité des sensations* [1754] (Londres, 1788)

Cordemoy, Géraud de: *Discours physique de la parole* (Paris, 1666¹, 1677²) [Engl. trans. 1668] [Facsimile of 1677 ed., with Introd. by H. E. Brekle, in " Grammatica Universalis " Series (Stuttgart, Frommann-Holzboog, 1970)]

Croce, Benedetto: *Storia dell'età barocca in Italia* (Bari, 1929)

Croll, Morris W.: " The Sources of the Euphuistic Rhetoric," in M. W. Croll and Harry Clemons, eds.: John Lyly, *Euphues: The Anatomy of Wit; Euphues and his England*, with an Introd. by Morris W. Croll (London and New York, 1916)

————: " Juste Lipse et le mouvement anti-cicéronien à la fin du XVIᵉ et au début du XVIIᵉ siècle," *Revue du Seizième Siècle*, II (1914), 200-242

————: " The Cadence of English Oratorical Prose," *Studies in Philology*, XVI (1919), 1-55

————: " 'Attic Prose ' in the Seventeenth Century," *Studies in Philology*, XVIII (1921), 79-128

————: "Attic Prose: Lipsius, Montaigne, Bacon," *Schelling Anniversary Papers by his Former Students* (New York, 1923), 117-150

————: "Muret and the History of 'Attic Prose,'" *PMLA,* XXXIX (1924), 254-309

————: "The Baroque Style in Prose," *Studies in English Philology: A Miscellany in h. of F. Klaeber,* eds. Kemp Malone and M. B. Ruud (Minneapolis, 1929), 427-456

————: (See, also, Patrick, J. Max)

Davidson, Hugh M.: *Audience, Words, and Art. Studies in Seventeenth-Century French Rhetoric* (Columbus, Ohio, 1965)

Devoto, Giacomo: *Profilo di storia linguistica* (Florence, 1953)

Dockhorn, Klaus: *Die Rhetorik als Quelle des vorromantischen Irrationalismus in der Literatur und Geistesgeschichte,* Nachrichten der Ak. der Wiss., 5 (Göttingen, 1949)

Domergue, François Urbain: *Grammaire générale analytique* (Paris, 1799)

Donzé, Roland: *La Grammaire générale et raisonnée de Port-Royal. Contribution à l'histoire des idées grammaticales en France* (Bern, 1967)

Du Bos, Jean-Baptiste: *Réflexions critiques sur la poésie et sur la peinture* (Paris, 1719, 2 vols.; Paris, Pissot, 1770, 3 vols., facsimile reprint Geneva, Slatkine Reprints, 1967, in 1 vol.)

Du Marsais, César Chesneau: *Logique et Principes de Grammaire* (Paris, 1769)

————: *Œuvres* (7 vols., Paris, 1797) [Facsimiles, from this ed., of the *Exposition d'une méthode, Véritables principes de la Grammaire,* and *Des Tropes,* with Introd. by H. E. Brekle, in the "Grammatica Universalis" Series (Stuttgart, Frommann-Holzboog, 1971)]

Elwert, W. Theodor, ed.: *Problemi di Lingua e Letteratura italiana del Settecento. Atti del Quarto Congresso dell'Associazione Internazionale per gli Studi di Lingua e Letteratura Italiana,* Mainz and Köln, 1962 (Wiesbaden, 1965)

Fish, Harold: "The Puritans and the Reform of Prose Style," *ELH,* XIX (1952), 229-248

Folena, Gianfranco: "Le Origini e il significato del rinnovamento linguistico nel Settecento italiano," in Elwert, *Problemi,* pp. 392-427

François, Alexis: *Histoire de la langue française cultivée des origines à nos jours* (2 tomes, Geneva, 1959)

————: "Précurseurs français de la grammaire affective," *Mélanges Bally* (1939), 369-377

Frank, Thomas: "Aspetti della questione della lingua nell'Inghilterra del Settecento: La ricerca di uno standard," *Filologia e Letteratura,* XIV (1968), 242-267

Fubini, Mario: *Dal Muratori al Baretti. Studi sulla critica e sulla cultura del Settecento,* pp. 1-51 "L. A. Muratori letterato e scrittore";

pp. 52-191 "Le osservazioni del Muratori al Petrarca e la critica letteraria nell'età dell'Arcadia " (Bari, 1954²)

————: *Stile e umanità di G. B. Vico* (Bari, 1946)

————, ed.: *La Cultura illuministica in Italia* (Torino, E. R. I., 1964²)

Funke, Otto: *Die Frühzeit der englischen Grammatik . . . von Bullokar bis Wallis* (Bern, 1941)

Gamaches, É. S. de: *Les Agrémens du langage réduits à leurs principes* (Paris, 1718)

Gass, Karl Eugen: *Antoine de Rivarol (1753-1801) und der Ausgang der französischen Aufklärung* (Hagen, Westf., 1938)

Gibbons, Thomas: *Rhetoric* (London, 1767)

Gibert, Belthasar: *Jugemens des sçavans sur les auteurs qui ont traité de la Rhétorique* [. . .] (2 tomes, Paris, 1713-14)

Gillet, Fr.-P.: "Discours sur le génie de la langue françoise," *Plaidoyers et autres œuvres* (Paris, 1718)

Gilman, Margaret: *The Idea of Poetry in France, from Houdar de la Motte to Baudelaire* (Cambridge, Mass., 1958)

Gordon, Ian A.: *The Movement of English Prose* (Bloomington, Ind., 1967)

Grana, Gianni: "Lingua italiana e lingua francese nella polemica Galeani Napione—Cesarotti," in Elwert, *Problemi*, pp. 338-353

Hall, Robert A., jr.: *The Italian "Questione della Lingua": An Interpretative Essay* (Chapel Hill, N. C., 1942)

Hamilton, K. G.: *The Two Harmonies. Poetry and Prose in the Seventeenth Century* (Oxford, 1963)

Harnois, Guy: *Les Théories du langage en France de 1660 à 1821* (Paris, [1928?])

Havers, Wilhelm: *Handbuch der erklärenden Syntax* (Heidelberg, 1931)

Hazard, Paul: *La Pensée européenne au XVIIIᵉ siècle, de Montesquieu à Lessing* (Paris, 1946, 3 vols.; 1963, 1 vol.)

————: *La Crise de la conscience européenne (1680-1715)* (Paris, 1935, 3 vols.)

Herczeg, Giulio [Gyula]: "La Struttura del periodo nel Settecento," in Elwert, *Problemi*, pp. 353-373

Howell, W. S.: *Logic and Rhetoric*: See Renaissance Section

Jones, Richard Foster: "Science and English Prose Style in the Third Quarter of the Seventeenth Century," *PMLA*, XLV (1930), 977-1009

————: "Science and Language in England of the Mid-Seventeenth Century," *JEGP*, XXXI (1932), 315-331

————: *Ancients and Moderns: A Study of the Background of the Battle of the Books* (St. Louis, 1936, 1961²)

————: *The Triumph of the English Language* (Stanford, Ca., 1953)

———— *et al.*: *The Seventeenth Century*: studies in the history of English thought and literature from Bacon to Pope, by Richard Foster Jones and others writing in his honor (Stanford, Ca., 1951; London, 1969)

Kukenheim, Louis: *Esquisse historique de la linguistique française et de ses rapports avec la linguistique générale* (Leiden, 1962)

Labande-Jeanroy, Thérèse: *La question de la langue en Italie, de Baretti à Manzoni*: Strasbourg Diss. (Paris, 1925)

Lamy, Bernard: *La Rhétorique ou l'art de parler* (Paris, 1676 with title *De l'art de parler*; ibid., A. Pralard, 1688³; definitive ed. Paris, 1701⁴) [Ed. Paris, 1715⁴ now available in Sussex Reprints Series (Univ. of Sussex Libr., Brighton, Eng., 1969)]

[Lancelot, Claude, and Antoine Arnauld]: *Grammaire générale et raisonnée* (Paris, 1660)

————: *Id.* (The Scolar Press, Menston, Eng., 1967) [Facsimile of the 1660 ed., with ch. xix of the 1664² ed.]

Lawson, John: *Lectures Concerning Oratory delivered in Trinity College* (Dublin—London, 1759)

Le Gras (sieur): *La Rethorique* [sic] *françoise* (Paris, 1671¹, 1673²)

Le Hir, Yves: *Rhétorique et stylistique de la Pléiade au Parnasse* (Paris, 1960)

Le Laboureur, Jean: *Avantages de la langue françoise sur la langue latine* (Paris, 1669)

Lentzen, Manfred: "Malherbes aüsseres und inneres Verhältnis zur stoischen Philosophie," *Die Neueren Sprachen*, LXVI, 2-XVI N. F. (1967), 66-84

Marzot, Giulio: *L'Ingegno e il Genio del Seicento* (Florence, 1944), "Seneca scrittore nel Seicento," 133-169

————: *Il Gran Cesarotti* (Florence, 1949)

————: *L'Italia letteraria durante la Controriforma* (Rome, 1962)

Mascardi, Agostino: *Dell'arte istorica*, ed. A. Bartoli (Florence, 1859)

Mazzoni, Guido: *Tra libri e carte: Studi letterari* (Rome, 1887), "La Questione della lingua nel secolo XVIII," pp. 115-168

Monk, Samuel Holt: *The Sublime, a Study of Critical Theories in Eighteenth-Century England* (New York, 1935; reprinted Ann Arbor, 1960)

Mornet, Daniel: *Histoire de la clarté française* (Paris, 1929)

Morpurgo Tagliabue, Guido: "Aristotelismo e Barocco," in *Retorica e Barocco. Atti del III Congresso Intern. di Studi Umanistici*, 1954 (Rome, 1955), 119-195

Mortier, Roland: "Unité ou scission du siècle des lumières?", *Studies on Voltaire and the Eighteenth Century*, XXVI (1963), 1207-1221

Mourot, Jean: "Sur la ponctuation de Diderot," *Le Français Moderne*, XX (1952), 287-294

Munteano, Basile: *Constantes dialectiques en littérature et en histoire: Problèmes, Recherches, Perspectives* (Paris, 1967), pp. 139-185, 251-272, 297-374

Muratori, L. A.: *Della perfetta poesia italiana* (2 vols., Modena, 1706)

Ogilvie, John: *Philosophical and Critical Observations on the Nature, Characters, and Various Species of Composition* (London, 1774)

Patrick, J. Max, and Robert O. Evans: *Style, Rhetoric, and Rhythm. Essays by Morris W. Croll* (Princeton, 1966)

Peacham, Henry: *The Garden of Eloquence* (London, 1577); 1593 ed. with Intr. by William G. Crane (Gainesville, Fla., Scholars' Facsimiles and Reprints, 1954)

Pizzorusso, Arnaldo: *Teorie letterarie in Francia: Ricerche Sei-Settecentesche* (Pisa, 1968)

————: *La Poetica di Fénelon* (Milan, 1959)

Puppo, Mario, ed.: *Discussioni linguistiche del Settecento* (Torino, 1957)

————: "Appunti sul Problema della costruzione della frase nel Settecento," *Bollettino dell'Istituto di Lingue Estere*, V (Genoa, 1957), 76-78

————: "L'Illuminismo e le polemiche sulla lingua italiana," in M. Fubini, ed., *La Cultura illuministica in Italia* (Torino, E. R. I., 1964²), 243-253

Raimondi, Ezio: *Letteratura barocca. Studi sul Seicento italiano* (Florence, 1961): esp. "Polemica intorno alla prosa barocca," 175-248

————, ed.: *Trattatisti e Narratori del Seicento* (Milan—Naples, 1960)

Ricken, Ulrich: "Rationalismus und Sensualismus in der Diskussion über die Wortstellung, in Werner Bahner, ed., *Literaturgeschichte als geschichtlicher Auftrag* (Festgabe Werner Krauss), pp. 97-122 (East-Berlin, Rütten und Loening, 1961)

————: "Condillacs *liaison des idées* und die *clarté* des Französischen," *Die neueren Sprachen*, XII (1964), 552-567

————: "La *Liaison des idées* selon Condillac et la *clarté* du français" (trans. of preceding t.), *Dix-huitième Siècle*, I (1969), 179-193

Rivarol, Antoine: *Discours sur l'universalité de la langue française*, ed. Th. Suran (Paris—Toulouse, 1930)

————: *Discours sur l'universalité de la langue française*, ed. Marcel Hervier (Paris, 1929) [first critical ed.]

————: *De l'Universalité de la langue française*, ed. Marcel Lob (Paris, 1964) [reproduction of 2^d ed., 1785]

————: *Les plus belles pages*, ed. J. Dutourd (Paris, 1963)

Rosiello, Luigi: "Le teorie linguistiche di Vico e Condillac," *Forum Italicum*, II (1968), 386-393

————: *Linguistica illuminista* (Bologna, 1967)

Rothe, Arnold: *Quevedo und Seneca. Untersuchungen zu den Frühschriften Quevedos* (Geneva, 1965)

Sahlin, Gunvor: *César Chesnau Du Marsais et son rôle dans l'évolution de la grammaire générale* (Paris, 1928)

Salinari, Giambattista: "Una polemica linguistica a Milano nel sec. XVIII," *Cultura Neolatina*, IV-V (1944-45), 61-92

Scaglione, Aldo: "L'Algarotti e la crisi letteraria del Settecento," *Convivium*, n. s., IV (1956), 1-26

————: "Nicola Boileau come fulcro nella fortuna del *Sublime*," *Convivium*, raccolta nuova (1950), 161-187

————: "La Responsabilità di Boileau per la fortuna del *Sublime* nel Settecento," *Convivium*, r. n. (1952), 166-195

Schalk, Fritz: *Studien zur französischen Aufklärung* (Munich, 1964), 9-33: "Wissenschaft der Sprache und Sprache der Wissenschaft im Ancien Régime"

Schiaffini, Alfredo: *Momenti di storia della lingua italiana* (Rome, 1953²), 91-132: "Aspetti della crisi linguistica italiana del Settecento"

Shaaber, M. A., ed.: *Seventeenth Century English Prose* (New York, 1957)

Smith, Adam: *Considerations Concerning the First Formation of Languages, The Philological Miscellany*, vol. I (1761)

Smith, John: *The Mystery of Rhetorick Unveiled* (London, 1688)

Snyders, Georges: *La Pédagogie en France aux XVIIᵉ et XVIIIᵉ siècles* (Paris, 1965)

Soave, Francesco: *Grammatica ragionata della lingua italiana* (Parma, 1770)

Spongano, Raffaele: *La Prosa di Galileo e altri scritti* (Messina—Florence, 1949)

Sprat, Thomas: *The History of the Royal Society of London for the Improving of Natural Knowledge* (London, 1667)

————: *Id.*, eds. J. I. Cope and H. W. Jones (St. Louis, Wash. U. P., 1959)

Thiébault, Dieudonné: *Grammaire philosophique, ou la métaphysique, la logique, et la grammaire, réunies en un seul corps de doctrine* (2 tomes, Paris, 1802) [Now in facsimile, with Introd. by H. E. Brekle, in the "Grammatica Universalis" Series (Stuttgart, Frommann-Holzboog, 1970)]

Toffanin, Giuseppe: *L'Arcadia. Saggio storico* (Bologna, 1958³)

Trabalza, Ciro: *Storia della grammatica italiana* (Milan, 1908; Bologna, 1963²)

Vairasse, Denis: *Grammaire méthodique* . . . (Paris, 1681)

Valdastri, Ildefonso: *Corso teoretico di logica e lingua italiana* (Guastalla, 1783²)

Vaugelas, Cl. Favre de: *Remarques sur la langue française* . . . , ed. J. Streicher (Paris, 1934)

Vickers, Brian: *Francis Bacon and Renaissance Prose* (Cambridge, Eng., 1968)

Viscardi, Antonio: " Il problema della costruzione nelle polemiche linguistiche del Settecento," *Paideia*, II (1947), 193-214

Vitale, Maurizio: *La Questione della lingua* (Palermo, 1960)

Wallace, K. R.: *Francis Bacon on Communication and Rhetoric* (Chapel Hill, N. C., 1943)

Wallerstein, Ruth C.: *Studies in Seventeenth-Century Poetic* (Madison, Wis., 1950)

Wallis, John: *Grammatica linguae anglicanae* (Oxford, 1653, . . . 1745)

Ward, John: *System of Oratory* (2 vols., London, 1759)

Wellek, René: *A History of Modern Criticism: 1750-1950, I: The Later Eighteenth Century* (New Haven, 1955)

Whately, Richard: *Elements of Rhetoric* (1828), ed. Douglas Ehninger (Carbondale, Ill., 1963)

Wilkins, John, bp. of Chester: *An Essay towards a Real Character and a Philosophical Language* (London, 1668)

Wilkins, Kathleen S.: *A Study of the Works of Claude Buffier.* " Studies on Voltaire and the Eighteenth Century, Vol. 66 " (Geneva, Institut et Musée Voltaire, 1969)

Williamson, George: *The Senecan Amble. A Study in Prose Form from Bacon to Collier* (Chicago, 1951)

————: *Seventeenth Century Contexts*, ch. v: " Strong Lines "; x: " The Rhetorical Pattern of Neo-Classical Wit " (pp. 120-131, 240-271) (London, 1960)

Winkel, Elisabeth: *La grammaire générale et raisonnée de Port-Royal*, Diss. (Bonn, 1921)

Winkler, Emil: *La doctrine grammaticale française d'après Maupas et Oudin* (Halle, 1912)

Withers, Philip: *Aristarchus, or the Principles of Composition* . . . (London, 1788 . . .)

Zeller, Hugo: *Die Grammatik in der grossen französischen Enzyklopädie*, Diss. Heidelberg (Weisswasser, 1930)

MODERN THEORY

Aarsleff, Hans: *The Study of Language in England, 1780-1860* (Princeton, 1967)

Albalat, Antoine: *Le Travail du Style enseigné par les corrections manuscrites des Grands Écrivains* (Paris, 1913⁷)

———: *L'Art d'Écrire enseigné en vint leçons* (Paris, 1911), esp. 8th lesson

———: *La Formation du style par l'assimilation des auteurs* (Paris, 1914⁹)

Antoine, Gérald: *La Coordination en français* (2 vols., Paris, 1958-62)

Ascoli, Graziadio Isaia: *Scritti sulla Questione della lingua* (Milan, 1967)

Aurner, Robert R.: "The History of Certain Aspects of the Structure of the English Sentence," *Philological Quarterly*, II (1923), 187-208

Bally, Charles: *Traité de stylistique française* (2 vols., Heidelberg, 1909²; Heidelberg—Paris, 1919-1921²; Geneva—Paris, 1951³; Geneva, 1963⁴, 1970⁵ vol. 1)

———: *Linguistique générale et linguistique française* (Bern, 1932, 1944², . . . 1965⁴)

Bastardas Parera, Juan: *Particularidades sintácticas del latín medieval: Cartularios españoles de los siglos VIII al XI* (Barcelona—Madrid, 1953)

Baugh, Albert Croll: *A History of the English Language* (New York, 1957²)

Baulier, Francis: "Contribution à l'étude de l'inversion du sujet après la conjonction *et*," *Le Français Moderne*, 24 (1956), 249-257

Bergaigne, Abel: "Essai sur la construction grammaticale considérée dans son développement historique, en Sanskrit, en Grec, en Latin, dans les langues romanes et dans les langues germaniques," *Mémoires de la Société de Linguistique de Paris*, III (Paris, 1878), 1-51, 124-154, 169-186; Index p. 422

Berrettoni, Pierangiolo: "Ricerche sulla posizione delle parole nella frase italica," *Annali d. Sc. Norm. Sup. di Pisa*, XXXVI (1967), 31-81

Blinkenberg, Andreas: *L'ordre des mots en français moderne* (2 vols., Copenhagen, 1928-1933)

Boillot, Félix Fr.: *Psychologie de la construction dans la phrase française moderne* (Paris, 1930)

Bowden, Edwin T.: *An Introduction to Prose Style* (New York, 1955, 1956 . . .)

Branca, Vittore, and T. Kardos, eds.: *Il Romanticismo. Atti del VI Congresso dell'Ass. Int. per gli Studi di Lingua e Lett. It.*, Budapest—Venice, 1967: Maria Corti, "Il Problema della lingua nel Romanticismo italiano," pp. 111-135 (Budapest, 1968)

Brøndal, Viggo: *Le Français langue abstraite* (Copenhagen, 1936)

Brooks, Cleanth, and Robert P. Warren: *Modern Rhetoric* (New York, 1958²), esp. pp. 280-294, and see Index under WO

Brown, Huntington: *Prose Styles. Five Primary Types*: Minnesota Monographs in the Humanities, I (Minneapolis, 1966)

Brugmann, Karl: *Abrégé de grammaire comparée des langues indo-européennes*, French tr. (Paris, 1905), pp. 715-728

Bruneau, Charles: " La Phrase des traducteurs au XVIe siècle," *Mélanges . . . Henri Chamard* (Paris, 1951), pp. 275-284

Brunot, Ferdinand: *La Pensée et la langue* (Paris, 1922), pp. 5, 32-35, 542

Buck, Carl D.: *Comparative Grammar of Greek and Latin* (Chicago, 1933)

Cernecca, Domenico: " L'inversione del soggetto nella frase dei *Promessi Sposi*," *Studia romanica et anglica zagrabiensia*, 15-16 (Zagreb, 1963), 49-98

———: " Struttura della frase e inversione del soggetto nella prosa della *Vita Nuova*," *Studia romanica et anglica zagrabiensia*, 19-20 (Zagreb, 1965), 137-160; reprinted as " L'Inversione del soggetto nella prosa della *Vita Nuova*," in *Atti del Congresso Internazionale di Studi Danteschi* (Florence, 1966), vol. II, pp. 186-212

Chomsky, Noam: *Cartesian Linguistics: A Chapter in the History of Rationalist Thought* (New York and London, 1966)

Colagrosso, Francesco: *Studii stilistici* (Livorno, 1909)

Coseriu, Eugenio: *Logicismo y antilogicismo en la gramática* (Montevideo, 1958²)

Cousin, Jean: *Bibliographie de la langue latine (1880-1948)*, pp. 197-211 (Paris, 1951)

Cunningham, J. V., ed.: *The Problem of Style* (Greenwich, Conn., 1966) [An Anthology of Statements by Ancient and Modern Critics]: see, e. g., James Sledd, " Some Notes on English Prose Style," pp. 185-204, from *A Short Introduction to English Grammar* (1959)

Dardano, Maurizio: *Lingua e tecnica narrativa del Duecento* (Rome, 1969)

Dauzat, Albert: *Histoire de la langue française* (Paris, 1930)

———: *Le Génie de la langue française* (Paris, 1943, rev. ed. 1947)

———, ed.: *Où en sont les études de français* (Paris, s. a.)

Delbrück, Berthold: *Die altindische Wortfolge aus dem Catapathabrahmana* (Halle a. S., 1878)

———; *Syntaktische Forschungen*, V: *Altindische Syntax* (Halle a. S., 1888)

———: *Vergleichende Syntax der indogermanischen Sprachen* (Strassburg, 1900), Part III, Ch. 38, pp. 38-112

De Mauro, Tullio: *Storia linguistica dell'Italia unita* (Bari, 1963)

Devoto, Giacomo: *Storia della lingua di Roma* (Bologna, 1944²)

Dover, Kenneth J.: *Greek Word Order* (Cambridge, 1960) [Contains detailed bibliography, pp. ix-xiii, of modern linguistic and philological work on Greek WO]

Drăganu, Nicolae: *Istoria sintaxei* (Bucarest, Institutul de linguistică română, 1945)

————: *Storia della sintassi generale*, trans. P. Bardelli Plomteux, ed. C. Tagliavini (Bologna, 1970)

Feix, Joseph: *Wortstellung und Satzbau in Petrons Roman* (Breslau, 1934)

Firbas, Jan: "Some Notes on the Problem of English Word Order from the point of view of actual Sentence Analysis" (in Czech), *Sborník Prací Filosofické Fakulty Brněnské University*, Řada Jazykovědná, [Un. of Brno,] V (1956), 93-107; "Some Thoughts on the Function of Word Order in Old English and Modern English" (in English), ibid., VI (1957), 72-98

Foulet, Lucien: "L'ordre des mots et l'analyse de la phrase," *Romania*, XLIX (1923), 118-126

————: *Petite syntaxe de l'ancien français* (Paris, 1919); 3d ed. (Paris, 1930), esp. pp. 36-44 and 306-329

Fowler, Henry Watson, and F. G. Fowler: *The King's English* (Oxford, 1931³)

Fraenkel, Eduard: "Kolon und Satz: Beobachtungen zur Gliederung des antiken Satzes," *Nachrichten der Gesellschaft der Wissenschaften zu Göttingen*, Philol.-Hist. Kl. (1932), 197-213; (1933), 319-354

Fries, Charles C.: *The Structure of English: An Introduction to the Construction of English Sentences* (New York, 1952)

Frisk, Hjalmar: *Studien zur griechischen Wortstellung* (Göteborg, 1933)

Godfrey, Robert G.: "A Medieval Controversy Concerning the Nature of a General Grammar," *General Linguistics*, VII (1967), 79-104

Gossen, Carl Theodor: *Studien zur syntaktischen und stilistischen Hervorhebung im modernen Italienisch* (Berlin, 1954), Ch. ii

Greenberg, Joseph H., ed.: *Universals of Language* (Cambridge, Mass.—London, Eng., 1963, 1966): J. H. G., "Some Universals of Grammar with particular reference to the Order of Meaningful Elements," 58-90 in 1963 ed., 73-113 in 1966 ed.

Gries, Konrad: "Latin Word Order," *Cl. J.*, XLVII (1951), 83-87

Guberina, Petar: *Valeur logique et valeur stylistique des propositions complexes: Théorie générale et application au français* (Zagreb, 1954²)

Harmer, L. C.: *The French Language Today. Its Characteristics and Tendencies* (London, 1954)

Hatzfeld, Helmut: *Bibliografía crítica de la nueva estilística, aplicada a las literaturas románicas* (Madrid, 1955) [enlarged ed. of Eng. original]

Hazlitt, William: "On the Prose Style of Poets" (1826), repr. in *Selected Essays of W. Hazlitt*, ed. Geoffrey Keynes (New York, 1930), 482-500

Herczeg, Giulio [Gyula]: "Valore stilistico dell'inversione del soggetto nella prosa moderna," *Lingua Nostra*, XVI, 4 (1955), 119-122

———: "La Struttura del periodo nel Settecento," in Elwert, *Problemi* [see Baroque-Enl. Section]

Hilberg, Isidor: *Die Gesetze der Wortstellung im Pentameter des Ovid* (Leipzig, 1894)

Hudson, Hoyt H.: "The Field of Rhetoric," *Quarterly Journal of Speech Education*, VIII (1923), 167-180; reprinted in *Historical Studies of Rhetoric and Rhetoricians*, ed. Raymond F. Howes (Ithaca, N. Y., 1961)

Jespersen, Otto: *A Modern English Grammar on Historical Principles* (8 vols., London, 1909-1949, reprinted 1954, 1958), Parts III and VII

———: *Growth and Structure of the English Language* (Oxford, 1938[9])

———: *The Philosophy of Grammar* (London, 1924 . . . 1958)

———: *Progress in Language, with Special Reference to English* (London, 1894)

Kellenberger, Hunter: *The Influence of Accentuation on French Word Order* (Princeton and Paris, 1932)

Kieckers, Friedrich Ernst: *Die Stellung des Verbs im Griechisch und in den verwandten Sprachen* (Strassburg, 1911)

Koll, Hans Georg: "Zur Stellung des Verbs im spätantiken und frühmittelalterlichen Latein," *Mittellateinisches Jahrbuch*, II (Festschrift für K. Langosch) (Köln, 1965), 241-272

Kollross, Josef: "Die Stellung des Subjektes zum Verbum in den Briefen des Guittone d'Arezzo," *Zeitschrift für romanische Philologie*, LIII (1933), 113-145; 225-257

Kolovrat, Georges de: *L'Inversion du complément direct et l'accent oratoire dans le Roman de Troie* (Nice, 1923)

Kroll, Wilhelm: *Die wissenschaftliche Syntax im lateinischen Unterricht* (Berlin, 1925[3], 1962[4])

———: *La Sintaxis científica en la enseñanza del Latín*, trans. of 3[d] German ed. (Madrid, 1935)

———: *Historia de la filología clásica*. Traducida y ampliada por P. Galindo Romeo (Barcelona, 1928)

Kuttner, Max: *Prinzipien der Wortstellung im Französischen* (Bielefeld, 1929)

Lanson, Gustave: *L'art de la prose* (Paris, 1908)

Le Bidois, Georges and Robert: *L'inversion du sujet dans la prose contemporaine, 1900-1950* (Paris, 1952)

————: *Syntaxe du français moderne* (2 vols., Paris, 1935-38, 1967²), Livre 9ᵉ, vol. II, pp. 1-115

Lerch, Eugen: *Französische Sprache und Wesensart* (Frankfurt a. Main, 1933)

————: *Historische französische Syntax* (3 vols., Leipzig, 1925-34), III (1934), 252 ff. and 379-461

————: "Vom Wesen des Satzes und von der Bedeutung der Stimmführung für die Satzdefinition," *Archiv für die gesamte Psychologie*, C (1938), 133-197

————: "Die Inversion im modernen Französisch," *Mélanges de Linguistique offerts à Ch. Bally* (Geneva, 1939), 347-366

Lorian, Alexandre: *L'ordre des propositions dans la phrase française contemporaine: La Cause* (Paris, 1966)

Loubet, Émile: *La Technique de la Composition française* (Paris, 1954)

Lucas, Frank Laurence: *Style* (London, 1955)

McKnight, George Harley: *Modern English in the Making* (New York—London, 1930)

Malblanc, Alfred: *Stylistique comparée du français et de l'allemand* (Paris, 1961)

Marouzeau, Jules: *L'ordre des mots dans la phrase latine.* I: *Les groupes nominaux* (Paris, 1922); II: *Le verbe* (Paris, 1938); III: *Les articulations de l'énoncé* (Paris, 1949); Vol. *complémentaire avec exercices d'application et bibliographie* (Paris, 1953)

————: *Traité de stylistique appliquée au latin* (Paris, 1935)

Meyer-Lübke, Wilhelm: *Grammaire des langues romanes*, French trans., vol. III (Paris, 1900)

Migliorini, Bruno: *Lingua e cultura*, "Galileo e la lingua italiana" (Rome, 1948)

Miles, Josephine: "Eras in English Poetry" (1955), reprinted in Seymour Chatman and Samuel R. Levin, eds., *Essays on the Language of Literature* (Boston, 1967), 175-196

Milic, Louis T.: "Against the Typology of Styles," in S. Chatman and S. R. Levin, eds., *Essays on the Language of Literature* (Boston, 1967), 442-450

————: *Style and Stylistics: An Analytical Bibliography* (New York, 1967) [see Index under "Sentence Structure," "Word-order," etc.]

Mounin, Georges: *Histoire de la linguistique, des origines au XXᵉ siècle* (Paris, 1967)

Muldowney, Sister Mary S.: *Word-Order in the Works of St. Augustine* (Washington, D. C., 1937)

Müller-Hauser, Marie-Louise: *La mise en relief d'une idée en français moderne*, Romanica Helvetica, 21 (Geneva-Erlenbach, 1943)

Panfilov, V. Z.: *Grammar and Logic*, Janua Linguarum, Ser. Minor, 63 (The Hague, 1968)

Paul, Hermann: *Prinzipien der Sprachgeschichte* (Halle a. S., 1880, . . . 1909⁴; . . . Tübingen, 1960), esp. §§ 87-88, pp. 124-127 of 4th ed.

Perelman, Chaim: *La Nouvelle Rhétorique. Traité de l'argumentation* (2 vols., Paris, 1958)

Poutsma, H.: *A Grammar of Late Modern English*. Part One: The Sentence. First and Second Half (Groningen, 1904, 1928²)

Regula, Mario: *Grammaire française explicative* (Heidelberg, 1957)

———, and J. Jernej: *Grammatica italiana descrittiva su basi storiche e psicologiche* (Bern and Munich, 1965)

Richards, I. A.: *The Philosophy of Rhetoric* (New York—London, 1936)

Richter, Elise: *Zur Entwicklung der romanischen Wortstellung aus der lateinischen* (Halle a. S., 1903)

———: " Grundlinien der Wortstellungslehre," *Zeitschrift für romanische Philologie*, XL (1919), 9-61

Ries, John: *Was ist Syntax? Ein kritischer Versuch* (Marburg i. M., 1894)

———: " Zur Wortgruppenlehre," *Beiträge zur Grundlegung der Syntax*, Heft 2 (Prague, 1928)

———: *Die Stellung von Subject und Prädicatsverbum im Hêliand . . .* (Strassburg, 1880)

———: *Die Wortstellung im Beowulf* (Halle, 1907)

Robbins, Charles J.: " Rhetoric and Latin Word Order," *The Classical Journal*, XLVII (1951-52), 78-83

Rohlfs, Gerhard: *Historische Grammatik der italienischen Sprache*, Bd. 3 (Berlin, 1954), pp. 208-223 on It. word order

Ruelle, Pierre: " L'Ordre complément direct—sujet—verbe dans la proposition énonciative indépendante," in *Mélanges de Grammaire Française offerts à M. Maurice Grevisse . . .* (Gembloux, 1966), pp. 307-322

Saintsbury, George: *A History of Criticism and Literary Taste in Europe* (3 vols., New York, 1905)

———: *A History of English Prose Rhythm* (London, 1912; repr. Bloomington, Ind., 1965)

Sandmann, Manfred: *Subject and Predicate* (Edinburgh, 1954)

Scaglione, Aldo D.: " Periodic Syntax and Flexible Meter in the *Divina Commedia*," *RPh*, XXI (1967), 1-22

———: *Ars Grammatica: A Bibliographic Survey, Two Essays on the Grammar of the Latin and Italian Subjunctive, and A Note on the Ablative Absolute* (The Hague—Paris, 1970)

Schiaffini, Alfredo: " Rivalutazione della retorica," *Zeitschrift für romanische Philologie*, LXXVIII (1962), 503-518

Schmidl, Alfons: *Die vulgärlateinische Wortstellung*, Diss. (Munich, 1933)

Schmidt, Hermann: *Die Inversion und ihre Anwendungen* (Munich, 1950)

Schwarze, Christoph: *Untersuchungen zum syntaktischen Stil der italienischen Dichtungssprache bei Dante* (Bad Homburg v. d. H., 1970)

Schwentner, Ernst: " Bibliographie zur indogermanischen Wortstellung," *Zeitschrift für vergleichende Sprachforschung,* LXXXI (1967), 159-160 [This extensive bibliography was first started with this same title in *Wörter und Sachen* (Heidelberg), VIII (1923), 179 ff., then again as " Bibliographie zur Wortfolge," ibid., IX (1926), 194-196, and again as " Bibliogr. zur indogerm. Wortst.," ibid., XIX (1938), 160-163]

Sechehaye, Albert: *Essai sur la structure logique de la phrase* (Paris, 1926)

Short, R. W.: " The Sentence Structure of Henry James," *American Literature,* XVIII (1946), 71-88

Spencer, Herbert: *Philosophy of Style,* together with an *Essay on Style,* ed. T. H. Wright, with an intr. and notes by Fred N. Scott (Boston, 1892)

————: *Literary Style and Music* (New York, 1951)

Spitzer, Leo: *Stilstudien:* " Zum Stil Marcel Prousts " (Munich, 1961²), II, 365-497

Starobinski, Jean: " La doppietta di Voltaire. La Filosofia di uno stile e lo stile di una filosofia," *Strumenti critici,* 1 (1966), 13-32

Stempel, Wolf Dieter: " Untersuchungen zur Satzverknüpfung im Altfranzösischen," *Archiv für das Studium der neueren Sprachen und Literaturen, Beiheft* 1 (Braunschweig, 1964)

Stevens, Edward B.: " Uses of Hyperbaton in Latin Poetry," *Classical Weekly,* XLVI (1953), 200-205

Stevenson, Robert Louis: *Some Technical Elements of Style in Literature,* Edinburgh ed. of S.'s works, III, 236-261 (*Miscellanies*)

Stolz, F., and J. H. Schmalz: *Lateinische Grammatik* (Munich, 1928): Wortstellung, pp. 610-618

Strunk, William, jr., and E. B. White: *The Elements of Style* (New York, 1959)

Sütterlin, Ludwig: *Das Wesen der sprachlichen Gebilde* (Heidelberg, 1902), ch. 7, pp. 144-176

Taine, Hippolyte: *Philosophie de l'Art* (Paris-New York, 1865)

Tesnière, Lucien: *Éléments de Syntaxe Structurale* (Paris, 1959)

Trager, George L., and Harry L. Smith: *An Outline of English Structure* (Norman, Okla., 1951)

Tucker, Susie I., ed.: *English Examined: Two Centuries of Comment on the Mother Tongue* (Cambridge, Eng., 1961)

Uitti, Karl D.: *Linguistics and Literary Theory* (Englewood Cliffs, N. J., 1969)

Ullman, B. L.: " Latin Word-Order," *The Classical Journal*, XIV (1918), 644-658

Ullmann, Stephen: " Valeurs stylistiques de l'inversion dans *L'Éducation Sentimentale*," *Le Français Moderne*, 20 (1952), 175-188

———: " Inversion as a Stylistic Device in the Contemporary French Novel," *Moderne Language Review*, 47 (1952), 165-180

———: " L'Inversion du sujet dans la prose romantique," *Le Français Moderne*, 23 (1955), 23-28

———: *Style in the French Novel* (Oxford, 1964), ch. iv: " Word-Order as a Device of Style," pp. 146-188

Vendryes, Joseph: *Le langage* (Paris, 1921), 162-183 on " langage affectif "

Visser, Frederic Theodor: *An Historical Syntax of the English Language* (3 vols., to be completed, Leiden, 1963-66-69)

Vossler, Karl: *Frankreichs Kultur im Spiegel seiner Sprachentwicklung* (Heidelberg, 1921)

———: " Neue Denkformen im Vulgärlatein," *Hauptfragen der Romanistik, Festschrift für Ph. A. Becker*, 179-191 (Heidelberg, 1922)

Walden, J. W. H.: " A Point of Order in Greek and Latin," *Harvard Studies in Classical Philology*, VII (1896), 223-233

Wartburg, Walther von: *Évolution et Structure de la langue française* (Leipzig, 1934, 1937²; Bern, 1946³, 1949⁴ . . . , 1958)

———: *La Posizione della lingua italiana* (Florence, 1940)

Weil, Henri: *De l'ordre des mots dans les langues anciennes comparées aux langues modernes: Question de grammaire générale.* " Recueil de Travaux . . . relatifs à la philologie et à l'histoire littéraire " . . . " M. Bréal," 3ᵉ fasc. (Paris, 1869²) [The Preface (dated 1879) to the 3d ed. (Paris, 1879) says it is a reproduction of the 2nd, which was the same as the 1st (1844) except for a few modifications and additions]

———: *The Order of Words in the Ancient Languages compared with that of the modern languages*, trans. with notes and additions by Ch. W. Super (based on 3d ed.) (Boston, 1887)

Weinrich, Harald: " Die *clarté* der französischen Sprache und die Klarheit der Franzosen," *Zeitschrift für romanische Philologie*, LXXVII (1961), 528-544

Wundt, Wilhelm: *Völkerpsychologie*, I, 2 (Leipzig, 1900), ch. 7, pp. 215-420

Wydler, Karl: *Zur Stellung des attributiven Adjektivs vom Latein bis zum Neufranzösischen* (Bern, 1956)

INDEX